AMC | COUPES/SEDANS/WAGONS 1975-88 REPAIR MANUAL

President	Dean F. Morgantini, S.A.E.
Vice President–Finance	Barry L. Beck
Vice President–Sales	Glenn D. Potere
Executive Editor	Kevin M. G. Maher, A.S.E.
Production Manager	Ben Greisler, S.A.E.
Production Assistant	Melinda Possinger
Project Managers	George B. Heinrich III, A.S.E., S.A.E., Will Kessler, A.S.E., S.A.E., James R. Marotta, A.S.E., S.T.S., Richard Schwartz, A.S.E., Todd W. Stidham
Schematics Editor	Christopher G. Ritchie
Editor	Thomas A. Mellon, A.S.E., S.A.E.

CHILTON™ *Automotive Books*
PUBLISHED BY **W. G. NICHOLS, INC.**

Manufactured in USA
© 1997 W. G. Nichols
1020 Andrew Drive
West Chester, PA 19380
ISBN 0-8019-9075-0
Library of Congress Catalog Card No. 97-65897
2345678901 7654321098

Contents

1 GENERAL INFORMATION AND MAINTENANCE

1-2 HOW TO USE THIS BOOK
1-3 TOOLS AND EQUIPMENT
1-7 SERVICING YOUR VEHICLE SAFELY
1-8 FASTENERS, MEASUREMENTS AND CONVERSIONS
1-14 SERIAL NUMBER IDENTIFICATION
1-24 ROUTINE MAINTENANCE
1-52 FLUIDS AND LUBRICANT
1-73 PUSHING AND TOWING
1-73 TRAILER TOWING
1-75 JUMP STARTING A DEAD BATTERY
1-76 JACKING
1-79 HOW TO BUY A USED VEHICLE

2 TUNE-UP AND PERFORMANCE MAINTENANCE

2-2 SPARK PLUGS AND WIRES
2-8 FIRING ORDER
2-11 POINT TYPE IGNITION
2-18 ELECTRONIC IGNITION
2-24 IGNITION TIMING
2-27 VALVE LASH
2-29 IDLE SPEED AND MIXTU

3 ENGINE AND ENGINE OVERHAUL

3-2 ENGINE ELECTRICAL
3-23 ENGINE MECHANICAL
3-112 EXHAUST SYSTEM

4 EMISSION CONTROLS

4-2 AIR POLLUTION
4-3 AUTOMOTIVE EMISSIONS
4-5 EMISSION CONTROLS
4-20 ELECTRONIC ENGINE CONTROLS
4-31 VACUUM DIAGRAMS

5 FUEL SYSTEM

5-2 BASIC FUEL SYSTEM DIAGNOSIS
5-2 FUEL SYSTEM
5-33 FUEL TANK

6 CHASSIS ELECTRICAL

6-2 UNDERSTANDING AND TROUBLESHOOTING ELECTRICAL SYSTEMS
6-12 HEATING AND AIR CONDITIONING
6-24 ENTERTAINMENT SYSTEMS
6-24 WINDSHIELD WIPERS
6-27 INSTRUMENT AND SWITCHES
6-34 SEAT BELT/STARTER INTERLOCK SYSTEMS
6-34 LIGHTING
6-44 CIRCUIT PROTECTION
6-45 TRAILER WIRING
6-46 WIRING DIAGRAMS

Contents

MANUAL TRANSMISSION	**7-37**	TRANSFER CASE
PACER OVERDRIVE UNIT	**7-39**	DRIVELINE
CLUTCH	**7-45**	EAGLE FRONT AXLE
AUTOMATIC TRANSMISSION	**7-46**	REAR AXLE

DRIVE TRAIN

7

WHEELS	**8-14**	REAR SUSPENSION
FRONT SUSPENSION	**8-19**	STEERING

SUSPENSION AND STEERING

8

BRAKE OPERATING SYSTEM	**9-31**	REAR DRUM BRAKES
FRONT DRUM BRAKES	**9-36**	PARKING BRAKE
FRONT DISC BRAKES		

BRAKES

9

EXTERIOR	**10-24**	INTERIOR

BODY AND TRIM

10

-41 GLOSSARY

GLOSSARY

-45 MASTER INDEX

MASTER INDEX

SAFETY NOTICE

Proper service and repair procedures are vital to the safe, reliable operation of all motor vehicles, as well as the personal safety of those performing repairs. This manual outlines procedures for servicing and repairing vehicles using safe, effective methods. The procedures contain many NOTES, CAUTIONS and WARNINGS which should be followed along with standard procedures to eliminate the possibility of personal injury or improper service which could damage the vehicle or compromise its safety.

It is important to note that the repair procedures and techniques, tools and parts for servicing motor vehicles, as well as the skill and experience of the individual performing the work vary widely. It is not possible to anticipate all of the conceivable ways or conditions under which vehicles may be serviced, or to provide cautions as to all of the possible hazards that may result. Standard and accepted safety precautions and equipment should be used when handling toxic or flammable fluids, and safety goggles or other protection should be used during cutting, grinding, chiseling, prying, or any other process that can cause material removal or projectiles.

Some procedures require the use of tools specially designed for a specific purpose. Before substituting another tool or procedure, you must be completely satisfied that neither your personal safety, nor the performance of the vehicle will be endangered.

Although information in this manual is based on industry sources and is complete as possible at the time of publication, the possibility exists that some car manufacturers made later changes which could not be included here. While striving for total accuracy, Chilton Book Company cannot assume responsibility for any errors, changes or omissions that may occur in the compilation of this data.

PART NUMBERS

Part numbers listed in this reference are not recommendations by Chilton for any product by brand name. They are references that can be used with interchange manuals and aftermarket supplier catalogs to locate each brand supplier's discrete part number.

SPECIAL TOOLS

Special tools are recommended by the vehicle manufacturer to perform their specific job. Use has been kept to a minimum, but where absolutely necessary, they are referred to in the text by the part number of the tool manufacturer. These tools can be purchased, under the appropriate part number, from your local dealer or regional distributor, or an equivalent tool can be purchased locally from a tool supplier or parts outlet. Before substituting any tool for the one recommended, read the SAFETY NOTICE at the top of this page.

ACKNOWLEDGMENTS

The Nichols Publishing Company expresses its appreciation to the American Motors Corporation, Detroit, Michigan for their generous assistance in the preparation of this book.

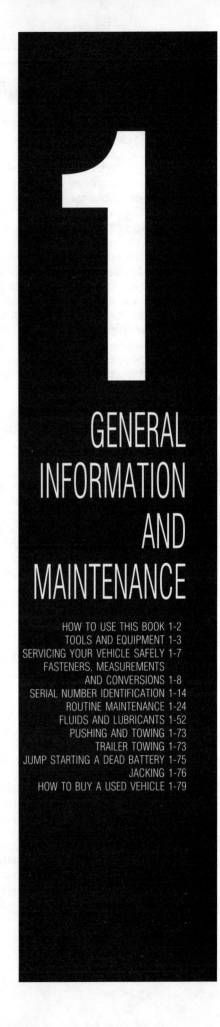

W TO USE THIS BOOK 1-2
ERE TO BEGIN 1-2
IDING TROUBLE 1-2
NTENANCE OR REPAIR? 1-2
IDING THE MOST COMMON MISTAKES 1-2
LS AND EQUIPMENT 1-3
CIAL TOOLS 1-6
VICING YOUR VEHICLE SAFELY 1-7
S 1-7
TS 1-8
TENERS, MEASUREMENTS AND
ONVERSIONS 1-8
TS, NUTS AND OTHER THREADED
ETAINERS 1-8
QUE 1-9
TORQUE WRENCHES 1-11
TORQUE ANGLE METERS 1-12
NDARD AND METRIC MEASUREMENTS 1-12
RIAL NUMBER IDENTIFICATION 1-14
ICLE 1-14
1975–80 MODELS 1-14
1981–88 MODELS 1-15
INE 1-16
4–21 ENGINE 1-16
4–150 ENGINE 1-16
4–151 ENGINE 1-16
6–232 & 258 ENGINES 1-17
8–304, 360, 401 ENGINES 1-17
NSMISSION 1-17
MANUAL 1-17
AUTOMATIC 1-17
UTINE MAINTENANCE 1-24
CLEANER 1-26
REMOVAL & INSTALLATION 1-26
L FILTER 1-28
REMOVAL & INSTALLATION 1-28
SYSTEM 1-29
REMOVAL & INSTALLATION 1-29
L VAPOR CANISTER 1-30
SERVICING 1-30
TERY 1-31
GENERAL MAINTENANCE 1-31
BATTERY FLUID 1-31
CABLES 1-33
CHARGING 1-34
REPLACEMENT 1-34
HAUST MANIFOLD HEAT VALVE 1-34
SERVICING 1-34
TS-35
INSPECTION 1-35
ADJUSTING 1-36
REMOVAL & INSTALLATION 1-36
SES-37
INSPECTION 1-37
REMOVAL & INSTALLATION 1-38
OTS-39
INSPECTION 1-39
CONDITIONING 1-39
SAFETY PRECAUTIONS 1-39
GENERAL SERVICING PROCEDURES 1-40
SYSTEM INSPECTION 1-41
ISOLATING THE COMPRESSOR 1-42
DISCHARGING, EVACUATING &
CHARGING 1-42
NDSHIELD WIPERS 1-43
ELEMENT (REFILL) CARE &
REPLACEMENT 1-43
ES AND WHEELS 1-47
TIRE ROTATION 1-47
TIRE DESIGN 1-48
TIRE STORAGE 1-48
INFLATION & INSPECTION 1-48
CARE OF SPECIAL WHEELS 1-50
UIDS AND LUBRICANTS 1-52
ID DISPOSAL 1-52
EL AND OIL RECOMMENDATIONS 1-53

ENGINE OIL 1-53
OIL LEVEL CHECK1-53
OIL & FILTER CHANGE 1-54
MANUAL TRANSMISSION 1-57
FLUID LEVEL CHECK 1-57
FLUID CHANGE 1-58
AUTOMATIC TRANSMISSION 1-59
FLUID LEVEL CHECK 1-59
FLUID & FILTER CHANGE 1-60
COOLANT 1-61
COOLANT LEVEL CHECK 1-61
DRAINING, FLUSHING & REFILLING 1-62
BRAKE MASTER CYLINDER 1-64
FLUID LEVEL CHECK 1-64
DRIVE AXLES 1-65
FLUID LEVEL CHECK 1-65
DRAIN & REFILL 1-66
TRANSFER CASE 1-67
MANUAL STEERING GEAR 1-67
POWER STEERING RESERVOIR 1-68
FRONT HUB AND WHEEL BEARINGS 1-69
ADJUSTMENT 1-69
PUSHING AND TOWING 1-73
TRAILER TOWING 1-73
GENERAL RECOMMENDATIONS 1-73
TRAILER WEIGHT 1-73
HITCH (TONGUE) WEIGHT 1-73
COOLING 1-74
ENGINE1-74
TRANSMISSION 1-74
HANDLING A TRAILER 1-74
JUMP STARTING A DEAD BATTERY 1-75
JUMP STARTING PRECAUTIONS 1-75
JUMP STARTING PROCEDURE 1-76
JACKING 1-76
JACKING PRECAUTIONS 1-77
BODY LUBRICATION AND MAINTENANCE 1-78
LOCK CYLINDERS 1-78
DOOR HINGES & HINGE CHECKS 1-78
TAILGATE 1-78
BODY DRAIN HOLES 1-78
HOW TO BUY A USED VEHICLE 1-79
TIPS 1-80
USED VEHICLE CHECKLIST 1-80
ROAD TEST CHECKLIST 1-82
COMPONENT LOCATIONS
MAINTENANCE COMPONENT LOCATIONS—
EARLY MODEL V8 ENGINE 1-24
MAINTENANCE COMPONENT LOCATIONS—
LATE MODEL INLINE ENGINE 1-25
SPECIFICATIONS CHARTS
STANDARD TORQUE SPECIFICATIONS AND
FASTENER MARKINGS 1-10
STANDARD AND METRIC CONVERSION
FACTORS 1-13
ENGINE APPLICATION CHART 1-17
MANUAL TRANSMISSION APPLICATION
CHART 1-18
AUTOMATIC TRANSMISSION APPLICATION
CHART 1-18
TRANSFER CASE APPLICATION CHART 1-19
FRONT DRIVE AXLE APPLICATION CHART 1-19
REAR AXLE APPLICATION CHART 1-19
MANUAL TRANSMISSION FLUID
RECOMMENDATIONS 1-58
TROUBLESHOOTING CHARTS
BASIC WHEEL PROBLEMS 1-51
BASIC TIRE PROBLEMS 1-51
TIRE SIZE COMPARISON CHART 1-52
OIL VISCOSITY SELECTOR 1-53
RECOMMENDED EQUIPMENT CHECKIST 1-75
CAPACITIES CHART 1-83
PREVENTIVE MAINTENANCE CHART 1-86
ENGLISH TO METRIC CONVERSION
CHARTS 1-88

1

GENERAL INFORMATION AND MAINTENANCE

HOW TO USE THIS BOOK 1-2
TOOLS AND EQUIPMENT 1-3
SERVICING YOUR VEHICLE SAFELY 1-7
FASTENERS, MEASUREMENTS
AND CONVERSIONS 1-8
SERIAL NUMBER IDENTIFICATION 1-14
ROUTINE MAINTENANCE 1-24
FLUIDS AND LUBRICANTS 1-52
PUSHING AND TOWING 1-73
TRAILER TOWING 1-73
JUMP STARTING A DEAD BATTERY 1-75
JACKING 1-76
HOW TO BUY A USED VEHICLE 1-79

HOW TO USE THIS BOOK

Chilton's Total Car Care manual is intended to help you learn more about the inner workings of your vehicle while saving you money on its upkeep and operation.

The beginning of the book will likely be referred to the most, since that is where you will find information for maintenance and tune-up. The other sections deal with the more complex systems of your vehicle. Operating systems from engine through brakes are covered to the extent that the average do-it-yourselfer becomes mechanically involved. This book will not explain such things as rebuilding a differential for the simple reason that the expertise required and the investment in special tools make this task uneconomical. It will, however, give you detailed instructions to help you change your own brake pads and shoes, replace spark plugs, and perform many more jobs that can save you money, give you personal satisfaction and help you avoid expensive problems.

A secondary purpose of this book is a reference for owners who want to understand their vehicle and/or their mechanics better. In this case, no tools at all are required.

Where to Begin

Before removing any bolts, read through the entire procedure. This will give you the overall view of what tools and supplies will be required. There is nothing more frustrating than having to walk to the bus stop on Monday morning because you were short one bolt on Sunday afternoon. So read ahead and plan ahead. Each operation should be approached logically and all procedures thoroughly understood before attempting any work.

All sections contain adjustments, maintenance, removal and installation procedures, and in some cases, repair or overhaul procedures. When repair is not considered practical, we tell you how to remove the part and then how to install the new or rebuilt replacement. In this way, you at least save the labor costs. Backyard repair of some components is just not practical.

Avoiding Trouble

Many procedures in this book require you to "label and disconnect . . ." a group of lines, hoses or wires. Don't be lulled into thinking you can remember where everything goes—you won't. If you hook up vacuum or fuel lines incorrectly, the vehicle will run poorly, if at all. If you hook up electrical wiring incorrectly, you may instantly learn a very expensive lesson.

You don't need to know the official or engineering name for each hose or line. A piece of masking tape on the hose and a piece on its fitting will allow you to assign your own label such as the letter A or a short name. As long as you remember your own code, the lines can be reconnected by matching similar letters or names. Do remember that tape will dissolve in gasoline or other fluids; if a component is to be washed or cleaned, use another method of identification. A permanent felt-tipped marker can be very handy for marking metal parts. Remove any tape or paper labels after assembly.

Maintenance or Repair?

It's necessary to mention the difference between maintenance and repair. Maintenance includes routine inspections, adjustment and replacement of parts which show signs of normal wear. Maintenance compensates for wear or deterioration. Repair implies that something has broken or is not working. A need for repair is often caused by lack of maintenance. Example: draining and refilling the automatic transmission fluid is maintenance recommended by the manufacturer at specific mileage intervals. Failure to do this can ruin the transmission/transaxle, requiring very expensive repairs. While no maintenance program can prevent items from breaking or wearing out, a general rule can be stated: MAINTENANCE IS CHEAPER THAN REPAIR.

Two basic mechanic's rules should be mentioned here. First, whenever the left side of the vehicle or engine is referred to, it meant to specify the driver's side. Conversely, the right side of the vehicle means the passenger's side. Second, most screws and bolts are removed by turning counterclockwise, and tightened by turning clockwise.

Safety is always the most important rule. Constantly be aware of the dangers involved in working on an automobile and take proper precautions. See the information in this section regarding SERVICING YOUR VEHICLE SAFELY and the SAFETY NOTICE on the acknowledgment page.

Avoiding the Most Common Mistakes

Pay attention to the instructions provided. There are 3 common mistakes in mechanical work:

1. **Incorrect order of assembly, disassembly or adjustment.** When taking something apart or putting it together, performing steps in the wrong order usually just costs you extra time; however, it CAN break something. Read the entire procedure before beginning disassembly. Perform everything in the order in which the instructions say you should, even if you can't immediately see a reason for it. When you're taking apart something that is very intricate, you might want to draw a picture of how it looks when assembled at one point in order to make sure you get everything back in its proper position. We will supply exploded views whenever possible. When making adjustments, perform them in the proper order; often, one adjustment affects another, and you cannot expect even satisfactory results unless each adjustment is made only when it cannot be changed by any other.

2. **Overtorquing (or undertorquing).** While it is more common for overtorquing to cause damage, undertorquing may allow a fastener to vibrate loose causing serious damage. Especially when dealing with aluminum parts, pay attention to torque specifications and utilize a torque wrench in assembly. If a torque figure is not available, remember that if you are using the right tool to perform the job, you will probably not have to strain yourself to get a fastener tight enough. The pitch of most threads is so slight that the tension you put on the wrench will be multiplied many times in actual force on what you are tightening. A good example of how critical torque is can be seen in the case of spark plug in

ation, especially where you are putting the plug into an alumi-... cylinder head. Too little torque can fail to crush the gasket, ...sing leakage of combustion gases and consequent overheating ...e plug and engine parts. Too much torque can damage the ...ads or distort the plug, changing the spark gap.

...here are many commercial products available for ensuring that ...eners won't come loose, even if they are not torqued just right ...ery common brand is Loctite®). If you're worried about getting ...ething together tight enough to hold, but loose enough to ...d mechanical damage during assembly, one of these products ...ht offer substantial insurance. Before choosing a threadlocking ...npound, read the label on the package and make sure the prod-...is compatible with the materials, fluids, etc. involved.

. Crossthreading. This occurs when a part such as a bolt ...crewed into a nut or casting at the wrong angle and forced. ...ssthreading is more likely to occur if access is difficult. It

helps to clean and lubricate fasteners, then to start threading with the part to be installed positioned straight in. Then, start the bolt, spark plug, etc. with your fingers. If you encounter resistance, un-screw the part and start over again at a different angle until it can be inserted and turned several times without much effort. Keep in mind that many parts, especially spark plugs, have tapered threads, so that gentle turning will automatically bring the part you're threading to the proper angle, but only if you don't force it or resist a change in angle. Don't put a wrench on the part until it's been tightened a couple of turns by hand. If you suddenly en-counter resistance, and the part has not seated fully, don't force it. Pull it back out to make sure it's clean and threading properly.

Always take your time and be patient; once you have some ex-perience, working on your vehicle may well become an enjoyable hobby.

OOLS AND EQUIPMENT

Naturally, without the proper tools and equipment it is impossi-...to properly service your vehicle. It would also be virtually im-...sible to catalog every tool that you would need to perform all ...he operations in this book. Of course, It would be unwise for ...amateur to rush out and buy an expensive set of tools on the ...ory that he/she may need one or more of them at some time. ...he best approach is to proceed slowly, gathering a good qual-...set of those tools that are used most frequently. Don't be mis-...by the low cost of bargain tools. It is far better to spend a lit-...more for better quality. Forged wrenches, 6 or 12-point ...kets and fine tooth ratchets are by far preferable to their less ...ensive counterparts. As any good mechanic can tell you, there ...few worse experiences than trying to work on a vehicle with ...d tools. Your monetary savings will be far outweighed by frus-...ion and mangled knuckles.

...Begin accumulating those tools that are used most frequently: ...se associated with routine maintenance and tune-up. In addi-...n to the normal assortment of screwdrivers and pliers, you ...uld have the following tools:

In addition to ratchets, a good set of wrenches and hex keys will be necessary

ll but the most basic procedures will require an ssortment of ratchets and sockets

A hydraulic floor jack and a set of jackstands are essential for lifting and supporting the vehicle

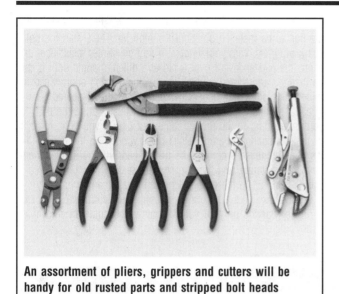

An assortment of pliers, grippers and cutters will be handy for old rusted parts and stripped bolt heads

Tools from specialty manufacturers such as Lisle® are designed to make your job easier . . .

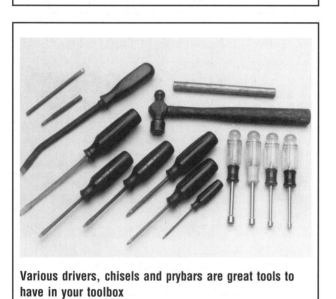

Various drivers, chisels and prybars are great tools to have in your toolbox

. . . these Torx® drivers and magnetic socket holders are just 2 examples of their handy products

Many repairs will require the use of a torque wrench to assure the components are properly fastened

Although not always necessary, using specialized brake tools will save time

few inexpensive lubrication tools will make maintenance easier

Dwell/tachometer unit (typical)

arious pullers, clamps and separator tools are needed or many larger, more complicated repairs

Inductive type timing light

A variety of tools and gauges should be used for spark plug gapping and installation

Compression gauge and a combination vacuum/fuel pressure test gauge

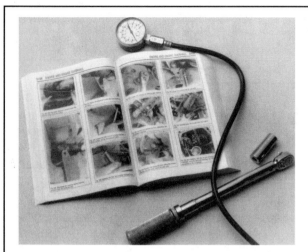

Proper information is vital, so always have a Chilton Total Car Care manual handy

• Wrenches/sockets and combination open end/box end wrenches in sizes from 1/8–3/4 in. or 3mm–19mm (depending on whether your vehicle uses standard or metric fasteners) and a 13/16 in. or 5/8 in. spark plug socket (depending on plug type).

➡**If possible, buy various length socket drive extensions. Universal-joint and wobble extensions can be extremely useful, but be careful when using them, as they can change the amount of torque applied to the socket.**

• Jackstands for support.
• Oil filter wrench.
• Spout or funnel for pouring fluids.
• Grease gun for chassis lubrication (unless your vehicle is not equipped with any grease fittings—for details, please refer to information on Fluids and Lubricants found later in this section).
• Hydrometer for checking the battery (unless equipped with a sealed, maintenance-free battery).
• A container for draining oil and other fluids.
• Rags for wiping up the inevitable mess.

In addition to the above items there are several others that are not absolutely necessary, but handy to have around. These include Oil Dry® (or an equivalent oil absorbent gravel—such as cat litter) and the usual supply of lubricants, antifreeze and fluids, although these can be purchased as needed. This is a basic list for routine maintenance, but only your personal needs and desire can accurately determine your list of tools.

After performing a few projects on the vehicle, you'll be amazed at the other tools and non-tools on your workbench. Some useful household items are: a large turkey baster or siphon, empty coffee cans and ice trays (to store parts), ball of twine, electrical tape for wiring, small rolls of colored tape for tagging lines or hoses, markers and pens, a note pad, golf tees (for plugging vacuum lines), metal coat hangers or a roll of mechanics's wire (to hold things out of the way), dental pick or similar long, pointed probe, a strong magnet, and a small mirror (to see into recesses and under manifolds).

A more advanced set of tools, suitable for tune-up work, can be drawn up easily. While the tools are slightly more sophisticated, they need not be outrageously expensive. There are seve inexpensive tach/dwell meters on the market that are every bit a good for the average mechanic as a professional model. Just b sure that it goes to a least 1200–1500 rpm on the tach scale a that it works on 4, 6 and 8-cylinder engines. (If you own one o more vehicles with a diesel engine, a special tachometer is required since diesels don't use spark plug ignition systems). Th key to these purchases is to make them with an eye towards adaptability and wide range. A basic list of tune-up tools could clude:

• Tach/dwell meter.
• Spark plug wrench and gapping tool.
• Feeler gauges for valve or point adjustment. (Even if your hicle does not use points or require valve adjustments, a feeler gauge is helpful for many repair/overhaul procedures).

A tachometer/dwell meter will ensure accurate tune-up work vehicles without electronic ignition. The choice of a timing ligh should be made carefully. A light which works on the DC curre supplied by the vehicle's battery is the best choice; it should h a xenon tube for brightness. On any vehicle with an electronic nition system, a timing light with an inductive pickup that clam around the No. 1 spark plug cable is preferred.

In addition to these basic tools, there are several other tools and gauges you may find useful. These include:

• Compression gauge. The screw-in type is slower to use, b eliminates the possibility of a faulty reading due to escaping pr sure.
• Manifold vacuum gauge.
• 12V test light.
• A combination volt/ohmmeter
• Induction Ammeter. This is used for determining whether o not there is current in a wire. These are handy for use if a wire broken somewhere in a wiring harness.

As a final note, you will probably find a torque wrench neces sary for all but the most basic work. The beam type models are perfectly adequate, although the newer click types (breakaway) a easier to use. The click type torque wrenches tend to be more e pensive. Also keep in mind that all types of torque wrenches should be periodically checked and/or recalibrated. You will hav to decide for yourself which better fits your purpose.

Special Tools

Normally, the use of special factory tools is avoided for repai procedures, since these are not readily available for the do-it-you self mechanic. When it is possible to perform the job with more commonly available tools, it will be pointed out, but occasionally a special tool was designed to perform a specific function and should be used. Before substituting another tool, you should be convinced that neither your safety nor the performance of the ve cle will be compromised.

Special tools can usually be purchased from an automotive parts store or from your dealer. In some cases special tools may be available directly from the tool manufacturer.

SERVICING YOUR VEHICLE SAFELY

It is virtually impossible to anticipate all of the hazards involved with automotive maintenance and service, but care and common sense will prevent most accidents.

The rules of safety for mechanics range from "don't smoke around gasoline," to "use the proper tool(s) for the job." The trick to avoiding injuries is to develop safe work habits and to take every possible precaution.

Do's

• Do keep a fire extinguisher and first aid kit handy.
• Do wear safety glasses or goggles when cutting, drilling, grinding or prying, even if you have 20–20 vision. If you wear glasses for the sake of vision, wear safety goggles over your regular glasses.
• Do shield your eyes whenever you work around the battery. Batteries contain sulfuric acid. In case of contact with the eyes or

Using the correct size wrench will help prevent the possibility of rounding off a nut

Screwdrivers should be kept in good condition to prevent injury or damage which could result if the blade slips from the screw

Power tools should always be properly grounded

NEVER work under a vehicle unless it is supported using safety stands (jackstands)

skin, flush the area with water or a mixture of water and baking soda, then seek immediate medical attention.
• Do use safety stands (jackstands) for any undervehicle service. Jacks are for raising vehicles; jackstands are for making sure the vehicle stays raised until you want it to come down. Whenever the vehicle is raised, block the wheels remaining on the ground and set the parking brake.
• Do use adequate ventilation when working with any chemicals or hazardous materials. Like carbon monoxide, the asbestos dust resulting from some brake lining wear can be hazardous in sufficient quantities.
• Do disconnect the negative battery cable when working on the electrical system. The secondary ignition system contains EXTREMELY HIGH VOLTAGE. In some cases it can even exceed 50,000 volts.
• Do follow manufacturer's directions whenever working with potentially hazardous materials. Most chemicals and fluids are poisonous if taken internally.

• Do properly maintain your tools. Loose hammerheads, mushroomed punches and chisels, frayed or poorly grounded electrical cords, excessively worn screwdrivers, spread wrenches (open end), cracked sockets, slipping ratchets, or faulty droplight sockets can cause accidents.

• Likewise, keep your tools clean; a greasy wrench can slip off a bolt head, ruining the bolt and often harming your knuckles in the process.

• Do use the proper size and type of tool for the job at hand. Do select a wrench or socket that fits the nut or bolt. The wrench or socket should sit straight, not cocked.

• Do, when possible, pull on a wrench handle rather than push on it, and adjust your stance to prevent a fall.

• Do be sure that adjustable wrenches are tightly closed on the nut or bolt and pulled so that the force is on the side of the fixed jaw.

• Do strike squarely with a hammer; avoid glancing blows.

• Do set the parking brake and block the drive wheels if the work requires a running engine.

Don'ts

• Don't run the engine in a garage or anywhere else without proper ventilation—EVER! Carbon monoxide is poisonous; it takes a long time to leave the human body and you can build up a deadly supply of it in your system by simply breathing in a little every day. You may not realize you are slowly poisoning yourself. Always use power vents, windows, fans and/or open the garage door.

• Don't work around moving parts while wearing loose clothing. Short sleeves are much safer than long, loose sleeves. Hard-toed shoes with neoprene soles protect your toes and give a better grip on slippery surfaces. Jewelry such as watches, fancy belt

buckles, beads or body adornment of any kind is not safe working around a vehicle. Long hair should be tied back under a hat or cap.

• Don't use pockets for toolboxes. A fall or bump can drive a screwdriver deep into your body. Even a rag hanging from your back pocket can wrap around a spinning shaft or fan.

• Don't smoke when working around gasoline, cleaning solvent or other flammable material.

• Don't smoke when working around the battery. When the battery is being charged, it gives off explosive hydrogen gas.

• Don't use gasoline to wash your hands; there are excellent soaps available. Gasoline contains dangerous additives which can enter the body through a cut or through your pores. Gasoline also removes all the natural oils from the skin so that bone dry hands will suck up oil and grease.

• Don't service the air conditioning system unless you are equipped with the necessary tools and training. When liquid or compressed gas refrigerant is released to atmospheric pressure it will absorb heat from whatever it contacts. This will chill or freeze anything it touches. Although refrigerant is normally non-toxic, R-12 becomes a deadly poisonous gas in the presence of an open flame. One good whiff of the vapors from burning refrigerant can be fatal.

• Don't use screwdrivers for anything other than driving screws! A screwdriver used as an prying tool can snap when you least expect it, causing injuries. At the very least, you'll ruin a good screwdriver.

• Don't use a bumper or emergency jack (that little ratchet, scissors, or pantograph jack supplied with the vehicle) for anything other than changing a flat! These jacks are only intended for emergency use out on the road; they are NOT designed as a maintenance tool. If you are serious about maintaining your vehicle yourself, invest in a hydraulic floor jack of at least a 1½ ton capacity and at least two sturdy jackstands.

FASTENERS, MEASUREMENTS AND CONVERSIONS

Bolts, Nuts and Other Threaded Retainers

Although there are a great variety of fasteners found in the modern car or truck, the most commonly used retainer is the threaded fastener (nuts, bolts, screws, studs, etc). Most threaded retainers may be reused, provided that they are not damaged in use or during the repair. Some retainers (such as stretch bolts or torque prevailing nuts) are designed to deform when tightened or in use and should not be reinstalled.

Whenever possible, we will note any special retainers which should be replaced during a procedure. But you should always inspect the condition of a retainer when it is removed and replace any that show signs of damage. Check all threads for rust or corrosion which can increase the torque necessary to achieve the desired clamp load for which that fastener was originally selected. Additionally, be sure that the driver surface of the fastener has not been compromised by rounding or other damage. In some cases a driver surface may become only partially rounded, allowing the driver to catch in only one direction. In many of these occurrences, a fastener may be installed and tightened, but the driver would not be able to grip and loosen the fastener again. (This

could lead to frustration down the line should that component ever need to be disassembled again).

If you must replace a fastener, whether due to design or damage, you must ALWAYS be sure to use the proper replacement. In all cases, a retainer of the same design, material and strength should be used. Markings on the heads of most bolts will help determine the proper strength of the fastener. The same material, thread and pitch must be selected to assure proper installation and safe operation of the vehicle afterwards.

Thread gauges are available to help measure a bolt or stud's thread. Most automotive and hardware stores keep gauges available to help you select the proper size. In a pinch, you can use another nut or bolt for a thread gauge. If the bolt you are replacing is not too badly damaged, you can select a match by finding another bolt which will thread in its place. If you find a nut which threads properly onto the damaged bolt, then use that nut to help select the replacement bolt. If however, the bolt you are replacing is so badly damaged (broken or drilled out) that its threads cannot be used as a gauge, you might start by looking for another bolt (from the same assembly or a similar location on your vehicle) which will thread into the damaged bolt's mounting. If so, the other bolt can be used to select a nut; the nut can then be used to select the replacement bolt.

Here are a few of the most common screw/bolt driver styles

A - Length
B - Diameter (major diameter)
C - Threads per inch or mm
D - Thread length
E - Size of the wrench required
F - Root diameter (minor diameter)

Threaded retainer sizes are determined using these measurements

There are many different types of threaded retainers found on vehicles

T - INTERNAL DRIVE
E - EXTERNAL

Special fasteners such as these Torx® head bolts are used by manufacturers to discourage people from working on vehicles without the proper tools

In all cases, be absolutely sure you have selected the proper replacement. Don't be shy, you can always ask the store clerk for help.

✳✳ WARNING

Be aware that when you find a bolt with damaged threads, you may also find the nut or drilled hole it was threaded into has also been damaged. If this is the case, you may have to drill and tap the hole, replace the nut or otherwise repair the threads. NEVER try to force a replacement bolt to fit into the damaged threads.

Torque

Torque is defined as the measurement of resistance to turning or rotating. It tends to twist a body about an axis of rotation. A common example of this would be tightening a threaded retainer

Standard Torque Specifications and Fastener Markings

In the absence of specific torques, the following chart can be used as a guide to the maximum safe torque of a particular size/grade of fastener.
- There is no torque difference for fine or coarse threads.
- Torque values are based on clean, dry threads. Reduce the value by 10% if threads are oiled prior to assembly.
- The torque required for aluminum components or fasteners is considerably less.

U.S. Bolts

SAE Grade Number	1 or 2			5			6 or 7		
Number of lines always 2 less than the grade number.									
Bolt Size (Inches)—(Thread)	Maximum Torque			Maximum Torque			Maximum Torque		
	Ft./Lbs.	Kgm	Nm	Ft./Lbs.	Kgm	Nm	Ft./Lbs.	Kgm	Nm
¼ — 20	5	0.7	6.8	8	1.1	10.8	10	1.4	13.5
— 28	6	0.8	8.1	10	1.4	13.6			
5/16 — 18	11	1.5	14.9	17	2.3	23.0	19	2.6	25.8
— 24	13	1.8	17.6	19	2.6	25.7			
⅜ — 16	18	2.5	24.4	31	4.3	42.0	34	4.7	46.0
— 24	20	2.75	27.1	35	4.8	47.5			
7/16 — 14	28	3.8	37.0	49	6.8	66.4	55	7.6	74.5
— 20	30	4.2	40.7	55	7.6	74.5			
½ — 13	39	5.4	52.8	75	10.4	101.7	85	11.75	115.2
— 20	41	5.7	55.6	85	11.7	115.2			
9/16 — 12	51	7.0	69.2	110	15.2	149.1	120	16.6	162.7
— 18	55	7.6	74.5	120	16.6	162.7			
⅝ — 11	83	11.5	112.5	150	20.7	203.3	167	23.0	226.5
— 18	95	13.1	128.8	170	23.5	230.5			
¾ — 10	105	14.5	142.3	270	37.3	366.0	280	38.7	379.6
— 16	115	15.9	155.9	295	40.8	400.0			
⅞ — 9	160	22.1	216.9	395	54.6	535.5	440	60.9	596.5
— 14	175	24.2	237.2	435	60.1	589.7			
1 — 8	236	32.5	318.6	590	81.6	799.9	660	91.3	894.8
— 14	250	34.6	338.9	660	91.3	849.8			

Metric Bolts

Relative Strength Marking	4.6, 4.8			8.8		
Bolt Markings						
Bolt Size Thread Size x Pitch (mm)	Maximum Torque			Maximum Torque		
	Ft./Lbs.	Kgm	Nm	Ft./Lbs.	Kgm	Nm
6 x 1.0	2–3	.2–.4	3–4	3–6	4–.8	5–8
8 x 1.25	6–8	.8–1	8–12	9–14	1.2–1.9	13–19
10 x 1.25	12–17	1.5–2.3	16–23	20–29	2.7–4.0	27–39
12 x 1.25	21–32	2.9–4.4	29–43	35–53	4.8–7.3	47–72
14 x 1.5	35–52	4.8–7.1	48–70	57–85	7.8–11.7	77–110
16 x 1.5	51–77	7.0–10.6	67–100	90–120	12.4–16.5	130–160
18 x 1.5	74–110	10.2–15.1	100–150	130–170	17.9–23.4	180–230
20 x 1.5	110–140	15.1–19.3	150–190	190–240	26.2–46.9	160–320
22 x 1.5	150–190	22.0–26.2	200–260	250–320	34.5–44.1	340–430
24 x 1.5	190–240	26.2–46.9	260–320	310–410	42.7–56.5	420–550

Standard and metric bolt torque specifications based on bolt strengths—WARNING: use only as a guide such as a nut, bolt or screw. Measuring torque is one of the most common ways to help assure that a threaded retainer has been properly fastened.

When tightening a threaded fastener, torque is applied in three distinct areas, the head, the bearing surface and the clamp load. About 50 percent of the measured torque is used in overcoming bearing friction. This is the friction between the bearing surface of the bolt head, screw head or nut face and the base material or washer (the surface on which the fastener is rotating). Approximately 40 percent of the applied torque is used in overcoming thread friction. This leaves only about 10 percent of the applied torque to develop a useful clamp load (the force which holds a joint together). This means that friction can account for as much as 90 percent of the applied torque on a fastener.

TORQUE WRENCHES

In most applications, a torque wrench can be used to assure proper installation of a fastener. Torque wrenches come in various designs and most automotive supply stores will carry a variety to suit your needs. A torque wrench should be used any time we supply a specific torque value for a fastener. A torque wrench can also be used if you are following the general guidelines in the accompanying charts. Keep in mind that because there is no worldwide standardization of fasteners, the charts are a general guideline and should be used with caution. Again, the general rule of "if you are using the right tool for the job, you should not have to strain to tighten a fastener" applies here.

Beam Type

The beam type torque wrench is one of the most popular types. It consists of a pointer attached to the head that runs the length of the flexible beam (shaft) to a scale located near the handle. As the wrench is pulled, the beam bends and the pointer indicates the torque using the scale.

Click (Breakaway) Type

Another popular design of torque wrench is the click type. To use the click type wrench you pre-adjust it to a torque setting. Once the torque is reached, the wrench has a reflex signalling fea-

Various styles of torque wrenches are usually available at your local automotive supply store

Example of a beam type torque wrench

A click type or breakaway torque wrench—note this one has a pivoting head

ture that causes a momentary breakaway of the torque wrench body, sending an impulse to the operator's hand.

Pivot Head Type

Some torque wrenches (usually of the click type) may be equipped with a pivot head which can allow it to be used in areas of limited access. BUT, it must be used properly. To hold a pivot head wrench, grasp the handle lightly, and as you pull on the handle, it should be floated on the pivot point. If the handle comes in contact with the yoke extension during the process of pulling, there is a very good chance the torque readings will be inaccurate because this could alter the wrench loading point. The design of the handle is usually such as to make it inconvenient to deliberately misuse the wrench.

➡**It should be mentioned that the use of any U-joint, wobble or extension will have an effect on the torque readings, no matter what type of wrench you are using. For the most accurate readings, install the socket directly on the wrench driver. If necessary, straight extensions (which hold a socket directly under the wrench driver) will have the least effect on the torque reading. Avoid any extension that alters the length of the wrench from the handle to the head/driving point (such as a crow's foot). U-joint or Wobble extensions can greatly affect the readings; avoid their use at all times.**

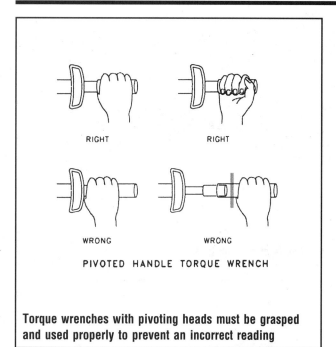

RIGHT RIGHT

WRONG WRONG

PIVOTED HANDLE TORQUE WRENCH

Torque wrenches with pivoting heads must be grasped and used properly to prevent an incorrect reading

Some specifications require the use of a torque angle meter (mechanical protractor)

The rigid case (direct reading) torque wrench uses a dial indicator to show torque

Rigid Case (Direct Reading)

A rigid case or direct reading torque wrench is equipped with a dial indicator to show torque values. One advantage of these wrenches is that they can be held at any position on the wrench without affecting accuracy. These wrenches are often preferred because they tend to be compact, easy to read and have a great degree of accuracy.

TORQUE ANGLE METERS

Because the frictional characteristics of each fastener or threaded hole will vary, clamp loads which are based strictly on

torque will vary as well. In most applications, this variance is not significant enough to cause worry. But, in certain applications, a manufacturer's engineers may determine that more precise clamp loads are necessary (such is the case with many aluminum cylinder heads). In these cases, a torque angle method of installation would be specified. When installing fasteners which are torque angle tightened, a predetermined seating torque and standard torque wrench are usually used first to remove any compliance from the joint. The fastener is then tightened the specified additional portion of a turn measured in degrees. A torque angle gauge (mechanical protractor) is used for these applications.

Standard and Metric Measurements

Throughout this manual, specifications are given to help you determine the condition of various components on your vehicle, or to assist you in their installation. Some of the most common measurements include length (in. or cm/mm), torque (ft. lbs., inch lbs. or Nm) and pressure (psi, in. Hg, kPa or mm Hg). In most cases, we strive to provide the proper measurement as determined by the manufacturer's engineers.

Though, in some cases, that value may not be conveniently measured with what is available in your toolbox. Luckily, many of the measuring devices which are available today will have two scales so the Standard or Metric measurements may easily be taken. If any of the various measuring tools which are available to you do not contain the same scale as listed in the specifications, use the accompanying conversion factors to determine the proper value.

The conversion factor chart is used by taking the given specification and multiplying it by the necessary conversion factor. For instance, looking at the first line, if you have a measurement in inches such as "free-play should be 2 in." but your ruler reads only in millimeters, multiply 2 in. by the conversion factor of 25.4 to get the metric equivalent of 50.8mm. Likewise, if the specification was given only in a Metric measurement, for example in Newton Meters (Nm), then look at the center column first. If the measurement is 100 Nm, multiply it by the conversion factor of 0.738 to get 73.8 ft. lbs.

CONVERSION FACTORS

LENGTH–DISTANCE

Inches (in.)	x 25.4	= Millimeters (mm)	x .0394	= Inches
Feet (ft.)	x .305	= Meters (m)	x 3.281	= Feet
Miles	x 1.609	= Kilometers (km)	x .0621	= Miles

VOLUME

Cubic Inches (in3)	x 16.387	= Cubic Centimeters	x .061	= in3
IMP Pints (IMP pt.)	x .568	= Liters (L)	x 1.76	= IMP pt.
IMP Quarts (IMP qt.)	x 1.137	= Liters (L)	x .88	= IMP qt.
IMP Gallons (IMP gal.)	x 4.546	= Liters (L)	x .22	= IMP gal.
IMP Quarts (IMP qt.)	x 1.201	= US Quarts (US qt.)	x .833	= IMP qt.
IMP Gallons (IMP gal.)	x 1.201	= US Gallons (US gal.)	x .833	= IMP gal.
Fl. Ounces	x 29.573	= Milliliters	x .034	= Ounces
US Pints (US pt.)	x .473	= Liters (L)	x 2.113	= Pints
US Quarts (US qt.)	x .946	= Liters (L)	x 1.057	= Quarts
US Gallons (US gal.)	x 3.785	= Liters (L)	x .264	= Gallons

MASS–WEIGHT

Ounces (oz.)	x 28.35	= Grams (g)	x .035	= Ounces
Pounds (lb.)	x .454	= Kilograms (kg)	x 2.205	= Pounds

PRESSURE

Pounds Per Sq. In. (psi)	x 6.895	= Kilopascals (kPa)	x .145	= psi
Inches of Mercury (Hg)	x .4912	= psi	x 2.036	= Hg
Inches of Mercury (Hg)	x 3.377	= Kilopascals (kPa)	x .2961	= Hg
Inches of Water (H_2O)	x .07355	= Inches of Mercury	x 13.783	= H_2O
Inches of Water (H_2O)	x .03613	= psi	x 27.684	= H_2O
Inches of Water (H_2O)	x .248	= Kilopascals (kPa)	x 4.026	= H_2O

TORQUE

Pounds–Force Inches (in–lb)	x .113	= Newton Meters (N·m)	x 8.85	= in–lb
Pounds–Force Feet (ft–lb)	x 1.356	= Newton Meters (N·m)	x .738	= ft–lb

VELOCITY

Miles Per Hour (MPH)	x 1.609	= Kilometers Per Hour (KPH)	x .621	= MPH

POWER

Horsepower (Hp)	x .745	= Kilowatts	x 1.34	= Horsepower

FUEL CONSUMPTION*

Miles Per Gallon IMP (MPG)	x .354	= Kilometers Per Liter (Km/L)
Kilometers Per Liter (Km/L)	x 2.352	= IMP MPG
Miles Per Gallon US (MPG)	x .425	= Kilometers Per Liter (Km/L)
Kilometers Per Liter (Km/L)	x 2.352	= US MPG

*It is common to covert from miles per gallon (mpg) to liters/100 kilometers (1/100 km), where mpg (IMP) x 1/100 km = 282 and mpg (US) x 1/100 km = 235.

TEMPERATURE

Degree Fahrenheit (°F)   = (°C x 1.8) + 32

Degree Celsius (°C)   = (°F – 32) x .56

Standard and metric conversion factors chart

SERIAL NUMBER IDENTIFICATION

Vehicle

The 13-digit Vehicle Identification Number (VIN) is attached to the left topside of the instrument panel, so that it is visible through the windshield.

1975–80 MODELS

◆ **See Figure 1**

First digit:
A, for American Motors
Second digit:
Last number of year, 5 for 1975
Third digit:
Transmission type
S: 3-Speed column
F: 3-Speed floor
A: Automatic-column
C: Automatic-floor
M: 4-Speed floor
Fourth digit:
Series
Fifth digit:
Body type
Sixth digit:
Trim class
Seventh digit:
Engine:
A, 6–258, 1 bbl.
B, 6–232, 1 bbl.
C, 6–232, 2 bbl.
E, 6–232, 1 bbl.
G, 6–232, 2 bbl.
H, 8–304, 2 bbl.
N, 8–360, 2 bbl.
P, 8–360, 4 bbl.
Z, 8–401, 4 bbl.
Remaining digits:
Vehicle serial number. Numbering was started at 100,001 each year at the Kenosha, Wisconsin plant and at 700,001 at the Brampton, Ontario plant.

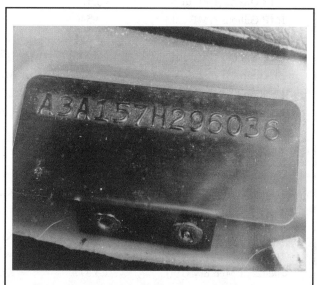

A 13-digit Vehicle Identification Number(VIN) is visible through the drivers side of the windshield

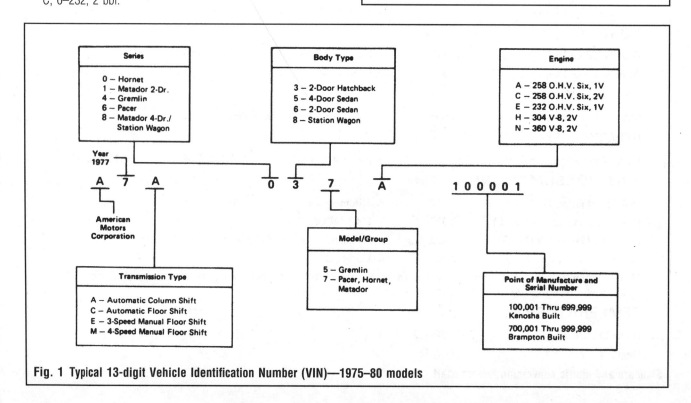

Fig. 1 Typical 13-digit Vehicle Identification Number (VIN)—1975–80 models

1981–88 MODELS

the dash panel visible through the windshield. To decode the VIN, see the accompanying illustration.

◆ **See Figure 2**

A seventeen digit Vehicle Identification Number (VIN) is embossed on a metal plate that is riveted to the upper left corner of

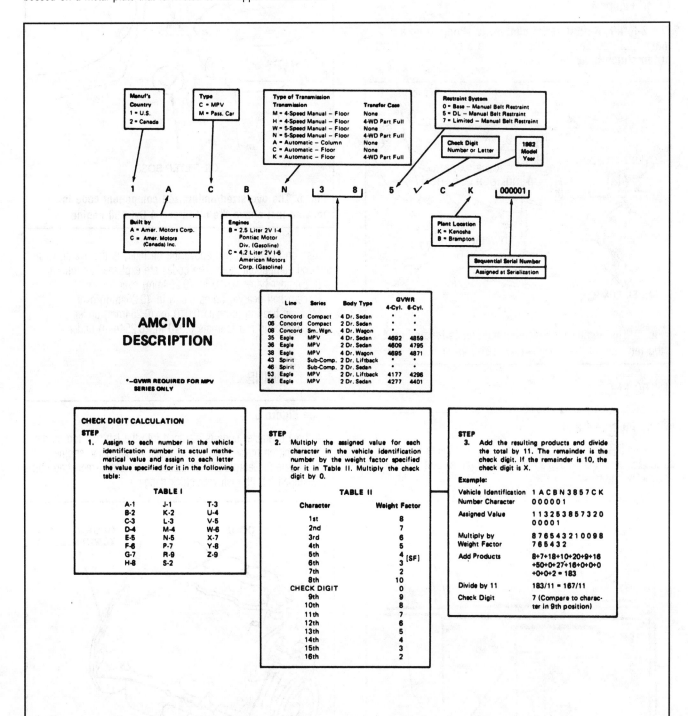

Fig. 2 Common 17-digit Vehicle Identification Number (VIN) decoding chart—1981–88 models

Engine

4–121 ENGINE

▶ See Figure 3

The 2-letter, 6-digit serial number is stamped on a machined pad on the left side of the block, just in front of the clutch housing.

Fig. 3 The engine identification number is located on the left side of the block—4 Cyl 121 engine

4–150 ENGINE

▶ See Figures 4 and 5

The engine serial number for the American Motors built 4–150 is located on a machined pad at the rear right side of the block, just below the head.

Fig. 4 The engine identification number is located on the right side of the block—4 Cyl 150 engine

Fig. 5 The oversized/undersized component code is located just above the oil filter—4 Cyl 150 engine

Also on the block, just above the oil filter, is the oversized/undersized component code. The codes are explained as follows:
B: cylinder bores 0.010 in. (0.254mm) over
C: camshaft bearing bores 0.010 in. (0.254mm) over
M: main bearing journals 0.010 in. (0.254mm) under
P: connecting rod journals 0.010 in. (0.254mm) under

4–151 ENGINE

▶ See Figure 6

A three character code is stamped into the left rear top corner of the block on these GM built engines. Additionally, engines built for sale in Georgia and Tennessee have a non-repeating number stamped into the left rear block flange.

Fig. 6 Location of the engine identification number and if applicable the stamp for vehicles built in Georgia and Tennessee—4 Cyl 151 engines

Engine Application Chart

| Engine | Actual Displacement | | | Type | Mfg. by | Years | Models |
	Cu. In.	CC	Liters				
4-121	120.96	1,982.2	2.0	OHC	Porsche	1977–79	Gremlin, Spirit, Concord
4-150	150.45	2,465.4	2.5	OHV	AMC	1984	All models
4-151	150.78	2,470.8	2.5	OHV	Chevrolet	1980–83	Spirit, Concord, Eagle, SX-4
6-232	231.91	3,800.3	3.8	OHV	AMC	1975	Except Matador
						1976–78	Gremlin, Hornet, Pacer, Concord
						1979	Spirit, Concord
6-258	258.08	4,229.2	4.2	OHV	AMC	1975–88	All models
8-304	303.92	4,980.3	5.0	OHV	AMC	1975	Except Pacer
						1976	Gremlin, Hornet, Matador
						1977–79	All models
8-360	359.80	5,896.1	5.9	OHV	AMC	1975	All models
						1976–78	Matador
8-401	401.11	6,572.9	6.6	OHV	AMC	1975–76	Matador

6–232 & 258 ENGINES

The American Motors engine code is, of course, found in the identification plate on the firewall. The second location is on a machined surface of the block between number 2 and 3 spark plugs. For further identification, the displacement is cast into the side of the block. The letter in the code identifies the engine by displacement (cu. in.), carburetor type and compression ratio.

On vehicles equipped with the 6–232 made prior to 1971, the engine code number is located on a machined surface, adjacent to the distributor. The letter contained in the code number denotes the cu. in. displacement of the engine. The letter, L, denotes 232 cu in. 8.5:1 compression ratio. The engine code letter is located on a boss directly above the oil filter.

On 6–232 engines built before 1971, the size code is stamped on a tag located on the left front side of the baffle above the intake manifold below the build date, and on the boss above the oil filter. The following chart explains just what the letters indicate on the 232 sixes made prior to 1971:

First Digit—Size of the bore: A, B, or C
Second Digit—Size of the main bearings: A, B, or C
Third Digit—Size of the connecting rod bearings: A, B, or C
A - Standard; B - 0.010 in. (0.254mm) undersized; C - 0.010 in. (0.254mm) oversized

All of the engines made after 1971 have the same undersize/oversize letter codes, located on the boss directly above the oil filter. The parts size code is as follows:

Letter B indicates 0.010 in. (0.254mm) oversized cylinder bore.
Letter M indicates 0.010 in. (0.254mm) undersized main bearings.
Letter P indicates 0.010 in. (0.254mm) undersized connecting rod bearings.
Letter C indicates 0.010 in. (0.254mm) oversized camshaft block bores.

8–304, 360, 401 ENGINES

On American Motors built V8 engines, the number is located on a tag attached to the right valve cover. For further identification, the displacement is cast into the side of the block. The letter in the code identifies the engine by displacement (cu. in.), carburetor type and compression ratio.

All of the engines made after 1971 have the same undersize/oversize letter codes, located on a tag next to the engine number. The parts size code is as follows:

Letter B indicates 0.010 in. (0.254mm) oversized cylinder bore.
Letter M indicates 0.010 in. (0.254mm) undersized main bearings.
Letter P indicates 0.010 in. (0.254mm) undersized connecting rod bearings.
Letters PM indicate a combination of the above specifications for P and M.
Letter C indicates 0.010 in. (0.254mm) oversized camshaft block bores.

Transmission

MANUAL

The transmission identification tag is attached to the rear of the transmission. It contains both the transmission manufacturer's and American Motor's part number. It is necessary to know both of these numbers when ordering replacement parts.

➤Be sure to attach the transmission identification tag it is original location when reassembling the transmission.

AUTOMATIC

Torque-Command

A 7-digit part number is stamped on the left-hand side of the transmission case, above the oil pan. A 4-digit number, indicating the date of manufacture, follows the part number.

➤If the date number is above 3500, add one for each day after 26 February 1971 to determine the date of manufacture. Hence, 3501 would be 27 February 1971, and 3809 would be 1 January 1972, etc. The final group of numbers is the transmission serial number.

Manual Transmission Application Chart

Transmission Types	Years	Models
HR-1	1978–79	All models w/4-121
Tremec T-150 3-sp	1975–76	All except 6-cylinder Gremlin
	1977–78	Standard on all 6-cylinder models
	1979	Spirit w/6-232
Warner SR-4 4-sp	1977–78	Optional on all 6-cylinder models
	1979	All except 6-232 Spirit & models w/4-121
	1980–82	Standard on all models*
Warner T-4 4-sp	1982–88	Standard on all models*
Warner T-5 5-sp	1982–88	Optional on all models
	1987	Standard on all models
Warner T-14 3-sp	1975–76	Gremlin w/ 6-cylinder engine

*1982 models may come equipped with either the SR-4 or T-4, depending on availability. Make sure you know which one you have, in as much as the SR-4 uses GL-5 85W-90 gear oil and the T-4 uses Dexron® II ATF fluid. The easiest way to tell is by shift pattern: The SR-4 reverse position is to the extreme left; the T-4 reverse is to the extreme right.

Automatic Transmission Application Chart

Transmission	Years	Models
Chrysler 727	1975–76	All w/8-360, 8-401
	1977	Optional on 8-304 HD
		All 8-360
	1978	Optional on 6-258 HD and Fleet uses
		All 8-360
Chrysler 904	1975–77	All w/6-cylinder
	1978–79	All 4- and 6-cylinder engines
	1980	All except Eagle
	1981	All 4-cylinder use a wide ratio version
		6-cylinder, except Eagle, use a standard ratio
	1982	All 4-cylinder models
		6-cylinder, except Eagle, use a lock-up torque converter
	1983	All 4-cylinder models
		6-cylinder, except Eagle and Concords built for fleet sales, use a lock-up torque converter
Chyrsler 998	1975–79	All w/8-304
	1980	All Eagle
	1981–82	6-cylinder Eagle
	1983	6-cylinder Eagle
		Concord sedan and wagon built for fleet sales use a lock-up torque converter
	1984	4-cylinder models use a wide ratio version
		6-cylinder models use a lock-up torque converter
	1985–88	All models use a lock-up torque converter

Transfer Case Application Chart

Transfer Case Type	Years	Fluid Used	Models
New Process NP-119	1980–81	Dexron® II ATF	All models
New Process NP-129	1982–85	Dexron® II ATF	All models
New Process NP-128	1986–88	Dexron® II ATF	All models

Front Drive Axle Application Chart

Axle Type	Years	Models
Dana 30	1970–88	All models

Rear Axle Application Chart

Models	Years	Code	Ring Gear Dia. (in.)	Ratio	Application
AMX	1978	K(V)	7⁹⁄₁₆	2.53	w/ 4-sp and AT, exc Cal and H.A.
		H(U)	7⁹⁄₁₆	2.73	Cal 4-sp
		F(T)	7⁹⁄₁₆	3.08	Cal At and H.A. 4-sp and AT
	1979	G(S)	7⁹⁄₁₆	3.31	All w/4-121, exc Cal
		E(R)	7⁹⁄₁₆	3.58	All Cal w/4-121
		K(V)	7⁹⁄₁₆	2.53	6-258 4-sp, exc Cal 6-258 AT, exc Cal and H.A. 8-304 AT, exc Cal and H.A.
		H(U)	7⁹⁄₁₆	2.73	6-258 Cal w/4-sp 6-258 & 8-304 Cal and H.A. w/AT
		C(O)	8⁷⁄₈	2.87	8-304 w/4-sp
	1980	F(T)	7⁹⁄₁₆	3.08	All w/4-151
		K(V)	7⁹⁄₁₆	2.53	6-258 w/4-sp, exc Cal 6-258 w/AT, exc Cal and H.A.
		H(U)	7⁹⁄₁₆	2.73	Cal 6-258 w/4-sp 6-258 Cal and H.A. w/AT

Rear Axle Application Chart

Models	Years	Code	Ring Gear Dia. (in.)	Ratio	Application
Concord	1978	H(U)	7⁹⁄₁₆	2.73	All 6-232 3-sp 6-258 Wagon w/AT exc Cal. & H.A. 6-258 Calif. w/4-sp
		K(V)	7⁹⁄₁₆	2.53	All 6-232 4-sp and AT 6-258 4-sp exc Cal. & H.A. 6-258 Sedan & Hatchback w/AT
		F(T)	7⁹⁄₁₆	3.08	6-258 H.A. w/4-sp 6-258 Cal. & H.A. w/4-sp
		X(Y)	8⁷⁄₈	2.56	8-304 Sdn & Wagon exc Cal and H.A.
		C(O)		2.87	8-304 Cal Sedan and Wagon 8-304 Hatchback exc Cal. & H.A.
		B(P)	8⁷⁄₈		8-304 Sedan & Wagon H.A. 8-304 Hatchback Cal and H.A.
	1979	G(S)	7⁹⁄₁₆	3.31	All w/4-121, exc Cal
		E(R)	7⁹⁄₁₆	3.58	All Cal w/4-121
		K(V)	7⁹⁄₁₆	2.53	All w/6-232, exc Wagon All 6-258 w/4-sp, exc Cal All 6-258 w/AT, exc Cal and H.A. All 8-304, exc Cal and H.A.
		H(U)	7⁹⁄₁₆	2.73	Wagon w/6-232 Cal 6-258 w/4-sp Cal and H.A. 6-258 w/AT Cal and H.A. 8-304
	1980	F(T)	7⁹⁄₁₆	3.08	All w/4-151
		K(V)	7⁹⁄₁₆	2.53	6-258 w/4-sp, exc Cal 6-258 w/AT, exc Cal and H.A.
		H(U)	7⁹⁄₁₆	2.73	Cal 6-258 w/4-sp 6-258 Cal and H.A. w/AT
	1981	F(T)	7⁹⁄₁₆	3.08	All w/4-151
		J	7⁹⁄₁₆	2.37	6-258 w/4-sp, exc H.A.
		K(V)	7⁹⁄₁₆	2.53	6-258 H.A. w/4-sp 6-258 w/AT, exc H.A.
		H(U)	7⁹⁄₁₆	2.73	6-258 H.A. w/AT
	1982	F(FF)	7⁹⁄₁₆	3.08	All w/4-151
		L(LL)	7⁹⁄₁₆	2.35	6-258 w/4- or 5-sp Std on 6-258 Cal w/AT
		M(MM)	7⁹⁄₁₆	2.21	Std on 6-258, exc Cal and H.A. Opt on Cal 6-258
		J(JJ)	7⁹⁄₁₆	2.73	6-258 H.A. w/AT 6-258 Trailer Towing option
	1983	L(LL)	7⁹⁄₁₆	2.35	Std. w/4- or 5-sp, exc Cal Opt w/AT, exc Cal and H.A.
		K(V)	7⁹⁄₁₆	2.53	Std on Cal w/4- or 5-sp or AT
		M(MM)	7⁹⁄₁₆	2.21	Std w/AT, exc Cal and H.A. Opt on Cal w/AT
		J(JJ)	7⁹⁄₁₆	2.73	Std on H.A. w/AT Trailer Towing Option
Eagle	1980	F(T)	7⁹⁄₁₆	3.08	Std, exc H.A.
		A(N)	7⁹⁄₁₆	3.54	Std w/H.A.; Opt, exc H.A.

Rear Axle Application Chart

Models	Years	Code	Ring Gear Dia. (in.)	Ratio	Application
Eagle (cont.)	1981	EE(FF)	7⁹⁄₁₆	3.54	All w/4-151
		H(U)	7⁹⁄₁₆	2.73	All 6-258, exc H.A.
		F(T)	7⁹⁄₁₆	3.08	6-258 H.A. w/4-sp
		G(S)	7⁹⁄₁₆	3.31	6-258 H.A. w/AT
	1982	J(JJ)	7⁹⁄₁₆	2.73	4-151 w/4- or 5-sp, exc Cal & H.A. Std on 6-258 w/4- or 5-sp Std on 6-258 H.A. w/AT
		L(LL)	7⁹⁄₁₆	2.35	Std on 6-258 w/AT, exc H.A. Opt on 6-258 w/4- or 5-sp, exc H.A.
		G(S)	7⁹⁄₁₆	3.31	Opt on H.A. w/AT
		F(FF)	7⁹⁄₁₆	3.08	Trailer Towing option w/6-258
		E(EE)	7⁹⁄₁₆	3.54	4-151 w/AT & all Cal and H.A.
	1983	E(EE)	7⁹⁄₁₆	3.54	All w/4-151
		J(JJ)	7⁹⁄₁₆	2.73	Std on all 6-258, exc Cal w/AT
		L(LL)	7⁹⁄₁₆	2.35	Opt on 6-258 w/4- or 5-sp, exc H.A. Opt on 6-258 w/AT, exc Cal & H.A. Std on Cal 6-258 w/AT
		F(FF)	7⁹⁄₁₆	3.08	Opt on 6-258 H.A. w/AT Trailer Towing Option w/4-dr
	1984	E(EE)	7⁹⁄₁₆	3.54	All w/4-150
		J(JJ)	7⁹⁄₁₆	2.73	6-258 w/4- or 5-sp Opt on 6-258 w/AT
		L(LL)	7⁹⁄₁₆	2.35	Std on 6-258 w/AT
		F(FF)	7⁹⁄₁₆	3.08	Trailer Towing Opt on 6-258 w/AT
	1985–88	J(JJ)	7⁹⁄₁₆	2.73	All models
Gremlin	1975–76	H	7⁹⁄₁₆	2.73	Std on 6-cylinder, exc Cal
		F	7⁹⁄₁₆	3.08	Std on Cal 6-cylinder Opt on 6-cylinder, exc Cal
		K	7⁹⁄₁₆	2.53	Opt on 6-cyl w/AT, exc Cal
		B	8⅞	3.15	Std on 8-304 w/MT Opt on 8-304 w/AT
		C	8⅞	2.87	Opt on 8-304 w/MT Std on 8-304 w/AT
	1977	H(U)	7⁹⁄₁₆	2.73	Std, exc. 4-sp & H.A.
		F(T)	7⁹⁄₁₆	3.08	Std on H.A. Opt, exc H.A.
		K	7⁹⁄₁₆	2.53	Std w/4-sp, exc H.A. Opt w/AT, exc H.A.
	1978	G(S)	7⁹⁄₁₆	3.31	Std w/4-121, exc Cal MT
		F(T)	7⁹⁄₁₆	3.08	Std w/4-121 Cal MT Std w/Cal 6-258 AT Std w/6-258 H.A.
		H(U)	7⁹⁄₁₆	2.73	Std w/6-232 3-sp Std w/Cal 6-258 4-sp
		K(V)	7⁹⁄₁₆	2.53	Std w/6-232 4-sp and AT Std w/6-258 exc Cal & H.A.
Hornet	1975–76	H	7⁹⁄₁₆	2.73	Std on 6-cylinder, exc Cal
		F	7⁹⁄₁₆	3.08	Std on Cal 6-cylinder Opt on 6-cylinder, exc Cal

Rear Axle Application Chart

Models	Years	Code	Ring Gear Dia. (in.)	Ratio	Application
Hornet (cont.)		K	7⁹⁄₁₆	2.53	Opt on 6-cyl w/AT, exc Cal
		B	8⁷⁄₈	3.15	Std on 8-304 w/MT Opt on 8-304 w/AT
		C	8⁷⁄₈	2.87	Opt on 8-304 w/MT Std on 8-304 w/AT
	1977	H(U)	7⁹⁄₁₆	2.73	Std on 6-cyl exc 4-sp & H.A.
		F(T)	7⁹⁄₁₆	3.08	Std on H.A. Opt on 6-cyl exc H.A.
		K(V)	7⁹⁄₁₆	2.53	Std w/4-sp, exc H.A. Opt on 6-cyl w/AT, exc H.A.
		C(O)	8⁷⁄₈	2.87	Std w/8-304
		B(P)	8⁷⁄₈	3.15	Opt w/8-304
Matador	1975–76	A	8⁷⁄₈	3.54	Std on 6-cyl Coupe w/MT Opt on 6-cyl Coupe w/AT Opt on 8-304 Coupe Opt on 8-360 Coupe Opt on 8-304 4-dr Opt on 8-360 4-dr
		B	8⁷⁄₈	3.15	Opt on 6-cyl Coupe w/MT Std on 6-cyl Coupe w/AT Opt on 8-304 Coupe Opt on 8-360 Coupe Std on 8-304 Cal 4-dr Opt on 8-304 4-dr, exc Cal Std on 8-360 Cal 4-dr Opt on 8-360 4-dr, exc Cal
		C	8⁷⁄₈	2.87	Std on 8-304 Coupe Std on 8-360 Coupe Std on 8-304 4-dr, exc Cal Std on 8-360 4-dr, exc Cal
	1977	B(P)	8⁷⁄₈	3.15	Std w/6-258 Opt w/8-304 Opt w/8-360, exc. H.A. Std w/8-360 H.A.
		A(N)	8⁷⁄₈	3.54	Opt w/6-258 Opt w/8-304 Opt w/8-360
		C(O)	8⁷⁄₈	2.87	Std w/8-304 and 8-360, exc Cal
	1978	B(P)	8⁷⁄₈	3.15	All 6-258 All Cal and H.A. V8
		C(O)	8⁷⁄₈	2.87	All V8 exc Cal and H.A.
Pacer	1975–76	H	7⁹⁄₁₆	2.73	Std, except Cal
		F	7⁹⁄₁₆	3.08	Std on Cal models Opt, exc Cal
		K	7⁹⁄₁₆	2.53	Opt, exc Cal
	1977	H(U)	7⁹⁄₁₆	2.73	Std, exc 4-sp & exc H.A.
		F(T)	7⁹⁄₁₆	3.08	Std on H.A. Opt, exc H.A.
		K(V)	7⁹⁄₁₆	2.53	Std w/4-sp, exc H.A. Opt w/AT, exc H.A.
	1978	H(U)	7⁹⁄₁₆	2.73	All 6-232 3-sp 6-258 w/AT, exc Cal and H.A. 6-258 Cal 4-sp

Rear Axle Application Chart

Models	Years	Code	Ring Gear Dia. (in.)	Ratio	Application
Pacer (cont.)		K(V)	7⁹⁄₁₆	2.53	All 6-232 4-sp and AT 6-258 4-sp, exc Cal and H.A.
		F(T)	7⁹⁄₁₆	3.08	6-258 all H.A. and Cal AT
	1979	K(V)	7⁹⁄₁₆	2.53	6-258 w/4-sp, exc Cal 6-258 w/AT, exc Cal and H.A. 8-304, exc Cal and H.A.
		H(U)	7⁹⁄₁₆	2.73	Cal 6-258 w/4-sp 6-258 Cal and H.A. w/AT 8-304 Cal and H.A.
	1980	K(V)	7⁹⁄₁₆	2.53	6-258 w/4-sp, exc Cal 6-258 w/AT, exc Cal and H.A.
		H(U)	7⁹⁄₁₆	2.73	Cal 6-258 w/4-sp 6-258 Cal and H.A. w/AT
Spirit	1979	F(T)	7⁹⁄₁₆	3.08	4-121 w/4-sp, exc H.A.
		G(S)	7⁹⁄₁₆	3.31	4-121 H.A. & all 4-121 w/AT
		H(U)	7⁹⁄₁₆	2.73	6-232 w/3-sp 6-258 Cal w/4-sp Cal and H.A. 6-258 w/AT 8-304 Cal and H.A.
		K(V)	7⁹⁄₁₆	2.53	6-232 w/4-sp or AT 6-258 w/4-sp, exc Cal 6-258 w/AT, exc Cal & H.A. 8-304, exc Cal and H.A.
	1980	F(T)	7⁹⁄₁₆	3.08	All w/4-151
		K(V)	7⁹⁄₁₆	2.53	6-258 w/4-sp, exc Cal 6-258 w/AT, exc Cal and H.A.
		H(U)	7⁹⁄₁₆	2.73	Cal 6-258 w/4-sp 6-258 Cal and H.A. w/AT
	1981	F(T)	7⁹⁄₁₆	3.08	All w/4-151
		J	7⁹⁄₁₆	2.37	6-258 w/4-sp, exc H.A.
		K(V)	7⁹⁄₁₆	2.53	6-258 H.A. w/4-sp 6-258 w/AT, exc H.A.
		H(U)	7⁹⁄₁₆	2.73	6-258 H.A. w/AT
	1982	F(FF)	7⁹⁄₁₆	3.08	All w/4-151
		L(LL)	7⁹⁄₁₆	2.35	6-258 w/4- or 5-sp Std on 6-258 Cal w/AT
		M(MM)	7⁹⁄₁₆	2.21	Std on 6-258, exc Cal and H.A. Opt on Cal 6-258
		J(JJ)	7⁹⁄₁₆	2.73	6-258 H.A. w/AT
	1983	L(LL)	7⁹⁄₁₆	2.35	Std w/4- or 5-sp, exc Cal Opt w/AT, exc Cal and H.A.
		K(V)	7⁹⁄₁₆	2.53	Std on Cal w/4- or 5-sp or AT
		M(MM)	7⁹⁄₁₆	2.21	Std w/AT, exc Cal and H.A. Opt on Cal w/AT
		J(JJ)	7⁹⁄₁₆	2.73	Std on H.A. w/AT

Letters in parenthesis indicate the code for the locking axle version, called Twin-Grip®
NOTE: a small number of 1982 axles were coded with 1981 codes, as follows:
    F as T
    E as EE and FF
    J as H and U

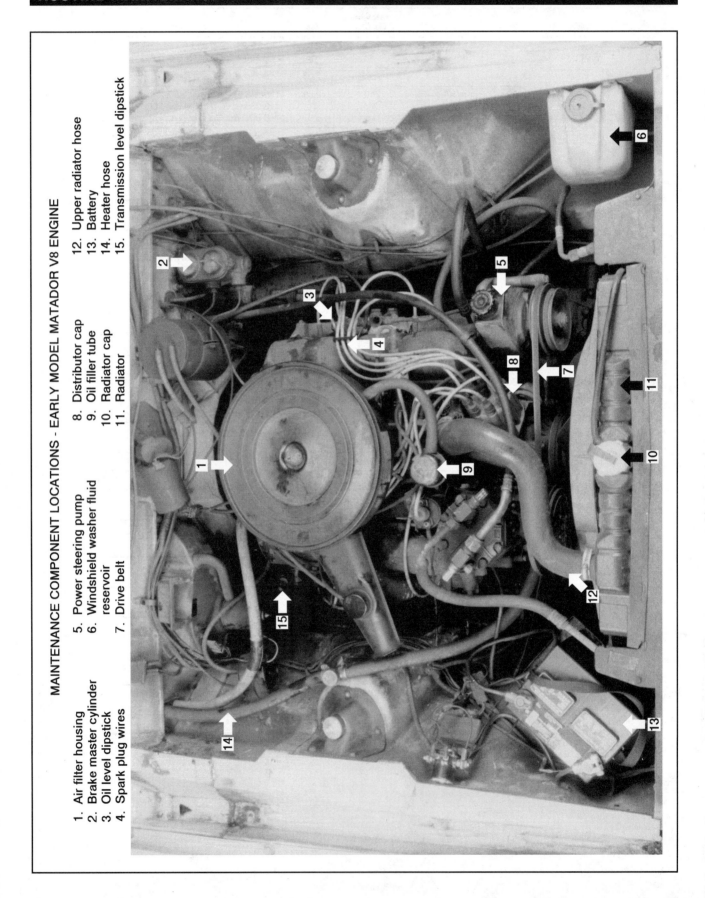

MAINTENANCE COMPONENT LOCATIONS - EARLY MODEL MATADOR V8 ENGINE

1. Air filter housing
2. Brake master cylinder
3. Oil level dipstick
4. Spark plug wires
5. Power steering pump
6. Windshield washer fluid reservoir
7. Drive belt
8. Distributor cap
9. Oil filler tube
10. Radiator cap
11. Radiator
12. Upper radiator hose
13. Battery
14. Heater hose
15. Transmission level dipstick

MAINTENANCE COMPONENT LOCATIONS - LATE MODEL EAGLE INLINE ENGINE

1. Heater hose
2. Air filter housing
3. Brake master cylinder
4. Transmission level dipstick
5. Spark plug wire
6. PCV valve
7. Distributor cap
8. Oil filler hole
9. Coolant over flow reservoir
10. Power steering pump
11. Radiator cap
12. Radiator
13. Drive belt
14. Upper radiator hose
15. Battery
16. Oil level dipstick
17. Windshield washer reservoir

Air Cleaner

REMOVAL & INSTALLATION

▶ **See Figures 7, 8, 9 and 10**

The air cleaner has a disposable element which should be replaced at the intervals shown in the 'Service Intervals' chart. It should be checked at every oil change. To check or replace the element:

1. Remove the wing nut at the top.
2. On a 4–151 or V8 engine, lift off the large disc under the wing nut. Remove the element.

3. On a six, detach the PCV hose at the valve cover. Don't pull the hose our of the air cleaner or you will damage it. Remove the whole top of the air cleaner and remove the element.

4. There are a couple of ways to clean the element. How well either works depends on the type of dirt trapped in the paper element. Dust and dirt can be removed by rapping the element on a flat surface or by blowing from the inside with an air hose. If the element still appears black or clogged, replace it. A clogged filter causes a rich fuel/air mixture and low gas mileage.

5. Wipe out the housing and install the new or rejuvenated element.

6. Reinstall the top of the unit and the wing nut.

Fig. 7 Exploded view of the air cleaner assembly—4 Cyl 151 engines

Fig. 8 Air cleaner assembly—6 Cyl 232 and 258

Fig. 9 Exploded view of the air cleaner assembly—8 Cyl engines

Fig. 10 Exploded view of the air cleaner assembly—4 Cyl 121 engine

Loosen the air cleaner cover wing nut by turning it counterclockwise . . .

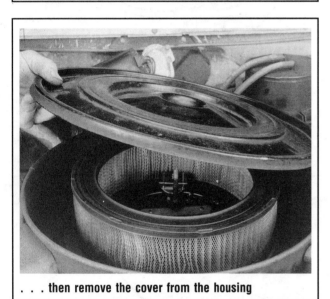

. . . then remove the cover from the housing

Remove the air filter element from the housing

Fuel Filter

REMOVAL & INSTALLATION

4–121, 4–150, 6–232, 6–258, 8–304, 360 and 401 Engines

♦ **See Figure 11**

All these engines have a throwaway cartridge filter in the line between the fuel pump and the carburetor. To replace it:
1. Remove the air cleaner as necessary.
2. Put an absorbent rag under the filter to catch spillage.
3. Remove the hose clamps.
4. Remove the filter and short attaching hoses.
5. Remove the hoses if they are to be reused.
6. Assemble the new filter and hoses.

Fig. 11 Make sure to position the arrow on the filter towards the engine—except 4 Cyl 151 engine

On fuel filters equipped with spring type clamps, use a pair of pliers to remove them

Disconnect the fuel lines and remove the filter from the vehicle

➡️**The original equipment wire hose clamps should be replaced with screw type band clamps for the best results.**

7. 1975 V8 and all 1976 and later filters have two outlets. The extra one is to return fuel vapors and bubbles to the tank so as to prevent vapor lock. The tank line outlet must be up.

8. Install the filter, tighten the clamps, start the engine, and check for leaks. Discard the rag and old filter safely.

4–151 Engine
♦ **See Figure 12**

The filter is located behind the large inlet nut in the carburetor. It is a small, paper, throwaway type.

✳✳ CAUTION

DO NOT perform a filter change on a hot engine!

Fig. 12 Components and location of the fuel filter—4 Cyl 151 engine

1. Place an absorbent rag under the carburetor inlet nut.
2. Hold the inlet nut with one wrench, while loosening the fuel line fitting with another. Remove the fuel line.
3. Unscrew the inlet nut and remove the nut, washer, spring and filter.
4. Installation is the reverse of removal. It's always best to use a new washer. Coat the threads of the inlet nut with a non-hardening, fuel-proof gasket cement. Do not overtighten the inlet nut! The threads are easily stripped in the carburetor. Hold the inlet nut with a wrench while tightening the fuel line fitting.

PCV System

PCV means Positive Crankcase Ventilation. This is a simple emission control system which routes crankcase fumes into the intake manifold or carburetor to be burned. A clogged PCV system will cause poor idle and rough running. There are two points of maintenance in this system: A valve and a filter. Maintenance intervals are shown in the 'Service Intervals' chart, but remember that this system can clog pretty quickly on an older engine that is using a little oil.

REMOVAL & INSTALLATION

Valve
♦ **See Figures 13, 14 and 15**

On a six, the PCV valve is at the cover end of a hose leading from just below the carburetor to the valve cover. On a 4–151 or V8, it is at the intake manifold end of a hose leading from the carburetor to the intake manifold.

1. Pull the valve from its grommet in the intake manifold (V8) or valve cover (six).

Fig. 13 Typical PCV system components—4 Cyl 121 engine

Fig. 14 PCV system assembly—6 Cyl 232 and 258 engines (4 Cyl 151 system is similar); 1980–82 models do not have the purge hose

Fig. 15 Common V8 engine PCV system

2. Loosen the hose clamp and pull the valve from the hose. The valve can be washed in kerosene, but the best plan is to replace it. If the valve seems really sludged up, check the hose, too.

3. Push the new or cleaned valve into its hose. Push the valve into its grommet. The condition of this grommet is important. If it leaks air, the engine will idle too fast because of a lean fuel/air mixture.

Filter

To clean the system filter:

1. On a six, remove the top of the air cleaner as explained previously under 'Air Cleaner.' Turn the top upside down and pull the filter out of the hose, inside the top. Don't pull the hose off first, or you'll damage it. Wash the filter in kerosene and replace it when dry. Replace the top of the air cleaner.

2. On a 4–151 or V8, remove the oil filter cap and wash it with kerosene. The cap contains the filter element. Replace it when dry.

Fuel Vapor Canister

SERVICING

▶ **See Figures 16 and 17**

The canister stores carburetor and fuel tank vapors while the engine is off, holding them to be drawn into the engine and burned when it starts. This system is on some models beginning 1971, and all models beginning 1973. Look for a black container

Fig. 16 Cross-sectional view of a typical fuel vapor control system

Fig. 17 Common fuel vapor canister and hoses used on American motors models

about the size and shape of a coffee tin can with some hoses attached in the engine compartment. The air filter in this canister should be changed at the intervals shown in the 'Service Intervals' chart. To change the filter:

1. Loosen the canister clamp screw and raise the canister enough that you can work under it. Remove it as necessary.

2. Pull out the old filter from the bottom of the canister.

3. Install a new filter, making sure that it covers the whole opening.

4. Replace the canister and tighten the clamp screws.

Battery

GENERAL MAINTENANCE

All batteries, regardless of type, should be carefully secured by a battery hold-down device. If this is not done, the battery terminals or casing may crack from stress applied to the battery during vehicle operation. A battery which is not secured may allow acid to leak out, making it discharge faster; such leaking corrosive acid can also eat away components under the hood. A battery that is not sealed must be checked periodically for electrolyte level. You cannot add water to a sealed maintenance-free battery (though not all maintenance-free batteries are sealed), but a sealed battery must also be checked for proper electrolyte level as indicated by the color of the built-in hydrometer "eye."

Keep the top of the battery clean, as a film of dirt can help completely discharge a battery that is not used for long periods. A solution of baking soda and water may be used for cleaning, but be careful to flush this off with clear water. DO NOT let any of the solution into the filler holes. Baking soda neutralizes battery acid and will de-activate a battery cell.

✳✳ CAUTION

Always use caution when working on or near the battery. Never allow a tool to bridge the gap between the negative and positive battery terminals. Also, be careful not to allow a tool to provide a ground between the positive cable/terminal and any metal component on the vehicle. Either of these conditions will cause a short circuit leading to sparks and possible personal injury.

Batteries in vehicles which are not operated on a regular basis can fall victim to parasitic loads (small current drains which are constantly drawing current from the battery). Normal parasitic loads may drain a battery on a vehicle that is in storage and not used for 6–8 weeks. Vehicles that have additional accessories such as a cellular phone, an alarm system or other devices that increase parasitic load may discharge a battery sooner. If the vehicle is to be stored for 6–8 weeks in a secure area and the alarm system, if present, is not necessary, the negative battery cable should be disconnected at the onset of storage to protect the battery charge.

Remember that constantly discharging and recharging will shorten battery life. Take care not to allow a battery to be needlessly discharged.

BATTERY FLUID

✳✳ CAUTION

Battery electrolyte contains sulfuric acid. If you should splash any on your skin or in your eyes, flush the affected area with plenty of clear water. If it lands in your eyes, get medical help immediately.

On non-maintenance free batteries, the level can be checked through the case on translucent batteries; the cell caps must be removed on other models

Check the specific gravity of the battery's electrolyte with a hydrometer

The fluid (sulfuric acid solution) contained in the battery cells will tell you many things about the condition of the battery. Because the cell plates must be kept submerged below the fluid level in order to operate, maintaining the fluid level is extremely important. And, because the specific gravity of the acid is an indication of electrical charge, testing the fluid can be an aid in determining if the battery must be replaced. A battery in a vehicle with a properly operating charging system should require little maintenance, but careful, periodic inspection should reveal problems before they leave you stranded.

Fluid Level

Check the battery electrolyte level at least once a month, or more often in hot weather or during periods of extended vehicle operation. On non-sealed batteries, the level can be checked either through the case on translucent batteries or by removing the cell caps on opaque-cased types. The electrolyte level in each cell should be kept filled to the split ring inside each cell, or the line marked on the outside of the case.

If the level is low, add only distilled water through the opening until the level is correct. Each cell is separate from the others, so each must be checked and filled individually. Distilled water should be used, because the chemicals and minerals found in most drinking water are harmful to the battery and could significantly shorten its life.

If water is added in freezing weather, the vehicle should be driven several miles to allow the water to mix with the electrolyte. Otherwise, the battery could freeze.

Although some maintenance-free batteries have removable cell caps for access to the electrolyte, the electrolyte condition and level on all sealed maintenance-free batteries must be checked using the built-in hydrometer "eye." The exact type of eye varies between battery manufacturers, but most apply a sticker to the battery itself explaining the possible readings. When in doubt, refer to the battery manufacturer's instructions to interpret battery condition using the built-in hydrometer.

➡**Although the readings from built-in hydrometers found in sealed batteries may vary, a green eye usually indicates a properly charged battery with sufficient fluid level. A dark**

Location of indicator on sealed battery

Check the appearance of the charge indicator on top of the battery before attempting a jump start; if it's not green or dark, do not jump start the car

A typical sealed (maintenance-free) battery with a built-in hydrometer—NOTE that the hydrometer eye may vary between battery manufacturers; always refer to the battery's label

eye is normally an indicator of a battery with sufficient fluid, but one which may be low in charge. And a light or yellow eye is usually an indication that electrolyte supply has dropped below the necessary level for battery (and hydrometer) operation. In this last case, sealed batteries with an insufficient electrolyte level must usually be discarded.

Specific Gravity

As stated earlier, the specific gravity of a battery's electrolyte level can be used as an indication of battery charge. At least once a year, check the specific gravity of the battery. It should be between 1.20 and 1.26 on the gravity scale. Most auto supply stores carry a variety of inexpensive battery testing hydrometers. These can be used on any non-sealed battery to test the specific gravity in each cell.

The battery testing hydrometer has a squeeze bulb at one end and a nozzle at the other. Battery electrolyte is sucked into the hydrometer until the float is lifted from its seat. The specific gravity is then read by noting the position of the float. If gravity is low in one or more cells, the battery should be slowly charged and checked again to see if the gravity has come up. Generally, if after charging, the specific gravity between any two cells varies more than 50 points (0.50), the battery should be replaced as it can no longer produce sufficient voltage to guarantee proper operation.

On sealed batteries, the built-in hydrometer is the only way of checking specific gravity. Again, check with your battery's manufacturer for proper interpretation of its built-in hydrometer readings.

CABLES

Once a year (or as necessary), the battery terminals and the cable clamps should be cleaned. Loosen the clamps and remove the cables, negative cable first. On batteries with posts on top, the use of a puller specially made for this purpose is recommended. These are inexpensive and available in most auto parts stores. Side terminal battery cables are secured with a small bolt.

Clean the cable clamps and the battery terminal with a wire brush, until all corrosion, grease, etc., is removed and the metal is shiny. It is especially important to clean the inside of the clamp

The underside of this special battery tool has a wire brush to clean post terminals

Place the tool over the terminals and twist to clean the post

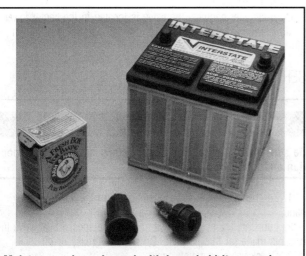

Maintenance is performed with household items and with special tools like this post cleaner

A special tool is available to pull the clamp from the post

Clean the battery terminals until the metal is shiny

The cable ends should be cleaned as well

(an old knife is useful here) thoroughly, since a small deposit of foreign material or oxidation there will prevent a sound electrical connection and inhibit either starting or charging. Special tools are available for cleaning these parts, one type for conventional top post batteries and another type for side terminal batteries.

Before installing the cables, loosen the battery hold-down clamp or strap, remove the battery and check the battery tray. Clear it of any debris, and check it for soundness (the battery tray can be cleaned with a baking soda and water solution). Rust should be wire brushed away, and the metal given a couple coats of anti-rust paint. Install the battery and tighten the hold-down clamp or strap securely. Do not overtighten, as this can crack the battery case.

After the clamps and terminals are clean, reinstall the cables, negative cable last; DO NOT hammer the clamps onto post batteries. Tighten the clamps securely, but do not distort them. Give the clamps and terminals a thin external coating of grease after installation, to retard corrosion.

Check the cables at the same time that the terminals are cleaned. If the cable insulation is cracked or broken, or if the ends are frayed, the cable should be replaced with a new cable of the same length and gauge.

CHARGING

✳ CAUTION

The chemical reaction which takes place in all batteries generates explosive hydrogen gas. A spark can cause the battery to explode and splash acid. To avoid serious personal injury, be sure there is proper ventilation and take appropriate fire safety precautions when connecting, disconnecting, or charging a battery and when using jumper cables.

A battery should be charged at a slow rate to keep the plates inside from getting too hot. However, if some maintenance-free batteries are allowed to discharge until they are almost "dead," they may have to be charged at a high rate to bring them back to "life." Always follow the charger manufacturer's instructions on charging the battery.

REPLACEMENT

When it becomes necessary to replace the battery, select one with a rating equal to or greater than the battery originally installed. Deterioration and just plain aging of the battery cables, starter motor, and associated wires makes the battery's job harder in successive years. The slow increase in electrical resistance over time makes it prudent to install a new battery with a greater capacity txxhan the old.

Exhaust Manifold Heat Valve

▸ **See Figure 18**

The exhaust manifold heat valve should be inspected and lubricated every 30,000 miles.

On 6-cylinder engines, the valve is located in the center lower portion of the exhaust manifold, on the left-hand side of the engine.

SERVICING

✳ CAUTION

Be sure that the manifold is cool before carrying out inspection and lubrication.

1. To check the heat valve operation, turn the valve shaft by hand.
2. Lubricate the heat valve with one of the special heat valve lubricants made for this purpose. Do not use grease or oil.
3. Check valve operation again.

COUNTERWEIGHT

Fig. 18 Typical exhaust manifold heat valve used on V8 engines—other models are similar

Belts

INSPECTION

Inspect the belts for signs of glazing or cracking. A glazed belt will be perfectly smooth from slippage, while a good belt will have a slight texture of fabric visible. Cracks will usually start at the inner edge of the belt and run outward. All worn or damaged drive belts should be replaced immediately. It is best to replace all drive belts at one time, as a preventive maintenance measure, during this service operation.

CONVENTIONAL "V" BELT   COGGED "V" BELT

"V" RIBBED BELT

There are typically 3 types of accessory drive belts found on vehicles today

An example of a healthy drive belt

Deep cracks in this belt will cause flex, building up heat that will eventually lead to belt failure

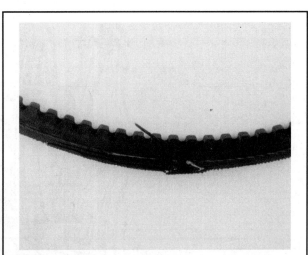

The cover of this belt is worn, exposing the critical reinforcing cords to excessive wear

Installing too wide a belt can result in serious belt wear and/or breakage

ADJUSTING

Belts are normally adjusted by loosening the bolts of the accessory being driven and moving that accessory on its pivot points until the proper tension is applied to the belt. The accessory is held in this position while the bolts are tightened. To determine proper belt tension, you can purchase a belt tension gauge or simply use the deflection method. To determine deflection, press inward on the belt at the midpoint of its longest straight run. The belt should deflect (move inward) ⅜ to ½ in. (9.525–12.7mm). Some long V-belts and most serpentine belts have idler pulleys which are used for adjusting purposes. Just loosen the idler pulley and move it to take up tension on the belt.

REMOVAL & INSTALLATION

♦ See Figures 19 thru 24

To remove a drive belt, simply loosen the accessory being driven and move it on its pivot point to free the belt. Then, remove the belt. If an idler pulley is used, it is often necessary, only, to loosen the idler pulley to provide enough slack the remove the belt.

It is important to note, however, that on engines with many driven accessories, several or all of the belts may have to be removed to get at the one to be replaced.

Fig. 20 Take the tension off the belt by pushing the component towards the engine, then remove the belt

Fig. 19 To adjust or replace a belt, loosen the mounting and adjusting bolts slightly

Fig. 21 Slip a new belt over the pulley.

Fig. 22 Pull or pry outwards on the component to tension the belt, then tighten the mounting bolts

Fig. 23 Use a ruler and a straight edge to measure belt deflection

Fig. 24 On most serpentine belts and some long V-belts an idler pulley is used for belt tension adjustment

Hoses

INSPECTION

Upper and lower radiator hoses along with the heater hoses should be checked for deterioration, leaks and loose hose clamps at least every 15,000 miles (24,000 km). It is also wise to check the hoses periodically in early spring and at the beginning of the fall or winter when you are performing other maintenance. A quick visual inspection could discover a weakened hose which might have left you stranded if it had remained unrepaired.

Whenever you are checking the hoses, make sure the engine and cooling system are cold. Visually inspect for cracking, rotting or collapsed hoses, and replace as necessary. Run your hand along the length of the hose. If a weak or swollen spot is noted when squeezing the hose wall, the hose should be replaced.

REMOVAL & INSTALLATION

1. Remove the radiator pressure cap.

✳✳ CAUTION

Never remove the pressure cap while the engine is running, or personal injury from scalding hot coolant or steam may result. If possible, wait until the engine has cooled to remove the pressure cap. If this is not possible, wrap a thick cloth around the pressure cap and turn it slowly to the stop. Step back while the pressure is released from the cooling system. When you are sure all the pressure has been released, use the cloth to turn and remove the cap.

2. Position a clean container under the radiator and/or engine draincock or plug, then open the drain and allow the cooling sys-

A soft spongy hose (identifiable by the swollen section) will eventually burst and should be replaced

The cracks developing along this hose are a result of age-related hardening

Hoses are likely to deteriorate from the inside if the cooling system is not periodically flushed

tem to drain to an appropriate level. For some upper hoses, only a little coolant must be drained. To remove hoses positioned lower on the engine, such as a lower radiator hose, the entire cooling system must be emptied.

✳✳ CAUTION

When draining coolant, keep in mind that cats and dogs are attracted by ethylene glycol antifreeze, and are quite likely to drink any that is left in an uncovered container or in puddles on the ground. This will prove fatal in sufficient quantity. Always drain coolant into a sealable container. Coolant may be reused unless it is contaminated or several years old.

3. Loosen the hose clamps at each end of the hose requiring replacement. Clamps are usually either of the spring tension type (which require pliers to squeeze the tabs and loosen) or of the

A hose clamp that is too tight can cause older hoses to separate and tear on either side of the clamp

screw tension type (which require screw or hex drivers to loosen). Pull the clamps back on the hose away from the connection.

4. Twist, pull and slide the hose off the fitting, taking care not to damage the neck of the component from which the hose is being removed.

➡**If the hose is stuck at the connection, do not try to insert a screwdriver or other sharp tool under the hose end in an effort to free it, as the connection and/or hose may become damaged. Heater connections especially may be easily damaged by such a procedure. If the hose is to be replaced, use a single-edged razor blade to make a slice along the portion of the hose which is stuck on the connection, perpendicular to the end of the hose. Do not cut deep so as to prevent damaging the connection. The hose can then be peeled from the connection and discarded.**

5. Clean both hose mounting connections. Inspect the condition of the hose clamps and replace them, if necessary.

To install:

6. Dip the ends of the new hose into clean engine coolant to ease installation.

7. Slide the clamps over the replacement hose, then slide the hose ends over the connections into position.

8. Position and secure the clamps at least ¼ in. (6.35mm) from the ends of the hose. Make sure they are located beyond the raised bead of the connector.

9. Close the radiator or engine drains and properly refill the cooling system with the clean drained engine coolant or a suitable mixture of ethylene glycol coolant and water.

10. If available, install a pressure tester and check for leaks. If a pressure tester is not available, run the engine until normal operating temperature is reached (allowing the system to naturally pressurize), then check for leaks.

✳✳ CAUTION

If you are checking for leaks with the system at normal operating temperature, BE EXTREMELY CAREFUL not to touch any moving or hot engine parts. Once temperature has been reached, shut the engine OFF, and check for leaks around the hose fittings and connections which were removed earlier.

Boots

INSPECTION

The CV (Constant Velocity) boots should be checked for damage each time the oil is changed and any other time the vehicle is raised for service. These boots keep water, grime, dirt and other damaging matter from entering the CV-joints. Any of these could cause early CV-joint failure which can be expensive to repair. Heavy grease thrown around the inside of the front wheel(s) and on the brake caliper/drum can be an indication of a torn boot. Thoroughly check the boots for missing clamps and tears. If the boot is damaged, it should be replaced immediately.

A torn boot should be replaced immediately

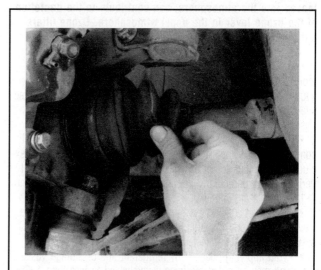

CV-boots must be inspected periodically for damage

Air Conditioning

➡**Be sure to consult the laws in your area before servicing the air conditioning system. In most areas, it is illegal to perform repairs involving refrigerant unless the work is done by a certified technician. Also, it is quite likely that you will not be able to purchase refrigerant without proof of certification.**

SAFETY PRECAUTIONS

There are two major hazards associated with air conditioning systems and they both relate to the refrigerant gas. First, the refrigerant gas (R-12) is an extremely cold substance. When exposed to air, it will instantly freeze any surface it comes in contact with, including your eyes. The other hazard relates to fire. Although normally non-toxic, the R-12 gas becomes highly poisonous in the presence of an open flame. One good whiff of the vapor formed by burning R-12 can be fatal. Keep all forms of fire (including cigarettes) well clear of the air conditioning system.

Because of the inherent dangers involved with working on air conditioning systems and R-12 refrigerant, these safety precautions must be strictly followed.

• Avoid contact with a charged refrigeration system, even when working on another part of the air conditioning system or vehicle. If a heavy tool comes into contact with a section of tubing or a heat exchanger, it can easily cause the relatively soft material to rupture.

• When it is necessary to apply force to a fitting which contains refrigerant, as when checking that all system couplings are securely tightened, use a wrench on both parts of the fitting involved, if possible. This will avoid putting torque on refrigerant tubing. (It is also advisable to use tube or line wrenches when tightening these flare nut fittings.)

➡ **R-12 refrigerant is a chlorofluorocarbon which, when released into the atmosphere, can contribute to the depletion of the ozone layer in the upper atmosphere. Ozone filters out harmful radiation from the sun.**

• Do not attempt to discharge the system without the proper tools. Precise control is possible only when using the service gauges and a proper A/C refrigerant recovery station. Wear protective gloves when connecting or disconnecting service gauge hoses.

• Discharge the system only in a well ventilated area, as high concentrations of the gas which might accidentally escape can exclude oxygen and act as an anesthetic. When leak testing or soldering, this is particularly important, as toxic gas is formed when R-12 contacts any flame.

• Never start a system without first verifying that both service valves are properly installed, and that all fittings throughout the system are snugly connected.

• Avoid applying heat to any refrigerant line or storage vessel. Charging may be aided by using water heated to less than 125°F (50°C) to warm the refrigerant container. Never allow a refrigerant storage container to sit out in the sun, or near any other source of heat, such as a radiator or heater.

• Always wear goggles to protect your eyes when working on a system. If refrigerant contacts the eyes, it is advisable in all cases to consult a physician immediately.

• Frostbite from liquid refrigerant should be treated by first gradually warming the area with cool water, and then gently applying petroleum jelly. A physician should be consulted.

• Always keep refrigerant drum fittings capped when not in use. If the container is equipped with a safety cap to protect the valve, make sure the cap is in place when the can is not being used. Avoid sudden shock to the drum, which might occur from dropping it, or from banging a heavy tool against it. Never carry a drum in the passenger compartment of a vehicle.

• Always completely discharge the system into a suitable recovery unit before painting the vehicle (if the paint is to be baked on), or before welding anywhere near refrigerant lines.

• When servicing the system, minimize the time that any refrigerant line or fitting is open to the air in order to prevent moisture or dirt from entering the system. Contaminants such as moisture or dirt can damage internal system components. Always replace O-rings on lines or fittings which are disconnected. Prior to installation coat, but do not soak, replacement O-rings with suitable compressor oil.

GENERAL SERVICING PROCEDURES

➡ **It is recommended, and possibly required by law, that a qualified technician perform the following services.**

The most important aspect of air conditioning service is the maintenance of a pure and adequate charge of refrigerant in the system. A refrigeration system cannot function properly if a significant percentage of the charge is lost. Leaks are common because the severe vibration encountered underhood in an automobile can easily cause a sufficient cracking or loosening of the air conditioning fittings; allowing, the extreme operating pressures of the system to force refrigerant out.

The problem can be understood by considering what happens to the system as it is operated with a continuous leak. Because the expansion valve regulates the flow of refrigerant to the evaporator, the level of refrigerant there is fairly constant. The receiver/drier stores any excess refrigerant, and so a loss will first appear there as a reduction in the level of liquid. As this level nears the bottom of the vessel, some refrigerant vapor bubbles will begin to appear in the stream of liquid supplied to the expansion valve. This vapor decreases the capacity of the expansion valve very little as the valve opens to compensate for its presence. As the quantity of liquid in the condenser decreases, the operating pressure will drop there and throughout the high side of the system. As the R-12 continues to be expelled, the pressure available to force the liquid through the expansion valve will continue to decrease, and, eventually, the valve's orifice will prove to be too much of a restriction for adequate flow even with the needle fully withdrawn.

At this point, low side pressure will start to drop, and a severe reduction in cooling capacity, marked by freeze-up of the evaporator coil, will result. Eventually, the operating pressure of the evaporator will be lower than the pressure of the atmosphere surrounding it, and air will be drawn into the system wherever there are leaks in the low side.

Because all atmospheric air contains at least some moisture, water will enter the system and mix with the R-12 and the oil. Trace amounts of moisture will cause sludging of the oil, and corrosion of the system. Saturation and clogging of the filter/drier, and freezing of the expansion valve orifice will eventually result. As air fills the system to a greater and greater extent, it will interfere more and more with the normal flows of refrigerant and heat.

From this description, it should be obvious that much of the repairman's focus in on detecting leaks, repairing them, and then restoring the purity and quantity of the refrigerant charge. A list of general rules should be followed in addition to all safety precautions:

• Keep all tools as clean and dry as possible.

• Thoroughly purge the service gauges/hoses of air and moisture before connecting them to the system. Keep them capped when not in use.

• Thoroughly clean any refrigerant fitting before disconnecting it, in order to minimize the entrance of dirt into the system.

• Plan any operation that requires opening the system beforehand, in order to minimize the length of time it will be exposed to open air. Cap or seal the open ends to minimize the entrance of foreign material.

• When adding oil, pour it through an extremely clean and dry tube or funnel. Keep the oil capped whenever possible. Do not use oil that has not been kept tightly sealed.

• Use only R-12 refrigerant. Purchase refrigerant intended for use only in automatic air conditioning systems.

• Completely evacuate any system that has been opened for service, or that has leaked sufficiently to draw in moisture and air. This requires evacuating air and moisture with a good vacuum pump for at least one hour. If a system has been open for a considerable length of time it may be advisable to evacuate the system for up to 12 hours (overnight).

• Use a wrench on both halves of a fitting that is to be disconnected, so as to avoid placing torque on any of the refrigerant lines.

• When overhauling a compressor, pour some of the oil into a clean glass and inspect it. If there is evidence of dirt, metal particles, or both, flush all refrigerant components with clean refrigerant before evacuating and recharging the system. In addition, if metal particles are present, the compressor should be replaced.

• Schrader valves may leak only when under full operating pressure. Therefore, if leakage is suspected but cannot be located, operate the system with a full charge of refrigerant and look for leaks from all Schrader valves. Replace any faulty valves.

Additional Preventive Maintenance

USING THE SYSTEM

The easiest and most important preventive maintenance for your A/C system is to be sure that it is used on a regular basis. Running the system for five minutes each month (no matter what the season) will help assure that the seals and all internal components remain lubricated.

ANTIFREEZE

In order to prevent heater core freeze-up during A/C operation, it is necessary to maintain a proper antifreeze protection. Use a hand-held antifreeze tester (hydrometer) to periodically check the condition of the antifreeze in your engine's cooling system.

➡**Antifreeze should not be used longer than the manufacturer specifies.**

RADIATOR CAP

For efficient operation of an air conditioned vehicle's cooling system, the radiator cap should have a holding pressure which meets manufacturer's specifications. A cap which fails to hold these pressures should be replaced.

CONDENSER

Any obstruction of or damage to the condenser configuration will restrict the air flow which is essential to its efficient operation. It is therefore a good rule to keep this unit clean and in proper physical shape.

➡**Bug screens which are mounted in front of the condenser, (unless they are original equipment), are regarded as obstructions.**

CONDENSATION DRAIN TUBE

This single molded drain tube expels the condensation, which accumulates on the bottom of the evaporator housing, into the engine compartment. If this tube is obstructed, the air conditioning performance can be restricted and condensation buildup can spill over onto the vehicle's floor.

SYSTEM INSPECTION

➡**R-12 refrigerant is a chlorofluorocarbon which, when released into the atmosphere, can contribute to the depletion of the ozone layer in the upper atmosphere. Ozone filters out harmful radiation from the sun.**

The easiest and often most important check for the air conditioning system consists of a visual inspection of the system components. Visually inspect the air conditioning system for refrigerant leaks, damaged compressor clutch, compressor drive belt tension and condition, plugged evaporator drain tube, blocked condenser fins, disconnected or broken wires, blown fuses, corroded connections and poor insulation.

A refrigerant leak will usually appear as an oily residue at the leakage point in the system. The oily residue soon picks up dust or dirt particles from the surrounding air and appears greasy. Through time, this will build up and appear to be a heavy dirt impregnated grease. Most leaks are caused by damaged or missing O-ring seals at the component connections, damaged charging valve cores or missing service gauge port caps.

For a thorough visual and operational inspection, check the following:

1. Check the surface of the radiator and condenser for dirt, leaves or other material which might block air flow.

2. Check for kinks in hoses and lines. Check the system for leaks.

3. Make sure the drive belt is under the proper tension. When the air conditioning is operating, make sure the drive belt is free of noise or slippage.

4. Make sure the blower motor operates at all appropriate positions, then check for distribution of the air from all outlets with the blower on **HIGH**.

➡**Keep in mind that under conditions of high humidity, air discharged from the A/C vents may not feel as cold as expected, even if the system is working properly. This is because the vaporized moisture in humid air retains heat more effectively than does dry air, making the humid air more difficult to cool.**

An antifreeze tester can be used to determine the freezing and boiling levels of the coolant

Make sure the air passage selection lever is operating correctly. Start the engine and warm it to normal operating temperature, then make sure the hot/cold selection lever is operating correctly.

ISOLATING THE COMPRESSOR

It is not necessary to discharge the system for compressor removal. The compressor can be isolated from the rest of the system, eliminating the need for recharging.

1. Connect a manifold gauge set.
2. Close both gauge hand valves and mid-position (crack) both compressor service valves.
3. Start the engine and turn on the air conditioning.
4. Turn the compressor suction valve slowly clockwise towards the front seated position. When the suction pressure drops to zero, stop the engine and turn off the air conditioning. Quickly front seat the valve completely.
5. Front seat the discharge service valve.
6. Loosen the oil level check plug to remove any internal pressure.

The compressor is now isolated and the service valves can now be removed.

DISCHARGING, EVACUATING & CHARGING

♦ See Figure 25

Discharging, evacuating and charging the air conditioning system must be performed by a properly trained and certified mechanic in a facility equipped with refrigerant recovery/recycling equipment that meets SAE standards for the type of system to be serviced.

If you don't have access to the necessary equipment, we recommend that you take your vehicle to a reputable service station to have the work done. If you still wish to perform repairs on the vehicle, have them discharge the system, then take your vehicle home and perform the necessary work. When you are finished, return the vehicle to the station for evacuation and charging. Just be sure to cap ALL A/C system fittings immediately after opening them and keep them protected until the system is recharged.

Fig. 25 Typical air conditioning system components and directional flow of the refrigerant

Windshield Wipers

ELEMENT (REFILL) CARE & REPLACEMENT

For maximum effectiveness and longest element life, the windshield and wiper blades should be kept clean. Dirt, tree sap, road tar and so on will cause streaking, smearing and blade deterioration if left on the glass. It is advisable to wash the windshield carefully with a commercial glass cleaner at least once a month. Wipe off the rubber blades with the wet rag afterwards. Do not attempt to move wipers across the windshield by hand; damage to the motor and drive mechanism will result.

To inspect and/or replace the wiper blade elements, place the wiper switch in the **LOW** speed position and the ignition switch in the **ACC** position. When the wiper blades are approximately vertical on the windshield, turn the ignition switch to **OFF.**

Examine the wiper blade elements. If they are found to be cracked, broken or torn, they should be replaced immediately. Replacement intervals will vary with usage, although ozone deterioration usually limits element life to about one year. If the wiper pattern is smeared or streaked, or if the blade chatters across the glass, the elements should be replaced. It is easiest and most sensible to replace the elements in pairs.

If your vehicle is equipped with aftermarket blades, there are several different types of refills and your vehicle might have any kind. Aftermarket blades and arms rarely use the exact same type blade or refill as the original equipment. Here are some typical aftermarket blades; not all may be available for your vehicle:

The Anco® type uses a release button that is pushed down to allow the refill to slide out of the yoke jaws. The new refill slides back into the frame and locks in place.

Some Trico® refills are removed by locating where the metal backing strip or the refill is wider. Insert a small screwdriver blade between the frame and metal backing strip. Press down to release the refill from the retaining tab.

Other types of Trico® refills have two metal tabs which are unlocked by squeezing them together. The rubber filler can then be withdrawn from the frame jaws. A new refill is installed by in-

Lexor® wiper blade and fit kit

Pylon® wiper blade and adaptor

Bosch® wiper blade and fit kit

Trico® wiper blade and fit kit

Tripledge® wiper blade and fit kit

On Trico® wiper blades, the tab at the end of the blade must be turned up . . .

To remove and install a Lexor® wiper blade refill, slip out the old insert and slide in a new one

. . . then the insert can be removed. After installing the replacement insert, bend the tab back

On Pylon® inserts, the clip at the end has to be removed prior to sliding the insert off

The Tripledge® wiper blade insert is removed and installed using a securing clip

BLADE REPLACEMENT

1. CYCLE ARM AND BLADE ASSEMBLY TO UP POSITION-ON THE WINDSHIELD WHERE REMOVAL OF BLADE ASSEMBLY CAN BE PERFORMED WITHOUT DIFFICULTY. TURN IGNITION KEY OFF AT DESIRED POSITION.

2. TO REMOVE BLADE ASSEMBLY, INSERT SCREWDRIVER IN SLOT, PUSH DOWN ON SPRING LOCK AND PULL BLADE ASSEMBLY FROM PIN (VIEW A)

3. TO INSTALL, PUSH THE BLADE ASSEMBLY ON THE PIN SO THAT THE SPRING LOCK ENGAGES THE PIN (VIEW A). BE SURE THE BLADE ASSEMBLY IS SECURELY ATTACHED TO PIN

VIEW A

NOTE: INSERT SCREWDRIVER 3.2 mm (1/8 INCH) OR LESS PAST THIS EDGE

TWIST CLOCKWISE

ELEMENT REPLACEMENT

1 INSERT SCREWDRIVER BETWEEN THE EDGE OF THE SUPER STRUCTURE AND THE BLADE BACKING DRIP (VIEW B) TWIST SCREWDRIVER SLOWLY UNTIL ELEMENT CLEARS ONE SIDE OF THE SUPER STRUCTURE CLAW

2 SLIDE THE ELEMENT INTO THE SUPER STRUCTURE CLAWS

VIEW B

4 INSERT ELEMENT INTO ONE SIDE OF THE END CLAWS (VIEW D) AND WITH A ROCKING MOTION PUSH ELEMENT UPWARD UNTIL IT SNAPS IN (VIEW E)

VIEW D

SLIDE ELEMENT STARTING AT THIS POINT

ELEMENT STOP (BOTH ENDS)

3. SLIDE THE ELEMENT INTO THE SUPER STRUCTURE CLAWS, STARTING WITH SECOND SET FROM EITHER END (VIEW C) AND CONTINUE TO SLIDE THE BLADE ELEMENT INTO ALL THE SUPER STRUCTURE CLAWS TO THE ELEMENT STOP (VIEW C)

VIEW C

VIEW E

Trico® wiper blade insert (element) replacement

BLADE REPLACEMENT

1. Cycle arm and blade assembly to a position on the windshield where removal of blade assembly can be performed without difficulty. Turn ignition key off at desired position.
2. To remove blade assembly from wiper arm, pull up on spring lock and pull blade assembly from pin (View A). Be sure spring lock is not pulled excessively or it will become distorted.
3. To install, push the blade assembly onto the pin so that the spring lock engages the pin (View A). Be sure the blade assembly is securely attached to pin.

ELEMENT REPLACEMENT

1. In the plastic backing strip which is part of the rubber blade assembly, there is an 11.11mm (7/16 inch) long notch located approximately one inch from either end. Locate either notch.
2. Place the frame of the wiper blade assembly on a firm surface with either notched end of the backing strip visible.
3. Grasp the frame portion of the wiper blade assembly and push down until the blade assembly is tightly bowed.
4. With the blade assembly in the bowed position, grasp the tip of the backing strip firmly, pulling up and twisting C.C.W. at the same time. The backing strip will then snap out of the retaining tab on the end of the frame.
5. Lift the wiper blade assembly from the surface and slide the backing strip down the frame until the notch lines up with the next retaining tab, twist slightly, and the backing strip will snap out. Continue this operation with the remaining tabs until the blade element is completely detached from the frame.
6. To install blade element, reverse the above procedure, making sure all six (6) tabs are locked to the backing strip before installing blade to wiper arm.

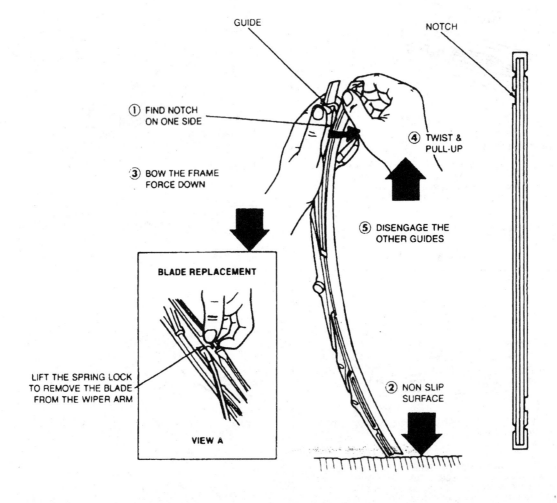

Tridon® wiper blade insert (element) replacement

serting the refill into the front frame jaws and sliding it rearward to engage the remaining frame jaws. There are usually four jaws; be certain when installing that the refill is engaged in all of them. At the end of its travel, the tabs will lock into place on the front jaws of the wiper blade frame.

Another type of refill is made from polycarbonate. The refill has a simple locking device at one end which flexes downward out of the groove into which the jaws of the holder fit, allowing easy release. By sliding the new refill through all the jaws and pushing through the slight resistance when it reaches the end of its travel, the refill will lock into position.

To replace the Tridon® refill, it is necessary to remove the wiper blade. This refill has a plastic backing strip with a notch about 1 in. (25mm) from the end. Hold the blade (frame) on a hard surface so that the frame is tightly bowed. Grip the tip of the backing strip and pull up while twisting counterclockwise. The backing strip will snap out of the retaining tab. Do this for the remaining tabs until the refill is free of the blade. The length of these refills is molded into the end and they should be replaced with identical types.

Regardless of the type of refill used, be sure to follow the part manufacturer's instructions closely. Make sure that all of the frame jaws are engaged as the refill is pushed into place and locked. If the metal blade holder and frame are allowed to touch the glass during wiper operation, the glass will be scratched.

Tires and Wheels

Common sense and good driving habits will afford maximum tire life. Fast starts, sudden stops and hard cornering are hard on tires and will shorten their useful life span. Make sure that you don't overload the vehicle or run with incorrect pressure in the tires. Both of these practices will increase tread wear.

➡**For optimum tire life, keep the tires properly inflated, rotate them often and have the wheel alignment checked periodically.**

Inspect your tires frequently. Be especially careful to watch for bubbles in the tread or sidewall, deep cuts or underinflation. Re-

place any tires with bubbles in the sidewall. If cuts are so deep that they penetrate to the cords, discard the tire. Any cut in the sidewall of a radial tire renders it unsafe. Also look for uneven tread wear patterns that may indicate the front end is out of alignment or that the tires are out of balance.

TIRE ROTATION

Tires must be rotated periodically to equalize wear patterns that vary with a tire's position on the vehicle. Tires will also wear in an uneven way as the front steering/suspension system wears to the point where the alignment should be reset.

Rotating the tires will ensure maximum life for the tires as a set, so you will not have to discard a tire early due to wear on only part of the tread. Regular rotation is required to equalize wear.

When rotating "unidirectional tires," make sure that they always roll in the same direction. This means that a tire used on the left

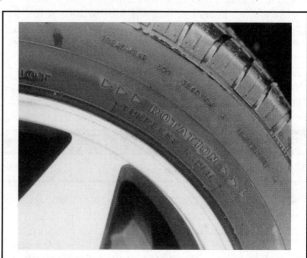

Unidirectional tires are identifiable by sidewall arrows and/or the word "rotation"

Common tire rotation patterns for 4 and 5-wheel rotations

side of the vehicle must not be switched to the right side and vice-versa. Such tires should only be rotated front-to-rear or rear-to-front, while always remaining on the same side of the vehicle. These tires are marked on the sidewall as to the direction of rotation; observe the marks when reinstalling the tire(s).

Some styled or "mag" wheels may have different offsets front to rear. In these cases, the rear wheels must not be used up front and vice-versa. Furthermore, if these wheels are equipped with uni-directional tires, they cannot be rotated unless the tire is re-mounted for the proper direction of rotation.

➡**The compact or space-saver spare is strictly for emergency use. It must never be included in the tire rotation or placed on the vehicle for everyday use.**

TIRE DESIGN

For maximum satisfaction, tires should be used in sets of four. Mixing of different types (radial, bias-belted, fiberglass belted) must be avoided. In most cases, the vehicle manufacturer has designated a type of tire on which the vehicle will perform best. Your first choice when replacing tires should be to use the same type of tire that the manufacturer recommends.

When radial tires are used, tire sizes and wheel diameters should be selected to maintain ground clearance and tire load capacity equivalent to the original specified tire. Radial tires should always be used in sets of four.

✳✳ CAUTION

Radial tires should never be used on only the front axle.

When selecting tires, pay attention to the original size as marked on the tire. Most tires are described using an industry size code sometimes referred to as P-Metric. This allows the exact identification of the tire specifications, regardless of the manufacturer. If selecting a different tire size or brand, remember to check the installed tire for any sign of interference with the body or suspension while the vehicle is stopping, turning sharply or heavily loaded.

Snow Tires

Good radial tires can produce a big advantage in slippery weather, but in snow, a street radial tire does not have sufficient tread to provide traction and control. The small grooves of a street tire quickly pack with snow and the tire behaves like a billiard ball on a marble floor. The more open, chunky tread of a snow tire will self-clean as the tire turns, providing much better grip on snowy surfaces.

To satisfy municipalities requiring snow tires during weather emergencies, most snow tires carry either an M + S designation after the tire size stamped on the sidewall, or the designation "all-season." In general, no change in tire size is necessary when buying snow tires.

Most manufacturers strongly recommend the use of 4 snow tires on their vehicles for reasons of stability. If snow tires are fitted only to the drive wheels, the opposite end of the vehicle may become very unstable when braking or turning on slippery surfaces. This instability can lead to unpleasant endings if the driver can't counteract the slide in time.

Note that snow tires, whether 2 or 4, will affect vehicle han-

P-Metric tire coding

dling in all non-snow situations. The stiffer, heavier snow tires will noticeably change the turning and braking characteristics of the vehicle. Once the snow tires are installed, you must re-learn the behavior of the vehicle and drive accordingly.

➡**Consider buying extra wheels on which to mount the snow tires. Once done, the "snow wheels" can be installed and removed as needed. This eliminates the potential damage to tires or wheels from seasonal removal and installation. Even if your vehicle has styled wheels, see if inexpensive steel wheels are available. Although the look of the vehicle will change, the expensive wheels will be protected from salt, curb hits and pothole damage.**

TIRE STORAGE

If they are mounted on wheels, store the tires at proper inflation pressure. All tires should be kept in a cool, dry place. If they are stored in the garage or basement, do not let them stand on a concrete floor; set them on strips of wood, a mat or a large stack of newspaper. Keeping them away from direct moisture is of paramount importance. Tires should not be stored upright, but in a flat position.

INFLATION & INSPECTION

The importance of proper tire inflation cannot be overemphasized. A tire employs air as part of its structure. It is designed around the supporting strength of the air at a specified pressure. For this reason, improper inflation drastically reduces the tires's ability to perform as intended. A tire will lose some air in day-to-day use; having to add a few pounds of air periodically is not necessarily a sign of a leaking tire.

Two items should be a permanent fixture in every glove compartment: an accurate tire pressure gauge and a tread depth gauge. Check the tire pressure (including the spare) regularly with a pocket type gauge. Too often, the gauge on the end of the air hose at your corner garage is not accurate because it suffers too much abuse. Always check tire pressure when the tires are cold, as pressure increases with temperature. If you must move the vehicle to check the tire inflation, do not drive more than a mile before checking. A cold tire is generally one that has not been driven for more than three hours.

A plate or sticker is normally provided somewhere in the vehicle (door post, hood, tailgate or trunk lid) which shows the proper pressure for the tires. Never counteract excessive pressure build-up by bleeding off air pressure (letting some air out). This will cause the tire to run hotter and wear quicker.

✳✳ CAUTION

Never exceed the maximum tire pressure embossed on the tire! This is the pressure to be used when the tire is at maximum loading, but it is rarely the correct pressure for everyday driving. Consult the owner's manual or the tire pressure sticker for the correct tire pressure.

Once you've maintained the correct tire pressures for several weeks, you'll be familiar with the vehicle's braking and handling personality. Slight adjustments in tire pressures can fine-tune these characteristics, but never change the cold pressure specification by more than 2 psi. A slightly softer tire pressure will give a softer ride but also yield lower fuel mileage. A slightly harder tire will give crisper dry road handling but can cause skidding on wet surfaces. Unless you're fully attuned to the vehicle, stick to the recommended inflation pressures.

All tires made since 1968 have built-in tread wear indicator bars that show up as ½ in. (13mm) wide smooth bands across the tire when 1/16 in. (1.5mm) of tread remains. The appearance of tread wear indicators means that the tires should be replaced. In fact, many states have laws prohibiting the use of tires with less than this amount of tread.

You can check your own tread depth with an inexpensive gauge or by using a Lincoln head penny. Slip the Lincoln penny (with Lincoln's head upside-down) into several tread grooves. If you can see the top of Lincoln's head in 2 adjacent grooves, the tire has less than 1/16 in. (1.5mm) tread left and should be replaced. You can measure snow tires in the same manner by using the "tails" side of the Lincoln penny. If you can see the top of the Lincoln memorial, it's time to replace the snow tire(s).

Tires with deep cuts, or cuts which show bulging should be replaced immediately

- DRIVE WHEEL HEAVY ACCELERATION
- OVERINFLATION

- HARD CORNERING
- UNDERINFLATION
- LACK OF ROTATION

Examples of inflation-related tire wear patterns

Tires should be checked frequently for any sign of puncture or damage

PROPERLY INFLATED

IMPROPERLY INFLATED

RADIAL TIRE

Radial tires have a characteristic sidewall bulge; don't try to measure pressure by looking at the tire. Use a quality air pressure gauge

CONDITION	RAPID WEAR AT SHOULDERS	RAPID WEAR AT CENTER	CRACKED TREADS	WEAR ON ONE SIDE	FEATHERED EDGE	BALD SPOTS	SCALLOPED WEAR
EFFECT							
CAUSE	UNDER-INFLATION OR LACK OF ROTATION	OVER-INFLATION OR LACK OF ROTATION	UNDER-INFLATION OR EXCESSIVE SPEED*	EXCESSIVE CAMBER	INCORRECT TOE	UNBALANCED WHEEL OR TIRE DEFECT*	LACK OF ROTATION OF TIRES OR WORN OR OUT-OF-ALIGNMENT SUSPENSION.
CORRECTION		ADJUST PRESSURE TO SPECIFICATIONS WHEN TIRES ARE COOL ROTATE TIRES		ADJUST CAMBER TO SPECIFICATIONS	ADJUST TOE-IN TO SPECIFICATIONS	DYNAMIC OR STATIC BALANCE WHEELS	ROTATE TIRES AND INSPECT SUSPENSION

*HAVE TIRE INSPECTED FOR FURTHER USE.

Common tire wear patterns and causes

CARE OF SPECIAL WHEELS

If you have invested money in magnesium, aluminum alloy or sport wheels, special precautions should be taken to make sure your investment is not wasted and that your special wheels look good for the life of the vehicle.

Special wheels are easily damaged and/or scratched. Occasionally check the rims for cracking, impact damage or air leaks. If any of these are found, replace the wheel. But in order to prevent this type of damage and the costly replacement of a special wheel, observe the following precautions:

• Use extra care not to damage the wheels during removal, installation, balancing, etc. After removal of the wheels from the vehicle, place them on a mat or other protective surface. If they are to be stored for any length of time, support them on strips of wood. Never store tires and wheels upright; the tread may develop flat spots.

• When driving, watch for hazards; it doesn't take much to crack a wheel.

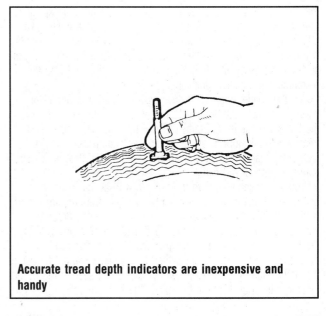

Accurate tread depth indicators are inexpensive and handy

Tread wear indicators will appear when the tire is worn

A penny works well for a quick check of tread depth

• When washing, use a mild soap or non-abrasive dish detergent (keeping in mind that detergent tends to remove wax). Avoid cleansers with abrasives or the use of hard brushes. There are many cleaners and polishes for special wheels.

• If possible, remove the wheels during the winter. Salt and sand used for snow removal can severely damage the finish of a wheel.

• Make certain the recommended lug nut torque is never exceeded or the wheel may crack. Never use snow chains on special wheels; severe scratching will occur.

Troubleshooting Basic Wheel Problems

Problem	Cause	Solution
The car's front end vibrates at high speed	• The wheels are out of balance • Wheels are out of alignment	• Have wheels balanced • Have wheel alignment checked/adjusted
Car pulls to either side	• Wheels are out of alignment • Unequal tire pressure • Different size tires or wheels	• Have wheel alignment checked/adjusted • Check/adjust tire pressure • Change tires or wheels to same size
The car's wheel(s) wobbles	• Loose wheel lug nuts • Wheels out of balance • Damaged wheel • Wheels are out of alignment • Worn or damaged ball joint • Excessive play in the steering linkage (usually due to worn parts) • Defective shock absorber	• Tighten wheel lug nuts • Have tires balanced • Raise car and spin the wheel. If the wheel is bent, it should be replaced • Have wheel alignment checked/adjusted • Check ball joints • Check steering linkage • Check shock absorbers
Tires wear unevenly or prematurely	• Incorrect wheel size • Wheels are out of balance • Wheels are out of alignment	• Check if wheel and tire size are compatible • Have wheels balanced • Have wheel alignment checked/adjusted

Troubleshooting Basic Tire Problems

Problem	Cause	Solution
The car's front end vibrates at high speeds and the steering wheel shakes	• Wheels out of balance • Front end needs aligning	• Have wheels balanced • Have front end alignment checked
The car pulls to one side while cruising	• Unequal tire pressure (car will usually pull to the low side) • Mismatched tires • Front end needs aligning	• Check/adjust tire pressure • Be sure tires are of the same type and size • Have front end alignment checked
Abnormal, excessive or uneven tire wear See "How to Read Tire Wear"	• Infrequent tire rotation • Improper tire pressure • Sudden stops/starts or high speed on curves	• Rotate tires more frequently to equalize wear • Check/adjust pressure • Correct driving habits
Tire squeals	• Improper tire pressure • Front end needs aligning	• Check/adjust tire pressure • Have front end alignment checked

Tire Size Comparison Chart

"Letter" sizes			Inch Sizes	Metric-inch Sizes		
"60 Series"	"70 Series"	"78 Series"	1965–77	"60 Series"	"70 Series"	"80 Series"
		Y78-12	5.50-12, 5.60-12 6.00-12	165/60-12	165/70-12	155-12
		W78-13	5.20-13	165/60-13	145/70-13	135-13
		Y78-13	5.60-13	175/60-13	155/70-13	145-13
			6.15-13	185/60-13	165/70-13	155-13, P155/80-13
A60-13	A70-13	A78-13	6.40-13	195/60-13	175/70-13	165-13
B60-13	B70-13	B78-13	6.70-13	205/60-13	185/70-13	175-13
			6.90-13			
C60-13	C70-13	C78-13	7.00-13	215/60-13	195/70-13	185-13
D60-13	D70-13	D78-13	7.25-13			
E60-13	E70-13	E78-13	7.75-13			195-13
			5.20-14	165/60-14	145/70-14	135-14
			5.60-14	175/60-14	155/70-14	145-14
			5.90-14			
A60-14	A70-14	A78-14	6.15-14	185/60-14	165/70-14	155-14
	B70-14	B78-14	6.45-14	195/60-14	175/70-14	165-14
	C70-14	C78-14	6.95-14	205/60-14	185/70-14	175-14
D60-14	D70-14	D78-14				
E60-14	E70-14	E78-14	7.35-14	215/60-14	195/70-14	185-14
F60-14	F70-14	F78-14, F83-14	7.75-14	225/60-14	200/70-14	195-14
G60-14	G70-14	G77-14, G78-14	8.25-14	235/60-14	205/70-14	205-14
H60-14	H70-14	H78-14	8.55-14	245/60-14	215/70-14	215-14
J60-14	J70-14	J78-14	8.85-14	255/60-14	225/70-14	225-14
L60-14	L70-14		9.15-14	265/60-14	235/70-14	
	A70-15	A78-15	5.60-15	185/60-15	165/70-15	155-15
B60-15	B70-15	B78-15	6.35-15	195/60-15	175/70-15	165-15
C60-15	C70-15	C78-15	6.85-15	205/60-15	185/70-15	175-15
	D70-15	D78-15				
E60-15	E70-15	E78-15	7.35-15	215/60-15	195/70-15	185-15
F60-15	F70-15	F78-15	7.75-15	225/60-15	205/70-15	195-15
G60-15	G70-15	G78-15	8.15-15/8.25-15	235/60-15	215/70-15	205-15
H60-15	H70-15	H78-15	8.45-15/8.55-15	245/60-15	225/70-15	215-15
J60-15	J70-15	J78-15	8.85-15/8.90-15	255/60-15	235/70-15	225-15
	K70-15		9.00-15	265/60-15	245/70-15	230-15
L60-15	L70-15	L78-15, L84-15	9.15-15			235-15
	M70-15	M78-15				255-15
		N78-15				

Note: Every size tire is not listed and many size comparisons are approximate, based on load ratings. Wider tires than those supplied new with the vehicle, should always be checked for clearance.

FLUIDS AND LUBRICANTS

Fluid Disposal

Used fluids such as engine oil, transmission fluid, antifreeze and brake fluid are hazardous wastes and must be disposed of properly. Before draining any fluids, consult with the local authorities; in many areas, waste oil, etc. is being accepted as a part of recycling programs. A number of service stations and auto parts stores are also accepting waste fluids for recycling.

Be sure of the recycling center's policies before draining any fluids, as many will not accept different fluids that have been mixed together, such as oil and antifreeze.

Fuel and Oil Recommendations

➡Be aware that your engine's fuel requirement can change with time, mainly due to carbon buildup changing the compression ratio. If your engine pings, knocks, or runs on, switch to a higher grade of fuel and check the ignition timing as soon as possible. Do not retard the timing from specification unless you still have trouble with the higher grade fuel, and then not more than 3°. Retarded timing will reduce power output and fuel mileage and increase engine temperature.

Only oils labeled SF are approved under warranty for use. Select the viscosity rating to be used by your type of driving and the temperature range anticipated before the next oil change.

The multi-viscosity oils offer the important advantage of being adaptable to temperature extremes. They can allow easy starts at low temperatures, yet still give good protection at high speeds and warm temperatures. This is a decided advantage in changeable climate or in long distance touring.

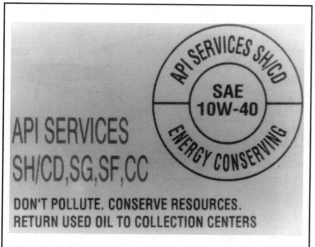

Look for the API oil identification label when choosing your engine oil

Oil Viscosity Selector

Lowest Temperature Expected (deg F)	Multi-Viscosity (SAE)	Single-Viscosity (SAE)
Above 32	10W-30 10W-40 10W-50 20W-50	20W-20
Above 0	10W-30 10W-40 10W-50	10W*
Below 0	5W-20 5W-30	10W*

*Do not run above 65 mph with SAE 10W; oil consumption will be excessive.

➡If your engine takes a long time in building up oil pressure after starting in warm weather, when using 10W-30 or 10W-40 oil, the problem can often be solved by switching to 20W-40. This is not specifically recommended by AMC, but it is a proven method.

Engine Oil

OIL LEVEL CHECK

✱✱ CAUTION

The EPA warns that prolonged contact with used engine oil may cause a number of skin disorders, including cancer! You should make every effort to minimize your exposure to used engine oil. Protective gloves should be worn when changing the oil. Wash your hands and any other exposed skin areas as soon as possible after exposure to used engine oil. Soap and water, or waterless hand cleaner should be used.

The engine oil should be checked on a regular basis, at least at every gas stop, or more often under severe usage. If the check is made at a gas stop, wait until the tank has been filled. If the level is checked immediately after stopping, a false low reading will result. The proper level is between the FULL and ADD marks on the dipstick, preferable at FULL.

1. Pull out the dipstick on the side of the engine. Do not take a reading yet, unless the engine has been off all night.
2. Wipe off the dipstick with a clean rag.
3. Replace the dipstick, count slowly to ten or do whatever you like for ten seconds, and remove it. Check the level on the dipstick.
4. If the level is at the ADD mark, adding one full quart at the filler (usually marked OIL) will bring it to the FULL mark. Never add a full quart if the level is not down to the ADD mark, because

Remove the engine dipstick from the tube, wipe it clean and reinsert it in the tube again . . .

. . . then remove the dipstick again, hold it horizontally and check the fluid level as indicated

. . . then turn the plug out by hand and drain the oil into a suitable container

this overfilling will result in possible damage to engine seals or rapid oil consumption. See 'Oil and Fuel Recommendations' later in this section for the proper oils.

➡**If you need to add oil when the level is down less than a full quart, you will have a problem storing partly full quart oil cans. The plastic covers that come with coffee cans are ideal for covering these cans.**

5. Replace the dipstick, seating it firmly.

OIL & FILTER CHANGE

⬥ **See Figures 26 thru 33**

The oil should always be changed while hot, so the dirt and particles will still be suspended in the oil when it drains out of the engine. Hot oil also flows better providing for a more complete removal of old oil. To change the oil and filter:

1. Run the engine until it reaches normal operating temperature.

Fig. 26 A crescent wrench may be used to loosen the oil pan drain plug but, a socket is preferred

To drain the engine oil, remove the pan drain plug with a wrench or socket . . .

Fig. 27 Turn the plug out by hand keeping inward pressure on it to prevent being burned with hot oil

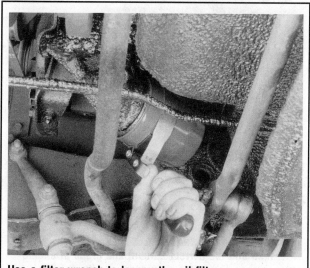

Use a filter wrench to loosen the oil filter

Before installing a new oil filter, lightly coat the rubber gasket with clean oil

After the filter has been loosened, twist the filter off by hand. Be careful of the hot oil!

Install the new filter and hand-tighten it only. Do not use a strap wrench to tighten the filter

Fig. 28 When removing the oil filter make sure that the gasket also comes off with it from the mounting base

Fig. 29 Install a new filter on the mounting base until it is snug then, tighten it another 1/2–1 turn

Fig. 30 Clean the dirt and debris from the area around the oil pan drain hole . . .

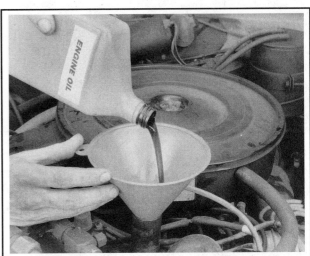

. . . then add the correct amount and grade of engine oil

Fig. 31 . . . then install the oil pan drain plug using a wrench

Fig. 32 After adding the oil remove the oil dipstick and check that the level is correct

2. Jack up the front of the car and support it on safety stands.

3. Slide a drain pan of at least 6 quarts capacity under the oil pan.

4. Loosen the drain plug. Put on a pair of gloves and turn the drain plug out by hand. By keeping an inward pressure on the plug as you unscrew it, oil won't escape past the threads and you can remove it without being burned by hot oil.

✳✳ CAUTION

When you are ready to release the plug, pull it away from the drain hole quickly, to avoid being burned by the hot oil.

5. Allow the oil to drain completely and then install the drain plug. Don't overtighten the plug, or you'll be buying a new pan or a trick replacement plug for stripped threads.

6. Using a strap wrench, remove the oil filter. Keep in mind that it's holding about one quart of dirty, hot oil.

To add oil to the crankcase, remove the oil filler cap . . .

Fig. 33 Exploded view of a typical oil filter and related components

7. Empty the old filter into the drain pan and dispose of the filter.

8. Using a clean rag, wipe off the filter adapter on the engine block. Be sure that the rag doesn't leave any lint which could clog an oil passage.

9. Coat the rubber gasket on the filter with fresh oil. Spin it onto the engine by hand; when the gasket touches the adapter surface, give it another ½–¾ turn. No more, or you'll squash the gasket and it may leak.

10. Recheck that the drain plug and oil filter are properly tightened. Remove the oil pan and lower the vehicle.

11. Locate and remove the oil filler cap and place a funnel in the filler opening.

12. Refer to the capacities chart in this section for your vehicle's specified amount of engine oil.

13. Refill the engine with the correct amount and viscosity of fresh oil.

14. As you add oil, check the level on the dipstick. It is normal for the level to be a bit above the full mark. Start the engine and allow it to idle for a few minutes.

✳✳ CAUTION

Do not run the engine above idle speed until it has built up oil pressure, indicated when the oil light goes out.

15. Shut off the engine, allow the oil to drain back into the crankcase, and check the oil level. Check around the filter and drain plug for any leaks, and correct as necessary.

Assuming that the recommended oils are used, the oil and filter should be changed at the intervals shown in the 'Service Intervals' chart. This interval should be halved under severe usage such as dusty conditions, trailer towing, prolonged high speeds, or repeated short trips in freezing temperatures.

✳✳ CAUTION

The EPA warns that prolonged contact with used engine oil may cause a number of skin disorders, including cancer! You should make every effort to minimize your exposure to used engine oil. Protective gloves should be worn when changing the oil. Wash your hands and any other exposed skin areas as soon as possible after exposure to used engine oil. Soap and water, or waterless hand cleaner should be used.

Manual Transmission

FLUID LEVEL CHECK

▶ **See Figures 34, 35 and 36**

The transmission level should be checked when the oil is changed. Since your hands are apt to be pretty oily at these

Manual Transmission Fluid Recommendations

Transmission	Fluid
HR-1	80W-90
SR-4	85W-90
T-150	80W-90
T-4	Dexron® II ATF
T-5	Dexron® II ATF
T-14	80W-90

Fig. 34 Typical manual transmission fill and drain plugs—drain plug at the bottom center

Fig. 35 Manual transmission fill and drain plugs, using a tailshaft bolt as the drain plug

Fig. 36 Drain bolt location for the Eagle models equipped a manual transmission

times, you shouldn't mind this job. To check the level, remove the filler plug in the right side of the transmission case from under the car. There is a similar plug in the overdrive case at the rear of the transmission. With the car level, oil should drip out. If it runs our in a steady stream, let it run until it just drips. Any fluid required can be pumped in with a suction gun. All transmissions use SAE 80W-90 Gear oil, except the 1982 T4 and T5. These use Dexron®II automatic transmission fluid.

Pacer 3-Speed with Overdrive

The overdrive unit shares a common supply of lubricant with the manual transmission. The fluid level is checked at the transmission fill plug in the same manner as for manual transmissions without overdrive. The fluid level should be checked every 5,000 miles.

If lubricant is required, use only API GL-4 SAE 80W-140 gear lubricant.

✳✳ CAUTION

Don't use antifriction or limited slip differential lubricant in the transmission/overdrive unit.

FLUID CHANGE

The manufacturer says that the transmission lubricant need never be changed, except for overhaul. However, if you bought your car used, or if you subject it to heavy duty use, you may want to change the lubricant. To do this, first drive the car until it is warm, then:

1. Wipe off the area around the drain and filler plugs for the transmission and overdrive. Remove both plugs and drain the oil into a container.

2. Replace the drain plug after cleaning off the threads.

3. Use a suction gun to fill the transmission or overdrive through the filler hole. The correct level is even with the bottom of the filler hoe. See 'Fluid level Checks,' earlier in the Chapter, for the proper lubricants.

Automatic Transmission

FLUID LEVEL CHECK

Check the level at oil change intervals. With the transmission at operating temperature, proceed as follows:

1. The normal operating temperature of 175°F is not obtained until the car has been driven several miles, making frequent starts and stops.
2. Park the car on a level surface. Set the parking brake.
3. With the engine idling, shift the selector lever through all gear positions.
4. Shift into Neutral.
5. Pull out the dipstick at the right rear of the engine. Wipe it off with a clean rag.
6. Replace the dipstick and push it in all the way.
7. Pull out the dipstick after ten seconds and take a reading.

Use a scraper to clean the old gasket residue from both mating surfaces

Remove the transmission dipstick to check the fluid level

Use a screwdriver to remove the transmission filter retainers . . .

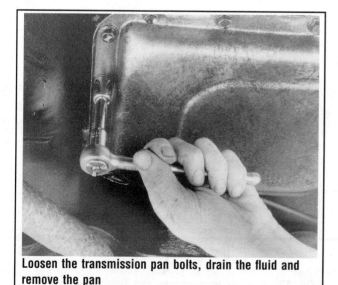

Loosen the transmission pan bolts, drain the fluid and remove the pan

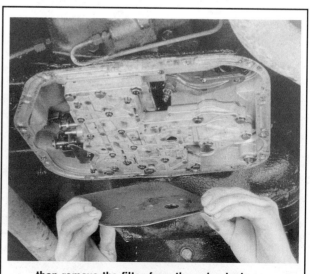

. . . then remove the filter from the valve body

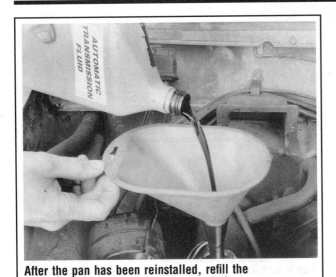

After the pan has been reinstalled, refill the transmission through the dipstick tube

The level should be between the FULL and ADD ONE PINT marks.

8. If the level is at or below the add one pint mark, add fluid through the dipstick tube to bring the level from add one pint to full. Be very cautious not to overfill the transmission.

➡The proper transmission fluid is AMC or DEXRON®II automatic transmission fluid.

FLUID & FILTER CHANGE

◗ See Figures 37 thru 42

The manufacturer says that the transmission fluid doesn't ever have to be changed, unless the car is used for heavy work such as trailering. In this case, the fluid is to be changed every 25,000 miles. A band adjustment is also required at the same interval for these cars.

➡See Section 6 for details of the band adjustment.

Fig. 37 Loosen the transmission pan bolts and drain the fluid

Fig. 38 Automatic transmission filter location. Do not disturb the valve body screws when removing the filter

Fig. 39 Unscrew the filter retainers and discard the old filter

Fig. 40 Clean the transmission pan thoroughly with a solvent and let it air dry

Fig. 41 Use a new gasket and install the transmission pan

Fig. 42 Transmission fluid may be added through the dipstick tube using a funnel and a flexible hose

1. Drive the car until it is thoroughly warm.
2. Unbolt the pan. It holds six or more quarts, so be ready.

➡**If the fluid removed smells burnt, serious transmission troubles, probably due to overheating should be suspected.**

3. Unscrew and discard the filter.
4. Install a new filter. The proper torque is 28 inch lbs., though the torque wrench isn't absolutely necessary here.
5. Clean out the pan, being extremely careful not to leave any lint from rags inside.
6. Replace the pan with a new gasket. Tighten the bolts to 11 ft. lb. in a crisscross pattern. The torque wrench isn't absolutely essential.
7. Pour six quarts of DEXRON®II or AMC automatic transmission fluid through the dipstick tube.
8. Start the engine in Neutral and let it idle for two minutes or more.
9. Hold you foot on the Brake and shift through D, 2 and R and back to N.

10. Add enough fluid to bring the level to the add one pint mark.
11. Operate the car until the transmission is thoroughly warmed up, then check the level as explained previously under 'Fluid Level Checks.' Add fluid as necessary.

Coolant

COOLANT LEVEL CHECK

The coolant level should be maintained 1½–2″ (38–51mm) below the bottom of the filler cap when the engine is cold. Since operating temperatures reach as high as +205°F (+96°C) for the four and six, and +190°F (+88°C) for the V8s, coolant could be forced out of the radiator if it is filled too high. The radiator coolant level should be checked regularly, such as every time you fill the vehicle with gas. Never open the radiator cap of an engine

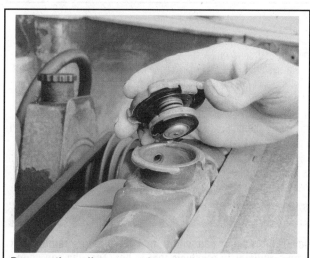

Remove the radiator cap when checking or adding to the coolant level

Loosen the draincock to drain the radiator

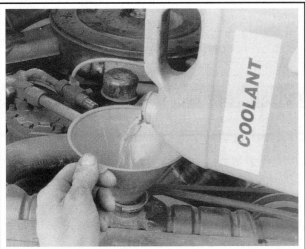

Use a funnel and add the correct coolant mixture to the system

that hasn't had sufficient time to cool or the pressure can blow off the cap and send out a spray of scalding water.

On systems with a coolant recovery tank, maintain the coolant level at the level marks on the recovery bottle.

For best protection against freezing and overheating, maintain an approximate 50% water and 50% ethylene glycol antifreeze mixture in the cooling system. Do not mix different brands of antifreeze to avoid possible chemical damage to the cooling system.

Avoid using water that is known to have a high alkaline content or is very hard, except in emergency situations. Drain and flush the cooling system as soon as possible after using such water.

> ✳✳ **CAUTION**
>
> **Cover the radiator cap with a thick cloth before removing it from a radiator in a vehicle that is hot. Turn the cap counterclockwise slowly until pressure can be heard escaping. Allow all pressure to escape from the radiator before completely removing the radiator cap. It is best to allow the engine to cool if possible, before removing the radiator cap.**

➡ **Never add cold water to an overheated engine while the engine is not running.**

After filling the radiator, run the engine until it reaches normal operating temperature, to make sure that the thermostat has opened and all the air is bled from the system.

DRAINING, FLUSHING & REFILLING

> ✳✳ **CAUTION**
>
> **When draining engine coolant, keep in mind that cats and dogs are attracted to ethylene glycol antifreeze and could drink any that is left in an uncovered container or in puddles on the ground. This will prove fatal in sufficient quan-**

tity. Always drain coolant into a sealable container. Coolant should be reused unless it is contaminated or is several years old.

To drain the cooling system, allow the engine to cool down **BEFORE ATTEMPTING TO REMOVE THE RADIATOR CAP.** Then turn the cap until it hisses. Wait until all pressure is off the cap before removing it completely.

> ✳✳ **CAUTION**
>
> **To avoid burns and scalding, always handle a warm radiator cap with a heavy rag.**

1. At the dash, set the heater TEMP control lever to the fully HOT position.

2. With the radiator cap removed, drain the radiator by loosening the petcock at the bottom of the radiator. Locate any drain plugs in the block and remove them. Flush the radiator with water until the fluid runs clear.

3. Close the petcock and replace the plug(s), then refill the system with a 50/50 mix of ethylene glycol antifreeze. Fill the system to ¾–1¼" (19.05–31.75mm) from the bottom of the filler neck. Reinstall the radiator cap.

➡ **If equipped with a fluid reservoir tank, fill it up to the MAX level.**

4. Operate the engine at 2,000 rpm for a few minutes and check the system for signs of leaks.

Radiator Cap Inspection

Allow the engine to cool sufficiently before attempting to remove the radiator cap. Use a rag to cover the cap, then remove by pressing down and turning counterclockwise to the first stop. If any hissing is noted (indicating the release of pressure), wait until the hissing stops completely, then press down again and turn counterclockwise until the cap can be removed.

> ✳✳ **CAUTION**
>
> **DO NOT attempt to remove the radiator cap while the engine is hot. Severe personal injury from steam burns can result.**

Check the condition of the radiator cap gasket and seal inside of the cap. The radiator cap is designed to seal the cooling system under normal operating conditions which allows the build up of a certain amount of pressure (this pressure rating is stamped or printed on the cap). The pressure in the system raises the boiling point of the coolant to help prevent overheating. If the radiator cap does not seal, the boiling point of the coolant is lowered and overheating will occur. If the cap must be replaced, purchase the new cap according to the pressure rating which is specified for your vehicle.

Prior to installing the radiator cap, inspect and clean the filler neck. If you are reusing the old cap, clean it thoroughly with clear water. After turning the cap on, make sure the arrows align with the overflow hose.

Be sure the rubber gasket on the radiator cap has a tight seal

Periodically remove all debris from the radiator fins

Cooling systems should be pressure tested for leaks periodically

NOTE: HEATER COOLANT FLOW CIRCUIT IS ALWAYS OPEN EXCEPT WHEN IN MAX. A/C OR OFF MODES

SHUT OFF VALVE A/C ONLY

HEATER

INTAKE MANIFOLD COOLANT FLOW "METERED" FROM REAR TO FRONT AND BELOW EXHAUST HEAT CROSSOVER

COOLANT FLOW - PUMP TO CYLINDER BLOCK, UP THROUGH CYLINDER HEADS TO INTAKE MANIFOLD WATER BOX TO RADIATOR — TO PUMP

BYPASS ★

★BYPASS
THERMOSTAT CLOSED — HIGH FLOW
THERMOSTAT OPEN — LOW FLOW

CYLINDER HEAD   BLOCK

Cutaway view of a typical cooling system flow

Brake Master Cylinder

FLUID LEVEL CHECK

▶ **See Figure 43**

The master cylinder is in the left rear of the engine compartment, on the firewall. With power brakes, there is a round container behind the cylinder. To check the fluid level as recommended at each oil change interval:

1. Clean off the area around the cap. Very small particles of dirt can cause serious difficulties in the brake system.

2. Remove the bolt retaining the cover, or, on later models, pry the wire retaining the cap to one side with a prytool. Take off the cover.

3. The proper level in each of the two reservoirs is within ¼ in. (6mm) of the top. Add fluid as necessary.

✳✳ CAUTION

Brake fluid dissolves paint.

4. Replace the cover. Replace the retaining bolt or snap the retaining wire back in place.

POWER BRAKE DIAPHRAGM

MASTER CYLINDER

Fig. 43 On the power brake system the master cylinder is mounted on the power brake diaphragm

In some cases it may be necessary to use a prytool to remove the brake master cylinder reservoir cover

Use an Allen wrench to loosen the rear axle filler plug

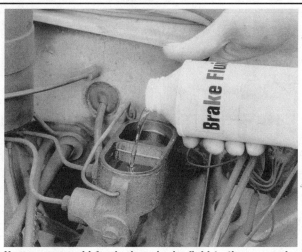

If necessary, add fresh clean brake fluid to the reservoir until the proper level is reached

Unscrew the filler plug and remove it from the opening

✳✳ CAUTION

Use only high quality brake fluid designated for disc brake systems, even if you don't have discs. Lesser fluids can boil during heavy braking, causing complete loss of braking power. Make sure that brake fluid containers are sealed tightly; brake fluid can absorb moisture from the air.

Drive Axles

FLUID LEVEL CHECK

It is recommended that the front or rear axle lubricant level be checked at each engine oil change. The filler plug may be located either on the front or the rear of the housing, depending on the axle used. Sometimes it is an allen head plug. When the unit is

Insert your finger in the plug opening and check that the fluid is level with the hole

If the level is low, add gear oil until the fluid is even with the opening

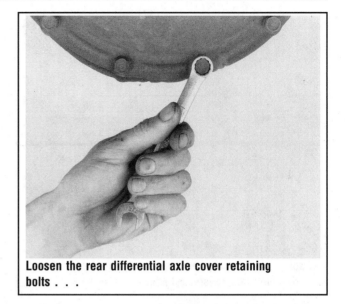

Loosen the rear differential axle cover retaining bolts . . .

warm, the level should be even with the plug hole; when cold, it may be a bit below. A finger makes a fine dipstick. Lubricant may be added with a suction gun. Standard differentials may use SAE 80W GL-5 gear lubricant or the special lubricant made for limited slip differentials. Limited slip differentials must use the special lubricant or they will be damaged. If you don't want to go to the trouble of finding our, then the obvious solution is to use the special limited slip stuff.

DRAIN & REFILL

▶ **See Figure 44**

1. Park the vehicle on the level with the axles at normal operating temperature.

Fig. 44 Location of the drive axle fill plugs and the correct fluid level on the Eagle front drive axle

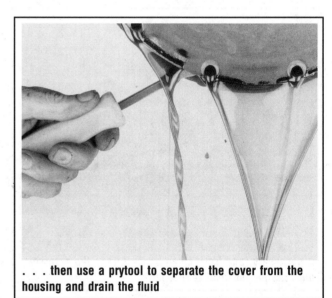

. . . then use a prytool to separate the cover from the housing and drain the fluid

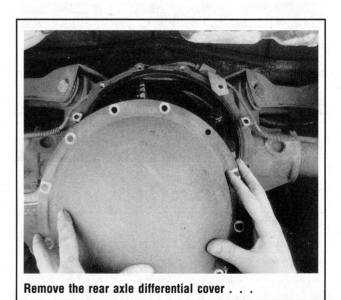

Remove the rear axle differential cover . . .

. . . then inspect the gears for signs of wear or damage

Remove the gasket from the cover and clean off any residue from both mating surfaces

2. Place a pan of at least 6 pints capacity under the differential housing.

3. Remove the filler plug.

4. If you have a drain plug, remove it. If not, unbolt and remove the differential cover.

5. Install the drain plug, or differential cover. Use a new gasket if the differential cover has been removed.

6. Install the drain plug and tighten it so it will not leak. Do not overtighten.

➡It is usually a good idea to replace the gasket at this time.

7. Refill the differential with the proper lubricant—do not overfill!

Transfer Case

♦ See Figure 45

Drain and fill the transfer case at the interval recommended in the Maintenance Intervals chart. The drain and fill plugs are on

Fig. 45 Correct fluid level and fill plug location on the transfer case

the front of the case. Fill the case until the fluid is at the fill plug hole. Recommended fluid is: 1982 and later: Dexron®II automatic transmission fluid 1980–81: 10W-30 engine oil.

Manual Steering Gear

♦ See Figure 46

The level of lubricant in the steering gear box doesn't need to be checked unless you notice leakage. An oily film is not important, but escaping grease is. To check the level:

1. Wipe off the gearbox until you can see one cover bolt between the words check lube. Sometimes there is a filler plug.

Fig. 46 Location of the manual steering gear fill hole

2. With the wheels turned all the way to the left, remove the cover bolt or filler plug.

❊❊ CAUTION

Don't remove the locknut in the center or you will mess up the gearbox adjustment. Don't take the cover off.

3. If you can see grease, there is enough. If not, fill the chassis grease through the hole.

4. Torque the cover bolt to 25–40 ft. lb. if you have a torque wrench. If not, just pull it down firmly but gently.

Power Steering Reservoir

▶ See Figure 47

The belt driven power steering pump/reservoir is located at the from of the engine. To check the level, as recommended at oil change intervals, proceed as follows:

1. Wipe off the cap and surrounding area, after stopping the engine with the wheels straight.

❊❊ CAUTION

Very small dirt particles can cause trouble in any hydraulic system.

2. Remove the cap.

3. If the cap has a dipstick, wipe it off with a clean rag, replace the cap, wait ten seconds, and take a reading. The level should be at FULL.

4. If you didn't get a dipstick, the level should be 1" below the top.

5. The correct fluid is DEXRON®II or AMC Automatic Transmission Fluid.

Fig. 47 The power steering pump cap/dipstick is located on top of the assembly

To check the power steering fluid level, unscrew the cap and remove the dipstick

Hold the dipstick horizontally and check the fluid level

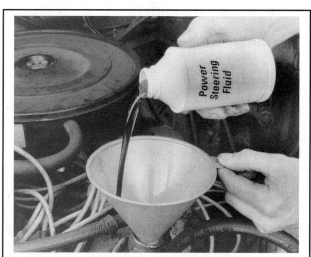

If necessary, add power steering fluid until the pump is properly filled

Front Hub and Wheel Bearings

ADJUSTMENT

Before handling the bearings, there are a few things that you should remember to do and not to do.

➡**Sodium based grease is not compatible with lithium based grease. Read the package labels and be careful not to mix the two types. If there is any doubt as to the type of grease used, completely clean the old grease from the bearing and hub before replacing.**

Remember to DO the following:
• Remove all outside dirt from the housing before exposing the bearing.
• Treat a used bearing as gently as you would a new one.
• Work with clean tools in clean surroundings.
• Use clean, dry canvas gloves, or at least clean, dry hands.
• Clean solvents and flushing fluids are a must.
• Use clean paper when laying out the bearings to dry.
• Protect disassembled bearings from rust and dirt. Cover them up.
• Use clean rags to wipe bearings.
• Keep the bearings in oil-proof paper when they are to be stored or are not in use.
• Clean the inside of the housing before replacing the bearing.

Do NOT do the following:
• Don't work in dirty surroundings.
• Don't use dirty, chipped or damaged tools.
• Try not to work on wooden work benches or use wooden mallets.
• Don't handle bearings with dirty or moist hands.
• Do not use gasoline for cleaning. Use a safe solvent.
• Do not spin dry bearings with compressed air. They will be damaged.
• Do not spin dirty bearings.
• Avoid using cotton waste or dirty cloths to wipe bearings.
• Try not to scratch or nick bearing surfaces.
• Do not allow the bearing to come in contact with dirt or rust at any time.

4-WD Models

1. Raise the front of the vehicle and place jackstands under the axle.
2. Remove the wheel.
3. Remove the front hub grease cap and driving hub snapring. On models equipped with locking hubs, remove the retainer knob hub ring, agitator knob, snapring, outer clutch retaining ring and actuating cam body.
4. Remove the splined driving hub and the pressure spring. This may require slight prying with a screwdriver.
5. Remove the external snapring from the sindle shaft and remove the hub shaft drive gear.
6. Remove the wheel bearing locknut, lockring, adjusting nut and inner lockring.
7. On vehicles with drum brakes, remove the hub and drum assembly. This may require that the brake adjusting wheel be backed off a few turns. The outer wheel bearing and spring retainer will come off with the hub.

8. On vehicles with disc brakes, remove the caliper and suspend it out of the way by hanging it from a suspension or frame member with a length of wire. Do not disconnect the brake hose, and be careful to avoid stretching the hose. Remove the rotor and hub assembly. The outer wheel bearing and, on vehicles with locking hubs, the spring collar, will come off with the hub.
9. Carefully drive out the inner bearing and seal from the hub, using a wood block.
10. Inspect the bearing races for excessive wear, pitting or grooves. If they are cracked or grooved, or if pitting and excess wear is present, drive them out with a drift or punch.
11. Check the bearing for excess wear, pitting or cracks, or excess looseness.

To install:

➡**If it is necessary to replace either the bearing or the race, replace both. Never replace just a bearing or a race. These parts wear in a mating pattern. If just one is replaced, premature failure of the new part will result.**

12. If the old parts are retained, thoroughly clean them in a safe solvent and allow them to dry on a clean towel. Never spin dry them with compressed air.
13. On vehicles with drum brakes, cover the spindle with a cloth and thoroughly brush all dirt from the brakes. Never blow the dirt off the brakes, due to the presence of asbestos in the dirt, which is harmful to your health when inhaled.
14. Remove the cloth and thoroughly clean the spindle.
15. Thoroughly clean the inside of the hub.
16. Pack the inside of the hub with wheel bearing grease. Add grease to the hub until it is flush with the inside diameter of the bearing cup.
17. Pack the bearing with the same grease. A needle shaped wheel bearing packer is best for this operation. If one is not available, place a large amount of grease in the palm of your hand and slide the edge of the bearing cage through the grease to pick up as much as possible, then work the grease in as best you can with your fingers.
18. If a new race is being installed, very carefully drive it into position until it bottoms all around, using a brass drift. Be careful to avoid scratching the surface.
19. Place the inner bearing in the race and install a new grease seal.
20. Place the hub assembly onto the spindle and install the inner lockring and outer bearing. Install the wheel bearing nut and torque it to 50 ft. lbs. while turning the wheel back and forth to seat the bearings. Back off the nut about ¼ turn (90°) maximum.
21. Install the lockwasher with the tab aligned with the keyway in the spindle and turn the inner wheel bearing adjusting nut until the peg on the nut engages the nearest hole in the lockwasher.
22. Install the outer locknut and torque it to 50 ft. lbs.
23. Install the spring collar, drive flange, snapring, pressure spring, and hub cap.
24. Install the caliper over the rotor.

2-WD Models
♦ See Figure 48

1. Raise the front of the vehicle and place jackstands under the axle.
2. Remove the wheel.
3. Remove the front hub grease cap.
4. Remove the cotter pin and locknut.

Fig. 48 Exploded view of the hub and wheel bearing assembly—1980–86 models

5. Pull out on the brake drum slightly to free the outer bearing and remove the bearing.

6. Remove the drum and hub.

7. Using an awl, puncture the inner seal and pry it out. Discard the seal.

8. Remove the inner bearing.

9. Inspect the bearing races for excessive wear, pitting or grooves. If they are cracked or grooved, or if pitting and excess wear is present, drive them out with a drift or punch.

10. Check the bearing for excess wear, pitting or cracks, or excess looseness.

To install:

➡**If it is necessary to replace either the bearing or the race, replace both. Never replace just a bearing or a race. These parts wear in a mating pattern. If just one is replaced, premature failure of the new part will result.**

11. If the old parts are retained, thoroughly clean them in a safe solvent and allow them to dry on a clean towel. Never spin dry them with compressed air.

12. On vehicles with drum brakes, cover the spindle with a cloth and thoroughly brush all dirt from the brakes. Never blow

Pry the dust cap from the hub taking care not to distort or damage its flange

Once the bent ends are cut, grasp the cotter pin and pull or pry it free of the spindle

If difficulty is encountered, gently tap on the pliers with a hammer to help free the cotter pin

With the nut and washer out of the way, the outer bearings may be removed from the hub

Loosen and remove the castellated nut from the spindle

Pull the hub and inner bearing assembly from the spindle

Remove the washer from the spindle

Use a small prytool to remove the old inner bearing seal

With the seal removed, the inner bearing may be withdrawn from the hub

Use a suitably sized driver to install the inner bearing seal to the hub

Thoroughly pack the bearing with fresh, high temperature wheel-bearing grease before installation

With new or freshly packed bearings, tighten the nut while gently spinning the wheel, then adjust the bearings

Apply a thin coat of fresh grease to the new inner bearing seal lip

After the bearings are adjusted, install the dust cap by gently tapping on the flange—DO NOT damage the cap by hammering on the center

the dirt off the brakes, due to the presence of asbestos in the dirt, which is harmful to your health when inhaled.

13. Remove the cloth and thoroughly clean the spindle.

14. Thoroughly clean the inside of the hub.

15. Pack the inside of the hub with EP wheel bearing grease. Add grease to the hub until it is flush with the inside diameter of the bearing cup.

16. Pack the bearing with the same grease. A needle shaped wheel bearing packer is best for this operation. If one is not available, place a large amount of grease in the palm of your hand and slide the edge of the bearing cage through the grease to pick up as much as possible, then work the grease in as best you can with your fingers.

17. If a new race is being installed, very carefully drive it into position until it bottoms all around, using a brass drift. Be careful to avoid scratching the surface.

18. Place the inner bearing in the race and install a new grease seal.

19. Place the hub assembly onto the spindle and install the outer bearing. Install the wheel bearing nut and tighten it until the hub binds while turning. Back off the nut about 1/6–1/4 turn to free the bearings. Install a new cotter pin.

20. Install the grease cap.

21. Install the wheel.

22. Lower the vehicle and install the hub cap.

PUSHING AND TOWING

Cars with automatic transmission may not be started by pushing or towing. Manual transmission cars may be started by pushing. The car need not be pushed very fast to start.

To push start a manual transmission car:

1. Make sure that the bumpers of the two cars align so as not to damage either one.

2. Turn on the ignition switch in the pushed car. Place the transmission in Second or Third gear and hold-down the clutch pedal.

3. Have the car pushed to a speed of 10–15 mph.

4. Ease up on the clutch and press down on the accelerator slightly at the same time. If the clutch is engaged abruptly, damage to the push vehicle may result.

The car should not be towed to start, since there is a chance of the towed vehicle ramming the tow car. Models with automatic should not be towed over 30 mph, for more than 15 miles. If these recommendations must be exceeded, remove the driveshaft to prevent automatic transmission damage.

TRAILER TOWING

General Recommendations

Your vehicle was primarily designed to carry passengers and cargo. It is important to remember that towing a trailer will place additional loads on your vehicles engine, drivetrain, steering, braking and other systems. However, if you decide to tow a trailer, using the prior equipment is a must.

Local laws may require specific equipment such as trailer brakes or fender mounted mirrors. Check your local laws.

Trailer Weight

The weight of the trailer is the most important factor. A good weight-to-horsepower ratio is about 35:1, 35 lbs. of Gross Combined Weight (GCW) for every horsepower your engine develops. Multiply the engine's rated horsepower by 35 and subtract the weight of the vehicle passengers and luggage. The number remaining is the approximate ideal maximum weight you should tow, although a numerically higher axle ratio can help compensate for heavier weight.

Hitch (Tongue) Weight

Calculate the hitch weight in order to select a proper hitch. The weight of the hitch is usually 9–11% of the trailer gross weight and should be measured with the trailer loaded. Hitches fall into various categories: those that mount on the frame and rear bumper, the bolt-on type, or the weld-on distribution type used for larger trailers. Axle mounted or clamp-on bumper hitches should never be used.

Check the gross weight rating of your trailer. Tongue weight is usually figured as 10% of gross trailer weight. Therefore, a trailer with a maximum gross weight of 2000 lbs. will have a maximum tongue weight of 200 lbs. Class I trailers fall into this category. Class II trailers are those with a gross weight rating of 2000–3000 lbs., while Class III trailers fall into the 3500–6000 lbs. category. Class IV trailers are those over 6000 lbs. and are for use with fifth wheel trucks, only.

When you've determined the hitch that you'll need, follow the manufacturer's installation instructions, exactly, especially when it comes to fastener torques. The hitch will subjected to a lot of

Calculating proper tongue weight for your trailer

stress and good hitches come with hardened bolts. Never substitute an inferior bolt for a hardened bolt.

Cooling

ENGINE

Overflow Tank

One of the most common, if not THE most common, problems associated with trailer towing is engine overheating. If you have a cooling system without an expansion tank, you'll definitely need to get an aftermarket expansion tank kit, preferably one with at least a 2 quart capacity. These kits are easily installed on the radiator's overflow hose, and come with a pressure cap designed for expansion tanks.

Flex Fan

Another helpful accessory for vehicles using a belt-driven radiator fan is a flex fan. These fans are large diameter units designed to provide more airflow at low speeds, by using fan blades that have deeply cupped surfaces. The blades then flex, or flatten out, at high speed, when less cooling air is needed. These fans are far lighter in weight than stock fans, requiring less horsepower to drive them. Also, they are far quieter than stock fans. If you do decide to replace your stock fan with a flex fan, note that if your vehicle has a fan clutch, a spacer will be needed between the flex fan and water pump hub.

Oil Cooler

Aftermarket engine oil coolers are helpful for prolonging engine oil life and reducing overall engine temperatures. Both of these factors increase engine life. While not absolutely necessary in towing Class I and some Class II trailers, they are recommended for heavier Class II and all Class III towing. Engine oil cooler systems usually consist of an adapter, screwed on in place of the oil filter, a remote filter mounting and a multi-tube, finned heat exchanger, which is mounted in front of the radiator or air conditioning condenser.

TRANSMISSION

An automatic transmission is usually recommended for trailer towing. Modern automatics have proven reliable and, of course, easy to operate, in trailer towing. The increased load of a trailer, however, causes an increase in the temperature of the automatic transmission fluid. Heat is the worst enemy of an automatic transmission. As the temperature of the fluid increases, the life of the fluid decreases.

It is essential, therefore, that you install an automatic transmission cooler. The cooler, which consists of a multi-tube, finned heat exchanger, is usually installed in front of the radiator or air conditioning compressor, and hooked in-line with the transmission cooler tank inlet line. Follow the cooler manufacturer's installation instructions.

Select a cooler of at least adequate capacity, based upon the combined gross weights of the vehicle and trailer.

Cooler manufacturers recommend that you use an aftermarket cooler in addition to, and not instead of, the present cooling tank in your radiator. If you do want to use it in place of the radiator cooling tank, get a cooler at least two sizes larger than normally necessary.

➡**A transmission cooler can, sometimes, cause slow or harsh shifting in the transmission during cold weather, until the fluid has a chance to come up to normal operating temperature. Some coolers can be purchased with or retrofitted with a temperature bypass valve which will allow fluid flow through the cooler only when the fluid has reached above a certain operating temperature.**

Handling A Trailer

Towing a trailer with ease and safety requires a certain amount of experience. It's a good idea to learn the feel of a trailer by practicing turning, stopping and backing in an open area such as an empty parking lot.

Recommended Equipment Checklist

Equipment	Class I Trailers Under 2,000 pounds	Class II Trailers 2,000-3,500 pounds	Class III Trailers 3,500-6,000 pounds	Class IV Trailers 6,000 pounds and up
Hitch	Frame or Equalizing	Equalizing	Equalizing	Fifth wheel Pick-up truck only
Tongue Load Limit**	Up to 200 pounds	200-350 pounds	350-600 pounds	600 pounds and up
Trailer Brakes	Not Required	Required	Required	Required
Safety Chain	3/16" diameter links	1/4" diameter links	5/16" diameter links	—
Fender Mounted Mirrors	Useful, but not necessary	Recommended	Recommended	Recommended
Turn Signal Flasher	Standard	Constant Rate or heavy duty	Constant Rate or heavy duty	Constant Rate or heavy duty
Coolant Recovery System	Recommended	Required	Required	Required
Transmission Oil Cooler	Recommended	Recommended	Recommended	Recommended
Engine Oil Cooler	Recommended	Recommended	Recommended	Recommended
Air Adjustable Shock Absorbers	Recommended	Recommended	Recommended	Recommended
Flex or Clutch Fan	Recommended	Recommended	Recommended	Recommended
Tires	***	***	***	***

NOTE: The information in this chart is a guide. Check the manufacturer's recommendations for your car if in doubt.

* Local laws may require specific equipment such as trailer brakes or fender mounted mirrors. Check your local laws. Hitch weight is usually 10-15% of trailer gross weight and should be measured with trailer loaded.

** Most manufacturer's do not recommend towing trailers of over 1,000 pounds with compacts. Some intermediates cannot tow Class III trailers.

*** Check manufacturer's recommendations for your specific car/ trailer combination.

— Does not apply

JUMP STARTING A DEAD BATTERY

Whenever a vehicle is jump started, precautions must be followed in order to prevent the possibility of personal injury. Remember that batteries contain a small amount of explosive hydrogen gas which is a by-product of battery charging. Sparks should always be avoided when working around batteries, especially when attaching jumper cables. To minimize the possibility of accidental sparks, follow the procedure carefully.

✳✳ CAUTION

NEVER hook the batteries up in a series circuit or the entire electrical system will go up in smoke, including the starter!

Vehicles equipped with a diesel engine may utilize two 12 volt batteries. If so, the batteries are connected in a parallel circuit (positive terminal to positive terminal, negative terminal to negative terminal). Hooking the batteries up in parallel circuit increases battery cranking power without increasing total battery volt-age output. Output remains at 12 volts. On the other hand, hooking two 12 volt batteries up in a series circuit (positive terminal to negative terminal, positive terminal to negative terminal) increases total battery output to 24 volts (12 volts plus 12 volts).

Jump Starting Precautions

• Be sure that both batteries are of the same voltage. Vehicles covered by this manual and most vehicles on the road today utilize a 12 volt charging system.

• Be sure that both batteries are of the same polarity (have the same terminal, in most cases NEGATIVE grounded).

• Be sure that the vehicles are not touching or a short could occur.

• On serviceable batteries, be sure the vent cap holes are not obstructed.

• Do not smoke or allow sparks anywhere near the batteries.

MAKE CONNECTIONS IN NUMERICAL ORDER

FIRST JUMPER CABLE

DO NOT ALLOW VEHICLES TO TOUCH

DISCHARGED BATTERY

SECOND JUMPER CABLE

MAKE LAST CONNECTION ON ENGINE, AWAY FROM BATTERY

BATTERY IN VEHICLE WITH CHARGED BATTERY

Connect the jumper cables to the batteries and engine in the order shown

- In cold weather, make sure the battery electrolyte is not frozen. This can occur more readily in a battery that has been in a state of discharge.
- Do not allow electrolyte to contact your skin or clothing.

Jump Starting Procedure

1. Make sure that the voltages of the 2 batteries are the same. Most batteries and charging systems are of the 12 volt variety.

2. Pull the jumping vehicle (with the good battery) into a position so the jumper cables can reach the dead battery and that vehicle's engine. Make sure that the vehicles do NOT touch.

3. Place the transmissions/transaxles of both vehicles in **Neutral** (MT) or **P** (AT), as applicable, then firmly set their parking brakes.

➡️**If necessary for safety reasons, the hazard lights on both vehicles may be operated throughout the entire procedure without significantly increasing the difficulty of jumping the dead battery.**

4. Turn all lights and accessories OFF on both vehicles. Make sure the ignition switches on both vehicles are turned to the **OFF** position.

5. Cover the battery cell caps with a rag, but do not cover the terminals.

6. Make sure the terminals on both batteries are clean and free of corrosion or proper electrical connection will be impeded. If necessary, clean the battery terminals before proceeding.

7. Identify the positive (+) and negative (−) terminals on both batteries.

8. Connect the first jumper cable to the positive (+) terminal of the dead battery, then connect the other end of that cable to the positive (+) terminal of the booster (good) battery.

9. Connect one end of the other jumper cable to the negative (−) terminal on the booster battery and the final cable clamp to an engine bolt head, alternator bracket or other solid, metallic point on the engine with the dead battery. Try to pick a ground on the engine that is positioned away from the battery in order to minimize the possibility of the 2 clamps touching should one loosen during the procedure. DO NOT connect this clamp to the negative (−) terminal of the bad battery.

✳✳ CAUTION

Be very careful to keep the jumper cables away from moving parts (cooling fan, belts, etc.) on both engines.

10. Check to make sure that the cables are routed away from any moving parts, then start the donor vehicle's engine. Run the engine at moderate speed for several minutes to allow the dead battery a chance to receive some initial charge.

11. With the donor vehicle's engine still running slightly above idle, try to start the vehicle with the dead battery. Crank the engine for no more than 10 seconds at a time and let the starter cool for at least 20 seconds between tries. If the vehicle does not start in 3 tries, it is likely that something else is also wrong or that the battery needs additional time to charge.

12. Once the vehicle is started, allow it to run at idle for a few seconds to make sure that it is operating properly.

13. Turn ON the headlights, heater blower and, if equipped, the rear defroster of both vehicles in order to reduce the severity of voltage spikes and subsequent risk of damage to the vehicles' electrical systems when the cables are disconnected. This step is especially important to any vehicle equipped with computer control modules.

14. Carefully disconnect the cables in the reverse order of connection. Start with the negative cable that is attached to the engine ground, then the negative cable on the donor battery. Disconnect the positive cable from the donor battery and finally, disconnect the positive cable from the formerly dead battery. Be careful when disconnecting the cables from the positive terminals not to allow the alligator clips to touch any metal on either vehicle or a short and sparks will occur.

JACKING

◆ **See Figures 49 and 50**

Your vehicle was supplied with a jack for emergency road repairs. This jack is fine for changing a flat tire or other short term procedures not requiring you to go beneath the vehicle. If it is used in an emergency situation, carefully follow the instructions provided either with the jack or in your owner's manual. Do not attempt to use the jack on any portions of the vehicle other than specified by the vehicle manufacturer. Always block the diagonally opposite wheel when using a jack.

A more convenient way of jacking is the use of a garage or floor jack.

Never place the jack under the radiator, engine or transmission components. Severe and expensive damage will result when the jack is raised. Additionally, never jack under the floorpan or bodywork; the metal will deform.

Whenever you plan to work under the vehicle, you must support it on jackstands or ramps. Never use cinder blocks or stacks of wood to support the vehicle, even if you're only going to be un-

Fig. 49 Jacking points—except Pacer and Eagle models

Fig. 50 Jacking points—Pacer models

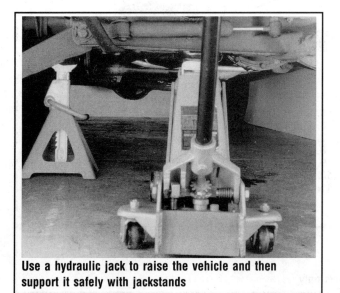

Use a hydraulic jack to raise the vehicle and then support it safely with jackstands

der it for a few minutes. Never crawl under the vehicle when it is supported only by the tire-changing jack or other floor jack.

➡ **Always position a block of wood or small rubber pad on top of the jack or jackstand to protect the lifting point's finish when lifting or supporting the vehicle.**

Small hydraulic, screw, or scissors jacks are satisfactory for raising the vehicle. Drive-on trestles or ramps are also a handy and safe way to both raise and support the vehicle. Be careful though, some ramps may be too steep to drive your vehicle onto without scraping the front bottom panels. Never support the vehicle on any suspension member (unless specifically instructed to do so by a repair manual) or by an underbody panel.

Jacking Precautions

The following safety points cannot be overemphasized:
• Always block the opposite wheel or wheels to keep the vehicle from rolling off the jack.

• When raising the front of the vehicle, firmly apply the parking brake.

• When the drive wheels are to remain on the ground, leave the vehicle in gear to help prevent it from rolling.

• Always use jackstands to support the vehicle when you are working underneath. Place the stands beneath the vehicle's jacking brackets. Before climbing underneath, rock the vehicle a bit to make sure it is firmly supported.

Body Lubrication and Maintenance

LOCK CYLINDERS

◆ **See Figures 51, 52 and 53**

Apply graphite lubricant sparingly through the key slot. Insert the key and operate the lock several times to be sure that the lubricant is worked into the lock cylinder.

DOOR HINGES & HINGE CHECKS

Spray a silicone lubricant on the hinge pivot points to eliminate any binding conditions. Open and close the door several times to be sure that the lubricant is evenly and thoroughly distributed.

TAILGATE

Spray a silicone lubricant on all of the pivot and friction surfaces to eliminate any squeaks or binds. Work the tailgate to distribute the lubricant.

BODY DRAIN HOLES

Be sure that the drain holes in the doors and rocker panels are cleared of obstruction. A small screwdriver can be used to clear them of any debris.

BRAKES

○ INSPECTION/LUBRICATION POINTS

1. Check front and rear axle differential fluid level
1. Drain and change front and rear axle differential oil
2. Brake and chassis inspection lubrication ①
3. Lubricate body components ①
4. Check exhaust system ②
5. Check transfer case oil
5. Drain and change transfer case oil
6. Drain and change automatic transmission oil
7. Check manual transmission fluid level
8. Lubricate front and rear propeller shafts ③
9. Check and lubricate steering linkage ④
10. Check tire pressure in spare tire
11. Check windshield washer reservoir fluid level

Fig. 51 Chassis inspection and lubrication points—Eagle models only

Fig. 52 Chassis inspection and lubrication points—except Eagle and Pacer models

Fig. 53 Chassis inspection and lubrication points—Pacer models only

HOW TO BUY A USED VEHICLE

Many people believe that a two or three year old used car or truck is a better buy than a new vehicle. This may be true as most new vehicles suffer the heaviest depreciation in the first two years and, at three years old, a vehicle is usually not old enough to present a lot of costly repair problems. But keep in mind, when buying a non-warranted automobile, there are no guarantees. Whatever the age of the used vehicle you might want to purchase, this section and a little patience should increase your chances of selecting one that is safe and dependable.

Tips

1. First decide what model you want, and how much you want to spend.

2. Check the used car lots and your local newspaper ads. Privately owned vehicles are usually less expensive, however, you may not get a warranty that, in many cases, comes with a used vehicle purchased from a lot. Of course, some aftermarket warranties may not be worth the extra money, so this is a point you will have to debate and consider based on your priorities.

3. Never shop at night. The glare of the lights make it easy to miss faults on the body caused by accident or rust repair.

4. Try to get the name and phone number of the previous owner. Contact him/her and ask about the vehicle. If the owner of a lot refuses this information, look for a vehicle somewhere else.

A private seller can tell you about the vehicle and maintenance. But remember, there's no law requiring honesty from private citizens selling used vehicles. There is a law that forbids tampering with or turning back the odometer mileage. This includes both the private citizen and the lot owner. The law also requires that the seller or anyone transferring ownership of the vehicle must provide the buyer with a signed statement indicating the mileage on the odometer at the time of transfer.

5. You may wish to contact the National Highway Traffic Safety Administration (NHTSA) to find out if the vehicle has ever been included in a manufacturer's recall. Write down the year, model and serial number before you buy the vehicle, then contact NHTSA (there should be a 1-800 number that your phone company's information line can supply). If the vehicle was listed for a recall, make sure the needed repairs were made.

6. Refer to the Used Vehicle Checklist in this section and check all the items on the vehicle you are considering. Some items are more important than others. Only you know how much money you can afford for repairs, and depending on the price of the vehicle, may consider performing any needed work yourself. Beware, however, of trouble in areas that will affect operation, safety or emission. Problems in the Used Vehicle Checklist break down as follows:

• Numbers 1–8: Two or more problems in these areas indicate a lack of maintenance. You should beware.

• Numbers 9–13: Problems here tend to indicate a lack of proper care, however, these can usually be corrected with a tune-up or relatively simple parts replacement.

• Numbers 14–17: Problems in the engine or transmission can be very expensive. Unless you are looking for a project, walk away from any vehicle with problems in 2 or more of these areas.

7. If you are satisfied with the apparent condition of the vehicle, take it to an independent diagnostic center or mechanic for a complete check. If you have a state inspection program, have it inspected immediately before purchase, or specify on the bill of sale that the sale is conditional on passing state inspection.

8. Road test the vehicle—refer to the Road Test Checklist in this section. If your original evaluation and the road test agree—the rest is up to you.

USED VEHICLE CHECKLIST

➡**The numbers on the illustrations refer to the numbers on this checklist.**

1. Mileage: Average mileage is about 12,000–15,000 miles per year. More than average mileage may indicate hard usage or could indicate many highway miles (which could be less detrimental than half as many tough around town miles).

2. Paint: Check around the tailpipe, molding and windows for overspray indicating that the vehicle has been repainted.

3. Rust: Check fenders, doors, rocker panels, window moldings, wheelwells, floorboards, under floormats, and in the trunk for signs of rust. Any rust at all will be a problem. There is no way to permanently stop the spread of rust, except to replace the part or panel.

➡**If rust repair is suspected, try using a magnet to check for body filler. A magnet should stick to the sheet metal parts of the body, but will not adhere to areas with large amounts of filler.**

4. Body appearance: Check the moldings, bumpers, grille, vinyl roof, glass, doors, trunk lid and body panels for general overall condition. Check for misalignment, loose hold-down clips, ripples, scratches in glass, welding in the trunk, severe misalignment of body panels or ripples, any of which may indicate crash work.

5. Leaks: Get down and look under the vehicle. There are no normal leaks, other than water from the air conditioner evaporator.

6. Tires: Check the tire air pressure. One old trick is to pump the tire pressure up to make the vehicle roll easier. Check the tread wear, then open the trunk and check the spare too. Uneven wear is a clue that the front end may need an alignment.

7. Shock absorbers: Check the shock absorbers by forcing downward sharply on each corner of the vehicle. Good shocks will not allow the vehicle to bounce more than once after you let go.

8. Interior: Check the entire interior. You're looking for an interior condition that agrees with the overall condition of the vehicle. Reasonable wear is expected, but be suspicious of new seat covers on sagging seats, new pedal pads, and worn armrests. These indicate an attempt to cover up hard use. Pull back the carpets and look for evidence of water leaks or flooding. Look for missing hardware, door handles, control knobs, etc. Check lights and signal operations. Make sure all accessories (air conditioner, heater, radio, etc.) work. Check windshield wiper operation.

9. Belts and Hoses: Open the hood, then check all belts and hoses for wear, cracks or weak spots.

10. Battery: Low electrolyte level, corroded terminals and/or cracked case indicate a lack of maintenance.

11. Radiator: Look for corrosion or rust in the coolant indicating a lack of maintenance.

12. Air filter: A severely dirty air filter would indicate a lack of maintenance.

Each of the numbered items should be checked when purchasing a used vehicle

13. Ignition wires: Check the ignition wires for cracks, burned spots, or wear. Worn wires will have to be replaced.

14. Oil level: If the oil level is low, chances are the engine uses oil or leaks. Beware of water in the oil (there is probably a cracked block or bad head gasket), excessively thick oil (which is often used to quiet a noisy engine), or thin, dirty oil with a distinct gasoline smell (this may indicate internal engine problems).

15. Automatic Transmission: Pull the transmission dipstick out when the engine is running. The level should read FULL, and the fluid should be clear or bright red. Dark brown or black fluid that has distinct burnt odor, indicates a transmission in need of repair or overhaul.

16. Exhaust: Check the color of the exhaust smoke. Blue smoke indicates, among other problems, worn rings. Black smoke can indicate burnt valves or carburetor problems. Check the exhaust system for leaks; it can be expensive to replace.

17. Spark Plugs: Remove one or all of the spark plugs (the most accessible will do, though all are preferable). An engine in good condition will show plugs with a light tan or gray deposit on the firing tip.

ROAD TEST CHECKLIST

1. Engine Performance: The vehicle should be peppy whether cold or warm, with adequate power and good pickup. It should respond smoothly through the gears.

2. Brakes: They should provide quick, firm stops with no noise, pulling or brake fade.

3. Steering: Sure control with no binding harshness, or looseness and no shimmy in the wheel should be expected. Noise or vibration from the steering wheel when turning the vehicle means trouble.

4. Clutch (Manual Transmission/Transaxle): Clutch action should give quick, smooth response with easy shifting. The clutch pedal should have free-play before it disengages the clutch. Start the engine, set the parking brake, put the transmission in first gear and slowly release the clutch pedal. The engine should begin to stall when the pedal is ½–¾ of the way up.

5. Automatic Transmission/Transaxle: The transmission should shift rapidly and smoothly, with no noise, hesitation, or slipping.

6. Differential: No noise or thumps should be present. Differentials have no normal leaks.

7. Driveshaft/Universal Joints: Vibration and noise could mean driveshaft problems. Clicking at low speed or coast conditions means worn U-joints.

8. Suspension: Try hitting bumps at different speeds. A vehicle that bounces excessively has weak shock absorbers or struts. Clunks mean worn bushings or ball joints.

9. Frame/Body: Wet the tires and drive in a straight line. Tracks should show two straight lines, not four. Four tire tracks indicate a frame/body bent by collision damage. If the tires can't be wet for this purpose, have a friend drive along behind you and see if the vehicle appears to be traveling in a straight line.

Capacities Chart
Gremlin, Hornet, Concord, Spirit

Year	Engine	Crank-case Incl. Filter (qt)	Transmission (pt.) 3-sp	4-sp	5-sp	Auto	Drive Axle (pt.)	Fuel Tank (gal.)	Cooling System (qt) w/AC	wo/AC
1975	6-232	5.0	①	—	—	17.0	②	③	11.0	11.5
	6-258	5.0	①	—	—	17.0	②	③	11.0	11.5
	8-304	5.0	3.5	—	—	17.0	4.0	③	16.0	16.0
1976	6-232	5.0	①	—	—	17.0	②	③	11.0	11.5
	6-232	5.0	①	—	—	17.0	②	③	11.0	11.5
	8-304	5.0	3.5	—	—	17.0	4.0	③	16.0	16.0
1977	4-121	4.5	—	2.4	—	14.2	3.0	15.0	6.5	6.5
	6-232	5.0	3.5	3.5	—	17.0	3.0	③	11.0	④
	6-258	5.0	3.5	3.5	—	17.0	3.0	③	11.0	④
	8-304	5.0	3.5	—	—	17.0	4.0	③	16.0	16.0
1978	4-121	4.5	—	2.4	—	14.2	3.0	15.0	6.5	6.5
	6-232	5.0	3.0	3.5	—	17.0	3.0	③	11.0	14.0
	6-258	5.0	3.0	3.5	—	17.0	3.0	③	11.0	④
	8-304	5.0	3.0	—	—	17.0	4.0	③	18.0	18.0
1979	4-121	4.5	2.5	2.8	—	14.2	3.0	13.0	6.5	6.5
	6-232	5.0	2.5	2.8	—	17.0	②	21.0	11.0	14.0
	6-258	5.0	2.5	2.8	—	17.0	②	21.0	11.0	14.0
	8-304	5.0	2.5	2.8	—	17.0	②	21.0	18.0	18.0
1980	4-151	4.0	—	3.3	—	17.0	3.0	21.0	6.5	6.5
	6-258	5.0	—	3.3	—	17.0	3.0	21.0	11.0	11.0
1981	4-151	3.0	—	3.5	—	14.2	3.0	21.0	6.5	6.5
	6-258	5.0	—	3.5	—	17.0	3.0	21.0	11.0	14.0
1982	4-151	3.0	—	3.5	4.0	14.2	3.0	⑤	6.5	6.5
	6-258	5.0	—	3.5	4.0	17.0	3.0	⑤	11.0	14.5
1983	4-151	3.0	—	3.5	4.0	14.2	3.0	⑤	6.5	6.5
	6-258	5.0	—	3.5	4.0	17.0	3.0	⑤	11.0	14.5

① wo/overdrive: 3.5
   w/overdrive: 4.5
② 7⁹⁄₁₆″ ring gear: 3.0
   8⅞″ ring gear: 4.0
③ Gremlin: 21
   Hornet & Concord: 22
④ Gremlin: 14.0
   Hornet & Concord: 11.5
⑤ Spirit: 21.0
   Concord: 22.0

Capacities Chart
Matador

Year	Engine	Crank-case Incl. Filter (qt)	Transmission (pt.)				Drive Axle (pt.)	Fuel Tank (gal.)	Cooling System (qt)	
			3-sp	4-sp	5-sp	Auto			w/AC	wo/AC
1975	6-232	5.0	3.5	—	—	17.0	②	③	11.0	11.5
	6-258	5.0	3.5	—	—	17.0	②	③	11.0	11.5
	8-304	5.0	3.5	—	—	17.0	4.0	③	16.0	16.0
1976	6-258	5.0	3.5	—	—	17.0	4.0	③	①	①
	8-304	5.0	3.5	—	—	17.0	4.0	③	16.0	②
	8-360	5.0	—	—	—	19.0	4.0	③	④	④
	8-401	5.0	—	—	—	19.0	4.0	③	④	④
1977	6-258	5.0	—	—	—	17.0	4.0	③	①	①
	8-304	5.0	3.5	—	—	17.0	4.0	③	16.0	②
	8-360	5.0	—	—	—	19.0	4.0	③	④	④
1978	6-258	5.0	—	—	—	17.0	4.0	③	①	①
	8-304	5.0	3.5	—	—	16.4	4.0	③	16.0	②
	8-360	5.0	—	—	—	16.4	4.0	③	④	④

① Coupe: 14.0
  Sedan and SW: 11.0 wo/air cond.; 11.5 w/air cond.; 13.5 w/coolant recovery system
② 16.5 wo/coolant recovery; 19.5 w/coolant recovery
③ Sedan and SW: 21.5
  Coupe: 24.5
④ Coupe: 17.5
  Sedan and SW: 15.5 wo/air cond.; 15.5 w/air cond.; 18.5 w/coolant recovery system

Pacer

Year	Engine	Crank-case Incl. Filter (qt)	Transmission (pt.)				Drive Axle (pt.)	Fuel Tank (gal.)	Cooling System (qt)	
			3-sp	4-sp	5-sp	Auto			w/AC	wo/AC
1975	6-232	5.0	①	—	—	17.0	3.0	22.0	11.0	11.5
	6-258	5.0	①	—	—	17.0	3.0	22.0	11.0	11.5
1976	6-232	5.0	①	3.5	—	17.0	3.0	22.0	14.0	14.0
	6-258	5.0	①	3.5	—	17.0	3.0	22.0	14.0	14.0
1977	6-232	5.0	3.5	3.5	—	17.0	3.0	22.0	14.0	14.0
	6-258	5.0	3.5	3.5	—	17.0	3.0	22.0	14.0	14.0
1978	6-232	5.0	3.0	3.5	—	17.0	3.0	20.0	14.0	14.0
	6-258	5.0	3.0	3.5	—	17.0	3.0	20.0	14.0	14.0
1979	6-258	5.0	2.5	2.8	—	17.0	3.0	21.0	14.0	14.0
1980	6-258	5.0	—	3.3	—	17.0	3.0	21.0	14.5	14.5

① wo/overdrive: 3.5
  w/overdrive: 4.5

Capacities Chart
Eagle

| Year | Engine | Crank-case Incl. Filter (qt) | Transmission (pts.) | | | Transfer Case (pt.) | Drive Axle (pt.) | | Fuel Tank (gal.) | Cooling System (qt) | |
			4-sp	5-sp	Auto		Front	Rear		w/AC	wo/AC
1980	6-258	5.0	3.3	—	17.0	①	2.5	3.0	22.0	14.0	14.0
1981	4-151	4.0	3.5	—	14.2	4.0	2.5	3.0	22.0	6.5	6.5
	6-258	5.0	3.5	—	17.0	4.0	2.5	3.0	22.0	14.0	14.0
1982	4-151	3.0	3.5	4.0	17.0	6.0	2.5	3.0	②	6.5	6.5
	6-258	5.0	3.5	4.0	17.0	6.0	2.5	3.0	②	14.0	14.0
1983	4-151	3.0	3.5	4.0	14.2	6.0	2.5	3.0	②	6.5	6.5
	6-258	5.0	3.5	4.0	17.0	6.0	2.5	3.0	②	14.0	14.0
1984	4-150	4.0	3.5	4.0	17.0	6.0③	2.5	3.0	22.0	9.0	9.0
	6-258	5.0	3.5	4.0	17.0	6.0③	2.5	3.0	22.0	14.0	14.0
1985	6-258	5.0	3.5	4.0	17.0	6.0③	2.5	3.0	22.0	14.0	14.0
1986 - 88	6-258	5.0	3.5	4.0	17.0	6.0③	2.5	3.0	22.0	14.0	14.0

① Transfer cases built prior to 3/80: 3.0
   Transfer cases built after 3/80: 4.0
② Sedan and SW: 22.0
   SX/4 and Kammback: 21.0
③ Select-Shift housing: 5.0 oz

Preventive Maintenance Chart

1975–76

Interval	Item	Service
Every 5,000 miles	Engine oil and filter	Change
	Steering gear	Check level
	Power steering reservoir	Check level
	Heat riser	Lubricate
	Differentials	Check level
	Manual transmission	Check level
	Transfer case	Check level
	Automatic transmission	Check level
	All chassis lube fittings	EP chasis lube
	Drive belts	Check
	Air cleaner	Change filter
Every 10,000 miles	Driveshaft splines	EP chassis lube
Every 15,000 miles	Front and rear wheel bearings	Clean and repack
	U-joints	EP chassis lube
	Fuel filter	Replace
	PCV valve	Replace
	Oil filler cap	Clean
	Timing and dwell	Check
	Point, condenser, rotor	Replace
	Spark plugs	Replace
	EGR valve port	Clean
Every 25,000 miles	Automatic transmission	Change fluid and filter
Every 30,000 miles	Differentials	Change fluid
	Manual transmission	Change fluid
	Spark plug wires	Change

1977–79

Interval	Item	Service
Every 5,000 miles	Engine oil and filter	Change
	Steering gear	Check level
	Power steering reservoir	Check level
	Hear riser	Lubricate
	Differentials	Check level
	Manual transmission	Check level
	Transfer case	Check level
	Automatic transmission	Check level
	Drive belts	Check
	Air cleaner	Change filter
Every 10,000 miles	Driveshaft splines	EP chassis lube
Every 15,000 miles	All chassis lube fittings	EP chassis lube
	U-joints	EP chassis lube
	Fuel filter	Replace
	PCV valve	Replace
	Oil filler cap	Clean
	Timing and dwell	Check
	Point, condenser, rotor	Replace
	Spark plugs	Replace
	ERG valve port	Clean
Every 25,000 miles	Automatic transmission	Change fluid and filter
Every 30,000 miles	Differentials	Change fluid
	Manual transmission	Change fluid
	Spark plug wires	Change
	Front wheel bearings	Clean and repack

Preventive Maintenance Chart
1980–86

Interval	Item	Service
Every 5,000 miles	Engine oil and filter	Change
	Steering gear	Check level
	Power steering reservoir	Check level
	Heat riser	Lubricate
	Differentials	Check level
	Manual transmission	Check level
	Transfer case	Check level
	Automatic transmission	Check level
	Air cleaner	Change filter
	Drive belts	Check
Every 10,000 miles	Driveshaft splines	EP chassis lube
Every 15,000 miles	All chassis lube fittings	EP chassis lube
	U-joints	EP chassis lube
	Fuel filter	Replace
	PCV valve	Replace
	Oil filler cap	Clean
	Spark plugs	Replace
	EGR valve port	Clean
Every 25,000 miles	Automatic transmission	Change fluid and filter
Every 30,000 miles	Differentials	Change fluid
	Manual transmission	Change fluid
	Spark plug wires	Change
	Front wheel bearings	Clean and repack
	Transfer case	Change fluid

1987–88

Interval	Item	Service
Every 5,000 miles	Engine oil and filter	Change
	Steering gear	Check level
	Power steering reservoir	Check level
	Differentials	Check level
	Manual transmission	Check level
	Transfer case	Check level
	Automatic transmission	Check level
	Air cleaner	Change filter
	Drive belts	Check
Every 15,000 miles	All chassis lube fittings	EP chassis lube
	U-joints	EP chassis lube
	Fuel filter	Replace
	PCV valve	Replace
	Oil filler cap	Clean
	Spark plugs	Replace
Every 30,000 miles	Spark plug wires	Change
	Front wheel bearings	Clean and repack
Every 48,000 miles	Manual transmission	Change fluid
	Differentials	Change fluid
	Automatic transmission	Change fluid and filter
	Transfer case	Change fluid

ENGLISH TO METRIC CONVERSION: MASS (WEIGHT)

Current **mass** measurement is expressed in pounds and ounces (lbs. & ozs.). The metric unit of mass (or weight) is the kilogram (kg). Even although this table does not show conversion of masses (weights) larger than 15 lbs, it is easy to calculate larger units by following the data immediately below.

To convert ounces (oz.) to grams (g): multiply th number of ozs. by 28
To convert grams (g) to ounces (oz.): multiply the number of grams by .035

To convert pounds (lbs.) to kilograms (kg): multiply the number of lbs. by .45
To convert kilograms (kg) to pounds (lbs.): multiply the number of kilograms by 2.2

lbs	kg	lbs	kg	oz	kg	oz	kg
0.1	0.04	0.9	0.41	0.1	0.003	0.9	0.024
0.2	0.09	1	0.4	0.2	0.005	1	0.03
0.3	0.14	2	0.9	0.3	0.008	2	0.06
0.4	0.18	3	1.4	0.4	0.011	3	0.08
0.5	0.23	4	1.8	0.5	0.014	4	0.11
0.6	0.27	5	2.3	0.6	0.017	5	0.14
0.7	0.32	10	4.5	0.7	0.020	10	0.28
0.8	0.36	15	6.8	0.8	0.023	15	0.42

ENGLISH TO METRIC CONVERSION: TEMPERATURE

To convert Fahrenheit (°F) to Celsius (°C): take number of °F and subtract 32; multiply result by 5; divide result by 9

To convert Celsius (°C) to Fahrenheit (°F): take number of °C and multiply by 9; divide result by 5; add 32 to total

Fahrenheit (F)		Celsius (C)		Fahrenheit (F)		Celsius (C)		Fahrenheit (F)		Celsius (C)	
°F	°C	°C	°F	°F	°C	°C	°F	°F	°C	°C	°F
−40	−40	−38	−36.4	80	26.7	18	64.4	215	101.7	80	176
−35	−37.2	−36	−32.8	85	29.4	20	68	220	104.4	85	185
−30	−34.4	−34	−29.2	90	32.2	22	71.6	225	107.2	90	194
−25	−31.7	−32	−25.6	95	35.0	24	75.2	230	110.0	95	202
−20	−28.9	−30	−22	100	37.8	26	78.8	235	112.8	100	212
−15	−26.1	−28	−18.4	105	40.6	28	82.4	240	115.6	105	221
−10	−23.3	−26	−14.8	110	43.3	30	86	245	118.3	110	230
−5	−20.6	−24	−11.2	115	46.1	32	89.6	250	121.1	115	239
0	−17.8	−22	−7.6	120	48.9	34	93.2	255	123.9	120	248
1	−17.2	−20	−4	125	51.7	36	96.8	260	126.6	125	257
2	−16.7	−18	−0.4	130	54.4	38	100.4	265	129.4	130	266
3	−16.1	−16	3.2	135	57.2	40	104	270	132.2	135	275
4	−15.6	−14	6.8	140	60.0	42	107.6	275	135.0	140	284
5	−15.0	−12	10.4	145	62.8	44	112.2	280	137.8	145	293
10	−12.2	−10	14	150	65.6	46	114.8	285	140.6	150	302
15	−9.4	−8	17.6	155	68.3	48	118.4	290	143.3	155	311
20	−6.7	−6	21.2	160	71.1	50	122	295	146.1	160	320
25	−3.9	−4	24.8	165	73.9	52	125.6	300	148.9	165	329
30	−1.1	−2	28.4	170	76.7	54	129.2	305	151.7	170	338
35	1.7	0	32	175	79.4	56	132.8	310	154.4	175	347
40	4.4	2	35.6	180	82.2	58	136.4	315	157.2	180	356
45	7.2	4	39.2	185	85.0	60	140	320	160.0	185	365
50	10.0	6	42.8	190	87.8	62	143.6	325	162.8	190	374
55	12.8	8	46.4	195	90.6	64	147.2	330	165.6	195	383
60	15.6	10	50	200	93.3	66	150.8	335	168.3	200	392
65	18.3	12	53.6	205	96.1	68	154.4	340	171.1	205	401
70	21.1	14	57.2	210	98.9	70	158	345	173.9	210	410
75	23.9	16	60.8	212	100.0	75	167	350	176.7	215	414

ENGLISH TO METRIC CONVERSION: LENGTH

To convert inches (ins.) to millimeters (mm): multiply number of inches by 25.4

To convert millimeters (mm) to inches (ins.): multiply number of millimeters by .04

Inches		Decimals	Milli-meters	Inches to millimeters		Inches		Decimals	Milli-meters	Inches to millimeters	
				inches	mm					inches	mm
	1/64	0.051625	0.3969	0.0001	0.00254		33/64	0.515625	13.0969	0.6	15.24
1/32		0.03125	0.7937	0.0002	0.00508	17/32		0.53125	13.4937	0.7	17.78
	3/64	0.046875	1.1906	0.0003	0.00762		35/64	0.546875	13.8906	0.8	20.32
1/16		0.0625	1.5875	0.0004	0.01016	9/16		0.5625	14.2875	0.9	22.86
	5/64	0.078125	1.9844	0.0005	0.01270		37/64	0.578125	14.6844	1	25.4
3/32		0.09375	2.3812	0.0006	0.01524	19/32		0.59375	15.0812	2	50.8
	7/64	0.109375	2.7781	0.0007	0.01778		39/64	0.609375	15.4781	3	76.2
1/8		0.125	3.1750	0.0008	0.02032	5/8		0.625	15.8750	4	101.6
	9/64	0.140625	3.5719	0.0009	0.02286		41/64	0.640625	16.2719	5	127.0
5/32		0.15625	3.9687	0.001	0.0254	21/32		0.65625	16.6687	6	152.4
	11/64	0.171875	4.3656	0.002	0.0508		43/64	0.671875	17.0656	7	177.8
3/16		0.1875	4.7625	0.003	0.0762	11/16		0.6875	17.4625	8	203.2
	13/64	0.203125	5.1594	0.004	0.1016		45/64	0.703125	17.8594	9	228.6
7/32		0.21875	5.5562	0.005	0.1270	23/32		0.71875	18.2562	10	254.0
	15/64	0.234375	5.9531	0.006	0.1524		47/64	0.734375	18.6531	11	279.4
1/4		0.25	6.3500	0.007	0.1778	3/4		0.75	19.0500	12	304.8
	17/64	0.265625	6.7469	0.008	0.2032		49/64	0.765625	19.4469	13	330.2
9/32		0.28125	7.1437	0.009	0.2286	25/32		0.78125	19.8437	14	355.6
	19/64	0.296875	7.5406	0.01	0.254		51/64	0.796875	20.2406	15	381.0
5/16		0.3125	7.9375	0.02	0.508	13/16		0.8125	20.6375	16	406.4
	21/64	0.328125	8.3344	0.03	0.762		53/64	0.828125	21.0344	17	431.8
11/32		0.34375	8.7312	0.04	1.016	27/32		0.84375	21.4312	18	457.2
	23/64	0.359375	9.1281	0.05	1.270		55/64	0.859375	21.8281	19	482.6
3/8		0.375	9.5250	0.06	1.524	7/8		0.875	22.2250	20	508.0
	25/64	0.390625	9.9219	0.07	1.778		57/64	0.890625	22.6219	21	533.4
13/32		0.40625	10.3187	0.08	2.032	29/32		0.90625	23.0187	22	558.8
	27/64	0.421875	10.7156	0.09	2.286		59/64	0.921875	23.4156	23	584.2
7/16		0.4375	11.1125	0.1	2.54	15/16		0.9375	23.8125	24	609.6
	29/64	0.453125	11.5094	0.2	5.08		61/64	0.953125	24.2094	25	635.0
15/32		0.46875	11.9062	0.3	7.62	31/32		0.96875	24.6062	26	660.4
	31/64	0.484375	12.3031	0.4	10.16		63/64	0.984375	25.0031	27	690.6
1/2		0.5	12.7000	0.5	12.70						

ENGLISH TO METRIC CONVERSION: TORQUE

To convert foot-pounds (ft. lbs.) to Newton-meters: multiply the number of ft. lbs. by 1.3

To convert inch-pounds (in. lbs.) to Newton-meters: multiply the number of in. lbs. by .11

in lbs	N-m	in lbs	N-m	in lbs	N-m	in lbs	N-m	in lbs	N-m
0.1	0.01	1	0.11	10	1.13	19	2.15	28	3.16
0.2	0.02	2	0.23	11	1.24	20	2.26	29	3.28
0.3	0.03	3	0.34	12	1.36	21	2.37	30	3.39
0.4	0.04	4	0.45	13	1.47	22	2.49	31	3.50
0.5	0.06	5	0.56	14	1.58	23	2.60	32	3.62
0.6	0.07	6	0.68	15	1.70	24	2.71	33	3.73
0.7	0.08	7	0.78	16	1.81	25	2.82	34	3.84
0.8	0.09	8	0.90	17	1.92	26	2.94	35	3.95
0.9	0.10	9	1.02	18	2.03	27	3.05	36	4.0

ENGLISH TO METRIC CONVERSION: TORQUE

Torque is now expressed as either foot-pounds (ft./lbs.) or inch-pounds (in./lbs.). The metric measurement unit for torque is the Newton-meter (Nm). This unit—the Nm—will be used for all SI metric torque references, both the present ft./lbs. and in./lbs.

ft lbs	N-m	ft lbs	N-m	ft lbs	N-m	ft lbs	N-m
0.1	0.1	33	44.7	74	100.3	115	155.9
0.2	0.3	34	46.1	75	101.7	116	157.3
0.3	0.4	35	47.4	76	103.0	117	158.6
0.4	0.5	36	48.8	77	104.4	118	160.0
0.5	0.7	37	50.7	78	105.8	119	161.3
0.6	0.8	38	51.5	79	107.1	120	162.7
0.7	1.0	39	52.9	80	108.5	121	164.0
0.8	1.1	40	54.2	81	109.8	122	165.4
0.9	1.2	41	55.6	82	111.2	123	166.8
1	1.3	42	56.9	83	112.5	124	168.1
2	2.7	43	58.3	84	113.9	125	169.5
3	4.1	44	59.7	85	115.2	126	170.8
4	5.4	45	61.0	86	116.6	127	172.2
5	6.8	46	62.4	87	118.0	128	173.5
6	8.1	47	63.7	88	119.3	129	174.9
7	9.5	48	65.1	89	120.7	130	176.2
8	10.8	49	66.4	90	122.0	131	177.6
9	12.2	50	67.8	91	123.4	132	179.0
10	13.6	51	69.2	92	124.7	133	180.3
11	14.9	52	70.5	93	126.1	134	181.7
12	16.3	53	71.9	94	127.4	135	183.0
13	17.6	54	73.2	95	128.8	136	184.4
14	18.9	55	74.6	96	130.2	137	185.7
15	20.3	56	75.9	97	131.5	138	187.1
16	21.7	57	77.3	98	132.9	139	188.5
17	23.0	58	78.6	99	134.2	140	189.8
18	24.4	59	80.0	100	135.6	141	191.2
19	25.8	60	81.4	101	136.9	142	192.5
20	27.1	61	82.7	102	138.3	143	193.9
21	28.5	62	84.1	103	139.6	144	195.2
22	29.8	63	85.4	104	141.0	145	196.6
23	31.2	64	86.8	105	142.4	146	198.0
24	32.5	65	88.1	106	143.7	147	199.3
25	33.9	66	89.5	107	145.1	148	200.7
26	35.2	67	90.8	108	146.4	149	202.0
27	36.6	68	92.2	109	147.8	150	203.4
28	38.0	69	93.6	110	149.1	151	204.7
29	39.3	70	94.9	111	150.5	152	206.1
30	40.7	71	96.3	112	151.8	153	207.4
31	42.0	72	97.6	113	153.2	154	208.8
32	43.4	73	99.0	114	154.6	155	210.2

ENGLISH TO METRIC CONVERSION: FORCE

Force is presently measured in pounds (lbs.). This type of measurement is used to measure spring pressure, specifically how many pounds it takes to compress a spring. Our present force unit (the pound) will be replaced in SI metric measurements by the Newton (N). This term will eventually see use in specifications for electric motor brush spring pressures, valve spring pressures, etc.

To convert pounds (lbs.) to Newton (N): multiply the number of lbs. by 4.45

lbs	N	lbs	N	lbs	N	oz	N
0.01	0.04	21	93.4	59	262.4	1	0.3
0.02	0.09	22	97.9	60	266.9	2	0.6
0.03	0.13	23	102.3	61	271.3	3	0.8
0.04	0.18	24	106.8	62	275.8	4	1.1
0.05	0.22	25	111.2	63	280.2	5	1.4
0.06	0.27	26	115.6	64	284.6	6	1.7
0.07	0.31	27	120.1	65	289.1	7	2.0
0.08	0.36	28	124.6	66	293.6	8	2.2
0.09	0.40	29	129.0	67	298.0	9	2.5
0.1	0.4	30	133.4	68	302.5	10	2.8
0.2	0.9	31	137.9	69	306.9	11	3.1
0.3	1.3	32	142.3	70	311.4	12	3.3
0.4	1.8	33	146.8	71	315.8	13	3.6
0.5	2.2	34	151.2	72	320.3	14	3.9
0.6	2.7	35	155.7	73	324.7	15	4.2
0.7	3.1	36	160.1	74	329.2	16	4.4
0.8	3.6	37	164.6	75	333.6	17	4.7
0.9	4.0	38	169.0	76	338.1	18	5.0
1	4.4	39	173.5	77	342.5	19	5.3
2	8.9	40	177.9	78	347.0	20	5.6
3	13.4	41	182.4	79	351.4	21	5.8
4	17.8	42	186.8	80	355.9	22	6.1
5	22.2	43	191.3	81	360.3	23	6.4
6	26.7	44	195.7	82	364.8	24	6.7
7	31.1	45	200.2	83	369.2	25	7.0
8	35.6	46	204.6	84	373.6	26	7.2
9	40.0	47	209.1	85	378.1	27	7.5
10	44.5	48	213.5	86	382.6	28	7.8
11	48.9	49	218.0	87	387.0	29	8.1
12	53.4	50	224.4	88	391.4	30	8.3
13	57.8	51	226.9	89	395.9	31	8.6
14	62.3	52	231.3	90	400.3	32	8.9
15	66.7	53	235.8	91	404.8	33	9.2
16	71.2	54	240.2	92	409.2	34	9.4
17	75.6	55	244.6	93	413.7	35	9.7
18	80.1	56	249.1	94	418.1	36	10.0
19	84.5	57	253.6	95	422.6	37	10.3
20	89.0	58	258.0	96	427.0	38	10.6

ENGLISH TO METRIC CONVERSION: LIQUID CAPACITY

Liquid or fluid capacity is presently expressed as pints, quarts or gallons, or a combination of all of these. In the metric system the liter (l) will become the basic unit. Fractions of a liter would be expressed as deciliters, centiliters, or most frequently (and commonly) as milliliters.

To convert pints (pts.) to liters (l): multiply the number of pints by .47
To convert liters (l) to pints (pts.): multiply the number of liters by 2.1
To convert quarts (qts.) to liters (l): multiply the number of quarts by .95

To convert liters (l) to quarts (qts.): multiply the number of liters by 1.06
To convert gallons (gals.) to liters (l): multiply the number of gallons by 3.8
To convert liters (l) to gallons (gals.): multiply the number of liters by .26

gals	liters	qts	liters	pts	liters
0.1	0.38	0.1	0.10	0.1	0.05
0.2	0.76	0.2	0.19	0.2	0.10
0.3	1.1	0.3	0.28	0.3	0.14
0.4	1.5	0.4	0.38	0.4	0.19
0.5	1.9	0.5	0.47	0.5	0.24
0.6	2.3	0.6	0.57	0.6	0.28
0.7	2.6	0.7	0.66	0.7	0.33
0.8	3.0	0.8	0.76	0.8	0.38
0.9	3.4	0.9	0.85	0.9	0.43
1	3.8	1	1.0	1	0.5
2	7.6	2	1.9	2	1.0
3	11.4	3	2.8	3	1.4
4	15.1	4	3.8	4	1.9
5	18.9	5	4.7	5	2.4
6	22.7	6	5.7	6	2.8
7	26.5	7	6.6	7	3.3
8	30.3	8	7.6	8	3.8
9	34.1	9	8.5	9	4.3
10	37.8	10	9.5	10	4.7
11	41.6	11	10.4	11	5.2
12	45.4	12	11.4	12	5.7
13	49.2	13	12.3	13	6.2
14	53.0	14	13.2	14	6.6
15	56.8	15	14.2	15	7.1
16	60.6	16	15.1	16	7.6
17	64.3	17	16.1	17	8.0
18	68.1	18	17.0	18	8.5
19	71.9	19	18.0	19	9.0
20	75.7	20	18.9	20	9.5
21	79.5	21	19.9	21	9.9
22	83.2	22	20.8	22	10.4
23	87.0	23	21.8	23	10.9
24	90.8	24	22.7	24	11.4
25	94.6	25	23.6	25	11.8
26	98.4	26	24.6	26	12.3
27	102.2	27	25.5	27	12.8
28	106.0	28	26.5	28	13.2
29	110.0	29	27.4	29	13.7
30	113.5	30	28.4	30	14.2

ENGLISH TO METRIC CONVERSION: PRESSURE

The basic unit of pressure measurement used today is expressed as pounds per square inch (psi). The metric unit for psi will be the kilopascal (kPa). This will apply to either fluid pressure or air pressure, and will be frequently seen in tire pressure readings, oil pressure specifications, fuel pump pressure, etc.

To convert pounds per square inch (psi) to kilopascals (kPa): multiply the number of psi by 6.89

Psi	kPa	Psi	kPa	Psi	kPa	Psi	kPa
0.1	0.7	37	255.1	82	565.4	127	875.6
0.2	1.4	38	262.0	83	572.3	128	882.5
0.3	2.1	39	268.9	84	579.2	129	889.4
0.4	2.8	40	275.8	85	586.0	130	896.3
0.5	3.4	41	282.7	86	592.9	131	903.2
0.6	4.1	42	289.6	87	599.8	132	910.1
0.7	4.8	43	296.5	88	606.7	133	917.0
0.8	5.5	44	303.4	89	613.6	134	923.9
0.9	6.2	45	310.3	90	620.5	135	930.8
1	6.9	46	317.2	91	627.4	136	937.7
2	13.8	47	324.0	92	634.3	137	944.6
3	20.7	48	331.0	93	641.2	138	951.5
4	27.6	49	337.8	94	648.1	139	958.4
5	34.5	50	344.7	95	655.0	140	965.2
6	41.4	51	351.6	96	661.9	141	972.2
7	48.3	52	358.5	97	668.8	142	979.0
8	55.2	53	365.4	98	675.7	143	985.9
9	62.1	54	372.3	99	682.6	144	992.8
10	69.0	55	379.2	100	689.5	145	999.7
11	75.8	56	386.1	101	696.4	146	1006.6
12	82.7	57	393.0	102	703.3	147	1013.5
13	89.6	58	399.9	103	710.2	148	1020.4
14	96.5	59	406.8	104	717.0	149	1027.3
15	103.4	60	413.7	105	723.9	150	1034.2
16	110.3	61	420.6	106	730.8	151	1041.1
17	117.2	62	427.5	107	737.7	152	1048.0
18	124.1	63	434.4	108	744.6	153	1054.9
19	131.0	64	441.3	109	751.5	154	1061.8
20	137.9	65	448.2	110	758.4	155	1068.7
21	144.8	66	455.0	111	765.3	156	1075.6
22	151.7	67	461.9	112	772.2	157	1082.5
23	158.6	68	468.8	113	779.1	158	1089.4
24	165.5	69	475.7	114	786.0	159	1096.3
25	172.4	70	482.6	115	792.9	160	1103.2
26	179.3	71	489.5	116	799.8	161	1110.0
27	186.2	72	496.4	117	806.7	162	1116.9
28	193.0	73	503.3	118	813.6	163	1123.8
29	200.0	74	510.2	119	820.5	164	1130.7
30	206.8	75	517.1	120	827.4	165	1137.6
31	213.7	76	524.0	121	834.3	166	1144.5
32	220.6	77	530.9	122	841.2	167	1151.4
33	227.5	78	537.8	123	848.0	168	1158.3
34	234.4	79	544.7	124	854.9	169	1165.2
35	241.3	80	551.6	125	861.8	170	1172.1
36	248.2	81	558.5	126	868.7	171	1179.0

ENGLISH TO METRIC CONVERSION: PRESSURE

The basic unit of pressure measurement used today is expressed as pounds per square inch (psi). The metric unit for psi will be the kilopascal (kPa). This will apply to either fluid pressure or air pressure, and will be frequently seen in tire pressure readings, oil pressure specifications, fuel pump pressure, etc.

To convert pounds per square inch (psi) to kilopascals (kPa): multiply the number of psi by 6.89

Psi	kPa	Psi	kPa	Psi	kPa	Psi	kPa
172	1185.9	216	1489.3	260	1792.6	304	2096.0
173	1192.8	217	1496.2	261	1799.5	305	2102.9
174	1199.7	218	1503.1	262	1806.4	306	2109.8
175	1206.6	219	1510.0	263	1813.3	307	2116.7
176	1213.5	220	1516.8	264	1820.2	308	2123.6
177	1220.4	221	1523.7	265	1827.1	309	2130.5
178	1227.3	222	1530.6	266	1834.0	310	2137.4
179	1234.2	223	1537.5	267	1840.9	311	2144.3
180	1241.0	224	1544.4	268	1847.8	312	2151.2
181	1247.9	225	1551.3	269	1854.7	313	2158.1
182	1254.8	226	1558.2	270	1861.6	314	2164.9
183	1261.7	227	1565.1	271	1868.5	315	2171.8
184	1268.6	228	1572.0	272	1875.4	316	2178.7
185	1275.5	229	1578.9	273	1882.3	317	2185.6
186	1282.4	230	1585.8	274	1889.2	318	2192.5
187	1289.3	231	1592.7	275	1896.1	319	2199.4
188	1296.2	232	1599.6	276	1903.0	320	2206.3
189	1303.1	233	1606.5	277	1909.8	321	2213.2
190	1310.0	234	1613.4	278	1916.7	322	2220.1
191	1316.9	235	1620.3	279	1923.6	323	2227.0
192	1323.8	236	1627.2	280	1930.5	324	2233.9
193	1330.7	237	1634.1	281	1937.4	325	2240.8
194	1337.6	238	1641.0	282	1944.3	326	2247.7
195	1344.5	239	1647.8	283	1951.2	327	2254.6
196	1351.4	240	1654.7	284	1958.1	328	2261.5
197	1358.3	241	1661.6	285	1965.0	329	2268.4
198	1365.2	242	1668.5	286	1971.9	330	2275.3
199	1372.0	243	1675.4	287	1978.8	331	2282.2
200	1378.9	244	1682.3	288	1985.7	332	2289.1
201	1385.8	245	1689.2	289	1992.6	333	2295.9
202	1392.7	246	1696.1	290	1999.5	334	2302.8
203	1399.6	247	1703.0	291	2006.4	335	2309.7
204	1406.5	248	1709.9	292	2013.3	336	2316.6
205	1413.4	249	1716.8	293	2020.2	337	2323.5
206	1420.3	250	1723.7	294	2027.1	338	2330.4
207	1427.2	251	1730.6	295	2034.0	339	2337.3
208	1434.1	252	1737.5	296	2040.8	240	2344.2
209	1441.0	253	1744.4	297	2047.7	341	2351.1
210	1447.9	254	1751.3	298	2054.6	342	2358.0
211	1454.8	255	1758.2	299	2061.5	343	2364.9
212	1461.7	256	1765.1	300	2068.4	344	2371.8
213	1468.7	257	1772.0	301	2075.3	345	2378.7
214	1475.5	258	1778.8	302	2082.2	346	2385.6
215	1482.4	259	1785.7	303	2089.1	347	2392.5

SPARK PLUGS AND WIRES 2-2
SPARK PLUGS 2-2
  SPARK PLUG HEAT RANGE 2-2
  REMOVAL & INSTALLATION 2-2
  INSPECTION & GAPPING 2-6
SPARK PLUG WIRES 2-7
  TESTING 2-7
  REMOVAL & INSTALLATION 2-7
FIRING ORDER 2-8
POINT TYPE IGNITION 2-11
BREAKER POINTS AND
  CONDENSER 2-11
  DESCRIPTION & OPERATION 2-11
  REMOVAL & INSTALLATION 2-12
  DWELL ADJUSTMENT 2-16
ELECTRONIC IGNITION 2-18
AMERICAN MOTORS BREAKERLESS
  INDUCTIVE DISCHARGE IGNITION
  SYSTEM 2-18
  COMPONENTS 2-18
  DESCRIPTION & OPERATION 2-18
  DIAGNOSIS & TESTING 2-19
  DISTRIBUTOR OVERHAUL 2-19
AMERICAN MOTORS SOLID STATE
  IGNITION (SSI) SYSTEM 2-20
  DESCRIPTION & OPERATION 2-20
  TESTING 2-20
DELCO HIGH ENERGY IGNITION (HEI)
  SYSTEM 2-21
  HEI SYSTEM PRECAUTIONS 2-21
  TROUBLESHOOTING THE HEI
    SYSTEM 2-22
  COMPONENT REPLACEMENT 2-23
IGNITION TIMING 2-24
TIMING 2-24
  INSPECTION & ADJUSTMENT 2-25
VALVE LASH 2-27
GENERAL INFORMATION 2-27
  ADJUSTMENT 2-27
IDLE SPEED AND MIXTURE 2-29
ADJUSTMENTS 2-29
  4-121 ENGINES 2-29
  4-151 ENGINES 2-29
  1975–79 6-CYLINDER AND V8
    ENGINES 2-30
  1980 6-CYLINDER AND V8
    ENGINES 2-33
  1981–82 6-CYLINDER AND V8
    ENGINES 2-33
  1983 4-150 ENGINES 2-34
  1983–84 6-258 ENGINE 2-34
SPECIFICATION CHARTS
HEI PLUG WIRE RESISTANCE
  CHART 2-7
TUNE-UP SPECIFICATIONS 2-9
TROUBLESHOOTING CHARTS
TROUBLESHOOTING BASIC POINT-
  TYPE IGNITION SYSTEM
  PROBLEMS 2-17

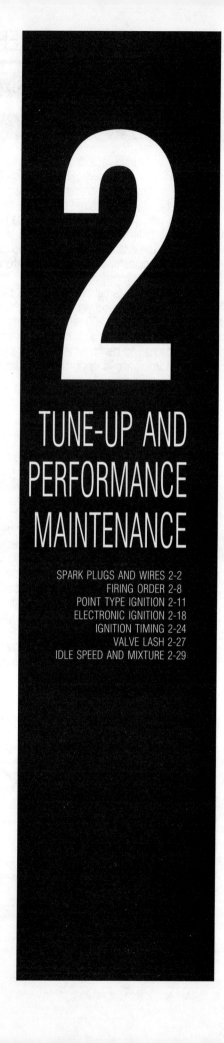

2

TUNE-UP AND PERFORMANCE MAINTENANCE

SPARK PLUGS AND WIRES 2-2
FIRING ORDER 2-8
POINT TYPE IGNITION 2-11
ELECTRONIC IGNITION 2-18
IGNITION TIMING 2-24
VALVE LASH 2-27
IDLE SPEED AND MIXTURE 2-29

SPARK PLUGS AND WIRES

Spark Plugs

A typical spark plug consists of a metal shell surrounding a ceramic insulator. A metal electrode extends downward through the center of the insulator and protrudes a small distance. Located at the end of the plug and attached to the side of the outer metal shell is the side electrode. The side electrode bends in at a 90° angle so that its tip is just past and parallel to the tip of the center electrode. The distance between these two electrodes (measured in thousandths of an inch or hundredths of a millimeter) is called the spark plug gap.

The spark plug does not produce a spark but instead provides a gap across which the current can arc. The coil produces anywhere from 20,000 to 50,000 volts (depending on the type and application) which travels through the wires to the spark plugs. The current passes along the center electrode and jumps the gap to the side electrode, and in doing so, ignites the air/fuel mixture in the combustion chamber.

SPARK PLUG HEAT RANGE

Spark plug heat range is the ability of the plug to dissipate heat. The longer the insulator (or the farther it extends into the engine), the hotter the plug will operate; the shorter the insulator (the closer the electrode is to the block's cooling passages) the cooler it will operate. A plug that absorbs little heat and remains too cool will quickly accumulate deposits of oil and carbon since it is not hot enough to burn them off. This leads to plug fouling and consequently to misfiring. A plug that absorbs too much heat will have no deposits but, due to the excessive heat, the electrodes will burn away quickly and might possibly lead to preignition or other ignition problems. Preignition takes place when plug tips get so hot that they glow sufficiently to ignite the air/fuel mixture before the actual spark occurs. This early ignition will usually cause a pinging during low speeds and heavy loads.

The general rule of thumb for choosing the correct heat range

THE SHORTER THE PATH, THE FASTER THE HEAT IS DISSIPATED AND THE COOLER THE PLUG

HEAVY LOADS, HIGH SPEEDS

SHORT Insulator Tip
Fast Heat Transfer
LOWER Heat Range
COLD PLUG

THE LONGER THE PATH, THE SLOWER THE HEAT IS DISSIPATED AND THE HOTTER THE PLUG

SHORT TRIP STOP-AND-GO

LONG Insulator Tip
Slow Heat Transfer
HIGHER Heat Range
HOT PLUG

Spark plug heat range

when picking a spark plug is: if most of your driving is long distance, high speed travel, use a colder plug; if most of your driving is stop and go, use a hotter plug. Original equipment plugs are generally a good compromise between the 2 styles and most people never have the need to change their plugs from the factory-recommended heat range.

REMOVAL & INSTALLATION

A set of spark plugs usually requires replacement after about 20,000–30,000 miles (32,000–48,000 km), depending on your style of driving. In normal operation plug gap increases about 0.001 in. (0.025mm) for every 2500 miles (4000 km). As the gap increases, the plug's voltage requirement also increases. It requires a greater voltage to jump the wider gap and about two to three times as much voltage to fire the plug at high speeds than at idle. The improved air/fuel ratio control of modern fuel injection combined with the higher voltage output of modern ignition sys-

PORCELAIN INSULATOR

INSULATOR CRACKS OFTEN OCCUR HERE

SHELL

ADJUST FOR PROPER GAP

SIDE ELECTRODE (BEND TO ADJUST GAP)

CENTER ELECTRODE: FILE FLAT WHEN ADJUSTING GAP; DO NOT BEND

Cross-section of a spark plug

Disengage the spark plug wire from the spark plug using a twisting motion. Pull on the boot only

Loosen the spark plug from the cylinder head . . .

. . . then remove it from the head

tems will often allow an engine to run significantly longer on a set of standard spark plugs, but keep in mind that efficiency will drop as the gap widdens (along with fuel economy and power).

When you're removing spark plugs, work on one at a time. Don't start by removing the plug wires all at once, because, unless you number them, they may become mixed up. Take a minute before you begin and number the wires with tape.

1. Disconnect the negative battery cable, and if the vehicle has been run recently, allow the engine to thoroughly cool.

2. Carefully twist the spark plug wire boot to loosen it, then pull upward and remove the boot from the plug. Be sure to pull on the boot and not on the wire, otherwise the connector located inside the boot may become separated.

3. Using compressed air, blow any water or debris from the spark plug well to assure that no harmful contaminants are allowed to enter the combustion chamber when the spark plug is removed. If compressed air is not available, use a rag or a brush to clean the area.

➡**Remove the spark plugs when the engine is cold, if possible, to prevent damage to the threads. If removal of the plugs is difficult, apply a few drops of penetrating oil or silicone spray to the area around the base of the plug, and allow it a few minutes to work.**

4. Using a spark plug socket that is equipped with a rubber insert to properly hold the plug, turn the spark plug counterclockwise to loosen and remove the spark plug from the bore.

❋❋ WARNING

Be sure not to use a flexible extension on the socket. Use of a flexible extension may allow a shear force to be applied to the plug. A shear force could break the plug off in the cylinder head, leading to costly and frustrating repairs.

To install:

5. Inspect the spark plug boot for tears or damage. If a damaged boot is found, the spark plug wire must be replaced.

6. Using a wire feeler gauge, check and adjust the spark plug gap. When using a gauge, the proper size should pass between the electrodes with a slight drag. The next larger size should not be able to pass while the next smaller size should pass freely.

7. Carefully thread the plug into the bore by hand. If resistance is felt before the plug is almost completely threaded, back the plug out and begin threading again. In small, hard to reach areas, an old spark plug wire and boot could be used as a threading tool. The boot will hold the plug while you twist the end of the wire and the wire is supple enough to twist before it would allow the plug to crossthread.

❋❋ WARNING

Do not use the spark plug socket to thread the plugs. Always carefully thread the plug by hand or using an old plug wire to prevent the possibility of crossthreading and damaging the cylinder head bore.

8. Carefully tighten the spark plug. If the plug you are installing is equipped with a crush washer, seat the plug, then tighten about ¼ turn to crush the washer. If you are installing a tapered seat plug, tighten the plug to specifications provided by the vehicle or plug manufacturer.

A normally worn spark plug should have light tan or gray deposits on the firing tip

A carbon fouled plug, identified by soft, sooty, black deposits, may indicate an improperly tuned vehicle. Check the air cleaner, ignition components and engine control system

A variety of tools and gauges are needed for spark plug service

Checking the spark plug gap with a feeler gauge

A physically damaged spark plug may be evidence of severe detonation in that cylinder. Watch that cylinder carefully between services, as a continued detonation will not only damage the plug, but could also damage the engine

An oil fouled spark plug indicates an engine with worn piston rings and/or bad valve seals allowing excessive oil to enter the chamber

Adjusting the spark plug gap

If the standard plug is in good condition, the electrode may be filed flat—**CAUTION**: do not file platinum plugs

This spark plug has been left in the engine too long, as evidenced by the extreme gap—Plugs with such an extreme gap can cause misfiring and stumbling accompanied by a noticeable lack of power

A bridged or almost bridged spark plug, identified by a build-up between the electrodes caused by excessive carbon or oil build-up on the plug

9. Apply a small amount of silicone dielectric compound to the end of the spark plug lead or inside the spark plug boot to prevent sticking, then install the boot to the spark plug and push until it clicks into place. The click may be felt or heard, then gently pull back on the boot to assure proper contact.

INSPECTION & GAPPING

Check the plugs for deposits and wear. If they are not going to be replaced, clean the plugs thoroughly. Remember that any kind of deposit will decrease the efficiency of the plug. Plugs can be cleaned on a spark plug cleaning machine, which can sometimes be found in service stations, or you can do an acceptable job of cleaning with a stiff brush. If the plugs are cleaned, the electrodes must be filed flat. Use an ignition points file, not an emery board or the like, which will leave deposits. The electrodes must be filed perfectly flat with sharp edges; rounded edges reduce the spark plug voltage by as much as 50%.

Check spark plug gap before installation. The ground electrode (the L-shaped one connected to the body of the plug) must be parallel to the center electrode and the specified size wire gauge (please refer to the Tune-Up Specifications chart for details) must pass between the electrodes with a slight drag.

➡**NEVER adjust the gap on a used platinum type spark plug.**

Always check the gap on new plugs as they are not always set correctly at the factory. Do not use a flat feeler gauge when measuring the gap on a used plug, because the reading may be inaccurate. A round-wire type gapping tool is the best way to check the gap. The correct gauge should pass through the electrode gap with a slight drag. If you're in doubt, try one size smaller and one larger. The smaller gauge should go through easily, while the larger one shouldn't go through at all. Wire gapping tools usually have a bending tool attached. Use that to adjust the side electrode until the proper distance is obtained. Absolutely never attempt to bend the center electrode. Also, be careful not to bend the side electrode too far or too often as it may weaken and break off within the engine, requiring removal of the cylinder head to retrieve it.

Spark Plug Wires

TESTING

▶ **See Figure 1**

Visually inspect the spark plug cables for burns, cuts, or breaks in the insulation. Check the spark plug boots and the nipples on the distributor cap and coil. Replace any damages wiring. If no physical damage is obvious, the wires can be checked with an ohmmeter for excessive resistance.

REMOVAL & INSTALLATION

When installing a new set of spark plug cables, replace the cables one at a time so there will be no mixup. Start by replacing the longest cable first. Install the boot firmly over the spark plug. Route the wire exactly the same as the original. Insert the nipple firmly into the tower on the distributor cap. Repeat the process for each cable.

Fig.1 When possible, use a special grasping tool for removing the spark plug wires

HEI Plug Wire Resistance Chart

Wire Length (inches)	Minimum Ohms	Maximum Ohms
Up to 15	3,000	10,000
15–25	4,000	15,000
25–35	6,000	20,000
Over 35		25,000

Fig. 2 HEI Spark plug wire resistance chart

Checking plug wire resistance through the distributor cap with an ohmmeter

Checking individual plug wire resistance with a digital ohmmeter

FIRING ORDER

♦ **See Figure 3, 4, 5, 6 and 7**

To avoid confusion, remove and tag the wires one at a time, for replacement.

Fig. 3 Porsche 4-121 engine
Firing order: 1–3–4–2
Distributor rotation: Clockwise

Fig. 4 Chevrolet 4-151 engine
Firing order: 1–3–4–2
Distributor rotation: Clockwise

Fig. 5 AMC 6-232 and 6-258 engines
Firing order: 1–5–3–6–2–4
Distributor rotation: Clockwise

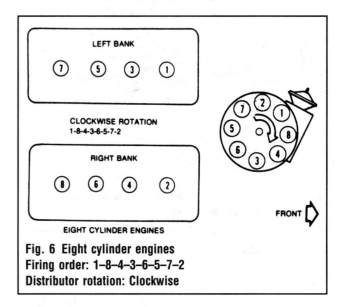

Fig. 6 Eight cylinder engines
Firing order: 1–8–4–3–6–5–7–2
Distributor rotation: Clockwise

Fig. 7 AMC 4-150 engine
Firing order: 1–2–3–4
Distributor rotation: Clockwise

Tune-up Specifications

Engine	Years	Spark Plugs Type	Gap (in.)	Distributor Point Gap (in.)	Dwell (deg.)	Ignition Timing (deg.) Man. Trans.	Auto. Trans.	Valve * Clearance In.	Exh.	Idle Speed MT	AT
4-121	1977	N-8L	0.035	0.018	47	12B	⑰	0.006–0.009	0.016–0.019	900	800
	1978	N-8L	0.035	0.018	47	12B	⑰	0.006–0.009	0.016–0.019	900	800
	1979	N-8L	0.035	0.018	47	12B	⑰	0.006–0.009	0.016–0.019	900	800
4-150	1984	RFN-14LY	0.035	Electronic		12B	12B	Hyd.	Hyd.	750	750
4-151	1980	R44TSX	0.060	Electronic		①	②	Hyd.	Hyd.	900	700
	1981	R44TSX	0.060	Electronic		③	④	Hyd.	Hyd.	900	700
	1982–83	R44TSX	0.060	Electronic		⑤	⑤	Hyd.	Hyd.	900	700
6-232	1975	N-12Y	0.035	Electronic		5B	5B	Hyd.	Hyd.	600	⑥
	1976	N-12Y	0.035	Electronic		8B	8B	Hyd.	Hyd.	850	⑥
	1977	N-12Y	0.035	Electronic		⑦	10B	Hyd.	Hyd.	⑧	⑥
	1978	N-13L	0.035	Electronic		8B	10B	Hyd.	Hyd.	600	550
	1979	N-13L	0.035	Electronic		8B	10B	Hyd.	Hyd.	600	550
6-258	1975	N-12Y	0.035	Electronic		3B	3B	Hyd.	Hyd.	600	⑥
	1976	N-12Y	0.035	Electronic		6B	8B	Hyd.	Hyd.	⑨	⑥
	1977	N-12Y	0.035	Electronic		⑩	⑪	Hyd.	Hyd.	600	⑥
	1978	1 bbl N-13L	0.035	Electronic		⑩	⑪	Hyd.	Hyd.	⑪	550
	1978	2 bbl N-13L	0.035	Electronic		6B	8B	Hyd.	Hyd.	600	600
	1979	1 bbl N-13L	0.035	Electronic		—	8B	Hyd.	Hyd.	—	700
	1979	2 bbl N-13L	0.035	Electronic		4B	8B	Hyd.	Hyd.	700	600
	1980	⑫	0.035	Electronic		6B	⑬	Hyd.	Hyd.	700	600
	1981	RFN-14LY	0.035	Electronic		⑭	⑮	Hyd.	hyd.	700	600
	1982–83	RFN-14LY	0.035	Electronic		⑯	⑯	Hyd.	Hyd.	750	650
	1984–88	RFN-14LY	0.035	Electronic		9B	9B	Hyd.	Hyd.	900	800
8-304	1975	N-12Y	0.035	Electronic		5B	5B	Hyd.	Hyd.	750	700

Tune-up Specifications

Engine	Years	Spark Plugs		Distributor		Ignition Timing (deg.)		Valve * Clearance		Idle Speed	
		Type	Gap (in.)	Point Gap (in.)	Dwell (deg.)	Man. Trans.	Auto. Trans.	In.	Exh.	MT	AT
8-304	1976	N-12Y	0.035	Electronic		5B	⑱	Hyd.	Hyd.	750	700
	1977–78	N-12Y	0.035	Electronic		—	⑱	Hyd.	Hyd.	—	⑥
	1979	N-12Y	0.035	Electronic		5B	8B	Hyd.	Hyd.	800	600
8-360	1975	N-12Y	0.035	Electronic		5B	5B	Hyd.	Hyd.	750	700
	1976	N-12Y	0.035	Electronic		—	⑱	Hyd.	Hyd.	—	700
	1977	N-12Y	0.035	Electronic		—	⑱	Hyd.	Hyd.	—	⑥
	1978	N-12Y	0.035	Electronic		—	10B	Hyd.	Hyd.	—	⑲
8-401	1975	N-12Y	0.035	Electronic		5B	5B	Hyd.	Hyd.	750	700
	1976	N-12Y	0.035	Electronic		—	⑱	Hyd.	Hyd.	—	700

NOTE: The specifications on the underhood sticker often reflect changes made during production. If the specifications on your vehicle's sticker disagree with the specifications in this chart, use the sticker specifications.

*Valve clearance is set on a hot engine.

① Except California: 10B
California: 12B
② Except California: 12B
California: 10B
③ Eagle, exc. Calif.: 11B
All other car models: 10B
④ Exc. Pacer and Calif. Eagle: 12B
Pacer and Calif. Eagle: 8B
⑤ Eagle, except Calif.: 12B
All California models: 8B
All High Altitude models: 15B
All other car models: 10B
⑥ Except Calif.: 550
Calif.: 700
⑦ Except Calif.: 8B
Calif.: 10B
⑧ Except Calif.: 600
Calif.: 850
⑨ Matador Coupe and Sedan: 600
All others: 850
⑩ Except High Altitude: 6B
High Altitude: 10B
⑪ Except High Altitude: 8B
High Altitude: 10B

⑫ Except Eagle: N-14LY
Eagle: N-13L
⑬ Except Pacer and Calif. Eagle: 10B
Pacer and Calif. Eagle: 8B
⑭ Concord and Spirit: 6B
Eagle, except Calif. and High Altitude: 8B
Calif., Eagles: 4B
High Altitude Eagles: 15B
⑮ Concord and Spirit: 6B
Eagle, except Calif. and High Altitude: 8B
Calif. Eagles: 6B
High Altitude Eagles: 15B
⑯ Concord and Spirit, except High Altitude: 15B
High Altitude Concord and Spirit: 19B
Eagle: 21B
⑰ Except Calif.: 12B
Calif.: 8B
⑱ Except Calif.: 10B
Calif.: 5B
⑲ Except Calif.: 600
Calif.: 650

POINT TYPE IGNITION

Breaker Points and Condenser

DESCRIPTION & OPERATION

♦ **See Figures 8 and 9**

The points function as a circuit breaker for the primary circuit of the ignition system. The ignition coil must boost the 12 volts of electrical pressure supplied by the battery to as much as 25,000 volts in order to fire the plugs. To do this, the coil depends on the points and the condenser to make a clean break in the primary circuit.

The coil has both primary and secondary circuits. When the ignition is turned on, the battery supplies voltage through the coil and onto the points. The points are connected to ground, completing the primary circuit. As the current passes through the coil, a magnetic field is created in the iron center core of the coil. As the cam in the distributor turns, the points open and the primary circuit collapses. The magnetic field in the primary circuit of the coil also collapses and cuts through the secondary circuit windings around the iron core. Because of the scientific phenomenon called electromagnetic induction, the battery voltage is increased to a level sufficient to fire the spark plugs.

When the points open, the electrical charge in the primary cir-

cuit jumps the gap created between the two open contacts of the points. If this electrical charge were not transferred elsewhere, the metal contacts of the points would melt and the gap between the points would start to change rapidly. If this gap is not maintained, the points will not break the primary circuit. If the primary circuit is not broken, the secondary circuit will not have enough voltage to fire the spark plugs.

The function of the condenser is to absorb excessive voltage from the points when they open and thus prevent the points from becoming pitted or burned.

It is interesting to note that the above cycle must be completed by the ignition system every time a spark plug fires. In a V8 engine, all of the spark plugs fire once for every two revolutions of the crankshaft. That means that in one revolution, 4 spark plugs fire once for every two revolutions of the crankshaft. That means that in one revolution, 4 spark plugs fire. So, when the engine is at an idle speed of 800 rpm, the points are opening and closing 3200 times a minute.

There are two ways to check the breaker point gap. It can be done with a feeler gauge or a dwell meter. Either way you set the points, you are basically adjusting the amount of time that the points remain open. The time is measured in degrees of distributor rotation. When you measure the gap between the breaker points with a feeler gauge, you are setting the maximum amount the points will open when the rubbing block on the points is on a high point of the distributor cam. When you adjust the points with

Fig. 8 Schematic of a common primary ignition circuit used on point type ignition systems

Fig. 9 Schematic of the secondary ignition system used on point type ignition systems

a dwell meter, you are adjusting the number of degrees that the points will remain closed before they start to open as a high point of the distributor cam approaches the rubbing block of the points.

When you replace a set of points, always replace the condenser at the same time.

When you change the point gap or dwell, you will also have changed the ignition timing. So, if the point gap or dwell is changed, the ignition timing must be adjusted also.

REMOVAL & INSTALLATION

♦ See Figures 10 thru 16

The usual procedure is to replace the condenser each time the point set is replaced. Although this is not always necessary, it is easy to do at this time and the cost is negligible. Every time you adjust or replace breaker points, the ignition timing must be checked and, if necessary, adjusted. No special equipment other than a feeler gauge is required for point replacement or adjustment, but a dwell meter is strongly advised.

1. Remove the distributor cap. You might have to unclip or detach some or all of the plug wires to remove the cap.
2. Clean the cap inside and out with a clean rag. Check for cracks and carbon paths. A carbon path shows up as a dark line, usually from one of the cap sockets inside terminals to a ground.

Check the condition of the carbon button inside the center of the cap and the inside terminals. Replace the cap as necessary.

3. Pull the rotor up and off the shaft. Clean off the metal outer tip if it is burned or corroded. Don't file it. Replace the rotor as necessary or if one came with your tune-up kit.

4. The factory says that the points don't need to be replaced if metal transfer from one contact to the other doesn't exceed 0.020 in. (0.51 mm). However, sad experience show that it is more economical and reliable in the long run to replace the point set while the distributor is open, than to have to do this at a later (and possible more inconvenient) time.

5. Pull off the two wire terminals from the point assembly. One wire comes from the condenser and the other comes from within the distributor. The terminals are usually held in place by spring tension only. There might be a clamp screw securing the terminals on some older versions. Loosen the point set hold-down screw(s). Be very careful not to drop any of these little screws inside the distributor. If this happens, the distributor will probably have to be removed to get at the screw. If the hold-down screw is lost elsewhere, it must be replaced with one that is no longer than the original to avoid interference with the distributor workings. Remove the point set, even if it is to be re-used.

6. If the points are to be reused, clean them with a few strokes or a special point file. This is done with the points removed to prevent tiny metal filings getting into the distributor.

Fig. 10 Exploded view of the distributor used on the 4-121 engine

CAP
ROTOR
DUST SHIELD
POINT ASSEMBLY
BREAKER PLATE
CONDENSER AND CONNECTOR ASSEMBLY
FLYWEIGHTS
WICK
HOUSING ASSEMBLY
VACUUM UNIT
LATCH
GEAR
PIN

Fig. 11 Remove the rotor by pulling it off the distributor shaft

Fig. 12 Disengage the wires from the point assembly terminals

Fig. 13 Unfasten the condenser retaining screw, then remove the condenser from the distributor housing

Fig. 14 Loosen the point assembly retaining screw, then remove the points

Fig. 15 To align the contact surfaces bend the stationary arm. Do not bend the moving arm

Fig. 16 Insert the correct size feeler gauge and adjust the point gap until a slight drag on the gauge is felt

7. Loosen the condenser hold-down screw and slide the condenser out of the clamp. This will save you a struggle with the clamp, condenser, and the tiny screw when you install the new one. If you have the type of clamp that is permanently fastened to the condenser, remove the screw and the condenser. Don't lose the screw.

8. Attend to the distributor cam lubricator. If you have the round kind, turn it around on its shaft at the first tune-up and replace it at the second. If you have the long kind, switch ends at the first tune-up and replace it at the second.

➡**Don't oil or grease the lubricator. The foam is impregnated with a special lubricant.**

If you didn't get any lubricator at all, of if it looks like someone took it off, don't worry. You don't really need it. Just rub a match head size dab of grease on the cam lobes.

9. Install the new condenser. If you left the clamp in place, just slide the new condenser into the clamp.

10. Replace the point set and leave the screw slightly loose. Replace the two wire terminals, making sure that the wired don't interfere with anything.

11. Check that the contacts meet squarely. If they don't, bend the tab supporting the fixed contact.

12. Turn the engine until a high point on the cam that opens the points contacts the rubbing block on the point arm. You can turn the engine by hand if you can get a wrench on the crankshaft pulley nut, or you can grasp the fan belt and turn the engine with the spark plugs removed.

✳✳ CAUTION

If you try turning the engine by hand, be very careful not to get your fingers pinched in the pulleys.

On a stick shift car, you can push it forward in high gear. Another alternative is to bump the starter switch or use a remote starter switch.

13. There is a screwdriver slot near the contacts. Insert a screwdriver and lever the points open or closed until they appear to be at about the gap specified in the Tune-Up Specifications.

14. Insert the correct size feel gauge and adjust the gap until you can push the gauge in and out between the contacts with a slight drag, but without distributing the point arm. This operation takes a bit of experience to obtain the correct feel. Check by trying the gauges 0.001–0.002 in. (0.025–0.051mm) larger and smaller than the setting size. The larger one should disturb the point arm, while the smaller one should not drag at all. Tighten the point set hold-down screw. Recheck the gap, because it often changes when the screw is tightened.

15. After all the point adjustments are complete, pull a white business card through (between) the contacts to remove any traces of oil. Oil will cause rapid contact burning.

➡**You can adjust dwell at this point, if you wish. Refer to Step 18.**

16. Push the rotor firmly down into place. It will only go on one way. Tighten the V8 rotor screws. If the rotor is not installed properly, it will probably break when the starter is operated.

17. Replace the distributor cap.

18. If a dwell meter is available, check the dwell.

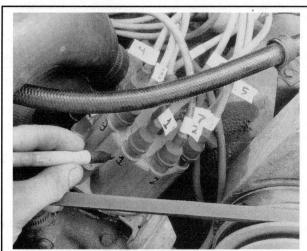

Tag the wires and matchmark their positions on the distributor cap towers . . .

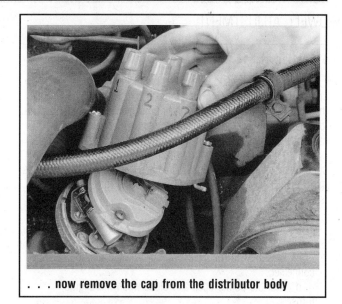

. . . now remove the cap from the distributor body

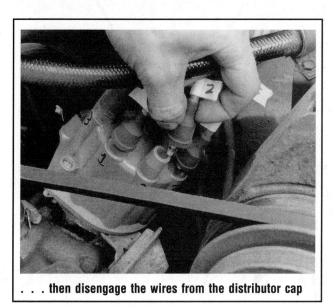

. . . then disengage the wires from the distributor cap

Unfasten the rotor retaining screws . . .

After all the wires have been disconnected, unfasten the distributor cap retainers . . .

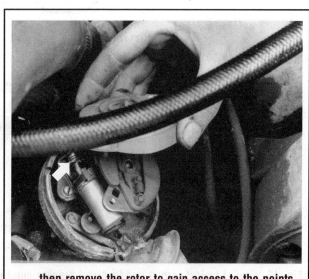

. . . then remove the rotor to gain access to the points

DWELL ADJUSTMENT

♦ See Figures 17 and 18

Dwell can be checked with the engine running or cranking. Decrease dwell by increasing the point gap; increase by decreasing the gap. Dwell angle is simply the number of degrees of distributor shaft rotation during which the points stay closed. Theoretically, if the point gap is correct, the dwell should also be correct or nearly so. Adjustment with a dwell meter produces more exact, consistent results since it is a dynamic adjustment. If dwell varies more than 3° from idle speed to 1750 engine rpm, the distributor is worn.

19. If the engine won't start, check:

    a. That all the spark plug wires are in place.

    b. That the rotor has been installed.

    c. That the two (or three) wires inside the distributor are connected.

    d. That the points open and close when the engine turns.

    e. That the gap is correct and the hold-down screw is tight.

20. After the first 200 miles or so on a new set of points, the point gap often closes up due to initial rubbing block wear. For best performance, recheck the dwell (or gap) at this time.

21. Since changing the gap affects the ignition point setting, the timing should be checked and adjusted as necessary after each point replacement or adjustment.

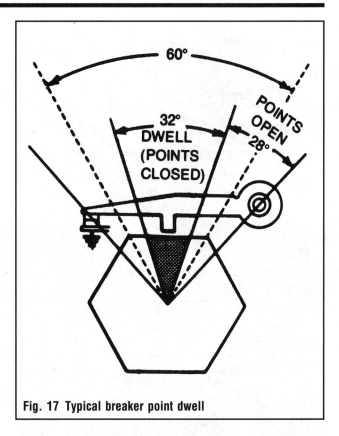

Fig. 17 Typical breaker point dwell

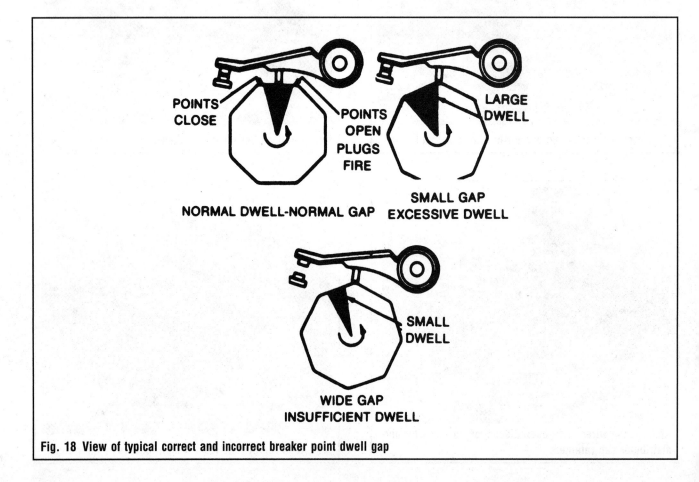

Fig. 18 View of typical correct and incorrect breaker point dwell gap

TROUBLESHOOTING BASIC POINT-TYPE IGNITION SYSTEM PROBLEMS

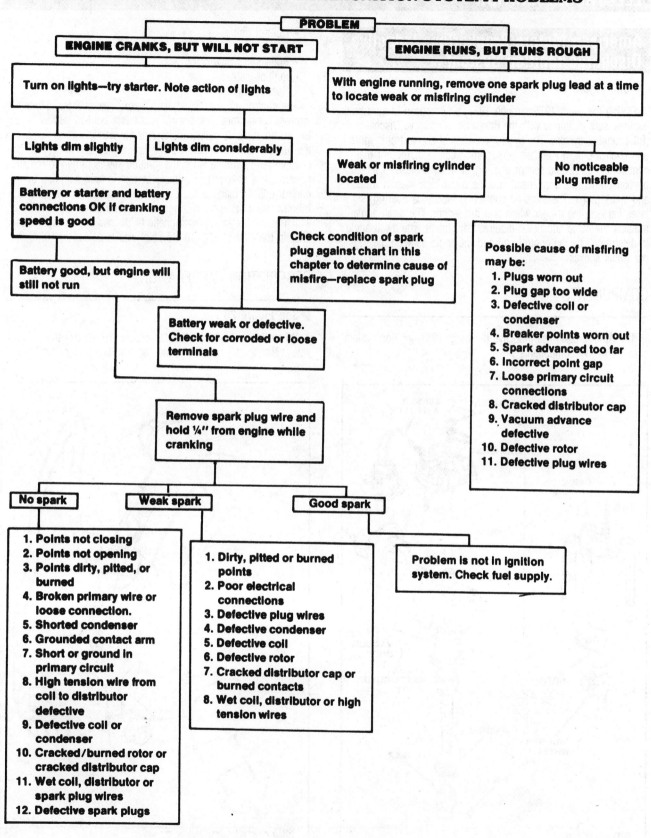

PROBLEM

ENGINE CRANKS, BUT WILL NOT START

Turn on lights—try starter. Note action of lights

Lights dim slightly

Lights dim considerably

Battery or starter and battery connections OK if cranking speed is good

Battery good, but engine will still not run

Battery weak or defective. Check for corroded or loose terminals

Remove spark plug wire and hold ¼" from engine while cranking

No spark

1. Points not closing
2. Points not opening
3. Points dirty, pitted, or burned
4. Broken primary wire or loose connection.
5. Shorted condenser
6. Grounded contact arm
7. Short or ground in primary circuit
8. High tension wire from coil to distributor defective
9. Defective coil or condenser
10. Cracked/burned rotor or cracked distributor cap
11. Wet coil, distributor or spark plug wires
12. Defective spark plugs

Weak spark

1. Dirty, pitted or burned points
2. Poor electrical connections
3. Defective plug wires
4. Defective condenser
5. Defective coil
6. Defective rotor
7. Cracked distributor cap or burned contacts
8. Wet coil, distributor or high tension wires

Good spark

Problem is not in ignition system. Check fuel supply.

ENGINE RUNS, BUT RUNS ROUGH

With engine running, remove one spark plug lead at a time to locate weak or misfiring cylinder

Weak or misfiring cylinder located

No noticeable plug misfire

Check condition of spark plug against chart in this chapter to determine cause of misfire—replace spark plug

Possible cause of misfiring may be:
1. Plugs worn out
2. Plug gap too wide
3. Defective coil or condenser
4. Breaker points worn out
5. Spark advanced too far
6. Incorrect point gap
7. Loose primary circuit connections
8. Cracked distributor cap
9. Vacuum advance defective
10. Defective rotor
11. Defective plug wires

ELECTRONIC IGNITION

American Motors Breakerless Inductive Discharge Ignition System

♦ **See Figure 19**

During the years 1975 through 1977, all American Motors built engines were equipped with the Breakerless Inductive Discharge (BID) ignition system. The system consists of an electronic ignition control unit, a standard type ignition coil, a distributor that contains an electronic sensor and trigger wheel instead of a cam, breaker points and condenser, and the usual high tension wires and spark plugs. There are no contacting (and thus wearing) surfaces between the trigger wheel and the sensor. The dwell angle remains the same and never requires adjustment. The dwell angle is determined by the control unit and the angle between the trigger wheel spokes.

COMPONENTS

The AMC breakerless inductive discharge (BID) ignition system consists of five components:

- Control unit
- Coil
- Breakerless distributor
- Ignition cables
- Spark plugs

The control unit is a solid state, epoxy sealed module with waterproof connectors. The control unit has a built-in current regulator, so no separate ballast resistor or resistance wire is needed in the primary circuit. Battery voltage is supplied to the ignition coil positive (+) terminal when the ignition key is turned to the ON position; low voltage coil primary current is also supplied by the control unit. In place of the points, cam, and condenser, the distributor has a sensor and trigger wheel. The sensor is a small coil which generates an electromagnetic field when excited by the oscillator in the control unit. This system was last used in 1977.

DESCRIPTION & OPERATION

♦ **See Figure 20**

When the ignition switch is turned on, the control unit is activated. The control unit then sends an oscillating signal to the sen-

BID distributor

Fig. 19 Exploded view of a Breakerless Inductive Discharge (BID) ignition system distributor

BID distributor sensor

Fig. 20 Location of the BID distributor sensor

sor, which cause the sensor to generate a magnetic field. When one of the trigger wheel teeth enters this field, the strength of the oscillation in the sensor is reduced. One the strength drops to a predetermined level, a demodulator circuit operates the control unit's switching transistor. The switching transistor is wired in series with the coil primary circuit; it switches the circuit off, inducing high voltage in the coil secondary winding when it gets the demodulator signal. From this point on, the BID ignition system works in the same manner as a conventional system.

DIAGNOSIS & TESTING

System Test

1. Check all the Breakerless Inductive Discharge (BID) ignition system electrical connections.
2. Disconnect the coil-to-distributor high tension lead from the distributor cap.
3. Using insulated pliers and a heavy glove, hold the end of the lead ½ in. (12.7mm) away from a ground. Crank the engine. If there is a spark, the trouble is not in the ignition system. Check the distributor cap, rotor, and wires.
4. Replace the spark plug lead. Turn the ignition switch off and disconnect the coil high tension cable from the center tower on the distributor cap. Place a paper clip around the cable ½–¾ in. (12.7–19.05mm) from the metal end. Ground the paper clip to the engine. Crank the engine. If there is spark, the distributor cap or rotor may be at fault.
5. Turn the ignition switch off and replace the coil wire. Make the spark test of Step 3 again. If there is no spark, check the coil high tension wire with an ohmmeter. It should show 5–10,000 ohms resistance. If not, replace it and repeat the spark test.
6. Detach the distributor sensor lead wire plug. Check the wire connector by trying a no. 16 (0.177 in. [4.5mm]) drill bit for a snug fit in the female terminals. Apply a light coat of Silicone Dielectric Compound or its equivalent to the male terminals. Fill the female cavities ¼ full. Reconnect the plug.
7. Repeat the test of Step 4.
8. If there was a spark in Step 7, detach the sensor lead plug and try a replacement sensor. Try the test again. If there is a spark, the sensor was defective.
9. Connect a multitester with a volt scale, between the coil positive terminal and an engine ground. With the ignition switch on, the volt scale should read battery voltage. If it is lower, there is a high resistance between the battery (through the ignition switch) and the coil.
10. Connect the multitester between the coil negative terminal and an engine ground. With the ignition switch on, the voltage should be 5–8 volts. If not, replace the coil. If you get a battery voltage reading, crank the engine slightly to move the trigger wheel tooth away from the sensor; voltage should drop to 5–8v.
11. Check the sensor resistance by connecting an ohmmeter to its leads. Resistance should be 1.6–2.4 ohms.

Coil Testing

Test the coil with a conventional coil checker or an ohmmeter. Primary resistance should be 1.25–1.40 ohms and secondary resistance should be 9–12K ohms. The open output circuit should be more than 20 kilovolts. Replace the coil if it doesn't meet specifications.

DISTRIBUTOR OVERHAUL

➡**If you must remove the sensor from the distributor for any reason, it will be necessary to have the special sensor positioning gauge in order to align it properly during installation.**

Disassembly

1. Scribe matchmarks on the distributor housing, rotor, and engine block. Disconnect the leads and vacuum lines from the distributor. Remove the distributor. Unless the cap is to be replaced, leave it connected to the spark plug cables and position it out of the way.
2. Remove the rotor and dust cap.
3. Place a small gear puller over the trigger wheel, so that its jaws grip the inner shoulders of the wheel and not its arms. Place a thick washer between the gear puller and the distributor shaft to act as a spacer; do not press against the smaller inner shaft.
4. Loosen the sensor hold-down screw with a small pair of needlenosed pliers; it has a tamper proof head. Pull the sensor lead grommet out of the distributor body and pull out the leads from around the spring pivot pin.
5. Release the sensor securing spring by lifting it. Make sure that it clears the leads. Slide the sensor off the bracket. Remember, a special gauge is required for sensor installation.
6. Remove the vacuum advance unit securing screw. Slide the vacuum unit out of the distributor. Remove it only if it is to be replaced.
7. Clean the vacuum unit and sensor brackets. Lubrication of these parts is not necessary.
   To assemble:
8. Install the vacuum unit, if it was removed.
9. Assemble the sensor, sensor guide, flat washer, and retaining screw. Tighten the screw only far enough to keep the assembly together; don't allow the screw to project below the bottom of the sensor.

➡**Replacement sensors come with a slotted head screw to aid in assembly. If the original sensor is being used, replace the tamperproof screw with a conventional one. Use the original washer.**

10. Secure the sensor on the vacuum advance unit bracket, making sure that the tip of the sensor is placed in the notch on the summing bar.
11. Position the spring on the sensor and route the leads around the spring pivot pin. Fit the sensor lead grommet into the slot on the distributor body. Be sure that the lead can't get caught in the trigger wheel.
12. Place the special sensor positioning gauge over the distributor shaft, so that the flat on the shaft is against the large notch on the gauge. Move the sensor until the sensor core fits into the small notch on the gauge. Tighten the sensor securing screw with the gauge in place (through the round hole in the gauge).
13. It should be possible to remove and install the gauge without any side movement of the sensor. Check this and remove the gauge.
14. Position the trigger wheel on the shaft. Check to see that the sensor core is centered between the trigger wheel legs and that the legs don't touch the core.
15. Bend a piece of 0.050" (1.27mm) gauge wire, so that it

has a 90° angle and one leg ½" (12.7mm) long. Use the gauge to measure the clearance between the trigger wheel legs and the sensor boss. Press the trigger wheel on the shaft until it just touches the gauge. Support the shaft during this operation.

16. Place 3 to 5 drops of SAE 20 oil on the felt lubricator wick.

17. Install the dust shield and rotor on the shaft.

18. Install the distributor on the engine using the matchmarks made during removal and adjust the timing. Use a new distributor mounting gasket.

American Motors Solid State Ignition (SSI) System

DESCRIPTION & OPERATION

♦ **See Figure 21**

AMC introduced Solid State Ignition (SSI) as a running change on some 1977 Canadian models. It is standard equipment on all 1978 and later American Motors built engines.

The system consists of a sensor and toothed trigger wheel inside the distributor, and a permanently sealed electronic control unit which determines dwell, in addition to the coil, ignition wires, and spark plugs.

Fig. 21 Exploded view of the American motors Solid State Ignition (SSI) system distributor components

The trigger wheel rotates on the distributor shaft. As one of its teeth nears the sensor magnet, the magnetic field shifts toward the tooth. When the tooth and sensor are aligned, the magnetic field is shifted to its maximum, signaling the electronic control unit to switch off the coil primary current. This starts an electronic timer inside the control unit, which allows the primary current to remain off only long enough for the spark plug to fire. The timer adjusts the amount of time primary current is off according to conditions, thus automatically adjusting dwell. There is also a special circuit within the control unit to detect and ignore spurious signals. Spark timing is adjusted by both mechanical (centrifugal) and vacuum advance.

A wire of 1.35 ohms resistance is spliced into the ignition feed to reduce voltage to the coil during running conditions. The resistance wire is bypassed when the engine is being started so that full battery voltage may be supplied to the coil. Bypass is accomplished by the I-terminal on the solenoid.

TESTING

Secondary Circuit

1. Disconnect the coil wire from the center of the distributor cap.

➡**Twist the rubber boot slightly in either direction, then grasp the boot and pull straight up. Do not pull on the wire, and do not use pliers.**

2. Hold the wire ⅜ in. (12.7mm) from a ground with a pair of insulated pliers and a heavy glove. As the engine is cranked, watch for a spark.

3. If a spark appears, reconnect the coil wire. Remove the wire from one spark plug, and test for a spark as above.

✳✳ CAUTION

Do not remove the spark plug wires from cylinder 3 on the 4-150, or cylinder 3 or 5 on a 1977-79 6-258 or 1 or 5 on a 1980 and later 6-258, or cylinders 3 or 4 of an 8-360, when performing this test, as sensor damage could occur.

4. If a spark occurs, the problem is in the fuel system or ignition timing. If no spark occurs, check for a defective rotor, cap, or spark plug wires.

5. If no spark occurs from the coil wire in Step 2, test the coil wire resistance with an ohmmeter. It should be 7,700–9,300Ω at +75°F (+24°C) or 12,000Ω maximum at +93°F (+34°C).

Primary Circuit

1. Turn the ignition **ON.** Connect a multitester to the coil positive (+) terminal and a ground. If the voltage is 5.5–6.5 volts, go to Step 2. If above 7 volts, go to Step 4. If below 5.5 volts, disconnect the condenser lead and measure. If the voltage is now 5.5–6.5 volts, replace the condenser. If not, go to Step 6.

2. With the multitester connected as in Step 1, read the voltage with the engine cranking. If battery voltage is indicated, the circuit is okay. If not, go to Step 3.

3. Check for a short or open in the starter solenoid I-terminal wire. Check the solenoid for proper operation.

4. Disconnect the wire from the starter solenoid I-terminal, with the ignition On and the multitester connected as in Step 1. If

the voltage drops to 5.5–6.5 volts, replace the solenoid. If not, connect a jumper between the coil negative (−) terminal and a ground. If the voltage drops to 5.5–6.5 volts, go to Step 5. If not, repair the resistance wire.

5. Check for continuity between the coil (−) terminal and D4, and D1 to ground. If the continuity is okay, replace the control unit. If not, check for an open wire and go back to Step 2.

6. Turn ignition **OFF.** Connect an ohmmeter between the + coil terminal and dash connector AV. If above 1.40 ohms, repair the resistance wire.

7. With the ignition Off, connect the ohmmeter between connector AV and ignition switch terminal 11. If less than 0.1 ohms, replace the ignition switch or repair the wire, whichever is the cause. If above 0.1 ohms, check connections; and check for defective wiring.

Coil

1. Check the coil for cracks, carbon tracks, etc., and replace as necessary.

2. Connect an ohmmeter across the coil + and − terminals, with the coil connector removed. If 1.13–1.23 ohms @ +75°F (+24°C), the coil is okay. If not, replace it.

Control Unit and Sensor

1. With the ignition **ON,** remove the coil high tension wire from the distributor cap and hold ½" (12.7mm) from ground with insulated pliers. Disconnect the 4-wire connector at the control unit. If a spark occurs (normal), go to Step 2. If not, go to Step 5.

2. Connect an ohmmeter to D2 and D3. If the resistance is 400–800 ohms (normal), go to Step 6. If not, go to Step 3.

3. Disconnect and reconnect the 3-wire connector at distributor. If the reading is now 400–800 ohms, go to Step 6. If not, disconnect the 3-wire connector and go to Step 4.

4. Connect the ohmmeter across B2 and B3. If 300–800 ohms, repair the harness between the 3-wire and 4-wire connectors. If not, replace the sensor.

5. Connect the ohmmeter between D1 and the battery negative terminal. If the reading is 0 (0.002 ohms or less), go to Step 2. If above 0.002 ohms, there is a bad ground in the cable or at the distributor. Repair the ground and retest.

6. Connect a multitester across D2 and D3. Crank the engine. If the needle fluctuates, the system is okay. If not, either the trigger wheel is defective, or the distributor is not turning. Repair or replace as required.

Ignition Feed-to-Control Unit Test

➡**Do not perform this test without first performing the Coil Primary Circuit Test.**

1. With the ignition **ON,** unplug the 2-wire connector at the module. Connect a multitester between F2 and ground. If the reading is battery voltage, replace the control unit and go to Step 3. If not, go to Step 2.

2. Repair the cause of the voltage reduction: either the ignition switch or a corroded dash connector. Check for a spark at the coil wire. If okay, stop. If not, replace the control unit and check for proper operation.

3. Reconnect the 2-wire connector at the control unit, and unplug the 4-wire connector at the control unit. Connect an ammeter between C1 and ground. If it reads 0.9–1.1 amps, the system is okay. If not, replace the module.

Delco High Energy Ignition (HEI) System

◆ See Figure 22

The General Motors High Energy Ignition (HEI) system is a pulse triggered, transistor controlled, inductive discharge ignition system. The entire HEI system is contained within the distributor cap.

The distributor, in addition to housing the mechanical and vacuum advance mechanisms, contains the ignition coil (except on some inline six engines), the electronic control module, and the magnetic triggering device. The magnetic pick-up assembly contains a permanent magnet, a pole piece with internal teeth, and a pick-up coil (not to be confused with the ignition coil).

In the HEI system, as in other electronic ignition systems, the breaker points have been replaced with an electronic switch—a transistor, which is located within the control module. This switching transistor performs the same function the points did in a conventional ignition system; it simply turns coil primary current on and off at the correct time. Essentially then, electronic and conventional ignition systems operate on the same principle.

The module which houses the switching transistor is controlled (turned on and off) by a magnetically generated impulse induced in the pick-up coil. When the teeth of the rotating timer align with the teeth of the pole piece, the induced voltage in the pick-up coil signals the electronic module to open the coil primary circuit. The primary current then decreases, and a high voltage is induced in the ignition coil secondary windings, which is then directed through the rotor and spark plug wires to fire the spark plugs.

In essence, then, the pick-up coil module system simply replaces the conventional breaker points and condenser. The condenser found within the distributor is for radio suppression purposes only and has nothing to do with the ignition process. The module automatically controls the dwell period, increasing it with increasing engine speed. Since dwell is automatically controlled, it cannot be adjusted. The module itself is non-adjustable and non-repairable and must be replaced if found defective.

HEI SYSTEM PRECAUTIONS

Before going on to troubleshooting, it might be a good idea to take note of the following precautions.

Timing Light Use

Inductive pick-up timing lights are the best kind to use with HEI. Timing lights which connect between the spark plug and the spark plug wire occasionally (not always) give false readings.

Spark Plug Wires

The plug wires used with HEI systems are of a different construction than conventional wires. When replacing them, make sure you get the correct wires, since conventional wires won't carry the voltage. Also handle them carefully to avoid cracking or splitting them and never pierce them.

Tachometer Use

Not all tachometers will operate or indicate correctly when used on an HEI system. While some tachometers may give a reading,

(EST) HEI DISTRIBUTOR

CAPACITOR

MAINSHAFT ASSEMBLY

7-TERMINAL MODULE

TO ECM CONNECTOR

COVER

COIL

CAP

ROTOR

HOUSING

Fig. 22 Exploded views of the High Energy Ignition (HEI) system distributor components

this does not necessarily mean the reading is correct. In addition, some tachometers hook up differently from others. If you can't figure out whether or not your tachometer will work on your truck, check with the tachometer manufacturer. Dwell readings have no significance at all.

HEI System Testers

Instruments designed specifically for testing HEI systems are available from several tool manufacturers. Some of these will even test the module itself. However, the test given in the following section will require only a multitester with volt and ohm scales.

TROUBLESHOOTING THE HEI SYSTEM

The symptoms of a defective component within the HEI system are exactly the same as those you would encounter in a conventional system. Some of these symptoms are:
• Hard or no starting
• Rough idle
• Poor fuel economy
• Engine misses under load or while accelerating

If you suspect a problem in the ignition system, there are certain preliminary checks which you should carry out before you begin to check the electronic portions of the system. First, it is extremely important to make sure that the vehicle's battery is in good condition. A defective or poorly charged battery will cause the various components of the ignition system to read incorrectly when tested.

Second, make sure all of the wiring connections are clean and tight, not only at the battery, but also at the distributor cap, coil and module.

Since the major difference between electronic and point type ignition systems is in the distributor area, it is imperative to check the secondary ignition wires first. If the secondary system checks out okay, then the problem is probably not in the ignition system. To check the secondary system, perform a simple spark test. Remove on of the spark plug wires from the plug and insert a makeshift extension made of conductive metal, in the wire boot. Hold the wire and extension about ¼ in. (6.35mm) away from the block and crank the engine. If a normal spark occurs, then the problem is most likely not in the ignition system. Check for fuel system problems, or fouled spark plugs.

If, however, there is no spark or a weak spark, then further ignition system testing will have to be done. Troubleshooting techniques fall into two categories, depending on the nature of the problem. The categories are (1) Engine cranks, but won't start, and (2) Engine runs, but runs rough or cuts out.

Engine Fails to Start

If the engine won't start, perform a spark test as described earlier. If no spark occurs, check for the presence of normal battery voltage at the battery (BAT) terminal in the distributor cap. The ignition switch must be in the on position for this test. Either a multitester or a test light may be used for this test. Connect the test light wire to ground and the probe end to the BAT terminal at the distributor. If the light comes on, you have voltage to the distributor. If the light fails to come on, this indicates an open circuit in the ignition primary wiring leading to the distributor. In this case, you will have to check wiring continuity back to the ignition switch using test light. If there is battery voltage at the BAT terminal, but no spark at the plugs, then the problem lies within the distributor assembly. Go on to the distributor components test section.

Engine Runs, but Runs Roughly or Cuts Out

1. Make sure the plug wires are in good shape first. There should be no obvious cracks or breaks. You can check the plug wires with an ohmmeter, but do not pierce the wires with a probe. Check the chart for the correct plug wire resistance.

2. If the plug wires are okay, remove the cap assembly, and check for moisture, cracks, chips, or carbon tracks, or any other high voltage leaks or failures. Replace the cap if you find any defects. Make sure the timer wheel rotates when the engine is cranked. If everything is all right so far, go on to the distributor components test section.

Distributor Components Testing

▶ **See Figure 23**

If the trouble has been narrowed down to the units within the distributor, the following tests can help pinpoint the defective component. An ohmmeter with both high and low ranges should be used. These tests are made with the cap assembly removed and the battery wire disconnected.

1. Connect an ohmmeter between the TACH and BAT terminals in the distributor cap. The primary coil resistance should be <1.0 ohms (zero or nearly zero).

2. To check the coil secondary resistance, connect an ohmmeter between the rotor button and the BAT terminal. Then connect the ohmmeter between the ground terminal and the rotor button. The resistance in both cases should be between 6,000 and 30,000 ohms.

3. Replace the coil only if the readings in steps 1 and 2 are infinite.

➡**These resistance checks will not disclose shorted coil windings. This condition can be detected only with scope analysis or a suitably designed coil tester. If these instru-**ments are unavailable, replace the coil with a known good coil as a final coil test.**

4. To test the pick-up coil, first disconnect the white and green module leads. Set the ohmmeter on the high scale and connect it between a ground and either the white or green lead. Any resistance measurement less than infinity requires replacement of the pick-up coil.

5. Pick-up coil continuity is tested by connecting the ohmmeter (on low range) between the white and green leads. Normal resistance is between 500 and 1500 ohms. Move the vacuum advance arm while performing this test. This will detect any break in coil continuity. Such a condition can cause intermittent misfiring. Replace the pick-up coil if the reading is outside the specific limits.

6. If no defects have been found at this time, and you still have a problem, then the module will have to be checked. If you do not have access to a module tester, the only possible alternative is a substitution test. If the module fails the substitution test, replace it.

COMPONENT REPLACEMENT

Integral Ignition Coil

1. Disconnect the feed and module wire terminal connectors from the distributor cap.

2. Remove the ignition set retainer.

3. Remove the 4 coil cover-to-distributor cap screws and coil cover.

4. Remove the 4 coil-to-distributor cap screws.

5. Using a blunt drift, press the coil wire spade terminals up out of distributor cap.

6. Lift the coil up out of the distributor cap.

7. Remove and clean the coil spring, rubber seal washer and coil cavity of the distributor cap.

8. Coat the rubber seal with a dielectric lubricant furnished in the replacement ignition coil package.

9. Reverse the above procedures to install.

Distributor Cap

1. Remove the feed and module wire terminal connectors from the distributor cap.

2. Remove the retainer and spark plug wires from the cap.

3. Depress and release the 4 distributor cap-to-housing retainers and lift off the cap assembly.

4. Remove the 4 coil cover screws and cover.

5. Using a finger or a blunt drift, push the spade terminals up out of the distributor cap.

6. Remove all 4 coil screws and lift the coil, coil spring, and rubber seal washer out of the cap coil cavity.

7. Using a new distributor cap, reverse the above procedures to assembly, being sure to clean and lubricate the rubber seal washer with dielectric lubricant.

Rotor

1. Disconnect the feed and module wire connectors from the distributor.

2. Depress and release the 4 distributor cap to housing retainers and lift off the cap assembly.

3. Remove the two rotor attaching screws and rotor.

4. Reverse the above procedure to install.

Fig. 23 Ohmmeter positions for testing the pick-up coil

Vacuum Advance

1. Remove the distributor cap and rotor as previously described.

2. Disconnect the vacuum hose from the vacuum advance unit.

3. Remove the two vacuum advance retaining screws, pull the advance unit outward, rotate, and disengage the operating rod from its tang.

4. Reverse the above procedure to install.

Module

♦ See Figure 24

1. Remove the distributor cap and rotor as previously described.

2. Disconnect the harness connector and pick-up coil spade connectors from the module. Be careful not to damage the wires when removing the connector.

3. Remove the two screws and module from the distributor housing.

4. Coat the bottom of the new module with dielectric lubricant supplied with the new module. Reverse the above procedure to install.

Fig. 24 Ensure the mating surfaces are coated with dielectric compound before installing the module

IGNITION TIMING

Timing

♦ See Figure 25

Ignition timing is the measurement, in degrees of crankshaft rotation, of the point at which the spark plugs fire in each of the cylinders. It is measured in degrees before or after Top Dead Center (TDC) of the compression stroke. Ignition timing is controlled by turning the distributor in the engine.

Ideally, the air/fuel mixture in the cylinder will be ignited by the spark plug just as the piston passes TDC of the compression stroke. If this happens, this piston will be beginning the power stroke just as the compressed and ignited air/fuel mixture starts to expand. The expansion of the air/fuel mixture then forces the piston down on the power stroke and turns the crankshaft.

Because it takes a fraction of a second for the spark plug to ignite the gases in the cylinder, the spark plug must fire a little before the piston reaches TDC. Otherwise, the mixture will not be completely ignited as the piston TDC and the full benefit of the explosion will not be used by the engine. The timing measurement is given in degrees of crankshaft rotation before the piston reaches TDC (BTDC). If the setting for the ignition timing is 5° BTDC, the spark plug must fire 5° before that piston reaches TDC. This only holds true, however, when the engine is at idle speed.

As the engine speed increases, the pistons go faster. The spark plugs have to ignite the fuel even sooner if it is to be completely ignited when the piston reaches TDC. To do this, the distributor has a means to advance the timing of the spark as the engine speed increases. In some vehicles that were made before 1972, the advancing of the spark in the distributor was accomplished by weights alone. Others have a vacuum diaphragm to assist the weights. It is necessary to disconnect the vacuum line to the distributor when the engine is being timed.

If the ignition is set too far advanced (BTDC), the ignition and expansion of the fuel in the cylinder will occur too soon and tend to force the piston down while it is still traveling up. This causes engine ping. If the engine is too far retarded after TDC (ATDC), the piston will have already passed TDC and started on its way down when the fuel is ignited. This will cause the piston to be forced down for only a portion of its travel. This will result in poor engine performance and lack of power.

The timing is best checked with a timing light. This device is connected in series with the no. 1 spark plug. The current that fires the spark plug also causes the light to flash.

When the engine is running, the timing light is aimed at the marks on the engine and crankshaft pulley.

There are three basic types of timing lights available. The first is a simple neon bulb with two wire connections. One wire connects to the spark plug terminal and the other plugs into the end of the spark plug wire for the No. 1 cylinder, thus connecting the light in series with the spark plug. This type of light is pretty dim and must be held very close to the timing marks to be seen. Sometimes a dark corner has to be sought out to see the flash at all. This type of light is very inexpensive. The second type operates from the car battery—two alligator clips connect to the battery terminals, while an adapter enables a third clip to be connected to the No. 1 spark plug and wire. This type is a bit more expensive, but it provides a nice bright flash that you can see even in bright sunlight. It is the type most often seen in professional shops. The third type replaces the battery power source with 110 volt current.

➡**Connect a tachometer to the BID or SSI ignition system in the conventional way; to the negative (distributor) side of the coil and to a ground. HEI distributor caps have a Tach terminal. Some tachometers may not work with a BID, SSI, or HEI ignition system and there is a possibility that some could be damaged. Check with the manufacturer of the tachometer to make sure it can be used.**

Fig. 25 View of the piston location with the timing at idle and 3000 rpm

Timing should be checked at each tune-up and any time the points are adjusted or replaced. The timing marks consist of a notch on the rim of the crankshaft pulley and a graduated scale attached to the engine front (timing) cover. A stroboscopic flash (dynamic) timing light must be used, as a static light is too inaccurate for emission controlled engines.

INSPECTION & ADJUSTMENT

Point Type Ignition

♦ See Figure 26

➡Some early engines have 6v ignition systems. Make sure your tach/dwell and timing light have 6v capability.

1. Locate the timing marks.
2. Clean off the timing marks so you can see them.
3. Mark the timing marks with a piece of chalk or white paint. Mark the one on the engine that will indicate correct timing when it is aligned with the mark on the pulley or flywheel.
4. Attach a tachometer to the engine.
5. Attach a timing light according to the manufacturer's instructions. If the timing light has three wires, one is attached to the no. 1 spark plug lead with an adapter. The other two are connected to the battery. The red one goes to the positive side of the battery and the black one to the negative terminal.
6. Disconnect the vacuum line to the distributor at the distributor. Plug the end of the hose.
7. Check to make sure that all of the wires clear the fan and then start the engine.
8. If there is an idle speed solenoid, disconnect it.
9. Aim the timing light at the timing marks. If the marks that you put on the pulley and the engine are aligned, the timing is correct. Turn off the engine and remove the tachometer and the timing light. If the marks are not in alignment, proceed to the following steps.
10. Turn off the engine.

11. Loosen the distributor lockbolt just enough so that the distributor can be turned with a little effort.
12. Start the engine. Keep the cords of the timing light clear of the fan.
13. With the timing light aimed at the pulley and the marks on the engine, turn the distributor in the direction of rotor rotation to retard the spark, and in the opposite direction of rotor rotation to advance the spark. Line up the marks on the pulley and the engine.
14. When the marks are aligned, tighten the distributor lockbolt and recheck the timing with the timing light to make sure that the distributor did not move when you tightened the distributor lockbolt.
15. Turn off the engine and remove the timing light.

Fig. 26 Timing mark location on the 4-121 engine

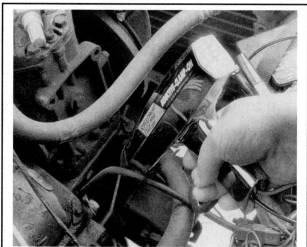

Use a timing light, like the one shown, to check the ignition timing

Electronic Ignition

♦ **See Figures 27, 28, 29 and 30**

1. Warm up the engine to normal operating temperature. Stop the engine and connect the timing light to the No. 1 (left front on V8, front on four or six) spark plug wire. Clean off the timing marks and mark the pulley notch and timing scale with white chalk.

2. Disconnect and plug the vacuum line at the distributor. This is done to prevent any distributor vacuum advance.

3. Start the engine and adjust the idle to 500 rpm with the carburetor idle speed screw on 1975–77 vehicles. On 1978 and later models, set the idle speed to the figure shown on the underhood sticker. This is done to prevent any distributor centrifugal ad-

Fig. 28 Timing mark location on the 6-232 and 6-258 engines

Fig. 27 Timing mark location on the 4-151 engine

Fig. 29 Timing mark location common to V8 engines

Fig. 30 Timing mark locations found on the 4-150 engine

vance. If there is a throttle stop solenoid, disconnect it electrically.

4. Aim the timing light at the pointer marks. Be careful not to touch the fan, because it may appear to be standing still. If the pulley notch isn't aligned with the proper timing mark (refer to the Tune-Up Specifications chart), the timing will have to be adjusted.

➡ **TDC or Top Dead Center corresponds to 0°. B, or BTDC, or Before Top Dead Center, may be shown as A for Advanced on a V8 timing scale. R on a V8 timing scale means Retarded, corresponding to ATDC, or After Top Dead Center.**

5. Loosen the distributor clamp locknut. You can buy trick wrenches that make this task a lot easier. Turn the distributor slowly to adjust the timing, holding it by the base and not the cap. Turn counterclockwise to advance timing (toward BTDC), and clockwise to retard (toward TDC or ATDC).

6. Tighten the locknut. Check the timing again, in case the distributor moved slightly as you tightened it.

7. Replace the distributor vacuum line and correct the idle speed to that specified in the Tune-Up Specifications chart.

8. Stop the engine and disconnect the timing light.

VALVE LASH

General Information

➡ **This applies to the 4-121 engine only.**

Valve adjustment is one factor which determines how far the intake and exhaust valves open into the cylinder. If the valve clearance is too large, part of the lift of the camshaft will be used in removing the excessive clearance, therefore the valves will not open far enough. This has two ill effects; one, the valve gear will become noisy as the excess clearance is taken up and, two, the engine will perform poorly. This is because intake valves which don't open the full distance will admit a smaller air/fuel mixture into the cylinders. Exhaust valves which aren't opening the full amount create a greater back pressure in the cylinder which prevents the proper air/fuel mixture from entering the cylinder.

If the valve clearance is too small, the intake and exhaust valves will not fully seat on the cylinder head when they close. When a valve seats on the cylinder head it does two things; it seals the combustion chamber so that none of the gases in the cylinder can escape and it cools itself by transferring some of the heat absorbed from the combustion process through the cylinder head and into the cooling system. Therefore, if the valve clearance is too small, the engine will run poorly (due to gases escaping from the combustion chamber), and the valves will overheat and eventually warp (since they cannot properly transfer heat unless they fully seat on the cylinder head).

While all valve adjustments must be as accurate as possible, it is better to have the valve adjustment slightly loose than tight, as burned valves can result from too tight an adjustment.

The valves are operated by an overhead camshaft, driven by a toothed rubber belt, connected to the crankshaft. The cam lobes contact 'bucket' type tappets, which are set over the valve and valve springs, and force the valve and springs to move downward, moving the valve from its seat on the cylinder head. Both intake and exhaust valves are manual adjusted by a wedge type screw angled into the tappet, perpendicular to the valve stem. A flat area is milled onto the screw, which contacts the valve stem end. The threaded area locks to a threaded area within the tappet. Each turn changes the clearance 0.002 in. (0.051mm). When tappet adjustment is done, the flat side of the adjusting screw must be toward the valve stem end at the completion of the adjustment.

ADJUSTMENT

◆ **See Figures 31, 32, 33 and 34**

➡ **Valve adjustment must be made with the engine at normal operating temperature.**

1. Remove the TAC hose, the cylinder head cover, the spark plug wires and distributor cap.

2. Rotate the crankshaft to bring the number one cylinder to TDC (the beginning of its firing stroke). The position of the distributor rotor will assist in determining this position.

➡ **There is a mark on the edge of the distributor housing at number one terminal position. Do not attempt to rotate the engine by turning the camshaft. Turn the crankshaft in the direction of normal rotation to avoid damage to the timing belt.**

Fig. 31 Cross-sectional view of the valve train assembly—4-121 engine

Fig. 32 Use a feeler gauge to measure the valve clearance—4-121 engine

Fig. 33 Sectional view of the valve adjusting screw—four cylinder 2.0L engine

Fig. 34 Checking the position of the screw in the tappet using tool J-26860 or its equivalent

3. With number one cylinder on TDC of its firing stroke, the clearance of the exhaust valves on cylinders number one and three, and of the intake valves on cylinders number one and two, can be checked.

➤The front valve in each pair per cylinder is the intake valve. If the clearance requires adjustment, a special too is required to move the adjusting screw.

4. Adjust the screw by turning one complete turn until it clicks, and continue until the proper clearance (0.006–0.009 in. [0.15–0.22mm] for intake, and 0.016–0.019 in. [0.40–0.48mm] for exhaust) is obtained.

5. After adjusting the clearance, use the special AMC gauge J-26860 to check the position of the screw in the tappet. If the gauge indicates the adjusting screw is turned too far into the tappet, the screw must be replaced. Five sizes of screws are available, identified by grooves on the end of the screws.

➤If the adjusting screws must be replaced, the tappets must be removed from the head. Note which tappets must be removed, then continue the adjustment procedure. When all eight adjustments are made, remove those tappets requiring screw replacement. Refer to camshaft removal and installation.

6. Rotate the crankshaft 360°. The distributor rotor should be 180° opposite the mark on the distributor housing.

7. The clearance can now be checked on the exhaust valves for cylinders two and four, and the intake valve on cylinders three and four.

8. Reinstall the head cover, using a new gasket.

9. Reinstall the distributor cap and spark plug wiring. Reinstall the TAC flexible hose.

IDLE SPEED AND MIXTURE

This section contains only tune-up adjustment procedures for fuel systems. Descriptions, adjustments, and overhaul procedures for fuel system components can be found in Section 5.

Adjustments

Some of these adjustments procedures require that the air cleaner be kept in place. A flexible screwdriver will probably be needed to reach the carburetor screws.

4-121 ENGINES

♦ **See Figure 35**

The 4-cylinder engine uses a staged, two barrel carburetor. The primary barrel is smaller than the secondary barrel, and mechanical linkage progressively open the secondary barrel. Idle speed and mixture setting procedures are as follows:

Fig. 35 Component locations on the Holley-Weber 5210 2-bbl carburetor

➤To compensate for temperature and fuel variations, while performing idle mixture adjustments, don't idle the engine over three minutes at a time. If settings are not completed within three minutes, operate the engine at 2000 rpm for one minute. Repeat as necessary until the proper adjustments are attained.

1. Note position of the screw head slot in the limiter cap.

2. Remove the limiter cap by installing a sheet metal screw in the center of the cap and turning the screw clockwise.

3. Reset the idle screw to its approximate original position.

4. Attach a tachometer. Start engine and warm to operating temperature.

5. A throttle stop solenoid is used to adjust curb idle. With the solenoid wire connected, turn the adjusting screw of the solenoid in or out to obtain the specified setting of 30 rpm above the specified rpm.

6. Disconnect the solenoid wire and adjust the solenoid off idle adjusting screw to obtain 500 rpm. Connect the solenoid wire.

7. Turn the mixture screw clockwise (lean) until a loss of rpm is indicated.

8. Turn the mixture screw counterclockwise until the highest rpm reading is obtained at the best lean idle setting.

9. As a final adjustment, turn the mixture screw clockwise (leaner) until the specified drop in engine rpm is obtained.

10. Install a replacement limiter cap on the idle mixture screw, with the tab positioned inside the slot on the carburetor body, while being careful not to move the mixture screw. Idle drop specifications for 1977–78 are 120 rpm, except for high altitude manual transmission models (75 rpm). For 1979 models they are 120 for manual transmissions and 45 for automatic transmissions.

4-151 ENGINES

♦ **See Figure 36**

The air cleaner should be removed and associated vacuum hoses plugged, choke open, A/C compressor clutch wire discon-

① PREPARE VEHICLE FOR ADJUSTMENTS - SEE EMISSION LABEL ON VEHICLE.
NOTE: IGNITION TIMING SET PER LABEL.

② SOLENOID ENERGIZED - A/T IN DRIVE, M/T IN NEUTRAL

④ TURN SOLENOID SCREW TO ADJUST CURB IDLE SPEED TO SPECIFIED RPM (SOLENOID ENERGIZED)

⑥ RECONNECT SOLENOID ELECTRICAL LEAD AFTER ADJUSTMENT

⑤ TURN IDLE SPEED SCREW TO SET BASIC IDLE SPEED TO SPECIFICATIONS (SOLENOID DE-ENERGIZED)

③ OPEN THROTTLE SLIGHTLY TO ALLOW SOLENOID PLUNGER TO FULLY EXTEND

Fig. 36 Adjustment points on the Rochester 2SE carburetor

nected (if equipped), and the deceleration valve supply hose plugged. Mixture is not adjustable.

1. Disconnect and plug the purge hose at the charcoal canister.

2. If equipped with a feedback system, connect a dwell meter to the single light blue wire which is taped to the mixture control solenoid wires at the carburetors. Set the meter on the six cylinder scale.

3. Connect a tachometer. There is a green wire above the heater fan motor for easy tachometer connection. Start the engine and allow it to reach normal operating temperature. On feedback models, the dwell meter should be fluctuating; the oscillation should be within 10° to 15° of needle movement. If not, the feedback system is not operating correctly and must be repaired.

4. Set the parking brake, shift automatic transmissions to Drive; if equipped with air conditioning, turn it on. Open the throttle to extend the solenoid plunger. Set idle speed by turning the solenoid idle screw. Turn off the A/C, if equipped.

5. Disconnect the anti-dieseling solenoid wire. Use the curb screw to adjust idle to specifications. Connect the solenoid wire.

1975–79 6-CYLINDER AND V8 ENGINES

▶ **See Figures 37, 38, 39, 40 and 41**

Beginning with the 1977 models, special carburetors, incorporating an altitude compensating circuit to increase the air flow are used on cars that are sold for use at elevations above 4,000 feet. The single barrel YF-1 is manually adjusted for altitude while the two barrel 2150-2 had a automatic compensator system, controlled by an aneroid, which is sensitive to atmospheric pressures. At high altitudes, where the atmospheric pressure is lower, the aneroid expands and opens an altitude compensating valve, allowing extra air to enter the carburetor and lean our the fuel/air mixture.

➡The aneroid is factory calibrated and is not adjustable. With a change of altitude operation, ignition timing and carburetor adjustments must be reset on all models.
This adjustment is performed with the air cleaner installed. Do not allow the engine to idle more than three minutes at a time. If the idle/mixture adjustment is not completed by the end of three minutes, run the engine for one minute at 2,000 rpm. Return to the specified rpm and continue the adjustment.

1. Adjust the idle screw(s) to the full rich stop(s). Note the position of the screw head slot inside the limited cap slots.

2. Carefully remove the idle limiter cap(s) by installing a sheet metal screw in the center of the cap and turning clockwise. Discard the old caps. Return the screws to their original positions.

3. Install a tachometer on the engine.

4. Start the engine and allow it to reach normal operating temperature.

5. Adjust the idle speed to 30 rpm above the specified idle speed. See the Tune-Up Specifications chart.

➡On most engines the idle speed is adjusted with the throttle stop solenoid. Use the following procedure for idle speed adjustment. When setting idle speed, put the manual transmission in Neutral and the automatic transmission in Drive.

a. With the solenoid wire connected, turn the nut on the solenoid plunger, idle speed adjusting screw, or the hex screw on the solenoid carriage in or out to obtain specified idle rpm.

b. Tighten the solenoid locknut, if so equipped.

c. Disconnect the solenoid wire and adjust curb idle speed screw to obtain 500 rpm.

d. Connect the solenoid wire.

Fig. 37 Carter YF carburetor adjustment points

CURB IDLE SCREW

IDLE MIXTURE SCREW AND LIMITER CAP

AIR HORN

AIR FLOW

COMPENSATION CHAMBER

PLUG— TURNED TO OUTER SEAT

TO IDLE CIRCUIT AND MAIN CIRCUIT

HIGH ALTITUDE MODE

AIR FLOW BLOCKED

PLUG— TURNED TO INNER SEAT

LOW ALTITUDE MODE

Fig. 38 Cross-sectional view of the six cylinder altitude compensator plug location and operation

FAST IDLE CAM ADJUSTING SCREW

FAST IDLE ADJUSTING SCREW

CHOKE HEAT TUBE CONNECTION

DIAPHRAGM STOP SCREW

Fig. 39 Adjustment point locations on the left side of the Autolite/Motorcraft 2100 carburetor

Fig. 40 Autolite/Motorcraft 4350 adjustment point locations

Fig. 41 Location of the components on the right side of the Autolite/Motorcraft 2100 carburetor

Use a screwdriver to adjust the idle screw until the proper RPM is reached

➡ On the Carter BBD 2bbl., the curb idle and fast idle screws are side by side; it is easy to get the wrong one when setting idle speed on cars without a throttle stop solenoid. The screw for idle speed is the longer of the two.

6. Starting from the full rich stop position, as noted in step 1, turn the mixture screw(s) clockwise (leaner) until the engine loses speed.

7. Turn the mixture screw(s) counterclockwise until the highest rpm reading is obtained.

➡ On engines with two mixture screws, turn both the screws an equal number of turns unless the engine demands otherwise.

8. If the idle speed has changed more than 30 rpm during the mixture adjustment, reset the idle to 30 rpm above the specified idle rpm as indicated in the 'Tune-Up Specifications' chart.

9. Turn the mixture adjustment screw(s) clockwise until the rpm drops as follows:
- 1975–76 6-cyl. automatic: 25 rpm
- 1975 6-cyl. manual: 25 rpm
- 1976 6-cyl. manual: 50 rpm
- 1975 6-cyl. manual w/EGR and catalytic converter: 35 rpm
- 1976 6-cyl. manual w/EGR: 50 rpm
- 1975–76 8-cyl. automatic: 20 rpm
- 1975 8-cyl. manual: 40 rpm
- 1976 8-cyl. manual: 100 rpm
- 1977–79 6-cyl. manual: 50 rpm
- 1977–78 6-cylinder automatic Matador: 175 rpm
- 1977–79 6-cyl. automatic high altitude: 25 rpm
- 1978–79 6-cyl. manual high altitude: 50 rpm
- 1978–79 6-cyl. 2-bbl automatic: 25 rpm
- 1977–79 6-cyl. 2-bbl manual: 50 rpm
- 1977–78 8-cyl. automatic: 20 rpm
- 1979 8-cyl. automatic: 40 rpm

10. Install new blue service idle limiter cap(s) over the idle mixture screw(s) with the limiter cap tang(s) positioned against the full rich stop(s). Be careful not to disturb the idle mixture setting while installing the cap(s). Press the cap(s) firmly into place.

1980 6-CYLINDER AND V8 ENGINES

♦ See Figure 42

The procedure for adjusting the idle speed and mixture is called the lean drop procedure and is made with the engine operating at normal operating temperature and the air cleaner in place as follows:

1. Turn the mixture screws to the full rich position with the tabs on the limiters against the stops. Note the position of the screw head slot inside the limiter cap slots.

2. Remove the idle limiter caps by threading a sheet metal screw in center of the cap and turning clockwise. Discard the limiter caps.

3. Reset the adjustment screws to the same position noted before the limiter caps were removed.

4. Start the engine and allow it to reach normal operating temperature.

5. Adjust the idle speed to 30 rpm above the specified rpm. See the Tune-Up Specifications chart. On 6-cylinder engines with a throttle stop solenoid, turn the solenoid in or out to obtain the specified rpm. On V8 engines with a throttle stop solenoid, turn the hex screw on the throttle stop solenoid carriage to obtain the specified rpm. This is done with the solenoid wire connected. Tighten the solenoid locknut, if so equipped. Disconnect the solenoid wire and adjust the curb idle speed screw to obtain an idle speed of 500 rpm. Reconnect the solenoid wire.

6. Starting from the full rich stop position, as was determined before the limiter caps were removed, turn the mixture adjusting screws clockwise (leaner) until a loss of engine speed is noticed.

7. Turn the screws counterclockwise (richer) until the highest rpm reading is obtained at the best lean idle setting. The best lean idle setting is on the lean side of the highest rpm setting without changing rpm.

8. If the idle speed changed more than 30 rpm during the mixture adjustment procedure, reset the idle speed to 30 rpm above

the specified rpm with the idle speed adjusting screw or the throttle stop solenoid and repeat the mixture adjustment.

9. Install new limiter caps over the mixture adjusting screws with the tabs positioned against the full rich stops. Be careful not to disturb the idle mixture setting while installing the caps.

1981–82 6-CYLINDER AND V8 ENGINES

♦ See Figure 43

Idle mixture screws on these carburetors are sealed with plugs or dowel pins. A mixture adjustment must be undertaken only when the carburetor is overhauled, the throttle body replaced, or the engine does not meet required emission standards. Since expensive testing equipment is needed to properly set the mixture, only the idle speed adjusting procedure is given below.

➡**The adjustment is made with the manual transmission in neutral and the automatic in drive. Therefore, make certain that the vehicle's parking brake is set firmly, and that the wheels are blocked. It may be a good idea to have someone in the vehicle with their foot on the brake.**

1. Connect a tachometer, start engine and warm it to normal operating temperature. The choke and intake manifold heater (6-cylinder engine only) must be off.

2. If the engine speed is not within the OK range, turn the curb idle adjustment screw to obtain the specified curb idle rpm.

3. For the 6-cylinder engine (BBD carburetor): Disconnect the vacuum hose from the vacuum actuator and holding solenoid wire connector. Adjust the curb (slow) idle speed adjustment screw to obtain the specified curb (slow) idle rpm, if it is not within the OK range. Refer to the Emission Control Information label, and the Tune-Up Specifications Chart. Apply a direct source of vacuum to the vacuum actuator. Turn the vacuum actuator adjustment screw on the throttle lever until the specified rpm is obtained (900 rpm for manual transmissions, and 800 rpm for automatic transmissions). Disconnect the manifold vacuum source from the vacuum actuator. With the jumper wire, apply battery voltage (12v) to energize the holding solenoid. Turn the A/C ON, if equipped.

➡**The throttle must be opened manually to allow the Sol-Vac throttle positioner to be extended.**

With the Sol-Vac throttle positioner extended, the idle speed should be 650 rpm for automatic transmission equipped vehicles and 750 rpm for manual transmission equipped vehicles. If the idle speed is not within tolerance, adjust the Sol-Vac (hex-head adjustment screw) to obtain the specified rpm. Remove the jumper wire from the Sol-Vac holding solenoid wire connector. Connect the Sol-Vac holding solenoid wire connector. Connect the original hose to the vacuum actuator.

4. For four and eight cylinder engines, turn the nut on the solenoid plunger or the hex screw on the solenoid carriage to obtain the specified idle rpm. Tighten the locknut, if equipped. Disconnect the solenoid wire connector and adjust the curb idle screw to obtain a 500 rpm idle speed. Connect the solenoid wire connector. If the model 2150 carburetor (8-cylinder engine), is equipped with a dashpot, fully depress the dashpot stem with the throttle at the curb idle position, and measure the clearance between the stem and throttle lever. The clearance should be 0.032 in. (0.8128mm). Adjust it by loosening the locknut and turning the dashpot.

Fig. 42 Adjustment points on the BBD 2-bbl adjustments

Fig. 43 On the 1976—79 2150 models; remove the 2 piece plugs and caps from the idle mixture screws

1983 4-150 ENGINES

1. Fully warm up the engine.

2. Check the choke fast idle adjustment: Disconnect and plug the EGR valve vacuum hose. Position the fast idle adjustment screw on the second step of the fast idle cam with the transmission in neutral. Adjust the fast idle speed to 2000 rpm for manual transmission and 2300 rpm for automatic transmission. Allow the throttle to return to normal curb idle and reconnect the EGR vacuum hose.

3. To adjust the Sol-Vac Vacuum Actuator: Remove the vacuum hose from the vacuum actuator and plug the hose. Connect an external vacuum source to the actuator and apply 10—15 in.Hg. of vacuum to the actuator. Shift the transmission to Neutral. Adjust the idle speed to the following rpm using the vacuum actuator adjustment screw on the throttle lever: 850 rpm for automatic transmission 950 rpm for manual transmission. The adjustment is made with all accessories turned OFF.

➡**The curb idle should always be adjusted after vacuum actuator adjustment.**

4. To adjust the curb idle: Remove the vacuum hose from the Sol-Vac vacuum actuator and plug the hose. Shift the transmis-

sion into Neutral. Adjust the curb idle using the 1/4 in. (6.35mm) hex-head adjustment screw on the end of the Sol-Vac unit. Set the speed to 750 rpm for manual transmission, 700 rpm for automatic transmission. Reconnect the vacuum hose to the vacuum actuator.

➡**Engine speed will vary 10–30 rpm during this mode due to the closed loop fuel control.**

5. To adjust the TRC (Anti-Diesel): The TRC screw is preset at the factory and should not require adjustment. However, to check adjustment, the screw should be 3/4 turn from closed throttle position.

1983–84 6-258 ENGINE

Sol-Vac Vacuum Actuator

1. Disconnect and plug the vacuum hose to the Sol-Vac vacuum actuator.

2. Disengage the Sol-Vac electrical connector. Connect an external vacuum source to the vacuum actuator and apply 10–15 in.Hg. of vacuum.

3. Open throttle for at least 3.0 seconds (1200 rpm); then close throttle.

4. Set the speed using the vacuum actuator adjustment screw on the throttle lever to obtain specified rpm.

5. Disconnect the external vacuum source. Reconnect the Sol-Vac vacuum hose and electrical connector.

Sol-Vac Holding Solenoid

‣ **See Figure 44**

➥**The Sol-Vac vacuum actuator adjustment should always precede the Sol-Vac solenoid adjustment.**

1. Disconnect and plug the vacuum hose at the Sol-Vac vacuum actuator.

2. Disengage the Sol-Vac electrical connector.

3. Energize the Sol-Vac holding solenoid with either of the two following methods:

    a. Apply battery voltage (12v) to the solenoid, or,

    b. Reconnect the Sol-Vac electrical connector and turn on the rear window defogger or turn on the air conditioner with the compressor disconnected.

4. Open throttle for at least 3.0 seconds (1,200 rpm) to allow the Sol-Vac holding solenoid to fully extend.

5. Set the speed using the ¼ in. (6.35mm) hex-head adjustment screw on the end of the Sol-Vac unit to obtain the specified rpm.

6. Reopen the throttle above 1,200 rpm to insure the correct holding position and reset the speed if necessary. Reconnect the vacuum hose to the Sol-Vac actuator. Reconnect the Sol-Vac electrical connector if disconnected.

1985–86 Models

➥**The carburetor choke and intake manifold heater must be OFF. This occurs when the engine coolant heats to approximately +160°F (71°C).**

1. Have the engine at normal operating temperature. Connect a tachometer to the ignition coil negative (TACH) terminal.

2. Remove the vacuum hose from the Sol-Vac vacuum actuator unit. Plug the vacuum hose. Disengage the holding solenoid wire connector.

3. Adjust the curb (slow) idle speed screw to obtain the correct curb idle speed. Refer to the specifications under Idle Speed or refer to the Emission Information label, under the hood, for the correct curb idle engine rpm.

4. Apply a direct source of vacuum to the vacuum actuator, using a hand vacuum pump or its equivalent. When the Sol-Vac throttle positioner is fully extended, turn the vacuum actuator adjustment screw on the throttler lever until the specified engine

Fig. 44 Location of the idle speed adjustment screw—Motorcraft 2100, 2150, 4300, 4300 (with TSP)

rpm is obtained. Disconnect the vacuum source from the vacuum actuator.

5. With a jumper wire, apply battery voltage (12v) to energize the holding solenoid.

➥**The holding wire connector can be installed and either the rear window defroster or the air conditioner (with the compressor clutch wire disconnected) can be turned on to energize the holding solenoid.**

6. Hold the throttle open manually to allow the throttle positioner to fully extend.

➥**Without the vacuum actuator, the throttle must be opened manually to allow the Sol-Vac throttle positioner to fully extend.**

7. If the holding solenoid idle speed is not within specifications, adjust the idle using the ¼ in. (6.35mm) hex-headed adjustment screw on the end of the Sol-Vac unit. Adjust to specifications.

8. Disconnect the jumper wire from the Sol-Vac holding solenoid wire connector, if used. Connect the wire connector to the Sol-Vac unit, if not connected. Install the original vacuum hose to the vacuum actuator.

9. Remove the tachometer and if disconnected, connect the compressor clutch wire. Install any other component that was previously removed.

Troubleshooting Engine Performance

Problem	Cause	Solution
Hard starting (engine cranks normally)	• Binding linkage, choke valve or choke piston	• Repair as necessary
	• Restricted choke vacuum diaphragm	• Clean passages
	• Improper fuel level	• Adjust float level
	• Dirty, worn or faulty needle valve and seat	• Repair as necessary
	• Float sticking	• Repair as necessary
	• Faulty fuel pump	• Replace fuel pump
	• Incorrect choke cover adjustment	• Adjust choke cover
	• Inadequate choke unloader adjustment	• Adjust choke unloader
	• Faulty ignition coil	• Test and replace as necessary
	• Improper spark plug gap	• Adjust gap
	• Incorrect ignition timing	• Adjust timing
	• Incorrect valve timing	• Check valve timing; repair as necessary
Rough idle or stalling	• Incorrect curb or fast idle speed	• Adjust curb or fast idle speed
	• Incorrect ignition timing	• Adjust timing to specification
	• Improper feedback system operation	• Refer to Chapter 4
	• Improper fast idle cam adjustment	• Adjust fast idle cam
	• Faulty EGR valve operation	• Test EGR system and replace as necessary
	• Faulty PCV valve air flow	• Test PCV valve and replace as necessary
	• Choke binding	• Locate and eliminate binding condition
	• Faulty TAC vacuum motor or valve	• Repair as necessary
	• Air leak into manifold vacuum	• Inspect manifold vacuum connections and repair as necessary
	• Improper fuel level	• Adjust fuel level
	• Faulty distributor rotor or cap	• Replace rotor or cap
	• Improperly seated valves	• Test cylinder compression, repair as necessary
	• Incorrect ignition wiring	• Inspect wiring and correct as necessary
	• Faulty ignition coil	• Test coil and replace as necessary
	• Restricted air vent or idle passages	• Clean passages
	• Restricted air cleaner	• Clean or replace air cleaner filler element
	• Faulty choke vacuum diaphragm	• Repair as necessary
Faulty low-speed operation	• Restricted idle transfer slots	• Clean transfer slots
	• Restricted idle air vents and passages	• Clean air vents and passages
	• Restricted air cleaner	• Clean or replace air cleaner filter element
	• Improper fuel level	• Adjust fuel level
	• Faulty spark plugs	• Clean or replace spark plugs
	• Dirty, corroded, or loose ignition secondary circuit wire connections	• Clean or tighten secondary circuit wire connections
	• Improper feedback system operation	• Refer to Chapter 4
	• Faulty ignition coil high voltage wire	• Replace ignition coil high voltage wire
	• Faulty distributor cap	• Replace cap
Faulty acceleration	• Improper accelerator pump stroke	• Adjust accelerator pump stroke
	• Incorrect ignition timing	• Adjust timing
	• Inoperative pump discharge check ball or needle	• Clean or replace as necessary
	• Worn or damaged pump diaphragm or piston	• Replace diaphragm or piston

Troubleshooting Engine Performance (cont.)

Problem	Cause	Solution
Faulty acceleration (cont.)	• Leaking carburetor main body cover gasket	• Replace gasket
	• Engine cold and choke set too lean	• Adjust choke cover
	• Improper metering rod adjustment (BBD Model carburetor)	• Adjust metering rod
	• Faulty spark plug(s)	• Clean or replace spark plug(s)
	• Improperly seated valves	• Test cylinder compression, repair as necessary
	• Faulty ignition coil	• Test coil and replace as necessary
	• Improper feedback system operation	• Refer to Chapter 4
Faulty high speed operation	• Incorrect ignition timing	• Adjust timing
	• Faulty distributor centrifugal advance mechanism	• Check centrifugal advance mechanism and repair as necessary
	• Faulty distributor vacuum advance mechanism	• Check vacuum advance mechanism and repair as necessary
	• Low fuel pump volume	• Replace fuel pump
	• Wrong spark plug air gap or wrong plug	• Adjust air gap or install correct plug
	• Faulty choke operation	• Adjust choke cover
	• Partially restricted exhaust manifold, exhaust pipe, catalytic converter, muffler, or tailpipe	• Eliminate restriction
	• Restricted vacuum passages	• Clean passages
	• Improper size or restricted main jet	• Clean or replace as necessary
	• Restricted air cleaner	• Clean or replace filter element as necessary
	• Faulty distributor rotor or cap	• Replace rotor or cap
	• Faulty ignition coil	• Test coil and replace as necessary
	• Improperly seated valve(s)	• Test cylinder compression, repair as necessary
	• Faulty valve spring(s)	• Inspect and test valve spring tension, replace as necessary
	• Incorrect valve timing	• Check valve timing and repair as necessary
	• Intake manifold restricted	• Remove restriction or replace manifold
	• Worn distributor shaft	• Replace shaft
	• Improper feedback system operation	• Refer to Chapter 4
Misfire at all speeds	• Faulty spark plug(s)	• Clean or replace spark plug(s)
	• Faulty spark plug wire(s)	• Replace as necessary
	• Faulty distributor cap or rotor	• Replace cap or rotor
	• Faulty ignition coil	• Test coil and replace as necessary
	• Primary ignition circuit shorted or open intermittently	• Troubleshoot primary circuit and repair as necessary
	• Improperly seated valve(s)	• Test cylinder compression, repair as necessary
	• Faulty hydraulic tappet(s)	• Clean or replace tappet(s)
	• Improper feedback system operation	• Refer to Chapter 4
	• Faulty valve spring(s)	• Inspect and test valve spring tension, repair as necessary
	• Worn camshaft lobes	• Replace camshaft
	• Air leak into manifold	• Check manifold vacuum and repair as necessary
	• Improper carburetor adjustment	• Adjust carburetor
	• Fuel pump volume or pressure low	• Replace fuel pump
	• Blown cylinder head gasket	• Replace gasket
	• Intake or exhaust manifold passage(s) restricted	• Pass chain through passage(s) and repair as necessary
	• Incorrect trigger wheel installed in distributor	• Install correct trigger wheel

Troubleshooting Engine Performance (cont.)

Problem	Cause	Solution
Power not up to normal	• Incorrect ignition timing	• Adjust timing
	• Faulty distributor rotor	• Replace rotor
	• Trigger wheel loose on shaft	• Reposition or replace trigger wheel
	• Incorrect spark plug gap	• Adjust gap
	• Faulty fuel pump	• Replace fuel pump
	• Incorrect valve timing	• Check valve timing and repair as necessary
	• Faulty ignition coil	• Test coil and replace as necessary
	• Faulty ignition wires	• Test wires and replace as necessary
	• Improperly seated valves	• Test cylinder compression and repair as necessary
	• Blown cylinder head gasket	• Replace gasket
	• Leaking piston rings	• Test compression and repair as necessary
	• Worn distributor shaft	• Replace shaft
	• Improper feedback system operation	• Refer to Chapter 4
Intake backfire	• Improper ignition timing	• Adjust timing
	• Faulty accelerator pump discharge	• Repair as necessary
	• Defective EGR CTO valve	• Replace EGR CTO valve
	• Defective TAC vacuum motor or valve	• Repair as necessary
	• Lean air/fuel mixture	• Check float level or manifold vacuum for air leak. Remove sediment from bowl
Exhaust backfire	• Air leak into manifold vacuum	• Check manifold vacuum and repair as necessary
	• Faulty air injection diverter valve	• Test diverter valve and replace as necessary
	• Exhaust leak	• Locate and eliminate leak
Ping or spark knock	• Incorrect ignition timing	• Adjust timing
	• Distributor centrifugal or vacuum advance malfunction	• Inspect advance mechanism and repair as necessary
	• Excessive combustion chamber deposits	• Remove with combustion chamber cleaner
	• Air leak into manifold vacuum	• Check manifold vacuum and repair as necessary
	• Excessively high compression	• Test compression and repair as necessary
	• Fuel octane rating excessively low	• Try alternate fuel source
	• Sharp edges in combustion chamber	• Grind smooth
	• EGR valve not functioning properly	• Test EGR system and replace as necessary
Surging (at cruising to top speeds)	• Low carburetor fuel level	• Adjust fuel level
	• Low fuel pump pressure or volume	• Replace fuel pump
	• Metering rod(s) not adjusted properly (BBD Model Carburetor)	• Adjust metering rod
	• Improper PCV valve air flow	• Test PCV valve and replace as necessary
	• Air leak into manifold vacuum	• Check manifold vacuum and repair as necessary
	• Incorrect spark advance	• Test and replace as necessary
	• Restricted main jet(s)	• Clean main jet(s)
	• Undersize main jet(s)	• Replace main jet(s)
	• Restricted air vents	• Clean air vents
	• Restricted fuel filter	• Replace fuel filter
	• Restricted air cleaner	• Clean or replace air cleaner filter element
	• EGR valve not functioning properly	• Test EGR system and replace as necessary
	• Improper feedback system operation	• Refer to Chapter 4

ENGINE ELECTRICAL 3-2
UNDERSTANDING ELECTRICITY 3-2
  BASIC CIRCUITS 3-2
  TROUBLESHOOTING 3-3
BATTERY, STARTING AND CHARGING
  SYSTEMS 3-4
  BASIC OPERATING PRINCIPLES 3-4
IGNITION COIL 3-5
  REMOVAL & INSTALLATION 3-5
IGNITION MODULE 3-6
  REMOVAL & INSTALLATION 3-6
DISTRIBUTOR 3-6
  REMOVAL 3-6
  INSTALLATION 3-8
ALTERNATOR 3-11
  ALTERNATOR PRECAUTIONS 3-11
  REMOVAL & INSTALLATION 3-11
  BELT TENSION ADJUSTMENT 3-14
REGULATOR 3-14
  REMOVAL & INSTALLATION 3-14
STARTER 3-14
  REMOVAL & INSTALLATION 3-14
  COMPONENT REPLACEMENT 3-15
  OVERHAUL 3-19
BATTERY 3-23
  REMOVAL & INSTALLATION 3-23
ENGINE MECHANICAL 3-23
DESCRIPTION 3-23
  4-121 ENGINE 3-23
  4-150 ENGINE 3-25
  4-151 ENGINE 3-25
  6-232 AND 258 ENGINES 3-27
  8-304, 360 AND 401 ENGINES 3-27
ENGINE OVERHAUL TIPS 3-27
  TOOLS 3-28
  INSPECTION TECHNIQUES 3-28
  OVERHAUL TIPS 3-29
  REPAIRING DAMAGED THREADS 3-29
CHECKING ENGINE COMPRESSION 3-30
ENGINE 3-34
  REMOVAL & INSTALLATION 3-34
ROCKER SHAFTS AND ROCKER
  STUDS 3-39
  REMOVAL & INSTALLATION 3-39
THERMOSTAT 3-42
  REMOVAL & INSTALLATION 3-42
INTAKE MANIFOLD 3-43
  REMOVAL & INSTALLATION 3-43
EXHAUST MANIFOLD 3-48
  REMOVAL & INSTALLATION 3-48
AIR CONDITIONING COMPRESSOR 3-51
  REMOVAL & INSTALLATION 3-51
RADIATOR 3-53
  REMOVAL & INSTALLATION 3-53
WATER PUMP 3-56
  REMOVAL & INSTALLATION 3-56
CYLINDER HEAD 3-61
  REMOVAL & INSTALLATION 3-61
VALVES AND SPRINGS 3-66
  REMOVAL 3-66
  INSPECTION & REFACING 3-69
  REFACING 3-70
  LAPPING 3-71
  VALVE SPRING TESTING 3-71
  INSTALLATION 3-72
VALVE SEATS 3-72
  INSPECTION AND REFACING 3-72

OIL PAN 3-72
  REMOVAL & INSTALLATION 3-72
OIL PUMP 3-75
  REMOVAL & INSTALLATION 3-75
CRANKSHAFT PULLEY (VIBRATION
  DAMPER) 3-78
  REMOVAL & INSTALLATION 3-78
TIMING CASE COVER 3-79
  REMOVAL & INSTALLATION 3-79
TIMING CHAIN/GEAR AND SPROCKET/
  PULLEY 3-85
  REMOVAL & INSTALLATION 3-85
TIMING BELT 3-89
  REMOVAL & INSTALLATION 3-89
SPROCKETS 3-93
  REMOVAL & INSTALLATION 3-93
CAMSHAFT 3-93
  REMOVAL & INSTALLATION 3-93
PISTONS AND CONNECTING RODS 3-98
  REMOVAL 3-98
  PISTON PIN REPLACEMENT 3-99
  INSPECTION 3-100
  MEASURING THE OLD PISTONS 3-102
  SELECTING NEW PISTONS 3-102
  CYLINDER HONING 3-102
  CHECKING CYLINDER BORE 3-103
  RING TOLERANCES 3-104
  PISTON RING REPLACEMENT 3-105
  INSTALLATION 3-105
REAR MAIN BEARING OIL SEAL 3-107
  REMOVAL & INSTALLATION 3-107
CRANKSHAFT 3-109
  REMOVAL 3-109
  CLEANING & INSPECTION 3-110
  INSTALLATION 3-111
FLYWHEEL/FLEXPLATE AND RING
  GEAR 3-112
  REMOVAL & INSTALLATION 3-112
EXHAUST SYSTEM 3-112
GENERAL INFORMATION 3-112
MUFFLER 3-113
  REMOVAL & INSTALLATION 3-113
FRONT EXHAUST PIPE (HEAD PIPE) 3-113
  REMOVAL & INSTALLATION 3-113
REAR EXHAUST PIPE OR TAILPIPE 3-113
  REMOVAL & INSTALLATION 3-113
CATALYTIC CONVERTER 3-114
  REMOVAL & INSTALLATION 3-114
SPECIFICATION CHARTS
ALTERNATOR AND REGULATOR
  SPECIFICATIONS 3-14
STARTER SPECIFICATIONS 3-22
GENERAL ENGINE SPECIFICATIONS 3-31
VALVE SPECIFICATIONS 3-32
CAMSHAFT SPECIFICATIONS 3-32
CRANKSHAFT AND CONNECTING ROD
  SPECIFICATIONS 3-33
PISTON AND RING SPECIFICATIONS 3-33
TORQUE SPECIFICATIONS 3-34
USING A VACUUM GAUGE 3-116
TROUBLESHOOTING CHARTS
ENGINE MECHANICAL PROBLEMS 3-117
ENGINE PERFORMANCE 3-120

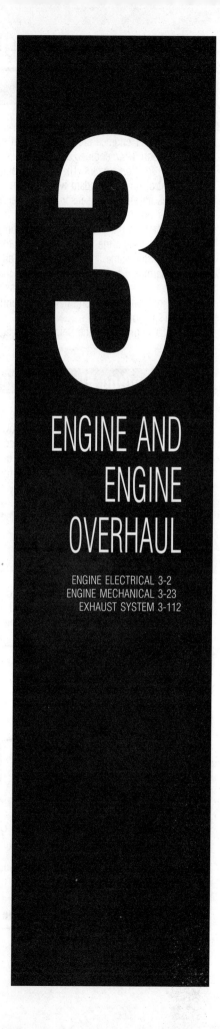

3

ENGINE AND ENGINE OVERHAUL

ENGINE ELECTRICAL 3-2
ENGINE MECHANICAL 3-23
EXHAUST SYSTEM 3-112

ENGINE ELECTRICAL

A conventional point-type ignition system is used on all 4-121 engines. All other engines are equipped with electronic ignition.

1975 through 1977 engines use the Breakerless Inductive Discharge (BID) ignition system. The system consists of an electronic ignition control unit, a standard type ignition coil, a distributor that contains an electronic sensor and trigger wheel instead of a cam, breaker points and condenser, and the usual high tension wires and spark plugs. There are no contacting (and thus wearing) surfaces between the trigger wheel and the sensor. The dwell angle remains the same and never requires adjustment. The dwell angle is determined by the control unit and the angle between the trigger wheel spokes. In 1978 the system was modified to include a different ignition module and distributor, and was renamed Solid State Ignition (SSI).

The 4-151 engine uses the Delco-Remy High Energy Ignition (HEI) system.

Understanding Electricity

For any electrical system to operate, there must be a complete circuit. This simply means that the power flow from the battery must make a full circle. When an electrical component is operating, power flows from the battery to the components, passes through the component (load) causing it to function, and returns to the battery through the ground path of the circuit. This ground may be either another wire or a metal part of the vehicle (depending upon how the component is designed).

BASIC CIRCUITS

Perhaps the easiest way to visualize a circuit is to think of connecting a light bulb (with two wires attached to it) to the battery. If one of the two wires was attached to the negative post (−) of the battery and the other wire to the positive post (+), the circuit would be complete and the light bulb would illuminate. Electricity could follow a path from the battery to the bulb and back to the battery. It's not hard to see that with longer wires on our light bulb, it could be mounted anywhere on the vehicle. Further, one wire could be fitted with a switch so that the light could be turned on and off. Various other items could be added to our primitive circuit to make the light flash, become brighter or dimmer under certain conditions, or advise the user that it's burned out.

Ground

Some automotive components are grounded through their mounting points. The electrical current runs through the chassis of the vehicle and returns to the battery through the ground (−) cable; if you look, you'll see that the battery ground cable connects between the battery and the body of the vehicle.

Load

Every complete circuit must include a "load" (something to use the electricity coming from the source). If you were to connect a wire between the two terminals of the battery (DON'T do this, but take our word for it) without the light bulb, the battery would attempt to deliver its entire power supply from one pole to another almost instantly. This is a short circuit. The electricity is taking a short cut to get to ground and is not being used by any load in the circuit. This sudden and uncontrolled electrical flow can cause great damage to other components in the circuit and can develop a tremendous amount of heat. A short in an automotive wiring harness can develop sufficient heat to melt the insulation on all the surrounding wires and reduce a multiple wire cable to one sad lump of plastic and copper. Two common causes of shorts are broken insulation (thereby exposing the wire to contact with surrounding metal surfaces or other wires) or a failed switch (the pins inside the switch come out of place and touch each other).

Here is an example of a simple automotive circuit. When the switch is closed, power from the positive battery terminal flows through the fuse, the switch and then the load (light bulb). The light illuminates and the circuit is completed through the return conductor and the vehicle ground. If the light did not work, the tests could be made with a voltmeter or test light at the battery, fuse, switch or bulb socket

Damaged insulation can allow wires to break (causing an open circuit) or touch (causing a short circuit)

Switches and Relays

Some electrical components which require a large amount of current to operate also have a relay in their circuit. Since these circuits carry a large amount of current (amperage or amps), the thickness of the wire in the circuit (wire gauge) is also greater. If this large wire were connected from the load to the control switch on the dash, the switch would have to carry the high amperage load and the dash would be twice as large to accommodate wiring harnesses as thick as your wrist. To prevent these problems, a relay is used. The large wires in the circuit are connected from the battery to one side of the relay and from the opposite side of the relay to the load. The relay is normally open, preventing current from passing through the circuit. An additional, smaller wire is connected from the relay to the control switch for the circuit. When the control switch is turned on, it grounds the smaller wire to the relay and completes its circuit. The main switch inside the relay closes, sending power to the component without routing the main power through the inside of the vehicle. Some common circuits which may use relays are the horn, headlights, starter and rear window defogger systems.

Protective Devices

It is possible for larger surges of current to pass through the electrical system of your vehicle. If this surge of current were to reach the load in the circuit, it could burn it out or severely damage it. To prevent this, fuses, circuit breakers and/or fusible links are connected into the supply wires of the electrical system. These items are nothing more than a built-in weak spot in the system. It's much easier to go to a known location (the fusebox) to see why a circuit is inoperative than to dissect 15 feet of wiring under the dashboard, looking for what happened.

When an electrical current of excessive power passes through the fuse, the fuse blows (the conductor melts) and breaks the circuit, preventing the passage of current and protecting the components.

A circuit breaker is basically a self repairing fuse. It will open the circuit in the same fashion as a fuse, but when either the short is removed or the surge subsides, the circuit breaker resets itself and does not need replacement.

A fuse link (fusible link or main link) is a wire that acts as a

fuse. One of these is normally connected between the starter relay and the main wiring harness under the hood. Since the starter is usually the highest electrical draw on the vehicle, an internal short during starting could direct about 130 amps into the wrong places. Consider the damage potential of introducing this current into a system whose wiring is rated at 15 amps and you'll understand the need for protection. Since this link is very early in the electrical path, it's the first place to look if nothing on the vehicle works, but the battery seems to be charged and is properly connected.

TROUBLESHOOTING

Electrical problems generally fall into one of three areas:
• The component that is not functioning is not receiving current.
• The component is receiving power but is not using it or is using it incorrectly (component failure).
• The component is improperly grounded.

A 12 volt test light is useful when checking parts of a circuit for power

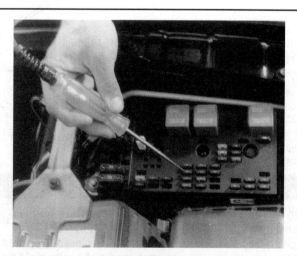

Here, someone is checking a circuit by making sure there is power to the component's fuse

The circuit can be can be checked with a test light and a jumper wire. The test light is a device that looks like a pointed screwdriver with a wire on one end and a bulb in its handle. A jumper wire is simply a piece of wire with alligator clips or special terminals on each end. If a component is not working, you must follow a systematic plan to determine which of the three causes is the villain.

1. Turn ON the switch that controls the item not working.

➡**Some items only work when the ignition switch is turned ON.**

2. Disconnect the power supply wire from the component.

3. Attach the ground wire of a test light or a voltmeter to a good metal ground.

4. Touch the end probe of the test light (or the positive lead of the voltmeter) to the power wire; if there is current in the wire, the light in the test light will come on (or the voltmeter will indicate the amount of voltage). You have now established that current is getting to the component.

5. Turn the ignition or dash switch **OFF** and reconnect the wire to the component.

If there was no power, then the problem is between the battery and the component. This includes all the switches, fuses, relays and the battery itself. The next place to look is the fusebox; check carefully either by eye or by using the test light across the fuse clips. The easiest way to check is to simply replace the fuse. If

Jumper wires with various connectors are handy for quick electrical testing

the fuse is blown, and upon replacement, immediately blows again, there is a short between the fuse and the component. This is generally (not always) a sign of an internal short in the component. Disconnect the power wire at the component again and replace the fuse; if the fuse holds, the component is the problem.

✳✳ WARNING

DO NOT test a component by running a jumper wire from the battery UNLESS you are certain that it operates on 12 volts. Many electronic components are designed to operate with less voltage and connecting them to 12 volts could de-

stroy them. Jumper wires are best used to bypass a portion of the circuit (such as a stretch of wire or a switch) that **DOES NOT contain a resistor and is suspected to be bad.**

If all the fuses are good and the component is not receiving power, find the switch for the circuit. Bypass the switch with the jumper wire. This is done by connecting one end of the jumper to the power wire coming into the switch and the other end to the wire leaving the switch. If the component comes to life, the switch has failed.

✳✳ WARNING

Never substitute the jumper for the component. The circuit needs the electrical load of the component. If you bypass it, you will cause a short circuit.

Checking the ground for any circuit can mean tracing wires to the body, cleaning connections or tightening mounting bolts for the component itself. If the jumper wire can be connected to the case of the component or the ground connector, you can ground the other end to a piece of clean, solid metal on the vehicle. Again, if the component starts working, you've found the problem.

A systematic search through the fuse, connectors, switches and the component itself will almost always yield an answer. Loose and/or corroded connectors, particularly in ground circuits, are becoming a larger problem in modern vehicles. The computers and on-board electronic (solid state) systems are highly sensitive to improper grounds and will change their function drastically if one occurs.

Remember that for any electrical circuit to work, ALL the connections must be clean and tight.

➡**For more information on Understanding and Troubleshooting Electrical Systems, please refer to Section 6 of this manual.**

Battery, Starting and Charging Systems

BASIC OPERATING PRINCIPLES

Battery

The battery is the first link in the chain of mechanisms which work together to provide cranking of the automobile engine. In most modern vehicles, the battery is a lead/acid electrochemical device consisting of six 2v subsections (cells) connected in series so the unit is capable of producing approximately 12v of electrical pressure. Each subsection consists of a series of positive and negative plates held a short distance apart in a solution of sulfuric acid and water.

The two types of plates are of dissimilar metals. This sets-up a chemical reaction, and it is this reaction which produces current flow from the battery when its positive and negative terminals are connected to an electrical accessory such as a lamp or motor. The continued transfer of electrons would eventually convert the sulfuric acid to water, and make the two plates identical in chemical composition. As electrical energy is removed from the battery, its voltage output tends to drop. Thus, measuring battery voltage and battery electrolyte composition are two ways of checking the ability of the unit to supply power. During engine cranking, electrical energy is removed from the battery. However, if the charging circuit is in good condition and the operating conditions are normal, the power removed from the battery will be replaced by the alternator which will force electrons back through the battery, reversing the normal flow, and restoring the battery to its original chemical state.

Starting System

The battery and starting motor are linked by very heavy electrical cables designed to minimize resistance to the flow of current. Generally, the major power supply cable that leaves the battery goes directly to the starter, while other electrical system needs are supplied by a smaller cable. During starter operation, power flows from the battery to the starter and is grounded through the vehicle's frame/body or engine and the battery's negative ground strap.

The starter is a specially designed, direct current electric motor capable of producing a great amount of power for its size. One thing that allows the motor to produce a great deal of power is its tremendous rotating speed. It drives the engine through a tiny pinion gear (attached to the starter's armature), which drives the very large flywheel ring gear at a greatly reduced speed. Another factor allowing it to produce so much power is that only intermittent operation is required of it. Thus, little allowance for air circulation is necessary, and the windings can be built into a very small space.

The starter solenoid is a magnetic device which employs the small current supplied by the start circuit of the ignition switch. This magnetic action moves a plunger which mechanically engages the starter and closes the heavy switch connecting it to the battery. The starting switch circuit usually consists of the starting switch contained within the ignition switch, a neutral safety switch or clutch pedal switch, and the wiring necessary to connect these in series with the starter solenoid or relay.

The pinion, a small gear, is mounted to a one way drive clutch. This clutch is splined to the starter armature shaft. When the ignition switch is moved to the **START** position, the solenoid plunger slides the pinion toward the flywheel ring gear via a collar and spring. If the teeth on the pinion and flywheel match properly, the pinion will engage the flywheel immediately. If the gear teeth butt one another, the spring will be compressed and will force the gears to mesh as soon as the starter turns far enough to allow them to do so. As the solenoid plunger reaches the end of its travel, it closes the contacts that connect the battery and starter, then the engine is cranked.

As soon as the engine starts, the flywheel ring gear begins turning fast enough to drive the pinion at an extremely high rate of speed. At this point, the one-way clutch begins allowing the pinion to spin faster than the starter shaft so that the starter will not operate at excessive speed. When the ignition switch is released from the starter position, the solenoid is de-energized, and a spring pulls the gear out of mesh interrupting the current flow to the starter.

Some starters employ a separate relay, mounted away from the starter, to switch the motor and solenoid current on and off. The relay replaces the solenoid electrical switch, but does not eliminate the need for a solenoid mounted on the starter used to mechanically engage the starter drive gears. The relay is used to reduce the amount of current the starting switch must carry.

Charging System

The automobile charging system provides electrical power for operation of the vehicle's ignition system, starting system and all electrical accessories. The battery serves as an electrical surge or storage tank, storing (in chemical form) the energy originally produced by the engine driven generator. The system also provides a means of regulating output to protect the battery from being overcharged and to avoid excessive voltage to the accessories.

The storage battery is a chemical device incorporating parallel lead plates in a tank containing a sulfuric acid/water solution. Adjacent plates are slightly dissimilar, and the chemical reaction of the two dissimilar plates produces electrical energy when the battery is connected to a load such as the starter motor. The chemical reaction is reversible, so that when the generator is producing a voltage (electrical pressure) greater than that produced by the battery, electricity is forced into the battery, and the battery is returned to its fully charged state.

Newer automobiles use alternating current generators or alternators, because they are more efficient, can be rotated at higher speeds, and have fewer brush problems. In an alternator, the field usually rotates while all the current produced passes only through the stator winding. The brushes bear against continuous slip rings. This causes the current produced to periodically reverse the direction of its flow. Diodes (electrical one way valves) block the flow of current from traveling in the wrong direction. A series of diodes is wired together to permit the alternating flow of the stator to be rectified back to 12 volts DC for use by the vehicle's electrical system.

The voltage regulating function is performed by a regulator. The regulator is often built in to the alternator; this system is termed an integrated or internal regulator.

Ignition Coil

REMOVAL & INSTALLATION

Except 4-151 Engines

1. Disconnect the battery ground.
2. Disconnect the two small and one large wire from the coil.
3. Disconnect the condenser connector from the coil, if equipped.
4. Unbolt and remove the coil.
5. Installation is the reverse of removal.

4-151 Engines

1980–81 MODELS

♦ **See Figure 1**

1. Remove the distributor cap.
2. Remove the three coil cover attaching screws and lift off the cover.
3. Remove the four coil attaching screws and lift off the coil.
4. Installation is the reverse of removal.

Fig. 1 Common ignition coil used on the 4-151 engine—1980–81

1982–83 MODELS
▶ See Figure 2

1. Disconnect the harness at the coil.
2. Pulling on the boot, only, pull the coil-to-distributor cap wire from the coil.
3. Remove the three coil mounting screws and lift off the coil.
4. Installation is the reverse of removal.

Fig. 2 Remove the harness from the ignition coil—except 4–151 engine

Ignition Module

REMOVAL & INSTALLATION

▶ See Figure 3

The ignition module is mounted next to the battery on all models. It is a sealed, weatherproof unit.

Removing the module, on all models, is a matter of simply removing the fasteners that attach it to the fender or firewall and pulling apart the connectors. When unplugging the connectors, pull them apart with a firm, straight pull, never pry them apart! To pry them will cause damage. When reconnecting them, coat the mating ends with silicone dielectric grease to waterproof the connection. Press the connectors together firmly to overcome any vacuum lock caused by the grease.

➡ **If the locking tabs weaken or break, don't replace the unit. Just secure the connection with electrical tape or tie straps.**

Fig. 3 The ignition control module used on all models except 1987 4—150 engines

Distributor

REMOVAL

▶ See Figure 4

1. Remove the high tension wires from the distributor cap terminal towers, noting their positions to assure correct reassembly. For diagrams of firing orders and distributor wiring, refer to the tune-up and troubleshooting section.
2. Remove the primary lead from the terminal post at the side of the distributor.

CAP

ROTOR

CENTRIFUGAL
ADVANCE
MECHANISM

TRIGGER
WHEEL

MAIN
SHAFT

SNAP
RING

PICKUP COIL
AND PLATE

VACUUM
ADVANCE
MECHANISM

ELECTRONIC
MODULE

ELECTRONIC
MODULE-TO-
IGNITION COIL
CONNECTOR

IGNITION
COIL
CONNECTOR

HOUSING

O-RING

WASHER

PIN

GEAR

Fig. 4 Exploded view of a common HEI distributor

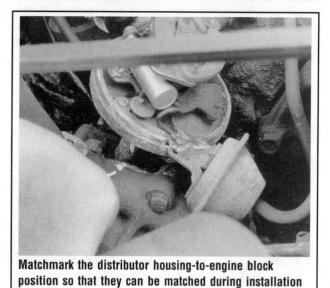

Matchmark the distributor housing-to-engine block
position so that they can be matched during installation

Disconnect the hose from the vacuum advance unit

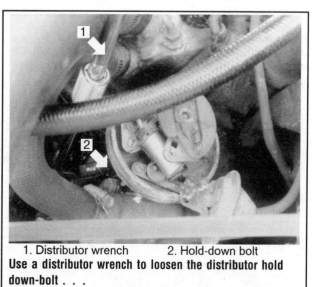

1. Distributor wrench   2. Hold-down bolt
Use a distributor wrench to loosen the distributor hold
down-bolt . . .

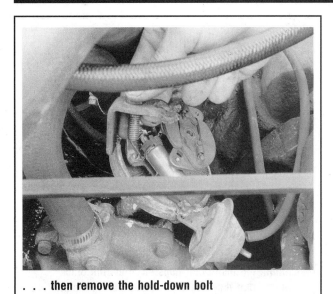

. . . then remove the hold-down bolt

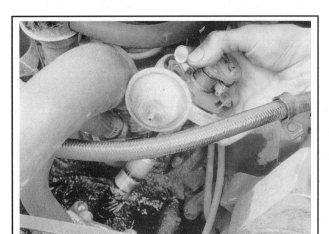

Grasp the distributor and pull it straight up and out from the engine

➡**The wire connector on 1978 and later models will contain a special conductive grease. Do not remove it. The same grease will also be found on the metal parts of the rotor.**

3. Disconnect the vacuum line if there is one.

4. Remove the two distributor cap retaining hooks or screws and remove the distributor cap.

5. Note the position of the rotor in relation to the base. Scribe a mark on the base of the distributor and on the engine block to facilitate reinstallation. Align the marks with the direction the metal tip of the rotor is pointing.

6. Remove the bolt that holds the distributor to the engine.

7. Lift the distributor assembly from the engine.

INSTALLATION

Engine Not Rotated

EXCEPT 4-150 ENGINES

➧ **See Figures 5 and 6**

1. Insert the distributor shaft and assembly into the engine. Line up the mark on the distributor and the one on the engine with the metal tip of the rotor. Make sure that the vacuum advance diaphragm is pointed in the same direction as it was pointed originally. This will be done automatically if the marks on the engine and the distributor are line up with the rotor.

2. Install the distributor hold-down bolt and clamp. Leave the screw loose enough so that you can move the distributor with heavy hand pressure.

3. Connect the primary wire to the distributor side of the coil. Install the distributor cap on the distributor housing. Secure the distributor cap with the spring clips or the screw type retainers, whichever is used.

4. Install the spark plug wires. Make sure that the wires are pressed all of the way into the top of the distributor cap and firmly onto the spark plugs.

5. Adjust the point cam dwell and set the ignition timing. Refer to the tune-up section.

➡**If the engine was turned while the distributor was removed, or if the marks were not drawn, it will be necessary to initially time the engine. Follow the procedure below.**

Engine Rotated

EXCEPT 4-150 ENGINES

1. If the engine has been rotated while the distributor was out, you'll have to first put the engine on No. 1 cylinder at Top Dead Center firing position. You can either remove the valve cover or No. 1 spark plug to determine engine position. Rotate the engine with a socket wrench on the nut at the center of the front pulley in the normal direction of rotation. Either feel for air being expelled forcefully through the spark plug hole or watch for the engine to rotate up to the Top Center mark without the valves moving (both valves will be closed). If the valves are moving as you approach TDC or there is no air being expelled through the plug hole, turn the engine another full turn until you get the appropriate indication as the engine approaches TDC position.

2. Start the distributor into the engine with the matchmarks between the distributor body and the engine lined up. Turn the rotor slightly until the matchmarks on the bottom of the distributor body and the bottom of the distributor shaft near the gear are aligned.

Then, insert the distributor all the way into the engine. If you have trouble getting the distributor and camshaft gears to mesh, turn the rotor back and forth very slightly until the distributor can be inserted easily. If the rotor is not now lined up with the position of No. 1 plug terminal, you'll have to pull the distributor back out slightly, shift the position of the rotor appropriately, and then reinstall it.

Fig. 5 Exploded view of the distributor used on the 4-151 engine—1980-81 models

Fig. 6 Exploded view of the distributor used on the 4–151 engine—1982–83 models

3. Align the matchmarks between the distributor and engine. Install the distributor mounting bolt and tighten it finger-tight. Reconnect the vacuum advance line and distributor wiring connector, and reinstall the gasket and cap. Reconnect the negative battery cable. Adjust the ignition timing as described in Chapter 2. Then, tighten the distributor mounting bolt securely.

4-150 ENGINES

▶ **See Figures 7, 8, 9 and 10**

1. Rotate the engine until the No. 1 piston is at TDC compression.
2. Using a flat bladed screwdriver, in the distributor hole, rotate the oil pump gear so that the slot in the oil pump shaft is

1. Pin
2. Gear
3. Washer
4. Distributor body
5. Vacuum advance mechanism
6. Wick
7. Washers
8. Pick-up coil
9. Retainer
10. Trigger wheel
11. Pin
12. Rotor
13. Cap

Fig. 7 Exploded view of the distributor components used on the 4–150 engine—1984 models

A. Oil pump gear slot
B. Front face of engine block
C. 3 o'clock position

Fig. 8 The oil pump shaft must be in position before distributor installation—4-150 engine

1. Front face of engine block
2. Rotor pre-positioned
3. 5 o'clock position (approx.)

Fig. 9 The distributor rotor and shaft must be in the position before installation—4-150 engine

A. Front face of engine block
B. Rotor position when properly installed

Fig. 10 Location of the rotor when the distributor is properly installed—4-150 engine

Alternator

A variety of alternators were used:
- 1975: Motorola and Delco
- 1976: 6-cyl.—Delco
8-cyl.—Motorcraft
- 1977-78: 4- & 6-cyl.—Delco
8-cyl.—Motorcraft
- 1979: 4- & 6-cyl.—Delco
8-cyl.—Bosch
- 1980: All Delco, exc. Eagle with heated rear window (Bosch)
- 1981-88: All Delco

The alternator needs no lubrication or adjustments except for drive belt tension.

ALTERNATOR PRECAUTIONS

Certain safety precautions should be observed concerning the alternator:

1. Do not polarize the unit.
2. Do not short across or ground any of the terminals.
3. Never operate the unit with the output terminal disconnected.
4. Make sure that the battery is installed with the correct polarity.
5. When connecting a booster battery or a charger, always connect positive terminal to positive terminal and negative terminal to negative terminal.
6. Disconnect the battery ground cable when working on any electrical equipment.

slightly past the 3:00 o'clock position, relative to the length of the engine block.

3. With the distributor cap removed, install the distributor with the rotor at the 5:00 o'clock position, relative to the oil pump gear shaft slot. When the distributor is completely in place, the rotor should be at the 6:00 o'clock position. If not, remove the distributor and perform the entire procedure again.

4. Tighten the lockbolt.

7. If any electric welding is done on the car, disconnect the alternator completely.

REMOVAL & INSTALLATION

▶ **See Figure 11**

1. Disconnect the battery cables.

➡**Always disconnect the ground cable first, and connect it last, and then you needn't fear sparks.**

2. Remove the adjusting bolt.
3. Take off the drive belt.
4. Disconnect the alternator wires or wiring plug.
5. Remove the mounting bolts and the alternator.
6. Reverse the procedure for installation.
7. Adjust the drive belt.

- Alternator "BAT" terminal to ground (1).
- Alternator No. 1 terminal to ground (2).
- Alternator No. 2 terminal to ground (3).

Fig. 11 Location of the electrical terminals on a common Delco alternator

Loosen the negative battery cable clamp retaining bolt . . .

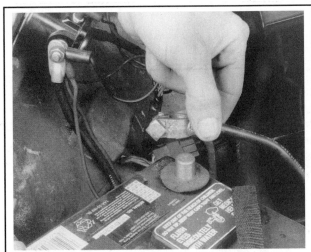

. . . then remove the negative battery cable from the terminal

Remove the alternator adjustment bolt . . .

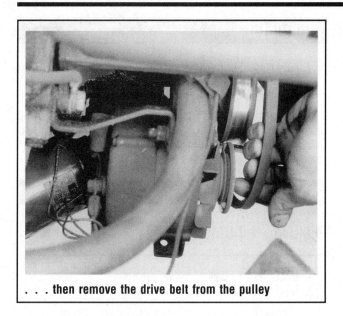

. . . then remove the drive belt from the pulley

Use a back-up wrench to hold the nut and a ratchet and socket to unfasten the mounting bolt

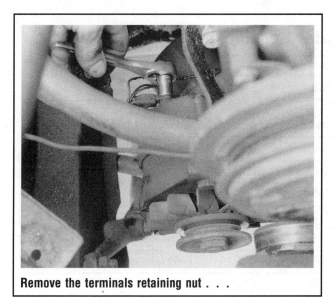

Remove the terminals retaining nut . . .

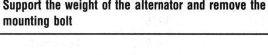

Support the weight of the alternator and remove the mounting bolt

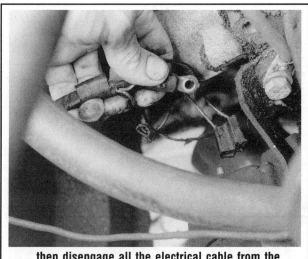

. . . then disengage all the electrical cable from the alternator

Remove the alternator from the engine

BELT TENSION ADJUSTMENT

The alternator drive belt, or any engine V-belt, is correctly tensioned when the longest span of belt between pulleys can be depressed about ½″ (12.7mm) in the middle by moderate thumb pressure. To adjust, loosen the slotted adjusting bracket bolt. If the alternator hinge bolt(s) is very tight, it may be necessary to loosen it slightly to more the alternator. V8 engines have a hole in the alternator bracket, so that you can insert a big screwdriver and pry out on the alternator. Some V8s have a square hole into which you can insert a ½″ square socket drive. The best way is to pull the alternator out by hand to avoid overtightening.

✲✲ WARNING

Be careful not to overtighten the belt, as this will damage the alternator bearings.

Regulator

REMOVAL & INSTALLATION

The regulator is sealed at the factory and thus cannot be adjusted. It is mounted to the fender well inside the engine compartment. To remove it, simply unplug it and remove the sheet metal screws holding it in place.

Starter

REMOVAL & INSTALLATION

1. Disconnect the battery ground cable.
2. Disconnect the leads from the starter.

Alternator and Regulator Specifications

Engine	Year	Manufacturer	Field Current @ 12V (amps)	Output (amps)	Manufacturer	Volts @ 75° F
		Alternator			**Regulator**	
4-121	1977–79	Delco-Remy	4.0–5.0	37 ③	Delco-Remy	13.7–14.2
4-150	1984	Delco-Remy	4.0–5.0	56 ①	Delco-Remy	13.9–14.9
4-151	1980–83	Delco-Remy	4.0–5.0	42 ②	Delco-Remy	12.0–15.5
6-232, 258	1975	Delco-Remy	1.8–2.5	37 ③ '	Delco-Remy	13.7–14.2
	1976–79	Delco-Remy	4.0–5.0	37 ②	Delco-Remy	12.0–15.5
6-258	1980–88	Delco-Remy	4.0–5.0	42 ②	Delco-Remy	13.9–14.9
8-304	1975	Motorola	1.8–2.5	37 ④	Motorola	12.7–15.3
	1976–77	Motorcraft	2.5–3.0	40 ⑤	Motorcraft	13.1–14.8
	1978–79	Delco-Remy	4.0–5.0	37 ②	Delco-Remy	12.0–15.5
8-360	1975	Motorola	1.8–2.5	37 ④	Motorola	12.7–15.3
	1976–77	Motorcraft	2.5–3.0	40 ⑤	Motorcraft	13.1–14.8
	1978	Delco-Remy	4.0–5.0	37 ②	Delco-Remy	12.0–15.5
8-401	1975	Motorola	1.8–2.5	37 ④	Motorola	12.7–15.3
	1976	Motorcraft	2.5–3.0	40 ⑤	Motorcraft	13.1–14.8

① Optional 68 and 78
② Optional 56, 63, 78 and 85
③ Optional 55 and 63
④ Optional 51 and 62
⑤ Optional 60
⑥ Optional 40 amp

Unfasten the electrical connection retaining nut . . .

. . . then remove the starter motor from the vehicle

. . . then disengage the electrical connection from the starter motor

Unfasten the starter motor retaining bolts . . .

3. Unbolt and remove the starter.
4. Reverse the procedure on installation.

COMPONENT REPLACEMENT

Starter Drive

AUTOLITE

▶ **See Figure 12**

1. Remove the cover of the starter drive's actuating lever arm. Remove the through bolts, starter drive gear housing, and the return spring of the drive gear's actuating lever.
2. Remove the pivot pin which retains the starter gear actuating lever and remove the lever and armature.
3. Remove the stopring retainer. Remove and discard the stopring which holds the drive gear to the armature shaft and then remove the drive gear assembly.

To install:

1. Lightly Lubriplate® the armature shaft splines and install the starter drive gear assembly on the shaft. Install a new stopring and stopring retainer.
2. Position the starter drive gear actuating lever to the frame and starter drive assembly. Install the pivot pin.
3. Fill the starter drive gear housing one quarter full of grease.
4. Position the drive actuating lever return spring and the drive gear housing to the frame, then install and tighten the through bolts. Be sure that the stopring retainer is properly seated in the drive housing.

DELCO-REMY

▶ **See Figure 13, 14 and 15**

1. Remove the through bolts.
2. Remove the starter drive housing.
3. Slide the two piece thrust collar off the end of the armature shaft.
4. Slide a standard ½ in. (12.7mm) pipe coupling, or other spacer, onto the shaft so the end of the coupling butts against the edge of the retainer.

Fig. 12 Exploded view of the Autolite starter used on all models except the 4–150 and 151 engines

1. Frame—commutator end
2. Brush and holder pkg.
3. Brush
4. Brush holder
5. Housing—drive end
6. Frame and field asm.
7. Solenoid switch
8. Armature
9. Drive asm.
10. Plunger
11. Shift lever
12. Plunger return springer
13. Shift lever shaft
14. Lock washer
15. Screw—Brush attaching
16. Screw—field lead to switch
17. Screw—Switch attaching
18. Washer—brake
19. Thru bolt
20. Bushing—commutator end
21. Bushing—drive end
22. Pinion stop collar
23. Thrust collar
24. Grommet
25. Grommet
26. Plunger pin
27. Pinion stop retainer ring
28. Lever shaft retaining ring

Fig. 13 Exploded view of the Delco starter used on the 4–151 engine

1. Drive end housing
2. Drive yoke return spring
3. Bushing
4. Washer
5. Retainer
6. Snapring
7. Pinion gear drive mechanism
8. Drive yoke
9. Solenoid contact point actuator
10. Moveable pole shoe
11. Armature
12. Frame
13. Solenoid contact point assembly
14. Drive yoke cover
15. Hold-in coil terminal
16. Field winding screw
17. Sleeve
18. Field winding
19. Terminal
20. Insulated brush
21. Ground brush
22. Pole shoe
23. Brush holder and insulator
24. Springs
25. Insulator
26. Bushing
27. Brush end plate
28. Terminal screw
29. Through bolt

Fig. 14 Components of the Delco starter used on the 4—150 engine

Fig. 15 Use two pair of pliers to install the starter drive snap ring

5. Tap the end of the coupling with a hammer, driving the retainer toward the armature end of the snapring.

6. Remove the snapring from its groove in the shaft with pliers. Slide the retainer and the starter drive from the armature.

To install:

1. Lubricate the drive end of the shaft with silicone lubricant.

2. Slide the drive gear assembly onto the shaft, with the gear facing outward.

3. Slide the retainer onto the shaft with the cupped surface facing away from the gear.

4. Stand the whole starter assembly on a block of wood with the snapring positioned on the upper end of the shaft. Drive the snapring down with a small block of wood and a hammer. Slide the snapring into its groove.

5. Install the thrust collar onto the shaft with the shoulder next to the snapring.

6. With the retainer on one side of the snapring and the thrust collar on the other side, squeeze them together with a pair of pliers until the ring seats in the retainer. On models without a thrust collar, use a washer. Remember to remove the washer before installing the starter in the engine.

PRESTOLITE

1. Slide the thrust collar off the armature shaft.

2. Using a standard ½ in. (12.7mm) pipe connector, drive the snapring retainer off the shaft.

3. Remove the snapring from the groove, and then remove the drive assembly.

To install:

1. Lubricate the drive end and splines with Lubriplate®.

2. Install the clutch assembly onto the shaft.

3. Install the snapring retainer with the cupped surface facing toward the end of the shaft.

4. Install the snapring into the groove. Use a new snapring if necessary.

5. Install the thrust collar onto the shaft with the shoulder against the snapring.

6. Force the retainer over the snapring in the same manner as was used for the Delco-Remy starters.

Solenoid or Relay

REMOTE MOUNTED

1. Disconnect the negative battery cable.
2. Unfasten the electrical connection attaching nut.
3. Disengage all the electrical connections.
4. Unfasten the relay bracket bolts and remove the relay.
5. Installation is the reverse of removal.

Unfasten the electrical terminals retaining nut . . .

. . . and slide the electrical connections off the stud

Unplug the remaining electrical connections

Unfasten the bracket retaining bolts . . .

. . . then remove the relay from the vehicle

AUTOLITE

To remove the solenoid from the starter, remove all of the leads to the solenoid, remove the connecting lever, and remove the attaching bolts that hold the solenoid assembly to the starter housing. Remove the solenoid assembly from the starter housing.

To install the solenoid assembly, reverse the above procedure.

DELCO-REMY

1. Remove the leads from the solenoid.
2. Remove the drive housing of the starter motor.
3. Remove the shift lever pin and bolt from the shift lever.
4. Remove the attaching bolts that hold the solenoid assembly to the housing of the starter motor.
5. Remove the starter solenoid from the starter housing.
6. To install the solenoid, reverse the above procedure.

PRESTOLITE

1. Remove the leads from the solenoid assembly.
2. Remove the attaching bolts that hold the solenoid to the starter housing.
3. Remove the bolt from the shift lever.
4. Remove the solenoid assembly from the starter housing.
5. Reverse the procedure for installation.

OVERHAUL

Autolite/Motorcraft

1. Remove the cover screw, the cover through-bolts, the starter drive end housing and the starter drive plunger lever return spring.
2. Remove the starter gear plunger lever pivot pin, the lever and the armature. Remove the stop ring retainer and the stop ring from the armature shaft (discard the ring), then the starter drive gear assembly.
3. Remove the brush end plate, the insulator assembly and the brushes from the plastic holder, then lift out the brush holder. For reassembly, note the position of the brush holder with respect to the end terminal.
4. Remove the two ground brush-to-frame screws.
5. Bend up the sleeve's edges which are inserted in the frame's rectangular hole, then remove the sleeve and the retainer. Detach the field coil ground wire from the copper tab.
6. Remove the three coil retaining screws. Cut the field coil connection at the switch post lead, then remove the pole shoes and the coils from the frame.
7. Cut the positive brush leads from the field coils (as close to the field connection point as possible).
8. Check the armature and the armature windings for broken or burned insulation, open circuits or grounds.
9. Check the commutator for runout. If it is rough, has flat spots or is more than 0.005 in. (0.127mm) out of round, reface the commutator face.
10. Inspect the armature shaft and the two bearings for scoring and excessive wear, then replace (if necessary).
11. Inspect the starter drive. If the gear teeth are pitted, broken or excessively worn, replace the starter drive.

➡**The factory brush length is ½ in. (12.7mm); the wear limit is ¼ in. (6.35mm).**

To install:

12. Install the starter terminal, the insulator, the washers and the nut in the frame.

➡**Be sure to position the screw slot perpendicular to the frame end surface.**

13. Position the coils and the pole pieces, with the coil leads in the terminal screw slot, then install the screws. When tightening the pole screws, strike the frame with several sharp hammer blows to align the pole shoes, then stake the screws.

14. Install the solenoid coil and the retainer, then bend the tabs to hold the coils to the frame.

15. Using resin core solder and a 300 watt iron, solder the field coils and the solenoid wire to the starter terminal. Check for continuity and ground connections of the assembled coils.

16. Position the solenoid coil ground terminal over the nearest ground screw hole and the ground brushes-to-starter frame, then install the screws.

17. Apply a thin coating of Lubriplate® on the armature shaft splines. Install the starter motor drive gear assembly-to-armature shaft, followed by a new stop ring and retainer. Install the armature in the starter frame.

18. Position the starter drive gear plunger lever to the frame and the starter drive assembly, then install the pivot pin. Place some grease into the end housing bore. Fill it about ¼ full, then position the drive end housing to the frame.

19. Install the brush holder and the brush springs. The positive brush leads should be positioned in their respective brush holder slots, to prevent grounding problems.

20. Install the brush end plate. Be certain that the end plate insulator is in the proper position on the end plate. Install the two starter frame through-bolts and torque them to 55–75 inch lbs.

21. Install the starter drive plunger lever cover and tighten the retaining screw.

Delco-Remy

1. Detach the field coil connectors from the motor solenoid terminal.

➡**If equipped, remove the solenoid mounting screws.**

2. Remove the through-bolts, the commutator end frame, the field frame and the armature assembly from drive housing.

3. Remove the overrunning clutch from the armature shaft as follows:

 a. Slide the two piece thrust collar off the end of the armature shaft.

 b. Slide a standard ½″ (12.7mm) pipe coupling or other spacer onto the shaft, so that the coupling end butts against the retainer edge.

 c. Using a hammer, tap the coupling end, driving the retainer towards the armature end of the snapring.

 d. Using snapring pliers, remove the snapring from its groove in the shaft, then slide the retainer and the clutch from the shaft.

4. Disassemble the field frame brush assembly by releasing the V-spring and removing the support pin. The brush holders, the brushes and the springs can now be pulled out as a unit and the leads disconnected.

➡**On the integral frame units, remove the brush holder from the brush support and the brush screw.**

5. If equipped, separate the solenoid from the lever housing.

6. Clean the parts with a rag. Do not immerse the parts in a solvent.

Immersion in a solvent will dissolve the grease that is packed in the clutch mechanism. It will damage the armature and the field coil insulation.

7. Test the overrunning clutch action. The pinion should turn freely in the overrunning direction but must not slip in the cranking direction. Check that the pinion teeth have not been chipped, cracked or excessively worn. Replace the unit (if necessary).

8. Inspect the armature commutator. If the commutator is rough or out of round, it should be machined and undercut.

➡**Undercut the insulation between the commutator bars by 1/32 in. (0.79375mm). The undercut must be the full width of the insulation and flat at the bottom. A triangular groove will not be satisfactory. Most late model starter motor use a molded armature commutator design. No attempt to undercut the insulation should be made or serious damage may result to the commutator.**

To install:

9. Install the brushes into the holders, then install solenoid (if equipped).

10. Assemble the insulated and the grounded holder together. Using the V-spring, position and assemble the unit on the support pin. Push the holders and the spring to bottom of the support, then rotate the spring to engage the slot in the support. Attach the ground wire to the grounded brush and the field lead wire to the insulated brush, then repeat this procedure for other brush sets.

11. Assemble the overrunning clutch to the armature shaft as follows:

 a. Lubricate the drive end of the shaft with silicone lubricant.

 b. Slide the clutch assembly onto the shaft with the pinion outward.

 c. Slide the retainer onto the shaft with the cupped surface facing away from the pinion.

 d. Stand the armature up on a wood surface with the commutator downward. Position the snapring on the upper end of the shaft and drive it onto the shaft with a small block of wood and a hammer, then slide the snapring into groove.

 e. Install the thrust collar onto the shaft with the shoulder next to snapring.

 f. With the retainer on one side of the snapring and the thrust collar on the other side, squeeze two sets together (with pliers) until the ring seats in the retainer. On models without a thrust collar use a washer. Remember to remove the washer before continuing.

12. Lubricate the drive end bushing with silicone lubricant, then slide the armature and the clutch assembly into place, while engaging the shift lever with the clutch.

➡**On the non-integral starters, the shift lever may be installed in the drive gear housing first.**

13. Position the field frame over the armature and apply sealer (silicone) between the frame and the solenoid case. Position the frame against the drive housing, making sure the brushes are not damaged in the process.

14. Lubricate the commutator end bushing with silicone lubricant, place a washer on the armature shaft and slide the commutator end frame onto the shaft. Install the through-bolts and tighten.

15. Reconnect the field coil connections to the solenoid motor terminal. Install the solenoid mounting screws (if equipped).

16. Check the pinion clearance. It should be 0.010–0.140 in. (0.254–3.556mm) with the pinion in the cranking position, on all models.

Bosch

▶ **See Figure 16**

1. Disconnect the field coil wire from the solenoid terminal.
2. Remove the solenoid and work the plunger off the shift fork.
3. Remove the two end shield bearing cap screws, the cap and the washers.

4. Remove the two commutator end frame cover through-bolts, the cover, the two brushes and the brush plate.

5. Slide the field frame off over the armature. Remove the shift lever pivot bolt, the rubber gasket and the metal plate.

6. Remove the armature assembly and the shift lever from the drive end housing. Press the stop collar off the snapring, then remove the snapring, the clutch assembly, the clutch assembly and the drive end housing from the armature.

7. The brushes that are worn more than ½ the length of new brushes or are oil soaked, should be replaced. The new brushes are $^{11}/_{16}$ in. (17.4625mm) long.

8. Do not immerse the starter clutch unit in cleaning solvent. Solvent will wash the lubricant from the clutch.

9. Place the drive unit on the armature shaft, then, while holding the armature, rotate the pinion.

1. Bushing	10. Bearing pedestal	19. Seal ring
2. Screw	11. Sealing rubber	20. Shim
3. Shield	12. Planetary gear system	21. Shim
4. Solenoid switch	13. Armature	22. Retaining washer
5. Retainer	14. Stator frame	23. Closure cap
6. Stop ring	15. Brush holder	24. Hexagon screw
7. Bushing	16. Gasket	25. Screw
8. Overrunning clutch drive	17. Commutator end shield	
9. Fork	18. Bushing	

Fig. 16 Exploded view of the Bosch starter motor used on the 4–150 engine—1986 models

➡The drive pinion should rotate smoothly in one direction only. The pinion may not rotate easily but as long as it rotates smoothly it is in good condition. If the clutch unit does not function properly or if the pinion is worn, chipped or burred, replace the unit.

To install:

10. Lubricate the armature shaft and the splines with SAE 10W or 30W oil.

11. Fit the drive end housing onto the armature, then install the clutch, the stop collar and the snapring onto the armature.

12. Install the shift fork pivot bolt, the rubber gasket and the metal plate. Slide the field frame into position and install the brush holder and the brushes.

13. Position the commutator end frame cover and the through-bolts.

14. Install the shim and the armature shaft lock. Check the end-play, which should be 0.002–0.012 in. (0.05–0.30mm), then install the bearing cover.

15. Assemble the plunger to the shift fork, then install the solenoid with its mounting bolts. Connect the field wire to the solenoid.

Prestolite

1. To remove the solenoid, remove the screw from the field coil connector and solenoid mounting screws. Rotate the solenoid 90° and remove it along with the plunger return spring.

2. For further service, remove the two through-bolts, then remove the commutator end frame and washer.

3. To replace the clutch and drive assembly proceed as follows:

   a. Remove the thrust washer or the collar from the armature shaft.

   b. Slide a ⅝ in. (15.875mm) deep socket or a piece of pipe of suitable size over the shaft and against the retainer as a driving tool. Tap the tool to remove the retainer off the snapring.

   c. Remove the snapring from the groove in the shaft. Check and make sure the snapring isn't distorted. If it is, it will be necessary to replace it with a new one upon reassembly.

   d. Remove the retainer and clutch assembly from the armature shaft.

4. The shift lever may be disconnected from the plunger at this time by removing the roll pin.

5. On models with the standard starter, the brushes may be removed by removing the brush holder pivot pin which positions one insulated and one grounded brush. Remove the brush and spring and replace the brushes as necessary.

6. On models with the smaller 5MT starter, remove the brush and holder from the brush support, then remove the screw from the brush holder and separate the brush and holder. Replace the brushes as necessary.

7. Installation is the reverse of removal. Assemble the armature and clutch and drive assembly as follows:

   a. Lubricate the drive end of the armature shaft and slide the clutch assembly onto the armature shaft with the pinion away from the armature.

   b. Slide the retainer onto the shaft with the cupped side facing the end of the shaft.

   c. Install the snapring into the groove on the armature shaft.

   d. Install the thrust washer on the shaft.

   e. Position the retainer and thrust washer with the snapring in between. Using two pliers, grip the retainer and thrust washer or collar and squeeze until the snapring is forced into the retainer and is held securely in the groove in the armature shaft.

   f. Lubricate the drive gear housing bushing.

   g. Engage the shift lever yoke with the clutch and slide the complete assembly into the drive gear housing.

➡When the starter motor has been disassembled or the solenoid has been replaced, it is necessary to check the pinion clearance. Pinion clearance must be correct to prevent the buttons on the shift lever yoke from rubbing on the clutch collar during cranking.

Checking Pinion Clearance

1. Disconnect the motor field coil connector from the solenoid motor terminal and insulate it carefully.

2. Connect one 12 volt battery lead to the solenoid switch terminal and the other to the starter frame.

3. Flash a jumper lead momentarily from the solenoid motor terminal to the starter frame. This will shift the pinion into cranking position and it will remain there until the battery is disconnected.

Push the pinion back as far as possible to take up any move-

Starter Specifications

Engine	Year	Manufacturer	Lock Test		Torque (ft. lb.)	No-Load Test			Brush Spring Tension (oz.)
			Amps	Volts		Amps	Volts	RPM	
4-121	1977–79	Bosch	Not Recommended			69	12.0	10,834	N.A.
4-150	1984	Delco	Not Recommended			67	12.0	8,500	30–40
4-151	1980–83	Delco	Not Recommended			70	9.0	11,900	N.A.
6-232, 6-258	1975–78	Autolite	600	3.4	13.0	65	12.0	9,250	35–40
6-258	1979–81	Motorcraft	Not Recommended			77	12.0	9,250	35–40
	1982–88	Motorcraft	Not Recommended			67	12.0	7,868	35–40
8-304	1975–79	Autolite	600	3.4	13.0	65	12.0	9,250	35–40
8-360	1975–78	Autolite	600	3.4	13.0	65	12.0	9,250	35–40
8-401	1975–76	Autolite	600	3.4	13.0	65	12.0	9,250	35–40

N.A.: Information Not Available

ment, and check the clearance with a feeler gauge. The clearance should be 0.010–0.140 in. (0.254–3.556mm).

5. There is no means for adjusting pinion clearance on the starter motor. If clearance does not fall within the limits, check for improper installation and replace all worn parts.

Battery

REMOVAL & INSTALLATION

1. Remove the hold-down screws from the battery box. Loosen the nuts that secure the cable ends to the battery terminals. Lift the battery cables from the terminals with a twisting motion.

2. If there is a battery cable puller available, make use of it. Lift the battery from the vehicle.

3. Before installing the battery in the vehicle, make sure that the battery terminals are clean and free from corrosion. Use a battery terminal cleaner on the terminals and on the inside of the battery cable ends. If a cleaner is not available, use a heavy sandpaper to remove the corrosion. A mixture of baking soda and water will neutralize any acid. Place the battery in the vehicle. Install the cables on the terminals. Tighten the nuts on the cable ends. Smear a light coating of grease on the cable ends and the tops of the terminals. This will prevent buildup of oxidized acid on the terminals and the cable ends. Install and tighten the nuts of the battery box.

ENGINE MECHANICAL

Description

4-121 ENGINE

▶ **See Figures 17 and 18**

During the 1977 model year, a four cylinder 2 liter (121 CID) engine, manufactured by Volkswagen, was introduced for the

Gremlin. The engine is of overhead camshaft design, belt driven from the crankshaft. The cylinder head is cast aluminum alloy and has removable camshaft bearing caps. Valve lash is controlled by manual adjustment of a tapered adjusting screw, located at the base of the tappet, under the camshaft. The intake and exhaust manifolds are on the opposite sides of the cylinder head. The block is of cast iron and the crankshaft is set into five main bearings. Three grooved aluminum alloy pistons are used with full floating piston pins. The oil pump is located at the front of the block and is driven by the crankshaft.

Fig. 17 Exploded view of the block assembly—4–121 engine

Fig. 18 Exploded view of the cylinder head components—4-121 engine

4-150 ENGINE

The 4-150 engine was first used in 1984 models, replacing the 4-151, is a new design, developed from existing technology at work in the venerable 6-258. It is a four cylinder, overhead valve configuration with cast iron head and block. The crankshaft rides in 5 main bearings. Both manifolds are on the left side of the engine. The engine is thoroughly conventional in all respects.

4-151 ENGINE

▶ **See Figures 19 and 20**

Beginning in 1980, the 151 cubic inch engine, manufactured by Pontiac, replaced the 121. The 151 is an inline 4-cylinder engine with a cast iron cylinder head and block. The pistons are made of light weight cast aluminum. The cylinder head is of a crossflow design for more efficient combustion. The cam shaft, gear driven by the crankshaft, operates the overhead valves through hydraulic lifters and pushrods.

1. Drive plate and ring gear (automatic trans)	13. Dowel	26. Timing gear cover oil seal
2. Oil filter	14. Cylinder block	27. Crankshaft pulley hub
3. Push rod cover and bolts	15. Pilot and/or converter bushing	28. Crankshaft pulley
4. Piston	16. Rear oil seal	29. Crankshaft pulley hub bolt
5. Piston ring	17. Crankshaft	30. Crankshaft pulley bolt
6. Piston pin	18. Block core plug	31. Crankshaft timing gear
7. Connecting rod	19. Timing gear oil nozzle	32. Camshaft thrust plate screw
8. Connecting rod bolt	20. Main bearings	33. Camshaft thrust plate
9. Dowel	21. Main bearing caps	34. Camshaft
10. Oil level indicator and tube	22. Connecting rod bearing cap	35. Camshaft bearing
11. Block drain	23. Connecting rod bearing	36. Oil pump driveshaft retainer plate, gasket and bolt
12. Flywheel and ring gear (manual trans)	24. Crankshaft gear	
	25. Timing gear cover (front)	

Fig. 19 Block assembly component locations —4–151 engine

1. PCV valve
2. Oil filler cap
3. Intake manifold attaching bolts
4. Intake manifold
5. Rocker arm capscrew
6. Rocker arm
7. Valve spring retainer assembly
8. Cylinder head cover (rocker cover)
9. Coolant hose fitting
10. Intake manifold gasket
11. Cylinder head
12. Cylinder head stud bolt
13. Valve spring
14. Push rod guide
15. Cylinder head plug
16. Cylinder head core plug
17. Exhaust manifold
18. Exhaust manifold bolt
19. Oil level indicator tube attaching screw
20. Exhaust manifold heat shroud (heat shield)
21. Exhaust manifold to exhaust pipe stud
22. Valves
23. Push rod
24. Tappet
25. Exhaust manifold gasket
26. Cylinder head gasket

Fig. 20 Exploded view of the cylinder head—4–151 engine

6-232 AND 258 ENGINES

◆ See Figures 21 and 22

The 232 and 258 sixes are virtually identical in construction. The design was originally adopted in 1966 and has remained unchanged. They employ a cast iron cylinder head and block and are long stroke cycle, giving them a good torque curve for low end power. The engines are overhead valve with a seven main bearing crankshaft.

8-304, 360 AND 401 ENGINES

All the AMC V8s are similar in design, having five main bearing crankshafts and overhead valves with hydraulic lifters. The head and block are cast iron.

Engine Overhaul Tips

Most engine overhaul procedures are fairly standard. In addition to specific parts replacement procedures and specifications for your individual engine, this section is also a guide to acceptable rebuilding procedures. Examples of standard rebuilding practice are given and should be used along with specific details concerning your particular engine.

Competent and accurate machine shop services will ensure maximum performance, reliability and engine life. In most instances it is more profitable for the do-it-yourself mechanic to remove, clean and inspect the component, buy the necessary parts and deliver these to a shop for actual machine work.

On the other hand, much of the rebuilding work (crankshaft, block, bearings, piston rods, and other components) is well within the scope of the do-it-yourself mechanic's tools and abilities. You will have to decide for yourself the depth of involvement you desire in an engine repair or rebuild.

Fig. 21 Cylinder head components—6–232 and 258 engines

1. Piston rings
2. Piston
3. Piston pin
4. Block
5. Camshaft bearing
6. Camshaft
7. Connecting rod
8. Camshaft sprocket
9. Crankshaft sprocket
10. Timing chain
11. Timing case cover
12. Cover gasket
13. Vibration damper
14. Pulley
15. Main bearing
16. Crankshaft
17. Upper seal
18. Lower seal
19. Flywheel
20. Ring gear
21. Main bearing cap
22. Connecting rod bearing cap
23. Converter drive plate and spacer
(with auto. trans.)

Fig. 22 Exploded view of the cylinder block—6–232 and 258 engines

TOOLS

The tools required for an engine overhaul or parts replacement will depend on the depth of your involvement. With a few exceptions, they will be the tools found in a mechanic's tool kit (see Section 1 of this manual). More in-depth work will require some or all of the following:
• A dial indicator (reading in thousandths) mounted on a universal base
• Micrometers and telescope gauges
• Jaw and screw-type pullers
• Scraper
• Valve spring compressor
• Ring groove cleaner
• Piston ring expander and compressor
• Ridge reamer
• Cylinder hone or glaze breaker
• Plastigage®
• Engine stand
The use of most of these tools is illustrated in this chapter.

Many can be rented for a one-time use from a local parts jobber or tool supply house specializing in automotive work.

Occasionally, the use of special tools is called for. See the information on Special Tools and the Safety Notice in the front of this book before substituting another tool.

INSPECTION TECHNIQUES

Procedures and specifications are given in this chapter for inspecting, cleaning and assessing the wear limits of most major components. Other procedures such as Magnaflux® and Zyglo® can be used to locate material flaws and stress cracks. Magnaflux® is a magnetic process applicable only to ferrous materials. The Zyglo® process coats the material with a fluorescent dye penetrant and can be used on any material.

Checking for suspected surface cracks can be more readily made using spot check dye. The dye is sprayed onto the suspected area, wiped off and the area sprayed with a developer. Cracks will show up brightly.

OVERHAUL TIPS

Aluminum has become extremely popular for use in engines, due to its low weight. Observe the following precautions when handling aluminum parts:

• Never hot tank aluminum parts (the caustic hot tank solution will eat the aluminum.

• Remove all aluminum parts (identification tag, etc.) from engine parts prior to the tanking.

• Always coat threads lightly with engine oil or anti-seize compounds before installation, to prevent seizure.

• Never overtorque bolts or spark plugs especially in aluminum threads.

Stripped threads in any component can be repaired using any of several commercial repair kits (Heli-Coil®, Microdot®, Keenserts®, etc.).

When assembling the engine, any parts that will be exposed to frictional contact must be prelubed to provide lubrication at initial start-up. Any product specifically formulated for this purpose can be used, but engine oil is not recommended as a prelube in most cases.

When semi-permanent (locked, but removable) installation of bolts or nuts is desired, threads should be cleaned and coated with Loctite® or another similar, commercial non-hardening sealant.

REPAIRING DAMAGED THREADS

Several methods of repairing damaged threads are available. Heli-Coil® (shown here), Keenserts® and Microdot® are among the most widely used. All involve basically the same principle—drilling out stripped threads, tapping the hole and installing a pre-wound insert—making welding, plugging and oversize fasteners unnecessary.

Two types of thread repair inserts are usually supplied: a standard type for most inch coarse, inch fine, metric course and metric fine thread sizes and a spark lug type to fit most spark plug

Standard thread repair insert (left), and spark plug thread insert

Drill out the damaged threads with the specified size bit. Be sure to drill completely through the hole or to the bottom of a blind hole

Damaged bolt hole threads can be replaced with thread repair inserts

Using the kit, tap the hole in order to receive the thread insert. Keep the tap well oiled and back it out frequently to avoid clogging the threads

Screw the insert onto the installer tool until the tang engages the slot. Thread the insert into the hole until it is ¼–½ turn below the top surface, then remove the tool and break off the tang using a punch

port sizes. Consult the individual tool manufacturer's catalog to determine exact applications. Typical thread repair kits will contain a selection of prewound threaded inserts, a tap (corresponding to the outside diameter threads of the insert) and an installation tool. Spark plug inserts usually differ because they require a tap equipped with pilot threads and a combined reamer/tap section. Most manufacturers also supply blister-packed thread repair inserts separately in addition to a master kit containing a variety of taps and inserts plus installation tools.

Before attempting to repair a threaded hole, remove any snapped, broken or damaged bolts or studs. Penetrating oil can be used to free frozen threads. The offending item can usually be removed with locking pliers or using a screw/stud extractor. After the hole is clear, the thread can be repaired, as shown in the series of accompanying illustrations and in the kit manufacturer's instructions.

A screw-in type compression gauge is more accurate and easier to use without an assistant

Checking Engine Compression

A noticeable lack of engine power, excessive oil consumption and/or poor fuel mileage measured over an extended period are all indicators of internal engine war. Worn piston rings, scored or worn cylinder bores, blown head gaskets, sticking or burnt valves and worn valve seats are all possible culprits here. A check of each cylinder's compression will help you locate the problems.

As mentioned in the Tools and Equipment section of Chapter 1, a screw-in type compression gauge is more accurate that the type you simply hold against the spark plug hole, although it takes slightly longer to use. It's worth it to obtain a more accurate reading. Follow the procedures below.

1. Warm up the engine to normal operating temperature.
2. Remove all spark plugs.
3. Disconnect the high tension lead from the ignition coil.
4. On fully open the throttle either by operating the carburetor throttle linkage by hand or by having an assistant floor the accelerator pedal.
5. Screw the compression gauge into the no. 1 spark plug hole until the fitting is snug.

➡**Be careful not to crossthread the plug hole. On aluminum cylinder heads use extra care, as the threads in these heads are easily ruined.**

6. Ask an assistant to depress the accelerator pedal fully. Then, while you read the compression gauge, ask the assistant to crank the engine two or three times in short bursts using the ignition switch.
7. Read the compression gauge at the end of each series of cranks, and record the highest of these readings. Repeat this procedure for each of the engine's cylinders. Compare the highest reading of each cylinder to the compression pressure specification in the Tune-Up Specifications chart in Chapter 2. The specs in this chart are maximum values.

A cylinder's compression pressure is usually acceptable if it is not less than 80% of maximum. The difference between any two cylinders should be no more than 12–14 pounds.

8. If a cylinder is unusually low, pour a tablespoon of clean engine oil into the cylinder through the spark plug hole and repeat the compression test. If the compression comes up after adding the oil, it appears that the cylinder's piston rings or bore are damaged or worn. If the pressure remains low, the valves may not be seating properly (a valve job is needed), or the head gasket may be blown near that cylinder. If compression in any two adjacent cylinders is low, and if the addition of oil doesn't help the compression, there is leakage past the head gasket. Oil and coolant water in the combustion chamber can result from this problem. There may be evidence of water droplets on the engine dipstick when a head gasket has blown.

General Engine Specifications

Engine	Years	Fuel System Type	SAE net Horsepower @ rpm	SAE net Torque ft. lb. @ rpm	Bore x Stroke	Comp. Ratio	Oil Press. (psi.) @ 2000 rpm
4-121	1977–79	2-bbl	80 @ 5,000	105 @ 2,800	3.410 x 3.320	8.1:1	30
4-150	1984	1-bbl	83 @ 4,200	116 @ 2,600	3.876 x 3.188	9.2:1	40
4-151	1980–83	2-bbl	99 @ 4,000	134 @ 2,400	4.000 x 3.000	8.4:1	38
6-232	1975–78	1-bbl	100 @ 3,600	185 @ 1,800	3.750 x 3.500	8.0:1	50
6-258	1975–76	1-bbl	110 @ 3,500	195 @ 2,000	3.750 x 3.895	8.0:1	50
	1977–88	2-bbl	114 @ 3,600	196 @ 2,000	3.750 x 3.895	8.0:1	50
	1987	2-bbl	112 @ 3,000	210 @ 2,000	3.750 x 3.895	8.6:1	50
8-304	1975	2-bbl	150 @ 4,200	245 @ 2,500	3.750 x 3.753	8.4:1	50
	1976	2-bbl	120 @ 3,200	220 @ 2,200	3.750 x 3.753	8.4:1	50
	1977	2-bbl	121 @ 3,450	219 @ 2,000	3.750 x 3.753	8.4:1	50
	1978	2-bbl	130 @ 3,200	238 @ 2,000	3.750 x 3.753	8.4:1	50
	1979	2-bbl	125 @ 3,200	220 @ 2,400	3.750 x 3.753	8.4:1	50
8-360	1975	2-bbl	175 @ 4,000	285 @ 2,400	4.080 x 3.440	8.25:1	46
		4-bbl	195 @ 4,400	295 @ 2,900	4.080 x 3.440	8.25:1	46
		DE	220 @ 4,400	315 @ 3,100	4.080 x 3.440	8.25:1	46
	1976	2-bbl	140 @ 4,000	260 @ 2,400	4.080 x 3.440	8.25:1	46
		4-bbl	180 @ 4,400	280 @ 2,800	4.080 x 3.440	8.25:1	46
	1977	2-bbl	129 @ 3,700	245 @ 1,600	4.080 x 3.440	8.25:1	46
	1978	2-bbl	140 @ 3,350	278 @ 2,000	4.080 x 3.440	8.25:1	46
8-401	1975	4-bbl	255 @ 4,600	345 @ 3,300	4.165 x 3.680	8.25:1	46
	1976	4-bbl	215 @ 4,200	320 @ 2,800	4.165 x 3.680	8.25:1	46

1-bbl: one barrel carburetor
2-bbl: two barrel carburetor
DE: 4-bbl w/Dual Exhaust

Valve Specifications

Engine	Seat Angle (deg)	Face Angle (deg)	Spring Test Pressure (lbs. @ in.)	Spring Installed Height (in.)	Stem to Guide Clearance (in.)		Stem Diameter (in.)	
					Intake	Exhaust	Intake	Exhaust
4-121	45	45.33	①	②	0.0280–0.0330	0.0370–0.0410	0.3526–0.3531	0.3522–0.3528
4-150	45	44	212 @ 1.203	1.625	0.0010–0.0030	0.0010–0.0030	0.3110–0.3120	0.3110–0.3120
4-151	46	45	176 @ 1.250	1.660	0.0010–0.0027	0.0010–0.0027	0.3422	0.3422
6-232	③	④	⑤	⑥	0.0010–0.0030	0.0010–0.0030	0.3715–0.3725	0.3715–0.3725
6-258	③	④	⑦	⑧	0.0010–0.0030	0.0010–0.0030	0.3715–0.3725	0.3715–0.3725
8-304, 360, 401	③	④	218 @ 1.359 ⑨	1.812 ⑨	0.0010–0.0030	0.0010–0.0030	0.3715–0.3725	0.3715–0.3725

① Intake outer spring: 166.46 @ 1.30
Intake inner spring: 39.02 @ 1.09
Exhaust outer spring: 160.28 @ 1.32
Exhaust inner spring: 37.15 @ 1.11
② Inner spring: 1.49
Outer spring: 1.70
③ Intake: 30
Exhaust: 44.5
④ Intake: 29
Exhaust: 44
⑤ With rotators: 218 @ 1.875
Without rotators: 195 @ 1.437
⑥ Intake: 1.786
Exhaust: 2.110

⑦ 1975–76: with rotators, 218 @ 1.875
without rotators: 195 @ 1.437
1977–78: 208 @ 1.386
1979–88: Intake, 195 @ 1.411
Exhaust, 220 @ 1.188
⑧ 1975–78: 1.786
1979–84: Intake, 1.786
Exhaust, 1.625
1985–88: 1.786
⑨ 1975–76 Police Special package for the 8-360 and 401:
Intake: 270 @ 1.38
Exhaust: 270 @ 1.19
Installed height: 1.625

Camshaft Specifications
(All specifications in inches)

Engine	Journal Diameter					Bearing Clearance	Lobe Lift		End Play
	1	2	3	4	5		Int.	Exh.	
4-121	1.2579–1.2569	1.0220–1.0212	1.0220–1.0212	1.0220–1.0212	1.0220–1.0212	①	0.396	0.366	0.002–0.006
4-150	2.0300–2.0290	2.0200–2.0190	2.0100–2.0009	2.0000–1.9990	—	0.0010–0.0030	0.2650	0.2650	0
4-151	1.8690	1.8690	1.8690	—	—	0.0007–0.0027	0.3980	0.3980	0.0015–0.0050
6-232	2.0300–2.0290	2.0200–2.0190	2.0100–2.0090	2.0000–1.9990	—	0.0010–0.0030	0.2540	0.2540	0
6-258	2.0300–2.0290	2.0200–2.0190	2.0100–2.0090	2.0000–1.9990	—	0.0010–0.0030	②	②	0
8-304, 360, 401	2.1205–2.1195	2.0905–2.0895	2.0605–2.0595	2.0305–2.0295	2.0005–1.9995	0.0010–0.0030	0.2660 ③	0.2660 ③	0

① #1: 0.002–0.004
#2–5: 0.002–0.003
② 1-bbl: 0.2540
2-bbl thru 1984: 0.2480
1985–88: 0.2531
③ 8-401: 0.286

Crankshaft and Connecting Rod Specifications

(All specifications in inches)

	Crankshaft				Connecting Rod		
Engine	Main Bearing Journal Dia.	Main Bearing Oil Clearance	Shaft End Play	Thrust on No.	Journal Dia.	Oil Clearance	Side Clearance
4-121	2.5177– 2.5185	0.0012– 0.0035	0.0039– 0.0075	3	1.8701– 1.9567	0.0009– 0.0032	0.002– 0.012
4-150	2.4996– 2.5001	0.0010– 0.0025	0.0015– 0.0065	2	2.0934– 2.0955	0.0010– 0.0030	0.010– 0.019
4-151	2.2988	0.0005– 0.0022	0.0035– 0.0085	5	1.8690	0.0007– 0.0027	0.006– 0.022
6-232	2.4986– 2.5001	0.0010– 0.0020	0.0015– 0.0065	3	2.0934– 2.0955	0.0010– 0.0020	0.005– 0.014
6-258	2.4986– 2.5001	①	0.0015– 0.0065	3	2.0934– 2.0955	②	③
8-304, 360, 401	④	⑤	0.0030– 0.0080	3	2.0934– 2.0955	0.0010– 0.0020	0.006– 0.018

① 1975–80: 0.0010–0.0030
   1981: #1—0.0005–0.0026
       #2,3,4,5,6—0.0005–0.0030
       #7—0.0011–0.0035
   1982–88: 0.0010–0.0025
② 1975–76: 0.0010–0.0030
   1977–81: 0.0010–0.0025
   1982–88: 0.0010–0.0030

③ 1975–80: 0.005–0.014
   1981–88: 0.010–0.019
④ #1,2,3,4: 2.7474–2.7489
   #5: 2.7464–2.7479
⑤ #1,2,3,4—0.0010–0.0020
   #5—0.0020–0.0030

Piston and Ring Specifications

(All specifications in inches)

	Ring Gap			Ring Side Clearance			
Engine	#1 Compr.	#2 Compr.	Oil Control	#1 Compr.	#2 Compr.	Oil Control	Piston * Clearance
4-121	0.0098– 0.0177	0.0098– 0.0177	0.0098– 0.0157	0.0012– 0.0024	0.0012– 0.0024	0.0012– 0.0024	0.0007– 0.0017
4-150	0.0100– 0.0200	0.0100– 0.0200	0.0100– 0.0250	0.0017– 0.0032	0.0017– 0.0032	0.0010– 0.0080	0.0009– 0.0017
4-151	0.0027– 0.0033	0.0090– 0.0190	0.0150– 0.0550	0.0025– 0.0033	0.0025– 0.0033	0.0025– 0.0033	0.0025– 0.0033
6-232	0.0100– 0.0200	0.0100– 0.0200	0.0150– 0.0550	0.0015– 0.0030	0.0015– 0.0030	0.0010– 0.0080	0.0009– 0.0017
6-258	0.0100– 0.0200	0.0100– 0.0200	0.0100– 0.0250	①	①	0.0010– 0.0080	0.0009– 0.0017
8-304	0.0100– 0.0200	0.0100– 0.0200	0.0100– 0.0250	0.0015– 0.0030	0.0015– 0.0030	0.0011– 0.0080	0.0010– 0.0018
8-360	0.0100– 0.0200	0.0100– 0.0200	0.0150– 0.0450	0.0015– 0.0030	0.0015– 0.0035	0.0000– 0.0070	0.0012– 0.0020 ②
8-401	0.0100– 0.0200	0.0100– 0.0200	0.0150– 0.0550	0.0015– 0.0030	0.0015– 0.0035	0.0000– 0.0070	0.0012– 0.0020 ③

* Measured at the skirt
① 1975–80: 0.0015–0.0030
   1981–88: 0.0017–0.0032
② Police Special package: 0.0016–0.0024
③ Police Special package: 0.0014–0.0022

Torque Specifications
(All specifications in ft. lb.)

Engine	Cyl. Head	Conn. Rod	Main Bearing	Crankshaft Damper	Flywheel	Manifold	
						Intake	Exhaust
4-121	65 cold 80 hot	41	①	181	65	18	18
4-150	80–90	30–35	75–85	75–85	50 ②	20–25	20–25
4-151	93–97	28–32	63–67	155–165	53–57	Bolt: 40 Nut: 30	Bolt: 40 Nut: 30
6-232	100–110	25–30	75–85	50–60	100–110	40–45	23–28
6-258	③	30–35	75–85	75–85	100–110	20–25	④
8-304	100–110	25–30	95–105	53–58	100–110	40–45	23–27
8-360	100–110	25–30	95–105	53–58	100–110	40–45	23–27
8-401	100–120	35–40	95–105	70–90	95–120	37–47	20–30

① #1–4: 58
  #5: 47
② Plus a 60° turn
③ 1975–80: 105
  1981–88: 85
④ 1975–79: 23
  1980 and later (See illustration in text): Bolts #1 thru 11: 23
                       Bolts #12 & 13: 50

Engine

REMOVAL & INSTALLATION

4-121 Engine

➡It is recommended by the manufacturer that the engine be removed from the car separately, and the transmission remain in the car.

1. Mark the hinge locations and remove the hood.
2. Drain the coolant and remove the air cleaner and TAC hose.

When removing nuts, bolts and other parts, place them in a tray or other container

✳✳ CAUTION

When draining engine coolant, keep in mind that cats and dogs are attracted to ethylene glycol antifreeze and could drink any that is left in an uncovered container or in puddles on the ground. This will prove fatal in sufficient quantity. Always drain coolant into a sealable container. Coolant should be reused unless it is contaminated or is several years old.

3. Detach the negative cable at the alternator bracket and battery.
4. Remove the fuel and vacuum lines from the engine. Plug the fuel line.
5. Disconnect the necessary wiring, the throttle cable, and automatic transmission valve linkage.
6. If your car has air conditioning, the system must be bled, the hoses disconnected, and the condenser moved. See Section 1.
7. Raise the car, disconnect and remove the starter motor and exhaust pipe support bracket. Unbolt the exhaust pipe from the manifold.
8. Remove the torque convertor nuts and fluid cooler lines, if the car has automatic transmission.
9. Disconnect the wiring at the backup lamp switch and from the alternator.
10. Remove the lower radiator hose and heater hose from the radiator.
11. Remove all the bell housing bolts, except the top center bolt.
12. Lower the car and remove the top radiator hose and the cold air induction manifold at the radiator.
13. Remove the radiator screws, move the radiator one inch to the left, rotate, and lift the radiator and shroud assembly out of the car. With air conditioning, first remove the condenser attaching bolts and more the condenser away from the radiator.

14. Remove any other heater hoses and wiring that are still attached to the car.

15. With power steering, disconnect the hoses from the steering gear. Remove the transmission filler tube support screws with automatic transmission.

16. Remove the engine support cushion nuts on both sides of the engine and attach a lifting device.

17. With the engine partially raised, support the transmission and remove the center bolt from the transmission bell housing. Carefully remove the engine from the car.

To install:

➡**When mating the engine to the transmission bell housing, install three bolts for a more secure mounting until the engine is bolted into place.**

18. With the engine partially raised, support the transmission and install the center bolt in the transmission bell housing. Carefully install the engine in the car.

19. Install the engine support cushion nuts on both sides of the engine and remove the lifting device.

20. With power steering, connect the hoses to the steering gear. Install the transmission filler tube support screws with automatic transmission.

21. Install the heater hoses and any wiring that was disconnected from the car.

22. Install the radiator and the condenser.

23. Lower the car and install the top radiator hose and the cold air induction manifold at the radiator.

24. Install all remaining bell housing bolts.

25. Install the lower radiator hose.

26. Connect the wiring at the backup lamp switch and alternator.

27. Install the torque convertor nuts and fluid cooler lines, if the car has automatic transmission.

28. Raise the car, install the starter motor and exhaust pipe support bracket. Connect the exhaust pipe at the manifold.

29. If your car has air conditioning, evacuate, charge and leak test the system. See Section 1.

30. Connect any remaining wiring, the throttle cable, and automatic transmission valve linkage.

31. Connect the fuel and vacuum lines at the engine.

32. Attach the negative cable at the alternator bracket and battery.

33. Fill the cooling system and install the air cleaner and TAC hose.

34. Install the hood.

4-150 Engine

1. Disconnect the battery ground cable.
2. Remove the air cleaner.
3. Remove the hood.
4. Drain the coolant.

✳✳ CAUTION

When draining the coolant, keep in mind that cats and dogs are attracted by the ethylene glycol antifreeze, and are quite likely to drink any that is left in an uncovered container or in puddles on the ground. This will prove fatal in

sufficient quantity. Always drain the coolant into a sealable container. Coolant should be reused unless it is contaminated or several years old.

5. Remove the lower radiator hose.
6. Remove the upper radiator hose.
7. Disconnect the coolant recovery hose.
8. Remove the fan shroud.
9. Disconnect the automatic transmission coolant lines.
10. Have the refrigerant discharged by a certified technician.

✳✳ CAUTION

Please refer to Section 1 before discharging the compressor or disconnecting air conditioning lines. Damage to the air conditioning system or personal injury could result. Consult your local laws concerning refrigerant discharge and recycling. In many areas it may be illegal for anyone but a certified technician to service the A/C system. Always use an approved recovery station when discharging the air conditioning.

11. Disconnect and remove the condenser. Cap all openings at once!

12. Remove the radiator.

13. Remove the fan and install a 5⁄16 in. × 1⁄2 in. (7.9375mm × 12.7mm) capscrew through the pulley and into the water pump flange to maintain the pulley-to-pump alignment.

14. Disconnect the heater hoses.

15. Disconnect the throttle linkage.

16. Disconnect the cruise control linkage.

17. Disconnect the oil pressure sending unit wire.

18. Disconnect the temperature sending unit wire.

19. Disconnect and tag all vacuum hoses connected to the engine.

20. Remove the air conditioning compressor.

21. Remove the power steering hoses at the gear.

22. Drain the power steering reservoir.

23. Remove the power brake vacuum check valve from the booster.

24. Raise and support the front end on jackstands.

25. Disconnect and tag the starter wires.

26. Remove the starter.

27. Disconnect the exhaust pipe at the manifold.

28. Remove the flywheel housing access cover.

29. On vehicles equipped with automatic transmission, matchmark the converter and flywheel and remove the attaching bolts.

30. Remove the upper flywheel housing-to-engine bolts and loosen the lower ones.

31. Remove the engine mount cushion-to-engine compartment bolts.

32. Attach a shop crane to the lifting eyes on the engine.

33. Raise the engine off the front supports.

34. Place a floor jack under the flywheel housing.

35. Remove the remaining flywheel housing bolts.

36. Lift the engine out of the vehicle.

37. Mount the engine on a work stand or cradle. Never let it rest on the oil pan.

✳✳ CAUTION

The EPA warns that prolonged contact with used engine oil may cause a number of skin disorders, including cancer! You should make every effort to minimize your exposure to used engine oil. Protective gloves should be worn when changing the oil. Wash your hands and any other exposed skin areas as soon as possible after exposure to used engine oil. Soap and water, or waterless hand cleaner should be used.

To install:

38. Lower the engine into place in the vehicle.
39. Lubricate the manual transmission input shaft with chassis lube before insertion into clutch splines.
40. Install the flywheel housing bolts. Torque the top flywheel housing-to-engine bolts to 27 ft.lb. and the bottom ones to 43 ft.lb.
41. Install the engine mount cushion-to-engine compartment bolts. Torque the front bracket support bolts to 33 ft.lb.
42. Remove the shop crane.
43. On vehicles equipped with automatic transmission, install the converter attaching bolts.
44. Install the flywheel housing access cover.
45. Connect the exhaust pipe at the manifold.
46. Install the starter.
47. Connect the wires.
48. Raise and support the front end on jackstands.
49. Install the power brake vacuum check valve on the booster.
50. Fill the power steering reservoir.
51. Connect the power steering hoses at the gear.
52. Install the air conditioning compressor.
53. Connect all vacuum hoses.
54. Connect all wires.
55. Connect the throttle linkage.
56. Connect the cruise control linkage.
57. Connect the heater hoses.
58. Install the fan.
59. Install the radiator.
60. Install the condenser.
61. Have the system charged by a certified technician.
62. Install the fan shroud.
63. Connect the automatic transmission coolant lines.
64. Install the upper radiator hose.
65. Connect the coolant recovery hose.
66. Install the lower radiator hose.
67. Fill the cooling system.
68. Install the hood.
69. Install the air cleaner.
70. Connect the battery ground cable.

4-151 Engine

✳✳ CAUTION

The EPA warns that prolonged contact with used engine oil may cause a number of skin disorders, including cancer! You should make every effort to minimize your exposure to used engine oil. Protective gloves should be worn when changing the oil. Wash your hands and any other exposed skin areas as soon as possible after exposure to used engine oil. Soap and water, or waterless hand cleaner should be used.

1. Disconnect the battery.
2. Remove the air cleaner.
3. Jack up the vehicle and support it on jackstands.
4. Disconnect the exhaust pipe from the manifold.
5. Disconnect the oxygen sensor.
6. Disconnect the wires from the starter.
7. Unbolt the starter and remove it from the vehicle.
8. Disconnect the wires from the distributor and oil pressure sending unit.
9. Remove the engine mount nuts.
10. On vehicles with manual transmission, remove the clutch slave cylinder and flywheel inspection plate.
11. Remove the clutch or converter housing-to-engine bolts.
12. On vehicle with automatic transmission, disconnect the converter from the drive plate.
13. Lower the vehicle.
14. Support the transmission with a jack.
15. Tag all hoses at the carburetor and remove them.
16. Disconnect the mixture control solenoid wire from the carburetor, (not all vehicles have these).
17. Disconnect the wires from the alternator.
18. Disconnect the throttle cable from the bracket and the carburetor.
19. Disconnect the choke and solenoid wires at the carburetor.
20. Disconnect the temperature sender wire.
21. Drain the radiator at the drain cock, then remove the lower hose.

✳✳ CAUTION

When draining engine coolant, keep in mind that cats and dogs are attracted to ethylene glycol antifreeze and could drink any that is left in an uncovered container or in puddles on the ground. This will prove fatal in sufficient quantity. Always drain coolant into a sealable container. Coolant should be reused unless it is contaminated or is several years old.

22. Remove the upper radiator hose and the heater hoses.
23. Remove the fan shroud, and radiator.
24. Remove the power steering hoses at the pump.
25. Attach a shop crane to the engine and lift it out of the vehicle.

➡The manual transmission may have to be raised slightly to allow a smooth separation.

To install:

26. Lower the engine into the vehicle.
27. On vehicle with automatic transmission, connect the converter to the drive plate.
28. Install the clutch or converter housing-to-engine bolts. Torque the bolts to 35 ft. lbs.
29. On vehicles with manual transmission, Install the clutch slave cylinder and flywheel inspection plate. Torque the slave cylinder bolts to 18 ft. lbs.
30. Install the engine mount nuts. Torque them to 34 ft. lbs.
31. Connect the wires to the distributor and oil pressure sending unit.

32. Install the starter. Torque the mounting bolts to 27 ft. lbs.; the bracket nut to 40 inch lbs.

33. Connect the wires to the starter.

34. Connect the oxygen sensor.

35. Connect the exhaust pipe at the manifold. Torque the nuts to 35 ft. lbs.

36. Install the power steering hoses at the pump.

37. Install the fan shroud, and radiator.

38. Install the upper radiator hose and the heater hoses.

39. Connect the temperature sender wire.

40. Connect the choke and solenoid wires at the carburetor.

41. Connect the throttle cable at the bracket and the carburetor.

42. Connect the wires to the alternator.

43. Connect the mixture control solenoid wire at the carburetor (not all vehicles have these).

44. Install all hoses at the carburetor.

45. Lower the vehicle.

46. Install the air cleaner.

47. Connect the battery.

48. Fill the cooling system.

6 and 8 Cylinder Engines

▶ See Figure 23

➡The engine is removed without the transmission on all models except the Pacer.

✵✵ CAUTION

The EPA warns that prolonged contact with used engine oil may cause a number of skin disorders, including cancer! You should make every effort to minimize your exposure to used engine oil. Protective gloves should be worn when changing the oil. Wash your hands and any other exposed skin areas as soon as possible after exposure to used engine oil. Soap and water, or waterless hand cleaner should be used.

1. Mark the hood hinge locations, disconnect the underhood light, if equipped, and remove the hood.

2. Drain the coolant and engine oil. Remove the filter on the Pacer.

✵✵ CAUTION

When draining engine coolant, keep in mind that cats and dogs are attracted to ethylene glycol antifreeze and could drink any that is left in an uncovered container or in puddles on the ground. This will prove fatal in sufficient quantity. Always drain coolant into a sealable container. Coolant should be reused unless it is contaminated or is several years old.

Fig. 23 A lifting device may be fabricated to support the engine weight when removing the mounts

3. Disconnect and remove the battery and air cleaner. On Pacers, first run the wipers to the center of the windshield.

4. Disconnect and tag the alternator, ignition coil distributor temperature and oil sender wiring. On Pacers, also disconnect the brake warning switch wiring.

5. If equipped with TCS, remove the switch bracket and vacuum solenoid wire harness.

6. Disconnect and plug the hose from the fuel pump. On Pacers, also disconnect the automatic transmission fluid cooler line.

7. Disconnect the engine ground strap at the block and the starter cable at the starter. Remove the right front engine support cushion-to-bracket bolt.

8. If your car has air conditioning, the system must be bled, the hoses disconnected, and the system removed. Have this service performed by a certified technician.

✳✳ CAUTION

Please refer to Section 1 before discharging the compressor or disconnecting air conditioning lines. Damage to the air conditioning system or personal injury could result. Consult your local laws concerning refrigerant discharge and recycling. In many areas it may be illegal for anyone but a certified technician to service the A/C system. Always use an approved recovery station when discharging the air conditioning.

9. Disconnect the return hose from the fuel filter. TAC hose from the manifold, carburetor vent hose, heater or A/C vacuum hose and/or power brake hose at intake manifold, and power brake vacuum check valve from booster, if equipped.

10. Disconnect the throttle cable and throttle valve rod, if equipped.

11. Disconnect the radiator and heater hoses from the engine, automatic transmission cooler lines from the radiator, radiator shroud, fan, and spacer, and remove the radiator.

12. Install a $5/16$ in. $\times$ $1/2$ in. bolt through the fan pulley into the water pump flange to maintain alignment (all but Pacer).

13. With power steering, disconnect the hoses, drain the reservoir, and cap the fittings. With power brakes, remove the vacuum check valve from the booster.

14. On Pacers only, remove the carburetor and plug the fitting, remove the valve cover(s) and remove the vibration damper.

15. With automatic transmission, remove the filler tube.

16. Jack and support the front of the car. Remove the starter.

17. With automatic transmission on all except the Pacer, remove the converter cover, converter bolts (rotate the crankshaft for access), and the exhaust pipe/transmission linkage support.

With manual transmission on all but the Pacer, remove the clutch cover, bellcrank inner support bolts and springs, the bellcrank, outer bellcrank-to-strut retainer, and disconnect the back-up lamp wire harness at the firewall for access later.

On Pacers disconnect the transmission and clutch linkage, speedometer cable at the transmission remove the driveshaft (plug the transmission), and support the transmission with a jack. Remove the rear crossmember.

18. Attach the lifting device and support the engine. Remove the engine mount bolts.

19. Disconnect the exhaust pipe from the manifold.

20. On all but the Pacer, remove the upper converter or clutch housing bolts and loosen the lower bolts. Raise the car and move the jackstands to the jack pad area. Remove the A/C idler pulley

and bracket, if equipped. Lift the engine off the front supports, support the transmission, remove the lower transmission cover attaching bolts, and lift the engine out of the car.

On Pacers, lift the engine slightly and remove the front support cushions. Remove the transmission support, raise the front of the car so that the bottom of the bumper is three feet from the floor, and partially remove the engine/transmission assembly until the rear of the cylinder head clears the cowl Lower the car and remove the engine.

To install:

21. On installation with manual transmission, insert the transmission shaft into the clutch spline and align the clutch housing to the engine. Install and tighten the lower housing bolts.

With automatic transmission, align the converter housing to the engine and loosely install the bottom housing bolts. Then install the next higher bolts and tighten all four bolts.

With both transmissions, next, lower the engine onto the mounts, and install the mounting bolts.

On Pacers raise the car with a jack as in Step 20. Lower the engine/transmission assembly into the compartment. Raise the transmission into position with a jack and install the rear crossmember.

22. On all but the Pacer, install the upper converter or clutch housing bolts and loosen the lower bolts. Raise the car and move the jackstands to the jack pad area. Install the A/C idler pulley and bracket, if equipped. Lift the engine off the front supports, support the transmission, install the lower transmission cover attaching bolts, and lift the engine out of the car.

On Pacers, lift the engine slightly and install the front support cushions. Install the transmission support, raise the front of the car so that the bottom of the bumper is three feet from the floor, and partially install the engine/transmission assembly until the rear of the cylinder head clears the cowl Lower the car and install the engine.

23. Connect the exhaust pipe from the manifold.

24. Install the engine mount bolts.

25. With automatic transmission on all except the Pacer, install the converter cover, converter bolts (rotate the crankshaft for access), and the exhaust pipe/transmission linkage support.

With manual transmission on all but the Pacer, install the clutch cover, bellcrank inner support bolts and springs, the bellcrank, outer bellcrank-to-strut retainer, and connect the back-up lamp wire harness at the firewall.

On Pacers connect the transmission and clutch linkage, speedometer cable at the transmission and install the driveshaft. Install the rear crossmember.

26. Install the starter.

27. With automatic transmission, install the filler tube.

28. On Pacers only, install the carburetor, valve cover(s) and vibration damper.

29. With power steering, connect the hoses. With power brakes, install the vacuum check valve on the booster.

30. Install the fan, spacer, and radiator. Connect the radiator and heater hoses, automatic transmission cooler lines and install the radiator shroud.

31. Connect the throttle cable and throttle valve rod, if equipped.

32. Connect the return hose to the fuel filter. Connect the TAC hose to the manifold, carburetor vent hose, heater or A/C vacuum hose and/or power brake hose at intake manifold, and power brake vacuum check valve to booster, if equipped.

33. Have the system evacuated, charged and leak tested by a certified technician.

34. Connect the engine ground strap at the block and the starter cable at the starter. Install the right front engine support cushion-to-bracket bolt.

35. Connect the hose at the fuel pump. On Pacers, also connect the automatic transmission fluid cooler line.

36. If equipped with TCS, install the switch bracket and vacuum solenoid wire harness.

37. Connect the alternator, ignition coil distributor temperature and oil sender wiring. On Pacers, also connect the brake warning switch wiring.

38. Install and connect the battery and install the air cleaner.

39. Fill the cooling system and engine oil.

40. Install the hood. Connect the underhood light, if equipped.

Rocker Shafts and Rocker Studs

REMOVAL & INSTALLATION

4-150 Engine

▶ **See Figure 24**

1. Remove the rocker arm cover. The cover seal is RTV sealer. Break the seal with a clean putty knife or razor blade. Don't attempt to remove the cover until the seal is broken. To remove the cover, pry where indicated at the bolt holes.

2. Remove the two capscrews at each bridge and pivot assembly. It's best to remove the capscrews alternately, a little at a time each to avoid damage to the bridge.

Fig. 24 To remove the bridge and cap assemblies from the rockers, unfasten the retaining bolts

3. Remove the bridges, pivots and rocker arms. Keep them in order.

4. Install the rocker arms and bridge and pivot assemblies. Tighten the capscrews to 19 ft.lb.

5. Clean the mating surfaces of the cover and head.

6. Run a ⅛ in. (3.175mm) bead of RTV sealer around the mating surface of the head. Install the cover within 10 minutes! Don't allow any of the RTV material to drop into the engine! In the engine it will form and set and possibly block and oil passage. Torque the cover bolts to 36–60 in.lb.

4-151 Engines

▶ **See Figure 25**

1. Remove the rocker arm cover.

2. Remove the rocker arm capscrew and ball.

3. Remove the rocker arm.

4. Install rocker arms. Tighten the capscrews to 20 ft.lb. DO NOT OVERTORQUE!

5. Clean the mating surfaces of the cover and head.

6. Install the cover. Tighten the bolts to 36–60 in.lb.

Fig. 25 View of the rocker arm assembly—4–151 engine

6-Cylinder 232, 258 and 8-Cylinder 304 Engines

▶ **See Figures 26, 27, 28 and 29**

On these engines the rocker arms pivot on a bridged pivot that is secured with two capscrews. The bridged pivots maintain proper rocker arm-to-valve tip alignment.

Fig. 26 Check the rocker arm retaining nuts for stress cracks

Fig. 27 Visually inspect the rocker arm-to-shaft contact area

Fig. 28 Exploded view of the V8 valve train components—1973 models

Fig. 29 Valve train components used on 6-cylinder engines

1. Remove the rocker cover and gasket.
2. Remove the two capscrews at each bridged pivot, backing off each capscrew one turn at a time to avoid breaking the bridge.
3. Remove each bridged pivot and corresponding pair of rocker arms and place them on a clean surface in the same order as they are removed.

➡Bridged pivots, capscrews, rockers, and pushrods must all be reinstalled in their original positions.

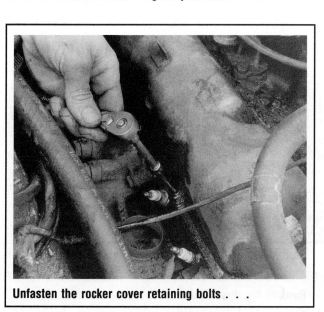

Unfasten the rocker cover retaining bolts . . .

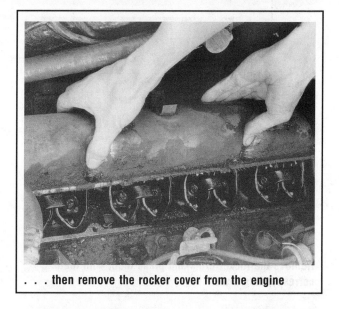

. . . then remove the rocker cover from the engine

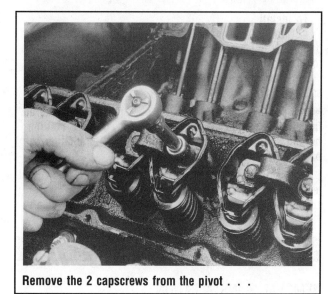

Remove the 2 capscrews from the pivot . . .

1. Bridged pivot   2. Retaining bolt   3. Rocker arm
. . . then remove the bridged pivot from the assembly

Remove the rocker arms and place them with their corresponding pivots

Remove the thermostat housing retaining bolts . . .

To install:

4. Clean all the parts in a suitable solvent and use compressed air to blow out the oil passages in the pushrods and the rocker arms. Replace any excessively worn parts.

5. Install rocker arms, pushrods and bridged pivots in the same positions from which they were removed.

➡Be sure that the bottom end of each pushrod is centered in the plunger which they were removed. Be sure that the bottom end of each pushrod is centered in the plunger cap of each hydraulic valve tappet.

6. Install the capscrews and tighten them one turn at a time, alternating between the two screws on each bridge. Tighten the capscrews to 21 ft.lb. on the Sixes and 10 ft.lb. on the 304 V8.

7. Install the rocker cover(s) with new gasket(s).

Thermostat

REMOVAL & INSTALLATION

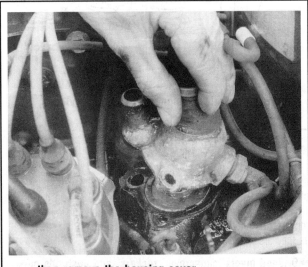

. . . then remove the housing cover

✳✳ CAUTION

When draining engine coolant, keep in mind that cats and dogs are attracted to ethylene glycol antifreeze and could drink any that is left in an uncovered container or in puddles on the ground. This will prove fatal in sufficient quantity. Always drain coolant into a sealable container. Coolant should be reused unless it is contaminated or is several years old.

The thermostat is located in the water outlet housing at the front or on top of the engine. On the V8 the water outlet housing is located in the front of the intake manifold.

To remove the thermostats from all of these engines.

1. Drain the cooling system. It is not necessary to disconnect or remove any of the hoses.

2. Remove the two attaching screws and lift the housing from the engine.

3. Remove the thermostat and the gasket.

Remove the thermostat from the engine block

To install:

4. Place the thermostat in the housing with the spring inside the engine.

5. Install a new gasket with a small amount of sealing compound applied to both sides.

6. The bleed hose on the thermostats used on 6-cylinder engines must be installed up (at 12 o'clock), to prevent 'burping' caused by trapped air.

7. Install the water outlet and tighten the attaching bolts to 30 ft. lbs.

8. Refill the cooling system.

Intake Manifold

REMOVAL & INSTALLATION

4-121 Engine

◆ **See Figure 30**

1. Drain the cooling system.

✳✳ CAUTION

When draining engine coolant, keep in mind that cats and dogs are attracted to ethylene glycol antifreeze and could drink any that is left in an uncovered container or in puddles on the ground. This will prove fatal in sufficient quantity. Always drain coolant into a sealable container. Coolant should be reused unless it is contaminated or is several years old.

2. Disconnect the EGR tube at the exhaust manifold and remove the air cleaner assembly.

Fig. 30 Exploded view of the intake manifold assembly—4–121 engine

3. Disconnect the fuel and vacuum lines and plug the main fuel line to avoid gasoline leakage.

4. Remove the accelerator cable and the air hose from the diverter valve.

5. Remove the fuel pump and the power brake cylinder vacuum hose. Loosen the air conditioner compressor mounting bracket, if so equipped. Do not discharge the system.

6. Remove the water inlet and outlet hoses from the manifold and the PCV hose at the block.

7. Remove the wires from the carburetor, accessories and from the ignition coil.

8. Remove the manifold bracket lower screw, loosen and remove the manifold nuts, and remove the manifold and lift bracket from the engine.

9. Remove the gasket and clean the mating surfaces on the manifold and the cylinder head.

To install:

10. Install the new gasket on the cylinder head.

11. Install the manifold and lift bracket on the engine. Don't tighten the manifold retaining nuts until the EGR tube is connected to the exhaust manifold. Install, but don't tighten, the manifold bracket lower screw.

12. Install the wires on the carburetor, accessories and ignition coil.

13. Install the water inlet and outlet hoses on the manifold and connect the PCV hose at the block.

14. Install the fuel pump and the power brake cylinder vacuum hose. Tighten the air conditioner compressor mounting bracket, if so equipped.

15. Install the accelerator cable and connect the air hose at the diverter valve.

16. Connect the fuel and vacuum lines.

17. Connect the EGR tube at the exhaust manifold and Install the air cleaner assembly. Then tighten the manifold retaining nuts to 18 ft.lb. torque and the bracket lower screw to 30 ft. lbs.

18. Fill the cooling system.

19. Operate the engine for 3 to 5 minutes and check for leaks.

4-150 Engine

◆ **See Figure 31**

➡It may be necessary to remove the carburetor from the intake manifold before the manifold is removed.

1. Disconnect the negative battery cable. Drain the radiator.

✳✳ CAUTION

When draining engine coolant, keep in mind that cats and dogs are attracted to ethylene glycol antifreeze and could drink any that is left in an uncovered container or in puddles on the ground. This will prove fatal in sufficient quantity. Always drain coolant into a sealable container. Coolant should be reused unless it is contaminated or is several years old.

2. Remove the air cleaner. Disconnect the fuel pipe and, if necessary, remove the carburetor.

3. Disconnect the coolant hoses from the intake manifold.

4. Disconnect the throttle cable from the bell crank.

5. Disconnect the PCV valve vacuum hose from the intake manifold.

1. Heat stove
2. Intake manifold
3. Gasket

Fig. 31 Intake manifold component locations—4–150 engine

6. If equipped, remove the vacuum advance CTO valve vacuum hoses.

7. Disconnect the system coolant temperature sender wire connector (located on the intake manifold). Disconnect the air temperature sensor wire, if equipped.

8. Disconnect the vacuum hose from the EGR valve.

9. On vehicles equipped with power steering remove the power steering pump and its mounting bracket. Do not detach the power steering pump hoses.

10. Disconnect the intake manifold electric heater wire connector, as required.

11. Disconnect the throttle valve linkage, if equipped with automatic transmission.

12. Disconnect the EGR valve tube from the intake manifold.

13. Remove the intake manifold attaching screws, nuts and clamps. Remove the intake manifold. Discard the gasket.

14. Clean the mating surfaces of the manifold and cylinder head.

➡ **If the manifold is being replaced, ensure all fittings, etc., are transferred to the replacement manifold.**

To install:

15. Install the intake manifold. Install the intake manifold attaching screws, nuts and clamps. Torque manifold fasteners to 23 ft. lbs.

16. Connect the EGR valve tube to the intake manifold.

17. Connect the throttle valve linkage, if equipped with automatic transmission.

18. Connect the intake manifold electric heater wire connector, as required.

19. On vehicles equipped with power steering install the power steering pump and its mounting bracket.

20. Connect the vacuum to from the EGR valve.

21. Connect the system coolant temperature sender wire con-

nector (located on the intake manifold). Connect the air temperature sensor wire, if equipped.

22. If equipped, install the vacuum advance CTO valve vacuum hoses.

23. If removed, install the carburetor and tighten the mounting bolts to 14 ft. lbs.

24. Connect the PCV valve vacuum hose to the intake manifold.

25. Connect the throttle cable to the bell crank.

26. Connect the fuel pipe.

27. Connect the coolant hoses to the intake manifold.

28. Install the air cleaner.

29. Connect the negative battery cable.

30. Fill the cooling system.

4-151 Engine

▶ **See Figure 32**

1. Remove the negative cable.
2. Remove the air cleaner and the PCV valve hose.

✳✳ CAUTION

DO NOT remove the block drain plugs or loosen the radiator draincock with system hot and under pressure because serious burns from the coolant can occur.

3. Drain the cooling system.

✳✳ CAUTION

When draining engine coolant, keep in mind that cats and dogs are attracted to ethylene glycol antifreeze and could drink any that is left in an uncovered container or in puddles on the ground. This will prove fatal in sufficient quantity. Always drain coolant into a sealable container. Coolant should be reused unless it is contaminated or is several years old.

4. Tag and remove the vacuum hoses (ensure the distributor vacuum advance hose is removed).

Fig. 32 Intake manifold bolt tightening sequence—4–151 engine

5. Disengage the fuel pipe and electrical wire connections from the carburetor.

6. Disconnect the carburetor throttle linkage. Remove the carburetor and the carburetor spacer.

7. Remove the bell crank and throttle linkage brackets and move them to one side for clearance.

8. Remove the heater hose at the intake manifold.

9. Remove the alternator. Note the position of spacers for installation.

10. Remove the manifold-to-cylinder head bolts and remove the manifold.

To install:

11. Position the replacement gasket and install the replacement manifold on the cylinder head. Start all bolts.

12. Tighten all bolts with 37 ft. lbs.

13. Connect the heater hose to the intake manifold.

14. Install the bell crank and throttle linkage brackets.

15. Connect the carburetor throttle linkage to the brackets and bell crank.

16. Install the carburetor spacer and tighten the bolts with 15 ft. lbs.

17. Install the carburetor and gasket. Tighten the nuts with 15 ft. lbs.

18. Install the fuel pipe and engage the electrical wire connections. Install the vacuum hoses.

19. Install the battery negative cable.

✷✷ CAUTION

Use extreme caution when the engine is operating. Do not stand in a direct line with the fan. Do not put your hands near pulleys, belts or fan. Do not wear loose clothing.

20. Refill the cooling system. Start the engine and inspect for leaks.

21. Install the air cleaner and the PCV valve hose.

6-232 and 258 Engines

▶ **See Figures 33, 34, 35 and 36**

The intake manifold and exhaust manifold are mounted externally on the left side of the engine and are attached to the cylinder head. The intake and exhaust manifolds are removed as a unit. On some engines, an exhaust gas recirculation valve is mounted on the side of the intake manifold.

1. Remove the air cleaner and carburetor.

2. Disconnect the accelerator cable from the accelerator bell-crank.

3. Disconnect the Positive Crankcase System (PCS) vacuum hose from the intake manifold.

4. Disconnect the distributor vacuum hose and electrical wires at the Transmission Controlled Spark (TCS) solenoid vacuum valve.

5. Remove the TCS solenoid vacuum valve and bracket from the intake manifold. In some cases it might not be necessary to remove the TCS unit.

6. If so equipped, disconnect the EGR valve vacuum hoses.

7. Remove the power steering mounting bracket and pump and set it aside without disconnecting the hoses.

8. Remove the EGR valve, if so equipped.

9. Disconnect the exhaust pipe from the manifold flange. Disconnect the spark Coolant Temperature Override (CTO) hoses and remove the oxygen sensor.

Fig. 33 Exploded view of the intake and exhaust manifold assembly—6-cylinder engines

Fig. 34 Intake and exhaust manifold components—1981–82 6-cylinder engines

Fig. 35 Intake manifold bolt tightening sequence—6-cylinder engines through 1980

Fig. 36 Intake manifold bolt tightening sequence—1981–82 6-cylinder engines

10. Remove the manifold attaching bolts, nuts and clamps.

11. Separate the intake manifold and exhaust manifold from the engine as an assembly. Discard the gasket.

12. If either manifold is to be replaced, they should be separated at the heat riser area.

To install:

13. Clean the mating surfaces of the manifolds and the cylinder head before replacing the manifolds. Replace them in reverse order of the above procedure with a new gasket. Tighten the bolts and nuts to the specified torque in the proper sequence.

14. Connect the exhaust pipe to the manifold flange. Torque the nuts to 20 ft. lbs. Connect the spark CTO hoses and install the oxygen sensor.

15. Install the EGR valve, if so equipped.

16. Install the power steering mounting bracket and pump.

17. If so equipped, connect the EGR valve vacuum hoses.

18. Install the TCS solenoid vacuum valve and bracket to the intake manifold.

19. Connect the distributor vacuum hose and electrical wires at the TCS solenoid vacuum valve.

20. Connect the PCS vacuum hose to the intake manifold.

21. Connect the accelerator cable to the accelerator bellcrank.

22. Install the air cleaner and carburetor.

8-304, 360 and 401 Engines

1. Drain the coolant from the radiator.

✳✳ CAUTION

When draining engine coolant, keep in mind that cats and dogs are attracted to ethylene glycol antifreeze and could drink any that is left in an uncovered container or in puddles on the ground. This will prove fatal in sufficient quantity. Always drain coolant into a sealable container. Coolant should be reused unless it is contaminated or is several years old.

2. Remove the air cleaner assembly.

3. Disconnect the spark plug wires. Remove the spark plug wire brackets from the valve covers, and the bypass valve bracket.

Unscrew the air cleaner assembly cover retaining nut . . .

. . . then remove the cover

Remove the air filter element . . .

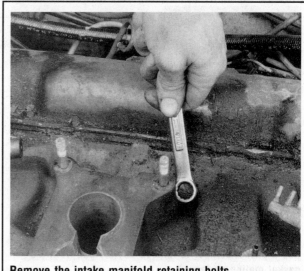

Remove the intake manifold retaining bolts . . .

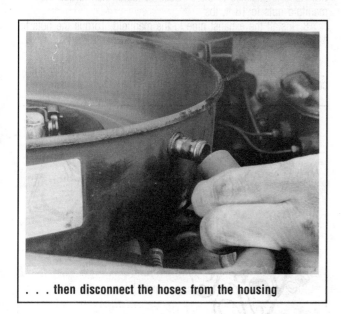

. . . then disconnect the hoses from the housing

. . . then remove the intake manifold assembly

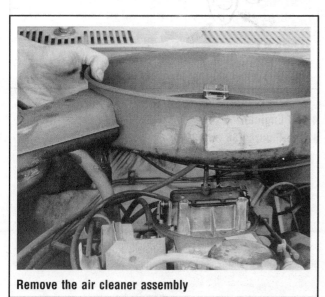

Remove the air cleaner assembly

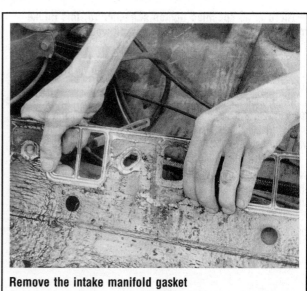

Remove the intake manifold gasket

Use a gasket scraper to remove any residue from the gasket mating surfaces

4. Disconnect the upper radiator hose and the by-pass hose from the intake manifold. Disconnect the heater hose from the rear of the manifold.

5. Disconnect the ignition coil bracket and lay the coil aside.

6. Disconnect the TCS solenoid vacuum valve from the right side valve cover.

7. Disconnect all lines, hoses, linkages and wires from the carburetor and intake manifold and TCS components as required.

8. Disconnect the air delivery hoses at the air distribution manifolds.

9. Disconnect the air pump diverter valve and lay the valve and the bracket assembly, including the hoses, forward of the engine.

10. Remove the intake manifold after removing the cap bolts that hold it in place. Remove and discard the side gaskets and the end seals.

To install:

11. Clean the mating surfaces of the intake manifold and the cylinder head before replacing the intake manifold. Use new gaskets and tighten the cap bolts to the correct torque. Install in reverse order of the above procedure.

→**There is no specified tighten sequence for this intake manifold. Start at the center bolts and work outward.**

12. Connect the air pump diverter valve.

13. Connect the air delivery hoses at the air distribution manifolds.

14. Connect all lines, hoses, linkages and wires to the carburetor and intake manifold and TCS components as required.

15. Install the TCS solenoid vacuum valve to the right side valve cover.

16. Install the ignition coil bracket.

17. Connect the upper radiator hose and the by-pass hose to the intake manifold. Connect the heater hose to the rear of the manifold.

18. Connect the spark plug wires. Install the spark plug wire brackets on the valve covers, and the bypass valve bracket.

19. Install the air cleaner assembly.

20. Fill the cooling system.

Exhaust Manifold

REMOVAL & INSTALLATION

4-121 Engine

▶ **See Figure 37**

1. Remove the TAC cold air induction manifold assembly and components.

2. Disconnect the EGR tube from the manifold.

3. Remove the exhaust pipe from the manifold.

4. Remove the manifold retaining nuts and washers.

5. Remove the manifold and gasket from the engine.

6. Clean the mating surfaces of the manifold and the head.

To install:

7. Install a new gasket on the head and install the manifold. Install, but do not tighten, the exhaust manifold nuts until the EGR tube is attached to the exhaust manifold, then torque the manifold nuts to 18 ft. lbs.

8. Install the exhaust pipe to the manifold. Torque the nuts to 18 ft. lbs.

9. Connect the EGR tube to the manifold.

10. Install the TAC cold air induction manifold assembly and components.

EXHAUST MANIFOLD

EGR OUTLET

GASKET

Fig. 37 Typical exhaust manifold used on 4–121 engines

4-150 Engine

▶ **See Figures 38 and 39**

1. Remove the intake manifold.

2. Disconnect the EGR tube.

3. Disconnect the exhaust pipe at the manifold.

4. Disconnect the oxygen sensor wire.

5. Support the manifold and remove the nuts from the studs.

To install:

6. If a new manifold is being installed, transfer the oxygen sensor. Torque the sensor to 35 ft. lbs.

Fig. 38 Exhaust manifold bolt tightening sequence—4–150 engine

7. Thoroughly clean the gasket mating surfaces of the manifold and head.

8. Install the manifold, using a new gasket. Torque the nuts to 23 ft. lbs.

9. Connect the oxygen sensor wire.

10. Connect the exhaust pipe at the manifold.

11. Connect the EGR tube.

12. Install the intake manifold.

➡**On some 1984 4-150 engines, the manifold end studs can be bent or broken if the manifold is misaligned. To remedy this:**

a. Remove the manifold.

b. Replace any bent or broken studs.

c. Using a straightedge, check the flatness of the manifold mating surface. If a 0.015 in. (0.38mm) flat feeler gauge can be inserted between the straightedge and the manifold, at any point, replace the manifold.

Fig. 39 Exhaust manifold modification on the 4–150 engine

d. Modify the original or replacement manifold by grinding the mounting flanges as shown in the accompanying illustration.

e. Install the manifold.

4-151 Engine

▶ **See Figure 40**

1. Remove the air cleaner and the hot air tube.
2. Remove the Pulsair system from the exhaust manifold.
3. Disconnect the exhaust pipe from the manifold at the flange. Spray the bolts first with penetrating sealer, if necessary.
4. Remove the engine oil dipstick bracket bolt.
5. Remove the exhaust manifold bolts and remove the manifold from the head.

Fig. 40 Exhaust manifold bolt tightening sequence—4-151 engine

To install:

6. Place a new gasket against the cylinder head, then install the exhaust manifold over it. Start all the bolts into the head finger-tight.
7. Torque the exhaust manifold bolts to 37 ft. lbs. in two stages, using the torque sequence illustrated.
8. The remainder of installation is the reverse removal.

6-Cylinder Engines

The exhaust manifold is removed along with the intake manifold. Refer to the intake manifold procedure in this section.

V8 Engines

EXCEPT 1975–76 GREMLIN AND HORNET WITH AIR PUMP

➡**The mating surfaces of both the exhaust manifold and the cylinder head are machined smooth, thus eliminating any need for a gasket between them.**

1. Disconnect the wires from the spark plugs after marking them for firing order.
2. On models equipped with air injection, disconnect the air delivery hoses from the injection manifold. Remove the injection manifold and nozzles from the exhaust manifold.
3. Disconnect the exhaust pipe from the exhaust manifold flange.

4. Remove the bolts and washers used to retain the manifold.
5. Remove the shields from the spark plugs. On 1977 and later Hornets and Concords only, before removing the right side manifold, remove the transmission filler tube bolt and tube.
6. Remove the exhaust manifold from the cylinder head.
7. Clean the machined surfaces of the manifold and head.

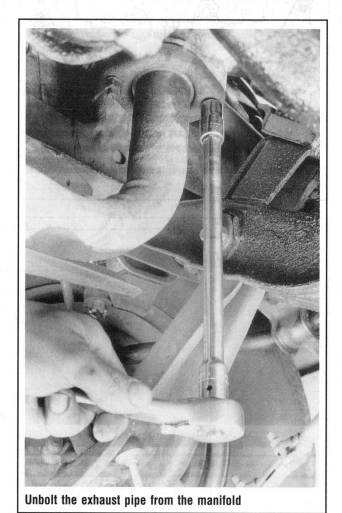

Unbolt the exhaust pipe from the manifold

Unfasten the exhaust manifold retaining bolts . . .

. . . then remove the manifold from the engine

To install:

8. Install the exhaust manifold on the cylinder head.

9. Install the shields on the spark plugs. On 1977 and later Hornets and Concords only, install the transmission filler tube bolt and tube. Use a new O-ring when installing the tube.

10. Connect the exhaust pipe from the exhaust manifold flange.

11. On models equipped with air injection, install the injection manifold and nozzles on the exhaust manifold. Connect the air delivery hoses at the injection manifold.

12. Connect the wires at the spark plugs.

1975–76 GREMLIN AND HORNET WITH AIR PUMP

The exhaust manifold on the left side may be removed in the same manners detailed for other V8 engines; however, the right side manifold on Gremlins and Hornets equipped with air pumps must be removed in the following order:

1. Raise the car and securely support it with jackstands.

2. Disconnect the exhaust pipe from the manifold flange.

3. Support the engine at the vibration damper, by placing a jack with a block of wood on its lifting pad underneath it.

4. Remove the bolts which secure the engine mounting bracket on the right side.

5. Remove the air cleaner assembly, including the tube which runs to the manifold heat stove.

6. Disconnect the battery cables. Remove the spark plug leads after marking them for installation.

7. Disconnect the air supply hose from the air injection manifold.

8. Remove the air injection tubes from the exhaust manifold.

9. On cars with automatic transmissions, remove the dipstick and the screw which secures the transmission dipstick tube.

10. Working from the rear, unscrew the exhaust manifold mounting bolts.

11. Raise the engine. Remove the exhaust manifold and the air injection manifold as an assembly.

12. Clean the joining surfaces of the manifold and cylinder head. Be careful not to nick or scratch either surface.

To install:

13. Install the exhaust manifold and the air injection manifold as an assembly.

14. On cars with automatic transmissions, install the dipstick and the screw which secures the transmission dipstick tube.

15. Install the air injection tubes.

16. Connect the air supply hose at the air injection manifold.

17. Connect the battery cables. Install the spark plug leads.

18. Install the air cleaner assembly, including the tube which runs to the manifold heat stove.

19. Install the bolts which secure the engine mounting bracket on the right side.

20. Remove the jack.

21. Connect the exhaust pipe at the manifold flange.

22. Raise the car and securely support it with jackstands.

Air Conditioning Compressor

REMOVAL & INSTALLATION

4-121 Engine

1. Isolate the compressor. Refer to Section 1 for this procedure.

2. Remove both service valves and cap the valves and compressor ports immediately.

3. Loosen the power steering pump and remove the drive belt.

4. Remove the power steering pump and brackets and lay the pump aside, without disconnecting the hoses.

5. Loosen the idler pulley eccentric and remove the compressor drive pulley.

6. Disconnect the clutch wire.

7. Unbolt and remove the compressor.

8. Install the compressor.

9. Disconnect the clutch wire.

10. Install the compressor drive pulley and adjust the belt tension.

11. Install the power steering pump and brackets.

12. Install and adjust the power steering drive belt.

13. Install both service valves and remove the caps.

14. Purge the compressor of air and open the service valves. Refer to Section 1 for this procedure.

4-151 Engine

1. Isolate the compressor. Refer to Section 1 for this procedure.

2. Remove both service valves and cap the valves and compressor ports immediately.

3. Loosen and remove the drive belt.

4. Disconnect the clutch wire.

5. Unbolt and remove the compressor.

6. Install the compressor.

7. Connect the clutch wire.

8. Install and adjust the drive belt.

9. Install both service valves and remove the caps.

10. Purge the compressor of air and open the service valves. Refer to Section 1 for this procedure.

1975–80 6-Cylinder Engines and 1981 (Non-California) 6-Cylinder Engines

♦ **See Figures 41, 42 and 43**

1. Isolate the compressor. Refer to Section 1 for this procedure.

2. Remove both service valves and cap the valves and compressor ports immediately.

Fig. 41 Compressor mounting bracket components on the 6–258 engine1977–80 and 1981 models, except California

Fig. 42 Compressor mounting bracket and retainers—6–1981 California and all 1982–87 6–258 engines

Fig. 43 Exploded view of the compressor mounting and retainers—V8 engines

3. Remove the alternator belt and adjusting bolt.

4. Remove the upper alternator mounting bolt and loosen the lower mounting bolt.

5. Remove the idler pulley.

6. Disconnect the compressor clutch wire. Remove the compressor mounting nuts and lift out the compressor. BE CAREFUL; IT'S HEAVY!

7. For installation, install the compressor, alternator and belt, idler pulley, and adjust the drive belts.

8. Install the service valves and purge the compressor of air. Open the valves.

9. Connect the clutch wire.

1981 California Models, 1982–87 4-150 and 6-258 Models

1. Isolate the compressor. Refer to Section 1 for this procedure.

2. Disconnect the battery ground.

3. Remove the discharge and suction hoses from the compressor and cap all openings immediately.

4. Loosen the alternator and remove the drive belts.

5. Remove the alternator from its brackets and set it out of the way.

6. Unbolt and remove the compressor.

7. For installation, install the compressor and alternator, connect the hoses and install and tension the drive belts. Connect the compressor clutch wire. Open the valves.

8-304, 360 and 401 Engines

1. Isolate the compressor. Refer to Section 1 for this procedure.

2. Remove both service valves and cap the valves and compressor ports immediately.

3. Loosen the alternator and remove the drive belts.

4. Remove the alternator mounting bracket.

5. Remove the compressor clutch wire.

6. Remove the compressor and mounting bracket as an assembly.

7. For installation, install the compressor and mounting bracket, install the alternator bracket, connect the clutch wire, install the belts, idler pulley, and adjust the drive belts.

8. Install the service valves and purge the compressor of air. Open the valves.

Radiator

REMOVAL & INSTALLATION

◗ See Figure 44

1. Raise the hood and remove the radiator cap. Be sure the engine is cold.

2. Drain the radiator. If the coolant appears to be clean, drain it into a clean container and save it for re-use.

Fig. 44 Exploded view of the cooling system components used on 4–121 engine

✳✳ **CAUTION**

When draining engine coolant, keep in mind that cats and dogs are attracted to ethylene glycol antifreeze and could drink any that is left in an uncovered container or in puddles on the ground. This will prove fatal in sufficient quantity. Always drain coolant into a sealable container. Coolant should be reused unless it is contaminated or is several years old.

3. Remove the upper and lower radiator hoses. Disconnect the coolant recovery hose, if so equipped.

4. On four cylinder models, remove the ambient air intake from the radiator support.

5. On four cylinder air conditioned models, remove the charcoal canister and the bracket.

6. Remove the fan shroud, if so equipped.

7. On automatic transmission models, disconnect and plug the fluid cooler lines. Remove battery on Pacers for access.

. . . then disconnect the upper hose from the radiator

Loosen the radiator petcock to drain the coolant

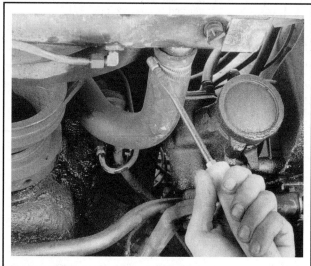

Loosen the lower radiator hose clamp . . .

Loosen the upper radiator hose clamp . . .

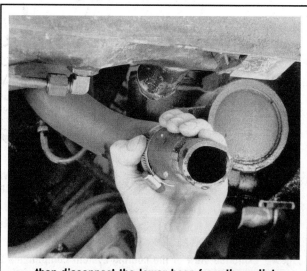

. . . then disconnect the lower hose from the radiator

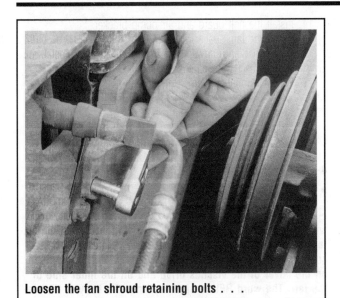

Loosen the fan shroud retaining bolts . . .

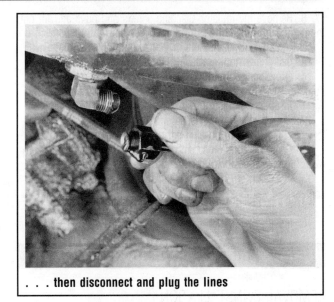

. . . then disconnect and plug the lines

. . . then move the fan shroud back and rest it on the cooling fan

Unscrew the radiator mounting bolts . . .

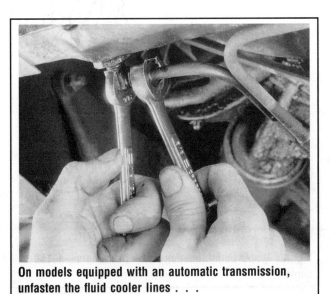

On models equipped with an automatic transmission, unfasten the fluid cooler lines . . .

. . . then remove the radiator from the vehicle

8. Remove the radiator attaching screws and bolts and lift out the radiator.

To install:

9. Install the radiator.

10. On automatic transmission models, connect and plug the fluid cooler lines. Install battery on Pacers.

11. Install the fan shroud, if so equipped.

12. On 4-121 air conditioned models, install the charcoal canister and the bracket.

13. On 4-121 models, install the ambient air intake from the radiator support.

14. Install the upper and lower radiator hoses. Connect the coolant recovery hose, if so equipped.

15. Fill the cooling system.

16. Install the radiator cap.

Water Pump

REMOVAL & INSTALLATION

The water pump is a centrifugal unit having a non-adjustable packless seal. It is non-serviceable and must be replace of defective. No maintenance is required.

4-121 Engine

1. Drain the cooling system. Disconnect the negative (−) cable from the battery. Remove the fan shroud.

❄❄ CAUTION

When draining engine coolant, keep in mind that cats and dogs are attracted to ethylene glycol antifreeze and could drink any that is left in an uncovered container or in puddles on the ground. This will prove fatal in sufficient quantity. Always drain coolant into a sealable container. Coolant should be reused unless it is contaminated or is several years old.

2. Rotate the crankshaft until the camshaft and crankshaft are at Top Dead Center (TDC) for number one cylinder.

3. If equipped with power steering, loosen the pump and remove the belt. Loosen the air conditioner idler pulley and remove the belt, if so equipped.

4. Loosen the alternator and air pump.

5. Remove the fan, spacer, and pulley.

6. Remove the belt guard and air pump bracket.

7. Remove the camshaft and drive belt idler pulley.

8. Disconnect all the hoses from the pump except the hose from the thermostat.

9. Remove the water pump attaching bolts and pull the pump out of the hose from the thermostat.

To install:

10. Clean the gasket from the block, install a new gasket on the pump or block.

11. Insert the pump into the thermostat hose, install the pump attaching bolts and torque the small bolts to 7 ft.lb. and the large bolts to 16 ft.lb.

12. Connect all the hoses at the pump.

13. Install the camshaft and drive belt idler pulley.

14. Install the belt guard and air pump bracket.

15. Install the fan, spacer, and pulley.

16. If equipped with power steering, install the belt. Install the air conditioner belt, if so equipped.

17. Fill the cooling system. Connect the negative (−) battery cable.

18. Install the fan shroud.

19. Operate engine for 3 to 5 minutes with the heater on to check for leaks and correct fluid level.

4-150 Engine

▶ See Figure 45

➡Some 4-150 engines with air conditioning are equipped with a serpentine drive belt and have a reverse rotating water pump coupled with a viscous fan drive assembly. The components are identified by the words REVERSE stamped on the cover of the viscous drive and on the inner side of the fan. The word REV is also cast into the body of the water pump.

1. Drain the cooling system.

❄❄ CAUTION

When draining engine coolant, keep in mind that cats and dogs are attracted to ethylene glycol antifreeze and could drink any that is left in an uncovered container or in puddles on the ground. This will prove fatal in sufficient quantity. Always drain coolant into a sealable container. Coolant should be reused unless it is contaminated or is several years old.

2. Disconnect the hoses at the pump.

3. Remove the drive belts.

4. Remove the power steering pump bracket.

5. Remove the fan and shroud.

6. Unbolt and remove the pump.

1. Water pump
2. Gasket

Fig. 45 Water pump location and its retainers—4–150 engine

To install:

7. Clean the mating surfaces thoroughly.

8. Using a new gasket, install the pump and torque the bolts to 13 ft.lb.

9. Install all other parts in reverse order of removal.

4-151 Engine

▶ See Figure 46

1. Drain the cooling system.

✳✳ CAUTION

When draining engine coolant, keep in mind that cats and dogs are attracted to ethylene glycol antifreeze and could drink any that is left in an uncovered container or in puddles on the ground. This will prove fatal in sufficient quantity. Always drain coolant into a sealable container. Coolant should be reused unless it is contaminated or is several years old.

2. Remove all drive belts.
3. Remove the fan and pump pulley.
4. Unbolt and remove the pump from the engine.

To install:

5. Clean the gasket surfaces, coat the new gasket with non-hardening type sealer and position the gasket on the block.

6. Coat the threaded areas of the bolts with waterproof sealer and install the pump. Torque the bolts to 25 ft. lbs.

7. Install the pulley and fan. Tighten the fan and hub bolts to 18 ft.lb.

8. Install the drive belts. The belts should be adjusted so that a ½ in. (12.7mm) deflection is present when they are depressed mid-point along their longest straight run.

6-232 and 258 Engines

▶ See Figures 47 and 48

1. Drain the cooling system.

✳✳ CAUTION

When draining engine coolant, keep in mind that cats and dogs are attracted to ethylene glycol antifreeze and could drink any that is left in an uncovered container or in puddles on the ground. This will prove fatal in sufficient quantity. Always drain coolant into a sealable container. Coolant should be reused unless it is contaminated or is several years old.

Fig. 46 Exploded view of the cooling system components—4–150 engine

Fig. 47 Early model cooling system components commonly found on 6-cylinder engines

2. Disconnect all hoses at the pump.
3. Remove the drive belts.
4. Remove the fan shroud attaching screws.
5. Unbolt the fan and fan drive assembly and remove along with the shroud. On some models it may be easier to turn the shroud ½ turn.
6. Unbolt and remove the pump.

➡️**Engines built for sale in California having a single, serpentine drive belt and viscous fan drive, have a reverse rotating pump and drive. These components are identified by the word REVERSE stamped on the drive cover and inner side of the fan, and REV cast into the water pump body. Never interchange standard rotating parts with these.**

To install:
7. Installation is the reverse of removal. Always use a new gasket coated with sealer. Torque the water pump bolts to 13 ft. lbs.; the fan bolts to 18 ft. lbs.

Fig. 48 Cooling system components used on late model 6-cylinder engines

8-304, 360 and 401 Engines

▶ See Figures 49 and 50

1. Drain the cooling system.

✳✳ CAUTION

When draining engine coolant, keep in mind that cats and dogs are attracted to ethylene glycol antifreeze and could drink any that is left in an uncovered container or in puddles on the ground. This will prove fatal in sufficient quantity. Always drain coolant into a sealable container. Coolant should be reused unless it is contaminated or is several years old.

2. Disconnect all hoses at the pump.
3. Loosen all drive belts.

4. Remove the shroud, but reinsert one bolt to hold the radiator.

5. Remove the fan and hub.

6. If the vehicle is equipped with A/C install a double nut on the compressor bracket-to-water pump stud and remove the stud.

7. Remove, but do not disconnect the alternator and bracket.

8. If so equipped, remove the nuts that attach the power steering pump to the rear half of the pump bracket.

9. Remove the two bolts that attach the front half to the rear half of the bracket.

10. Remove the remaining upper screw from the inner air pump support bracket, loosen the lower bolt and drop the bracket away from the power steering front bracket.

11. Remove the front half of the power steering bracket from the water pump mounting stud.

12. Unbolt and remove the water pump.

1. Radiator upper hose
2. Thermostat housing cover
3. Gasket
4. Thermostat
5. Gasket
6. Drive pulley
7. Viscous drive fan
8. Coolant recovery bottle
9. Radiator
10. Shroud
11. Bimetallic coil spring
12. Silicone fluid chamber
13. Stud
14. Hose (from heater)
15. Water pump
16. Bypass hose

Fig. 49 Exploded view of the cooling system components used on late model V8 engines

Fig. 50 Typical cooling system components found on early model V8 engines

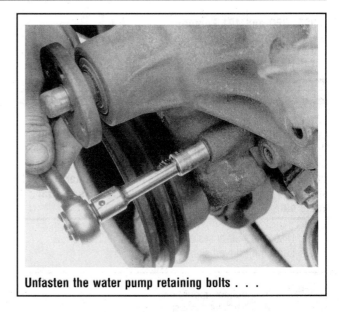

Unfasten the water pump retaining bolts . . .

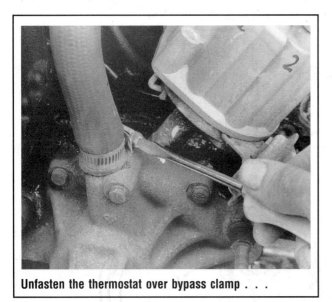

Unfasten the thermostat over bypass clamp . . .

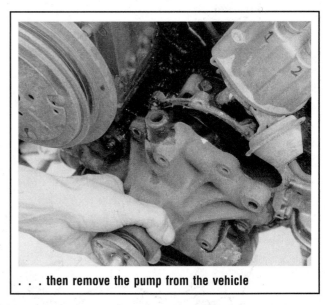

. . . then remove the pump from the vehicle

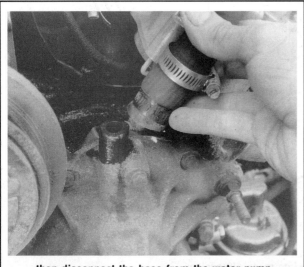

. . . then disconnect the hose from the water pump

To install:

13. Install the pump. Always use a new gasket coated with sealer. Torque the pump-to-timing case bolts to 48 in.lb. and the pump-to-blockbolts to 25 ft.lb.

14. Install the front half of the power steering bracket to the water pump mounting stud. Torque the power steering pulley nut to 60 ft.lb.

15. Install the upper screw from the inner air pump support bracket, and tighten the lower bolt.

16. If so equipped, install the nuts that attach the power steering pump to the rear half of the pump bracket.

17. Install the two bolts that attach the front half to the rear half of the bracket.

18. Install the alternator and bracket.

19. If the vehicle is equipped with A/C install a double nut on the compressor bracket-to-water pump stud and install the stud.

20. Install the fan and hub.

21. Install the shroud.

22. Adjust all drive belts.

23. Connect all hoses at the pump.
24. Fill the cooling system.

Cylinder Head

REMOVAL & INSTALLATION

• Don't loosen the head bolts until the engine is thoroughly cool, to prevent warping. Do not remove block drain plugs or loosen radiator draincock with the system hot and under pressure, as serious burns from coolant can occur.

• If the head sticks, operate the starter to loosen it by compression or rap it upward with a soft hammer. Do not force anything between the head and the block.

• Resurfacing (milling or grinding) the cylinder head will increase the compression ratio, and can affect the emission output, as well as the fuel octane requirement. For this reason the factory recommends replacing rather than resurfacing cylinder heads.

• Cylinder heads bolts should be retorqued after the first 500 miles or so unless a special AMC gasket is used. The special gasket doesn't require retorquing.

• It is important to note that each engine has its own head bolt tightening sequence and torque. Incorrect tightening procedure may cause head warpage and compression loss. Correct sequence and torque for each engine model is shown in this chapter.

• Make sure to blow any coolant out of the cylinder head bolt holes before reassembly to prevent inaccurate torque readings.

4-121 Engine
▶ See Figure 51

1. Drain the coolant from the system and disconnect the negative cable from the battery.

❊❊ CAUTION

When draining engine coolant, keep in mind that cats and dogs are attracted to ethylene glycol antifreeze and could drink any that is left in an uncovered container or in puddles on the ground. This will prove fatal in sufficient quantity. Always drain coolant into a sealable container. Coolant should be reused unless it is contaminated or is several years old.

2. Remove the air cleaner assembly, vacuum hoses and flexible hoses from the cylinder head area.
3. Remove the radiator hoses, radiator bypass hose and the heater hoses.
4. Remove the accessory drive belts, camshaft drive belt cover, and the camshaft drive belt. Loosen the compressor mounting bracket if equipped with A/C.
5. Remove the fan belt, fan blades, spacer and pulley. Remove the air pump and also the alternator pivot bolt. Do not disconnect the wire harness from the alternator.
6. Remove the air pump front bracket, and the exhaust pipe from the manifold. Remove the air hose from the diverter valve and remove the EGR tube to bell housing screw.
7. Disengage the remaining wires to the electrical units of the cylinder head, marking the wires for connection during assembly.
8. Disengage the fuel line at the bottom of the intake mani-

Fig. 51 Cylinder head bolt tightening sequence—4–121 engine

fold, and remove the screw from the bottom of the manifold bracket.

9. Disconnect the power brake vacuum hose. Remove the remaining fuel vapor control hoses, PCV hoses and the remaining vacuum lines.
10. Disconnect the accelerator cable.
11. Remove the coolant inlet and outlet hoses from the intake manifold.
12. Remove the cylinder head cover. Loosen and remove the head bolts. Loosen the bolts in the reverse order of the tightening sequence, in two passes. Remove the cylinder head, manifolds and carburetor as a unit.
13. Clean the machined surfaces of the cylinder head and the engine block. With a straight edge and feeler gauge, check the flatness of the mating surfaces. There should not be a distortion of over 0.002 in. (0.051mm) on both surfaces.
14. After the necessary services have been done to the cylinder head and/or the block assembly, prepare the mating surfaces by cleaning thoroughly.

❊❊ CAUTION

The EPA warns that prolonged contact with used engine oil may cause a number of skin disorders, including cancer! You should make every effort to minimize your exposure to used engine oil. Protective gloves should be worn when changing the oil. Wash your hands and any other exposed skin areas as soon as possible after exposure to used engine oil. Soap and water, or waterless hand cleaner should be used.

To install:
15. Install a new head gasket, and place the head on the block with the aid of locating dowels. Torque the cylinder head according to the torque sequence illustration, and in three stages.
16. Install the coolant inlet and outlet hoses on the intake manifold.
17. Connect the accelerator cable.
18. Connect the power brake vacuum hose. Install the fuel vapor control hoses, PCV hoses, and the vacuum lines.

19. Attach the fuel line at the bottom of the intake manifold, and install the screw in the bottom of the manifold bracket.

20. Connect the wires to the electrical units of the cylinder head.

21. Install the air pump front bracket, and the exhaust pipe at the manifold. Install the air hose at the diverter valve and install the EGR tube-to-bell housing screw.

22. Install the fan belt, fan blades, spacer and pulley. Install the air pump and also the alternator pivot bolt.

23. Install the accessory drive belts, camshaft drive belt cover, and the camshaft drive belt.

24. Install the radiator hoses, radiator bypass hose and the heater hoses.

25. Install the air cleaner assembly, vacuum hoses and flexible hoses at the cylinder head area.

26. Fill the cooling system and connect the negative battery cable.

27. Temporarily install the head cover. Start the engine and allow it to warm up for five minutes.

28. When the engine has warmed up to operating temperature, stop the engine and remove the top engine cover.

29. Following the head torque sequence, loosen the first head bolt ⅛ of a turn and retorque the bolt to 80 ft.lb. Proceed to the second bolt and repeat the procedure for each head bolt until all the bolts have been retorqued to the new specification.

30. Check the engine for leakage.

4-150 Engine

▶ **See Figures 52 and 53**

1. Disconnect the battery ground.
2. Drain the cooling system.

✳✳ CAUTION

When draining engine coolant, keep in mind that cats and dogs are attracted to ethylene glycol antifreeze and could drink any that is left in an uncovered container or in puddles on the ground. This will prove fatal in sufficient quantity. Always drain coolant into a sealable container. Coolant should be reused unless it is contaminated or is several years old.

3. Disconnect the hoses at the thermostat housing.
4. Remove the air cleaner.
5. Remove the rocker arm cover. The cover seal is RTV sealer. Break the seal with a clean putty knife or razor blade. Don't attempt to remove the cover until the seal is broken. To remove the cover, pry where indicated at the bolt holes.
6. Remove the rocker arms. Keep them in order!
7. Remove the pushrods. Keep them in order!
8. Remove the power steering pump bracket.
9. Suspend the pump out of the way.
10. Remove the intake and exhaust manifolds.
11. Remove the air conditioning compressor drive belt.
12. Loosen the alternator drive belt.
13. Remove the the compressor/alternator bracket mounting bolt.
14. Unbolt the compressor and suspend it out of the way. Do not disconnect the refrigerant lines!
15. Remove the spark plugs.
16. Disconnect the temperature sending unit wire.
17. Remove the head bolts.

Fig. 52 Cylinder head bolt tightening sequence—4–150 engine

Fig. 53 Some head bolts on 4–150 engines are defective. If they are broken they must be replaced

18. Lift the head off the engine and place it on a clean workbench.

19. Remove the head gasket.

➡**Some head bolts used on the spark plug side of the 1984 4-150 were improperly hardened and may break under the head during service or at head installation while torquing the bolts. Engines with the defective bolts are serial numbers 310U06 through 310U14. Whenever a broken bolts is found, replace all bolts on the spark plug side of the head with bolt #400 6593.**

20. Thoroughly clean the gasket mating surfaces. Remove all traces of old gasket material. Remove all carbon deposits from the combustion chambers. Lay a straightedge across the head and check for flatness. Total deviation should not exceed 0.001 in. (0.0254mm).

To install:

21. Do not apply sealant to the head or block. Coat both sides of the gasket with sealer. The gasket should be stamped **TOP** for installation. Place the gasket on the block.

22. Install the head on the block.

23. Coat the bolt labeled 8 in the torque sequence illustration, with Permatex #2®, or equivalent. Install all the bolts. Tighten the bolts in three equal steps, in the sequence shown, to 85 ft.lb. Torque #8 to 75 ft.lb.

24. Connect the temperature sending unit wire.

25. Install the spark plugs.

26. Install the compressor.

27. Install the compressor/alternator bracket mounting bolt.

28. Adjust the alternator drive belt.

29. Install the air conditioning compressor drive belt.

30. Install the intake and exhaust manifolds.

31. Install the power steering pump bracket.

32. Install the pushrods. Keep them in order!

33. Install the rocker arms. Keep them in order!

34. Thoroughly clean the mating surfaces of the head and rocker cover. Run a ⅛ in. (3.175mm) bead of RTV sealer along the length of the sealing surface of the head. Position the cover on the head within 10 minutes of applying the sealer. Torque the cover bolts, in a crisscross pattern, to 55 in.lb.

35. Install the air cleaner.

36. Connect the hoses at the thermostat housing.

37. Connect the battery ground.

38. Fill the cooling system.

4-151 Engine

▶ **See Figure 54**

➡ **The 4-151 rocker cover is sealed with RTV silicone gasket material. Do not use a conventional gasket.**

1. Drain the cooling system and disconnect the hoses at the thermostat housing.

✳✳ CAUTION

When draining engine coolant, keep in mind that cats and dogs are attracted by the ethylene glycol antifreeze and could drink any that is left in an uncovered container or in puddles on the ground. This will prove fatal in sufficient quantity. Always drain the coolant into a sealable container. Coolant should be reused unless it is contaminated or several years old.

2. Remove the cylinder head cover (valve cover), the gasket, the rocker arm assembly, and the pushrods.

3. Remove the intake and exhaust manifold from the cylinder head.

4. Disconnect the spark plug wires and remove the spark plugs to avoid damaging them.

5. Disconnect the temperature sending unit wire, ignition coil and bracket assembly and battery ground cable from the engine.

6. Remove the cylinder head bolts, the cylinder head and gasket from the block.

7. Thoroughly clean the gasket mating surfaces. Remove all traces of old gasket material. Remove all carbon deposits from the combustion chambers. Lay a straightedge across the head and check for flatness. Total deviation should not exceed 0.001 in. (0.0254mm).

To install:

8. Do not apply sealant to the head or block. Coat both sides of the gasket with sealer. The gasket should be stamped **TOP** installation. Place the gasket on the block.

9. Install the head on the block. Insert the bolts and tighten them, in sequence, to the proper torque.

10. Install the pushrods and the rocker arm assembly.

11. Install the intake and exhaust manifold on the cylinder head.

12. Install the spark plugs and connect the spark plug wires.

13. Connect the temperature sending unit wire, ignition coil and bracket assembly and battery ground cable at the engine.

14. Connect the hoses at the thermostat housing.

15. Thoroughly clean the mating surfaces of the head and rocker cover. Run a ⅛ in. (3.175mm) bead of RTV sealer along the length of the sealing surface of the head, inboard of the bolt holes. Position the cover on the head within 10 minutes of applying the sealer. Torque the cover bolts, in a crisscross pattern, to 55 in.lb.

16. Fill the cooling system.

6-232 and 258 Engines

▶ **See Figure 55**

➡ **On Pacers, run the wipers to the center of the windshield to ease valve cover removal.**

Fig. 54 Cylinder head bolt tightening sequence—4–151 engine

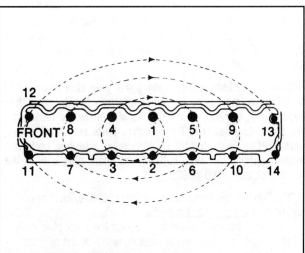

Fig. 55 Cylinder head bolt tightening sequence—6-cylinder engines

1. Drain the cooling system and disconnect the hoses at the thermostat housing.

✳✳ CAUTION

When draining engine coolant, keep in mind that cats and dogs are attracted to ethylene glycol antifreeze and could drink any that is left in an uncovered container or in puddles on the ground. This will prove fatal in sufficient quantity. Always drain coolant into a sealable container. Coolant should be reused unless it is contaminated or is several years old.

2. Remove the cylinder head cover (valve cover), the gasket, the rocker arm assembly, and the pushrods.

➡**The pushrods must be replaced in their original positions.**

3. Remove the intake and exhaust manifold from the cylinder head.

If equipped with power steering, remove the power steering pump bracket and air guard pump and set them aside. Don't disconnect the hoses.

4. Disconnect the spark plug wires and the spark plugs to avoid damaging them.

5. Disconnect the temperature sending unit wire, ignition coil and bracket assembly from the engine.

If the vehicle is equipped with air conditioning, remove the drive belt idler pulley bracket from the cylinder head. Loosen the alternator drive belt and remove the bolts from the compressor mounting bracket. Set the compressor aside, all hoses attached.

6. Remove the cylinder head bolts, the cylinder head and gasket from the block.

To install:

7. Thoroughly clean the gasket mating surfaces. Remove all traces of old gasket material. Remove all carbon deposits from the combustion chambers. Lay a straightedge across the head and check for flatness. Total deviation should not exceed 0.001 in. (0.0254mm).

8. Do not apply sealant to the head or block. Coat both sides of the gasket with sealer. The gasket should be stamped **TOP** for installation. Place the gasket on the block.

9. Install the head on the block. Insert the bolts and tighten them, in sequence, to the proper torque, in three progressive passes. Torque all bolts to 85 ft. lbs., except #11 in the torque sequence, which should be coated with sealer and torqued to 75 ft. lbs.

➡**Some head bolts used on the spark plug side of the 1984 6-258 were improperly hardened and may break under the head during service or at head installation while torquing the bolts. Engines with the defective bolts are serial numbers 310C06 through 310C14. Whenever a broken bolts is found, replace all seven bolts on the spark plug side of the head with bolt #400 6593.**

10. Connect the temperature sending unit wire, ignition coil and bracket assembly at the engine.

11. Install the spark plugs and connect the spark plug wires.

12. Install the intake and exhaust manifold on the cylinder head.

13. Install the the rocker arm assembly, and the pushrods.

➡**The pushrods must be replaced in their original positions.**

14. Install the cylinder head cover (valve cover) and the gasket.

15. Connect the hoses at the thermostat housing.

16. Fill the cooling system.

8-304, 360 and 401 Engines

▶ **See Figure 56**

1. Drain the cooling system and cylinder block.

✳✳ CAUTION

When draining engine coolant, keep in mind that cats and dogs are attracted to ethylene glycol antifreeze and could drink any that is left in an uncovered container or in puddles on the ground. This will prove fatal in sufficient quantity. Always drain coolant into a sealable container. Coolant should be reused unless it is contaminated or is several years old.

2. When removing the right cylinder head, it may be necessary to remove the heater core housing from the firewall.

3. Remove the valve cover(s) and gasket(s).

4. Remove the rocker arm assemblies and the pushrods.

➡**The valve train components must be replaced in their original positions.**

5. Remove the spark plugs to avoid damaging them.

6. Remove the intake manifold with the carburetor still attached.

7. Remove the exhaust pipes at the flange of the exhaust manifold. When replacing the exhaust pipes it is advisable to install new gaskets at the flange.

8. Loosen all of the drive belts.

9. Disconnect the battery ground cable and alternator bracket from the right cylinder head.

10. Disconnect the air pump and power steering pump brackets from the left cylinder head.

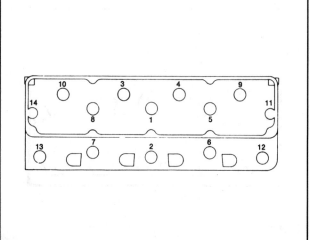

Fig. 56 Cylinder head bolt tightening sequence—V8 engines

Unfasten the cylinder head bolts in the designated bolts . . .

. . . then use a scraper to remove any remaining gasket material

. . . then remove the cylinder head from the engine block

Use a torque wrench to tighten the cylinder head bolts in sequence to the proper specification

Remove the cylinder head gasket . . .

11. Remove the cylinder head bolts and lift the head(s) from the cylinder block.

12. Remove the cylinder head gasket from the head or the block.

✳✳ CAUTION

The EPA warns that prolonged contact with used engine oil may cause a number of skin disorders, including cancer! You should make every effort to minimize your exposure to used engine oil. Protective gloves should be worn when changing the oil. Wash your hands and any other exposed skin areas as soon as possible after exposure to used engine oil. Soap and water, or waterless hand cleaner should be used.

To install:

13. Thoroughly clean the gasket mating surfaces. Remove all traces of old gasket material. Remove all carbon deposits from the combustion chambers. Lay a straightedge across the head and check for flatness. Total deviation should not exceed 0.001 in. (0.0254mm).

14. Do not apply sealant to the head or block. Coat both sides of the gasket with sealer. The gasket should be stamped **TOP** for installation. Place the gasket on the block.

15. Install the head on the block. Insert the bolts and tighten them, in sequence, to the proper torque, in three progressive passes. Torque all bolts to 80 ft.lb.

16. Connect the air pump and power steering pump brackets to the left cylinder head.

17. Connect the battery ground cable and alternator bracket to the right cylinder head.

Check the cylinder head for warpage along the center using a straightedge and a feeler gauge

Use a gasket scraper to remove the bulk of the old head gasket from the mating surface

An electric drill equipped with a wire wheel will expedite complete gasket removal

18. Adjust all of the drive belts.

19. Install the exhaust pipes at the flange of the exhaust manifold. When replacing the exhaust pipes it is advisable to install new gaskets at the flange.

20. Install the intake manifold with the carburetor still attached.

21. Install the spark plugs.

22. Install the rocker arm assemblies and the pushrods.

➡**The valve train components must be replaced in their original positions.**

23. Install the valve cover(s) and gasket(s).

24. Install the heater core housing on the firewall.

25. Fill the cooling system and cylinder block.

Valves and Springs

➡**Fabricate a valve arrangement board to use when you remove the valves, which will indicate the port in which each valve was originally installed (and which cylinder head on V8 models). Also note that the valve keys, rotators, caps, etc. should be arranged in a manner which will allow you to install them on the valve on which they were originally used.**

REMOVAL

4-121 Engine

▸ **See Figure 57**

1. Remove the cylinder head.

2. Make a wooden fixture according to the dimensions shown in the accompanying illustration. Attach the fixture to the bottom of the head with ⅜ in. × ¾ in. (10mm × 83mm) bolts and

Fig. 57 Fabricate a cylinder head fixture and attach it to the of the head—4–121 engine

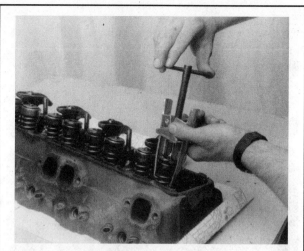

Use a valve spring compressor tool to relieve spring tension from the valve caps

nuts, to hold the valves against their seats while the valve springs are compressed.

3. Remove the camshaft from the head.

4. Loosely install a nut to one camshaft bearing stud next to each valve.

5. Lift the tappets from their bores, keeping them in order for installation.

6. Place a 21mm deep socket on each retainer and strike it sharply with a hammer to loosen the valve locks.

7. Using spring compressor J-26809, compress the valve springs. Remove the locks, retainers, springs and oil deflectors.

8. When all of the parts are removed from all the valves, remove the home made retaining tool and remove the valves. Keep them in order for installation.

Except 4-121 Engine

1. The head must be removed from the engine.

2. Remove the rocker arm assemblies.

3. Using a spring compressor, compress the valve springs and remove the keepers (locks). Relax the compressor and remove the washers or rotators, the springs, and the lower washers (on some engines). Keep all parts in order.

A magnet may be helpful in removing the valve keepers

Be careful not to lose the valve keepers

Remove the spring from the valve stem in order to access the seal

Remove the valve stem seal from the cylinder head

Invert the cylinder head and withdraw the valve from the cylinder head bore

INSPECTION & REFACING

♦ **See Figure 58**

1. Clean the valves with a wire wheel.
2. Inspect the valves for warping, cracks or wear.
3. The valves may be refaced if not worn or pitted excessively.
4. Using a valve guide cleaner chucked into a drill, clean all of the valve guides. Check the valve stem diameter and the guide diameter with micrometers. The guide must be reamed and an insert pressed in, or they may be knurled to bring up interior metal, restoring their diameter. Oversized valve stems are available to compensate for wear.

➡**AMC recommends that, if the 4-121 guides are worn excessively, the head should be replaced. Inserts are not available.**

5. Install each valve into its respective port (guide) of the cylinder head.

A dial gauge may be used to check valve stem-to-guide clearance

Fig. 58 Check the valve stem-to-guide clearance using a dial indicator

Valve stems may be rolled on a flat surface to check for bends

A wire wheel may be used to clean the combustion chambers of carbon deposits

Use a micrometer to check the valve stem diameter

6. Mount a dial indicator so that the stem is at 90° to the valve stem, as close to the valve guide as possible.

7. Move the valve off its seat, and measure the valve guide-to-stem clearance by rocking the stem back and forth to actuate the dial indicator.

8. In short, the refacing of valves and other such head work is most easily done at a machine shop. The quality and time saved easily justifies the cost.

9. Inspect the springs for obvious signs of wear. Check their installed height and tension using the values in the Valve Specifications Chart in this section.

REFACING

▶ **See Figures 59, 60, 61, 62 and 63**

✳✳ CAUTION

On the 4-121, reface only the intake valves. Never attempt to reface the exhaust valves. Exhaust valves are sodium-filled and refacing could be hazardous! When refacing the intake valves, the face width should not exceed 3.5mm.

Using a valve grinder, resurface the valves according to specifications in this chapter. All machine work should be performed by a competent, professional machine shop.

➡**Valve face angle is not always identical to valve seat angle.**

A minimum margin of 1/32 in. (0.79375mm) should remain after grinding the valve. The valve stem top should also be squared and resurfaced, by placing the stem in the V-block of the grinder, and turning it while pressing lightly against the grinding wheel. Be sure to chamfer the edge of the tip so that the squared edges don't dig into the rocker arm or cam.

Fig. 60 Valve grinding is usually performed with a machine

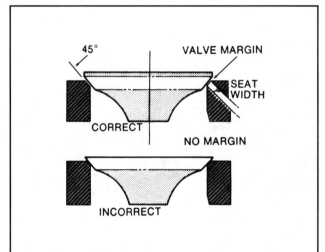

Fig. 61 Sectional view of incorrect and correct valve seat width and centering

Fig. 59 Typical critical valve dimensions

Fig. 62 Use a dial gauge to check the valve seat concentricity

Fig. 63 A hand reamer may be used on the valve seats

LAPPING

♦ See Figures 64 and 65

This procedure should be performed after the valves and seats have been machined, to insure that each valve mates to each seat precisely.

1. Invert the cylinder head, lightly lubricate the valve stems, and install the valves in the head as numbered.
2. Coat valve seats with fine grinding compound, and attach the lapping tool suction cup to a valve head.

➡Moisten the suction cup.

3. Rotate the tool between your palms, changing position and lifting the tool often to prevent grooving.
4. Lap the valve until a smooth, polished seat is evident.
5. Remove the valve and tool, and rinse away all traces of grinding compound.

Fig. 65 A homemade valve lapping tool can be fabricated

VALVE SPRING TESTING

♦ See Figures 66 and 66A

Place the spring on a flat surface next to a square. Measure the height of the spring, and rotate it against the edge of the square to measure distortion. If spring height varies (by comparison) by more than $\frac{1}{16}$ in. (1.5875mm) or if distortion exceeds $\frac{1}{16}$ in. (1.5875mm), replace the spring.

In addition to evaluating the spring as above, test the spring pressure at the installed and compressed (installed height minus valve lift) height using a valve spring tester. Spring pressure should be ± 1 lb. of all other springs in either position.

Fig. 64 Lapping the valves by hand

Use a caliper gauge to check the valve spring free-length

Check the valve spring for squareness on a flat service; a carpenter's square can be used

Fig. 66 A carpenters square may be used to check the spring free length and squareness

Fig. 66a Check the valve spring installed height using a spring testing tool

INSTALLATION

1. Coat all parts with clean engine oil. Install all parts in their respective locations. The spring is installed with the closely wound coils toward the valve head. Always use new valve seals.

2. Use a spring compressor to install the keepers and slowly release the compressor after the keepers are in place.

3. Release the spring compressor. Tap the end of the stem with a wood mallet to insure that the keepers are securely in place.

4. Install all other parts in reverse order of removal.

Valve Seats

INSPECTION AND REFACING

♦ See Figure 67

All engines have integral seats. Check the condition of the seats for excessive wear, pitting or cracks. Remove all traces of deposits from the seats. The seats may be refaced with a special grinding tool, to the dimensions shown in the Valve Specifications Chart.

Fig. 67 Installing the valve stem seals

Oil Pan

REMOVAL & INSTALLATION

➡It is much easier to remove the engine in most cases.

4-121 Engine

♦ See Figure 68

1. Raise the car and support it with stands. Drain the oil.

2. Install an engine lifting device and support weight of the engine, while removing the engine bracket to mount cushion nuts. Loosen the strut and bracket screws.

Fig. 68 Exploded view of the engine lubrication system components—4–121 engine

3. Raise the engine approximately 2 in. and remove the cross-member to sill attaching parts.

4. Remove the steering gear idler bracket from the frame rail.

5. Pry the crossmember down and insert wooden blocks between the crossmember and the side sill on both sides.

6. Remove the oil pan and clean the gasket from the mating surfaces of the block and oil pan.

To install:

7. Cement the gasket to the engine block; use sealer between side gaskets and end seals.

8. Install the oil pan. Tighten the side pan bolts to 80 in.lb. and the end bolts to 90 in.lb.

9. Install the steering gear idler bracket on the frame rail.

10. Remove the blocks and install the crossmember-to-sill attaching parts.

11. Tighten the strut and bracket screws. Install the engine bracket-to-mount cushion nuts.

12. Replace the engine oil.

4-150 Engine

♦ See Figure 69

1. Turn the steering wheel to full left lock. Support the engine with a hoist. Raise and support the car at the side sills. Disconnect the engine ground cable. Drain the oil.

2. Unbolt the steering idler arm at the side sill, and the engine cushions at the brackets.

3. Remove the sway bar, if equipped. Remove the front crossmember-to-side sill bolts and pull the crossmember down. Remove the right engine bracket. Loosen but do not remove the strut rods at the lower control arm.

4. Disconnect the exhaust pipe at the manifold.

5. Remove the starter.

6. Remove the bell housing access plate.

7. Unbolt and remove the oil pan.

1. Front seal
2. Rear seal
3. Gaskets

Fig. 69 Common oil pan, gasket and seal—4–150 engine

To install:

8. Clean the gasket surfaces thoroughly.

9. Install a replacement seal at the bottom of the timing case cover and at the rear bearing cap.

10. Using new gaskets coated with sealer, install the pan and torque the bolts to 10 ft. lbs.

11. Install all other parts in reverse order of removal.

4-151 Engine

♦ See Figure 70

1. Follow Steps 1 through 6 of the 4-121 procedure.

2. To install the pan, thoroughly clean all the gasket mating surfaces.

Fig. 70 Lubrication system components—4-151 engine

3. Install a new rear oil pan gasket in the rear main bearing cap. Apply a small quantity of RTV silicone sealer into the depressions where the rear pan gasket engages the block.

4. Install a new from oil pan gasket onto the timing gear cover. Press the tips into the holes in the cover.

5. Install the side gaskets onto the block, not the oil pan. Retain them with a thin film of grease. Apply a ¼ in. (6mm) long bead of RTV silicone sealer to the split lines of the front and side gaskets; the bead should be ⅛ in. (3mm) wide.

6. Install the oil pan onto the engine. The timing cover bolts should be installed last. They are installed at an angle; the holes will line up after the rest of the pan bolts have been snugged down. The bolts should be tightened to 6 ft. lbs. all around. The rest of installation is the reverse of removal.

6- and 8-Cylinder Engines

EXCEPT PACER

> ✳✳ **CAUTION**
>
> **The EPA warns that prolonged contact with used engine oil may cause a number of skin disorders, including cancer! You should make every effort to minimize your exposure to used engine oil. Protective gloves should be worn when changing the oil. Wash your hands and any other exposed skin areas as soon as possible after exposure to used engine oil. Soap and water, or waterless hand cleaner should be used.**

1. Turn the steering wheel to full left lock. Support the engine with a hoist. Raise and support the car at the side sills. Disconnect the engine ground cable.

2. Unbolt the steering idler arm at the side sill, and the engine cushions at the brackets.

3. Remove the sway bar, if equipped. Remove the front crossmember-to-side sill bolts and pull the crossmember down. Remove the right engine bracket. Loosen but do not remove the strut rods at the lower control arm.

4. Drain the engine oil.

5. Remove the starter.

6. Remove the oil pan bolts and pan. Remove the front and rear seats, and clean the gasket surfaces.

To install:

7. Install the new pan front seal to the timing cover, and apply sealer to end tabs. Cement new pan side gaskets to the block, and apply sealer to the ends of the gasket.

8. Coat the inside surface of the new rear seal with soap, and apply sealer to end tabs. Install the seal in the rear main cap.

9. Coat front and rear seal contact surfaces with engine oil, and install the pan. The remainder of the installation is the reverse of removal.

PACER

▶ **See Figure 71**

1. Drain the engine oil.

2. Install an engine lifting device and support the weight of the engine.

3. Disconnect the steering shaft flexible joint and hold it aside with a length of wire.

4. Raise and support the car.

5. Remove the front engine support through bolts.

6. Disconnect the front brake lines at the wheel cylinders.

7. Disconnect the upper ball joints from the spindles. Make sure the shock absorbers are attached securely.

8. Remove the upper control arm and move it aside.

9. Support the front crossmember with a jack.

10. Remove the nuts from the front crossmember rear mounts and swing the crossmember down and forward.

11. Follow Steps 5–9 of the preceding 6-cylinder and V8 procedure.

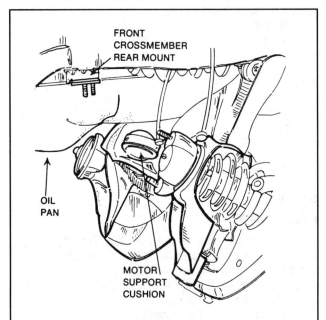

Fig. 71 Disconnect the front engine support mounts to gain access to the oil pan on Pacer models

To install:

12. Install and assemble the remaining components in the reverse order of removal, tightening the ¼ in. oil pan screws to 7 ft. lbs., the ⁵⁄₁₆ in. oil pan screws to 11 ft. lbs., the crossmember

attaching nuts to 50 ft. lbs., the upper control arm cross shaft bolt and nut to 60 ft. lbs., and the engine mount and steering shaft nuts to 25 ft. lbs. Fill the crankcase with oil and bleed the brakes.

Oil Pump

REMOVAL & INSTALLATION

> **✳✳ WARNING**
>
> **Anytime the oil pump cover is removed or the pump disassembled, the pump must be primed by filling the spaces around the gears with petroleum jelly. Do not use grease.**

4-121 Engine

♦ **See Figure 72**

The oil pump is on the lower front of the engine block. It consists of two gears with meshing teeth, one with internal teeth and the other with external teeth. Oil pressure is controlled by a pressure relief valve and spring assembly. The inner gear is driven by the crankshaft at twice the speed of distributor driven oil pumps. To service the oil pump assembly, removal is necessary. Proceed as follows:

1. Remove the fan shroud.
2. Raise the car and support it on stands.
3. Loosen the crankshaft pulley screws but don't remove them.

> **✳✳ CAUTION**
>
> **The EPA warns that prolonged contact with used engine oil may cause a number of skin disorders, including cancer! You should make every effort to minimize your exposure to used engine oil. Protective gloves should be worn when changing the oil. Wash your hands and any other exposed skin areas as soon as possible after exposure to used engine oil. Soap and water, or waterless hand cleaner should be used.**

4. Loosen and remove the power steering pump belt, air conditioner and alternator belt.
5. Remove the crankshaft pulley. Attach a crankshaft sprocket wrench using all of the pulley screws and remove the crankshaft screw.
6. Remove the camshaft drive sprocket from the crankshaft.
7. Remove the oil pump screws and the front oil pan screws and remove the oil pump by prying in the slots with a large screwdriver.

To install:

8. Replace the gasket and the crankshaft seal. Trim the edges of the gasket.
9. Rotate the crankshaft so the oil pump lugs are either vertical or horizontal.
10. Cut off the oil pan gasket flush with the front of the block.
11. Align the gears of the oil pump with the crankshaft lugs and carefully tap the pump on as far as possible.
12. Apply silicone sealant to the edges of the pump and the oil pan and to the pump sealing surfaces. Tighten the screws to 87 in.lbs.
13. Install the crankshaft seal with a seal installing tool.
14. Install the camshaft drive sprocket and the crankshaft accessory drive pulley, making sure the pins align with the holes. Install the crankshaft screw.
15. Install the camshaft drive belt, belt guard, accessory drive belts and the fan shroud. Start the engine and check for leaks or low oil pressure, and adjust the timing.

> **✳✳ WARNING**
>
> **An oil filter with a built-in bypass valve must be used on the 4-121 engine.**

4-150 Engine

♦ **See Figure 73**

> **✳✳ CAUTION**
>
> **The EPA warns that prolonged contact with used engine oil may cause a number of skin disorders, including cancer! You should make every effort to minimize your exposure to used engine oil. Protective gloves should be worn when changing the oil. Wash your hands and any other exposed skin areas as soon as possible after exposure to used engine oil. Soap and water, or waterless hand cleaner should be used.**

1. Disconnect the battery ground.
2. Raise and support the car on jackstands.
3. Drain the oil.
4. Disconnect the exhaust pipe at the manifold.
5. Remove the starter.
6. Remove the bellhousing access plate.
7. Unbolt and remove the oil pan.

Fig. 72 Exploded view of the oil pump components—4-121 engine

1. Bolts
2. Pump body
3. Gasket

Fig. 73 Oil pump components—4–150 engine

To install:

8. Clean the gasket surfaces thoroughly.

9. Install a replacement seal at the bottom of the timing case cover and at the rear bearing cap.

10. Using new gaskets coated with sealer, install the pan and torque the bolts to 10 ft. lbs.

11. Install all other parts in reverse order of removal.

4-151 Engine

▸ **See Figure 74**

✳✳ CAUTION

The EPA warns that prolonged contact with used engine oil may cause a number of skin disorders, including cancer! You should make every effort to minimize your exposure to used engine oil. Protective gloves should be worn when changing the oil. Wash your hands and any other exposed skin areas as soon as possible after exposure to used engine oil. Soap and water, or waterless hand cleaner should be used.

1. Remove the engine oil pan. Refer to the 4-151 oil pan removal procedure in this section.

2. Remove the two bolts and one nut, and carefully lower the pump.

Fig. 74 Exploded view of the oil pump assembly—4–151 engine

3. Install in reverse order. To ensure immediate oil pressure on start-up, the oil pump gear cavity can be packed with petroleum jelly.

6-232 and 258 Engines
▶ **See Figure 75**

The oil pump is driven by the distributor driveshaft. Oil pump replacement does not, however affect distributor timing because the drive gear remains in mesh with the camshaft gear.

1. Drain the oil and remove the oil pan.

2. Remove the oil pump attaching screws. Remove the pump and gasket from the engine block.

3. Installation is the reverse removal. Prime the pump before installation; use a new cover gasket.

8-304, 360 and 401 Engines
▶ **See Figure 76**

✳✳ CAUTION

The EPA warns that prolonged contact with used engine oil may cause a number of skin disorders, including cancer! You should make every effort to minimize your exposure to used engine oil. Protective gloves should be worn when changing the oil. Wash your hands and any other exposed skin areas as soon as possible after exposure to used engine oil. Soap and water, or waterless hand cleaner should be used.

Fig. 75 Oil pump and filter components and location—6-cylinder engines

Fig. 76 Exploded view of the oil pump components—V8 engines

The oil pump is located in, and is part of, the timing cover. The pump is driven by the distributor driveshaft. Oil pump replacement does not, however, affect distributor timing.

1. Remove the retaining bolts and separate the oil pump cover, complete with filter and gasket, from the timing cover.

2. The drive gear and shaft and the idler gear will slide out of the timing cover after removal of the pump cover.

3. Prime the pump before installation, and use a new gasket.

Crankshaft Pulley (Vibration Damper)

REMOVAL & INSTALLATION

♦ **See Figure 77**

1. Remove the fan shroud, as required. If necessary, drain the cooling system and remove the radiator. Remove drive belts from pulley.

✳✳ CAUTION

When draining engine coolant, keep in mind that cats and dogs are attracted to ethylene glycol antifreeze and could drink any that is left in an uncovered container or in puddles on the ground. This will prove fatal in sufficient quantity. Always drain coolant into a sealable container. Coolant should be reused unless it is contaminated or is several years old.

J-21791

Fig. 77 Use a puller to separate the damper from the crankshaft

2. On those engines with a separate pulley, remove the retaining bolts and separate the pulley from the vibration damper.

3. Remove the vibration damper/pulley retaining bolt from the crankshaft end.

4. Using a puller, remove the damper/pulley from the crankshaft.

5. Upon installation, align the key slot of the pulley hub to the crankshaft key. Complete the assembly in the reverse order of removal. Torque the retaining bolts to specifications.

Timing Case Cover

REMOVAL & INSTALLATION

4-150 Engine

➡ **Special tools are needed for this job.**

◗ **See Figures 78, 79, 80 and 81**

1. Remove the drive belts and fan shroud.
2. Unscrew the vibration damper bolts and washer.
3. Using a puller, remove the vibration damper.
4. Remove the fan assembly. If the fan is equipped with a fan clutch do not lay it down! If you lay it down, the fluid will leak out of the clutch and irreversibly damage the fan.
5. Disconnect the battery ground.

1. Pulley
2. Timing cover
3. Seal

Fig. 78 Timing cover assembly components—4–150 engine

Fig. 79 Typical oil pan gaskets—4–150 engine

Fig. 80 Install the timing cover centering tool on the crankshaft before tightening the cover bolts

Fig. 81 Use tool J-9163-2 to install the timing cover oil seal—4–150 engine

6. Remove the air conditioning compressor/alternator bracket assembly and lay it out of the way. Do not disconnect the refrigerant lines!
7. Unbolt the cover from the block and oil pan. Remove the cover and front seal.
8. Cut off the oil pan side gasket end tabs and oil pan front seal tabs (indicated by the arrows in the illustration).
To install:
9. Clean all gasket mating surfaces thoroughly.
10. Remove the seal from the cover.
11. Apply sealer to both sides of the new case cover gasket and position it on the block.
12. Cut the end tabs off the new oil pan side gaskets corresponding to those cut off the original gasket and attach the tabs to the oil pan with gasket cement.
13. Coat the front cover seal end tab recesses generously with RTV sealant and position the side seal in the cover.

14. Apply engine oil to the seal-to-pan contact surface.

15. Position the cover on the block.

16. Insert alignment tool J-22248 or its equivalent into the crankshaft opening in the cover.

17. Install the cover bolts. Tighten the cover-to-blockbolts to 5 ft. lbs.; the cover-to-pan bolts to 11 ft. lbs.

18. Remove the alignment tool and position the new front seal on the tool with the seal lip facing outward. Apply a light film of sealer to the outside diameter of the seal. Lightly coat the crankshaft with clean engine oil.

19. Position the tool and seal over the end of the crankshaft and insert the Draw Screw J-9163-2 or its equivalent into the installation tool.

20. Tighten the nut until the tool just contacts the cover.

21. Remove the tools and apply a light film of engine oil on the vibration damper hub contact surface of the seal.

22. With the key inserted in the keyway in the crankshaft, install the vibration damper, washer and bolt. Lubricate the bolt and tighten it to 108 ft.lb.

23. Install all other parts in reverse order of removal.

4-151 Engine

▶ **See Figures 82, 83, 84 and 85**

1. Disconnect the battery ground.

2. Remove the crankshaft pulley hub.

3. Remove the alternator bracket.

4. Remove the fan and radiator shroud.

5. Remove the oil pan-to-timing case cover bolts.

6. Pull the cover forward just enough to allow cutting the oil pan front seal flush with the block on both sides of the cover. Use a sharp knife or razor.

7. Remove the front cover.

To install:

8. Clean the gasket surface on the block and cover.

9. Cut the tabs from the new oil pan front seal.

10. Install the seal on the cover, pressing the tips into the holes provided in the cover.

11. Coat a new gasket with sealer and place on the cover.

12. Apply a ⅛ in. (3.175mm) bead of RTV sealant to the joint formed at the oil pan and block.

Fig. 83 Use a razor to cut the oil pan seal as indicated—4–151 engine

Fig. 84 Apply a 1/8 in. bead of sealer to the areas indicated on the block—4–151 engine

Fig. 82 Apply sealer to the locations indicated before installing the front cover—4–151 engine

Fig. 85 Place an alignment tool in the cover seal and tighten the bolts—4–151 engine

13. Install an aligning tool such as tool J-23042 or its equivalent in the timing case cover seal.

➡**It is important that an aligning tool is used to avoid seal damage and to ensure a tight, even seal fit.**

14. Position the cover on the block and partially retighten the two oil pan-to-cover bolts.

15. Install the remaining bolts, and tighten all bolts to 45 inch lbs.

16. Install all other parts in reverse order of removal. Tighten the fan assembly bolts to 18 ft. lbs.

6-232 and 258 Engines

COVER REMOVED

◆ See Figures 86, 87 and 88

1. Remove the drive belts, engine fan and hub assembly, the accessory pulley, and vibration damper.

2. Remove the oil pan to timing chain cover screws and the screws that attach the cover to the block.

3. Raise the timing chain cover just high enough to detach the retaining nibs of the oil pan neoprene seal from the bottom side of the cover. This must be done to prevent pulling the seal end tabs away from the tongues of the oil pan gaskets which would cause a leak.

4. Remove the timing chain cover and gasket from the engine.

5. Use a razor blade to cut off the oil pan seal end tabs flush with the front face of the cylinder block and remove the seal. Clean the timing chain cover, oil pan, and cylinder block surfaces.

To install:

6. Apply seal compound (Perfect Seal, or equivalent) to both sides of the replacement timing case cover gasket and position the gasket on cylinder block.

7. Cut the end tabs off the replacement oil pan gasket corresponding to the pieces cut off the original gasket. Cement these pieces on the oil pan.

8. Coat the oil pan seal end tabs generously with Permatex® No. 2 or equivalent, and position the seal on the timing case cover.

Fig. 87 Use tool J-9163 with the alignment tool to install the seal—6-cylinder 258 engine

Fig. 88 Remove the cover seal using tool J-9256 or its equivalent—6-cylinder 258 engine

9. Position the timing case cover on the engine. Place the timing case cover alignment tool and seal installer J-22248 or its equivalent in the crankshaft opening of the cover.

10. Install the cover-to-block screws and oil pan-to-cover screws. Tighten the cover-to-block screws to 60 inch lbs. and the oil pan-to-cover screws to 11 ft. lbs.

11. Remove the cover aligning tool and position the replacement oil seal aligning tool in the case. Position the replacement oil seal on the tool with the seal lip facing outward. Apply a light film of perfect seal, or equivalent, on the outside diameter of the seal.

12. Insert the draw screw from Tool J-9163 or its equivalent into the seal installing tool. Tighten the nut against the tool until the tool contacts the cover.

Fig. 86 Exploded view of the timing case cover and its related components—6-cylinder engine

13. Remove the tools and apply a light film of engine oil to the seal lip.

14. Install the vibration damper and tighten the retaining screw to 80 ft. lbs.

15. Install the damper pulley. Tighten the capscrews to 20 ft. lbs.

16. Install the engine fan and hub assembly.

17. Install the drive belt(s).

COVER INSTALLED

1. Remove the drive belts.
2. Remove the vibration damper pulley.
3. Remove the vibration damper.
4. Remove the oil seal with Tool J-9256 or its equivalent.
5. Position the replacement oil seal on the timing case cover alignment tool and seal installer J-22248 or its equivalent with the seal lip facing outward. Apply a light film of perfect seal, or equivalent, to the outside diameter of the seal.
6. Insert the draw screw from Tool J-9163 into the seal installing tool. Tighten the nut against the tool until the tool contacts the cover.
7. Remove the tools. Apply a light film of engine oil to the seal lip.
8. Install the vibration damper and tighten the retaining bolt to 80 ft. lbs.
9. Install the damper pulley. Tighten the capscrews to 20 ft. lbs.
10. Install the drive belt(s).

8-304, 360 and 401 Engines

♦ See Figure 89

1. Remove the negative battery cable.
2. Drain the cooling system and disconnect the radiator hoses and by-pass hose.

3. Remove all of the drive belts and the fan and spacer assembly.
4. Remove the alternator and the front portion of the alternator bracket as an assembly.
5. Disconnect the heater hose.
6. Remove the power steering pump and/or the air pump, and the mounting bracket as an assembly. Do not disconnect the power steering hoses.
7. Remove the distributor cap and note the position of the rotor. Remove the distributor. Refer to the distributor removal and installation procedure earlier in this manual.
8. Remove the fuel pump.
9. Remove the vibration damper and pulley.
10. Remove the two front oil pan bolts and the bolts which secure the timing chain cover to the engine block.

➡ The timing gear cover retaining bolts vary in length and must be installed in the same locations from which they were removed.

11. Remove the cover by pulling forward until it is free of the locating dowel pins.

Fig. 89 Exploded view of the timing cover assembly and related components on V8 models through 1976; 1977 models are similar except for seal location

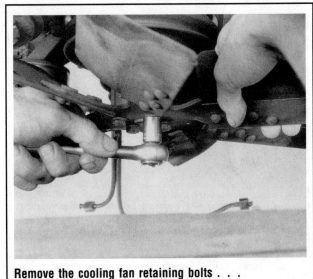

Remove the cooling fan retaining bolts . . .

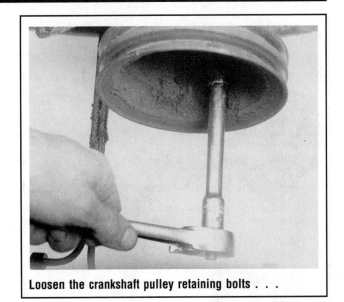

Loosen the crankshaft pulley retaining bolts . . .

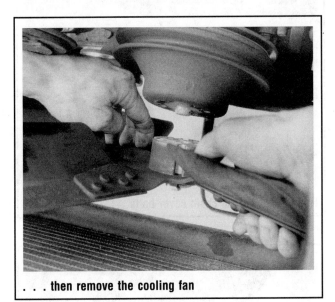

. . . then remove the cooling fan

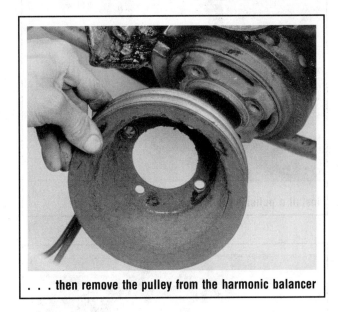

. . . then remove the pulley from the harmonic balancer

Remove the water pump pulley from the vehicle

1. Retaining bolt
2. Harmonic balancer

Remove the retaining bolt from the harmonic balancer

Install a puller on the harmonic balancer . . .

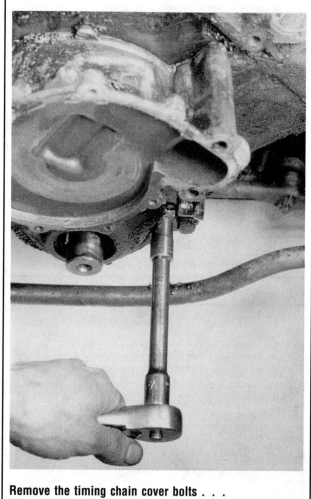

Remove the timing chain cover bolts . . .

. . . then remove the balancer from the engine

. . . then separate the cover from the engine block using a prytool

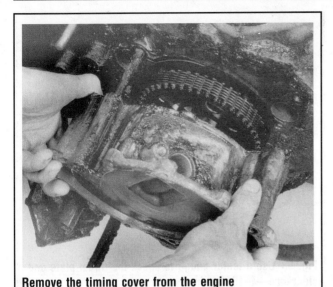

Remove the timing cover from the engine

To install:

12. Clean the gasket surface of the cover and the engine block.

13. Pry out the original seal from inside the timing chain cover and clean the seal bore.

14. Drive the new seal into place from the inside with a block of wood until it contacts the outer flange of the cover.

15. Apply a light film of motor oil to the lips of the new seal.

16. Before reinstalling the timing gear cover, remove the lower locating dowel pin from the engine block. The pin is required for correct alignment of the cover and must either be reused or a replacement dowel pin installed after the cover is in position.

✳✳ CAUTION

The EPA warns that prolonged contact with used engine oil may cause a number of skin disorders, including cancer! You should make every effort to minimize your exposure to used engine oil. Protective gloves should be worn when changing the oil. Wash your hands and any other exposed skin areas as soon as possible after exposure to used engine oil. Soap and water, or waterless hand cleaner should be used.

17. Cut both sides of the oil pan gasket flush with the engine block with a razor blade.

18. Trim a new gasket to correspond to the amount cut off at the oil pan.

19. Apply sealer to both sides of the new gasket and install the gasket on the timing case cover.

20. Install the new front oil pan seal.

21. Align the tongues of the new oil pan gasket pieces with the oil pan seal and cement them into place on the cover.

22. Apply a bead of sealer to the cutoff edges of the original oil pan gaskets.

23. Place the timing case cover into position and install the front oil pan bolts. Tighten the bolts slowly and evenly until the cover aligns with the upper locating dowel.

24. Install the lower dowel through the cover and drive it into the corresponding hole in the engine block.

25. Install the cover retaining bolts in the same locations from which they were removed. Tighten to 25 ft. lbs.

26. Assemble the remaining components in the reverse order of removal.

Timing Chain/Gear and Sprocket/Pulley

REMOVAL & INSTALLATION

4-150 Engine

▶ **See Figures 90, 91 and 92**

1. Remove the timing case cover.

2. Rotate the crankshaft so that the timing marks on the cam and crank sprockets align next to each other, as illustrated.

3. Remove the oil slinger from the crankshaft.

4. Remove the cam sprocket retaining bolt and remove the sprocket and chain. The crank sprocket may also be removed at this time. If the tensioner is to be removed, the oil pan must be removed first.

Fig. 90 Correct timing mark alignment—4–150 engine

Fig. 91 Install the timing chain and sprockets together—4–150 engines

Fig. 92 Timing chain tensioner components include the tensioner lever (1) and block (2)—4–150 engines

Fig. 93 Use a feeler gauge to check the thrust plate end clearance—4–151 engine

✳✳ CAUTION

The EPA warns that prolonged contact with used engine oil may cause a number of skin disorders, including cancer! You should make every effort to minimize your exposure to used engine oil. Protective gloves should be worn when changing the oil. Wash your hands and any other exposed skin areas as soon as possible after exposure to used engine oil. Soap and water, or waterless hand cleaner should be used.

To install:

5. Prior to installation, turn the tensioner lever to the unlock (down) position.

6. Pull the tensioner block toward the tensioner to compress the spring. Hold the block and turn the tensioner lever to the lock (up) position. The camshaft sprocket bolt should be torqued to 50 ft. lbs.

7. Install the sprockets and chain together, as a unit. Make sure the timing marks are aligned.

To verify that the timing chain is correctly installed:

a. Turn the crankshaft to place the camshaft timing mark at approximately the one o'clock position.

b. At this point, there should be a tooth on the crankshaft sprocket meshed with the chain at the three o'clock position.

c. Count the number of timing chain pins between the two timing marks on the right side (your right, facing the engine). There should be 20 pins.

8. Install the oil pan, slinger and timing cover.

4-151 Engine

♦ See Figures 93 and 94

➡Removal of the camshaft gear requires a special adapter #J-971 and the use of a press. Camshaft removal is necessary.

1. Place the adapter on the press and place the camshaft through the opening.

Fig. 94 Correct timing mark alignment—4–151 engine

2. Press the shaft out of the gear using a socket or other suitable tool.

✳✳ WARNING

The thrust plate must be in position so that the Woodruff key does not damage the gear when the shaft is pressed out.

3. To install the gear firmly support the shaft at the back of the front journal in an arbor press using pressplate adapters J-21474-13, J-21795-1, or their equivalents.

4. Place the gear spacer ring and thrust plate over the end of the shaft, and install the woodruff key in the shaft keyway.

5. Install the camshaft gear and press it onto the shaft until it bottoms against the gear spacer ring. The end clearance of the thrust plate should be 0.0015–0.0050 in. (0.0381–0.127mm). If

less than 0.0015 in. (0.0381mm), the spacer ring should be replaced.

6-232 and 258 Engines

▶ **See Figures 95 and 96**

1. Remove the drive belts, engine fan and hub assembly, accessory pulley, vibration damper and timing chain cover.
2. Remove the oil seal from the timing chain cover.
3. Remove the camshaft sprocket retaining bolt and washer.
4. Rotate the crankshaft until the timing mark on the crankshaft sprocket is closest to and in a center line with the timing pointer of the camshaft sprocket.
5. Remove the crankshaft sprocket, camshaft sprocket and timing chain as an assembly. Disassemble the chain and sprockets.

To install:

1. Assemble the timing chain, crankshaft sprocket and camshaft sprocket with the timing marks aligned.
2. Install the assembly to the crankshaft and the camshaft.

Fig. 95 Proper timing mark alignment—6-cylinder engines

Fig. 96 Place the camshaft sprocket mark at the one o'clock position and count the pins—6-cylinder engines

3. Install the camshaft sprocket retaining bolt and washer and tighten to 45–55 ft. lbs.
4. Install the timing chain cover and a new oil seal.
5. Install the vibration damper, accessory pulley, engine fan and hub assembly and drive belts. Tighten the belts to the proper tension.

8-304, 360 and 401 Engines

▶ **See Figures 97, 98 and 99**

❉❉ CAUTION

The EPA warns that prolonged contact with used engine oil may cause a number of skin disorders, including cancer! You should make every effort to minimize your exposure to used engine oil. Protective gloves should be worn when changing the oil. Wash your hands and any other exposed skin areas as soon as possible after exposure to used engine oil. Soap and water, or waterless hand cleaner should be used.

1. Remove the timing chain cover and gasket.
2. Remove the crankshaft oil slinger.
3. Remove the camshaft sprocket retaining bolt. and washer, distributor drive gear and fuel pump eccentric.
4. Rotate the crankshaft until the timing mark on the crankshaft sprocket is adjacent to, and on a center line with, the timing mark on the camshaft sprocket.
5. Remove the crankshaft sprocket, camshaft sprocket and timing chain as an assembly.
6. Clean all of the gasket surfaces.

Fig. 97 Correct timing mark installation—V8 engines

Fig. 98 Position the crankshaft sprocket mark on the center line and count the pins—V8 engines

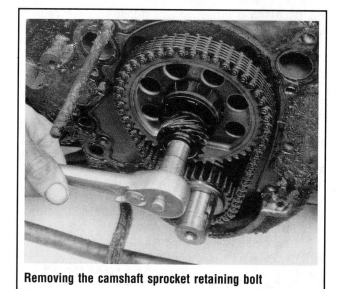

Removing the camshaft sprocket retaining bolt

To install:

1. Assemble the timing chain, crankshaft sprocket and camshaft sprocket with the timing marks on both sprockets aligned.

2. Install the assembly to the crankshaft and the camshaft.

3. Install the fuel pump eccentric, distributor drive gear, washer and retaining bolt. Tighten the bolt to 25–35 ft.lb.

4. Install the crankshaft oil slinger.

5. Install the timing chain cover using a new gasket and oil seal.

➡In mid-year 1979, a new timing chain, camshaft sprocket and crankshaft sprocket were phased into production on all V8 engines. These are offered as replacement parts for older engines. When installing any one of these parts on an older engine, all three parts must be installed. None of the new parts is usable in conjunction with the older parts. They must be installed as a set. To determine the necessity for a replacement of an older chain, perform the following deflection test:

1. Remove the timing case cover.

2. Rotate the sprockets until all slack is removed from the right side of the chain.

3. Locate the dowel on the lower left side of the engine and measure up ¾ in. (19.05mm). Make a mark.

4. Measure across the chain with a straight-edge from the mark to a point at the bottom of the camshaft sprocket.

5. Grab the chain at the point where the straightedge crosses it. Push the chain left (inward) as far as it will go. Make a mark on the block at this point. Push the chain to the right as far as it will go. Make another mark. Measure between the two marks. Total deflection should not exceed ⅞ in. (22.23mm).

6. Replace the chain and sprockets if deflection is not within specifications.

7. Replace the timing case cover.

Fig. 99 Check the timing chain for proper deflection—8-cylinder 304 engines

Timing Belt

REMOVAL & INSTALLATION

4-121 Engine

⬧ **See Figures 100, 101, 102, 103 and 104**

This engine used a toothed rubber belt to drive the camshaft. Belt tension is controlled by an adjustable idler pulley. The distributor is at the rear of the cylinder head and is driven by a gear pressed on the rear of the camshaft.

✳✳ WARNING

Do not turn the engine backwards. Damage to the drive belt teeth could result. Turn the engine by the crankshaft bolt, not the camshaft.

Check if the teeth are cracked or damaged

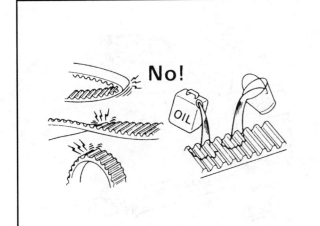

Do not bend, twist or turn the timing belt inside out. Never allow oil, water or steam to contact the belt

Inspect the timing belt for cracks, fraying, glazing or damage of any kind

Check for premature parting of the belt

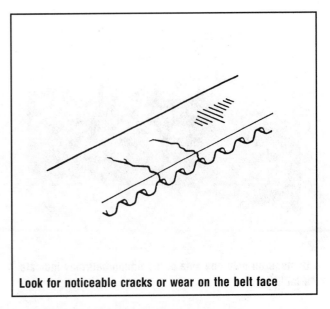

Look for noticeable cracks or wear on the belt face

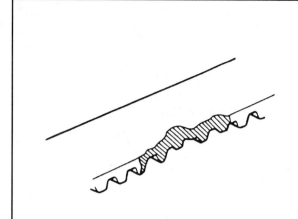

You may only have damage on one side of the belt; if so, the guide could be the culprit

ALWAYS replace the timing belt at the interval specified by the manufacturer

Foreign materials can get in between the teeth and cause damage

Fig. 100 Align the camshaft timing mark with the edge of the cylinder head—4–121 engine

Damage on only one side of the timing belt may indicate a faulty guide

Fig. 101 Align the timing marks on the crankshaft and intermediate shaft—4–121 engine

CAUTION

IF TIMING BELT WAS REMOVED OR REPLACED, RECHECK VALVE TIMING.

NOTE

ALL PARTS SHOWN IN THIS ILLUSTRATION CAN BE REMOVED AND INSTALLED WITH ENGINE IN CAR.

TIMING BELT SPROCKET ON CAMSHAFT
DO NOT REMOVE WHEN REPLACING TIMING BELT, DRIVE OR ADJUSTING VALVE TIMING

79 N·m (58 ft lb)

TENSIONER FOR TIMING BELT
CHECK FOR FREE MOVEMENT

TIMING BELT
CHECK FOR WEAR/ADJUSTING
INSTALLING: REMOVE WATER PUMP PULLEY

43 N·m (32 ft lb)

24 N·m (18 ft lb)

TIMING BELT COVER
BOLTS 10 N·m
(90 IN. LB.)

V-BELT
CHECK FOR WEAR
ADJUSTING TENSION

OIL SEAL FOR
INTERMEDIATE SHAFT

CRANKSHAFT PULLEY
NOTE POSITION WHEN
INSTALLING DRIVE BELT

OIL SEAL FOR CRANKSHAFT

79 N·m (58 ft lb)

TIMING BELT SPROCKET
ON INTERMEDIATE SHAFT

79 N·m (58 ft lb)

TIMING BELT SPROCKET
ON CRANKSHAFT

27 N·m (20 ft lb)
REMOVE ONLY WHEN SEPARATING V-BELT
PULLEY FROM DRIVE BELT SPROCKET

14 N·m (10 ft lb)

Fig. 102 Exploded view of the timing belt and related components—4–121 engine

Fig. 103 Removing the camshaft pulley from the 4–121 engine

1. Rotate the crankshaft in the normal direction of rotation, until the timing mark on the pulley is pointing to the zero position on the degree scale on the block. The timing mark on the rear of the camshaft pulley should be aligned with the pointer on the cylinder head cover.

2. Loosen the accessory pulley attaching bolts. Remove the V belts and the cam drive belt shield.

3. Loosen the adjuster retaining screw to allow the belt to slacken and remove the belt.

4. To replace the belt, install the belt on the crankshaft pulley, and position it on the tensioner pulley. Slip the belt over the camshaft pulley using hand pressure only, while maintaining the pulleys at their respective timing marks.

➡**Do not pry the belt with metal tools. The belt drive surface can be damaged and premature belt failure can result.**

5. Turn the offset adjusting nut on the tensioning pulley counterclockwise to increase the belt tension. The belt is properly tensioned when the drive side of the belt can be twisted 90° with finger pressure.

➡**When checking belt tension, apply tension on the crankshaft with a wrench, in a counterclockwise direction, to get all the slack on one side of the belt.**

Fig. 104 Sectional views of the different timing mark locations—4–121 engine

6. With pressure on the tensioning pulley nut, tighten the retaining nut to 29 ft. lbs. torque. Recheck the belt tension.

7. Install the drive belt shield. Install the alternator belts and adjust their tension. Tighten the accessory pulley bolts to 15 ft. lbs.

8. Start the engine and adjust the ignition timing.

Sprockets

REMOVAL & INSTALLATION

Camshaft

1. Remove the drive belt.

2. Insert a bar or other suitable tool through the camshaft pulley to prevent it from turning.

3. Remove the pulley retaining bolt. Remove the pulley, woodruff key, and washer from the camshaft.

4. To replace the pulley reverse the disassembly procedure. Hold the camshaft pulley and torque the retaining bolt to 58 ft. lbs.

5. Refer to Belt removal and installation procedure for installation and tensioning.

Crankshaft

1. Raise and support the from of the car with stands.

2. Remove the camshaft drive belt.

3. Remove the accessory drive pulley from the crankshaft pulley using a no. 40 Torx head bit to remove the pulley screws.

4. The sprocket retaining bolt can be loosened and removed from the crankshaft. Hold the pulley from turning while the bolt is loosened.

5. Remove the pulley from the crankshaft.

6. Install in the pulley so that the indexing hole in the pulley engages with the pin on the crankshaft.

7. Hold the pulley from turning. Install the retaining bolt and torque to 181 ft. lbs.

8. Install the drive belt. Refer to the belt removal and installation procedure for tensioning.

9. Replace the belt guard. Replace the accessory drive pulley and torque the attaching bolts to 15 ft. lbs.

10. Complete the assembly in the reverse order of disassembly. Start the engine and reset the ignition timing.

Camshaft

REMOVAL & INSTALLATION

➡Caution must be taken when performing this procedure. Camshaft bearings are coated with babbit material, which can be damaged by scraping the cam lobes across the bearing.

4-121 Engine
♦ See Figure 105

1. Remove the air cleaner assembly, and the distributor cap with the wires attached.

2. Remove the accessory belts, and the belt guard. Loosen and remove the camshaft drive belt.

Fig. 105 Location of the camshaft bearings—4–121 engine

3. Remove the distributor and housing assembly from the rear of the cylinder head.

4. Remove the cylinder head cover, and the camshaft pulley from the camshaft.

➡Use a tool to prevent the sprocket from turning while removing the retaining bolt, and protect the head surface by wrapping a cloth around the end of the tool.

5. Remove the bolts from number 5 camshaft bearing cap (rear cap), and them remove the retaining nuts from caps 1, 3, and 5. Next remove the nuts on bearing caps number 2 and 4, backing off each nut ¼ turn at a time to relieve tension on the camshaft. Remove the oil pipe retainers from the bolts on bearing caps number 2 and 4.

6. Remove all the camshaft bearing caps from the cylinder head. Keep them in order.

7. Remove the camshaft from the cylinder head.

➡The distributor drive fear should be removed from the camshaft with a puller. It can be replaced by driving the gear on the camshaft with the use of a block or wood and a hammer. Note the gear location before removal.

8. The tappets may be removed for service by lifting them our of their bores in the cylinder head.

To install:

9. On installation, lubricate the camshaft lobes and bearing surfaces and install the shaft into the cylinder head. Install the camshaft bearing caps on their respective seats, and install the retaining nuts on cap numbers 2 and 4, tightening to 13 ft. lbs.

10. Torque numbers 3 and 5 retaining nuts to 13 ft. lbs. Install the bolts in bearing cap number 5 and torque to 7 ft. lbs.

11. Install a replacement seal on the camshaft and tighten the number 1 bearing cap to 13 ft. lbs. torque. Install the oil pipe and tighten the nuts to 13 ft. lbs.

12. Install the camshaft sprocket and torque the retaining bolt to 58 ft. lbs., while holding the sprocket to prevent its turning.

13. Temporarily install the cylinder head cover and position the camshaft pulley timing mark in line with the indicator on the cylinder head cover.

14. Install the distributor and housing on the rear of the cylinder head, setting the rotor to the number one cylinder position.

15. Install the distributor cap and wiring, attach the vacuum line, and connect the primary wire.

16. Rotate the crankshaft to the TDC mark. Install the camshaft drive belt and adjust. Refer to Belt Removal and Installation.

17. Reassemble the drive belt guard, replace the accessory belts and adjust.

18. Remove the cylinder head cover and adjust the tappet to camshaft clearance.

19. Install the cylinder head cover and complete the assembly. Start the engine and adjust the ignition timing.

4-150 Engine

◆ See Figures 106, 107, 108 and 109

✻✻ CAUTION

Please refer to Section 1 before discharging the compressor or disconnecting air conditioning lines. Damage to the air conditioning system or personal injury could result. Consult your local laws concerning refrigerant discharge and recycling. In many areas it may be illegal for anyone but a certified technician to service the A/C system. Always use an approved recovery station when discharging the air conditioning.

1. Disconnect the battery ground.
2. Drain the cooling system.

✻✻ CAUTION

When draining engine coolant, keep in mind that cats and dogs are attracted to ethylene glycol antifreeze and could drink any that is left in an uncovered container or in puddles on the ground. This will prove fatal in sufficient quantity. Always drain coolant into a sealable container. Coolant should be reused unless it is contaminated or is several years old.

3. Remove the radiator, discharge the refrigerant system (refer to Section 1) and remove the condenser.

Fig. 106 Use tool J-21884 or its equivalent to remove the lifters from the 4–150 engine

Fig. 107 Check the face of the lifter for squareness and damage

Fig. 108 Carefully remove the camshaft from the engine block—4–150 engine

Fig. 109 Typical camshaft lobe measurements

4. Remove the fuel pump.

5. Matchmark the distributor and engine for installation. Note the rotor position by marking it on the distributor body. Unbolt and remove the distributor and wires.

6. Remove the rocker arm cover.

7. Remove the rocker arm assemblies.

8. Remove the pushrods.

➡**Keep everything in order for installation.**

9. Using a tool J-21884 or its equivalent, remove the hydraulic lifters.

10. Remove the pulley, vibration damper and timing case cover. Remove the crankshaft oil slinger.

➡**If the camshaft sprocket appears to have been rubbing against the cover, check the oil pressure relief holes in the rear cam journal for debris.**

11. Remove the timing chain and sprockets.

12. Slide the camshaft from the engine.

To install:

✳✳ CAUTION

The EPA warns that prolonged contact with used engine oil may cause a number of skin disorders, including cancer! You should make every effort to minimize your exposure to used engine oil. Protective gloves should be worn when changing the oil. Wash your hands and any other exposed skin areas as soon as possible after exposure to used engine oil. Soap and water, or waterless hand cleaner should be used.

13. Inspect all parts for wear and damage. Lubricate all moving parts with engine oil supplement.

14. Slide the camshaft into the engine, carefully, to avoid damage to the bearing surfaces.

15. Install the timing chain and sprockets. Make sure that all camshaft timing marks align. Torque the camshaft sprocket bolt to 50 ft. lbs.

16. Install the timing case cover.

17. Using a tool J-21884 or its equivalent, install the hydraulic lifters.

18. Install the pushrods.

19. Install the rocker arm assemblies.

20. Install the rocker arm cover.

21. Install the distributor and wires. When installing the distributor, make sure that all matchmarks align. It may be necessary to rotate the oil pump drive tang with a long bladed screwdriver to facilitate installation of the distributor.

➡**If the distributor is not installed correctly, or removed later, the complete installation procedure must be done again.**

22. Install the fuel pump.

23. Install the radiator.

24. Install the condenser and evacuate and charge the refrigerant system. Refer to section 1 for this procedure.

25. Fill the cooling system.

26. Connect the battery ground.

4-151 Engine

1. Remove the air cleaner.

2. Drain the cooling system.

✳✳ CAUTION

When draining engine coolant, keep in mind that cats and dogs are attracted to ethylene glycol antifreeze and could drink any that is left in an uncovered container or in puddles on the ground. This will prove fatal in sufficient quantity. Always drain coolant into a sealable container. Coolant should be reused unless it is contaminated or is several years old.

3. Remove the timing gear cover.

4. Disconnect the radiator hoses at the radiator. Remove the radiator.

5. Remove the two camshaft thrust plate screws through the holes in the camshaft gear.

6. Remove the tappets.

7. Remove the distributor, oil pump drive and fuel pump.

8. Remove the camshaft and gear assembly by pulling out through front of the block. Support the shaft carefully when removing it to prevent damaging the camshaft bearings.

To install:

9. Thoroughly coat the camshaft journals with a high quality engine oil supplement such as STP or its equivalent.

10. Install the camshaft assembly in engine block. Use care to prevent damaging the bearings or the camshaft.

11. Turn the crankshaft and camshaft so that the valve timing marks on the gear teeth are aligned. The engine is now in number four cylinder firing position. Install the camshaft thrust plate-to-block screws and tighten to 75 inch lbs.

12. Install the timing gear cover and gasket.

13. Line up the keyway in the hub with the key on crankshaft and slide the hub onto the shaft. Install the center bolt and tighten to 160 ft. lbs.

14. Install the valve tappets, pushrods, pushrod cover, oil pump shaft and gear assembly and the fuel pump. Install the distributor according to the following procedure:

    a. turn Turn the crankshaft 360° to the firing position of the number one cylinder (number one exhaust and intake valve tappets both on base circle [heel] of the camshaft and the timing notch on the vibration damper is indexed with the Top Dead Center mark [TDC] on the timing degree scale).

    b. Install the distributor and align the shaft so that the rotor arm points toward the number one cylinder spark plug contact.

15. Install the rocker arms and pivot balls over the pushrods. With the tappets on the base circle (heel) of camshaft, tighten the rocker arm capscrews to 20 ft. lbs. Do not overtighten.

16. Install the cylinder head cover.

17. Install the intake manifold.

18. Install the radiator and lower radiator hose.

19. Install the belt, fan and shroud. Tighten the fan bolts to 18 ft. lbs.

20. Install the upper radiator hose.

21. Tighten the belts.

6-232 and 258 Engines

♦ See Figures 110 thru 115

1. Drain the cooling system and remove the radiator. With air conditioning, remove the condenser and receiver assembly as a unit, without disconnecting any lines or discharging the system.

❈❈ CAUTION

When draining engine coolant, keep in mind that cats and dogs are attracted to ethylene glycol antifreeze and could drink any that is left in an uncovered container or in puddles on the ground. This will prove fatal in sufficient quantity. Always drain coolant into a sealable container. Coolant should be reused unless it is contaminated or is several years old.

2. Remove the valve cover and gasket, the rocker assemblies, pushrods, cylinder head and gasket and the lifters.

➡The valve train components must be replaced in their original locations.

3. Remove the drive belts, cooling fan, fan hub assembly, vibration damper and the timing chain cover.
4. Remove the fuel pump and distributor assembly, including the spark plug wires.
5. Rotate the crankshaft until the timing mark of the crankshaft sprocket is adjacent to, and on a center line with, the timing mark of the camshaft sprocket.
6. Remove the crankshaft sprocket, camshaft sprocket, and the timing chain as an assembly.
7. Remove the front bumper or grille as required and carefully slide out the camshaft.

Fig. 111 Cross-sectional view of a typical camshaft bearing removal and installation tool for OHV engines

Fig. 112 Use a feeler gauge to check the cam-shaft end-play

Fig. 110 Use a dial indicator to check the camshaft for straightness

Fig. 113 A dial indicator may be used to check the camshaft end play

Fig. 114 Use a dial indicator to check the camshaft gear backlash

Fig. 115 Measure the camshaft gear run-out with a dial indicator

To install:

8. Coat all parts with engine oil supplement.
9. Slide the camshaft into place.
10. Install the front bumper and/or grille.
11. Install the crankshaft sprocket, camshaft sprocket, and the timing chain as an assembly.
12. Rotate the crankshaft until the timing mark of the crankshaft sprocket is adjacent to, and on a center line with, the timing mark of the camshaft sprocket.
13. Install the fuel pump and distributor assembly, including the spark plug wires.
14. Install the drive belts.
15. Install the cooling fan and fan hub assembly.
16. Install the vibration damper.
17. Install the cylinder head and gasket and the lifters.
18. Install the rocker assemblies and pushrods.
19. Install the valve cover and gasket.
20. Install the the timing chain cover.
21. With air conditioning, install the condenser and receiver.

➡ The valve train components must be replaced in their original locations.

22. Install the radiator and fill the cooling system.

8-304, 360 and 401 Engines
◆ **See Figure 116**

1. Disconnect the battery cables.
2. Drain the radiator and both banks of the block. Remove the lower hose at the radiator, the by-pass hose at the pump, the thermostat housing and the radiator. With air conditioning, remove the condenser and receiver assembly as a unit, without disconnecting any lines or discharging the system.

✳✳ CAUTION

When draining engine coolant, keep in mind that cats and dogs are attracted to ethylene glycol antifreeze and could drink any that is left in an uncovered container or in puddles on the ground. This will prove fatal in sufficient quantity. Always drain coolant into a sealable container. Coolant should be reused unless it is contaminated or is several years old.

3. Remove the distributor, all wires, and the coil from the manifold.
4. Remove the intake manifold as an assembly.

1. Retaining bolt
2. Camshaft
3. Distributor drive gear
4. Fuel pump eccentric
5. Sprocket

Fig. 116 Exploded view of a typical camshaft used on the 8-cylinder 304, 360 and 401 engines

5. Remove the valve covers, rocker arms and pushrods.
6. Remove the lifters.

➡ The valve train components must be replaced in their original locations.

7. Remove the cooling fan and hub assembly, fuel pump, and heater hose at the water pump.
8. Remove the alternator and bracket as an assembly. Just move it aside, do not disconnect the wiring.
9. Remove the crankshaft pulley and the damper. Remove the lower radiator hose at the water pump.
10. Remove the timing chain cover.

11. Remove the distributor/oil pump drive gear, fuel pump eccentric, sprockets and the timing chain.

12. Remove the grille.

13. Remove the camshaft carefully by sliding it forward out of the engine.

To install:

14. Coat all parts with engine oil supplement.

15. Slide the camshaft, carefully, into the engine.

16. Install the grille.

17. Install the distributor/oil pump drive gear, fuel pump eccentric, sprockets and the timing chain.

18. Install the timing chain cover.

19. Install the crankshaft pulley and the damper.

20. Install the lower radiator hose at the water pump.

21. Install the alternator and bracket as an assembly.

22. Install the cooling fan and hub assembly.

23. Install the fuel pump.

24. Install the heater hose at the water pump.

25. Install the lifters.

➡**The valve train components must be replaced in their original locations.**

26. Install the valve covers, rocker arms and pushrods.

27. Install the intake manifold as an assembly.

28. Install the distributor, all wires, and the coil on the manifold.

29. Install the radiator.

30. With air conditioning, install the condenser and receiver assembly.

31. Install the thermostat and housing.

32. Install the by-pass hose at the pump.

33. Install the lower hose at the radiator.

34. Fill the cooling system.

35. Connect the battery cables.

Pistons and Connecting Rods

REMOVAL

◗ **See Figures 117, 118, 119, 120**

➡**In most cases, this procedure is easier with the engine out of the vehicle.**

1. Remove the head(s).

2. Remove the oil pan.

3. Rotate the engine to bring each piston, in turn, to the bottom of its stroke. With the piston bottomed, use a ridge reamer to remove the ridge at the top of the cylinder. Do not cut too deeply.

4. Matchmark the rods and caps. If the pistons are to be removed from the connecting rod, mark the cylinder number on the piston with a silver pencil or quick drying paint for proper cylinder identification and cap-to-rod location. Remove the connecting rod capnuts and lift off the rod caps, keeping them in order. Install a guide hose over the threads of the rod bolts. This is to prevent damage to the bearing journal and rod bolt threads.

5. Using a hammer handle, push the piston and rod assemblies up out of the block.

Fig. 117 A number stamp may be used to match the cylinders to the connecting rod

Fig. 118 Matchmark the connecting rod and cap to aid in installation

Fig. 119 Typical cylinder bore ridge

Fig. 120 Use a hammer handle or a wooden dowel to remove the piston from the bore

Place rubber hose over the connecting rod studs to protect the crank and bores from damage

PISTON PIN REPLACEMENT

▶ See Figures 121 and 122

Use care at all times when handling and servicing connecting rods and pistons. To prevent possible damage to these units, do not clamp the rod or piston in a vise since they may become distorted. Do not allow the pistons to strike against one another, against hard objects or bench surfaces, since distortion of the piston contour or nicks in the soft aluminum material may result.

1. Remove the piston rings using a suitable piston ring remover.

2. Remove the piston pin lockring, if used. Install the guide bushing of the piston pin removing and installing tool.

3. Install the piston and connecting rod assembly on a support, and place the assembly in an arbor press. Press the pin out of the connecting rod, using the appropriate piston pin tool.

4. Assembly is the reverse of disassembly. Use new lockrings where needed.

Fig. 121 If equipped, install the piston pin lock-rings

INSPECTION

Cylinder Block

◗ See Figure 123

Check the cylinder walls for evidence of rust, which would indicate a cracked block. Check the block face for distortion with a straightedge. Maximum distortion variance is 0.005 in. (0.127mm). The block cannot be planed, so it will have to be re-

Fig. 123 Use a straight edge to check the main bearing saddle

Fig. 122 Use an arbor press to install the piston pins

placed if too distorted. Using a micrometer, check the cylinders for out-of-roundness.

Connecting Rods and Bearings
▶ See Figures 124 and 125

Wash connecting rods in cleaning solvent and dry with compressed air. Check for twisted or bent rods and inspect for nicks or cracks. Replace connecting rods that are damaged.

Inspect journals for roughness and wear. Slight roughness may be removed with a fine grit polishing cloth saturated with engine oil. Burrs may be removed with a fine oil stone by moving the stone on the journal circumference. Do not move the stone back and forth across the journal. If the journals are scored or ridged, the crankshaft must be replaced.

Fig. 124 Check the connecting rod length by measuring between the points indicated (arrows)

Fig. 125 Use a prytool to spread the rods then insert a feeler gauge to measure side clearance

The connecting rod journals should be checked for out-of-round and correct size with a micrometer.

➡**Crankshaft rod journals will normally be standard size. If any undersized bearings are used, the size will be stamped on a counterweight.**

If plastic gauging material is to be used:
1. Clean oil from the journal bearing cap, connecting rod and outer and inner surfaces of the bearing inserts. Position the insert so that the tang is properly aligned with the notch in the rod and cap.
2. Place a piece of plastic gauging material in the center of lower bearing shell.
3. Remove the bearing cap and determine the bearing clearances by comparing the width of the flattened plastic gauging material at its widest point with the graduation on the container. The number within the graduation on the envelope indicates the clearance in thousandths of an inch or millimeters. If this clearance is excessive, replace the bearing and recheck the clearance with the plastic gauging material. Lubricate the bearing with engine oil before installation. Repeat the procedure on the remaining connecting rod bearings. All rods must be connected to their journals when rotating the crankshaft, to prevent engine damage.

Pistons
▶ See Figures 126 and 127

Clean varnish from piston skirts and pins with a cleaning solvent. Do not wire brush any part of the piston. Clean the ring grooves with a groove cleaner and make sure oil ring holes and slots are clean.

Inspect the piston for cracked ring lands, skirts or pin bosses, wavy or worn ring lands, scuffed or damaged skirts, eroded areas at the top of the piston. Replace pistons that are damaged or show signs of excessive wear. Inspect the grooves for nicks or burrs that might cause the rings to hang up.

Measure piston skirt (across center line of piston pin) and check piston clearance.

RING EXPANDER

Fig. 126 Use a ring expander to remove the piston rings

Fig. 127 A ring groove cleaner may be used to clean the ring grooves

MEASURING THE OLD PISTONS

Check used piston-to-cylinder bore clearance as follows:

1. Measure the cylinder bore diameter with a telescope gauge.
2. Measure the pistons for size or taper, measurements must be made with the piston pin removed.
3. Subtract the piston diameter from the cylinder bore diameter to determine piston-to-bore clearance.
4. Compare the piston-to-bore clearances obtained with those clearances recommended. Determine if the piston-to-bore clearance is in the acceptable range.
5. When measuring taper, the largest reading must be at the bottom of the skirt.

Measure the piston's outer diameter using a micrometer

SELECTING NEW PISTONS

1. If the used piston is not acceptable, check the service piston size and determine if a new piston can be selected. (Service pistons are available in standard, high limit and standard oversize.)

2. If the cylinder bore must be reconditioned, measure the new piston diameter, then hone the cylinder bore to obtain the preferred clearance.

3. Select a new piston and mark the piston to identify the cylinder for which it was fitted. (On some vehicles, oversize pistons may be found. These pistons will be 0.010 in (0.254mm) oversize).

CYLINDER HONING

◆ **See Figure 128**

1. When cylinders are being honed, follow the manufacturer's recommendations for the use of the hone.
2. Occasionally, during the honing operation, the cylinder bore should be thoroughly cleaned and the selected piston checked for correct fit.
3. When finish-honing a cylinder bore, the hone should be

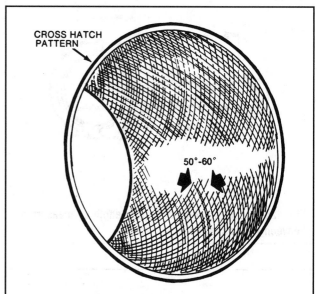

Fig. 128 The cylinder bore should look like this after it has been honed

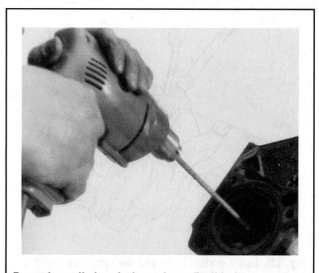

Removing cylinder glazing using a flexible hone

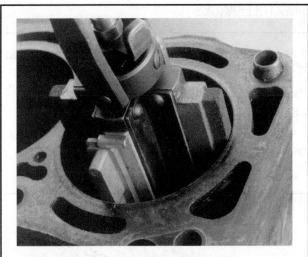

As with a ball hone, work the hone carefully up and down the bore to achieve the desired results

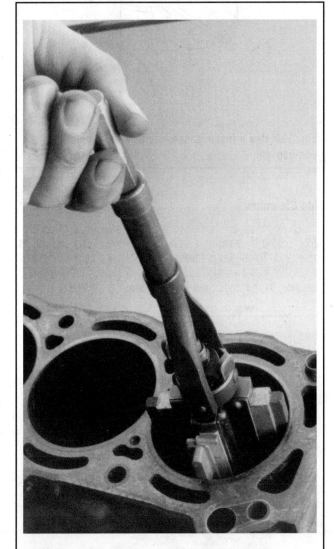

A solid hone can also be used to cross-hatch the cylinder bore

moved up and down at a sufficient speed to obtain a very fine uniform surface finish in a cross-hatch pattern of approximately 45–65° included angle. The finish marks should be clean but not sharp, free from imbedded particles and torn or folded metal.

4. Permanently mark the piston for the cylinder to which it has been fitted and proceed to hone the remaining cylinders.

➡**Handle the pistons with care. Do not attempt to force the pistons through the cylinders until the cylinders have been honed to the correct size. Pistons can be distorted through careless handling.**

5. Thoroughly clean the bores with hot water and detergent. Scrub well with a stiff bristle brush and rinse thoroughly with hot water. It is extremely essential that a good cleaning operation be performed. If any of the abrasive material is allowed to remain in the cylinder bores, it will rapidly wear the new rings and cylinder bores. The bores should be swabbed several times with light engine oil and a clean cloth and then wiped with a clean dry cloth. Clean the remainder of the cylinder block to remove the excess material spread during the honing operation.

CHECKING CYLINDER BORE

▶ **See Figures 129, 130 and 131**

Cylinder bore size can be measured with inside micrometers or a cylinder gauge. The most wear will occur at the top of the ring travel.

Reconditioned cylinder bores should be held to not more than 0.001 in. (0.025mm) taper.

If the cylinder bores are smooth, the cylinder walls should not be deglazed. If the cylinder walls are scored, the walls may have to be honed before installing new rings. It is important that reconditioned cylinder bores be thoroughly washed with a soap and water solution to remove all traces of abrasive material to eliminate premature wear.

CENTERLINE OF ENGINE

A—AT RIGHT ANGLE TO CENTERLINE OF ENGINE
B—PARALLEL TO CENTERLINE OF ENGINE

Fig. 129 Typical cylinder bore measuring points

A telescoping gauge may be used to measure the cylinder bore diameter

Fig. 130 Use a telescopic gauge to measure the cylinder bore . . .

Fig. 131 . . . then measure the telescopic gauge with a micrometer to determine cylinder bore size

RING TOLERANCES

When installing new rings, ring gap and side clearance should be checked as follows:

Piston Ring and Rail Gap

▶ **See Figure 132**

Each ring and rail gap must be measured with the ring or rail positioned squarely and at the bottom of the ring travel area of the bore.

Fig. 132 Use a feeler gauge to check the piston ring end-gap

Side Clearance

Each ring must be checked for side clearance in its respective piston groove by inserting a feeler gauge between the ring and its upper land. The piston grooves must be cleaned before checking the ring for side clearance specifications. To check oil ring side clearance, the oil rings must be installed on the piston.

Clean the piston grooves using a ring groove cleaner

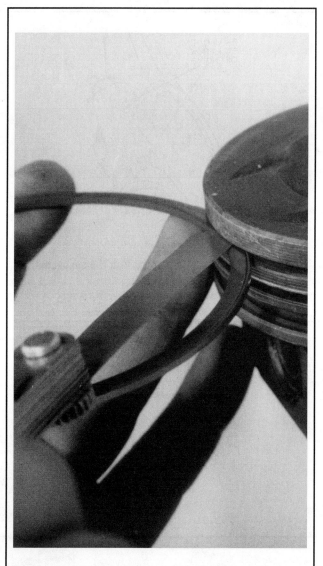

You can use a piece of an old ring to clean the piston grooves, BUT be careful, the ring is sharp

PISTON RING REPLACEMENT

For service ring specifications and detailed installation productions, refer to the instructions furnished with the parts package.

INSTALLATION

▶ See Figures 133 thru 140

1. Using a ring expander, install new rings in the grooves, with their gaps staggered to be 270° apart.
2. Using a straightedge, check the rods for straightness. Check, also, for cracks. Before assembling the block, it's a good idea to have the block checked for cracks with Magnaflux® or its equivalent.
3. Install the pins and retainers.
4. Coat the pistons with clean engine oil and apply a ring compressor. Position the assembly over the cylinder bore and slide

Fig. 133 Proper ring gap spacing

Most rings are marked to show which side should face upward

Checking the ring-to-ring groove clearance

Most pistons are marked to indicate positioning in the engine (usually a mark means the side facing front)

The notch on the the side of the bearing cap matches the groove on the bearing insert

USE A SHORT PIECE OF 3/8" HOSE AS A GUIDE

Fig. 134 Place lengths of rubber hose over the connecting rod studs to protect the crankshaft journals

PROJECTIONS FACE FRONT OF ENGINE

Fig. 135 Make sure the projections on the connecting rod face forward—4-121 engine

Installing the piston into the block using a ring compressor and the handle of a hammer

NOTCH TO FRONT OF ENGINE

NUMBERS ON ROD & CAP TO CAMSHAFT SIDE OIL SPURT HOLE SAME SIDE

Fig. 136 Typical connecting rod and piston—6 cylinder engine

Fig. 137 Ensure the numbers marked on the rods match and the squirt holes align—4–151 engine

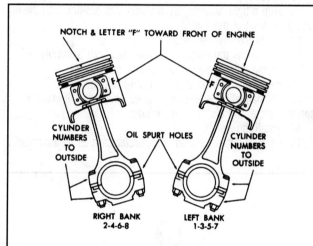

Fig. 138 Common piston and rod assemblies set-up prior to installation—V8 engines

Fig. 139 The arrow on the piston faces the front of the block—4-150 engine

Fig. 140 Check the rod side clearance with a feeler gauge

the piston into the cylinder slowly, taking care to avoid nicking the walls. The pistons will have a mark on the crown, such as a groove or notch or stamped symbol. This mark indicates the side of the piston which should face front. Lower the piston slowly, until it bottoms on the crankshaft. A good idea is to cover the rod studs with length of rubber hose to avoid nicking the crank journals. Assemble the rod caps at this time. Check the rod bearing clearances using Plastigage®, going by the instructions on the package.

5. Install the bearing caps with the stamped numbers matched. Tighten the caps to the figure shown in the Torque specifications chart. Refer to the accompanying illustrations for proper piston and rod installation.

Rear Main Bearing Oil Seal

REMOVAL & INSTALLATION

4-121 Engine

♦ See Figure 141

The rear main bearing oil seal consists of a single piece of formed neoprene with a single lip. To replace the seal, proceed as follows.

1. Remove the transmission assembly. If manual transmission, remove the pressure plate and flywheel.

2. Remove the crankshaft seal from its seat in the block, while exercising care not to scratch the seal contacting area of the crankshaft.

To install:

3. Install the seal, after lubricating the lip with engine oil, into the recess of the block, until the seal bottoms. The seal should be about 1/32 in. (0.79mm) below the surface of the block.

4. Install the flywheel and components. Install the transmission assembly, adjust as necessary, start the engine and check for oil leakage.

Fig. 141 Common rear main oil seal assembly—4–121 engine

4-150 Engine

See Figure 142

1. Remove the transmission.
2. Remove the flywheel.
3. Pry out the seal from around the crankshaft flange.

To install:

4. Coat the inner lip of the new seal with clean engine oil.
5. Gently tap the new seal into place, flush with the block, using a rubber or plastic mallet.
6. Install the flywheel.
7. Install the transmission.

Fig. 142 Location of the rear main seal—4–151 engines

4-151 Engine

See Figure 143

→The seal is a one-piece unit that can be removed and installed without removing the oil pan or crankshaft.

1. Raise and support the vehicle on jackstands.
2. Remove the transmission and transfer case as an assembly.
3. Disconnect and remove the starter.
4. On manual transmission vehicles, remove the flywheel inspection plate, and clutch slave cylinder.
5. Remove the flywheel or drive plate housing.
6. On manual transmission, remove the clutch assembly by backing out the bolts evenly around the pressure plate.
7. Remove the flywheel or drive plate. It is a good idea to match mark the flywheel location for assembly.
8. Using a small bladed screwdriver, pry the rear seal out from around the crankshaft hub. Be careful to avoid damaging the sealing groove or hub.

To install:

9. With a light hammer, tap the seal into position with the lip facing the front of the engine.
10. Install the flywheel or drive plate.
11. On manual transmission, install the clutch assembly by tightening the bolts evenly around the pressure plate.
12. Install the flywheel or drive plate housing.
13. On manual transmission vehicles, install the flywheel inspection plate, and clutch slave cylinder.
14. Install the starter.
15. Install the transmission and transfer case as an assembly.

Fig. 143 Use a prytool to remove the rear main seal from the crankshaft—4–151 engine

6- and 8-Cylinder Engines

♦ **See Figure 144**

This seal is a two piece neoprene type with a single lip.

1. Raise and support the vehicle on jackstands.
2. Remove the oil pan.
3. Remove the rear main bearing cap and discard the lower seal.
4. Loosen all remaining main bearing caps.
5. Using a center punch, carefully drive the upper half of the seal out of the block just far enough to graph with a pliers and pull out.
6. Remove the oil pan front and rear seals and the side gaskets.

Fig. 144 Coat the ends of the seal with RTV, the curved surface with soap and lip with engine oil

To install:

7. Clean all gasket surfaces.
8. Wipe clean the sealing surface of the crankshaft and coat it lightly with engine oil.
9. Coat the lip of the upper seal with engine oil and install it in the block. The lip faces forward.
10. Coat both end tabs of the lower seal with RTV silicone sealer. Do not get any RTV sealer on the seal lip.
11. Coat the outer curved surface of the seal with liquid soap. Coat the seal lip with engine oil.
12. Install the seal into the cap, pressing firmly.
13. Coat both chamferred edges of the cap with RTV sealer.

❊❊ WARNING

Do not allow any RTV sealer to get on the mating surfaces of the cap or block as this will affect bearing clearance.

14. Install the rear main cap.
15. Tighten all main bearing cap bolts gradually to 80 ft.lb.
16. Replace the oil pan.

Crankshaft

REMOVAL

4-121 Engine

➡**On engines equipped with automatic transmissions, mark the converter-to-flexplate position prior to disassembly.**

1. Remove the engine from the car.
2. Remove the rear main seal.
3. Install the engine on a work stand.
4. Remove the timing belt cover.
5. Remove the accessory drive pulley.
6. Loosen the tensioner and remove the timing belt.
7. Using tool J-26876 or its equivalent, remove the belt drive pulley from the crankshaft. Leave the pulley attached to the tool.
8. Remove the oil pump.
9. Remove the oil pan. Remove all traces of the gasket from the pan and block.
10. Remove the oil pick-up tube.
11. Matchmark and number the connecting rod bearing caps and remove the caps, two at a time, rotating the crankshaft to make them accessible. Place them on a clean work surface.
12. Number the main bearing caps and remove them. Place them on a clean work surface.
13. Lift out the crankshaft.

4-151 Engine

1. Remove the engine and mount it on a work stand.
2. Remove the spark plugs.
3. Remove the fan and pulley.
4. Remove the vibration damper and hub.
5. Remove the oil pan and oil pump.
6. Remove the timing case cover.
7. Remove the crankshaft timing gear.
8. Remove the connecting rod bearing caps. Mark each for reassembly.
9. Remove the main bearing caps, marking each for reassembly.
10. Remove the crankshaft.

4-150, 6- and 8-Cylinder Engines

♦ **See Figures 145 and 146**

1. Remove the engine from the vehicle and mount it on a work stand.
2. Drain the oil.
3. Remove the flywheel or torque converter, match marking the pieces for installation.
4. Remove all drive belts.
5. Remove the fan and hub assembly.
6. Remove the crankshaft pulley and vibration damper.
7. Remove the timing case cover.
8. Remove the oil pan.
9. Remove the oil pump and pickup.

Fig. 145 The upper bearing insert is removed or installed using a roll-out pin

Fig. 146 A bearing roll-out pin can be fabricated using these specifications

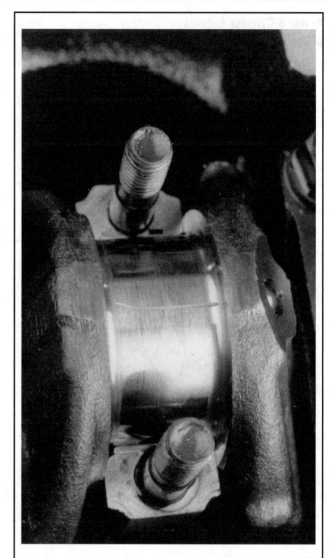

Apply a strip of gauging material to the bearing journal, then install and torque the cap

10. Remove the rod bearing caps, marking them for installation.

11. Remove the main bearing caps, marking them for installation.

12. Lift out the crankshaft.

➡A replacement oil pickup tube must be used. Do not attempt to install the original. Make sure the plastic button is inserted in the bottom of the pickup screen. Always use a new rear main seal. If new bearings are installed, check clearances with Plastigage®.

CLEANING & INSPECTION

1. Check the crankshaft for wear or damage to the bearing surfaces of the journals. Crankshafts that are damaged can be reconditioned by a professional machine shop.

2. Using a dial indicator, check the crankshaft journal runout. Measure the crankshaft journals with a micrometer to determine

After the cap is removed again, use the scale supplied with the gauge material to check clearances

the correct size rod and main bearings to be used. Whenever a new or reconditioned crankshaft is installed, new connecting rod bearings and main bearings should be installed.

3. Clean all oil passages in the block (and crankshaft if it is being reused).

→**A new rear main seal should be installed any time the crankshaft is removed or replaced.**

4. Wipe the oil from the crankshaft journal and the outer and inner surfaces of the bearing shell.

5. Place a piece of plastic gauging material in the center of the bearing.

6. Use a floor jack or other means to hold the crankshaft against the upper bearing shell. This is necessary to obtain accurate clearance readings when using plastic gauging material.

7. Install the bearing cap and bearing. Place engine oil on the cap bolts and install. Torque the bolts to specification.

8. Remove the bearing cap and determine the bearing clearance by comparing the width of the flattened plastic gauging material at its widest point with the graduations on the gauging material container. The number within the graduation on the envelope indicates the clearance in millimeters or thousandths of an inch. If the clearance is greater than allowed, replace both bearing shells as a set. Recheck the clearance after replacing the shells.

INSTALLATION

♦ **See Figure 147**

→**Main bearing clearances must be corrected by the use of selective upper and lower shells. UNDER NO CIRCUM-STANCES should the use of shims behind the shells to compensate for wear be attempted.**

1. Install new bearing upper halves in the block. If the crankshaft has been turned to resurface the journals, undersized bearing must be used to compensate. Lay the crankshaft in the block.

2. Install the lower bearing halves in the caps.

3. Use Plastigage® to check bearing fit.

4. When the bearings are properly fitted, install and torque the bearing caps.

A dial gauge may be used to check crankshaft end-play

Carefully pry the shaft back and forth while reading the dial gauge for play

Fig. 147 A prytool and a block of wood can be used to align the thrust bearing

5. Check crankshaft end-play to determine the need for thrust washers.

6. While you're at it, it's a good idea to replace the rear main seal at this time.

7. Install sufficient oil pan bolts in the block to align with the connecting rod bolts. Use rubber bands between the bolts to position the connecting rods as required. Connecting rod position can be adjusted by increasing the tension on the rubber bands with additional turns around the pan bolts or thread protectors.

8. Position the upper half of main bearings in the block and lubricate them with engine oil.

9. Position crankshaft keyway in the same position as removed and lower it into block. The connecting rods will follow the crank pins into the correct position as the crankshaft is lowered.

10. Lubricate the thrust flanges with clean engine oil or engine rebuilding oil. Install caps with the lower half of the bearings lubricated with engine oil. Lubricate the cap bolts with engine oil and install, but do not tighten.

11. With a block of wood, bump the shaft in each direction to align the thrust flanges of the main bearing. After bumping the shaft in each direction, wedge the shaft to the front and hold it while torquing the thrust bearing cap bolts.

➡**In order to prevent the possibility of cylinder block and/or main bearing cap damage, the main bearing caps are to be tapped into their cylinder block cavity using a wood or rubber mallet before the bolts are installed. Do not use attaching bolts to pull the main bearing caps into their seats. Failure to observe this information may damage the cylinder block or a bearing cap.**

12. Torque all main bearing caps to specification. Check crankshaft end-play, using a flat feeler gauge.

13. Remove the connecting rod bolt thread protectors and lubricate the connecting rod bearings with engine oil.

14. Install the connecting rod bearing caps in their original position. Torque the nuts to specification.

15. Install all parts in reverse order of removal. See related procedures in this chapter for component installation.

Flywheel/Flexplate and Ring Gear

➡**Flex plate is the term for a flywheel mated with an automatic transmission.**

REMOVAL & INSTALLATION

All Engines

➡**The ring gear is replaceable only on engines mated with a manual transmission. Engine with automatic transmissions have ring gears which are welded to the flexplate.**

1. Remove the transmission and transfer case.

2. Remove the clutch, if equipped, or torque converter from the flywheel. The flywheel bolts should be loosened a little at a time in a cross pattern to avoid warping the flywheel. On vehicles with manual transmission, replace the pilot bearing in the end of the crankshaft if removing the flywheel.

3. The flywheel should be checked for cracks and glazing. It can be resurfaced by a machine shop.

4. If the ring gear is to be replaced, drill a hole in the gear between two teeth, being careful not to contact the flywheel surface. Using a cold chisel at this point, crack the ring gear and remove it.

To install:

5. Polish the inner surface of the new ring gear and heat it in an oven to about 600°F (316°C). Quickly place the ring gear on the flywheel and tap it into place, making sure that it is fully seated.

➡**Never heat the ring gear past 800°F (426°C), or the tempering will be destroyed.**

6. Position the flywheel on the end of the crankshaft. Torque the bolts a little at a time, in a cross pattern, to the torque figure shown in the Torque Specifications Chart.

7. Install the clutch or torque converter.

8. Install the transmission and transfer case.

EXHAUST SYSTEM

General Information

➡**Safety glasses should be worn at all times when working on or near the exhaust system. Older exhaust systems will almost always be covered with loose rust particles which will shower you when disturbed. These particles are more than a nuisance and could injure your eye.**

Whenever working on the exhaust system always keep the following in mind:

• Check the complete exhaust system for open seams, holes loose connections, or other deterioration which could permit exhaust fumes to seep into the passenger compartment.

• The exhaust system is usually supported by free-hanging rubber mountings which permit some movement of the exhaust system, but does not permit transfer of noise and vibration into the passenger compartment. Do not replace the rubber mounts with solid ones.

• Before removing any component of the exhaust system, ALWAYS squirt a liquid rust dissolving agent onto the fasteners for ease of removal. A lot of knuckle skin will be saved by following this rule. It may even be wise to spray the fasteners and allow them to sit overnight.

❋❋ CAUTION

Allow the exhaust system to cool sufficiently before spraying a solvent exhaust fasteners. Some solvents are highly flammable and could ignite when sprayed on hot exhaust components.

• Annoying rattles and noise vibrations in the exhaust system are usually caused by misalignment of the parts. When aligning the system, leave all bolts and nuts loose until all parts are properly aligned, then tighten, working from front to rear.

• When installing exhaust system parts, make sure there is enough clearance between the hot exhaust parts and pipes and hoses that would be adversely affected by excessive heat. Also make sure there is adequate clearance from the floor pan to avoid possible overheating of the floor.

✳✳ CAUTION

When working on exhaust systems, ALWAYS wear protective goggles! Avoid working on a hot exhaust system!

Muffler

REMOVAL & INSTALLATION

➡**The following applies to exhaust systems using clamped joints. Most later model, original equipment systems use welded joints at the muffler. These joints will, of course, have to be cut.**

1. Raise and support the rear end on jackstands, placed under the frame, so that the axle hangs freely.
2. Remove the muffler clamps.
3. Remove the tailpipe hanger clamp.
4. Spray the joint liberally with a penetrant/rust dissolver compound such as Liquid Wrench®, WD-40®, or equivalent.
5. If the tailpipe cannot be pulled or twisted free from the muffler, drive a chisel between the muffler and tailpipe at several places to free it.
6. Disconnect the muffler hanger.
7. If the pipe leading into the muffler is not to be replaced,

1. Mufler   2. Clamp
Typical muffler assembly

and cannot be pulled free of the muffler, heat the joint with an oxyacetylene torch until it is cherry red. Place a block of wood against the front of the muffler and drive it rearward to disengage it from the pipe.

If the pipe is being replaced, use a chisel to free it.

✳✳ CAUTION

When using a torch, make certain that no combustibles or brake or fuel lines are in the immediate area of the torch.

To install:
8. When installing the new muffler, make sure that the locator slot and tab at the tailpipe joint index each other.
9. Drive the muffler onto the front pipe.
10. Position the system, without muffler clamps, under the car and install the hangers. Make certain that there is sufficient clearance between the system components and the floor pan and axle. Then, install the muffler clamps and tighten the hangers.

➡**Install the muffler clamps so that the shafts of the U-bolts covers the slots in the joint flanges.**

Front Exhaust Pipe (Head Pipe)

REMOVAL & INSTALLATION

1. Raise and support the front end on jackstands.
2. Disconnect any oxygen sensor wires or air injection pipes.
3. Disconnect the front pipe at the manifold(s).
4. Disconnect the rear end of the pipe from the muffler or catalytic converter.
To install:
5. Installation is the reverse of removal. Torque the pipe-to-manifold nuts to 17 ft.lb. on 4-cylinder engines, or 20 ft.lb. on the 6- and 8-cylinder engines. Make sure the pipe is properly aligned.

Rear Exhaust Pipe or Tailpipe

REMOVAL & INSTALLATION

➡**Some vehicle use an intermediate pipe, also called a rear exhaust pipe. This pipe connects the front pipe with the muffler, or runs between the converter and muffler.**

1. Raise and support the rear end on jackstands.
2. If just the intermediate pipe is being replaced, cut it at the joints and collapse and remove the remainder from the front pipe and muffler or converter. If adjoining parts are also being replaced, the pipe may be chiseled off.
3. If just the tailpipe is being replaced, cut it just behind the muffler and collapse and remove the remainder from the muffler flange. Remove the tailpipe hanger.

To install:

4. When installing any pipe, position it in the system and make sure that it is properly aligned and has sufficient clearance at the floor pan. Position U-bolts so that the bolt shafts cover any slots in the pipe flanges. When the system is correctly aligned, tighten all U-bolts and hangers.

Catalytic Converter

REMOVAL & INSTALLATION

1. Raise and support the rear end on jackstands.
2. Disconnect the downstream air injection tube at the converter.
3. On the 4-cylinder engine, the front pipe is bolted to the converter at a facing flange. On the 6 and 8-cylinder engines, the front pipe and converter are clamped together at a slip-fit joint. On all engines, the rear joint of the converter is a slip-fit.
4. To avoid damaging any components, it will probably be nec-

essary to heat any slip-fit joint with an oxyacetylene torch, until the joint is cherry red. Then, place a block of wood against the converter and drive it off of the pipe.

✱✱ CAUTION

When using a torch, make certain that no combustibles or brake or fuel lines are in the immediate area of the torch.

To install:

5. Position the replacement converter in the system and install the rear clamp. Hand-tighten the nuts.
6. On 4-cylinder engines: bolt the flanges together at the front end. Tighten the bolts to 25 ft. lbs. Tighten the rear clamp nuts to 45 ft. lbs.
7. On 6- and 8-cylinder engines, install the front clamp, make sure that the converter is properly positioned and tighten the front and rear clamp nuts to 45 ft. lbs.
8. Install the downstream air injection tube and tighten the clamps to 36–48 inch lbs.
9. Lower the car.

SPECIAL TOOLS

B.Vi. 28-01

Mot. 521-01

J-22248

Mot. 582

Mot. 251-01

J-9163

Mot. 252-01

Mot. 788

Mot. 853

Mot. 789

Mot. 851

B.Vi. 859

J-21884

Mot. 854

J-29114

Mot. 852

Mot. 861

Mot. LM

Mot. 855

Fig. 148 These tools or their equivalents may be needed when repairing or rebuilding your engine

USING A VACUUM GAUGE

White needle = steady needle   *Dark needle = drifting needle*

The vacuum gauge is one of the most useful and easy-to-use diagnostic tools. It is inexpensive, easy to hook up, and provides valuable information about the condition of your engine.

Indication: Normal engine in good condition

Gauge reading: Steady, from 17–22 in./Hg.

Indication: Sticking valve or ignition miss

Gauge reading: Needle fluctuates from 15–20 in./Hg. at idle

Indication: Late ignition or valve timing, low compression, stuck throttle valve, leaking carburetor or manifold gasket.

Gauge reading: Low (15–20 in./Hg.) but steady

Indication: Improper carburetor adjustment, or minor intake leak at carburetor or manifold

NOTE: Bad fuel injector O-rings may also cause this reading.

Gauge reading: Drifting needle

Indication: Weak valve springs, worn valve stem guides, or leaky cylinder head gasket (vibrating excessively at all speeds).

NOTE: A plugged catalytic converter may also cause this reading.

Gauge reading: Needle fluctuates as engine speed increases

Indication: Burnt valve or improper valve clearance. The needle will drop when the defective valve operates.

Gauge reading: Steady needle, but drops regularly

Indication: Choked muffler or obstruction in system. Speed up the engine. Choked muffler will exhibit a slow drop of vacuum to zero.

Gauge reading: Gradual drop in reading at idle

Indication: Worn valve guides

Gauge reading: Needle vibrates excessively at idle, but steadies as engine speed increases

Troubleshooting Engine Mechanical Problems

Problem	Cause	Solution
External oil leaks	• Cylinder head cover RTV sealant broken or improperly seated	• Replace sealant; inspect cylinder head cover sealant flange and cylinder head sealant surface for distortion and cracks
	• Oil filler cap leaking or missing	• Replace cap
	• Oil filter gasket broken or improperly seated	• Replace oil filter
	• Oil pan side gasket broken, improperly seated or opening in RTV sealant	• Replace gasket or repair opening in sealant; inspect oil pan gasket flange for distortion
	• Oil pan front oil seal broken or improperly seated	• Replace seal; inspect timing case cover and oil pan seal flange for distortion
	• Oil pan rear oil seal broken or improperly seated	• Replace seal; inspect oil pan rear oil seal flange; inspect rear main bearing cap for cracks, plugged oil return channels, or distortion in seal groove
	• Timing case cover oil seal broken or improperly seated	• Replace seal
	• Excess oil pressure because of restricted PCV valve	• Replace PCV valve
	• Oil pan drain plug loose or has stripped threads	• Repair as necessary and tighten
	• Rear oil gallery plug loose	• Use appropriate sealant on gallery plug and tighten
	• Rear camshaft plug loose or improperly seated	• Seat camshaft plug or replace and seal, as necessary
Excessive oil consumption	• Oil level too high	• Drain oil to specified level
	• Oil with wrong viscosity being used	• Replace with specified oil
	• PCV valve stuck closed	• Replace PCV valve
	• Valve stem oil deflectors (or seals) are damaged, missing, or incorrect type	• Replace valve stem oil deflectors
	• Valve stems or valve guides worn	• Measure stem-to-guide clearance and repair as necessary
	• Poorly fitted or missing valve cover baffles	• Replace valve cover
	• Piston rings broken or missing	• Replace broken or missing rings
	• Scuffed piston	• Replace piston
	• Incorrect piston ring gap	• Measure ring gap, repair as necessary
	• Piston rings sticking or excessively loose in grooves	• Measure ring side clearance, repair as necessary
	• Compression rings installed upside down	• Repair as necessary
	• Cylinder walls worn, scored, or glazed	• Repair as necessary

Troubleshooting Engine Mechanical Problems

Problem	Cause	Solution
Excessive oil consumption (cont.)	• Piston ring gaps not properly staggered	• Repair as necessary
	• Excessive main or connecting rod bearing clearance	• Measure bearing clearance, repair as necessary
No oil pressure	• Low oil level	• Add oil to correct level
	• Oil pressure gauge, warning lamp or sending unit inaccurate	• Replace oil pressure gauge or warning lamp
	• Oil pump malfunction	• Replace oil pump
	• Oil pressure relief valve sticking	• Remove and inspect oil pressure relief valve assembly
	• Oil passages on pressure side of pump obstructed	• Inspect oil passages for obstruction
	• Oil pickup screen or tube obstructed	• Inspect oil pickup for obstruction
	• Loose oil inlet tube	• Tighten or seal inlet tube
Low oil pressure	• Low oil level	• Add oil to correct level
	• Inaccurate gauge, warning lamp or sending unit	• Replace oil pressure gauge or warning lamp
	• Oil excessively thin because of dilution, poor quality, or improper grade	• Drain and refill crankcase with recommended oil
	• Excessive oil temperature	• Correct cause of overheating engine
	• Oil pressure relief spring weak or sticking	• Remove and inspect oil pressure relief valve assembly
	• Oil inlet tube and screen assembly has restriction or air leak	• Remove and inspect oil inlet tube and screen assembly. (Fill inlet tube with lacquer thinner to locate leaks.)
	• Excessive oil pump clearance	• Measure clearances
	• Excessive main, rod, or camshaft bearing clearance	• Measure bearing clearances, repair as necessary
High oil pressure	• Improper oil viscosity	• Drain and refill crankcase with correct viscosity oil
	• Oil pressure gauge or sending unit inaccurate	• Replace oil pressure gauge
	• Oil pressure relief valve sticking closed	• Remove and inspect oil pressure relief valve assembly
Main bearing noise	• Insufficient oil supply	• Inspect for low oil level and low oil pressure
	• Main bearing clearance excessive	• Measure main bearing clearance, repair as necessary
	• Bearing insert missing	• Replace missing insert
	• Crankshaft end-play excessive	• Measure end-play, repair as necessary
	• Improperly tightened main bearing cap bolts	• Tighten bolts with specified torque
	• Loose flywheel or drive plate	• Tighten flywheel or drive plate attaching bolts
	• Loose or damaged vibration damper	• Repair as necessary

Troubleshooting Engine Mechanical Problems

Problem	Cause	Solution
Connecting rod bearing noise	• Insufficient oil supply	• Inspect for low oil level and low oil pressure
	• Carbon build-up on piston	• Remove carbon from piston crown
	• Bearing clearance excessive or bearing missing	• Measure clearance, repair as necessary
	• Crankshaft connecting rod journal out-of-round	• Measure journal dimensions, repair or replace as necessary
	• Misaligned connecting rod or cap	• Repair as necessary
	• Connecting rod bolts tightened improperly	• Tighten bolts with specified torque
Piston noise	• Piston-to-cylinder wall clearance excessive (scuffed piston)	• Measure clearance and examine piston
	• Cylinder walls excessively tapered or out-of-round	• Measure cylinder wall dimensions, rebore cylinder
	• Piston ring broken	• Replace all rings on piston
	• Loose or seized piston pin	• Measure piston-to-pin clearance, repair as necessary
	• Connecting rods misaligned	• Measure rod alignment, straighten or replace
	• Piston ring side clearance excessively loose or tight	• Measure ring side clearance, repair as necessary
	• Carbon build-up on piston is excessive	• Remove carbon from piston
Valve actuating component noise	• Insufficient oil supply	• Check for: (a) Low oil level (b) Low oil pressure (c) Wrong hydraulic tappets (d) Restricted oil gallery (e) Excessive tappet to bore clearance
	• Rocker arms or pivots worn	• Replace worn rocker arms or pivots
	• Foreign objects or chips in hydraulic tappets	• Clean tappets
	• Excessive tappet leak-down	• Replace valve tappet
	• Tappet face worn	• Replace tappet; inspect corresponding cam lobe for wear
	• Broken or cocked valve springs	• Properly seat cocked springs; replace broken springs
	• Stem-to-guide clearance excessive	• Measure stem-to-guide clearance, repair as required
	• Valve bent	• Replace valve
	• Loose rocker arms	• Check and repair as necessary
	• Valve seat runout excessive	• Regrind valve seat/valves
	• Missing valve lock	• Install valve lock
	• Excessive engine oil	• Correct oil level

Troubleshooting Engine Performance

Problem	Cause	Solution
Hard starting (engine cranks normally)	• Faulty engine control system component	• Repair or replace as necessary
	• Faulty fuel pump	• Replace fuel pump
	• Faulty fuel system component	• Repair or replace as necessary
	• Faulty ignition coil	• Test and replace as necessary
	• Improper spark plug gap	• Adjust gap
	• Incorrect ignition timing	• Adjust timing
	• Incorrect valve timing	• Check valve timing; repair as necessary
Rough idle or stalling	• Incorrect curb or fast idle speed	• Adjust curb or fast idle speed (If possible)
	• Incorrect ignition timing	• Adjust timing to specification
	• Improper feedback system operation	• Refer to Chapter 4
	• Faulty EGR valve operation	• Test EGR system and replace as necessary
	• Faulty PCV valve air flow	• Test PCV valve and replace as necessary
	• Faulty TAC vacuum motor or valve	• Repair as necessary
	• Air leak into manifold vacuum	• Inspect manifold vacuum connections and repair as necessary
	• Faulty distributor rotor or cap	• Replace rotor or cap (Distributor systems only)
	• Improperly seated valves	• Test cylinder compression, repair as necessary
	• Incorrect ignition wiring	• Inspect wiring and correct as necessary
	• Faulty ignition coil	• Test coil and replace as necessary
	• Restricted air vent or idle passages	• Clean passages
	• Restricted air cleaner	• Clean or replace air cleaner filter element
Faulty low-speed operation	• Restricted idle air vents and passages	• Clean air vents and passages
	• Restricted air cleaner	• Clean or replace air cleaner filter element
	• Faulty spark plugs	• Clean or replace spark plugs
	• Dirty, corroded, or loose ignition secondary circuit wire connections	• Clean or tighten secondary circuit wire connections
	• Improper feedback system operation	• Refer to Chapter 4
	• Faulty ignition coil high voltage wire	• Replace ignition coil high voltage wire (Distributor systems only)
	• Faulty distributor cap	• Replace cap (Distributor systems only)
Faulty acceleration	• Incorrect ignition timing	• Adjust timing
	• Faulty fuel system component	• Repair or replace as necessary
	• Faulty spark plug(s)	• Clean or replace spark plug(s)
	• Improperly seated valves	• Test cylinder compression, repair as necessary
	• Faulty ignition coil	• Test coil and replace as necessary

Troubleshooting Engine Performance

Problem	Cause	Solution
Faulty acceleration (cont.)	• Improper feedback system operation	• Refer to Chapter 4
Faulty high speed operation	• Incorrect ignition timing • Faulty advance mechanism	• Adjust timing (if possible) • Check advance mechanism and repair as necessary (Distributor systems only)
	• Low fuel pump volume • Wrong spark plug air gap or wrong plug • Partially restricted exhaust manifold, exhaust pipe, catalytic converter, muffler, or tailpipe	• Replace fuel pump • Adjust air gap or install correct plug • Eliminate restriction
	• Restricted vacuum passages • Restricted air cleaner	• Clean passages • Cleaner or replace filter element as necessary
	• Faulty distributor rotor or cap	• Replace rotor or cap (Distributor systems only)
	• Faulty ignition coil • Improperly seated valve(s)	• Test coil and replace as necessary • Test cylinder compression, repair as necessary
	• Faulty valve spring(s)	• Inspect and test valve spring tension, replace as necessary
	• Incorrect valve timing	• Check valve timing and repair as necessary
	• Intake manifold restricted	• Remove restriction or replace manifold
	• Worn distributor shaft	• Replace shaft (Distributor systems only)
	• Improper feedback system operation	• Refer to Chapter 4
Misfire at all speeds	• Faulty spark plug(s) • Faulty spark plug wire(s) • Faulty distributor cap or rotor	• Clean or relace spark plug(s) • Replace as necessary • Replace cap or rotor (Distributor systems only)
	• Faulty ignition coil • Primary ignition circuit shorted or open intermittently • Improperly seated valve(s)	• Test coil and replace as necessary • Troubleshoot primary circuit and repair as necessary • Test cylinder compression, repair as necessary
	• Faulty hydraulic tappet(s) • Improper feedback system operation • Faulty valve spring(s)	• Clean or replace tappet(s) • Refer to Chapter 4 • Inspect and test valve spring tension, repair as necessary
	• Worn camshaft lobes • Air leak into manifold	• Replace camshaft • Check manifold vacuum and repair as necessary
	• Fuel pump volume or pressure low • Blown cylinder head gasket • Intake or exhaust manifold passage(s) restricted	• Replace fuel pump • Replace gasket • Pass chain through passage(s) and repair as necessary
Power not up to normal	• Incorrect ignition timing • Faulty distributor rotor	• Adjust timing • Replace rotor (Distributor systems only)

Troubleshooting Engine Performance

Problem	Cause	Solution
Power not up to normal (cont.)	• Incorrect spark plug gap • Faulty fuel pump • Faulty fuel pump • Incorrect valve timing • Faulty ignition coil • Faulty ignition wires • Improperly seated valves • Blown cylinder head gasket • Leaking piston rings • Improper feedback system operation	• Adjust gap • Replace fuel pump • Replace fuel pump • Check valve timing and repair as necessary • Test coil and replace as necessary • Test wires and replace as necessary • Test cylinder compression and repair as necessary • Replace gasket • Test compression and repair as necessary • Refer to Chapter 4
Intake backfire	• Improper ignition timing • Defective EGR component • Defective TAC vacuum motor or valve	• Adjust timing • Repair as necessary • Repair as necessary
Exhaust backfire	• Air leak into manifold vacuum • Faulty air injection diverter valve • Exhaust leak	• Check manifold vacuum and repair as necessary • Test diverter valve and replace as necessary • Locate and eliminate leak
Ping or spark knock	• Incorrect ignition timing • Distributor advance malfunction • Excessive combustion chamber deposits • Air leak into manifold vacuum • Excessively high compression • Fuel octane rating excessively low • Sharp edges in combustion chamber • EGR valve not functioning properly	• Adjust timing • Inspect advance mechanism and repair as necessary (Distributor systems only) • Remove with combustion chamber cleaner • Check manifold vacuum and repair as necessary • Test compression and repair as necessary • Try alternate fuel source • Grind smooth • Test EGR system and replace as necessary
Surging (at cruising to top speeds)	• Low fuel pump pressure or volume • Improper PCV valve air flow • Air leak into manifold vacuum • Incorrect spark advance • Restricted fuel filter • Restricted air cleaner • EGR valve not functioning properly • Improper feedback system operation	• Replace fuel pump • Test PCV valve and replace as necessary • Check manifold vacuum and repair as necessary • Test and replace as necessary • Replace fuel filter • Clean or replace air cleaner filter element • Test EGR system and replace as necessary • Refer to Chapter 4

Troubleshooting the Serpentine Drive Belt

Problem	Cause	Solution
Tension sheeting fabric failure (woven fabric on outside circumference of belt has cracked or separated from body of belt)	• Grooved or backside idler pulley diameters are less than minimum recommended • Tension sheeting contacting (rubbing) stationary object • Excessive heat causing woven fabric to age • Tension sheeting splice has fractured	• Replace pulley(s) not conforming to specification • Correct rubbing condition • Replace belt • Replace belt
Noise (objectional squeal, squeak, or rumble is heard or felt while drive belt is in operation)	• Belt slippage • Bearing noise • Belt misalignment • Belt-to-pulley mismatch • Driven component inducing vibration • System resonant frequency inducing vibration	• Adjust belt • Locate and repair • Align belt/pulley(s) • Install correct belt • Locate defective driven component and repair • Vary belt tension within specifications. Replace belt.
Rib chunking (one or more ribs has separated from belt body)	• Foreign objects imbedded in pulley grooves • Installation damage • Drive loads in excess of design specifications • Insufficient internal belt adhesion	• Remove foreign objects from pulley grooves • Replace belt • Adjust belt tension • Replace belt
Rib or belt wear (belt ribs contact bottom of pulley grooves)	• Pulley(s) misaligned • Mismatch of belt and pulley groove widths • Abrasive environment • Rusted pulley(s) • Sharp or jagged pulley groove tips • Rubber deteriorated	• Align pulley(s) • Replace belt • Replace belt • Clean rust from pulley(s) • Replace pulley • Replace belt
Longitudinal belt cracking (cracks between two ribs)	• Belt has mistracked from pulley groove • Pulley groove tip has worn away rubber-to-tensile member	• Replace belt • Replace belt
Belt slips	• Belt slipping because of insufficient tension • Belt or pulley subjected to substance (belt dressing, oil, ethylene glycol) that has reduced friction • Driven component bearing failure • Belt glazed and hardened from heat and excessive slippage	• Adjust tension • Replace belt and clean pulleys • Replace faulty component bearing • Replace belt
"Groove jumping" (belt does not maintain correct position on pulley, or turns over and/or runs off pulleys)	• Insufficient belt tension • Pulley(s) not within design tolerance • Foreign object(s) in grooves	• Adjust belt tension • Replace pulley(s) • Remove foreign objects from grooves

Troubleshooting the Serpentine Drive Belt

Problem	Cause	Solution
"Groove jumping" (belt does not maintain correct position on pulley, or turns over and/or runs off pulleys)	• Excessive belt speed • Pulley misalignment • Belt-to-pulley profile mismatched • Belt cordline is distorted	• Avoid excessive engine acceleration • Align pulley(s) • Install correct belt • Replace belt
Belt broken (Note: identify and correct problem before replacement belt is installed)	• Excessive tension • Tensile members damaged during belt installation • Belt turnover • Severe pulley misalignment • Bracket, pulley, or bearing failure	• Replace belt and adjust tension to specification • Replace belt • Replace belt • Align pulley(s) • Replace defective component and belt
Cord edge failure (tensile member exposed at edges of belt or separated from belt body)	• Excessive tension • Drive pulley misalignment • Belt contacting stationary object • Pulley irregularities • Improper pulley construction • Insufficient adhesion between tensile member and rubber matrix	• Adjust belt tension • Align pulley • Correct as necessary • Replace pulley • Replace pulley • Replace belt and adjust tension to specifications
Sporadic rib cracking (multiple cracks in belt ribs at random intervals)	• Ribbed pulley(s) diameter less than minimum specification • Backside bend flat pulley(s) diameter less than minimum • Excessive heat condition causing rubber to harden • Excessive belt thickness • Belt overcured • Excessive tension	• Replace pulley(s) • Replace pulley(s) • Correct heat condition as necessary • Replace belt • Replace belt • Adjust belt tension

Troubleshooting the Cooling System

Problem	Cause	Solution
High temperature gauge indication— overheating	· Coolant level low · Improper fan operation · Radiator hose(s) collapsed · Radiator airflow blocked · Faulty pressure cap · Ignition timing incorrect · Air trapped in cooling system · Heavy traffic driving · Incorrect cooling system component(s) installed · Faulty thermostat · Water pump shaft broken or impeller loose · Radiator tubes clogged · Cooling system clogged · Casting flash in cooling passages · Brakes dragging · Excessive engine friction · Antifreeze concentration over 68% · Missing air seals · Faulty gauge or sending unit · Loss of coolant flow caused by leakage or foaming · Viscous fan drive failed	· Replenish coolant · Repair or replace as necessary · Replace hose(s) · Remove restriction (bug screen, fog lamps, etc.) · Replace pressure cap · Adjust ignition timing · Purge air · Operate at fast idle in neutral intermittently to cool engine · Install proper component(s) · Replace thermostat · Replace water pump · Flush radiator · Flush system · Repair or replace as necessary. Flash may be visible by removing cooling system components or removing core plugs. · Repair brakes · Repair engine · Lower antifreeze concentration percentage · Replace air seals · Repair or replace faulty component · Repair or replace leaking component, replace coolant · Replace unit
Low temperature indication— undercooling	· Thermostat stuck open · Faulty gauge or sending unit	· Replace thermostat · Repair or replace faulty component
Coolant loss—boilover	· Overfilled cooling system · Quick shutdown after hard (hot) run · Air in system resulting in occasional "burping" of coolant · Insufficient antifreeze allowing coolant boiling point to be too low · Antifreeze deteriorated because of age or contamination · Leaks due to loose hose clamps, loose nuts, bolts, drain plugs, faulty hoses, or defective radiator	· Reduce coolant level to proper specification · Allow engine to run at fast idle prior to shutdown · Purge system · Add antifreeze to raise boiling point · Replace coolant · Pressure test system to locate source of leak(s) then repair as necessary

Troubleshooting the Cooling System (cont.)

Problem	Cause	Solution
Coolant loss—boilover	• Faulty head gasket • Cracked head, manifold, or block • Faulty radiator cap	• Replace head gasket • Replace as necessary • Replace cap
Coolant entry into crankcase or cylinder(s)	• Faulty head gasket • Crack in head, manifold or block	• Replace head gasket • Replace as necessary
Coolant recovery system inoperative	• Coolant level low • Leak in system • Pressure cap not tight or seal missing, or leaking • Pressure cap defective • Overflow tube clogged or leaking • Recovery bottle vent restricted	• Replenish coolant to FULL mark • Pressure test to isolate leak and repair as necessary • Repair as necessary • Replace cap • Repair as necessary • Remove restriction
Noise	• Fan contacting shroud • Loose water pump impeller • Glazed fan belt • Loose fan belt • Rough surface on drive pulley • Water pump bearing worn • Belt alignment	• Reposition shroud and inspect engine mounts (on electric fans inspect assembly) • Replace pump • Apply silicone or replace belt • Adjust fan belt tension • Replace pulley • Remove belt to isolate. Replace pump. • Check pulley alignment. Repair as necessary.
No coolant flow through heater core	• Restricted return inlet in water pump • Heater hose collapsed or restricted • Restricted heater core • Restricted outlet in thermostat housing • Intake manifold bypass hole in cylinder head restricted • Faulty heater control valve • Intake manifold coolant passage restricted	• Remove restriction • Remove restriction or replace hose • Remove restriction or replace core • Remove flash or restriction • Remove restriction • Replace valve • Remove restriction or replace intake manifold

NOTE: *Immediately after shutdown, the engine enters a condition known as heat soak. This is caused by the cooling system being inoperative while engine temperature is still high. If coolant temperature rises above boiling point, expansion and pressure may push some coolant out of the radiator overflow tube. If this does not occur frequently it is considered normal.*

AIR POLLUTION 4-2
NATURAL POLLUTANTS 4-2
INDUSTRIAL POLLUTANTS 4-2
AUTOMOTIVE POLLUTANTS 4-2
    TEMPERATURE INVERSION 4-2
    HEAT TRANSFER 4-3
AUTOMOTIVE EMISSIONS 4-3
EXHAUST GASES 4-3
    HYDROCARBONS 4-3
    CARBON MONOXIDE 4-4
    NITROGEN 4-4
    OXIDES OF SULFUR 4-4
    PARTICULATE MATTER 4-4
CRANKCASE EMISSIONS 4-5
EVAPORATIVE EMISSIONS 4-5
EMISSION CONTROLS 4-5
CRANKCASE EMISSION CONTROLS 4-5
    OPERATION 4-5
    TESTING 4-8
    REMOVAL & INSTALLATION 4-8
AIR INJECTION SYSTEM 4-9
    DESCRIPTION 4-9
    REMOVAL & INSTALLATION 4-10
    TROUBLESHOOTING 4-11
EXHAUST GAS RECIRCULATION (EGR)
  SYSTEM 4-11
    OPERATION 4-11
    REMOVAL & INSTALLATION 4-14
THERMOSTATICALLY CONTROLLED AIR
  CLEANER SYSTEM (TAC) 4-14
    OPERATION 4-14
    TROUBLESHOOTING 4-14
DISTRIBUTOR CONTROLS 4-15
    DUAL DIAPHRAGM DISTRIBUTOR
      TEST 4-15
VACUUM THROTTLE MODULATING
  SYSTEM (VTM) 4-15
    OPERATION 4-15
    TESTING 4-16
    ADJUSTMENT 4-16
TRANSMISSION CONTROLLED SPARK
  (TCS) SYSTEM 4-16
    OPERATION 4-16
    TESTING 4-17
ANTI-DIESELING SOLENOID 4-19
    TESTING 4-19
ELECTRIC ASSIST CHOKE 4-19
    OPERATION 4-19
    TESTING 4-19
FUEL TANK VAPOR EMISSION
  CONTROL SYSTEM 4-20
    OPERATION 4-20
    TROUBLESHOOTING 4-20
ELECTRONIC ENGINE
  CONTROLS 4-20
GENERAL INFORMATION 4-20
    COMPUTER CONTROLLED
      CATALYTIC CONVERTER (C-4)
      SYSTEM 4-21
    COMPUTER COMMAND CONTROL
      (CCC) SYSTEM 4-22

AMERICAN MOTORS FEEDBACK
  SYSTEM 4-23
    BASIC TROUBLESHOOTING 4-24
    ACTIVATING THE TROUBLE
      CODE 4-26
OXYGEN SENSOR 4-28
    REMOVAL & INSTALLATION 4-28
VACUUM SWITCH 4-28
    REMOVAL & INSTALLATION 4-28
CONTROL UNIT 4-28
    REMOVAL & INSTALLATION 4-28
MIXTURE CONTROL SOLENOID 4-28
    REMOVAL & INSTALLATION 4-28
STEPPER MOTOR 4-29
    REMOVAL & INSTALLATION 4-29
CATALYTIC CONVERTER 4-29
    OPERATION 4-29
CHOKE HEAT BY-PASS VALVE
  (CHBPV) 4-30
    OPERATION 4-30
FUEL RETURN SYSTEM 4-30
    OPERATION 4-30
VACUUM DIAGRAMS 4-31
COMPONENT LOCATIONS
  EMISSION COMPONENT
    LOCATIONS—EARLY MODEL V8
    ENGINE 4-6
  EMISSION COMPONENT
    LOCATIONS—LATE MODEL INLINE
    ENGINE 4-7
SPECIFICATION CHARTS
  EMISSION CONTROL SYSTEMS
    USAGE 4-8
  EMISSION CONTROLLED
    DISTRIBUTOR VACUUM
    APPLICATION CHART FOR VEHICLES
    EQUIPPED WITH TCS 4-18
TROUBLESHOOTING CHARTS
  EXPLANATION OF TROUBLE CODES
    GM C-4 AND CCC SYSTEMS 4-26

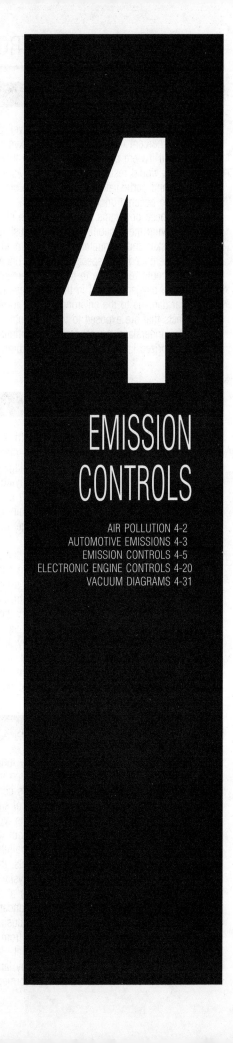

4

EMISSION CONTROLS

AIR POLLUTION 4-2
AUTOMOTIVE EMISSIONS 4-3
EMISSION CONTROLS 4-5
ELECTRONIC ENGINE CONTROLS 4-20
VACUUM DIAGRAMS 4-31

AIR POLLUTION

The earth's atmosphere, at or near sea level, consists approximately of 78 percent nitrogen, 21 percent oxygen and 1 percent other gases. If it were possible to remain in this state, 100 percent clean air would result. However, many varied sources allow other gases and particulates to mix with the clean air, causing our atmosphere to become unclean or polluted.

Some of these pollutants are visible while others are invisible, with each having the capability of causing distress to the eyes, ears, throat, skin and respiratory system. Should these pollutants become concentrated in a specific area and under certain conditions, death could result due to the displacement or chemical change of the oxygen content in the air. These pollutants can also cause great damage to the environment and to the many man made objects that are exposed to the elements.

To better understand the causes of air pollution, the pollutants can be categorized into 3 separate types, natural, industrial and automotive.

Natural Pollutants

Natural pollution has been present on earth since before man appeared and continues to be a factor when discussing air pollution, although it causes only a small percentage of the overall pollution problem. It is the direct result of decaying organic matter, wind born smoke and particulates from such natural events as plain and forest fires (ignited by heat or lightning), volcanic ash, sand and dust which can spread over a large area of the countryside.

Such a phenomenon of natural pollution has been seen in the form of volcanic eruptions, with the resulting plume of smoke, steam and volcanic ash blotting out the sun's rays as it spreads and rises higher into the atmosphere. As it travels into the atmosphere the upper air currents catch and carry the smoke and ash, while condensing the steam back into water vapor. As the water vapor, smoke and ash travel on their journey, the smoke dissipates into the atmosphere while the ash and moisture settle back to earth in a trail hundreds of miles long. In some cases, lives are lost and millions of dollars of property damage result.

Industrial Pollutants

Industrial pollution is caused primarily by industrial processes, the burning of coal, oil and natural gas, which in turn produce smoke and fumes. Because the burning fuels contain large amounts of sulfur, the principal ingredients of smoke and fumes are sulfur dioxide and particulate matter. This type of pollutant occurs most severely during still, damp and cool weather, such as at night. Even in its less severe form, this pollutant is not confined to just cities. Because of air movements, the pollutants move for miles over the surrounding countryside, leaving in its path a barren and unhealthy environment for all living things.

Working with Federal, State and Local mandated regulations and by carefully monitoring emissions, big business has greatly reduced the amount of pollutant introduced from its industrial sources, striving to obtain an acceptable level. Because of the mandated industrial emission clean up, many land areas and streams in and around the cities that were formerly barren of vege-

tation and life, have now begun to move back in the direction of nature's intended balance.

Automotive Pollutants

The third major source of air pollution is automotive emissions. The emissions from the internal combustion engines were not an appreciable problem years ago because of the small number of registered vehicles and the nation's small highway system. However, during the early 1950's, the trend of the American people was to move from the cities to the surrounding suburbs. This caused an immediate problem in transportation because the majority of suburbs were not afforded mass transit conveniences. This lack of transportation created an attractive market for the automobile manufacturers, which resulted in a dramatic increase in the number of vehicles produced and sold, along with a marked increase in highway construction between cities and the suburbs. Multi-vehicle families emerged with a growing emphasis placed on an individual vehicle per family member. As the increase in vehicle ownership and usage occurred, so did pollutant levels in and around the cities, as suburbanites drove daily to their businesses and employment, returning at the end of the day to their homes in the suburbs.

It was noted that a smoke and fog type haze was being formed and at times, remained in suspension over the cities, taking time to dissipate. At first this "smog," derived from the words "smoke" and "fog," was thought to result from industrial pollution but it was determined that automobile emissions shared the blame. It was discovered that when normal automobile emissions were exposed to sunlight for a period of time, complex chemical reactions would take place.

It is now known that smog is a photo chemical layer which develops when certain oxides of nitrogen (NOx) and unburned hydrocarbons (HC) from automobile emissions are exposed to sunlight. Pollution was more severe when smog would become stagnant over an area in which a warm layer of air settled over the top of the cooler air mass, trapping and holding the cooler mass at ground level. The trapped cooler air would keep the emissions from being dispersed and diluted through normal air flows. This type of air stagnation was given the name "Temperature Inversion."

TEMPERATURE INVERSION

In normal weather situations, surface air is warmed by heat radiating from the earth's surface and the sun's rays. This causes it to rise upward, into the atmosphere. Upon rising it will cool through a convection type heat exchange with the cooler upper air. As warm air rises, the surface pollutants are carried upward and dissipated into the atmosphere.

When a temperature inversion occurs, we find the higher air is no longer cooler, but is warmer than the surface air, causing the cooler surface air to become trapped. This warm air blanket can extend from above ground level to a few hundred or even a few thousand feet into the air. As the surface air is trapped, so are the pollutants, causing a severe smog condition. Should this stagnant air mass extend to a few thousand feet high, enough air movement with the inversion takes place to allow the smog layer to rise above ground level but the pollutants still cannot dissipate. This inversion can remain for days over an area, with the smog level only rising or lowering from ground level to a few hundred feet high. Meanwhile, the pollutant levels increase, causing eye irritation, respiratory problems, reduced visibility, plant damage and in some cases, even disease.

This inversion phenomenon was first noted in the Los Angeles, California area. The city lies in terrain resembling a basin and with certain weather conditions, a cold air mass is held in the basin while a warmer air mass covers it like a lid.

Because this type of condition was first documented as prevalent in the Los Angeles area, this type of trapped pollution was named Los Angeles Smog, although it occurs in other areas where a large concentration of automobiles are used and the air remains stagnant for any length of time.

HEAT TRANSFER

Consider the internal combustion engine as a machine in which raw materials must be placed so a finished product comes out. As in any machine operation, a certain amount of wasted material is formed. When we relate this to the internal combustion engine, we find that through the input of air and fuel, we obtain power during the combustion process to drive the vehicle. The by-product or waste of this power is, in part, heat and exhaust gases with which we must dispose.

AUTOMOTIVE EMISSIONS

Before emission controls were mandated on internal combustion engines, other sources of engine pollutants were discovered along with the exhaust emissions. It was determined that engine combustion exhaust produced approximately 60 percent of the total emission pollutants, fuel evaporation from the fuel tank and carburetor vents produced 20 percent, with the final 20 percent being produced through the crankcase as a by-product of the combustion process.

Exhaust Gases

The exhaust gases emitted into the atmosphere are a combination of burned and unburned fuel. To understand the exhaust emission and its composition, we must review some basic chemistry.

When the air/fuel mixture is introduced into the engine, we are mixing air, composed of nitrogen (78 percent), oxygen (21 percent) and other gases (1 percent) with the fuel, which is 100 percent hydrocarbons (HC), in a semi-controlled ratio. As the combustion process is accomplished, power is produced to move the vehicle while the heat of combustion is transferred to the cooling system. The exhaust gases are then composed of nitrogen, a diatomic gas (N_2), the same as was introduced in the engine, carbon dioxide (CO_2), the same gas that is used in beverage carbonation, and water vapor (H_2O). The nitrogen (N_2), for the most part, passes through the engine unchanged, while the oxygen (O_2) reacts (burns) with the hydrocarbons (HC) and produces the carbon dioxide (CO_2) and the water vapors (H_2O). If this chemical process would be the only process to take place, the exhaust emissions would be harmless. However, during the combustion process, other compounds are formed which are considered dangerous. These pollutants are hydrocarbons (HC), carbon monoxide (CO), oxides of nitrogen (NOx) oxides of sulfur (SOx) and engine particulates.

HYDROCARBONS

Hydrocarbons (HC) are essentially fuel which was not burned during the combustion process or which has escaped into the atmosphere through fuel evaporation. The main sources of incomplete combustion are rich air/fuel mixtures, low engine temperatures and improper spark timing. The main sources of hydrocarbon emission through fuel evaporation on most vehicles used to be the vehicle's fuel tank and carburetor float bowl.

To reduce combustion hydrocarbon emission, engine modifications were made to minimize dead space and surface area in the combustion chamber. In addition, the air/fuel mixture was made more lean through the improved control which feedback carburetion and fuel injection offers and by the addition of external controls to aid in further combustion of the hydrocarbons outside the engine. Two such methods were the addition of air injection systems, to inject fresh air into the exhaust manifolds and the installation of catalytic converters, units that are able to burn traces of hydrocarbons without affecting the internal combustion process or fuel economy.

To control hydrocarbon emissions through fuel evaporation, modifications were made to the fuel tank to allow storage of the fuel vapors during periods of engine shut-down. Modifications

The heat from the combustion process can rise to over 4000°F (2204°C). The dissipation of this heat is controlled by a ram air effect, the use of cooling fans to cause air flow and a liquid coolant solution surrounding the combustion area to transfer the heat of combustion through the cylinder walls and into the coolant. The coolant is then directed to a thin-finned, multi-tubed radiator, from which the excess heat is transferred to the atmosphere by 1 of the 3 heat transfer methods, conduction, convection or radiation.

The cooling of the combustion area is an important part in the control of exhaust emissions. To understand the behavior of the combustion and transfer of its heat, consider the air/fuel charge. It is ignited and the flame front burns progressively across the combustion chamber until the burning charge reaches the cylinder walls. Some of the fuel in contact with the walls is not hot enough to burn, thereby snuffing out or quenching the combustion process. This leaves unburned fuel in the combustion chamber. This unburned fuel is then forced out of the cylinder and into the exhaust system, along with the exhaust gases.

Many attempts have been made to minimize the amount of unburned fuel in the combustion chambers due to quenching, by increasing the coolant temperature and lessening the contact area of the coolant around the combustion area. However, design limitations within the combustion chambers prevent the complete burning of the air/fuel charge, so a certain amount of the unburned fuel is still expelled into the exhaust system, regardless of modifications to the engine.

were also made to the air intake system so that at specific times during engine operation, these vapors may be purged and burned by blending them with the air/fuel mixture.

CARBON MONOXIDE

Carbon monoxide is formed when not enough oxygen is present during the combustion process to convert carbon (C) to carbon dioxide (CO_2). An increase in the carbon monoxide (CO) emission is normally accompanied by an increase in the hydrocarbon (HC) emission because of the lack of oxygen to completely burn all of the fuel mixture.

Carbon monoxide (CO) also increases the rate at which the photo chemical smog is formed by speeding up the conversion of nitric oxide (NO) to nitrogen dioxide (NO_2). To accomplish this, carbon monoxide (CO) combines with oxygen (O_2) and nitric oxide (NO) to produce carbon dioxide (CO_2) and nitrogen dioxide (NO_2). ($CO + O_2 + NO \; CO_2 + NO_2$).

The dangers of carbon monoxide, which is an odorless and colorless toxic gas are many. When carbon monoxide is inhaled into the lungs and passed into the blood stream, oxygen is replaced by the carbon monoxide in the red blood cells, causing a reduction in the amount of oxygen supplied to the many parts of the body. This lack of oxygen causes headaches, lack of coordination, reduced mental alertness and, should the carbon monoxide concentration be high enough, death could result.

NITROGEN

Normally, nitrogen is an inert gas. When heated to approximately 2500°F (1371°C) through the combustion process, this gas becomes active and causes an increase in the nitric oxide (NO) emission.

Oxides of nitrogen (NOx) are composed of approximately 97–98 percent nitric oxide (NO). Nitric oxide is a colorless gas but when it is passed into the atmosphere, it combines with oxygen and forms nitrogen dioxide (NO_2). The nitrogen dioxide then combines with chemically active hydrocarbons (HC) and when in the presence of sunlight, causes the formation of photo-chemical smog.

Ozone

To further complicate matters, some of the nitrogen dioxide (NO_2) is broken apart by the sunlight to form nitric oxide and oxygen. (NO_2 + sunlight NO + O). This single atom of oxygen then combines with diatomic (meaning 2 atoms) oxygen (O_2) to form ozone (O_3). Ozone is one of the smells associated with smog. It has a pungent and offensive odor, irritates the eyes and lung tissues, affects the growth of plant life and causes rapid deterioration of rubber products. Ozone can be formed by sunlight as well as electrical discharge into the air.

The most common discharge area on the automobile engine is the secondary ignition electrical system, especially when inferior quality spark plug cables are used. As the surge of high voltage is routed through the secondary cable, the circuit builds up an electrical field around the wire, which acts upon the oxygen in the surrounding air to form the ozone. The faint glow along the cable with the engine running that may be visible on a dark night, is called the "corona discharge." It is the result of the electrical field

passing from a high along the cable, to a low in the surrounding air, which forms the ozone gas. The combination of corona and ozone has been a major cause of cable deterioration. Recently, different and better quality insulating materials have lengthened the life of the electrical cables.

Although ozone at ground level can be harmful, ozone is beneficial to the earth's inhabitants. By having a concentrated ozone layer called the "ozonosphere," between 10 and 20 miles (16–32 km) up in the atmosphere, much of the ultra violet radiation from the sun's rays are absorbed and screened. If this ozone layer were not present, much of the earth's surface would be burned, dried and unfit for human life.

OXIDES OF SULFUR

Oxides of sulfur (SOx) were initially ignored in the exhaust system emissions, since the sulfur content of gasoline as a fuel is less than $\frac{1}{10}$ of 1 percent. Because of this small amount, it was felt that it contributed very little to the overall pollution problem. However, because of the difficulty in solving the sulfur emissions in industrial pollutions and the introduction of catalytic converter to the automobile exhaust systems, a change was mandated. The automobile exhaust system, when equipped with a catalytic converter, changes the sulfur dioxide (SO_2) into sulfur trioxide (SO_3).

When this combines with water vapors (H_2O), a sulfuric acid mist (H_2SO_4) is formed and is a very difficult pollutant to handle since it is extremely corrosive. This sulfuric acid mist that is formed, is the same mist that rises from the vents of an automobile battery when an active chemical reaction takes place within the battery cells.

When a large concentration of vehicles equipped with catalytic converters are operating in an area, this acid mist may rise and be distributed over a large ground area causing land, plant, crop, paint and building damage.

PARTICULATE MATTER

A certain amount of particulate matter is present in the burning of any fuel, with carbon constituting the largest percentage of the particulates. In gasoline, the remaining particulates are the burned remains of the various other compounds used in its manufacture. When a gasoline engine is in good internal condition, the particulate emissions are low but as the engine wears internally, the particulate emissions increase. By visually inspecting the tail pipe emissions, a determination can be made as to where an engine defect may exist. An engine with light gray or blue smoke emitting from the tail pipe normally indicates an increase in the oil consumption through burning due to internal engine wear. Black smoke would indicate a defective fuel delivery system, causing the engine to operate in a rich mode. Regardless of the color of the smoke, the internal part of the engine or the fuel delivery system should be repaired to prevent excess particulate emissions.

Diesel and turbine engines emit a darkened plume of smoke from the exhaust system because of the type of fuel used. Emission control regulations are mandated for this type of emission and more stringent measures are being used to prevent excess emission of the particulate matter. Electronic components are being introduced to control the injection of the fuel at precisely the proper time of piston travel, to achieve the optimum in fuel ignition and fuel usage. Other particulate after-burning components are being tested to achieve a cleaner emission.

Good grades of engine lubricating oils should be used, which meet the manufacturers specification. Cut-rate oils can contribute to the particulate emission problem because of their low flash or ignition temperature point. Such oils burn prematurely during the combustion process causing emission of particulate matter.

The cooling system is an important factor in the reduction of particulate matter. The optimum combustion will occur, with the cooling system operating at a temperature specified by the manufacturer. The cooling system must be maintained in the same manner as the engine oiling system, as each system is required to perform properly in order for the engine to operate efficiently for a long time.

Crankcase Emissions

Crankcase emissions are made up of water, acids, unburned fuel, oil fumes and particulates. These emissions are classified as hydrocarbons (HC) and are formed by the small amount of unburned, compressed air/fuel mixture entering the crankcase from the combustion area (between the cylinder walls and piston rings) during the compression and power strokes. The head of the compression and combustion help to form the remaining crankcase emissions.

Since the first engines, crankcase emissions were allowed into the atmosphere through a road draft tube, mounted on the lower side of the engine block. Fresh air came in through an open oil filler cap or breather. The air passed through the crankcase mixing with blow-by gases. The motion of the vehicle and the air blowing past the open end of the road draft tube caused a low pressure area (vacuum) at the end of the tube. Crankcase emissions were simply drawn out of the road draft tube into the air.

To control the crankcase emission, the road draft tube was deleted. A hose and/or tubing was routed from the crankcase to the intake manifold so the blow-by emission could be burned with the air/fuel mixture. However, it was found that intake manifold vacuum, used to draw the crankcase emissions into the manifold, would vary in strength at the wrong time and not allow the proper emission flow. A regulating valve was needed to control the flow of air through the crankcase.

Testing, showed the removal of the blow-by gases from the crankcase as quickly as possible, was most important to the longevity of the engine. Should large accumulations of blow-by gases remain and condense, dilution of the engine oil would oc-

cur to form water, soots, resins, acids and lead salts, resulting in the formation of sludge and varnishes. This condensation of the blow-by gases occurs more frequently on vehicles used in numerous starting and stopping conditions, excessive idling and when the engine is not allowed to attain normal operating temperature through short runs.

Evaporative Emissions

Gasoline fuel is a major source of pollution, before and after it is burned in the automobile engine. From the time the fuel is refined, stored, pumped and transported, again stored until it is pumped into the fuel tank of the vehicle, the gasoline gives off unburned hydrocarbons (HC) into the atmosphere. Through the redesign of storage areas and venting systems, the pollution factor was diminished, but not eliminated, from the refinery standpoint. However, the automobile still remained the primary source of vaporized, unburned hydrocarbon (HC) emissions.

Fuel pumped from an underground storage tank is cool but when exposed to a warmer ambient temperature, will expand. Before controls were mandated, an owner might fill the fuel tank with fuel from an underground storage tank and park the vehicle for some time in warm area, such as a parking lot. As the fuel would warm, it would expand and should no provisions or area be provided for the expansion, the fuel would spill out of the filler neck and onto the ground, causing hydrocarbon (HC) pollution and creating a severe fire hazard. To correct this condition, the vehicle manufacturers added overflow plumbing and/or gasoline tanks with built in expansion areas or domes.

However, this did not control the fuel vapor emission from the fuel tank. It was determined that most of the fuel evaporation occurred when the vehicle was stationary and the engine not operating. Most vehicles carry 5–25 gallons (19–95 liters) of gasoline. Should a large concentration of vehicles be parked in one area, such as a large parking lot, excessive fuel vapor emissions would take place, increasing as the temperature increases.

To prevent the vapor emission from escaping into the atmosphere, the fuel systems were designed to trap the vapors while the vehicle is stationary, by sealing the system from the atmosphere. A storage system is used to collect and hold the fuel vapors from the carburetor (if equipped) and the fuel tank when the engine is not operating. When the engine is started, the storage system is then purged of the fuel vapors, which are drawn into the engine and burned with the air/fuel mixture.

EMISSION CONTROLS

Crankcase Emission Controls

OPERATION

▶ See Figure 1

The crankcase emission control equipment consists of a Positive Crankcase Ventilation valve (PCV), a closed or open oil filler cap and hoses to connect this equipment.

When the engine is running, a small portion of the gases which are formed in the combustion chamber during combustion,

leak by the piston rings and enter the crankcase. Since these gases are under pressure, they tend to escape from the crankcase and enter the atmosphere. If these gases were allowed to remain in the crankcase for any length of time, they would contaminate the engine oil and cause sludge to build up. If the gases were allowed to escape into the atmosphere, they would pollute the air, as they contain unburned hydrocarbons. The crankcase emission control equipment recycles these gases back into the engine combustion chamber where they are burned.

Crankcase gases are recycled in the following manner: while the engine is running, clean filtered air is drawn into the crankcase either directly through the oil filler cap, or through the carbu-

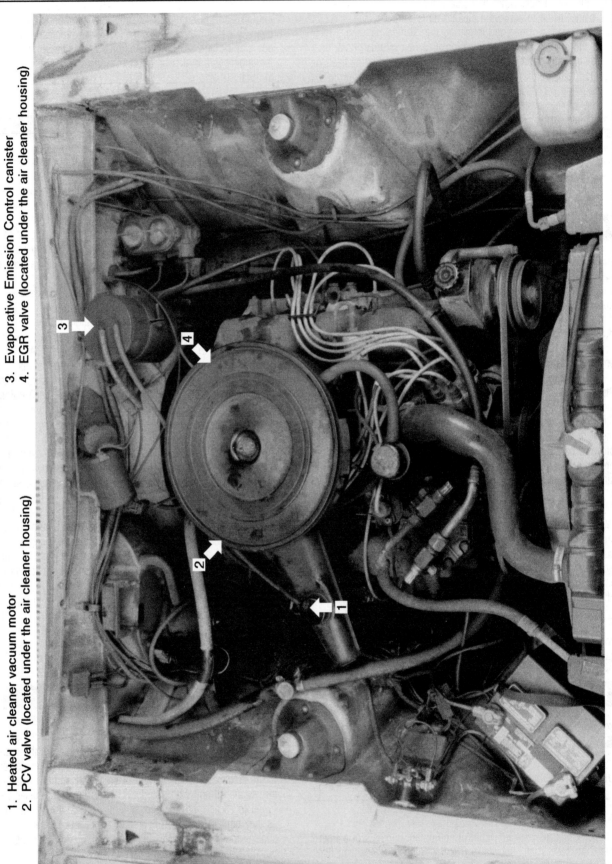

EMISSION COMPONENT LOCATIONS - EARLY MODEL MATADOR V8 ENGINE

1. Heated air cleaner vacuum motor
2. PCV valve (located under the air cleaner housing)
3. Evaporative Emission Control canister
4. EGR valve (located under the air cleaner housing)

EMISSION COMPONENT LOCATIONS - LATE MODEL EAGLE INLINE ENGINE

1. Vacuum switching valves
2. Vacuum delay valves
3. Heated air cleaner vacuum motors
4. PCV valve
5. Evaporative emissions control canister

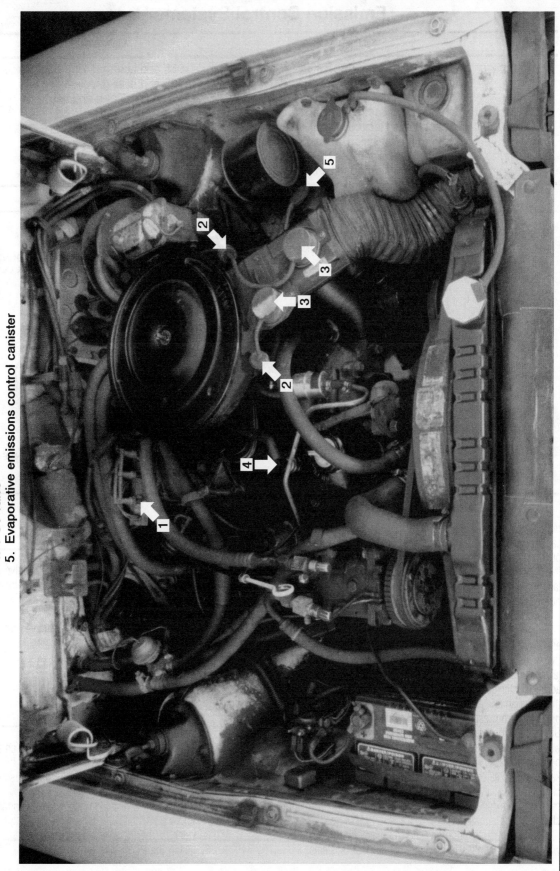

Emission Control Systems Usage

System	Application
Positive Crankcase Ventilation	1965 and later gasoline engines
Air injection	1965 and later gasoline engines
Thermostatically controlled air cleaner	All 1971 and later engines
Transmission controlled spark (TCS)	All AMC engines
Exhaust Gas Recirculation (EGR)	All 1971 and later engines
Evaporative emission control canister	All 1971 and later engines
Catalytic Converter	1979 and later gasoline engines
Vacuum throttle modulation	1975 and later gasoline engines

Fig. 1 Common Positive Crankcase Ventilation (PCV) system used on AMC vehicles-inline engine shown

retor air filter and then through a hose leading to the oil filler cap. As the air passes through the crankcase, it picks up the combustion gases and carries them out of the crankcase, up through the PCV valve and into the intake manifold. After they enter the intake manifold, they are drawn into the combustion chamber and burned.

The most critical component in the system is the PCV valve. This vacuum controlled valve regulates the amount of gases which are recycled into the combustion chamber. At low engine speeds, the valve is partially closed, limiting the flow of gases into the intake manifold. As engine speed increases, the valve opens to admit greater quantities of the gases into the intake manifold. If the valve should become blocked or plugged, the gases will be prevented from escaping from the crankcases by the normal route. Since these gases are under pressure, they will find their own way out of the crankcase. This alternate route is usually a weak oil seal or gasket in the engine. As the gas escapes by the gasket, it also creates an oil leak. Besides causing oil leaks, a clogged PCV valve also allows these gases to remain in the crankcase for an extended period of time, promoting the formation of sludge in the engine.

The above explanation and the troubleshooting procedure which follows applies to all engines with PCV systems.

TESTING

With the engine running, pull the PCV valve and hose from the engine. Block off the end of the valve with your finger. The engine speed should drop at least 50 rpm when the end of the valve is blocked. If the engine speed does not drop at least 50 rpm, then the valve is defective and should be replaced.

REMOVAL & INSTALLATION

1. Pull the PCV valve and hose from the engine.
2. Remove the PCV valve from the hose. Inspect the inside of the PCV valve from the hose. If it is dirty, disconnect it from the intake manifold and clean it.
3. If the PCV valve hose was removed, connect it to the intake manifold.
4. Connect the PCV valve to its hose.
5. Install the PCV valve on the engine.

Check the PCV valve for vacuum at idle

Air Injection System

DESCRIPTION

The exhaust emission air injection system consists of a belt driven air pump which directs compressed air through connecting hoses to a steel distribution manifold into stainless steel injection tubes in the exhaust port adjacent to each exhaust valve. The air, with its normal oxygen content, reacts with the hot, but incompletely burned exhaust gases and permits further combustion in the exhaust port or manifold.

Air Pump
▶ **See Figures 2, 3 and 4**

The air injection pump is a positive displacement vane type which is permanently lubricated and requires little periodic maintenance. The only serviceable parts on the air pump are the filter,

exhaust tube, and relief valve. The relief valve relieves the air flow when the pump pressure reaches a preset level. This occurs at high engine rpm. This serves to prevent damage to the pump and to limit maximum exhaust manifold temperatures.

Pump Air Filter

The air filter attached to the pump is a replaceable element type. The filter should be replaced every 12,000 miles under normal conditions and sooner under off-road use. Some models draw their air supply through the carburetor air filter.

Air Delivery Manifold
▶ **See Figure 5**

The air delivery manifold distributes the air from the pump to each of the air delivery tubes in a uniform manner. A check valve is integral with the air delivery manifold. Its function is to prevent the reverse flow of exhaust gases to the pump should the pump fail. This reverse flow would damage the air pump and connecting hose.

Air Injection Tubes

The air injection tubes are inserted into the exhaust ports. The tubes project into the exhaust ports, directing air into the vicinity of the exhaust valve.

Anti-Backfire Valve

The anti-backfire diverter valve prevents engine backfire by briefly interrupting the air being injected into the exhaust manifold during periods of deceleration or rapid throttle closure. The valve opens when a sudden increase in manifold vacuum overcomes the diaphragm spring tension. With the valve in the open position, the air flow from the air pump is directed to the atmosphere.

On the 1972 6-232 engine, the anti-backfire valve is what is commonly called a gulp valve. During rapid deceleration the valve is opened by the sudden high vacuum condition in the intake manifold and gulps air into the intake manifold.

Both of these valves prevent backfiring in the exhaust manifold. Both valves also prevent an over right fuel mixture from being burned in the exhaust manifold, which would cause backfiring and possible damage to the engine.

Fig. 2 Exploded view of the air pump mounting—4–150 engine

Fig. 3 Common air pump system used on all models except 8-cylinder engines

Fig. 4 Exploded view of the air injection system components used on 8-cylinder engines

Fig. 5 Location of the air diverter valve and manifold—4–150 engine

REMOVAL & INSTALLATION

Air Pump

✳✳ WARNING

Never place the pump is a vise or attempt to dismantle it. The pump has no internal parts that are replaceable and it is serviced as a unit. Never pry or hammer on the pump housing.

1. Loosen the bolts on the pump pulley.
2. Loosen the air pump attachment racket. On V8 models with air conditioning, loosen the power steering pump to aid in drive belt removal.
3. Detach the air supply hoses at the pump.
4. Remove the drivebelt and pulley from the hub.
5. Unfasten the bolts on the bracket and remove the pump.

To install:

1. Place the pump on its mounting bracket and install, but so not tighten the attachment volts.
2. With the rotor shaft used as a center, fit the pulley into the hub and install the drive belt over the pulley.
3. Tighten the pulley attachment bolts, using care not to snap them off.
4. Adjust the pump until the belt is secure. Tighten the mounting bolts and the adjusting screw to 18–22 ft. lbs. Do not overtighten.
5. Attach the hoses and clamps.

Air Pump Relief Valve

1. Use a gear pulley and a steel bridge to remove the relief valve from the pump.
2. Remove the pressure plug from the new relief valve assembly.
3. Insert the relief valve into it housing mounting hole.
4. Place a block of wood over the valve. Use a hammer to tap the valve until it lightly registers against the housing. Use care not to distort the housing.
5. Press the pressure plug into the center of the relief valve.

Centrifugal Filter Fan

➡**Never attempt to clean the filter fan. It is impossible to remove the fan without destroying it.**

1. Remove the air pump from the car, as detailed above.
2. Gently pry the outer disc off and pull off the remaining portion. Be careful that no fragments from the fan enter the pump air intake.

To install:

3. Install a new filter fan pulling it into place with the pump pulley and attaching bolts.
4. Alternately tighten the bolts so that the fan is drawn down evenly. Be sure that the outer edge of the fan fits into the pump housing.

✳✳ WARNING

Never hammer or press the fan into place; damage to it and the pump will result.

5. Install the pump on the car.

➡**For the first 20–30 minutes of operation, the fan may squeal until its lip has worn in. This is normal and does not indicate a damaged pump.**

Exhaust Tube

1. Remove the exhaust tube by grasping it (never the pump body) in a vise or a pair of pliers. Pull the tube out with a gentle twisting motion.
2. Install the new exhaust tube by tapping it into the hole with a hammer and a wooden block. Be careful not to damage its end.
3. Tap it until 7/8 in. (22.23mm) of the tube remains above the pump cover.

➡**Do not clamp the pump in a vise while installing the exhaust tube.**

By-Pass (Diverter Valve)

1. Disconnect the hoses from the valve.
2. Remove the screws that attach the valve bracket to the engine. Remove the valve and bracket assembly.
3. Installation is the reverse of removal.

Air Injection Manifold and Check Valve Assembly

6-232 AND 258 ENGINES

1. Remove the intake/exhaust manifold assembly, after disconnecting the hoses from the air injection manifold.
2. Place the assembly in a vise and unfasten the retaining nuts on the air injection manifold at each cylinder exhaust port.
3. Lightly tap the injection tubes, then pull the injection manifold away from the exhaust manifold.
4. If the tubes have become fused to the injection manifold, remove them by applying heat while rotating them with pliers.

To install:

1. Insert new air injection tubes into the exhaust manifold.

➡**The shorter tubes of into the Nos. 3 and 4 cylinders.**

2. Using a new gasket, assemble the exhaust/intake manifold to the engine.
3. Using new gaskets, install the air injection manifold on to the exhaust manifold in the reverse order of removal.

V8 ENGINES

1. Detach the air delivery hose at the check valve.
2. Unfasten the air injection manifold attachment nuts from the cylinder head. Carefully, ease the air injection manifold away from the heat.

➡**On some models it may be necessary to lower the bottom steering shaft clamp to gain access to the left rear mounting bolt; or to disconnect the right engine support and raise the engine to remove the right air injection manifold assembly.**

3. On newer cars, the air injection tubes and the manifold are removed as an assembly.
4. On older models, or if the tubes are hard to remove, use a screw extractor to twist the tube out gradually.

➡**Some interference may be encountered because of the normal carbon buildup on the tubes. Injection tubes which are removed with a screw extractor must be replaced with new ones.**

5. Installation is the reverse of removal.

TROUBLESHOOTING

✳✳ WARNING

Do not hammer on, pry, or bend the pump housing while tightening the drive belt or testing the pump.

Belt Tension and Air Leaks

1. Check the pump drive belt tension. There should be about 1/2 in. (12.7mm) play in the longest span of belt between pulleys.
2. Turn the pump by hand. If it has seized, the belt will slip, producing noise. Disregard any chirping, squealing, or rolling sounds from inside the pump; these are normal when it is turned by hand.
3. Check the hoses and connections for leaks. Hissing or a blast of air is indicative of a leak. Soapy water, applied lightly around the area in question, is a good method for detecting leaks.

Air Output Tests

1. Disconnect the air supply hose at the antibackfire valve.
2. Connect a vacuum pressure gauge to the air supply hose.

➡**If there are two hoses plug the second one.**

3. With the engine at normal operating temperature, increase the idle speed and watch the gauge.

Exhaust Gas Recirculation (EGR) System

OPERATION

◆ **See Figures 6, 7, 8, 9 and 10**

The Exhaust Gas Recirculation (EGR) system consists of a diaphragm actuated flow control valve (EGR valve), coolant tempera-

Fig. 6 Common EGR system components—1975–79 8-cylinder engines

Fig. 7 Location of the EGR system components—1975–79 6 cylinder engines

Fig. 8 Typical EGR system used on 8 cylinder engines—1980–88 models

Fig. 9 EGR system used the 4–151 engine

ture override switch, low temperature vacuum signal modulator, high temperature vacuum signal modulator.

All 1977 and later California units have a back pressure sensor which modulates EGR signal vacuum according to the rise or fall of exhaust pressure in the manifold. A restrictor plate is not used in these applications.

The purpose of the EGR system is to limit the formation of nitrogen oxides by diluting the fresh air intake charge with a metered amount of exhaust gas, thereby reducing the peak temperatures of the burning gases in the combustion chambers.

Fig. 10 EGR system component locations—1980–82 6 cylinder engines

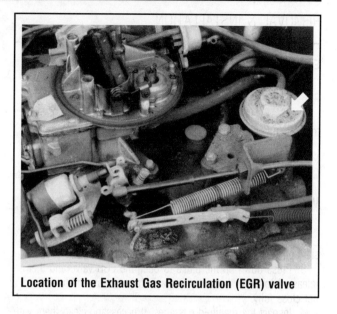

Location of the Exhaust Gas Recirculation (EGR) valve

Some EGR valves may be tested using a vacuum pump by watching for diaphragm movement

EGR Valve

The EGR valve is mounted on a machined surface at the rear of the intake manifold on the V8s and on the side of the intake manifold on the sixes.

The valve is held in a normally closed position by a coil spring located above the diaphragm. A special fitting is provided at the carburetor to route ported (above the throttle plates) vacuum through hose connections to a fitting located above the diaphragm on the valve. A passage in the intake manifold directs exhaust gas from the exhaust crossover passage (V8) or from below the riser area (Sixes) to the EGR valve. When the diaphragm is actuated by vacuum, the valve opens and meters exhaust gas through another passage in the intake manifold to the floor of the intake manifold below the carburetor.

Coolant Temperature Override Switch

This switch is located in the intake manifold at the coolant passage adjacent to the oil filler tube on the V8s or at the left side of the engine block (formerly the drain plug) on the Sixes. The outer port of the switch is open and not used. The inner port is connected by a hose to fitting at the carburetor. The center port is connected to the EGR valve. When coolant temperature is below 115°F (46°C) (160°F [71°C] on the 8-304 with manual transmission), the center port of the switch is closed and no vacuum signal is applied to the EGR valve. Therefore, no exhaust gas will flow through the valve. When the coolant temperature reaches 115°F (46°C), both the center port and the inner port of the switch are open and a vacuum signal is applied to the EGR valve. This vacuum signal is, however, subject to regulation by the low and high temperature signal modulators.

Low Temperature Vacuum Signal Modulator

This unit is located just to the right of the radiator behind the grill opening. The low temperature vacuum signal modulator vacuum hose is connected by a plastic T-fitting to the EGR vacuum signal hose. The modulator is open when ambient temperatures are below 60°F (16°C). This causes a weakened vacuum signal to the EGR valve and a resultant decrease in the amount of exhaust gas being recirculated.

High Temperature Vacuum Signal Modulator

This unit is located at the right front fender inner panel. The high temperature vacuum signal modulator is connected to the EGR vacuum signal hose by a plastic T-fitting. The modulator opens when the underhood air temperatures reach 115°F (46°C) and it causes a weakened vacuum signal to the EGR valve, thus reducing the amount of exhaust gases being recirculated.

REMOVAL & INSTALLATION

EGR Valve

1. Remove the air cleaner assembly from the carburetor.
2. Unfasten the vacuum line from the top of the EGR valve.
3. Loosen and remove the two screws which secure the valve to the manifold.
4. Remove the EGR valve, complete with its gasket.
5. Installation of the EGR valve is the reverse of its removal. Always use a new gasket. Tighten the valve securing bolts to 13 ft. lbs.

Valve and Passage Cleaning

1. Remove the EGR valve.
2. Use a wire brush to clean all the deposits from the stainless steel pintle.
3. Press down on the pintle to open the EGR valve and them release it to close the valve. Replace the valve assembly if it will not close fully.
4. Inspect the manifold passages. If necessary, clean them with a spiral wire brush.

➡**On 6-cylinder engines, deposits will build up most rapidly in the upper passage. If the deposits cannot be removed with the wire brush, use a ⁹⁄₁₆ in. (14mm) drill bit. Rotate the drill by hand, after coating it with heavy grease.**

5. Install the EGR valve with a new gasket.

Thermostatically Controlled Air Cleaner System (TAC)

OPERATION

This system consists of a heat shroud which is integral with the right side exhaust manifold, a hot air hose and a special air cleaner assembly equipped with a thermal sensor and a vacuum motor and air valve assembly.

The thermal sensor incorporates an air bleed valve which regulates the amount of vacuum applied to the vacuum motor, controlling the air valve position to supply either heated air from the exhaust manifold or air from the engine compartment.

During the warm-up period when underhood temperatures are low, the air bleed valve is closed and sufficient vacuum is applied to the vacuum motor to hold the air valve in the closed (heat on) position.

As the temperature of the air entering the air cleaner approaches approximately 115°F (46°C), the air bleed valve opens to decrease the amount of vacuum applied to the vacuum motor. The diaphragm spring in the vacuum motor then moves the air valve into the open (heat off) position, allowing only underhood air to enter the air cleaner.

The air valve in the air cleaner will also open, regardless of air temperature, during heavy acceleration to obtain maximum air flow through the air cleaner.

TROUBLESHOOTING

Non Vacuum-Operated Air Door Test

▶ **See Figure 11**

1. Unfasten the temperature sensing valve and snorkle assembly from the air cleaner. Place it in a container of cold water. Make sure that the thermostat is completely covered with water.
2. Place a thermometer, of known accuracy, in the water. Heat the water slowly and watch the temperature.
3. At 105°F or less, the door should be closed (manifold heat position).
4. Continue heating the water until it reaches 130°F. The door should be fully open to the outside air position.
5. If the door does not open at or near this temperature, check it for binding or a detached spring. If the door doesn't open or close properly, the sensor is defective and must be replaced.

➡**This usually requires that the entire snorkle assembly must be replaced.**

Fig. 11 Sectional view of the non-vacuum controlled thermostatic air cleaner operation

Vacuum-Operated Air Door Test

▶ **See Figure 12**

1. Either start with a cold engine or remove the air cleaner from the engine for at least half an hour. While cooling the air cleaner, leave the hood open.

2. Tape a thermometer, of know accuracy, to the inside of the air cleaner so that it is near the temperature sensor unit. Install the air cleaner on the engine but do not fasten its securing nut.

3. Start the engine. With the engine cold and the outside temperature less than 90°F, the door should be in the 'heat-on' position (closed to outside air).

➡**Due to the position of the air cleaner on some cars, a mirror may be necessary when observing the position of the air door.**

4. Operate the throttle rapidly to ½–¾ of its opening and release it. The air door should open to allow outside air to enter and then close again.

5. Allow the engine to warm up to normal temperature. Watch the door. When it opens to the outside air, remove the cover from the air cleaner. The temperature should be over 90°F and no more than 130°F; 115°F is about normal. If the door does not work within these temperature ranges, or fails to work at all, check for linkage or door binding.

If there is no binding and the air door is not working, proceed with the vacuum test below. If these indicate no faults in the vacuum motor and the door is not working, the temperature sensor is defective and must be replaced.

Vacuum Motor Test

➡**Be sure that the vacuum hose that runs between the temperature switch and the vacuum motor is not pinched by the**

Fig. 12 View of a vacuum controlled thermostatic air cleaner operation

retaining clip under the air cleaner. This could prevent the air door from closing.

1. Check all of the vacuum lines and fittings for leaks. Correct any leaks. If none are found, proceed with the test.

2. Remove the hose which runs from the sensor to the vacuum motor. Run a hose directly from the manifold vacuum source to the vacuum motor.

3. If the motor closes the air door, it is functioning properly and the temperature sensor is defective.

4. If the motor does not close the door and no binding is present in its operations, the vacuum motor is defective and must be replaced.

➡**If an alternate vacuum source is applied to the motor, insert a vacuum gauge in the line by using a T-fitting. Apply at least 9 in.Hg of vacuum in order to operate the motor.**

Distributor Controls

DUAL DIAPHRAGM DISTRIBUTOR TEST

1. Connect a timing light to the engine. Check the ignition timing.

➡**First disconnect any spark control devices, distributor vacuum valves, etc. If these are left connected, inaccurate results may be obtained.**

2. Remove the retard hose from the distributor and plug it. Increase the engine speed. The timing should advance. It if fails to do so, then the vacuum unit is faulty and must be replaced.

3. Check the timing with the engine at normal idle speed. Unplug the retard hose and connect it to the vacuum unit. The timing should instantly be retarded from 4–10. If this does not occur, the retard diaphragm has a leak and the vacuum unit must be replaced.

Vacuum Throttle Modulating System (VTM)

OPERATION

▶ **See Figure 13**

This system is designed to reduce the level of hydrocarbon emission during rapid throttle closure at high speed. It is used on some 49 states models, and all models with a V8 engine.

The system consists of a deceleration valve located at the right front of the intake manifold, and a throttle modulating diaphragm located at the carburetor base. The valve and the diaphragm are connected by a vacuum hose and the valve is connected to direct manifold vacuum. During deceleration, manifold vacuum acts to delay, slightly, the closing of the throttle plate.

Fig. 13 Common vacuum throttle modulating system components and their locations

TESTING

➡**Timing, idle speed and air fuel mixture should be correct before beginning this test.**

1. Connect a vacuum gauge to the distributor vacuum advance line.
2. If the carburetor has a dashpot, tape its plunger down so that it cannot touch the throttle lever at idle.
3. Speed the engine up to about 2000 rpm and retain this speed for about ten seconds.
4. Release the throttle, allowing the engine to return to normal idle.
5. The vacuum reading should rise to about 20 in.Hg and stay there for one second. It should take about three seconds for the reading to return to normal, the valve should be adjusted.

To check for a leaking valve diaphragm:

1. Remove the vacuum gauge and connect it to the manifold vacuum line with a T-connector.
2. Clamp shut the valve-to-distributor vacuum line and, with the engine at normal idle speed, check the vacuum reading.
3. Clamp the line shut between the deceleration valve and the T-connection. Check the vacuum gauge reading again.
4. If the second reading is higher than the first, the valve diaphragm is leaking and the valve should be replaced.

ADJUSTMENT

Deceleration Valve

If the deceleration valve test indicted a need for adjustment, proceed as follows:

1. Remove the cover to gain access to the adjusting screw.
2. If an increase in valve opening time is desired, turn the adjusting screw counterclockwise.
3. If a decrease in time is desired, turn the adjusting screw clockwise.

➡**Each complete turn of the adjusting screw equals ½ in. Hg.**

4. After finishing the adjustments, retest the valve. If the valve cannot be adjusted, it is defective and must be replaced.

Throttle Modulating Diaphragm

1. Run the engine to normal operating temperature and set the idle speed to specification. Shut off the engine.
2. Position the throttle lever against the curb idle adjusting screw.
3. Measure the clearance between the throttle modulating diaphragm plunger and the throttle lever. A clearance of 1/16 in. (1.5875mm) should exist.
4. Adjust the clearance, if necessary, by loosening the jam nut and turning the diaphragm assembly.

Transmission Controlled Spark (TCS) System

OPERATION

◆ **See Figures 14, 15 and 16**

The purpose of this system is to reduce the emission of oxides of nitrogen by lowering the peak combustion pressure and temperature during the power stroke.

Ambient Temperature Override Switch

This switch, located at the firewall, senses ambient temperatures and completes the electrical circuit from the battery to the solenoid vacuum valve when the ambient temperatures are above 63°F (17°C).

Fig. 14 Electrical schematic of the Transmission Controlled Spark (TCS) system operation

Fig. 15 TCS system component locations—6 cylinder engines

Fig. 16 TCS system schematic and component locations used on 8 cylinder engines

Solenoid Vacuum Valve

This valve is attached to the ignition coil bracket at the right side of the engine (V8 engines) or to a bracket at the rear of the intake manifold (Sixes). When the valve is energized, carburetor vacuum is blocked off and the distributor vacuum line is vented to the atmosphere through a port in the valve, resulting in no vacuum advance. When the valve is de-energized, vacuum is applied to the distributor resulting in normal vacuum advance.

Solenoid Control Switch

This switch is located in the transmission valve body. It opens or closes in relation to car speed and gear range. When the transmission is in high gear, the switch opens and breaks the ground circuit to the solenoid vacuum valve. In lower gear ranges the switch closes and completes the ground circuit to the solenoid vacuum valve. With a manual transmission, the switch is operated by the transmission shifter shaft. With automatic transmissions, the switch is controlled by the speedometer gear speed. Under speeds of 25 mph, the switch is activated.

Coolant Temperature Override Switch

This switch is used only on the 8-304 engine. It is threaded into the thermostat housing. The switch reacts to coolant temperatures to route either intake manifold or carburetor vacuum to the distributor vacuum advance diaphragm.

When the coolant temperature is below 160°F (71°C), intake manifold vacuum is applied through a hose connection to the distributor advance diaphragm, resulting in the full vacuum advance.

When the coolant temperature is above 160°F (71°C), intake manifold vacuum is blocked off and carburetor vacuum is then applied through the solenoid vacuum valve to the distributor advance diaphragm, resulting in decreased vacuum advance.

The relationship between distributor vacuum advance and the operation of the TCS system and coolant temperature override switch can be determined by referring to the Emission Control Distributor Vacuum Application Charts.

TESTING

System Test

MANUAL TRANSMISSION

1. Connect a vacuum gauge between the distributor and the solenoid vacuum valve, using a T-connector.

➡**This won't work unless the temperature switch on the front crossmember is above 63°F.**

2. Start the engine. With the transmission in Neutral, the vacuum gauge should ready zero.

3. Increase engine speed to between 1000–1500 rpm with the clutch pedal depressed. The vacuum reading should remain at zero.

4. With the clutch still depressed, place the transmission in High gear. Increase engine speed, as before. The vacuum gauge should now read at least 6 in. Hg. If it does not, proceed further with testing.

5. Unfasten the transmission switch lead from the solenoid vacuum valve terminal. Connect the lead in series with a low amperage test lamp and the positive side of the battery.

6. Move the shift lever through all of the gears. The test lamp should remain on until high gear is entered.

7. If the lamp stays on when the transmission is in High, either the switch is defective or the circuit is grounded. If it fails to come on at all, the switch is defective or the circuit has a loose wire.

8. If the transmission switch is functioning properly but the system check indicates that something is still wrong, check the temperature switch.

AUTOMATIC TRANSMISSION

➡**The spark control system is controlled by a switch which operates on transmission governor oil pressure.**

1. Disconnect the electrical lead from the terminal of the governor pressure switch.

➡**The switch may easily be reached with the hood opened. On sixes, the switch is located on the right rear of the cylinder block; on V8's, it is attached to a bracket at the rear of the right-hand rocker cover.**

2. Connect a 12V test light in series, between the lead and the terminal on the switch.

✳✳ WARNING

Use a low amperage test light, so that the switch contacts will not be damaged.

3. Raise the car, block the front wheels (if they are not off the ground), and securely support it so that the rear wheels are free to turn.

4. Apply the service brakes. Start the engine. The test light should glow.

5. Place the gear selector in Drive, release the brake pedal and slowly depress the gas pedal.

6. Watch the speedometer and the test light; between 33–37 mph the switch should open and the test light should go out.

7. If the light does not go out within this speed range, adjust the switch by turning the 1/16 in. allen screw on the switch terminal. Turn the screw clockwise to increase or counter-clockwise to decrease the switch cut-out sped. The switch should be adjusted to open at 35 mph.

8. If the switch cannot be adjusted, replace it.

9. If the switch is working properly, but the TCS system is not working, the solenoid vacuum valve is probably defective.

Transmission Switch

1. Leave the rear wheels of the car off the ground as in the system test above.

2. Disconnect the transmission switch leads. Connect a low amperage test lamp in series with the switch and the positive side of the battery.

3. Accelerate to the speed specified in Step 3 of the system test and watch the test lamp. It should remain on until the specified speed is reached. If the lamp fails to go out or if it does not light at all, the switch is defective and must be replaced.

4. If the switch is working properly, reconnect it and go on with the next test.

Vacuum Advance Solenoid

1. Disconnect the vacuum advance solenoid leads. Connect a vacuum gauge to the solenoid hose as in the system test.

2. Place the transmission in Neutral and start the engine. Increase engine speed. The gauge should indicate the presence of a vacuum.

3. Connect the hot lead to a 12 volt power source. Ground the other lead. Increase the engine speed again. The solenoid should energize, resulting in a vacuum reading of zero.

Emission Controlled Distributor Vacuum Application Chart for Vehicles Equipped with TCS

Manual Transmission Gear		Automatic Transmission Vehicle Speed (mph)	Ambient Temperature Deg. F	Coolant Temperature Deg. F	Vacuum Applied to Distributor
3-sp	4-sp				
1–2	1–2–3	Under 25	Below 63	Below 160	Manifold
1–2	1–2–3	Under 25	Below 63	Above 160	Ported
1–2	1–2–3	Under 25	Above 63	Above 160	None
1–2	1–2–3	Under 25	Above 63	Below 160	Manifold
3	4	25–30	Below 63	Below 160	Manifold
3	4	25–30	Below 63	Above 160	Ported
3	4	25–30	Above 63	Above 160	Ported
3	4	25–30	Above 63	Below 160	Manifold

4. Replace the vacuum advance solenoid if it is faulty. If it is not, reconnect the wiring and go on with the next appropriate test.

Ambient Temperature Override Switch

1. Disconnect the ambient temperature switch leads.
2. Replace the switch in the circuit with a jumper wire.
3. Repeat the system test. If the vacuum gauge now reads zero or below the specified speed, i.e., the solenoid energized, the temperature switch is defective.
4. If the switch proves not to be defective when tested in Step 3, reconnect it after removing the jumper lead.
5. Cool the switch, using either ice, cold water, or an aerosol spray, to below 63°F. Repeat the system test. If there is no vacuum below the specified speed, the switch is stuck closed and must be replaced.

Anti-Dieseling Solenoid

TESTING

➡**Anti-dieseling solenoids are also referred to as, 'throttle stop' or 'idle stop' solenoids.**

1. Turn the ignition key **ON** and open the throttle. The solenoid plunger should extend (solenoid energized).
2. Turn the ignition **OFF.** The plunger should retract, allowing the throttle to close.

➡**With the anti-dieseling solenoid deenergized, the carburetor idle speed adjusting screw must make contact with the throttle shaft to prevent the throttle plates from jamming in the throttle bore when the engine is turned off.**

3. If the solenoid is functioning properly and the engine is still dieseling, check for one of the following:
    a. High idle or engine shut off speed.
    b. Engine timing not set to specifications. Correct any of these problems, as necessary.
4. If the solenoid fails to function as outlined in steps 1–2, disconnect the solenoid leads; the solenoid should de-energize. If it does not, it is jammed and must be replaced.
5. Connect the solenoid to a 12 volt power source and to ground. Open the throttle so that the plunger can extend. If it does not, the solenoid is defective.
6. If the solenoid is functioning correctly and no other source of trouble can be found, the fault probably lies in the wiring between the solenoid and the ignition switch or in the ignition switch itself.

Electric Assist Choke

OPERATION

An electric assist choke is used to more accurately match the choke operation to engine requirements. It provides extra heat to the choke bimetal spring to speed up the choke valve opening after the underhood air temperature reaches 95°F ± 15°F (35°C). Its purpose is to reduce the emission of carbon monoxide (CO) during the engine's warmup period.

A special AC terminal is provided at the alternator to supply a 7 volt power source for the electric choke. A thermostatic switch within the choke cover closes when the underhood air temperature reaches 95°F ± 15°F (35°C) and allows current to flow to a ceramic heating element. The circuit is completed through the choke cover ground strap and choke housing to the engine. As the heating element warms up, heat is absorbed by an attached metal plate which in turn heats the choke bimetal spring.

After the engine is turned off, the thermostatic switch remains closed until the underhood temperature drops below approximately 65°F (18°C). Therefore, the heating element will immediately begin warming up when the engine is restarted, if the underhood temperature is above 65°F (18°C).

TESTING

1. Detach the electrical lead from the choke cap.
2. Use a jumper lead to connect the terminal on the choke cap and the wire terminal, so that the electrical circuit is still completed.
3. Start the engine.
4. Hook up a test light between the connector on the choke lead and ground.
5. The test light should glow. If it does not, current is not being supplied to the electrically assisted choke.
6. Connect the test light between the terminal on the alternator and the terminal on the choke cap. If the light now glows, replace the lead, since it is not passing current to the choke assist.

✳✳ CAUTION

Do not ground the terminal on the alternator while performing Step 6.

7. If the light still does not glow, the fault lies somewhere in the electrical system.

If the electrically assisted choke receives power, but still does not appear to be functioning properly, reconnect the choke lead and proceed with the rest of the test.

8. Tape the bulb end of a thermometer to the metallic portion of the choke housing.
9. If the electrically assisted choke operates below 55°F (13°C), it is defective and must be replaced.
10. Allow the engine to warm up to between 80°F and 110°F (27–43°C); at these temperatures the choke should operate for about 1½ minutes.
11. If it does not operate for this length of time, check the bimetallic spring to see if it is connected to the tang on the choke lever.
12. If the spring is connected and the choke is not operating properly, replace the cap assembly.

Fuel Tank Vapor Emission Control System

OPERATION

A closed fuel tank system is used on some 1975–78, and all 1979 and later models, to route raw fuel vapor from the fuel tank into the PCV system (sixes) or air cleaner snorkle (V8s), where it is burned along with the fuel/air mixture. The system prevents raw fuel vapors from entering the atmosphere.

The fuel vapor system consists of internal fuel tank venting, a vacuum-pressure fuel tank filler cap, an expansion tank or charcoal filled canister, liquid limit fill valve, and internal carburetor venting.

Fuel vapor pressure in the fuel tank forces the vapor through vent lines to the expansion tank or charcoal filled storage canister. The vapor then travels through a single vent line to the limit fill valve, which regulates the vapor flow to the valve cover or air cleaner.

Limit Fill Valve

This valve is essentially a combination vapor flow regulator and pressure relief valve. It regulates vapor flow from the fuel tank vent line into the valve cover. The valve consists of a housing, a spring loaded diaphragm and a diaphragm cover. As tank vent pressure increases, the diaphragm lifts, permitting vapor to flow through. The pressure at which this occurs is 4–6 in. H_2O column. This action regulates the flow of vapors under severe conditions, but generally prohibits the flow of vapor during normal temperature operation, thus minimizing driveability problems.

Liquid Check Valve

The liquid check valve prevents liquid fuel from entering the vapor lines leading to the storage canister. The check valve incorporates a float and needle valve assembly. If liquid fuel should enter the check valve, the float will rise and force the needle upward to close the vent passage. With no liquid fuel present in the check valve, fuel vapors pass freely from the tank, through the check valve, and on to the storage canister.

TROUBLESHOOTING

There are several things to check for it a malfunction of the evaporative emission control system is suspected.

Location of the Evaporative Emission Control canister

1. Leaks may be traced by using an infrared hydrocarbon tester. Run the test probe along the lines and connections. The meter will indicate the presence of a leak by a high hydrocarbon (HC) reading. This method is much more accurate than a visual inspection which would indicate only the presence of a leak large enough to pass liquid.

2. Leaks may be caused by any of the following, so always check these areas when looking for them:
   a. Defective or worn lines.
   b. Disconnected or pinched lines.
   c. Improperly routed lines.
   d. A defective filler cap.

➡️**If it becomes necessary to replace any of the lines used in the evaporative emission control system, use only hoses which are fuel resistant or are marked 'EVAP'.**

3. If the fuel tank has collapsed, it may be the fault of clogged or pinched vent lines, a defective vapor separator, or a plugged or incorrect fuel filler cap.

4. To test the filler cap, clean it and place it against the mouth. Blow into the relief valve housing. If the cap passes pressure with light blowing or if it fails to release with hard blowing, it is defective and must be replaced.

ELECTRONIC ENGINE CONTROLS

General Information

▶ **See Figure 17**

The GM designed Computer Controlled Catalytic Converter System (C-4 System), was introduced in 1979 and used on 4–151 engines through 1980. The C-4 System primarily maintains the ideal air/fuel ratio at which the catalytic converter is most effective. Some versions of the system also control ignition timing of the distributor.

The Computer Command Control System (CCC system), introduced on some 1980 California models and used on all 1981 and later carbureted car lines, is an expansion of the C-4 system. The CCC system monitors up to fifteen engine/vehicle operating conditions which uses to control up to nine engine and emission control systems. In addition to maintaining the ideal air/fuel ratio for the catalytic converter and adjusting ignition timing, the CCC system also controls the air management system so that the catalytic converter can operate at the highest efficiency possible. The system also controls the lockup on the transmission torque converter

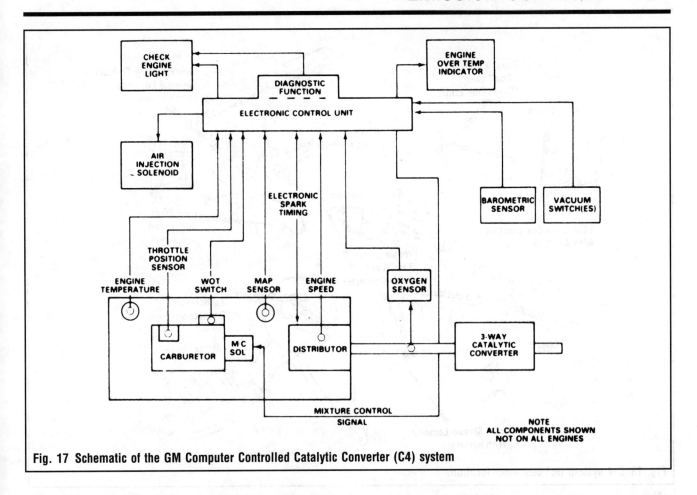

Fig. 17 Schematic of the GM Computer Controlled Catalytic Converter (C4) system

clutch (certain automatic transmission models only), adjust idle speed over a wide range of conditions, purges the evaporative emissions charcoal canister, controls the EGR valve operation and operates the Early Fuel Evaporative (EFE) system. Not all engines use all of the above sub systems.

There are two operation modes for both the C-4 System and the CCC system: closed loop and open loop fuel control. Closed loop fuel control means the oxygen sensor is controlling the carburetor's air/fuel mixture ratio. Under open loop fuel control operating conditions (wide open throttle, engine and/or oxygen sensor cold), the oxygen has no effect on the air/fuel mixture.

➡**On some engines, the oxygen sensor will cool off while the engine is idling, putting the system into open loop operation. To restore closed loop operation, run the engine at part throttle and accelerate from idle to part throttle a few times.**

COMPUTER CONTROLLED CATALYTIC CONVERTER (C-4) SYSTEM

♦ **See Figure 18**

Major components of the system include an Electronic Control Module (ECM), an oxygen sensor, and electronically controlled variable mixture carburetor, and a three-way oxidation/reduction catalytic converter.

The oxygen sensor generates a voltage which varies with exhaust gas oxygen content. Lean mixtures (more oxygen) reduce

voltage; rich mixtures (less oxygen) increase voltage. Voltage output is sent to the ECM.

An engine temperature sensor installed in the engine coolant outlet monitors coolant temperatures. Vacuum control switches and throttle position sensors also monitor engine conditions and supply signals to the ECM.

The Electronic Control Module (ECM) monitors the voltage input of the oxygen sensor along with information from other input signals. It processes these signals and generates a control signal sent to the carburetor. The control signal cycles between ON (lean command) and OFF (rich command). The amount of ON and OFF time is a function of the input voltage sent to the ECM by the oxygen sensor. The ECM has a calibration unit called a Programmable Read Only Memory (PROM) which contains the specific instructions for a given engine application. In other words, the PROM assembly is a replaceable component which plugs into a socket on the ECM and requires a special tool for removal and installation.

➡**Electronic Spark Timing (EST) allows continuous spark timing adjustments to be made by the ECM. Engines with EST can easily be identified by the absence of vacuum and mechanical spark advance mechanisms on the distributor. Engines with EMR systems may be recognized by the presence of five connectors, instead of the HEI module's usual four.**

To maintain good idle and driveability under all conditions, other input signals are used to modify the ECM output signal. Besides the sensors and switches already mentioned, these input sig-

Trouble Code "Test" Lead (Green Connector)

"Check Engine" Light Connector

Connect Bat. + To Blank Terminal For Long Term Memory

"Check Engine" Light Connector

ECM Connectors

Fuse Block Connection

ECM Glove Box Location With Air Cond.

Trouble Code "Test" Lead (Green Connector)

Tachometer Connection Point

A

View A

ECM Shroud Location With Heater

Fig. 18 C-4 system test connector locations

nals include the Manifold Absolute Pressure (MAP) or vacuum sensors and the Barometric Pressure (BARO) sensor. The MAP or vacuum sensors sense changes in manifold vacuum, while the BARO sensor senses changes in barometric pressure. One important function of the BARO sensor is the maintenance of good engine performance at various altitudes. These sensors act as throttle position sensors on some engines. See the following paragraph for description.

A Rochester Dualjet carburetor is used with the C-4 system. It may be an E2SE, E2SME, E4MC or E4ME model, depending on engine application. An electronically operated mixture control solenoid is installed in the carburetor float bowl. The solenoid controls the air/fuel mixture metered to the idle and main metering systems. Air metering to the idle system is controlled by an idle air bleed valve. It follows the movement of the mixture solenoid to control the amount of air bled into the idle system, enriching or leaning out the mixture as appropriate. Air/fuel mixture enrichment occurs when the fuel valve is open and the air bleed is closed. All cycling of this system, which occurs ten times per second, is controlled by the ECM. A throttle position switch informs the ECM of open or closed throttle operation. A number of different switches are used, varying with application. The 4-cylinder engine (151 cu. in.) uses two vacuum switches to sense open throttle and closed throttle operation.

COMPUTER COMMAND CONTROL (CCC) SYSTEM

▶ See Figure 19

The Computer Command Control (CCC) has many components in common with the C-4 system (although they should probably not be interchanged between systems). These include the Electronic Control Module (ECM), which is capable of monitoring and adjusting more sensors and components than the ECM used on the C-4 System, an oxygen sensor, an electronically controlled variable mixture carburetor, a three-way catalytic converter, throttle position and coolant sensors, a Barometric Pressure (BARO) Sensor, a Manifold Absolute Pressure (MAP) sensor, a "check engine" light on the instrument cluster, and an Electronic Spark Control (ESC) which retards ignition spark under some conditions (detonation, etc.).

Components used almost exclusively by the CCC System include the Air Injection Reaction (AIR) management system, charcoal canister purge solenoid, EGR valve control, Vehicle Speed Sensor (VSS) located in the instrument cluster, transmission torque converter clutch solenoid (automatic transmission models only), idle speed control, and early fuel evaporate (EFE) system.

See the operation descriptions under C-4 system for those com-

Fig. 19 GM Computer Command Control (CCC) system components

ponents (except the ECM) the CCC system shares with the C-4 System.

The CCC system ECM, in addition to monitoring sensors and sending a control signal to the carburetor, also control the following components or sub systems: charcoal canister urge, AIR management system, idle speed control, automatic transmission converter lockup, distributor ignition timing, EGR valve control, EFE control, and the air conditioner compressor clutch operation. The CCC ECM is equipped with a PROM assembly similar to the one used in the C-4 ECM. See above description.

The AIR management system is an emission control which provides additional oxygen either to the catalyst or the cylinder head ports (in some cases exhaust manifold). An AIR management system, composed of an air switching valve and/or an air control valve, controls the air pump flow and is itself controlled by the ECM. A complete description of the AIR system is given elsewhere in this unit repair section. The major difference between the CCC AIR system and the systems used on other cars is that the flow of air from the air pump is controlled electrically by the ECM, rather than the vacuum signal.

The charcoal canister purge control is an electrically operated solenoid valve controlled by the ECM. When energized, the purge control solenoid blocks vacuum from reaching the canister purge valve. When the ECM de-energized the purge control solenoid, vacuum is allowed to reach the canister and operate the purge valve. This releases the fuel vapors collected in the canister into the induction system.

The EGR valve control solenoid is activated by the ECM in similar fashion to the canister purge solenoid. When the engine is cold, the ECM energized the solenoid, which blocks the vacuum

signal to the EGR valve. When the engine is warm, the ECM de-energized the solenoid and the vacuum signal is allowed to reach and activate the EGR valve.

The Transmission Converter Clutch (TCC) lock is controlled by the ECM through an electrical solenoid in the automatic transmission. When the vehicle speed sensor in the instrument panel signals the ECM that the vehicle has reached the correct speed, the ECM energizes the solenoid which allows the torque converter to mechanically couple the engine to the transmission. When the brake pedal is pushed or during deceleration, passing, etc., the ECM returns the transmission to fluid drive.

The Early Fuel Evaporative (EFE) system is used on some engines to provide rapid heat to the engine induction system to promote smooth start-up and operation. There are two types of system: vacuum servo and electrically heated. They use different means to achieve the same end, which is to pre-heat the incoming air/fuel mixture. They are controlled by the ECM.

AMERICAN MOTORS FEEDBACK SYSTEM

▶ **See Figures 20 and 21**

American Motors introduced feedback systems on all cars (except Eagle) in 1980. Two different, but similar, systems are used. The four cylinder engine used the G.M. C-4 feedback system, which is covered earlier in this section. Component usage is identical to that of the 4–151 engine, including an oxygen sensor, a vacuum switch (which is closed at idle and partial throttle positions), a wide open throttle switch, a coolant temperature sensor

Fig. 20 Computerized Emission Control (CEC) system wiring schematic—4 cylinder engine

(set to open at 150°F [66°C]), and Electronic Control Module (ECM) equipped with modular Programmable Read Only memory (PROM), and a mixture control solenoid installed in the air horn on the E2SE carburetor. A 'Check Engine' light is included on the instrument panel as a service and diagnostic indicator.

The 6-cylinder engine is equipped with a Computerized Emission Control (CEC) System.

In 1980 CEC components include an oxygen sensor; two vacuum switches (one ported and one manifold) to detect three operating conditions; idle, partial throttle, and wide open throttle; a coolant temperature switch; a Micro Computer Unit (MCU), the control unit for the system which monitors all data and sends an output signal to the carburetor; and a stepper motor installed in the main body of the BBD carburetor, which varies the position of the two metering pins controlling the size of the air bleed orifices in the carburetor. The MCU also interrupts signals from the distributor (rpm voltage) to monitor engine rpm.

On 1981 and later models with CEC, the number of sensors has been increased. Three vacuum operated electric switches, two mechanically operated switches, one engine coolant switch and an air temperature operated switch are used to detach and send engine operating data to the MCU concerning the following engine operating conditions: cold engine start-up and operation; wide open throttle; idle (closed throttle); and partial and deep throttle.

Both AMC systems are conventional in operation. As in other feedback systems, two modes of operation are possible; open loop and closed loop. Open loop operation occurs during engine starting, cold engine operation, cold oxygen sensor operation, engine idling, wide open throttle operation, and low battery voltage

operation. In open loop, a fixed air/fuel mixture signal is provided by the ECM or MCU to the carburetor, and oxygen sensor data is ignored. Closed loop operation occurs at all other times, and in this mode all signals are used by the control unit to determine the optimum air/fuel mixture.

BASIC TROUBLESHOOTING

➡**The following explains how to activate the Trouble Code signal light in the instrument cluster and gives an explanation of what each code means. This is not a full C-4 of CCC System troubleshooting and isolation procedure.**

Before suspecting the C-4 or CCC System or any of its components as faulty, check the ignition system including distributor, timing, spark plugs and wires. Check the engine compression, air cleaner, and emission control components not controlled by the ECM. Also check the intake manifold, vacuum hoses and hose connectors for leaks and the carburetor for tightness.

The following systems could indicate a possible problem with the C-4 or CCC System.

1. Detonation.
2. Stalls or rough idle, cold.
3. Stalls or rough idle, hot.
4. Missing.
5. Hesitation.
6. Surges.
7. Poor gasoline mileage.

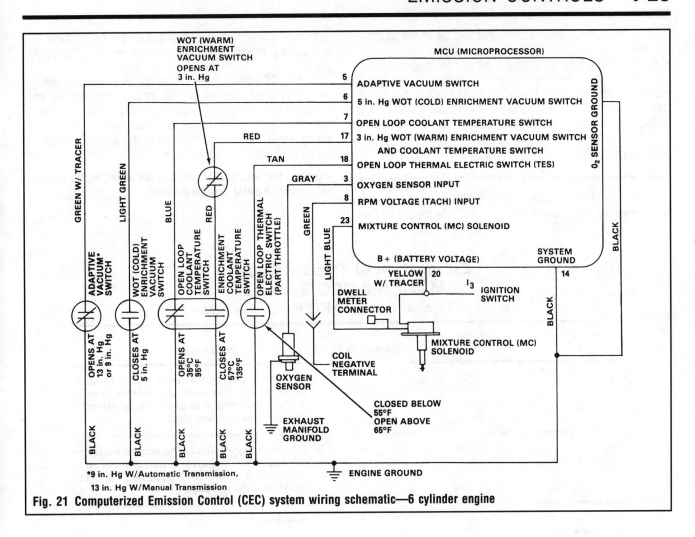

Fig. 21 Computerized Emission Control (CEC) system wiring schematic—6 cylinder engine

8. Sluggish or spongy.
9. Hard Starting, cold.
10. Hard starting, hot.
11. Objectionable exhaust odors.
12. Cuts out.

As a bulb and system check, the 'Check Engine' light will come on when the ignition switch is turned to the ON position but the engine is not started. The 'Check Engine' light will also produce the trouble code or codes by a series of flashes which translate as follows. When the diagnostic test lead (C-4) or terminal (CCC) under the dash is grounded, with the ignition in the ON position and the engine not running, the 'Check Engine' light will flash once, pause, then flash twice in rapid succession. This is a code 12, which indicates that the diagnostic system is working. After a longer pause, the code 12 will repeat itself two more times. The cycle will then repeat itself until the engine is started or the ignition is turned OFF.

When the engine is started, the 'Check Engine' light will remain on for a few seconds, then turn OFF. If the 'Check Engine' light remains on, the self-diagnostic system has detected a problem. If the test lead (C-4) or test terminal (CCC) is then grounded, the trouble code will flash three times. If more than one problem is found, each trouble code will flash three times. Trouble codes will flash in numerical order (lowest code number to highest). The trouble codes series will repeat as long as the test lead or terminal is grounded.

A trouble code indicates a problem with a given circuit. For ex-

ample, trouble code 14 indicated a problem in the cooling sensor circuit. This includes the coolant sensor, its electrical harness, and the Electronic Control Module (ECM).

Since the self-diagnostic system cannot diagnose every possible fault in the system, the absence of a trouble code does not mean the system is trouble free. To determine problems within the system which do not activate a trouble code, a system performance check must be made. This job should be left to a qualified technician.

In the case of a intermittent fault in the system, the 'Check Engine' light will go out when the fault goes away, but the trouble code will remain in the memory of the ECM. Therefore, if a trouble code can be obtained even though the 'Check Engine' light is not on, the trouble code must be evaluated. It must be determined if the fault is intermittent or if the engine must be at certain operating conditions (under load, etc.) before the 'Check Engine' light will come on. Some trouble codes will not be recorded in the ECM until the engine has been operated at part throttle for about 5 to 18 minutes.

On the C-4 System, the ECM erases all trouble codes every time the ignition is turned OFF. In the case of intermittent faults, a long term memory is desirable. This can be produced by connecting the orange connector/lead from terminal 'S' of the ECM directly to the battery (or to a 'hot' fuse panel terminal). This terminal must be disconnected after diagnosis is complete or it will drain the battery.

On the CCC System, a trouble code will be stored until terminal 'R' of the ECM has been disconnected from the battery for 10 seconds.

An easy way to erase the computer memory on the CCC System is to disconnect the battery terminals from the battery. If this method is used, don't forget to reset clocks and electronic preprogramable radios. Another method is to remove the fuse marked ECM in the fuse panel. Not all models have such a fuse.

ACTIVATING THE TROUBLE CODE

On the C-4 System, activate the trouble code by grounding the trouble code test lead. Use the illustration to locate the test lead under the instrument panel (usually a white and black wire or a wire with a green connector). Run a jumper wire from the lead to ground.

On the CCC System, locate the test terminal under the instrument panel. Ground the test lead. On many systems, the test lead is situated side by side with a ground terminal. In addition, on some models, the partition between the test terminal and the ground terminal has a cut out section so that a spade terminal can be used to connect the two terminals.

➡ **Ground the test lead or terminal according to the instructions given in Basic Troubleshooting.**

Explanation of Trouble Codes
GM C-4 and CCC Systems
Ground test lead or terminal AFTER engine is running.

Trouble Code	Applicable System	Notes	Possible Problem Area
12	C-4, CCC		No tachometer or reference signal to computer (ECM). This code will only be present while a fault exists, and will not be stored if the problem is intermittent.
13	C-4, CCC		Oxygen sensor circuit. The engine must run for about five minutes at part throttle (and under road load—CCC equipped cars) before this code will show.
13 & 14 (at same time)	C-4		See code 43.
14	C-4, CCC		Shorted coolant sensor circuit. The engine has to run 2 minutes before this code will show.
15	C-4, CCC		Open coolant sensor circuit. The engine has to operate for about five minutes at part throttle (some models) before this code will show.
21	C-4		Shorted wide open throttle switch and/or open closed-throttle switch circuit (when used).
	C-4, CCC		Throttle position sensor circuit. The engine must be run up to 10 seconds (25 seconds—CCC System) below 800 rpm before this code will show.
21 & 22 (at same time)	C-4		Grounded wide open throttle switch circuit.
22	C-4		Grounded closed throttle or wide open throttle switch circuit.
23	C-4, CCC		Open or grounded carburetor mixture control (M/C) solenoid circuit.

Explanation of Trouble Codes (cont.)
GM C-4 and CCC Systems

Ground test lead or terminal AFTER engine is running.

Trouble Code	Applicable System	Notes	Possible Problem Area
24	CCC		Vehicle speed sensor (VSS) circuit. The car must operate up to five minutes at road speed before this code will show.
32	C-4, CCC		Barometric pressure sensor (BARO) circuit output low.
32 & 55 (at same time)	C-4		Grounded +8V terminal or V(REF) terminal for barometric pressure sensor (BARO), or faulty ECM computer.
34	C-4		Manifold absolute pressure (MAP) sensor output high (after ten seconds and below 800 rpm).
	CCC		Manifold absolute pressure (MAP) sensor circuit or vacuum sensor circuit. The engine must run up to five minutes below 800 RPM before this code will set.
35	CCC		Idle speed control (ISC) switch circuit shorted (over ½ throttle for over two seconds).
41	CCC		No distributor reference pulses to the ECM at specified engine vacuum. This code will store in memory.
42	CCC		Electronic spark timing (EST) bypass circuit grounded.
43	C-4		Throttle position sensor adjustment (on some models, engine must run at part throttle up to ten seconds before this code will set).
44	C-4, CCC		Lean oxygen sensor indication. The engine must run up to five minutes in closed loop (oxygen sensor adjusting carburetor mixture), at part throttle and under road load (drive car) before this code will set.
44 & 55 (at same time)	C-4, CCC		Faulty oxygen sensor circuit.
45	C-4, CCC	Restricted air cleaner can cause code 45.	Rich oxygen sensor system indication. The engine must run up to five minutes in closed loop (oxygen sensor adjusting carburetor mixture), at part throttle under road load before this code will set.
51	C-4, CCC		Faulty calibration unit (PROM) or improper PROM installation in electronic control module (ECM). It takes up to thirty seconds for this code to set.

Explanation of Trouble Codes (cont.)
GM C-4 and CCC Systems
Ground test lead or terminal AFTER engine is running.

Trouble Code	Applicable System	Notes	Possible Problem Area
52 & 53	C-4		"Check Engine" light off: Intermittent ECM computer problem. "Check Engine" light on: Faulty ECM computer (replace).
52	C-4, CCC		Faulty ECM computer.
53	CCC		Faulty ECM computer.
54	C-4, CCC		Faulty mixture control solenoid circuit and/or faulty ECM computer.
55	C-4		Faulty throttle position sensor or ECM computer. Faulty ECM computer.
55	CCC		Grounded +8 volt supply (terminal 19 of ECM computer connector), grounded 5 volt reference (terminal 21 of ECM computer connector), faulty oxygen sensor circuit or faulty ECM computer.

Oxygen Sensor

REMOVAL & INSTALLATION

1. Disconnect the two wire plug.
2. Remove the sensor from the exhaust manifold on the four cylinder, or the exhaust pipe on the six.
3. Clean the threads in the manifold or pipe.
4. Coat the threads of the replacement sensor with an electrically conductive antiseize compound. Do not use a conventional antiseize compound, which may electrically insulate the sensor.
5. Install the sensor. Installation torque is 25 ft.lb. for the four cylinder, 31 ft.lb. for the 6-cylinder.
6. Connect the sensor lead. Do not push the rubber boot into the sensor body more than ½ in. (12.7mm) above the base.
7. If the sensors' pigtail is broken, replace the sensor. The wires cannot be spliced or soldered.

Vacuum Switch

REMOVAL & INSTALLATION

The vacuum switches are mounted in a bracket bolted to the left inner fender panel in the engine compartment. They are not replaceable individually; the complete unit must be replaced.
1. Tag all the vacuum hoses, then disconnect them from switches. Disconnect the electrical plugs. The four cylinder has two plugs and the six has one.

2. Remove the switch and bracket assembly from the fender panel.
3. Installation is the reverse.

Control Unit

REMOVAL & INSTALLATION

The control unit, whether ECM or MCU is mounted in the passenger compartment, beneath the right side of the instrument panel.
1. The ECM is installed in a mounting bracket; remove it from the bracket. The MCU is attached with bolts; remove the bolts and remove the unit.
2. Disconnect the electrical plugs.
3. Installation is the reverse. The 4-cylinder ECM is electrically insulated from the chassis; do not ground the ECM bracket!

Mixture Control Solenoid

REMOVAL & INSTALLATION

The E2SE mixture control solenoid is installed in the air horn.
1. Remove the air cleaner case.
2. Disconnect the solenoid electrical plug.

3. Remove the solenoid retaining screw.
4. Remove the solenoid from the air horn.
5. Before installation, coat the rubber seal on the end of the stem with silicone grease or light engine oil. Install the solenoid, accurately aligning the stem with the recess at the bottom of the bowl. Use a new gasket. Connect the electrical plug and install the air cleaner.

Stepper Motor

REMOVAL & INSTALLATION

The BBD stepper motor is installed in the side of the main body of the carburetor.
1. Remove the air cleaner case.
2. Disconnect the electrical plug.
3. Remove the retaining screw and remove the motor from the side of the carburetor. Be careful not to drop the metering pins or the spring when removing the motor.
4. Installation is the reverse.

Catalytic Converter

OPERATION

▶ See Figures 22 and 23

The catalytic converter is a muffler like device inserted in the exhaust system. Exhaust gases flow through the converter where a chemical change takes place, reducing carbon monoxide and hydrocarbons to carbon dioxide and water; the latter two elements being harmless. The catalysts promoting this reaction are platinum and palladium coated beads of alumina. Because of the chemical reaction which does take place in the converter, the temperature of the converter during operation is higher than the exhaust gases when they leave the engine. However, insulation keeps the outside skin of the converter about the same temperature as the muffler. An improperly adjusted carburetor or ignition problem which would permit unburned fuel to enter the converter could produce excessive heat. Excessive heat in the converter could result in bulging or other distortion of the converter's shape. If the converter is heat damaged and must be replaced, the ignition or carburetor problem must be corrected for.

Fig. 22 Exhaust system with a pellet type catalytic converter used on 4 cylinder engines

Fig. 23 Exhaust system with a dual bed monolithic type catalytic converter used on 6 cylinder engines

Choke Heat By-Pass Valve (CHBPV)

OPERATION

➡This system is found on 1976–79 V8 models.

When the engine is first started and begins to warm up, heated air from the exhaust crossover passage in the intake manifold is routed through a heat tube to the choke housing containing the thermostatic spring for regulating the choke flap. A thermostatic by-pass valve, which is integral with the choke heat tube, helps prevent premature choke valve opening during the early part of the warmup period. This is important when ambient temperatures are relatively low and adverse driveability could occur if the choke was opened too soon.

The thermostatic by-pass valve regulates the temperature of the hot airflow to the choke housing by allowing outside unheated air to enter the heat tube. A thermostatic disc in the valve is calibrated to close the valve at 75°F (24°C) and open it at 55°F (13°C).

Fuel Return System

OPERATION

♦ See Figures 24, 25 and 26

The purpose of the fuel return system is to reduce high temperature fuel vapor problems. The system consists of a fuel return

Fig. 24 Schematic of the fuel return system hoses—6 cylinder engines

line to the fuel tank and special fuel filter with an extra outlet nipple to which the return line is connected. During normal operation, a small amount of fuel is returned to the fuel tank. During periods of high underhood temperatures, vaporized fuel in the fuel line is returned to the fuel tank and not passed through the carburetor.

➡The extra nipple on the special fuel filter should be positioned upward to ensure proper operation of the system.

Fig. 25 Schematic of the fuel return system hoses—4 cylinder engines

Fig. 26 An inline check valve is used in the fuel return system

VACUUM DIAGRAMS

Following are vacuum diagrams for most of the engine and emissions package combinations covered by this manual. Because vacuum circuits will vary based on various engine and vehicle options, always refer first to the vehicle emission control information label, if present. Should the label be missing, or should vehicle be equipped with a different engine from the vehicle's original equipment, refer to the diagrams below for the same or similar configuration.

If you wish to obtain a replacement emissions label, most manufacturers make the labels available for purchase. The labels can usually be ordered from a local dealer.

Fig. 27 PCV system hose routing—1975 6 cylinder engine

Fig. 28 EGR system hose routing—1975 6 cylinder engine (Federal)

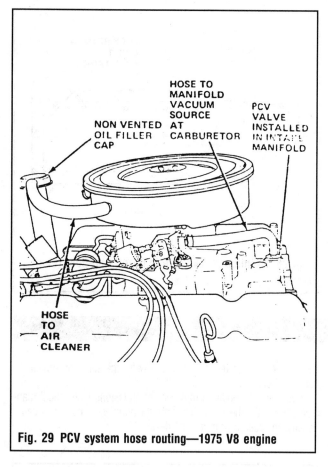

Fig. 29 PCV system hose routing—1975 V8 engine

Fig. 31 EGR system hose routing—1975 6 cylinder engines (California)

Fig. 30 EGR system hose routing—1975 V8 engine (Federal)

Fig. 32 EGR system hose routing—1976 6 cylinder engine (California)

Fig. 33 EGR system hose routing—1975–76 V8 engine (California)

Fig. 35 CTO system hose routing—1975–76 models (49 States)

Fig. 34 TCS system hose routing—1975–76 V8 engine (California)

Fig. 36 Vacuum control check valve hose routing—1977 V8 engine (California)

Fig. 37 EGR system hose routing—1976 6 cylinder engine

Fig. 39 TCS system hose routing—1977 6 cylinder engine

Fig. 38 Vacuum control check valve hose routing—1977 6 cylinder engine (California)

Fig. 40 TCS system hose routing—1977 V8 engine

Fig. 41 PCV system hose routing—1978 4 cylinder engine

Fig. 42 PCV system hose routing—1978 6 cylinder engine

Fig. 43 PCV system hose routing—1978 V8 engine

Fig. 44 TCS system hose routing—1978 6 cylinder engine

Fig. 46 EGR system hose routing—1978 4 cylinder engine

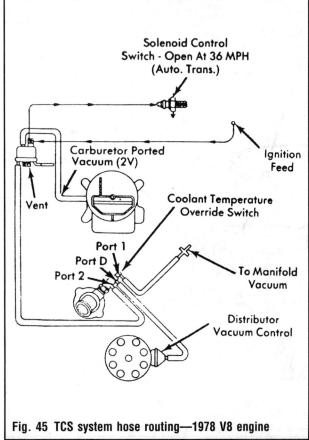

Fig. 45 TCS system hose routing—1978 V8 engine

Fig. 47 EGR system hose routing—1978 6 cylinder engine

Fig. 48 EGR system hose routing—1978 V8 engine

Fig. 49 CTO system hose routing—1978 4 cylinder engine

Fig. 50 Vacuum hose schematic—1979 Spirit and Concord 4–121 engines (49 States)

Fig. 51 Vacuum hose schematic—1979 Spirit and Concord 4–121 engines with M/T (California)

Fig. 52 Vacuum hose schematic—1979 Pacer, Spirit and Concord 6–232 engines (49 States)

Fig. 53 Vacuum hose schematic—1979 Pacer, Spirit and Concord 6–258 engines with M/T. EGR valve orifice plate is deleted on A/T (49 States)

Fig. 54 Vacuum hose schematic—1979 2 bbl. 6–258 engine with A/T

Fig. 55 Vacuum hose schematic—1979 1 bbl.6–258 engine with A/T

Fig. 56 Vacuum hose schematic—1979 Spirit 8–304 engine with M/T (49 States)

Fig. 57 Vacuum hose schematic—1979 Pacer, Spirit and Concord 8–304 engine with A/T. EGR valve orifice plate and the non-linear valve are deleted on M/T (49 States)

Fig. 58 Vacuum hose schematic—1980 4 cylinder engine (49 States)

Fig. 59 Vacuum hose schematic—1980 4 cylinder engine with A/T and without A/C (49 States)

Fig. 60 Vacuum hose schematic—1980 4 cylinder engine with A/T and A/C (49 States)

Fig. 61 Vacuum hose schematic—1980 4 cylinder engine with M/T (California)

Fig. 62 Vacuum hose schematic—1980 4 cylinder engine with A/T (California)

Fig. 63 Vacuum hose schematic—1980 6 cylinder engine with A/T (49 States)

Fig. 64 Vacuum hose schematic—1980 6 cylinder engine with M/T (49 States)

Fig. 65 Vacuum hose schematic—1980 6 cylinder engine with A/T (California)

Fig. 66 Vacuum hose schematic—1980 6 cylinder engine with M/T (California)

Fig. 67 Vacuum hose schematic—1980 Eagle with a 3.08 axle (49 States)

Fig. 68 Vacuum hose schematic—1980 Eagle with a 3.54 axle (49 States)

Fig. 69 Vacuum hose schematic—1980 Eagle (Hilly terrain)

Fig. 70 Vacuum hose schematic—1980 Eagle (California)

Fig. 71 Vacuum hose schematic—1981 Spirit and Concord 4–151 engine with M/T and without A/C (49 States)

Fig. 72 Vacuum hose schematic—1981 Spirit and Concord 4–151 engine with A/T and without A/C (49 States)

Fig. 73 Vacuum hose schematic—1981 Spirit and Concord 4-151 engine with M/T and A/C (49 States)

Fig. 74 Vacuum hose schematic—1981 Spirit and Concord 4-151 engine with A/T and A/C (49 States)

Fig. 75 Vacuum hose schematic—1981 Spirit and Concord 4–151 engine with M/T (California)

Fig. 76 Vacuum hose schematic—1981 Spirit and Concord 4–151 engine with A/T (California)

Fig. 77 Vacuum hose schematic—1981 Eagle 4–151 engine with M/T and without A/C (49 States)

Fig. 78 Vacuum hose schematic—1981 Eagle 4–151 engine with M/T and A/C (49 States)

Fig. 79 Vacuum hose schematic—1981 Eagle 4-151 engine with A/T and without A/C (49 States)

Fig. 80 Vacuum hose schematic—1981 Eagle 4-151 engine with A/T and without A/C (49 States)

Fig. 81 Vacuum hose schematic—1981 Eagle 4–151 engine with M/T (California)

Fig. 82 Vacuum hose schematic—1981 Eagle 4–151 engine with A/T (California)

Fig. 83 Vacuum hose schematic—1981 Spirit and Concord 6–258 engine with M/T

Fig. 84 Vacuum hose schematic—1981 Spirit and Concord 6–258 engine with A/T

Fig. 85 Vacuum hose schematic—1981 Eagle 6–258 engine with M/T (49 States)

Fig. 86 Vacuum hose schematic—1981 Eagle 6–258 engine with A/T (49 States)

Fig. 87 Vacuum hose schematic—1981 Eagle 6-258 engine with M/T (California)

Fig. 88 Vacuum hose schematic—1981 Eagle 6-258 engine with A/T (California)

Fig. 89 Vacuum hose schematic—1981 Eagle 6-258 engine with A/T (High altitude)

Fig. 90 Vacuum hose schematic—1982 Spirit and Concord 4-151 engine with M/T and without A/C (49 State, Canada and High altitude)

Fig. 91 Vacuum hose schematic—1982 Spirit and Concord 4–151 engine with M/T and A/C (49 State, Canada and High altitude)

Fig. 92 Vacuum hose schematic—1982 Spirit and Concord 4–151 engine with A/T and without A/C (49 State and Canada)

Fig. 93 Vacuum hose schematic—1982 Spirit and Concord 4–151 engine with M/T and without A/C (California)

Fig. 94 Vacuum hose schematic—1982 Spirit and Concord 4–151 engine with M/T and A/C (California)

Fig. 95 Vacuum hose schematic—1982 Spirit and Concord 4–151 engine with A/T and without A/C (California)

Fig. 96 Vacuum hose schematic—1982 Eagle and Eagle SX4 4–151 engine with M/T and without A/C (California)

Fig. 97 Vacuum hose schematic—1982 Eagle and Eagle SX4 4–151 engine with M/T and A/C (California)

Fig. 98 Vacuum hose schematic—1982 Eagle and Eagle SX4 4–151 engine without A/C

Fig. 99 Vacuum hose schematic—1982 Eagle and Eagle SX4 4–151 engine with A/C (49 state, Canada and High altitude)

Fig. 100 Vacuum hose schematic—1982 Eagle and Eagle SX4 4–151 engine without A/C (Canada)

Fig. 101 Vacuum hose schematic—1982 Eagle SX4 4–151 engine with A/T and without A/C (California)

Fig. 102 Vacuum hose schematic—1982 Eagle and Eagle SX4 6–258 engine with M/T (Canada)

Fig. 103 Vacuum hose schematic—1982 Spirit and Concord 6–258 engine with M/T, Eagle and Eagle SX4 (High altitude)

Fig. 104 Vacuum hose schematic—1982 Eagle and Eagle SX4 6–258 engine with M/T (49 State)

Fig. 105 Vacuum hose schematic—1982 Spirit and Concord 6-258 engine with A/T (California)

Fig. 106 Vacuum hose schematic—1982 Eagle and Eagle SX4 6-258 engine with A/T (California)

Fig. 107 Vacuum hose schematic—1982 Eagle, Eagle SX4, Spirit and Concord 6–258 engine with A/T (49 State, Canada and High altitude); Eagle and Eagle SX4 (California)

Fig. 108 Vacuum hose schematic—1984 SJ Eagle 4 cylinder engine

Fig. 109 Vacuum hose schematic—1984–88 SJ Eagle 6 cylinder engine

BASIC FUEL SYSTEM
  DIAGNOSIS 5-2
FUEL SYSTEM 5-2
FUEL PUMP 5-2
  REMOVAL & INSTALLATION 5-2
  TESTING 5-3
CARBURETORS 5-4
  REMOVAL & INSTALLATION 5-4
  OVERHAUL 5-6
CARTER YF CARBURETOR 5-6
  DESCRIPTION 5-6
  ADJUSTMENTS 5-9
CARTER BBD 2-BBL
  CARBURETOR 5-10
  ADJUSTMENT 5-10
AUTOLITE/MOTORCRAFT 2100 AND
  2150 CARBURETORS 5-14
  DESCRIPTION 5-14
  ADJUSTMENT 5-14
AUTOLITE/MOTORCRAFT 4300 AND
  4350 4-BBL CARBURETORS 5-20
  DESCRIPTION 5-20
  ADJUSTMENTS 5-22
ROCHESTER E2SE CARBURETOR 5-23
  ADJUSTMENTS 5-25
HOLLEY 5210-C CARBURETOR 5-26
  ADJUSTMENTS 5-26
CARTER YFA CARBURETOR 5-28
  ADJUSTMENT 5-29
FUEL TANK 5-33
TANK ASSEMBLY 5-33
  DRAINING 5-33
  REMOVAL & INSTALLATION 5-33
FUEL TANK SENDING UNIT 5-34
  REMOVAL & INSTALLATION 5-34
SPECIFICATION CHARTS
  CARBURETOR SPECIFICATIONS 5-30
TROUBLESHOOTING CHARTS
  BASIC FUEL SYSTEM
    PROBLEMS 5-33

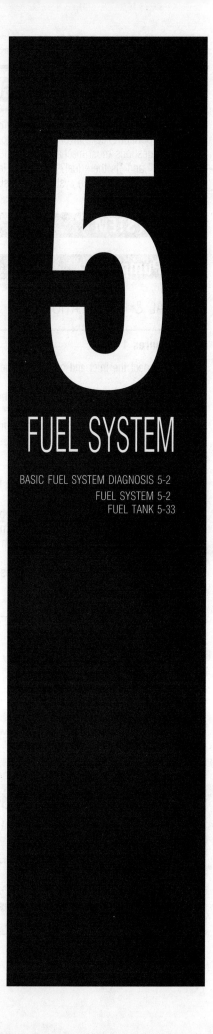

5

FUEL SYSTEM

BASIC FUEL SYSTEM DIAGNOSIS 5-2
FUEL SYSTEM 5-2
FUEL TANK 5-33

BASIC FUEL SYSTEM DIAGNOSIS

When there is a problem starting or driving a vehicle, two of the most important checks involve the ignition and the fuel systems. The questions most mechanics attempt to answer first, "is there spark?" and "is there fuel?" will often lead to solving most basic problems. For ignition system diagnosis and testing, please refer to the information on engine electrical components and ignition systems found earlier in this manual. If the ignition system checks out (there is spark), then you must determine if the fuel system is operating properly (is there fuel?).

FUEL SYSTEM

Fuel Pump

REMOVAL & INSTALLATION

▶ **See Figures 1 and 2**

1. Disconnect the inlet and outlet fuel lines, and any vacuum lines.
2. Remove the two fuel pump body attaching nuts and lock-washers.
3. Pull the pump and gasket, or O-ring, free of the engine. Make sure that the mating surfaces of the fuel pump and the engine are clean.

To install:

4. Cement a new gasket to the mounting flange of the fuel pump.
5. Position the fuel pump on the engine block so that the lever of the fuel pump rests on the fuel pump cam of the camshaft.
6. Secure the fuel pump to the block with the two cap screws and lock washers.
7. Connect the intake and outlet fuel lines to the fuel pump, and any vacuum lines.

Fig. 2 Exploded view of the fuel pump components—4–151 engine

Fig. 1 Common fuel pump assembly used on all models except the 4–151 engines

Use a pair of pliers to disengage the spring type fuel return line clamp . . .

. . . then separate the hose from the fuel pump

Use an extension to reach the fuel pump retaining bolts

Use a flare nut wrench to loosen the inlet line nut . . .

. . . then gently pull the line from the fuel pump being careful not to bend or kink it

✳✳ WARNING

When installing the 4–121 engine fuel pump, be sure that the pushrod is positioned properly against the actuating lever or the pump may be damaged when the screws are tightened.

TESTING

▶ See Figure 3

Volume Check

Disconnect the fuel line from the carburetor. Place the open end in a suitable container. Start the engine and operate it at normal idle speed. The pump should deliver at least one pint in 30 seconds.

INLET LINE
(FROM FUEL PUMP)

Fig. 3 Connect a fuel pressure gauge as shown to check pump volume and pressure

Pressure Check

1. Disconnect the fuel line at the carburetor.
2. Disconnect the fuel return line from the fuel filter if so equipped, and plug the nipple on the filter.
3. Install a T-fitting on the open end of the fuel line and refit the line to the carburetor.
4. Plug a pressure gauge into the remaining opening of the T-fitting.
5. The hose leading to the pressure gauge should not be any longer than 6 in. (152.5mm).
6. Start the engine and let it run at idle speed.
7. Bleed any air out of the hose between the gauge and the T-fitting.
8. On pumps with a fuel return line, the line must be plugged.
9. Start the engine. Fuel pressures are as follows:

4–121 Engine: 4.00–6.00psi @ idle
4–150 Engine: 4.00–5.00psi @ idle
4–151 Engine: 6.50–8.00psi @ idle
6–232 Engine: 3.00–5.00psi @ idle
6–258 Engine: 3.00–5.00psi @ idle
8–304 Engine: 4.00–6.00psi @ idle
8–360 Engine: 4.00–6.00psi @ idle
8–401 Engine: 4.00–6.00psi @ idle

Carburetors

REMOVAL & INSTALLATION

1. Remove the air cleaner.
2. Disconnect the fuel and vacuum lines. It might be a good idea to tag them to avoid confusion when the time comes to put them back.
3. Disconnect the choke rod.
4. Disconnect the accelerator linkage.
5. Disconnect the automatic transmission linkage.
6. Unbolt and remove the carburetor.
7. Remove the base gasket.

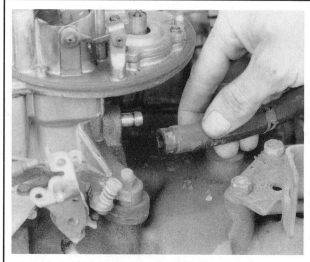

After releasing the clamp, disconnect the hose

Using a flare nut wrench and a back-up wrench, disengage the fuel line nut . . . .

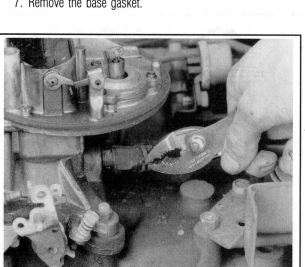

To remove the carburetor, disconnect the hoses. Some are secured with clamps

. . . then disconnect the fuel line from the carburetor

Disengage the transmission linkage from the throttle lever assembly . . .

. . . then disengage the linkage from the throttle shaft assembly

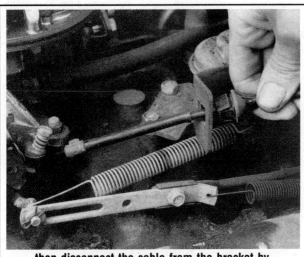

. . . then disconnect the cable from the bracket by compressing the square tabs

Unfasten the carburetor retaining bolts. Use an extension if necessary

Use a pair of pliers to remove the throttle linkage retaining pin . . .

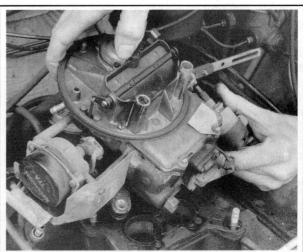

Remove the carburetor from the intake manifold assembly

To install:

8. Make sure that the carburetor and manifold sealing surfaces are clean.

9. Install a new carburetor base gasket.

10. Install the carburetor and start the fuel and vacuum lines.

11. Bolt down the carburetor evenly.

12. Tighten the fuel and vacuum lines.

13. Connect the accelerator and automatic transmission linkage. If the transmission linkage was disturbed, it will have to be adjusted. The procedure is in Section 7.

14. Connect the choke rod.

15. Install the air cleaner. Adjust the idle speed and mixture as described in Section 2. Depending on the vintage, it may not be necessary (or possible) to adjust the idle mixture.

OVERHAUL

Whenever wear or dirt causes a carburetor to perform poorly, there are two possible solutions to the problem. The simplest is to trade on the old unit for a rebuilt one. The other, cheaper alternative is to buy an overhaul kit and rebuild the original kit. Some of the better overhaul kits contain complete step-by-step instructions along with exploded views and gauges. Other kits, intended for the professional, have only a few general overhaul hints. The second type can be moderately confusing to the novice, especially since a kit may have extra parts so that one kit can cover several variations of the same carburetor. In any event, it is not a good idea to dismantle any carburetor without at least replacing all the gaskets. The carburetor adjustments should all be checked during or after overhaul.

➡**Before you go to the parts store for a rebuilding kit, make sure that you know what make and model your carburetor is.**

Efficient carburetion depends greatly on careful cleaning and inspection during overhaul, since dirt, gum, water, or varnish in or on the carburetor parts are often responsible for poor performance.

Overhaul your carburetor in a clean, dust free area. Carefully disassemble the carburetor, referring often to the exploded views. Keep all similar and lookalike parts segregated during disassembly and cleaning to avoid accidental interchange during assembly. Make a note of all jet sizes.

When the carburetor is disassembled, wash all parts (except diaphragms, electric choke units, pump plunger, and any other plastic, leather, fire, or rubber parts) in clean carburetor solvent. Do not leave parts in the solvent any longer than is necessary to sufficiently loosen the deposits. Excessive cleaning may remove the special finish from the float bowl and choke valve bodies, leaving these parts unfit for service. Rinse all parts in clean solvent and blow them dry with compressed air or allow them to air dry. Wipe clean all cork, plastic, leather, and fiber parts with a clean, lint-free cloth.

Blow out all passages and jets with compressed air and be sure that there are no restrictions or blockages. Never use wire or similar tools to clean jets, fuel passages, or air bleeds. Clean all jets and valves separately to avoid accidental interchange.

Check all parts for wear or damage. If wear or damage is found, replace the complete assembly.

2. Check the float hinge pin for wear and the float(s) for dents or distortion. Replace the float if fuel has leaked into it.

3. Check the throttle and choke shaft bores for wear or an out-of-round condition. Damage or wear to the throttle arm, shaft, or shaft bore will require replacement of the throttle body. These parts require a close tolerance of fit; wear may allow air leakage, which could affect starting and idling.

➡**Throttle shafts and bushings are not included in overhaul kits. They can be purchased separately.**

4. Inspect the idle mixture adjusting needles for burrs or grooves. Any such condition requires replacement of the needle, since you will not be able to obtain a satisfactory idle.

5. Test the accelerator pump check valves. They should pass air one way but not the other. Test for proper seating by blowing and sucking on the valve. Replace the valve as necessary. If the valve is satisfactory, wash the valve again to remove breath moisture.

6. Check the bowl cover for warped surfaces with a straightedge.

7. Closely inspect the valves and seats for wear and damage, replacing as necessary.

8. After the carburetor is assembled, check the choke valve for freedom of operation.

Carburetor overhaul kits are recommended for each overhaul. These kits contain all gaskets and new parts to replace those that deteriorate most rapidly. Failure to replace all parts supplied with the kit (especially gaskets) can result in poor performance later.

Some carburetor manufacturers supply overhaul kits of three basic types: minor repair; major repair; and gasket kits. Basically, they contain the following:

Minor Repair Kits
- All gaskets
- Float needle valve
- Volume control screw
- All diaphragms
- Spring for the pump diaphragm

Major Repair Kits
- All jets and gaskets
- All diaphragms
- Float needle valve
- Volume control screw
- Pump ball valve
- Main jet carrier
- Float
- Complete intermediate rod
- Intermediate pump lever
- Complete injector tube
- Some cover hold-down screws and washers

Gasket Kits
- All gaskets

After cleaning and checking all components, reassemble the carburetor, using new parts and referring to the exploded view. When reassembling, make sure that all screws and jets are tight in their seats, but do not overtighten as the tips will be distorted. Tighten all screws gradually, in rotation. Do not tighten needle valves into their seats; uneven jetting will result. Always use new gaskets. BE sure to adjust the float level when reassembling.

Carter YF Carburetor

DESCRIPTION

◆ **See Figures 4, 5 and 6**

The YF carburetor is a single barrel downdraft carburetor with a diaphragm type accelerator pump and diaphragm operated metering rods.

1. Air horn
2. Choke
3. Screw
4. Shaft
5. Piston
6. Pin
7. Coil housing baffle plate
8. Coil housing gasket
9. Choke cover
10. Solenoid and bracket
11. Coil housing retainer
12. Coil housing screw
13. Upper pump spring retainer
14. Upper pump spring
15. Metering rod arm
16. Diaphragm lifter link
17. Washer
18. Diaphragm spring
19. Diaphragm housing screw ④
20. Diaphragm housing
21. Washer
22. Spacer
23. Diaphragm
24. Discharge ball weight
25. Discharge ball
26. Body flange screw ③
27. Fast idle cam
28. Fast idle cam screw
29. Main body
30. Body gasket
31. Idle screw limiter cap
32. Idle mixture screw
33. Spring
34. Throttle body
35. Wave washer

36. Arm
37. Screw
38. Pump connector link
39. Throttle shaft arm
40. Retainer
41. Lever
42. Metering rod jet
43. Low speed jet
44. Float
45. Float pin

46. Needle pin
47. Needle spring
48. Needle, needle seat, gasket
49. Choke connector rod
50. Choke connector rod retainer
51. Lever
52. Metering rod
53. Air horn gasket
54. Screw ②
55. Chamber

56. Gasket
57. Spring
58. Lifter
59. Bellcrank
60. Retainer
61. Spring
62. Air horn screw (short)
63. Air horn screw (long)
64. Stud support
65. Screw

Fig. 4 Exploded view of the Carter YF carburetor with the altitude compensator

Fig. 5 Exploded view of the Carter YF carburetor without the altitude compensator

1. Air horn	22. Spacer	43. Low speed jet
2. Choke	23. Diaphragm	44. Float
3. Screw	24. Discharge ball weight	45. Float pin
4. Shaft	25. Discharge ball	46. Needle pin
5. Piston	26. Body flange screw ③	47. Needle spring
6. Pin	27. Fast idle cam	48. Needle, needle seat, gasket
7. Solenoid and bracket	28. Fast idle cam screw	49. Choke connector rod
8. Coil housing screw	29. Main body	50. Choke connector rod retainer
9. Coil housing retainer	30. Body gasket	51. Lever
10. Choke cover	31. Idle screw limiter cap	52. Metering rod
11. Coil housing gasket	32. Idle mixture screw	53. Air horn gasket
12. Coil housing baffle plate	33. Spring	54. Spring
13. Upper pump spring retainer	34. Throttle body	55. Lifter
14. Upper pump spring	35. Wave washer	56. Bellcrank
15. Metering rod arm	36. Arm	57. Retainer
16. Diaphragm lifter link	37. Screw	58. Spring
17. Washer	38. Pump connector link	59. Air horn screw (short)
18. Diaphragm spring	39. Throttle shaft arm	60. Air horn screw (long)
19. Diaphragm housing screw ④	40. Retainer	61. Stud support
20. Diaphragm housing	41. Lever	62. Screw
21. Washer	42. Metering rod jet	

Fig. 6 Component list for the Carter YF carburetor without the altitude compensator

ADJUSTMENTS

Float Level

1. Invert the air horn assembly and check the clearance from the top of the float to the surface of the air horn with a T-scale. The air horn should be held at eye level when gauging and the float arm should be resting on the needle pin.

2. Do not exert pressure on the needle valve when measuring or adjusting the float. Bend the float arm as necessary to adjust the float level.

Float Drop

1. Hold the air horn up with the float hanging free.

2. Measure the distance between the top of the float at the extreme out end and the air horn under surface.

3. Adjust by bending the tab at the rear of the float lever.

Metering Rod

1. Back out the idle speed adjusting screw until the throttle plate is seated fully in its bore.

2. Press down on the upper end of the diaphragm shaft until the diaphragm bottoms in the vacuum chamber.

3. The metering rod should contact the bottom of the metering rod well and lifter link at the outer end nearest the springs and at the supporting link. The eyelet of the rod should slide freely on the pin of the metering rod arm.

4. On models not equipped with an adjusting screw, adjust by bending the metering rod pin tab.

5. On models with an adjusting screw, turn the screw until the metering rod just bottoms in the body casting. For final adjustment, turn the screw one additional turn clockwise.

Fast Idle Cam

1. Open the throttle side enough to allow full closing of the choke valve. Be sure that the fast idle screw is not contacting the fast idle cam.

2. Close the throttle valve and the fast idle cam should revolve to the fast idle position.

3. If adjustment is necessary, bend the choke rod at its upper angle.

4. Position the fast idle screw on the second step of the fast idle cam and against the shoulder of the high step. Measure the specified clearance between the lower edge of the choke plate and the air horn wall. Bent the choke rod to adjust.

5. Fast idle speed may be checked with the engine warmed up. Speed adjustment is made by bending the choke rod at the lower angle. The speed is given with the adjusting screw on the second step and against the highest step. Adjustment is made with the adjusting screw.

➡**EGR hoses must be blocked off and TCS solenoid vacuum valve wires must be disconnected to do this.**

Choke Unloader

With the throttle valve held wide open and the choke valve held in the closed position, bend the unloader lug on the choke trip lever to obtain the specified clearance between the lower edge of the choke valve and the air horn wall.

Automatic Choke

1. Loosen the choke cover retaining screws.

2. Turn the choke over so that the index mark on the cover lines up with the specified mark on the choke housing. Never set it more than two graduations in either direction of the specified setting.

Electrically Assisted Choke

Starting with the 1976 models, some single barrel Carter YF carburetors use an electrically assisted choke to reduce hydrocarbon and carbon monoxide exhaust emissions during warm-up.

Once underhood temperatures reach 95°F (15°F), a bimetallic switch located in the choke cap closes, allowing a ceramic heating element to draw power from a special tap on the alternator.

This causes the choke valve to open faster than normal, thus reducing CO emission during engine warm-up.

After the engine is shut off, the bimetallic switch remains closed until underhood temperature drops below 65°F. Thus, if the engine is turned off for only a short time or if the ambient temperature is above 65°F, the choke will function for only a limited period of time.

TESTING

1. Detach the electrical lead from the choke cap.

2. Use a jumper lead to connect the terminal on the choke cap and the wire terminal, so that the electrical circuit is still completed.

3. Start the engine.

4. Hook up a test light between the connector on the choke lead and ground.

5. The test light should glow. If it does not, current is not being supplied to the electrically assisted choke.

6. Connect the test light between the terminal on the alternator and the terminal on the choke cap. If the light now glows, replace the lead, since it is not passing current to the choke assist.

✷✷ CAUTION

Do not ground terminal on the alternator while performing Step 6.

7. If the light still does not glow, the fault lies somewhere in the electrical system. Check the system out.

If the electrically assisted choke receives power, but still does not appear to be functioning properly, reconnect the choke lead and proceed with the rest of the test.

8. Tape the bulb end of a thermometer to the metallic portion of the choke housing.

9. If the electrically assisted choke operates below 55°F (13°C), it is defective and must be replaced.

10. Allow the engine to warm-up to between 80°F and 110°F (27–43°C); at these temperatures the choke should operate for about 1½ minutes.

11. If it does not operate for this length of time, check the bimetallic spring to see if it is connected to the tang on the choke lever.

12. If the spring is connected and the choke is not operating properly, replace the cap assembly.

REMOVAL & INSTALLATION

1. Unfasten the electrical lead from the choke cover.

2. Remove the choke cover retaining screws and clamp.

3. Remove the choke cover and gasket from the carburetor.

4. Installation is performed in the reverse order of removal. Adjust the choke cover.

Carter BBD 2-BBL Carburetor

◗ **See Figures 7 and 8**

ADJUSTMENT

Float Level

◗ **See Figure 9**

Float Adjustment

1. Remove the carburetor air horn.

2. Gently hold the lip of the float against its needle to raise the float.

3. Measure float level by placing a straightedge across the float bowl. Float level should be maintained at 0.250 in. (6.35mm), plus or minus 0.032 in. (0.81mm). Release the floats.

4. If necessary, adjust by bending the float lips as required.

➡**Do not bend float lip while it is resting against the needle as this may deform the synthetic needle tip and cause a false setting.**

5. Install the air horn.

Fast Idle

◗ **See Figure 10**

➡**Perform this adjustment with the carburetor installed on the engine. If the car is equipped with a Transmission Controlled Spark (TCS) system and/or an Exhaust Gas Recirculation (EGR) system, be sure that both are disconnected before attempting to set fast idle speed.**

1. Start engine and allow it to reach normal operating temperature.

2. Connect a tachometer to the engine.

3. Set the fast idle adjusting screw so that it contacts the second step of the fast idle cam and rests against the shoulder of the high step.

4. Rotate the fast idle adjusting screw until a fast idle speed of 1700 rpm is obtained.

5. Remove the tach and return the engine to normal idle speed after the adjustment is completed.

Automatic Choke

➡**This adjustment may be made with the carburetor either on or off the engine.**

1. Loosen the choke cover retaining screws.

2. Rotate the choke cover in the direction of its arrow to the specified setting. Refer to the carburetor specification charts.

3. Tighten the retaining screws.

4. If the car stumbles or stalls at the specified choke setting during engine warm-up, adjust the setting to (richer or leaner) until the car runs properly.

➡**Never set the choke more than two notches in either direction of the recommended setting.**

Choke Unloader

1. Hold the throttle in the wide open position and apply pressure on the choke plate toward the closed position.

2. Measure the distance between the lower edge of the choke plate and the air horn wall (see the 'Carburetor Specifications' chart).

3. If necessary, adjust by bending the unloader tang where it contacts the fast idle cam. Bend toward the cam to increase clearance, and away from the cam to decrease clearance.

➡**Do not bend the unloader tang down from the horizontal plane. After adjusting, make sure that the unloader tang maintains at least a 0.070 in. (1.78mm) clearance from the flange of the main body at wide open throttle position.**

4. Operate the throttle and make sure that the unloader does not bind against the carburetor or linkage. Also make sure the wide open throttle can be reached by fully depressing the gas pedal. If not, remove excess padding from beneath the floor mat or reposition the throttle cable bracket.

Initial Choke Valve

1. Remove the choke cover.

2. Using a vacuum source which holds a minimum of 19 in. Hg, pull the diaphragm in against its stop.

3. Open the throttle valve slightly so that the fast idle screw locates on the high step of the cam.

4. Hold the choke bimetallic coil tang in the closed position and measure the clearance between the choke plate and the air horn wall. The distance should be 0.128 in. (3.25mm), plus or minus 0.010 in. (0.254mm).

5. Adjust as necessary by bending the 'S' shaped section of the diaphragm connector link.

Vacuum Step-Up Piston Gap

◗ **See Figure 11**

1. Remove the step-up piston cover plate and gasket from the carburetor air horn.

2. Adjust the gap in the step-up piston to 0.040 in. (1.016mm), plus or minus 0.015 in. (0.38mm) using the allen head screw on top of the piston. Turning the screw clockwise richens the fuel mixture and turning counterclockwise leans it out.

3. Back off the curb idle adjustment until the throttle valves are fully closed, then rotate the idle screw inward one complete turn. Make a note of the number of turns so that the idle screw can be returned to its original position.

4. While keeping moderate pressure on the rod lifter tab, fully depress the step-up piston and tighten the rod lifter lockscrew.

5. Release the piston and rod lifter, and return the curb idle screw to its original position.

6. Install the step-up piston cover plate and gasket.

Accelerator Pump

◗ **See Figure 12**

1. Back off the curb idle screw until the throttle valves (plates) are completely closed. Then, open the choke valve (plate) so that the fast idle cam permits the throttle valves to seat in their bores. Make sure that the accelerator pump 'S' link is located in the outer hole of the pump arm.

2. Turn the curb idle screw clockwise until it just contacts its stop, and then continue to rotate two complete turns.

3. Measure the distance between the surface of the air horn and the top of the accelerator pump shaft. This distance should be 0.500 in. (12.7mm).

4. Adjust the pump travel as necessary, by loosening the pump arm adjusting lockscrew and rotating the sleeve until the proper measurement is obtained. Then, tighten the lockscrew.

WITH AUTOMATIC TRANSMISSION

Fig. 7 Exploded view of the Carter BBD carburetor components

1. Diaphragm connector link
2. Screw
3. Choke vacuum diaphragm
4. Hose
5. Valve
6. Metering rod
7. S-link
8. Pump arm
9. Gasket
10. Rollover check valve
11. Screw
12. Lock
13. Rod lifter
14. Bracket
15. Nut
16. Solenoid
17. Screw
18. Air horn retaining screw (short)
19. Air horn retaining screw (long)
20. Pump lever
21. Venturi cluster screw
22. Idle fuel pick-up tube
23. Gasket
24. Venturi cluster
25. Gasket
26. Check ball (small)
27. Float
28. Fulcrum pin
29. Baffle
30. Clip
31. Choke link
32. Screw
33. Fast idle cam
34. Gasket
35. Thermostatic choke shaft
36. Spring
37. Screw
38. Pump link
39. Clip
40. Gasket
41. Limiter cap
42. Screw
43. Throttle body
44. Choke housing
45. Baffle
46. Gasket
47. Retainer
48. Choke coil
49. Lever
50. Choke rod
51. Clip
52. Needle and seat assembly
53. Main body
54. Main metering jet
55. Check ball (large)
56. Accelerator pump plunger
57. Fulcrum pin retainer
58. Gasket
59. Spring
60. Air horn
61. Lever

Fig. 8 Component list for the Carter BBD carburetor

A. Apply slight pressure
B. Bend to adjust
C. Float
D. Gasket

Fig. 9 Carter BBD carburetor float adjustment points

1. Gap
2. Adjustment screw
3. Vacuum piston
4. Metering rods

Fig. 11 Carter BBD carburetor vacuum piston components

GAUGE

HOLD CLOSED BY PRESSURE ON THERMOSTAT COIL TANG

SCREW SET ON SECOND CAM STEP

MAKE ADJUSTMENT BY BENDING HERE

Fig. 10 Adjusting the fast idle cam on the Carter BBD carburetor

D. Flange
E. Gauge
F. Adjusting screw

Fig. 12 Carter BBD carburetor accelerator pump adjustment

Autolite/Motorcraft 2100 and 2150 Carburetors

DESCRIPTION

♦ **See Figures 13, 14, 15 and 16**

The Model 2100 and 2150 2-barrel carburetors have an air horn assembly that covers the main body and houses the choke plate and the internal fuel bowl vents. The throttle plate, accelerator pump assembly, power valve assembly, and fuel bowl are contained in the main body. The automatic choke is also attached to the main body. Each bore contains a main and booster venturi, a main fuel discharge, an accelerating pump discharge, an idle fuel discharge, and a throttle plate. They are used on V8 engines.

ADJUSTMENT

Float Level

DRY

The dry float level measurement is a preliminary check and must be followed by a wet float level measurement with the carburetor mounted on the engine.

1. With the air horn removed and the fuel inlet needle seated

1. Modulator cover
2. Modulator retaining screw ③
3. Pivot pin
4. Modulator arm
5. Choke valve retaining screw ②
6. Choke valve
7. Choke shaft
8. Air horn
9. Air horn retaining screw ④
10. Air horn gasket
11. Float and lever assembly

12. Float shaft retainer
13. Float shaft
14. Needle retaining clip
15. Curb idle adjusting screw
16. Curb idle adjusting screw spring
17. Throttle shaft and lever assembly
18. Dashpot
19. Dashpot locknut
20. Dashpot bracket
21. Dashpot bracket retaining screw
22. Adjusting screw

Fig. 13 Exploded view of the Motorcraft 2100 carburetor components

23. Carriage
24. Electric solenoid
25. Mounting bracket
26. Throttle valve retaining screw ④
27. Throttle valve ②
28. Needle and seat assembly
29. Needle seat gasket
30. Main jet ②
31. Main body
32. Elastomer valve
33. Pump return spring
34. Pump diaphragm
35. Pump lever pin
36. Pump cover
37. Pump rod
38. Pump rod retainer
39. Pump lever
40. Bowl vent bellcrank
41. Fuel inlet fitting
42. Power valve gasket
43. Power valve
44. Power valve cover gasket
45. Power valve cover
46. Power valve cover
    retaining screw ④
47. Idle limiter cap ②
48. Idle mixture screw ②
49. Idle mixture screw spring ②
50. Retainer
51. Retainer
52. Fast idle lever retaining nut
53. Fast idle lever pin
54. Retainer

55. Lever and shaft
56. Fast idle cam rod
57. Choke shield
58. Choke shield retaining screw ②
59. Piston passage plug
60. Heat passage plug
61. Choke cover retaining clamp
62. Choke cover retaining screw ③
63. Choke cover
64. Choke cover gasket
65. Thermostat lever retaining screw
66. Thermostat lever
67. Choke housing retaining screw ③
68. Choke housing
69. Choke shaft bushing
70. Fast idle speed adjusting screw
71. Fast idle lever
72. Fast idle cam
73. Choke housing gasket
74. Pump discharge check ball
75. Pump discharge weight
76. Booster venturi gasket
77. Booster venturi assembly
78. Air distribution plate
79. Pump discharge screw
80. Retainer
81. Choke rod
82. Choke lever retaining screw
83. Choke plate lever
84. Choke rod seal
85. Stop screw
86. Modulator return spring
87. Modulator diaphragm assembly

Fig. 14 Component list for the Motorcraft 2100 carburetor

Fig. 15 Exploded view of the Motorcraft 2150 carburetor components

1. Compensator choke shaft
2. Retainer
3. Compensator choke valve
4. Choke valve screw
5. Compensator choke rod
6. Choke valve
7. Choke shaft
8. Air horn
9. Air horn retaining screw ④
10. Air horn gasket
11. Float shaft retainer
12. Float and lever assembly
13. Float shaft
14. Needle retaining clip
15. Curb idle adjusting screw
16. Curb idle adjusting screw spring
17. Throttle shaft and lever assembly
18. Dashpot
19. Dashpot locknut
20. Dashpot bracket
21. Dashpot bracket
      retaining screw
22. Adjusting screw
23. Carriage
24. Electric solenoid
25. Mounting bracket
26. Throttle valve
      retaining screw ④
27. Throttle valve ②
28. Needle and seat assembly
29. Needle seat gasket
30. Main jet ②
31. Main body
32. Elastomer valve
33. Pump return spring
34. Pump diaphragm
35. Pump lever pin
36. Pump cover
37. Pump rod
38. Pump rod retainer
39. Pump lever
40. Pump cover retaining screw ④
41. Fuel inlet fitting
42. Power valve gasket
43. Power valve
44. Power valve cover gasket
45. Power valve cover
46. Power valve cover
      retaining screw ④
47. Idle limiter cap ②
48. Idle mixture
      screw ②

49. Idle mixture
      screw spring ②
50. Retainer
51. Retainer
52. Fast idle lever
      retaining nut
53. Fast idle lever pin
54. Retainer
55. Thermostatic
      choke shaft
56. Fast idle cam rod
57. Choke shield
58. Choke shield retaining screw ②
59. Piston passage plug
60. Heat passage plut
61. Choke cover retaining clamp
62. Choke cover retaining screw ③
63. Choke cover
64. Choke cover gasket
65. Thermostat lever retaining screw
66. Thermostat lever
67. Choke housing retaining screw ③
68. Choke housing
69. Choke shaft bushing
70. Fast idle cam lever adjusting screw
71. Choke diaphragm
72. Hose
73. Link
74. Screw
75. Fast idle speed adjusting screw
76. Fast idle lever
77. Fast idle cam
78. Choke housing gasket
79. Pump discharge check ball
80. Pump discharge weight
81. Booster venturi gasket
82. Booster venturi assembly
83. Air distribution plate
84. Pump discharge screw
85. Retainer
86. Choke rod
87. Gasket
88. Compensation chamber
89. Gasket
90. Screw
91. Aneroid
92. Screw
93. Choke lever retaining screw
94. Choke plate lever
95. Choke rod seal

Fig. 16 Component list for the Motorcraft 2150 carburetor

lightly, gently raise the float and measure the distance between the main body gasket surface (gasket removed) and the top of the float.

2. If necessary, bend the float tab to obtain the correct level.

Wet

♦ **See Figure 17**

1. Remove the screws that hold the air horn to the main body and break the seal between the air horn and main body. Leave the air horn and gasket loosely in place on top of the main body.

Fig. 17 Adjusting the float level (wet) on the Motorcraft 2150 carburetor

2. Start the engine and allow it to idle for at least 3 minutes.

3. After the engine has idled long enough to stabilize the fuel level, remove the air horn assembly.

4. With the engine idling, use a T-scale to measure the distance surface to the surface of the fuel. The scale must be held at least ¼ in. (6mm) away from any vertical surface to ensure proper measurement.

5. If any adjustment is required, stop the engine to avoid a fire from fuel spraying on the engine.

6. Bend the float tab upward to raise the level and downward to lower the level.

❊❊ WARNING

Be sure to hold the fuel inlet needle off its seat when bending the float tab so as not to damage the Viton tip.

7. Each time the float level is changed, the air horn must be temporarily positioned and the engine started to stabilize the fuel level before again checking it.

Initial Choke Valve Clearance

1. Remove the choke shield.

2. Loosen the choke cover screws. Rotate the cover ¼ turn counterclockwise.

Disconnect the choke shield bolts . . .

. . . then remove the shield from the choke assembly

Loosen the choke cover screws . . .

. . . then rotate the cover a 1/4 of a turn counterclockwise

Fig. 18 Motorcraft 2100 carburetor fast idle cam index setting

3. Disconnect the choke heat inlet tube. Align the fast idle speed adjusting screw with the indexed (second) step of the fast idle cam.

4. Start the engine without moving the accelerator linkage.

5. Turn the fast idle cam lever adjusting screw out 3 full turns. Measure the clearance between the lower edge of the choke valve and the air horn wall.

6. Adjust by grasping the modulator arm with a pair of pliers and twisting with a second pair of pliers. Twist to the front to increase the clearance and toward the rear to decrease the clearance.

✳✳ WARNING

Be very careful not to damage the nylon piston rod of the modulator assembly.

7. Stop the engine and connect the heat tube. Turn the fast idle cam lever in 3 full turns.

8. Don't reset the choke cover until the fast idle cam linkage adjustment is done.

Fast Idle Cam
▶ See Figure 18

1. Push down on the fast idle cam lever until the fast idle screw is in contact with the second step of the fast idle cam and against the shoulder of the high step.

2. The specified clearance should be present between the lower edge of the choke valve and the air horn wall.

3. The adjustment is made by turning the fast idle cam lever screw.

4. The choke cover may now be adjusted.

Choke Unloader (Dechoke)
▶ See Figures 19 and 20

1. With the throttle held completely open, move the choke valve to the closed position.

2. Measure the distance between the lower edge of the choke valve and the air horn wall.

3. Adjust by bending the tang on the fast idle speed lever which is located on the throttle shaft.

➡Final unloader adjustment must be performed on the car and the throttle should be opened by using the accelerator pedal of the car. This is to be sure that full throttle operation is achieved.

Fig. 19 Choke unloader adjustment on the Motorcraft 2150 carburetor

Fig. 20 Check the choke unloader/fast idle cam clearance here—Motorcraft 2150 carburetor

Accelerator Pump

♦ **See Figure 21**

The accelerator pump operating rod must be positioned in the proper holes of the accelerator pump lever and the throttle overtravel lever to assure contact pump travel. If adjusting is required, additional holes are provided in the throttle overtravel lever.

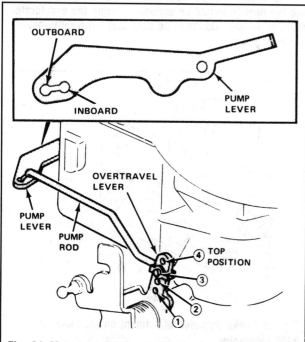

Fig. 21 Motorcraft 2100 and 2150 carburetor accelerator pump adjustment points

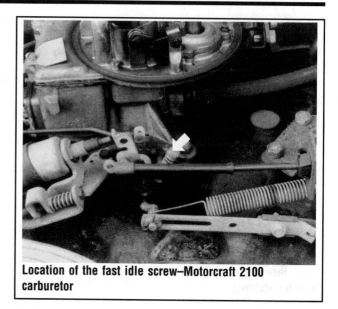

Location of the fast idle screw—Motorcraft 2100 carburetor

Fast Idle

Adjust the fast idle setting with the engine at operating temperature. The fast idle screw should be resting against the second step of the fast idle cam. Adjust by turning the fast idle screw.

Autolite/Motorcraft 4300 and 4350 4-BBL Carburetors

DESCRIPTION

♦ **See Figure 22**

The model 4300 and 4350 4-barrel carburetors are composed of three main assemblies: the air horn, the main body, and the throttle body. The air horn assembly serves as the fuel bowl cover as well as the housing for the choke valve and shaft. It contains the accelerator pump linkage, fuel inlet seat, float and lever, booster venturi, and internal fuel bowl vents.

The main body houses the fuel metering passages, accelerator pump mechanism, and the power valve.

The throttle body contains the primary and secondary throttle valve and shafts, the curb idle adjusting screw, the fast idle adjusting screw, the idle mixture adjusting screws, and the automatic choke assembly. It is used on V8 engines.

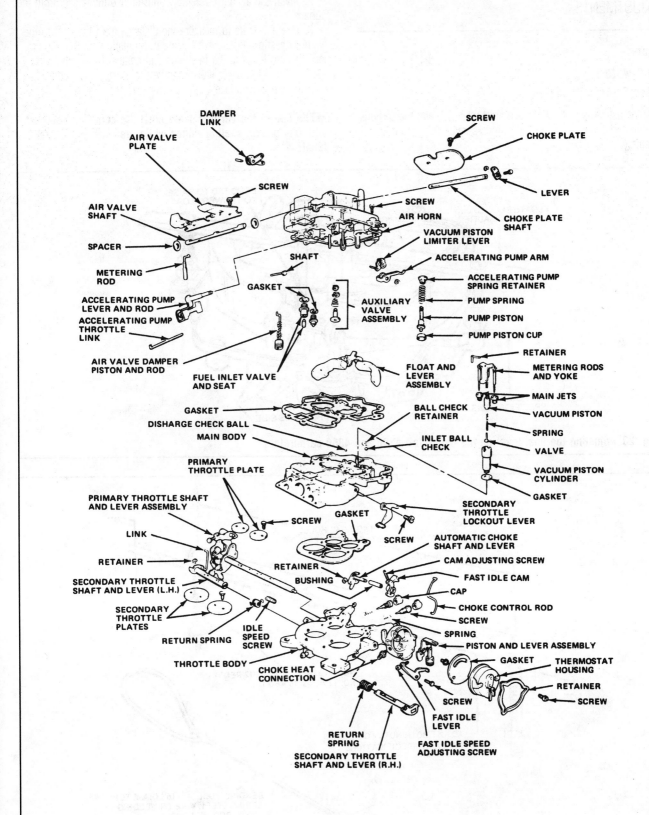

Fig. 22 Exploded view of the Motorcraft 4350 carburetor components

ADJUSTMENTS

Float

4300 MODEL

◆ See Figures 23 and 24

1. Adjustments to the fuel level are best made with the carburetor removed from the engine and the carburetor cleaned upon disassembly.

2. Invert the air horn assembly and remove the gasket from the surface.

3. Use a T-scale to measure the distance from the float to the air horn casting. Position the scale horizontally over the flat surface of both floats at the free ends and parallel to the air horn casting. Hold the lower end of the vertical scale in full contact with the smooth surface of the air horn.

➡**The end of the vertical scale must not come into contact with any gasket sealing ridges while measuring the float level.**

Fig. 23 Adjusting the float level on the Motorcraft 4300 and 4350 carburetors

Fig. 24 Fabricate float gauge bending tools by following the illustration—Motorcraft 4300 and 4350 carburetors

4. The free end of each float should just touch the horizontal scale, if one float is lower than the other; twist the float and lever assembly slightly to correct.

5. Adjust the float level by bending the tab which contact the needle and seat assembly.

4350 MODEL

1. Invert the air horn assembly and remove the gasket.

2. Measure the distance from the floats to the air horn rim using a T-scale. Position the horizontal scale over the flat surface of both floats at the free ends, parallel to the air horn casting. Hold the lower end of the vertical scale in full contact with the smooth area of the casting, midway between the main discharge nozzles.

➡**Do not allow the end of the vertical scale to contact any gasket sealing ridge while measuring the float setting.**

3. The free end of the floats should just touch the horizontal scale. Float-to-air horn casting distance should be 29/64 in. (11.5mm). Bend the vertical tab on the float arm to adjust the distance.

Initial Choke Valve Clearance

1. Remove the choke thermostatic spring housing.

2. Bend a wire gauge (0.035 in. [0.89mm] diameter) at a 90° angle about 1.8 in. (45.7mm) from one end.

3. Block the throttle open so that the fast idle screw does not contact the fast idle cam.

4. Insert the bend end of the wire gauge between the lower edge of the piston slot and the upped edge of the righthand slot in the choke housing.

5. Pull the choke piston lever counterclockwise until the gauge is snug in the piston slot. Hold the wire in place by exerting light pressure in a rearward direction on the choke piston lever. Check the distance from the lower edge of the choke valve to the air horn wall.

6. Adjustment is done by loosening the hex head screw (lefthand thread) on the choke valve shaft and rotating the choke shaft.

Fast Idle Cam

4300 MODEL

1. Loosen the screws on the choke thermostatic spring cover and rotate the housing 1/4 turn counterclockwise. Tighten the screws.

2. Open the throttle and allow the choke valve to close completely.

3. Push down on the fast idle cam counterweight until the fast idle screw is in contact with the second step of the cam and against the high step.

4. Measure the clearance between the lower edge of the choke valve and the air horn wall.

5. Adjust the turning the fast idle cam adjusting screw.

6. Return the housing to its original position.

4350 MODEL

1. Run the engine to normal operating temperature. Connect an accurate tachometer to the engine.

2. Disconnect and plug the EGR and TCS vacuum lines.

3. Position the fast idle screw against the first step of the fast idle screw. Adjust the fast idle screw to give a reading of 1600 rpm.

4. Return the linkage to its normal position, unplug and reconnect the vacuum lines.

Choke Unloader (Dechoke)

1. Open the throttle fully and hold it in this position.

2. Rotate the choke valve toward the closed position.

3. Check the clearance between the lower edge of the choke valve and the air horn wall.

4. Adjust by bending the unloader tang on the fast idle speed lever toward the cam to increase the clearance and away to decrease the clearance.

➡**Do not bend the unloader tang down from the horizontal. After adjustment, there should be at least 0.070 in. (1.78mm) clearance from the choke housing with the throttle fully open.**

Accelerator Pump Stroke

The accelerator pump should not need adjustment as its stroke is preset in compliance with exhaust emission control standards. If for any reason the stroke must be altered, it may be done by repositioning the link in the desired holes.

Fast Idle Speed

The fast idle speed is adjusted with the engine at operating temperature and the fast idle screw on the second step of the fast idle cam. Adjust by turning the fast idle screw in or out as required.

➡**To adjust the fast idle speed, you must plug the EGR valve vacuum line and disconnect the TCS solenoid wire.**

Dashpot

Some carburetors are equipped with a dashpot to prevent stalling. The dashpot adjustment procedure for these carburetors is as follows:

1. Be sure that the throttle valves are closed tightly and that the diaphragm stem is fully depressed.

2. Measure the clearance between the dashpot stem and the throttle lever with a feeler gauge. For the proper clearance specification, see the chart.

3. If the clearance is not correct, adjust it by loosening the locknut and rotating the dashpot until the proper clearance is obtained. Tighten the locknut.

Rochester E2SE Carburetor

◆ **See Figure 25**

This carburetor is used on the 4–151 engine.

MIXTURE CONTROL SOLENOID (E2SE ONLY)

GASKET

AIR VALVE

AIR HORN AND GASKET

FLOAT BOWL ASSEMBLY

NEEDLE SEAT ASSEMBLY

INLET FUEL FILTER ASSEMBLY

ELECTRIC STAT COVER AND COIL

THROTTLE PLATE (2)

THROTTLE BODY

INSULATOR

AIR HORN GASKET

VENT SCREEN

CHOKE VALVE

PUMP LEVER

VACUUM BREAK AND BRACKET

IDLE SPEED SOLENOID

VACUUM HOSE

VACUUM BREAK LEVER

VACUUM BREAK ROD

AIR VALVE ROD

CHOKE LINK

ACCELERATOR PUMP AND SPRING

PUMP DISCHARGE AND BALL RETAINER

IDLE SPEED ADJUSTMENT SCREW AND SPRING

FAST IDLE CAM

INTERMEDIATE CHOKE ROD

PUMP ROD

THROTTLE BODY LEVER ASSEMBLY

INTAKE MANIFOLD GASKET

INTAKE MANIFOLD ADAPTER

Fig. 25 Exploded view of the Rochester E2SE/2SE carburetor components

ADJUSTMENTS

Float

▶ **See Figure 26**

1. Remove the air horn.
2. Hold the float retainer and push down lightly on the float.
3. Using a T-scale, at a point ³⁄₁₆ in. (4.76mm) from the end of the float, measure the distance from the top surface of the float bowl to the top of the float. The distance should be 0.208 in. (5.28mm) with manual trans., 0.256 in. (6.5mm) with automatic trans., and 0.208 in. (5.28mm) for all Calif. E2SE models.
4. Bend the float arm as necessary to adjust.

Fig. 26 Adjusting the float level on the Rochester 2SE and E2SE carburetors

Fast Idle

▶ **See Figures 27 and 28**

1. Make sure the choke coil adjustment is correct and that the fast idle speed is correct.
2. Obtain a Choke Angle Gauge, tool #J-26701-1 or its equivalent. Rotate the degree scale to the 0° mark opposite the pointer.
3. With the choke valve completely closed, place the magnet on the tool squarely on the choke plate. Rotate the bubble unit until it is centered.
4. Rotate the degree scale until the 25° mark is opposite the pointer. On carburetors with choke cover sticker number 70172, the angle is 18°.
5. Place the fast idle screw on the second step of the cam.
6. Close the choke plate by pushing on the intermediate choke lever.
7. Push the vacuum brake lever toward the open choke position until the lever is against the rear tang on the choke lever.
8. Adjust by bending the fast idle cam rod until the bubble is centered.

1. Idle speed screw
2. Vacuum diaphagm
3. Fast idle screw
4. Fast idle cam

Fig. 27 Adjustment point locations—Rochester 2SE carburetor

Fig. 28 Fast idle cam adjustment on the Rochester 2SE/E2SE carburetors

Choke Setting

▶ **See Figure 29**

➡**Once the rivets and choke cover are removed, a choke cover retainer kit is necessary for assembly.**

1. Remove the rivets, retainers, choke cover and coil following the instructions found in the cover retainer kit.
2. Position the fast idle adjustment screw on the highest step of the fast idle cam.
3. Push on the intermediate choke lever and close the choke plate.
4. Insert the proper plug gauge, 0.050–0.080 in. (1.27–2.03mm) for manual trans. and 0.85 in. (21.6mm) for automatic trans., in the hole adjacent to the coil lever. The edge of the lever should barely contact the plug gauge.
5. Bend the intermediate choke rod to adjust.

Fig. 29 Adjusting the choke lever on the Rochester 2SE/E2SE carburetors

Choke Unloader

♦ **See Figure 30**

1. Obtain a Carburetor Choke Angle Gauge, tool #J-26701-1 or its equivalent. Rotate the scale on the gauge until the 0 mark is opposite the pointer.
2. Close the choke plate completely and set the magnet squarely on top of it.
3. Rotate the bubble until it is centered.
4. Rotate the degree scale until the 32° mark is opposite the pointer. On carburetors with choke cover sticker number 70172 the setting is 19°.
5. Hold the primary throttle valve wide open.
6. Bend the throttle lever tang until the bubble is centered.

Fig. 30 Choke unloader adjustment on the Rochester 2SE/E2SE carburetors

Holley 5210-C Carburetor

♦ **See Figure 31**

This carburetor is used on the 4–121 engine.

ADJUSTMENTS

Float Level

1. With the carburetor air horn inverted, and the float tang resting lightly on the inlet needle, insert the specified gauge between the air horn and the float.
2. Bend the float tang is an adjustment is needed.

Fast Idle Cam

1. Place the fast idle screw on the second step of the fast idle cam and against the shoulder of the high step.
2. Place the specified drill or gauge on the down side of the choke plate.
3. To adjust, bend the choke lever tang.

Choke Plate Pulldown (Vacuum Break)

1977–79 MODELS

1. Remove the three hex headed screws and ring which retain the choke cover.

✳✳ CAUTION

Do not remove the choke water housing screw if adjusting on the car. Pull the choke assembly back out of the way.

2. Push the diaphragm shaft against the stop. Push the coil lever clockwise.
3. Insert the specified size gauge on the down side of the primary choke plate.
4. Take the slack out of the linkage and turn the adjusting screw with a 5/32 in. Allen wrench.

1980 MODELS

1. Attach a hand vacuum pump to the vacuum break diaphragm; apply vacuum and seat the diaphragm.
2. Push the fast idle cam lever down to close the choke plate.
3. Take any slack out of the linkage in the open choke position.
4. Insert the specified gauge between the lower edge of the choke plate and the air horn wall.
5. If the clearance is incorrect, turn the vacuum break adjusting screw, located in the break housing, to adjust.

Secondary Vacuum Break

1977–78 MODELS

1. Remove the three screws and the choke coil assembly.
2. Place the cam follower on the highest step of the fast idle cam.
3. Seat the diaphragm by applying an outside source of vacuum.
4. Push the inside choke coil lever counterclockwise for 1977; clockwise for 1978, to close the choke valve.
5. Place a gauge of the size specified in the chart between the lower edge of the choke valve and the air horn wall.

Fig. 31 Exploded view of the Holley 5210-C carburetor components

6. Bend the vacuum break rod to adjust.
7. Replace and adjust the choke.

Choke Unloader

1. Position the throttle lever at the wide open position.
2. Insert a gauge of the size specified in the chart between the lower edge of the choke valve and the air horn wall.
3. Bend the unloader tang for adjustment.

Secondary Throttle Stop Screw

1. Back off the screw until it doesn't touch the throttle lever.
2. Turn the screw in until it touches the secondary throttle lever. Turn it in ¼ turn more.

Fast Idle Speed

1. The engine must be normal operating temperature with the air cleaner off.
2. With the engine running, position the fast idle screw on the second step against the shoulder of the high step. Plug the EGR Port on the carburetor.
3. Adjust the speed by turning the fast idle screw.

Carter YFA Carburetor

▸ **See Figure 32**

This carburetor is used on the 4–150.

1. Vacuum break	7. Idle mixture screw with O-ring	13. Mixture control solenoid
2. Air horn	8. Throttle plate	14. Low speed jet
3. Choke plate	9. Main body	15. Accelerator pump vent valve
4. Sole-vac throttle positioner	10. Accelerator pump check ball and weight	16. Wide open throttle (WOT) switch
5. Choke assembly	11. Main metering jet	17. Throttle shaft and lever
6. Accelerator pump assembly	12. Float assembly	18. Throttle body

Fig. 32 Exploded view of the Carter YFA carburetor components

ADJUSTMENT

Float and Fuel Level
◗ **See Figure 33**

1. Remove the top of the carburetor and the gasket.
2. Invert the carburetor top and check the clearance from the top of the float to the bottom edge of the air horn with a float level gauge. Hold the carburetor top at eye level when making the check. The float arm should be resting on the inlet needle pin. To adjust, bend the float arm. Do not bend the tab at the end of the arm! See the Carburetor Specifications chart for the correct clearance.

Fig. 33 Measuring the float clearance on the Carter YFA carburetor

Fast Idle Linkage
◗ **See Figure 34**

➡**This adjustment is performed with the air cleaner removed.**

1. Run the engine to normal operating temperature. Connect a tachometer according to the maker's instructions.
2. Disconnect and plug the EGR valve vacuum hose.
3. Position the fast idle adjustment screw on the second stop of the fast idle cam with the transmission in neutral.
4. Adjust the fast idle speed to 2300 rpm for auto. trans. and 2000 rpm for man. trans.
5. Idle the engine and reconnect the EGR hose.

Initial Choke Valve Clearance

1. Position the fast idle screw on the top step of the fast idle cam.
2. Using a vacuum pump, seat the choke vacuum break.
3. Apply light closing pressure in the choke plate to position the plate as far closed as possible without forcing it.

Fig. 34 Location of the fast idle adjustment screw (1) on the Carter YFA carburetor

4. Measure the distance between the air horn wall and the choke plate. If it is not that specified in the Carburetor Specifications Chart, bend the choke vacuum break link until it is.

Choke Setting

➡**Once the rivets and choke cover are removed, a choke cover retainer kit is necessary for assembly.**

1. Remove the rivets, retainers, choke cover and coil following the instructions found in the cover retainer kit.
2. Position the fast idle adjustment screw on the highest stop of the fast idle cam.
3. Push on the intermediate choke lever and close the choke plate.
4. Insert the proper plug gauge, 0.050–0.080 in. (1.27–2.032mm) for manual trans. and 0.85 in. (21.59mm) for automatic trans., in the hole adjacent to the coil lever. The edge of the lever should barely contact the plug gauge.
5. Bend the intermediate choke rod to adjust.

Unloader

1. Obtain a Carburetor Choke Angle Gauge tool #J-26701-A or its equivalent. Rotate the scale on the gauge until the 0 mark is opposite the pointer.
2. Close the choke plate completely and set the magnet squarely on top of it.
3. Rotate the bubble until it is centered.
4. Rotate the degree scale until the 32° mark is opposite the pointer. On carburetors with choke cover sticker number 70172 the setting is 19°.
5. Hold the primary throttle valve wide open.
6. Bend the throttle lever tang until the bubble is centered.

Metering Rod

▶ **See Figure 35**

1. Remove the air horn and gasket.
2. Make sure that the idle speed adjustment screw allows the throttle plate to close tightly in the bore.
3. Press down on the top of the pump diaphragm shaft until it bottoms.
4. In this position, adjust the metering rod by turning the adjusting screw counterclockwise, until the metering rod lightly bottoms in the main metering jet.
5. Turn the adjusting screw 1 full turn more.
6. Install the air horn and gasket, and adjust the curb idle speed.

B. Diaphragm shaft
C. Adjustment screw

Fig. 35 Adjusting the metering rod on the Carter YFA carburetor

Carburetor Specification Charts
Carter BBD

Engine	Years	Float Level Dry (in.)	Step-Up Piston Gap (in.)	Fast Idle Cam Setting (in.)	Fast Idle rpm	Choke Unloader (in.)	Initial Choke Valve Clearance (in.)	Automatic Choke Setting
6-258	1977–78	¼	³⁄₆₄	³⁄₃₂	1,700	⁹⁄₆₄	⅛	2 rich
	1979	¼	0.035	0.110	①	0.280	②	1 rich
	1980	¼	③	0.080–0.110	④	0.280	⑤	⑥
	1981	¼	⑦	0.080–0.110	⑧	0.280	⑨	⑥
	1982	¼	0.035	0.095	1,850	0.280	0.140	1 rich
	1983–84	¼	0.035	0.095	⑧	0.280	0.140	1 rich
	1985–88	¼	0.035	0.095	⑧	0.280	0.140	TR

TR: Tamper Resistant
① Except High Altitude: 1,600
   High Altitude: 1,500
② MT: 0.150
   AT: 0.140
③ Except High Altitude Eagle 0.035
   High Altitude Eagle: 0.025
④ MT: 1,700
   AT: 1,950
⑤ Eagle w/AT, except High Altitude: 0.128
   All w/MT: 0.140
   High Altitude Eagle w/AT and all 2-wd w/AT: 0.150

⑥ All w/MT: 1 rich
   High Altitude Eagle: Index
   All others: 2 rich
⑦ Eagle w/MT, except Calif.: 0.025
   All others: 0.035
⑧ MT: 1,700
   AT: 1,850
⑨ High Altitude Eagle: 0.140
   All others: 0.128

Carter YF

Engine	Years	Float Level (in.)	Float Drop (in.)	Dashpot Setting (in.)	Fast Idle rpm	Choke Unloader (in.)	Initial Choke Valve Clearance (in.)	Automatic Choke Setting
6-232, 258	1975	0.476	1.375	0.075	1,600	0.275	0.205	①
	1976	0.476	1.375	0.075	1,600	0.275	0.205	①
	1977	0.476	1.375	—	②	0.275	0.215 ④	③
	1978	0.476	1.375	—	②	0.275	0.215 ④	③
	1979	0.476	1.375	—	②	0.275	0.215	1 rich

① MT: 2 rich
　AT: 1 rich
② MT: 1,500
　AT: 1,600
③ Except Calif., and High Altitude w/AT: 1 rich
　Calif.: Index
　High Altitude w/AT: 2 rich
④ High Altitude: 0.221

Carter YFA

Engine	Years	Float Level (in.)	Initial Choke Valve Clearance (in.)	Fast Idle Cam Setting (in.)	Choke Unloader (in.)	Fast Idle Speed rpm	Automatic Choke Setting
4-150	1984	39/64	15/64	11/64	15/64	2,000 MT 2,300 AT	TR

MT: Manual Transmission
AT: Automatic Tranmission
TR: Tamper Resistant

Rochester 2SE/E2SE

Engine	Years	Float Level (in.)	Choke Coil Lever (in.)	Fast Idle Cam Clearance (in.)	Choke Vacuum Break (in.) Primary	Secondary	Choke Unloader (in.)	Air Valve Rod (deg.)
4-151	1980–83	①	5/64	1/8	9/64	②	17/64	2

① 2SE/E2SE Man. Trans. and Calif.: 13/64
　2SE Auto. Trans.: 1/4
　E2SE Auto. Trans.: 13/64
② Man. Trans.: 3/64–5/64
　Auto. Trans.: 5/64

Autolite/Motorcraft 2100

Engine	Years	Float Level Dry (in.)	Float Level Wet (in.)	Dashpot Setting (in.)	Fast Idle rpm	Choke Unloader (in.)	Initial Choke Valve Clearance (in.)	Automatic Choke Setting
8-304	1975	2/5	25/32	9/64	2,200	9/32	0.130	2 rich

Motorcraft 2100/2150

Engine	Years	Float Level Dry (in.)	Float Level Wet (in.)	Fast Idle Cam Setting (in.)	Fast Idle rpm	Choke Unloader (in.)	Initial Choke Valve Clearance (in.)	Automatic Choke Setting
8-304, 360	1976	①	②	③	1,600	0.250	④	⑤
	1977	0.313	0.780	⑥	⑦	0.250	④	⑧
	1978	0.555	0.780	⑨	⑪	⑫	⑬	⑩
	1979	0.313	0.780	0.113	⑭	0.300	0.125	1 rich

① MT: 0.547
　AT: 0.476
② AT: 0.780
　MT: 0.937
③ AT: 0.130
　MT: 0.120
④ AT, except High Altitude: 0.140
　High Altitude AT: 0.104
　MT: 0.130
⑤ AT: 1 rich
　MT: 2 rich
⑥ Except Calif. and High Altitude: 0.136
　Calif.: 0.130
　High Altitude: 0.089
⑦ Except Calif. 8-304: 1,600
　Calif. 8-304: 1,800

⑧ 8-360, all High Altitude, and Calif. 8-304: 1 rich
　All others: Index
⑨ Except Calif. and High Altitude: 0.126
　Calif.: 0.120
　High Altitude: 0.078
⑩ 8-304, except High Altitude: Index
　8-360, except High Altitude: 1 rich
　High Altitude: 2 rich
⑪ Except Calif. 8-304 and High Altitude 8-360: 1,600
　Calif. 8-304 and High Altitude 8-360: 1,800
⑫ Except High Altitude: 0.250
　High Altitude: 0.170 min.
⑬ Except High Altitude: 0.136
　High Altitude: 0.089
⑭ MT: 1,500
　AT: 1,600

Autolite 4350

Engine	Years	Float Level (in.)	Aux. Inlet (in.)	Fast Idle Cam Setting (in.)	Fast Idle rpm	Choke Unloader (in.)	Initial Choke Valve Clearance (in.)	Automatic Choke Setting
8-401	1975–76	0.050	0.900	0.135	1,600	0.325	0.130	2 rich

Troubleshooting Basic Fuel System Problems

Problem	Cause	Solution
Engine cranks, but won't start (or is hard to start) when cold	• Empty fuel tank • Incorrect starting procedure • Defective fuel pump • No fuel in carburetor • Clogged fuel filter • Engine flooded • Defective choke	• Check for fuel in tank • Follow correct procedure • Check pump output • Check for fuel in the carburetor • Replace fuel filter • Wait 15 minutes; try again • Check choke plate
Engine cranks, but is hard to start (or does not start) when hot— (presence of fuel is assumed)	• Defective choke	• Check choke plate
Rough idle or engine runs rough	• Dirt or moisture in fuel • Clogged air filter • Faulty fuel pump	• Replace fuel filter • Replace air filter • Check fuel pump output
Engine stalls or hesitates on acceleration	• Dirt or moisture in the fuel • Dirty carburetor • Defective fuel pump • Incorrect float level, defective accelerator pump	• Replace fuel filter • Clean the carburetor • Check fuel pump output • Check carburetor
Poor gas mileage	• Clogged air filter • Dirty carburetor • Defective choke, faulty carburetor adjustment	• Replace air filter • Clean carburetor • Check carburetor
Engine is flooded (won't start accompanied by smell of raw fuel)	• Improperly adjusted choke or carburetor	• Wait 15 minutes and try again, without pumping gas pedal • If it won't start, check carburetor

FUEL TANK

Tank Assembly

DRAINING

✳✳ CAUTION

Disconnect the battery before beginning the draining operation.

➡️**If the vehicle is not equipped with a darin plug, use the following procedure to remove the fuel.**

1. Using a 10 ft. (305cm) piece of ⅜ in. (9.5mm) hose, cut a flap slit 18 in. 945cm) from one end.
2. Install a pipe nipple, of slightly larger diameter than the hose, into the opposite end of the hose.
3. Install the nipple end of the hose into the fuel tank with the natural curve of the hose pointing downward. Keep feeding the hose in until the nipple hits the bottom of the tank.
4. Place the other end of the hose in a suitable container and insert a air hose pointing it in the downward direction of the slit and inject airinto the line.

➡️**If the vehicle is to be stored, always drain the fuel from the complete fuel system including the carburetor or throttle body, fuel pump supply, fuel injection pump, fuel lines, and tank.**

REMOVAL & INSTALLATION

1. Drain the fuel tank into a suitable container.
2. Raise the rear of the vehicle and support it with jackstands.
3. Disengage the sending unit electrical connection.
4. Tag and disconnect the fuel outlet, inlet and vapor hoses.
5. On vehicles equipped, disconnect the fuel return hose.
6. Remove the tank retaining straps and stone shield.
7. Support the tank and remove it from the vehicle.

To install:

8. Apply a coating of grease to the filler tube and slide the tank onto the filler tube.
9. Install the tank, and the stone shield, then tighten the retaining strap bolts.
10. Engage the sending unit electrical connections.
11. Install all the hoses disconnected during removal.
12. Lower the vehicle, fill the tank and check for fuel leaks.

Fuel Tank Sending Unit

REMOVAL & INSTALLATION

1. With the entine turned **OFF,** relieve the fuel pressure.
2. Disconnect the negative battery cable.
3. Raise and support the rear of the vehicle on jackstands.
4. Drain the fuel tank, then remove it.
5. Using a hammer and a drift punch, drive the fuel lever sending device and pump assembly locking ring (located on top of the fuel tank) counterclockwise. Lift the assembly from the tank and remove the sending device.
   To install:
6. Connect the fuel pump to the hose.

➡**Be careful that you don't fold or twist the strainer when installing the sending unit, or you'll restrict fuel flow.**

7. Install a new o-ring on the pump assembly. Install the sending unit and then position them into the fuel tank.
8. Turn the locking ring clockwise until it's tight.
9. Install the fuel tank and connect the battery cable.

A special tool is usually available to remove or install the fuel pump locking cam

A brass drift and a hammer can be used to loosen the fuel pump locking cam

Once the locking cam is released it can be removed to free the fuel pump

UNDERSTANDING AND TROUBLESHOOTING ELECTRICAL SYSTEMS 6-2
SAFETY PRECAUTIONS 6-2
UNDERSTANDING BASIC ELECTRICITY 6-2
THE WATER ANALOGY 6-2
CIRCUITS 6-2
AUTOMOTIVE CIRCUITS 6-3
SHORT CIRCUITS 6-3
TROUBLESHOOTING 6-3
BASIC TROUBLESHOOTING THEORY 6-4
TEST EQUIPMENT 6-4
TESTING 6-6
WIRING HARNESSES 6-8
WIRING REPAIR 6-8
ADD-ON ELECTRICAL EQUIPMENT 6-12
HEATING AND AIR CONDITIONING 6-12
BLOWER MOTOR 6-12
REMOVAL & INSTALLATION 6-12
HEATER CORE 6-14
REMOVAL & INSTALLATION 6-14
CONTROL HEAD 6-18
REMOVAL & INSTALLATION 6-18
ENTERTAINMENT SYSTEMS 6-24
RADIO 6-24
REMOVAL & INSTALLATION 6-24
WINDSHIELD WIPERS 6-24
MOTOR 6-24
REMOVAL & INSTALLATION 6-24
WIPER LINKAGE 6-27
REMOVAL & INSTALLATION 6-27
INSTRUMENT AND SWITCHES 6-27
INSTRUMENT CLUSTER 6-27
REMOVAL & INSTALLATION 6-27
PRINTED CIRCUIT BOARD 6-32
REMOVAL & INSTALLATION 6-32
SEAT BELT/STARTER INTERLOCK SYSTEMS 6-34
DISABLING THE INTERLOCK SYSTEM 6-34
LIGHTING 6-34
HEADLIGHTS 6-34
REMOVAL & INSTALLATION 6-34
SIGNAL AND MARKER LIGHTS 6-35
REMOVAL & INSTALLATION 6-35
CIRCUIT PROTECTION 6-44
FUSE LINK 6-44
FUSE BOX LOCATION 6-45
TRAILER WIRING 6-45
WIRING DIAGRAMS 6-46
TROUBLESHOOTING CHARTS
TROUBLESHOOTING THE HEATER 6-13
BASIC WINDSHIELD WIPER PROBLEMS 6-27
BASIC DASH GAUGE PROBLEMS 6-33
BASIC LIGHTING PROBLEMS 6-42

BASIC TURN SIGNAL AND FLASHER PROBLEMS 6-43

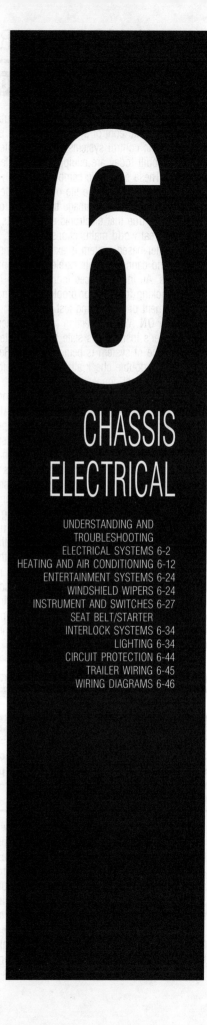

6

CHASSIS ELECTRICAL

UNDERSTANDING AND TROUBLESHOOTING ELECTRICAL SYSTEMS 6-2
HEATING AND AIR CONDITIONING 6-12
ENTERTAINMENT SYSTEMS 6-24
WINDSHIELD WIPERS 6-24
INSTRUMENT AND SWITCHES 6-27
SEAT BELT/STARTER INTERLOCK SYSTEMS 6-34
LIGHTING 6-34
CIRCUIT PROTECTION 6-44
TRAILER WIRING 6-45
WIRING DIAGRAMS 6-46

UNDERSTANDING AND TROUBLESHOOTING ELECTRICAL SYSTEMS

Over the years import and domestic manufacturers have incorporated electronic control systems into their production lines. In fact, electronic control systems are so prevalent that all new cars and trucks built today are equipped with at least one on-board computer. These electronic components (with no moving parts) should theoretically last the life of the vehicle, provided that nothing external happens to damage the circuits or memory chips.

While it is true that electronic components should never wear out, in the real world malfunctions do occur. It is also true that any computer-based system is extremely sensitive to electrical voltages and cannot tolerate careless or haphazard testing/service procedures. An inexperienced individual can literally cause major damage looking for a minor problem by using the wrong kind of test equipment or connecting test leads/connectors with the ignition switch **ON**. When selecting test equipment, make sure the manufacturer's instructions state that the tester is compatible with whatever type of system is being serviced. Read all instructions carefully and double check all test points before installing probes or making any test connections.

The following section outlines basic diagnosis techniques for dealing with automotive electrical systems. Along with a general explanation of the various types of test equipment available to aid in servicing modern automotive systems, basic repair techniques for wiring harnesses and connectors are also given. Read the basic information before attempting any repairs or testing. This will provide the background of information necessary to avoid the most common and obvious mistakes that can cost both time and money. Although the replacement and testing procedures are simple in themselves, the systems are not, and unless one has a thorough understanding of all components and their function within a particular system, the logical test sequence these systems demand cannot be followed. Minor malfunctions can make a big difference, so it is important to know how each component affects the operation of the overall system in order to find the ultimate cause of a problem without replacing good components unnecessarily. It is not enough to use the correct test equipment; the test equipment must be used correctly.

Safety Precautions

✳✳ CAUTION

Whenever working on or around any electrical or electronic systems, always observe these general precautions to prevent the possibility of personal injury or damage to electronic components.

• Never install or remove battery cables with the key **ON** or the engine running. Jumper cables should be connected with the key **OFF** to avoid power surges that can damage electronic control units. Engines equipped with computer controlled systems should avoid both giving and getting jump starts due to the possibility of serious damage to components from arcing in the engine compartment if connections are made with the ignition **ON**.

• Always remove the battery cables before charging the battery. Never use a high output charger on an installed battery or attempt to use any type of "hot shot" (24 volt) starting aid.

• Exercise care when inserting test probes into connectors to in-sure good contact without damaging the connector or spreading the pins. Always probe connectors from the rear (wire) side, NOT the pin side, to avoid accidental shorting of terminals during test procedures.

• Never remove or attach wiring harness connectors with the ignition switch **ON**, especially to an electronic control unit.

• Do not drop any components during service procedures and never apply 12 volts directly to any component (like a solenoid or relay) unless instructed specifically to do so. Some component electrical windings are designed to safely handle only 4 or 5 volts and can be destroyed in seconds if 12 volts are applied directly to the connector.

• Remove the electronic control unit if the vehicle is to be placed in an environment where temperatures exceed approximately 176°F (80°C), such as a paint spray booth or when arc/gas welding near the control unit location.

Understanding Basic Electricity

Understanding the basic theory of electricity makes electrical troubleshooting much easier. Several gauges are used in electrical troubleshooting to see inside the circuit being tested. Without a basic understanding, it will be difficult to understand testing procedures.

THE WATER ANALOGY

Electricity is the flow of electrons—hypothetical particles thought to constitute the basic stuff of electricity. Many people have been taught electrical theory using an analogy with water. In a comparison with water flowing in a pipe, the electrons would be the water. As the flow of water can be measured, the flow of electricity can be measured. The unit of measurement is amperes, frequently abbreviated amps. An ammeter will measure the actual amount of current flowing in the circuit.

Just as the water pressure is measured in units such as pounds per square inch, electrical pressure is measured in volts. When a voltmeter's two probes are placed on two live portions of an electrical circuit with different electrical pressures, current will flow through the voltmeter and produce a reading which indicates the difference in electrical pressure between the two parts of the circuit.

While increasing the voltage in a circuit will increase the flow of current, the actual flow depends not only on voltage, but on the resistance of the circuit. The standard unit for measuring circuit resistance is an ohm, measured by an ohmmeter. The ohmmeter is somewhat similar to an ammeter, but incorporates its own source of power so that a standard voltage is always present.

CIRCUITS

An actual electric circuit consists of four basic parts. These are: the power source, such as a generator or battery; a hot wire, which conducts the electricity under a relatively high voltage to the component supplied by the circuit; the load, such as a lamp, motor, resistor or relay coil; and the ground wire, which carries the current back to the source under very low voltage. In such a circuit the bulk of the resistance exists between the point where the hot wire is connected to the load, and the point where the load is grounded. In an automobile, the vehicle's frame or body, which is made of steel, is used as a part of the ground circuit for many of the electrical devices.

Remember that, in electrical testing, the voltmeter is connected in parallel with the circuit being tested (without disconnecting any wires) and measures the difference in voltage between the locations of the two probes; that the ammeter is connected in series with the load (the circuit is separated at one point and the ammeter inserted so it becomes a part of the circuit); and the ohmmeter is self-powered, so that all the power in the circuit should be off and the portion of the circuit to be measured contacted at either end by one of the probes of the meter.

For any electrical system to operate, it must make a complete circuit. This simply means that the power flow from the battery must make a complete circle. When an electrical component is operating, power flows from the battery to the component, passes through the component causing it to perform it to function (such as lighting a light bulb) and then returns to the battery through the ground of the circuit. This ground is usually (but not always) the metal part of the vehicle on which the electrical component is mounted.

Perhaps the easiest way to visualize this is to think of connecting a light bulb with two wires attached to it to your vehicle's battery. The battery in your vehicle has two posts (negative and positive). If one of the two wires attached to the light bulb was attached to the negative post of the battery and the other wire was attached to the positive post of the battery, you would have a complete circuit. Current from the battery would flow out one post, through the wire attached to it and then to the light bulb, where it would pass through causing it to light. It would then leave the light bulb, travel through the other wire, and return to the other post of the battery.

AUTOMOTIVE CIRCUITS

The normal automotive circuit differs from this simple example in two ways. First, instead of having a return wire from the bulb to the battery, the light bulb return the current to the battery through the chassis of the vehicle. Since the negative battery cable is attached to the chassis and the chassis is made of electrically conductive metal, the chassis of the vehicle can serve as a ground wire to complete the circuit. Secondly, most automotive circuits contain switches to turn components on and off.

Some electrical components which require a large amount of current to operate also have a relay in their circuit. Since these circuits carry a large amount of current, the thickness of the wire in the circuit (gauge size) is also greater. If this large wire were connected from the component to the control switch on the instrument panel, and then back to the component, a voltage drop would occur in the circuit. To prevent this potential drop in voltage, an electromagnetic switch (relay) is used. The large wires in the circuit are connected from the vehicle battery to one side of the relay, and from the opposite side of the relay to the component. The relay is normally open, preventing current from passing through the circuit. An additional, smaller wire is connected from the relay to the control switch for the circuit. When the control switch is turned on, it grounds the smaller wire from the relay and completes the circuit.

SHORT CIRCUITS

If you were to disconnect the light bulb (from the previous example of a light-bulb being connected to the battery by two wires) from the wires and touch the two wires together (please take our word for this; don't try it), the result will be a shower of sparks. A similar thing happens (on a smaller scale) when the power supply wire to a component or the electrical component itself becomes grounded before the normal ground connection for the circuit. To prevent damage to the system, the fuse for the circuit blows to interrupt the circuit—protecting the components from damage. Because grounding a wire from a power source makes a complete circuit—less the required component to use the power—the phenomenon is called a short circuit. The most common causes of short circuits are: the rubber insulation on a wire breaking or rubbing through to expose the current carrying core of the wire to a metal part of the car, or a shorted switch.

Some electrical systems on the vehicle are protected by a circuit breaker which is, basically, a self-repairing fuse. When either of the described events takes place in a system which is protected by a circuit breaker, the circuit breaker opens the circuit the same way a fuse does. However, when either the short is removed from the circuit or the surge subsides, the circuit breaker resets itself and does not have to be replaced as a fuse does.

Troubleshooting

When diagnosing a specific problem, organized troubleshooting is a must. The complexity of a modern automobile demands that you approach any problem in a logical, organized manner. There are certain troubleshooting techniques that are standard:

1. Establish when the problem occurs. Does the problem appear only under certain conditions? Were there any noises, odors, or other unusual symptoms?

2. Isolate the problem area. To do this, make some simple tests and observations; then eliminate the systems that are working properly. Check for obvious problems such as broken wires, dirty connections or split/disconnected vacuum hoses. Always check the obvious before assuming something complicated is the cause.

3. Test for problems systematically to determine the cause once the problem area is isolated. Are all the components functioning properly? Is there power going to electrical switches and motors? Is there vacuum at vacuum switches and/or actuators? Is there a mechanical problem such as bent linkage or loose mounting screws? Performing careful, systematic checks will often turn up most causes on the first inspection without wasting time checking components that have little or no relationship to the problem.

4. Test all repairs after the work is done to make sure that the problem is fixed. Some causes can be traced to more than one component, so a careful verification of repair work is important in order to pick up additional malfunctions that may cause a problem to reappear or a different problem to arise. A blown fuse, for example, is a simple problem that may require more than another fuse to repair. If you don't look for a problem that caused a fuse to blow, a shorted wire (for example) may go undetected.

Experience has shown that most problems tend to be the result of a fairly simple and obvious cause, such as loose or corroded connectors or air leaks in the intake system. This makes careful inspection of components during testing essential to quick and accurate troubleshooting.

BASIC TROUBLESHOOTING THEORY

Electrical problems generally fall into one of three areas:
• The component that is not functioning is not receiving current.
• The component itself is not functioning.
• The component is not properly grounded.

Problems that fall into the first category are by far the most complicated. It is the current supply system to the component which contains all the switches, relay, fuses, etc.

The electrical system can be checked with a test light and a jumper wire. A test light is a device that looks like a pointed screwdriver with a wire attached to it. It has a light bulb in its handle. A jumper wire is a piece of insulated wire with an alligator clip attached to each end.

If a light bulb is not working, you must follow a systematic plan to determine which of the three causes is the villain.

1. Turn on the switch that controls the inoperable bulb.
2. Disconnect the power supply wire from the bulb.
3. Attach the ground wire to the test light to a good metal ground.
4. Touch the probe end of the test light to the end of the power supply wire that was disconnected from the bulb. If the bulb is receiving current, the test light will go on.

➡**If the bulb is one which works only when the ignition key is turned on (turn signal), make sure the key is turned on.**

If the test light does not go on, then the problem is in the circuit between the battery and the bulb. As mentioned before, this includes all the switches, fuses, and relays in the system. Turn to a wiring diagram and find the bulb on the diagram. Follow the wire that runs back to the battery. The problem is an open circuit between the battery and the bulb. If the fuse is blown and, when replaced, immediately blows again, there is a short circuit in the system which must be located and repaired. If there is a switch in the system, bypass it with a jumper wire. This is done by connecting one end of the jumper wire to the power supply wire into the switch and the other end of the jumper wire to the wire coming out of the switch. If the test light illuminates with the jumper wire installed, the switch or whatever was bypassed is defective.

➡**Never substitute the jumper wire for the bulb, as the bulb is the component required to use the power from the power source.**

5. If the bulb in the test light goes on, then the current is getting to the bulb that is not working in the car. This eliminates the first of the three possible causes. Connect the power supply wire and connect a jumper wire from the bulb to a good metal ground. Do this with the switch which controls the bulb works with jumper wire installed, then it has a bad ground. This is usually caused by the metal area on which the bulb mounts to the vehicle being coated with some type of foreign matter.

6. If neither test located the source of the trouble, then the light bulb itself is defective.

The above test procedure can be applied to any of the components of the chassis electrical system by substituting the component that is not working for the light bulb. Remember that for any electrical system to work, all connections must be clean and tight.

TEST EQUIPMENT

➡**Pinpointing the exact cause of trouble in an electrical system can sometimes only be accomplished by the use of special test equipment. The following describes different types of commonly used test equipment and explains how to use them in diagnosis. In addition to the information covered below, the tool manufacturer's instructions booklet (provided with the tester) should be read and clearly understood before attempting any test procedures.**

Jumper Wires

Jumper wires are simple, yet extremely valuable, pieces of test equipment. They are basically test wires which are used to bypass sections of a circuit. The simplest type of jumper wire is a length of multi-strand wire with an alligator clip at each end. Jumper wires are usually fabricated from lengths of standard automotive wire and whatever type of connector (alligator clip, spade connector or pin connector) that is required for the particular vehicle be-

Example of using a jumper wire to bypass a switch during a diagnostic test

Checking for a bad ground connection with a jumper wire

ing tested. The well equipped tool box will have several different styles of jumper wires in several different lengths. Some jumper wires are made with three or more terminals coming from a common splice for special purpose testing. In cramped, hard-to-reach areas it is advisable to have insulated boots over the jumper wire terminals in order to prevent accidental grounding, sparks, and possible fire, especially when testing fuel system components.

Jumper wires are used primarily to locate open electrical circuits, on either the ground (−) side of the circuit or on the hot (+) side. If an electrical component fails to operate, connect the jumper wire between the component and a good ground. If the component operates only with the jumper installed, the ground circuit is open. If the ground circuit is good, but the component does not operate, the circuit between the power feed and component may be open. By moving the jumper wire successively back from the lamp toward the power source, you can isolate the area of the circuit where the open is located. When the component stops functioning, or the power is cut off, the open is in the segment of wire between the jumper and the point previously tested.

You can sometimes connect the jumper wire directly from the battery to the hot terminal of the component, but first make sure the component uses 12 volts in operation. Some electrical components, such as fuel injectors, are designed to operate on about 4 volts and running 12 volts directly to the injector terminals can cause damage.

By inserting an in-line fuse holder between a set of test leads, a fused jumper wire can be used for bypassing open circuits. Use a 5 amp fuse to provide protection against voltage spikes. When in doubt, use a voltmeter to check the voltage input to the component and measure how much voltage is normally being applied.

✳✳ CAUTION

Never use jumpers made from wire that is of lighter gauge than that which is used in the circuit under test. If the jumper wire is of too small a gauge, it may overheat and possibly melt. Never use jumpers to bypass high resistance loads in a circuit. Bypassing resistances, in effect, creates a short circuit. This may, in turn, cause damage and fire. Jumper wires should only be used to bypass lengths of wire.

Unpowered Test Lights

The 12 volt test light is used to check circuits and components while electrical current is flowing through them. It is used for voltage and ground tests. Twelve volt test lights come in different styles but all have three main parts; a ground clip, a probe, and a light. The most commonly used 12 volt test lights have pick-type probes. To use a 12 volt test light, connect the ground clip to a good ground and probe wherever necessary with the pick. The pick should be sharp so that it can be probed into tight spaces.

✳✳ CAUTION

Do not use a test light to probe electronic ignition spark plug or coil wires. Never use a pick-type test light to probe wiring on computer controlled systems unless specifically instructed to do so. Any wire insulation that is pierced by the test light probe should be taped and sealed with silicone after testing.

Like the jumper wire, the 12 volt test light is used to isolate opens in circuits. But, whereas the jumper wire is used to bypass the open to operate the load, the 12 volt test light is used to locate the presence of voltage in a circuit. If the test light glows, you know that there is power up to that point; if the 12 volt test light does not glow when its probe is inserted into the wire or connector, you know that there is an open circuit (no power). Move the test light in successive steps back toward the power source until the light in the handle does glow. When it glows, the open is between the probe and point which was probed previously.

➡**The test light does not detect that 12 volts (or any particular amount of voltage) is present; it only detects that some voltage is present. It is advisable before using the test light to touch its terminals across the battery posts to make sure the light is operating properly.**

Self-Powered Test Lights

The self-powered test light usually contains a 1.5 volt penlight battery. One type of self-powered test light is similar in design to the 12 volt unit. This type has both the battery and the light in the handle, along with a pick-type probe tip. The second type has the light toward the open tip, so that the light illuminates the contact point. The self-powered test light is a dual purpose piece of test equipment. It can be used to test for either open or short circuits when power is isolated from the circuit (continuity test). A powered test light should not be used on any computer controlled system or component unless specifically instructed to do so. Many engine sensors can be destroyed by even this small amount of voltage applied directly to the terminals.

Voltmeters

A voltmeter is used to measure voltage at any point in a circuit, or to measure the voltage drop across any part of a circuit. It can also be used to check continuity in a wire or circuit by indicating current flow from one end to the other. Analog voltmeters usually have various scales on the meter dial and a selector switch to allow the selection of different voltages. The voltmeter has a positive and a negative lead. To avoid damage to the meter, always connect the negative lead to the negative (−) side of the circuit (to ground or nearest the ground side of the circuit) and connect the positive lead to the positive (+) side of the circuit (to the power source or the nearest power source). Note that the negative voltmeter lead will always be black and that the positive voltmeter will always be some color other than black (usually red).

Depending on how the voltmeter is connected into the circuit, it has several uses. A voltmeter can be connected either in parallel or in series with a circuit and it has a very high resistance to current flow. When connected in parallel, only a small amount of current will flow through the voltmeter current path; the rest will flow through the normal circuit current path and the circuit will work normally. When the voltmeter is connected in series with a circuit, only a small amount of current can flow through the circuit. The circuit will not work properly, but the voltmeter reading will show if the circuit is complete or not.

Ohmmeters

The ohmmeter is designed to read resistance (which is measured in ohms or Ω) in a circuit or component. Although there are several different styles of ohmmeters, all analog meters will usually have a selector switch which permits the measurement of different ranges of resistance (usually the selector switch allows the multiplication of the meter reading by 10, 100, 1000, and 10,000). A calibration knob allows the meter to be set at zero for accurate measurement. Since all ohmmeters are powered by an internal battery, the ohmmeter can be used as a self-powered test light. When the ohmmeter is connected, current from the ohmmeter flows through the circuit or component being tested. Since the ohmmeter's internal resistance and voltage are known values, the amount of current flow through the meter depends on the resistance of the circuit or component being tested.

The ohmmeter can be used to perform a continuity test for opens or shorts (either by observation of the meter needle or as a self-powered test light), and to read actual resistance in a circuit. It should be noted that the ohmmeter is used to check the resistance of a component or wire while there is no voltage applied to the circuit. Current flow from an outside voltage source (such as the vehicle battery) can damage the ohmmeter, so the circuit or component should be isolated from the vehicle electrical system before any testing is done. Since the ohmmeter uses its own voltage source, either lead can be connected to any test point.

➡**When checking diodes or other solid state components, the ohmmeter leads can only be connected one way in order to measure current flow in a single direction. Make sure the positive (+) and negative (−) terminal connections are as described in the test procedures to verify the one-way diode operation.**

In using the meter for making continuity checks, do not be concerned with the actual resistance readings. Zero resistance, or any ohm reading, indicates continuity in the circuit. Infinite resistance indicates an open in the circuit. A high resistance reading where there should be none indicates a problem in the circuit. Checks for short circuits are made in the same manner as checks for open circuits except that the circuit must be isolated from both power and normal ground. Infinite resistance indicates no continuity to ground, while zero resistance indicates a dead short to ground.

Ammeters

An ammeter measures the amount of current flowing through a circuit in units called amperes or amps. Amperes are units of electron flow which indicate how fast the electrons are flowing through the circuit. Since Ohms Law dictates that current flow in a circuit is equal to the circuit voltage divided by the total circuit resistance, increasing voltage also increases the current level (amps). Likewise, any decrease in resistance will increase the amount of amps in a circuit. At normal operating voltage, most circuits have a characteristic amount of amperes, called "current draw" which can be measured using an ammeter. By referring to a specified current draw rating, measuring the amperes, and comparing the two values, one can determine what is happening within the circuit to aid in diagnosis. An open circuit, for example, will not allow any current to flow so the ammeter reading will be zero. More current flows through a heavily loaded circuit or when the charging system is operating.

An ammeter is always connected in series with the circuit being tested. All of the current that normally flows through the circuit must also flow through the ammeter; if there is any other path for the current to follow, the ammeter reading will not be accurate. The ammeter itself has very little resistance to current flow and therefore will not affect the circuit, but it will measure current

draw only when the circuit is closed and electricity is flowing. Excessive current draw can blow fuses and drain the battery, while a reduced current draw can cause motors to run slowly, lights to dim and other components to not operate properly. The ammeter can help diagnose these conditions by locating the cause of the high or low reading.

Multimeters

Different combinations of test meters can be built into a single unit designed for specific tests. Some of the more common combination test devices are known as Volt/Amp testers, Tach/Dwell meters, or Digital Multimeters. The Volt/Amp tester is used for charging system, starting system or battery tests and consists of a voltmeter, an ammeter and a variable resistance carbon pile. The voltmeter will usually have at least two ranges for use with 6, 12 and/or 24 volt systems. The ammeter also has more than one range for testing various levels of battery loads and starter current draw. The carbon pile can be adjusted to offer different amounts of resistance. The Volt/Amp tester has heavy leads to carry large amounts of current and many later models have an inductive ammeter pickup that clamps around the wire to simplify test connections. On some models, the ammeter also has a zero-center scale to allow testing of charging and starting systems without switching leads or polarity. A digital multimeter is a voltmeter, ammeter and ohmmeter combined in an instrument which gives a digital readout. These are often used when testing solid state circuits because of their high input impedance (usually 10 megohms or more).

The tach/dwell meter that combines a tachometer and a dwell (cam angle) meter is a specialized kind of voltmeter. The tachometer scale is marked to show engine speed in rpm and the dwell scale is marked to show degrees of distributor shaft rotation. In most electronic ignition systems, dwell is determined by the control unit, but the dwell meter can also be used to check the duty cycle (operation) of some electronic engine control systems. Some tach/dwell meters are powered by an internal battery, while others take their power from the vehicle battery in use. The battery powered testers usually require calibration (much like an ohmmeter) before testing.

TESTING

Open Circuits

To use the self-powered test light or a multimeter to check for open circuits, first isolate the circuit from the vehicle's 12 volt power source by disconnecting the battery or wiring harness connector. Connect the test light or ohmmeter ground clip to a good ground and probe sections of the circuit sequentially with the test light. (start from either end of the circuit). If the light is out/or there is infinite resistance, the open is between the probe and the circuit ground. If the light is on/or the meter shows continuity, the open is between the probe and end of the circuit toward the power source.

Short Circuits

By isolating the circuit both from power and from ground, and using a self-powered test light or multimeter, you can check for shorts to ground in the circuit. Isolate the circuit from power and ground. Connect the test light or ohmmeter ground clip to a good ground and probe any easy-to-reach test point in the circuit. If the light comes on or there is continuity, there is a short somewhere in the circuit. To isolate the short, probe a test point at either end of the isolated circuit (the light should be on/there should be continuity). Leave the test light probe engaged and open connectors, switches, remove parts, etc., sequentially, until the light goes out/continuity is broken. When the light goes out, the short is between the last circuit component opened and the previous circuit opened.

➡**The battery in the test light and does not provide much current. A weak battery may not provide enough power to illuminate the test light even when a complete circuit is made (especially if there are high resistances in the circuit). Always make sure that the test battery is strong. To check the battery, briefly touch the ground clip to the probe; if the light glows brightly the battery is strong enough for testing. Never use a self-powered test light to perform checks for opens or shorts when power is applied to the electrical system under test. The 12 volt vehicle power will quickly burn out the light bulb in the test light.**

Available Voltage Measurement

Set the voltmeter selector switch to the 20V position and connect the meter negative lead to the negative post of the battery. Connect the positive meter lead to the positive post of the battery and turn the ignition switch **ON** to provide a load. Read the voltage on the meter or digital display. A well charged battery should register over 12 volts. If the meter reads below 11.5 volts, the battery power may be insufficient to operate the electrical system properly. This test determines voltage available from the battery and should be the first step in any electrical trouble diagnosis procedure. Many electrical problems, especially on computer controlled systems, can be caused by a low state of charge in the battery. Excessive corrosion at the battery cable terminals can cause a poor contact that will prevent proper charging and full battery current flow.

Normal battery voltage is 12 volts when fully charged. When the battery is supplying current to one or more circuits it is said to be "under load." When everything is off the electrical system is under a "no-load" condition. A fully charged battery may show about 12.5 volts at no load; will drop to 12 volts under medium load; and will drop even lower under heavy load. If the battery is partially discharged the voltage decrease under heavy load may be excessive, even though the battery shows 12 volts or more at no load. When allowed to discharge further, the battery's available voltage under load will decrease more severely. For this reason, it is important that the battery be fully charged during all testing procedures to avoid errors in diagnosis and incorrect test results.

Voltage Drop

When current flows through a resistance, the voltage beyond the resistance is reduced (the larger the current, the greater the reduction in voltage). When no current is flowing, there is no voltage drop because there is no current flow. All points in the circuit which are connected to the power source are at the same voltage as the power source. The total voltage drop always equals the total source voltage. In a long circuit with many connectors, a series of small, unwanted voltage drops due to corrosion at the connectors can add up to a total loss of voltage which impairs the operation of the normal loads in the circuit. The maximum allowable voltage drop under load is critical, especially if there is more than one high resistance problem in a circuit because all voltage drops are cumulative. A small drop is normal due to the resistance of the conductors.

INDIRECT COMPUTATION OF VOLTAGE DROPS

1. Set the voltmeter selector switch to the 20 volt position.
2. Connect the meter negative lead to a good ground.
3. While operating the circuit, probe all loads in the circuit with the positive meter lead and observe the voltage readings. A drop should be noticed after the first load. But, there should be little or no voltage drop before the first load.

DIRECT MEASUREMENT OF VOLTAGE DROPS

1. Set the voltmeter switch to the 20 volt position.
2. Connect the voltmeter negative lead to the ground side of the load to be measured.
3. Connect the positive lead to the positive side of the resistance or load to be measured.
4. Read the voltage drop directly on the 20 volt scale.

Too high a voltage indicates too high a resistance. If, for example, a blower motor runs too slowly, you can determine if perhaps there is too high a resistance in the resistor pack. By taking voltage drop readings in all parts of the circuit, you can isolate the problem. Too low a voltage drop indicates too low a resistance. Take the blower motor for example again. If a blower motor runs too fast in the MED and/or LOW position, the problem might be isolated in the resistor pack by taking voltage drop readings in all parts of the circuit to locate a possibly shorted resistor.

HIGH RESISTANCE TESTING

1. Set the voltmeter selector switch to the 4 volt position.
2. Connect the voltmeter positive lead to the positive post of the battery.
3. Turn on the headlights and heater blower to provide a load.
4. Probe various points in the circuit with the negative voltmeter lead.
5. Read the voltage drop on the 4 volt scale. Some average maximum allowable voltage drops are:
- FUSE PANEL: 0.7 volts
- IGNITION SWITCH: 0.5 volts
- HEADLIGHT SWITCH: 0.7 volts
- IGNITION COIL (+): 0.5 volts
- ANY OTHER LOAD: 1.3 volts

➡**Voltage drops are all measured while a load is operating; without current flow, there will be no voltage drop.**

Resistance Measurement

The batteries in an ohmmeter will weaken with age and temperature, so the ohmmeter must be calibrated or "zeroed" before taking measurements. To zero the meter, place the selector switch in its lowest range and touch the two ohmmeter leads together. Turn the calibration knob until the meter needle is exactly on zero.

➡**All analog (needle) type ohmmeters must be zeroed before use, but some digital ohmmeter models are automatically calibrated when the switch is turned on. Self-calibrating digital ohmmeters do not have an adjusting knob, but its a good idea to check for a zero readout before use by touching the leads together. All computer controlled systems require the use of a digital ohmmeter with at least 10 megohms impedance for testing. Before any test procedures are attempted, make sure the ohmmeter used is compatible with the electrical system or damage to the on-board computer could result.**

To measure resistance, first isolate the circuit from the vehicle power source by disconnecting the battery cables or the harness connector. Make sure the key is **OFF** when disconnecting any components or the battery. Where necessary, also isolate at least one side of the circuit to be checked in order to avoid reading parallel resistances. Parallel circuit resistances will always give a lower reading than the actual resistance of either of the branches. When measuring the resistance of parallel circuits, the total resistance will always be lower than the smallest resistance in the circuit. Connect the meter leads to both sides of the circuit (wire or component) and read the actual measured ohms on the meter scale. Make sure the selector switch is set to the proper ohm scale for the circuit being tested to avoid misreading the ohmmeter test value.

✳✳ WARNING

Never use an ohmmeter with power applied to the circuit. Like the self-powered test light, the ohmmeter is designed to operate on its own power supply. The normal 12 volt automotive electrical system current could damage the meter!

Wiring Harnesses

The average automobile contains about ½ mile of wiring, with hundreds of individual connections. To protect the many wires from damage and to keep them from becoming a confusing tangle, they are organized into bundles, enclosed in plastic or taped together and called wiring harnesses. Different harnesses serve different parts of the vehicle. Individual wires are color coded to help trace them through a harness where sections are hidden from view.

Automotive wiring or circuit conductors can be in any one of three forms:
1. Single strand wire
2. Multi-strand wire
3. Printed circuitry

Single strand wire has a solid metal core and is usually used inside such components as alternators, motors, relays and other devices. Multi-strand wire has a core made of many small strands of wire twisted together into a single conductor. Most of the wiring in an automotive electrical system is made up of multi-strand wire, either as a single conductor or grouped together in a harness. All wiring is color coded on the insulator, either as a solid color or as a colored wire with an identification stripe. A printed circuit is a thin film of copper or other conductor that is printed on an insulator backing. Occasionally, a printed circuit is sandwiched between two sheets of plastic for more protection and flexibility. A complete printed circuit, consisting of conductors, insulating material and connectors for lamps or other components is called a printed circuit board. Printed circuitry is used in place of individual wires or harnesses in places where space is limited, such as behind instrument panels.

Since automotive electrical systems are very sensitive to changes in resistance, the selection of properly sized wires is critical when systems are repaired. A loose or corroded connection or a replacement wire that is too small for the circuit will add extra resistance and an additional voltage drop to the circuit. A ten percent voltage drop can result in slow or erratic motor operation, for

example, even though the circuit is complete. The wire gauge number is an expression of the cross-section area of the conductor. The most common system for expressing wire size is the American Wire Gauge (AWG) system.

Gauge numbers are assigned to conductors of various cross-section areas. As gauge number increases, area decreases and the conductor becomes smaller. A 5 gauge conductor is smaller than a 1 gauge conductor and a 10 gauge is smaller than a 5 gauge. As the cross-section area of a conductor decreases, resistance increases and so does the gauge number. A conductor with a higher gauge number will carry less current than a conductor with a lower gauge number.

➡**Gauge wire size refers to the size of the conductor, not the size of the complete wire. It is possible to have two wires of the same gauge with different diameters because one may have thicker insulation than the other.**

12 volt automotive electrical systems generally use 10, 12, 14, 16 and 18 gauge wire. Main power distribution circuits and larger accessories usually use 10 and 12 gauge wire. Battery cables are usually 4 or 6 gauge, although 1 and 2 gauge wires are occasionally used. Wire length must also be considered when making repairs to a circuit. As conductor length increases, so does resistance. An 18 gauge wire, for example, can carry a 10 amp load for 10 feet without excessive voltage drop; however if a 15 foot wire is required for the same 10 amp load, it must be a 16 gauge wire.

An electrical schematic shows the electrical current paths when a circuit is operating properly. It is essential to understand how a circuit works before trying to figure out why it doesn't. Schematics break the entire electrical system down into individual circuits and show only one particular circuit. In a schematic, no attempt is made to represent wiring and components as they physically appear on the vehicle; switches and other components are shown as simply as possible. Face views of harness connectors show the cavity or terminal locations in all multi-pin connectors to help locate test points.

If you need to backprobe a connector while it is on the component, the order of the terminals must be mentally reversed. The wire color code can help in this situation, as well as a keyway, lock tab or other reference mark.

WIRING REPAIR

Soldering is a quick, efficient method of joining metals permanently. Everyone who has the occasion to make wiring repairs should know how to solder. Electrical connections that are soldered are far less likely to come apart and will conduct electricity much better than connections that are only "pig-tailed" together. The most popular (and preferred) method of soldering is with an electrical soldering gun. Soldering irons are available in many sizes and wattage ratings. Irons with higher wattage ratings deliver higher temperatures and recover lost heat faster. A small soldering iron rated for no more than 50 watts is recommended, especially on electrical systems where excess heat can damage the components being soldered.

There are three ingredients necessary for successful soldering; proper flux, good solder and sufficient heat. A soldering flux is necessary to clean the metal of tarnish, prepare it for soldering and to enable the solder to spread into tiny crevices. When soldering, always use a rosin core solder which is non-corrosive and will not attract moisture once the job is finished. Other types of flux (acid core) will leave a residue that will attract moisture and cause the wires to corrode. Tin is a unique metal with a low melting point. In a molten state, it dissolves and alloys easily with many metals. Solder is made by mixing tin with lead. The most common proportions are 40/60, 50/50 and 60/40, with the percentage of tin listed first. Low priced solders usually contain less tin, making them very difficult for a beginner to use because more heat is required to melt the solder. A common solder is 40/60 which is well suited for all-around general use, but 60/40 melts easier and is preferred for electrical work.

Soldering Techniques

Successful soldering requires that the metals to be joined be heated to a temperature that will melt the solder, usually 360–460°F (182–238°C). Contrary to popular belief, the purpose of the soldering iron is not to melt the solder itself, but to heat the parts being soldered to a temperature high enough to melt the solder when it is touched to the work. Melting flux-cored solder on the soldering iron will usually destroy the effectiveness of the flux.

➡**Soldering tips are made of copper for good heat conductivity, but must be "tinned" regularly for quick transference of heat to the project and to prevent the solder from sticking to the iron. To "tin" the iron, simply heat it and touch the flux-cored solder to the tip; the solder will flow over the hot tip. Wipe the excess off with a clean rag, but be careful as the iron will be hot.**

After some use, the tip may become pitted. If so, simply dress the tip smooth with a smooth file and "tin" the tip again. Flux-cored solder will remove oxides but rust, bits of insulation and oil or grease must be removed with a wire brush or emery cloth. For maximum strength in soldered parts, the joint must start off clean and tight. Weak joints will result in gaps too wide for the solder to bridge.

If a separate soldering flux is used, it should be brushed or swabbed on only those areas that are to be soldered. Most solders contain a core of flux and separate fluxing is unnecessary. Hold the work to be soldered firmly. It is best to solder on a wooden board, because a metal vise will only rob the piece to be soldered of heat and make it difficult to melt the solder. Hold the soldering tip with the broadest face against the work to be soldered. Apply solder under the tip close to the work, using enough solder to give a heavy film between the iron and the piece being soldered, while moving slowly and making sure the solder melts properly. Keep the work level or the solder will run to the lowest part and favor the thicker parts, because these require more heat to melt the solder. If the soldering tip overheats (the solder coating on the face of the tip burns up), it should be retinned. Once the soldering is completed, let the soldered joint stand until cool. Tape and seal all soldered wire splices after the repair has cooled.

Wire Harness Connectors

Most connectors in the engine compartment or that are otherwise exposed to the elements are protected against moisture and dirt which could create oxidation and deposits on the terminals.

These special connectors are weather-proof. All repairs require the use of a special terminal and the tool required to service it. This tool is used to remove the pin and sleeve terminals. If removal is attempted with an ordinary pick, there is a good chance that the terminal will be bent or deformed. Unlike standard blade type terminals, these weather-proof terminals cannot be straightened once they are bent. Make certain that the connectors are properly seated and all of the sealing rings are in place when connecting leads. On some models, a hinge-type flap provides a backup or secondary locking feature for the terminals. Most secondary locks are used to improve connector reliability by retaining the terminals if the small terminal lock tangs are not positioned properly.

Molded-on connectors require complete replacement of the connection. This means splicing a new connector assembly into the harness. All splices should be soldered to insure proper contact. Use care when probing the connections or replacing terminals in them as it is possible to short between opposite terminals. If this happens to the wrong terminal pair, it is possible to damage certain components. Always use jumper wires between connectors for circuit checking and never probe through weatherproof seals.

Open circuits are often difficult to locate by sight because corrosion or terminal misalignment are hidden by the connectors. Merely wiggling a connector on a sensor or in the wiring harness may correct the open circuit condition. This should always be considered when an open circuit or a failed sensor is indicated. Intermittent problems may also be caused by oxidized or loose connections. When using a circuit tester for diagnosis, always probe connections from the wire side. Be careful not to damage sealed connectors with test probes.

All wiring harnesses should be replaced with identical parts, using the same gauge wire and connectors. When signal wires are spliced into a harness, use wire with high temperature insulation only. It is seldom necessary to replace a complete harness. If replacement is necessary, pay close attention to insure proper harness routing. Secure the harness with suitable plastic wire clamps to prevent vibrations from causing the harness to wear in spots or contact any hot components.

➡**Weatherproof connectors cannot be replaced with standard connectors. Instructions are provided with replacement connector and terminal packages. Some wire harnesses have mounting indicators (usually pieces of colored tape) to mark where the harness is to be secured.**

In making wiring repairs, its important that you always replace damaged wires with wiring of the same gauge as the wire being replaced. The heavier the wire, the smaller the gauge number. Wires are color-coded to aid in identification and whenever possible the same color coded wire should be used for replacement. A wire stripping and crimping tool is necessary to install solderless terminal connectors. Test all crimps by pulling on the wires; it should not be possible to pull the wires out of a good crimp.

Wires which are open, exposed or otherwise damaged are repaired by simple splicing. Where possible, if the wiring harness is accessible and the damaged place in the wire can be located, it is best to open the harness and check for all possible damage. In an inaccessible harness, the wire must be bypassed with a new insert, usually taped to the outside of the old harness.

When replacing fusible links, be sure to use fusible link wire,

NOT ordinary automotive wire. Make sure the fusible segment is of the same gauge and construction as the one being replaced and double the stripped end when crimping the terminal connector for a good contact. The melted (open) fusible link segment of the wiring harness should be cut off as close to the harness as possible, then a new segment spliced in as described. In the case of a damaged fusible link that feeds two harness wires, the harness connections should be replaced with two fusible link wires so that each circuit will have its own separate protection.

➡️**Most of the problems caused in the wiring harness are due to bad ground connections. Always check all vehicle ground connections for corrosion or looseness before performing any power feed checks to eliminate the chance of a bad ground affecting the circuit.**

Hard-Shell Connectors

Unlike molded connectors, the terminal contacts in hard-shell connectors can be replaced. Weatherproof hard-shell connectors with the leads molded into the shell have non-replaceable terminal ends. Replacement usually involves the use of a special terminal removal tool that depresses the locking tangs (barbs) on the connector terminal and allows the connector to be removed from the rear of the shell. The connector shell should be replaced if it shows any evidence of burning, melting, cracks, or breaks. Replace individual terminals that are burnt, corroded, distorted or loose.

➡️**The insulation crimp must be tight to prevent the insulation from sliding back on the wire when the wire is pulled. The insulation must be visibly compressed under the crimp tabs, and the ends of the crimp should be turned in for a firm grip on the insulation.**

The wire crimp must be made with all wire strands inside the crimp. The terminal must be fully compressed on the wire strands with the ends of the crimp tabs turned in to make a firm grip on the wire. Check all connections with an ohmmeter to insure a good contact. There should be no measurable resistance between the wire and the terminal when connected.

Fusible Links

The fuse link is a short length of special, Hypalon (high temperature) insulated wire, integral with the engine compartment wiring harness and should not be confused with standard wire. It is several wire gauges smaller than the circuit which it protects. Under no circumstances should a fuse link replacement repair be made using a length of standard wire cut from bulk stock or from another wiring harness.

To repair any blown fuse link use the following procedure:

1. Determine which circuit is damaged, its location and the cause of the open fuse link. If the damaged fuse link is one of three fed by a common No. 10 or 12 gauge feed wire, determine the specific affected circuit.

2. Disconnect the negative battery cable.

3. Cut the damaged fuse link from the wiring harness and discard it. If the fuse link is one of three circuits fed by a single feed wire, cut it out of the harness at each splice end and discard it.

4. Identify and procure the proper fuse link with butt connectors for attaching the fuse link to the harness.

➡️**Heat shrink tubing must be slipped over the wire before crimping and soldering the connection.**

5. To repair any fuse link in a 3-link group with one feed:
   a. After cutting the open link out of the harness, cut each of the remaining undamaged fuse links close to the feed wire weld.
   b. Strip approximately ½ in. (13mm) of insulation from the detached ends of the two good fuse links. Insert two wire ends into one end of a butt connector, then carefully push one stripped end of the replacement fuse link into the same end of the butt connector and crimp all three firmly together.

➡️**Care must be taken when fitting the three fuse links into the butt connector as the internal diameter is a snug fit for three wires. Make sure to use a proper crimping tool. Pliers, side cutters, etc. will not apply the proper crimp to retain the wires and withstand a pull test.**

   c. After crimping the butt connector to the three fuse links, cut the weld portion from the feed wire and strip approximately ½ in. (13mm) of insulation from the cut end. Insert the stripped end into the open end of the butt connector and crimp very firmly.
   d. To attach the remaining end of the replacement fuse link, strip approximately ½ in. (13mm) of insulation from the wire end of the circuit from which the blown fuse link was removed, and firmly crimp a butt connector or equivalent to the stripped wire. Then, insert the end of the replacement link into the other end of the butt connector and crimp firmly.
   e. Using rosin core solder with a consistency of 60 percent tin and 40 percent lead, solder the connectors and the wires at the repairs then insulate with electrical tape or heat shrink tubing.

6. To replace any fuse link on a single circuit in a harness, cut out the damaged portion, strip approximately ½ in. (13mm) of insulation from the two wire ends and attach the appropriate replacement fuse link to the stripped wire ends with two proper size butt connectors. Solder the connectors and wires, then insulate.

7. To repair any fuse link which has an eyelet terminal on one end such as the charging circuit, cut off the open fuse link behind the weld, strip approximately ½ in. (13mm) of insulation from the cut end and attach the appropriate new eyelet fuse link to the cut stripped wire with an appropriate size butt connector. Solder the connectors and wires at the repair, then insulate.

8. Connect the negative battery cable to the battery and test the system for proper operation.

➡️**Do not mistake a resistor wire for a fuse link. The resistor wire is generally longer and has print stating, "Resistor-don't cut or splice."**

When attaching a single No. 16, 17, 18 or 20 gauge fuse link to a heavy gauge wire, always double the stripped wire end of the fuse link before inserting and crimping it into the butt connector for positive wire retention.

REMOVE EXISTING VINYL TUBE SHIELDING
REINSTALL OVER FUSE LINK BEFORE CRIMPING
FUSE LINK TO WIRE ENDS

TAPE

TAPE OR STRAP

TYPICAL REPAIR USING THE SPECIAL #17 GA. (9.00" LONG-YELLOW) FUSE LINK REQUIRED FOR THE AIR/COND.
CIRCUITS (2) #687E and #261A LOCATED IN THE ENGINE COMPARTMENT

FUSE LINK

TAPE OR STRAP

TYPICAL REPAIR FOR ANY IN-LINE FUSE LINK USING THE SPECIFIED GAUGE FUSE LINK FOR THE SPECIFIC CIRCUIT

TAPE

TYPICAL REPAIR USING THE EYELET TERMINAL FUSE LINK OF THE SPECIFIED GAUGE FOR ATTACHMENT TO A CIRCUIT WIRE END

TAPE

(3) FUSE LINKS

TYPICAL REPAIR ATTACHING THREE LIGHT GAUGE
FUSE LINKS TO A SINGLE HEAVY GAUGE FEED WIRE

TAPE

BUTT CONNECTOR
FOR 10 OR 12 GA. WIRE

S

DOUBLED WIRE CRIMPED

TAPE

#10 OR 12 GA. WIRE

LIGHT GAUGE WIRE

'BUTT CONNECTOR
FOR #14 OR 16 WIRE

S

S

FUSIBLE LINK REPAIR PROCEDURE

**General fusible link repair—never replace a fusible link with regular wire or a fusible link rated at a higher amperage
than the one being replaced**

Add-On Electrical Equipment

The electrical system in your vehicle is designed to perform under reasonable operating conditions without interference between components. Before any additional electrical equipment is installed, it is recommended that you consult your dealer or a reputable repair facility that is familiar with the vehicle and its systems.

If the vehicle is equipped with mobile radio equipment and/or mobile telephone, it may have an effect upon the operation of any on-board computer control modules. Radio Frequency Interference (RFI) from the communications system can be picked up by the vehicle's wiring harnesses and conducted into the control module, giving it the wrong messages at the wrong time. Although well shielded against RFI, the computer should be further protected by taking the following measures:

• Install the antenna as far as possible from the control module. For instance, if the module is located behind the center console area, then the antenna should be mounted at the rear of the vehicle.

• Keep the antenna wiring a minimum of eight inches away from any wiring running to control modules and from the module itself. NEVER wind the antenna wire around any other wiring.

• Mount the equipment as far from the control module as possible. Be very careful during installation not to drill through any wires or short a wire harness with a mounting screw.

• Insure that the electrical feed wire(s) to the equipment are properly and tightly connected. Loose connectors can cause interference.

• Make certain that the equipment is properly grounded to the vehicle. Poor grounding can damage expensive equipment.

HEATING AND AIR CONDITIONING

The following procedures for servicing the components of the heater apply to those cars which have air conditioning as well as those without it.

Blower Motor

REMOVAL & INSTALLATION

Matador

1. Disconnect the motor wires, inside the engine compartment.
2. Remove the attaching screws from the motor mounting plate.
3. Remove the motor and fan assembly.
4. Installation is the reverse of removal.

Gremlin, Hornet, Concord, Spirit and Eagle

1. Drain about two quarts of coolant from the radiator.

Unfasten motor case-to-firewall retainers . . .

When removing the blower motor assembly, first disengage the electrical connection

. . . then remove the assembly from the vehicle

✳✳ CAUTION

When draining engine coolant, keep in mind that cats and dogs are attracted to ethylene glycol antifreeze and could drink any that is left in an uncovered container or in puddles on the ground. This will prove fatal in sufficient quantity. Always drain coolant into a sealable container. Coolant should be reused unless it is contaminated or is several years old.

2. Disconnect the heater hoses from the heater core tubes the plug the core tubes.
3. Disconnect the blower wires.
4. Remove the cover retaining nut and remove the motor and fan assembly.
5. To install, reverse the removal procedure.

Pacer

MODELS WITHOUT AIR CONDITIONING

1. Disconnect the negative battery cable.
2. Remove the right side windshield finish molding.
3. Remove the instrument panel crash pad.
4. Remove the right scuff plate and cowl trim panel.
5. Remove the lower instrument panel-to-right A-pillar attaching screws.
6. Pull the instrument panel to the rear and replace the lower attaching screw in the right A-pillar. Allow the instrument panel to rest on the screw.
7. Remove the heater core housing attaching nuts and screws.
8. Remove the vacuum hoses from the heater core housing clip and set the lines aside.
9. Disconnect the blend-air door cable from the heater core housing.
10. Pull the heater core housing forward and set atop the upper control arm.

11. Remove the blower motor ground wire at the relay.
12. Disconnect the wires at the blower motor resistor.
13. Remove the blower motor housing brace.
14. Loosen the heater housing-to-dash panel attaching nuts.
15. Pull the blower housing to the rear and downward.
16. Disconnect the vacuum hoses from the vacuum motors.
17. Remove the blower housing.
18. Remove the blower housing cover.
19. Disconnect the white blower wire inside the housing.
20. Remove the blower motor mounting plate-to-housing screws and remove the blower motor assembly.
21. Remove the blower fan from the motor shaft and remove the mounting plate from the motor housing.
22. Install the blower motor in the reverse order of removal.

MODELS WITH AIR CONDITIONING

1. Disconnect the negative battery cable.
2. Remove the right scuff plate and cowl trim panel.
3. Remove the radio overlay cover.
4. Remove the instrument panel crash pad.
5. Remove the instrument panel-to-right A-pillar attaching screws.
6. Remove the two upper instrument panel-to-lower instrument panel attaching screws above the glove box.
7. Disconnect the blend-air door cable from the heater core housing.
8. Remove the housing brace-to-floorpan screw.
9. Disconnect the wire at the blower motor resistor.
10. Disconnect the vacuum hoses from the vacuum motors.
11. Remove the heater core housing attaching nuts and screw.
12. Remove the vacuum hoses from the housing clip and set the lines aside.
13. Pull the heater core housing forward and set it atop the upper control arm.
14. Remove the floor outlet duct.
15. Disconnect the wires from the blower motor relay.
16. Remove the blower housing attaching screw located in the engine compartment on the dash panel.

Troubleshooting the Heater

Problem	Cause	Solution
Blower motor will not turn at any speed	• Blown fuse • Loose connection • Defective ground • Faulty switch • Faulty motor • Faulty resistor	• Replace fuse • Inspect and tighten • Clean and tighten • Replace switch • Replace motor • Replace resistor
Blower motor turns at one speed only	• Faulty switch • Faulty resistor	• Replace switch • Replace resistor
Blower motor turns but does not circulate air	• Intake blocked • Fan not secured to the motor shaft	• Clean intake • Tighten security
Heater will not heat	• Coolant does not reach proper temperature • Heater core blocked internally • Heater core air-bound • Blend-air door not in proper position	• Check and replace thermostat if necessary • Flush or replace core if necessary • Purge air from core • Adjust cable
Heater will not defrost	• Control cable adjustment incorrect • Defroster hose damaged	• Adjust control cable • Replace defroster hose

17. Loosen the evaporator housing-to-dash panel attaching screw.

18. Remove the blower housing-to-dash panel attaching screw.

19. Pull the blower housing to the rear and downward.

20. Pull the right side of the instrument panel to the rear and remove the blower housing from under the panel.

21. Remove the floor door vacuum motor attaching screws and motor to gain access to the blower housing cover attaching screws.

22. Remove the blower housing cover attaching screws and remove the cover.

23. Remove the blower motor mounting plate and remove the blower motor assembly.

24. Remove the blower fan from the motor shaft and the mounting plate from the body of the motor.

25. Install the motor in reverse order of removal.

Heater Core

REMOVAL & INSTALLATION

Matador

▶ **See Figures 1 and 2**

1. Disconnect the negative battery cable.
2. Drain about 2 quarts of coolant from the cooling system.

✳✳ CAUTION

When draining the coolant, keep in mind that cats and dogs are attracted by the ethylene glycol antifreeze, and are

Fig. 1 Exploded view of the heater assembly on Matador models equipped with air conditioning

Fig. 2 Exploded view of the Matador heater assembly on models without air conditioning

quite likely to drink any that is left in an uncovered container or in puddles on the ground. This will prove fatal in sufficient quantity. Always drain the coolant into a sealable container. Coolant should be reused unless it is contaminated or several years old.

---

3. Disconnect the heater hoses from the heater core in the engine compartment and plug the core tubes.

4. On air conditioned cars, disconnect the blend-air damper cable at the heater core housing and remove the fuse panel. On non-A/C cars, disconnect the blend-air damper door and fresh air door cables.

5. Remove the lower instrument finish panel and remove the glove box door and liner.

6. Remove the right windshield pillar and corner finish moldings for access to the upper right heater core housing mounting screws.

7. On air conditioned cars, remove the vacuum motor hoses.

8. Remove the remaining heater core housing attaching screws.

9. On air conditioned cars, remove the capscrew retaining the instrument panel to the right body pillar. Pull the right side of the instrument panel slightly rearward.

10. Remove the heater core housing and heater core. Remove the heater core from the housing.

11. Install the heater core and housing in the reverse order of removal.

Gremlin, Hornet, Concord, Spirit and Eagle
▶ See Figure 3

1. Disconnect the negative battery cable and drain 2 qts. of coolant.

2. Disconnect the heater hoses and plug the hoses and core fittings.

Fig. 3 Exploded view of the heater assembly on models without air conditioning except Matador and Pacer

3. Disconnect the blower wires and remove the motor and fan assembly.

4. Remove the housing attaching nut from the stud in the engine compartment.

5. Remove the package shelf, if so equipped.

6. Disconnect the wire at the resistor, located below the glove box.

7. Remove the instrument panel center bezel, air outlet, and duct on A/C models.

8. Disconnect the air and defroster cables from the damper levers.

9. Remove the right side windshield pillar molding, the instrument panel upper sheet metal screws and the cap screw at the right door post.

10. Remove the right cowl trim panel and door sill plate.

11. Remove the right kick panel and heater housing attaching screws.

12. Pull the right side of the instrument panel outward slightly and remove the housing.

13. Remove the core, defroster and blower housing.

14. Remove the core from the housing.

15. Installation is the reverse of removal.

Pacer

✳✳ CAUTION

When draining the coolant, keep in mind that cats and dogs are attracted by the ethylene glycol antifreeze, and are quite likely to drink any that is left in an uncovered container or in puddles on the ground. This will prove fatal in sufficient quantity. Always drain the coolant into a sealable container. Coolant should be reused unless it is contaminated or several years old.

▶ See Figures 4 and 5

1. Drain about two quarts of coolant from the radiator.

2. Disconnect the heater hoses from the heater core tubes and install plugs in the heater hoses.

3. Remove the vacuum hoses from the heater core housing cover clip and move the lines aside.

4. Remove the heater core housing cover screws.

5. Disconnect the overcenter spring from the cover and remove the cover.

Fig. 4 Exploded view of the heater assembly on Pacer models without air conditioning

Fig. 5 Exploded view of the heater assembly on Pacer models with air conditioning

6. Remove the heater core-to-housing attaching screws and remove the heater core.

7. Install the heater core in the reverse order of removal.

Control Head

REMOVAL & INSTALLATION

Matador

1975–77 MODELS

1. Disconnect the battery ground cable.
2. Remove the instrument cluster bezel.
3. Remove the clock or clock opening cover.
4. If equipped, remove the fuel economy gauge.
5. Remove the control head attaching screws.
6. Pull the control head out slightly and disconnect the cables, vacuum hoses and wires. It's a good idea to label the hoses and wires so that you'll remember where they go.
7. Installation is the reverse of removal. Adjust the cables as necessary.

1978 MODELS

1. Disconnect the battery ground cable.
2. Remove the right side remote mirror control.
3. Remove the instrument cluster bezel.
4. Remove the clock or clock opening cover.

5. If equipped, remove the fuel economy gauge.
6. Remove the control head attaching screws.
7. Pull the control head out slightly and disconnect the cables, vacuum hoses and wires. It's a good idea to label the hoses and wires so that you'll remember where they go.
8. Installation is the reverse of removal. Adjust the cables as necessary.

➡The fan switch attaching screw is accessible on the back of the panel after panel removal.

1975–77 Hornet, 1975–78 Gremlin and 1978 Gremlin and AMX Models

WITHOUT AIR CONDITIONING

1. Disconnect the battery ground cable.
2. Remove the instrument panel center housing.
3. Remove the radio.
4. Remove the control head attaching screws.
5. Pull the control head out slightly and disconnect the cables, vacuum hoses and wires. It's a good idea to label the hoses and wires so that you'll remember where they go.
6. Installation is the reverse of removal. Adjust the cables as necessary.

WITH AIR CONDITIONING

◆ See Figure 6

1. Disconnect the battery ground cable.
2. Remove the instrument panel center housing.
3. Remove the AC thermostat control knob and attaching nut.

Fig. 6 Control head and vacuum line components on all 1975–78 models except Pacer with A/C

4. Remove the control head attaching screws.

5. Remove the center upper discharge duct.

6. Remove the radio.

7. Pull the control head out slightly and disconnect the cables, vacuum hoses and wires. It's a good idea to label the hoses and wires so that you'll remember where they go.

8. Installation is the reverse of removal. Adjust the cables as necessary.

1979–80 AMX, 1979–83 Spirit and Concord and 1980–88 Eagle

WITHOUT AIR CONDITIONING

▶ **See Figure 7**

1. Disconnect the battery ground cable.

2. Remove the instrument panel center housing.

3. Remove the control head attaching screws.

4. Pull the control head out slightly and disconnect the cables, vacuum hoses and wires. It's a good idea to label the hoses and wires so that you'll remember where they go.

5. Installation is the reverse of removal. Adjust the cables as necessary.

➡**On 1980–88 models, the control cables must be attached with the colored tape in the center of the clips that are attached to the control head.**

Fig. 7 Control head and related components on all except Pacer models without A/C

WITH AIR CONDITIONING

▶ **See Figure 8**

1. Disconnect the battery ground cable.
2. Remove the instrument panel center housing.
3. Remove the control head attaching screws.
4. Remove the center upper discharge duct.
5. Remove the radio.
6. Pull the control head out slightly and disconnect the cables,

vacuum hoses and wires. It's a good idea to label the hoses and wires so that you'll remember where they go.

➡**The fan switch attaching screw is accessible on the back of the panel after panel removal.**

7. Installation is the reverse of removal. Adjust the cables as necessary.

Fig. 8 Control head and vacuum line components on all 1979–88 models with A/C except Pacer

Pacer

1977–7 MODELS8

▶ **See Figures 9 and 10**

1. Disconnect the battery ground cable.
2. Remove the instrument panel center housing.
3. Remove the radio.

4. Remove the control head attaching screws.
5. Pull the control head out slightly and disconnect the cables, vacuum hoses and wires. It's a good idea to label the hoses and wires so that you'll remember where they go.
6. Installation is the reverse of removal. Adjust the cables as necessary.

Fig. 9 Exploded view of the control head and its related components on Pacer models with A/C through 1979

PANEL DOOR AND WATER VALVE VACUUM SWITCH

DEFROST DOOR CABLE CLIP

FLOOR DOOR CABLE CLIP

FAN SWITCH

TEMPERATURE DOOR CABLE CLIP

CONTROL PANEL

Fig. 10 Control head and its related components on Pacer models without A/C through 1979

1979–80 MODELS

▶ **See Figure 11**

1. Disconnect the battery ground cable.
2. Remove the radio.

3. Remove the control panel attaching screws.
4. Pull the control panel out and disconnect the vacuum hoses, wires and cables. Tag them for proper installation.
5. Installation is the reverse of removal. Adjust the cables as necessary.

BLOWER MOTOR RESISTOR

BLOWER MOTOR RELAY

BLOWER CONTROL SWITCH

TEMPERATURE CONTROL LEVER

BLEND-AIR DOOR CABLE

THERMOSTAT CABLE

TURNBUCKLE

CONTROL ASSEMBLY

CONTROL PANEL LAMP ASSEMBLY

PUSHBUTTONS

VACUUM CONTROL SWITCH

Fig. 11 Exploded view of the control head components on 1980 Pacer models with A/C

ENTERTAINMENT SYSTEMS

Radio

The following precautions should be observed when working on a car radio:

1. Always observe the proper polarity of the connections; i.e., positive (+) goes to the power source and negative (−) to ground (negative ground electrical system).

2. Never operate the radio without a speaker; damage to the output transistors will result. If a replacement speaker is used, be sure that it is the correct impedance (ohms) for the radio. The impedance is stamped on the case of AMC radios.

3. If a new antenna or antenna cable is used, adjust the antenna trimmer for the best reception of a weak AM station around 1400 kc; the trimmer is located either behind the tuning knob or on the bottom of the radio case.

REMOVAL & INSTALLATION

Matador

1. Disconnect the negative battery cable. Remove the knobs from the radio and unfasten the control shafts retaining nuts.

2. Remove the bezel securing screws, and remove the bezel.

3. Loosen, but do not remove, the upper radio securing screw.

4. Raise the rear of the radio to separate its bracket from the upper securing screw.

5. Pull the radio forward slightly, and disconnect all of the leads from it. Remove the radio.

6. Radio installation is performed in the reverse order of removal. Adjust the antenna trimmer.

AMX, Concord, Eagle, Gremlin, Hornet and Spirit

1. Disconnect the battery ground cable.

2. On Gremlins and Hornets through 1977, remove the package tray and the ash tray and bracket.

3. Pull off the radio knobs and remove shaft retaining nuts.

4. Remove the bezel retaining screws and remove the bezel. On 1978 and later models with A/C, remove the center housing of the instrument panel.

5. Disconnect the speaker, antenna, and power leads, and remove the radio.

6. Installation is the reverse of removal.

Pacer

1. Disconnect the negative battery cable.

2. Remove the radio knobs, attaching nuts, cluster bezel, and overlay cover.

3. Loosen the radio-to-instrument panel attaching screw.

4. Lift the rear of the radio and pull forward slightly. Disconnect the electrical connections and the antenna and remove the radio.

5. Installation is the reverse of removal.

WINDSHIELD WIPERS

Motor

REMOVAL & INSTALLATION

AMX, Concord, Eagle, Gremlin, Hornet, Spirit and Matador (Sedan and Wagon)

▶ See Figure 12

1. Remove the wire arms and blades.

2. Remove the screws holding the motor adapter plate to the dash panel.

3. Separate the wiper wiring harness connector at the motor.

4. Pull the motor and linkage out of the opening to expose the drive link-to-crank stud retaining clip. Raise up the lock tab of the clip with a screwdriver and slide the clip off the stud. Remove the wiper motor assembly.

5. Install the windshield wiper motor in the reverse order of removal.

Matador Coupe

1. Remove the wire arm/blade assemblies.

2. Open the hood and remove the cowl screen from the cowl opening.

3. Separate the linkage drive arm from the motor arm crankpin, by unfastening the retaining clip.

4. Disconnect the two multiconnectors from the motor.

5. Remove the wiper motor securing screws and withdraw the motor from the opening.

➡ **If the output arm hangs up on the firewall panel during motor removal, rotate the arm clockwise by hand, so that it clears the panel opening.**

6. Installation is performed in the reverse order of removal. Prior to installation, make sure that the output arm is in the 'park' position. Tighten the motor retaining screws to 90–120 in. lbs.

Pacer

1. Remove the vacuum canister mounting bracket and canister.

2. Disconnect the linkage drive arm from the motor output arm crankpin by removing the retaining clip.

Fig. 12 Exploded view of a typical wiper motor and transmission used on AMC models

1. Nut
2. Drive crank
3. Seal
4. Bracket
5. Screw
6. Ground strap
7. Spring washer
8. Plain washer
9. Grommet
10. Gear housing
11. Shaft
12. Switch washer
13. Switch lever
14. Output gear and shaft
15. End play spring
16. Idler gear and pinion
17. Gasket
18. Screw
19. Cover
20. Push nut
21. Brushes and harness
22. End head
23. Armature
24. Ball
25. Motor housing
26. Bolt
27. Screw
28. Brush
29. Spring
30. Parking lever pin
31. Screw
32. Seal

When removing the wiper motor from the vehicle, first disengage the electrical connection

. . . slide the assembly out and use a wrench to unfasten the drive link-to-crank retainer

Remove the wiper motor adapter-to-dash panel retainers . . .

Disengage the wiper motor from the linkage and remove the motor

3. On vehicles equipped with air conditioning:
  a. Remove the two nuts on the left side of the heater housing.
  b. Remove the one nut on the right side on the heater housing.
  c. Remove the screw from the heater housing support.
4. On vehicles not equipped with air conditioning:
  a. Remove the two nuts and one screw on the left side of the heater housing.
  b. Remove the one nut on the right side of the heater housing.

  c. Remove the screw from the heater housing support. Pull the heater housing forward.
5. Remove the wiper motor mounting plate attaching screws and remove the wiper motor assembly from the cowl.
6. Disconnect the two wire connectors from the wiper motor.
7. Remove the wiper motor attaching screws and remove the wiper motor.
8. Install the wiper motor in the reverse order of removal.

Troubleshooting Basic Windshield Wiper Problems

Problem	Cause	Solution
Electric Wipers		
Wipers do not operate— Wiper motor heats up or hums	• Internal motor defect • Bent or damaged linkage • Arms improperly installed on linking pivots	• Replace motor • Repair or replace linkage • Position linkage in park and reinstall wiper arms
Wipers do not operate— No current to motor	• Fuse or circuit breaker blown • Loose, open or broken wiring • Defective switch • Defective or corroded terminals • No ground circuit for motor or switch	• Replace fuse or circuit breaker • Repair wiring and connections • Replace switch • Replace or clean terminals • Repair ground circuits
Wipers do not operate— Motor runs	• Linkage disconnected or broken	• Connect wiper linkage or replace broken linkage
Vacuum Wipers		
Wipers do not operate	• Control switch or cable inoperative • Loss of engine vacuum to wiper motor (broken hoses, low engine vacuum, defective vacuum/fuel pump) • Linkage broken or disconnected • Defective wiper motor	• Repair or replace switch or cable • Check vacuum lines, engine vacuum and fuel pump • Repair linkage • Replace wiper motor
Wipers stop on engine acceleration	• Leaking vacuum hoses • Dry windshield • Oversize wiper blades • Defective vacuum/fuel pump	• Repair or replace hoses • Wet windshield with washers • Replace with proper size wiper blades • Replace pump

Wiper Linkage

REMOVAL & INSTALLATION

1. Remove the wiper arms and blades.
2. Remove the screws retaining the right and left pivot shaft bodies to the cowl.

3. Disconnect the linkage drive arm from the motor output arm crankpin by removing the retaining clip.
4. Remove the pivot shaft body assembly.
5. Position the pivot shaft body assembly on the car.
6. Install the retaining screws and tighten them to 50–70 in. lbs.
7. Connect the linkage drive arm to the motor output arm crankpin and install the retaining clip.

INSTRUMENT AND SWITCHES

Instrument Cluster

REMOVAL & INSTALLATION

Pacer

▶ **See Figure 13**

1. Disconnect the negative battery cable.
2. Remove the instrument cluster bezel with a straight, firm pull.

3. Remove the radio control knobs and retaining nuts. Remove the radio overlay retaining screws.
4. Remove the headlight switch overlay retaining screws. Pull the headlight switch overlay back and disconnect the speedometer cable.
5. Remove the instrument cluster retaining screws. Tilt the cluster down and disconnect the instrument panel wire harness connectors.
6. If equipped with automatic transmission, disconnect the gear selector dial cable from the steering column.
7. Remove the cluster assembly.
8. Reverse the above procedure to install.

Fig. 13 Common instrument panel and components used on Pacer models

1975–76 Gremlin and Hornet

▶ **See Figure 14**

1. Disconnect the battery negative cable.
2. Cover the steering column with a cloth to prevent scratching of painted surfaces.
3. Remove the package tray (if equipped) and disconnect the speedometer cable.
4. Remove the control knobs and retaining nuts from the wiper control and headlight switches.

5. Remove the screws attaching the instrument cluster housing to the instrument panel.
6. Rotate the instrument cluster forward, disconnect all electrical connections and lamps, disconnect the vacuum line from the fuel economy gauge (if equipped), and remove the cluster.

To install:

7. Position the instrument cluster on the instrument panel and connect all electrical connections and lamps, connect the vacuum line to the fuel economy gauge (if equipped).

Fig. 14 Exploded view of the instrument panel and components used on all models except Matador and Pacer

8. Install the cluster housing-to-instrument panel attaching screws.

9. Install the wiper control and headlight switch retaining nuts and control knobs.

10. Connect the speedometer cable and install the package tray.

11. Remove the protective cloth cover from the steering column.

12. Connect the battery negative cable.

1975–76 Matador

▶ **See Figure 15**

1. Remove the radio control knobs and attaching nuts.
2. Remove the remote mirror control attaching nut (if equipped).
3. Remove the ten bezel attaching screws.
4. Tilt the bezel toward the interior of the car and disconnect all electrical connections.
5. Remove the bezel.
6. Remove the clock, clock opening cover, or fuel economy gauge.
7. Reach through the clock access opening and disconnect the speedometer cable from the cluster.
8. If equipped with automatic transmission, remove the lower instrument finish panel.
9. Disconnect the shift quadrant control cable from the steering column (if equipped).
10. Remove the instrument cluster mounting screws.
11. Tilt the cluster toward interior of car, disconnect all electrical connections, and remove the instrument cluster.

To install:

12. Position the instrument cluster in the panel and connect all electrical connections.
13. Install the cluster mounting screws.
14. Connect the shift quadrant control cable (if equipped).

➡ **Adjust the shift quadrant cable as outlined in the Torque-Command Transmission section.**

15. Install the lower instrument finish panel (if removed).
16. Reach through the clock access opening and connect the speedometer cable.
17. Install the clock, clock opening cover, or fuel economy gauge.
18. Position the bezel and connect all electrical connections.
19. Install the ten bezel attaching screws.
20. Install the radio attaching nuts and control knobs.
21. Install the remote mirror control attaching nut (if equipped).

➡ **The control knob aligning tabs must fit in the control shaft slots when installing the control knobs.**

1977 Gremlin and Hornet

1. Disconnect the battery negative cable.
2. Remove the package tray (if equipped) to gain access to the speedometer cable.
3. Cover the steering column with a cloth to prevent scratches.

4. Disconnect the speedometer cable (screw-on type).
5. Remove the top and side screws from the instrument panel and tilt the cluster forward slightly to gain access for disconnecting the headlamp switch and the wiper control harness connectors.

PRINTED CIRCUIT BOARD

FUEL AND TEMPERATURE GAUGES

INDICATOR BULB LENS

SPEEDOMETER

MASK

GEAR SELECTOR DIAL (AUTO. TRANS)

CLUSTER HOUSING

LENS

Fig. 15 Typical instrument cluster components—Matador models

➡️**Lift the two locking tabs to disconnect the headlamp switch connector.**

6. Disconnect the fiber-optic ashtray lamp, if equipped.
7. Disconnect the harness connectors and remove the instrument cluster assembly.

To install:

8. Position the instrument cluster on the instrument panel and connect all the electrical connections and lamps.

➡️**Be sure to connect the headlamp switch ground wire.**

9. Connect the fiber optic ashtray lamp to the cluster, if removed.
10. Install the cluster housing to the instrument panel with the attaching screws.
11. Connect the speedometer cable and install the package tray.
12. Remove the protective cloth cover from the steering column.
13. Connect the battery negative cable.
14. Reset the clock, if equipped.

1977–78 Matador

1. Remove the radio control knobs and attaching nuts.
2. Remove the right remote mirror control attaching nut, if equipped.
3. Remove the bezel attaching screws.
4. Tilt the bezel toward interior of car and disconnect all electrical connections.
5. Remove the bezel. Cover the steering column with a cloth to prevent scratching the column.
6. Remove the clock housing attaching screws, pull the assembly away from the cluster, and disconnect the bulbs and electrical leads. Remove the assembly.
7. Using the clock access opening, disconnect the speedometer cable by depressing the locking tab and moving the cable away from the instrument cluster.
8. Disconnect the gear selector dial cable from the steering column.
9. Remove the cluster mounting screws and disconnect the electrical connections.
10. Remove the cluster.

To install:

11. Position the cluster and connect the electrical components.
12. Install the cluster mounting screws.
13. Connect the gear selector dial cable.
14. Connect the speedometer cable.
15. Connect the clock electrical connector and install the bulbs and clock (or cover).
16. Install the instrument cluster bezel.
17. Install the right mirror remote control, if removed.
18. Install the radio attaching nuts and control knobs.
19. Connect the battery negative cable.
20. Reset the clock, if equipped.

1978 Gremlin, Concord

1. Disconnect the battery negative cable.
2. Cover the steering column to protect against scratching.

3. Remove the bezel attaching screws across the top, above radio and behind the glove box door.
4. Tip the bezel outward at the top and disengage the tabs along the bottom edge.
5. Unplug the glove box lamp connector, if equipped.
6. Depress the speedometer cable locking tab and move the cable away from the cluster.
7. Push down on the three illumination lamp housings above the bezel until the lamp housings are clear from the instrument panel.
8. Disconnect the headlamp switch and wiper control connectors and the switch illumination lamp.

➡️**Lift the two locking tabs to disconnect the headlamp switch connector.**

9. Twist and remove the cluster illumination lamp sockets.
10. Disconnect the instrument cluster connectors.
11. Remove the clock or tachometer screws, if equipped. It is not necessary to remove the clock adjusting knob.
12. Disconnect the clock or tachometer feed wires from the circuit board, if equipped.
13. Remove the cluster housing and circuit board-to-bezel screws.
14. Remove the cluster housing and circuit board assembly from bezel. If equipped with a clock or tachometer, move it aside as required.

To install:

15. Position the instrument cluster on the instrument cluster bezel. Move the clock or tachometer aside as required.
16. Install the cluster housing mounting screws.

➡️**The clock ground wire terminal must contact the foil on the circuit board beneath the clock mounting boss.**

17. Connect the clock or tachometer feed wires to the circuit board, if removed.
18. Install the clock or tachometer screws.
19. Connect the instrument cluster connectors.
20. Install the cluster illumination lamp sockets.
21. Connect the headlamp and wiper switch connectors and the switch illumination lamp.
22. Align the tabs at the bottom of the bezel with the openings, and raise the bezel. It may be necessary to press down on the illumination housings for clearance. Do not push the bezel into the final position.
23. Connect the speedometer cable.
24. Connect the glove box lamp wires, if removed.
25. Push the bezel forward into the installed position and install the screws.
26. Remove the protective cloth, connect the battery and reset the clock, if equipped.

1979–86 All Models

1. Disconnect the battery negative cable.
2. Cover the steering column to protect against scratching.
3. Remove the lower steering column cover.
4. Unscrew the speedometer cable connector from the speedometer.

5. Remove the gear selector dial actuator cable from the steering column shift shroud, if the automobile is equipped with a column shift automatic transmission.

6. Remove the bezel attaching screws across the top, above the radio and behind the glove box door.

7. Tip the bezel outward at the top and disengage the tabs along the bottom edge.

8. Unplug the glove box lamp connector, if equipped.

9. Push down on the three illumination lamp housings above the bezel until the lamp housings clear the instrument panel.

10. Disconnect the headlamp switch and wiper control connectors and the switch illumination lamp.

➡**Lift the two locking tabs to disconnect the headlamp switch connector.**

11. Twist and remove the cluster illumination lamp sockets.

12. Disconnect the instrument cluster connectors.

13. Remove the clock or tachometer screws, if equipped. It is not necessary to remove the clock adjusting knob.

14. Disconnect the clock or tachometer feed wires from the circuit board, if equipped.

15. Remove the cluster housing and circuit board-to-bezel screws.

16. Remove the cluster housing and circuit board assembly from the bezel. If equipped with a clock or tachometer, move it aside as required.

To install:

17. Position the instrument cluster on the instrument cluster bezel. Move the clock or tachometer aside as required.

18. Install the cluster housing mounting screws.

➡**The clock ground and feed wire terminals must contact the foil beneath the circuit board mounting screws.**

19. Connect the clock or tachometer feed wires to the circuit board, if removed.

20. Install the clock or tachometer screws.

21. Connect the instrument cluster connectors.

22. Install the cluster illumination lamp sockets.

23. Connect the headlamp and wiper switch connectors and the switch illumination lamp.

24. If the automobile is equipped with a column shift automatic transmission, use a piece of wire to fish the gear selector dial actuator cable through the grommet in the instrument panel reinforcement and attach it to the shift column shroud. Adjust the cable, if necessary.

25. Align the tabs at the bottom of the bezel with the openings, and raise the bezel. It may be necessary to press down on the illumination housings for clearance. Do not push the bezel into the final position.

26. Connect the glove box lamp wires, if removed.

27. Push the bezel forward into the installed position and install the screws.

➡**Make sure the gear selector dial actuator cable is adjusted in neutral.**

28. Connect the speedometer cable and tighten it securely.

29. Install the lower steering column cover.

30. Remove the protective cloth, connect the battery and reset the clock, if equipped.

Printed Circuit Board

Current is supplied to the instruments and the instrument panel lights through a printed circuit which is attached to the rear of the instrument cluster. The disconnect plug is part of the panel wiring harness and connects to pins attached to the printed circuit. A keyway located on the printed circuit board insures that the plug is always mounted correctly.

❋❋ CAUTION

Never pry under the plug to remove it, or damage to the printed circuit will result.

An instrument voltage regulator is wired in series with the gauges to supply a constant five volts to them. It is integral with the temperature gauge.

REMOVAL & INSTALLATION

1. Disconnect the cable from the negative (−) battery terminal.

2. Cover the steering column with a clean cloth, so that it will not be scratched.

3. If equipped with a parcel shelf, unfasten the two screws which secure it at either end, remove the screws which secure it to the center support bracket and withdraw the shelf from underneath the instrument panel.

4. Working from underneath the dash, disconnect the speedometer cable.

5. Remove the knobs from the headlight and wiper switches.

6. Remove the 5 screws that are located around the cluster bezel and partially withdraw the cluster/bezel assembly from the panel.

7. Disconnect all of the wiring and lights from the back of the cluster and remove the cluster/bezel assembly the rest of the way.

8. Installation is performed in the reverse order of removal.

Troubleshooting Basic Dash Gauge Problems

Problem	Cause	Solution
Coolant Temperature Gauge		
Gauge reads erratically or not at all	• Loose or dirty connections • Defective sending unit	• Clean/tighten connections • Bi-metal gauge: remove the wire from the sending unit. Ground the wire for an instant. If the gauge registers, replace the sending unit.
	• Defective gauge	• Magnetic gauge: disconnect the wire at the sending unit. With ignition ON gauge should register COLD. Ground the wire; gauge should register HOT.
Ammeter Gauge—Turn Headlights ON (do not start engine). Note reaction		
Ammeter shows charge Ammeter shows discharge Ammeter does not move	• Connections reversed on gauge • Ammeter is OK • Loose connections or faulty wiring • Defective gauge	• Reinstall connections • Nothing • Check/correct wiring • Replace gauge
Oil Pressure Gauge		
Gauge does not register or is inaccurate	• On mechanical gauge, Bourdon tube may be bent or kinked	• Check tube for kinks or bends preventing oil from reaching the gauge
	• Low oil pressure	• Remove sending unit. Idle the engine briefly. If no oil flows from sending unit hole, problem is in engine.
	• Defective gauge	• Remove the wire from the sending unit and ground it for an instant with the ignition ON. A good gauge will go to the top of the scale.
	• Defective wiring	• Check the wiring to the gauge. If it's OK and the gauge doesn't register when grounded, replace the gauge.
	• Defective sending unit	• If the wiring is OK and the gauge functions when grounded, replace the sending unit
All Gauges		
All gauges do not operate	• Blown fuse • Defective instrument regulator	• Replace fuse • Replace instrument voltage regulator
All gauges read low or erratically	• Defective or dirty instrument voltage regulator	• Clean contacts or replace
All gauges pegged	• Loss of ground between instrument voltage regulator and car • Defective instrument regulator	• Check ground • Replace regulator
Warning Lights		
Light(s) do not come on when ignition is ON, but engine is not started	• Defective bulb • Defective wire	• Replace bulb • Check wire from light to sending unit
	• Defective sending unit	• Disconnect the wire from the sending unit and ground it. Replace the sending unit if the light comes on with the ignition ON.
Light comes on with engine running	• Problem in individual system • Defective sending unit	• Check system • Check sending unit (see above)

SEAT BELT/STARTER INTERLOCK SYSTEMS

Disabling the Interlock System

Since the legal requirement for seat belt/starter interlock systems was dropped during the 1975 model year, those systems installed on cars built earlier may now be legally disconnected. However, the seat belt warning light is still required to operate.

1. Remove the pink wire and terminal from the two terminal connector at the emergency starter relay, located on the right inner fender panel, under the hood.

2. Cut off the pink wire close to the taped junction of the wire harness.

3. Remove the yellow wire and terminal.

4. Install the yellow wire into the two terminal connector at the location where the pink wire and terminal was removed from the three terminal connector at the starter relay.

5. From under the right side of the dash and along the right side of the glove box area, locate the interlock logic module and remove it from its bracket. Cut off the yellow with black tracer wire close to the taped junction of the wire harness and cut off the remaining end as close to the logic module as possible. Reinstall the logic module on its dash bracket.

6. The warning light should be off when the occupied seat belt is buckled and the car placed in gear with the ignition switch on.

➡**Most models require the seating of both the driver and front seat passenger, prior to buckling of the belts or turning of the ignition system, due to the programming of the logic module for the seat belt warning light to go out. These series can be identified by a buff colored logic module. Other series are equipped with a green colored logic module which allows non-sequential operation and independent use of the seat belts.**

LIGHTING

Headlights

REMOVAL & INSTALLATION

1. Remove the headlight cover (surrounding trim panel).

➡**The screws directly above and to one side of the headlight are for adjusting the vertical and horizontal headlight aim. Don't confuse these with the headlight cover retaining screws.**

2. Loosen the screws holding the headlight retainer ring in place.

3. Rotate the retainer ring to disengage the ring from the screws. Remove the ring.

4. Pull the headlight out and pull the wire plug off the back.

There are currently only 3 types of headlights commonly in use on U.S. cars:

   a. Four lamp system high beam.

   b. Four lamp system combined high and low beam.

   c. Two lamp system combined high and low beam.

To install:

5. Push the plug onto the new headlight. Position the headlight. There are lugs on the headlight to make it impossible to put it in wrong.

6. Replace the retainer ring and tighten the screws.

7. Replace the headlight cover.

To remove the headlight, unfasten the headlight trim cover screws and remove the cover

Loosen but do not remove the headlight retainer ring screws . . .

Turn the retaining ring so that the head of the screws can fit through the slots and remove the ring

1. Headlight   2. Electrical connection

Slide the headlight forward and disengage the wiring and remove it from the vehicle

➡When aiming the headlights, each combined high and low beam should be within 6 in. (152.4mm) to the right of the vertical centerline of the light and within 2 in. (51mm) above or below the horizontal centerline, at a distance of 25 ft. (8m). The high beams of a four lamp system should be within 2 in. (51mm) below the horizontal centerline and within 6 in. (152.4mm) right or left from the vertical centerline. Some state inspection laws may not allow this much leeway in adjustment.

Signal and Marker Lights

REMOVAL & INSTALLATION

Front Parking and Turn Signal Lights

◆ **See Figure 16**

1. Twist and remove the bulb socket from the rear of the light housing assembly.

2. Remove the bulb from the socket by turning it counterclockwise.

3. Installation is the reverse of removal.

Side Marker Lights

1. Unfasten the marker lens retaining screws.

2. Slide the marker lens away from the body panel and twist the bulb socket to disengage it from the lens.

3. Remove the bulb by turning it counterclockwise or pulling it from the socket.

4. Installation is the reverse of removal.

Fig. 16 Exploded view of the headlamp, parking, turn signal and side marker lamps—Spirit, Concord and Eagle

To remove the front side marker light bulb, unfasten the lens retaining screws

Remove the bulb from the socket by pulling it straight out

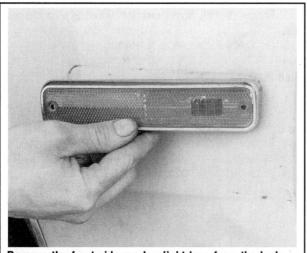

Remove the front side marker light lens from the body panel

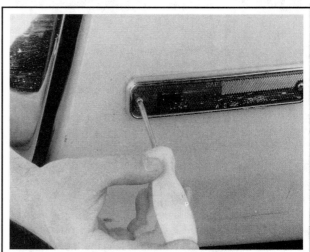

To gain access to the rear side marker light bulb you must first remove the lens retaining screws . . .

Remove the bulb and socket assembly from the front side marker light lens

. . . then separate the rear side marker light lens from the body

Remove the bulb and socket assembly from the rear side marker light lens

To replace the rear turn, brake, parking or back-up bulb, first remove the lens assembly retaining screws

Remove the bulb from the socket by pulling it straight out

Remove the lens assembly to gain access to the bulbs

Rear Turn, Brake, Parking and Back-up Lights

EARLY MODEL VEHICLES

1. Remove the light lens retaining screws.
2. Remove the lens assembly from the vehicle.
3. Grasp the bulb and turn it counterclockwise to remove it from the socket assembly.
4. Installation is the reverse of removal.

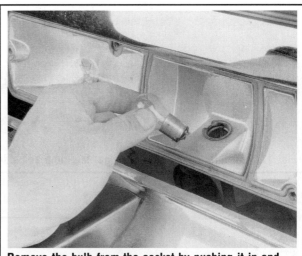

Remove the bulb from the socket by pushing it in and turning it counterclockwise

LATE MODEL VEHICLES

▶ See Figures 17, 18 and 19

The rear turn, brake, parking and back-up lights are usually contained in one unit.

1. To gain access to the unit remove the rear deck or trim panel in the trunk.

2. Slide the marker lens away from the body panel and twist the bulb socket to disengage it from the lens.

3. Remove the bulb from the socket by turning it counterclockwise.

4. Installation is the reverse of removal.

TAIL, STOP AND REAR DIRECTIONAL LAMP BULB

HOUSING

BACK UP LAMP BULB

LENS

SIDE MARKER BULB

SIDE MARKER

GASKET

Fig. 17 Rear turn signal, back-up, stop, tail lamp and side marker light components—Spirit sedan and Eagle Kamback

Fig. 18 Rear turn signal, back-up, stop, tail lamp and side marker light components—Spirit liftback and Eagle SX/4

Fig. 19 Rear turn signal, back-up, stop, tail lamp and side marker light components—Concord and Eagle Sedan and wagon

Dome Light

1. Remove the dome light cover.
2. Remove the bulb assembly by gently pulling it from its socket.
3. Installation is the reverse of removal.

License Plate lamp

1. Remove the lamp housing retaining screws or bolts.
2. Remove the lens.
3. Replace the bulb.
4. Installation is the reverse of removal.

To gain access to the dome light bulb assembly, first remove the dome light cover . . .

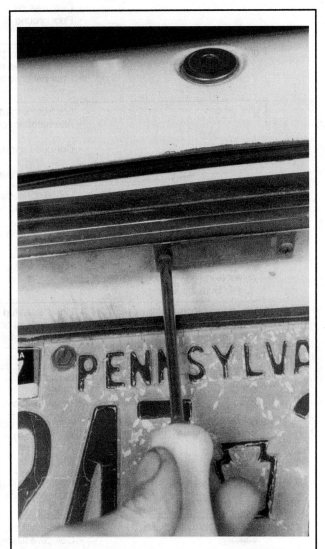

Remove the license plate lamp lens retaining screws to access the bulb assembly

. . . then remove the bulb from the socket

Troubleshooting Basic Lighting Problems

Problem	Cause	Solution
Lights		
One or more lights don't work, but others do	• Defective bulb(s) • Blown fuse(s) • Dirty fuse clips or light sockets • Poor ground circuit	• Replace bulb(s) • Replace fuse(s) • Clean connections • Run ground wire from light socket housing to car frame
Lights burn out quickly	• Incorrect voltage regulator setting or defective regulator • Poor battery/alternator connections	• Replace voltage regulator • Check battery/alternator connections
Lights go dim	• Low/discharged battery • Alternator not charging • Corroded sockets or connections • Low voltage output	• Check battery • Check drive belt tension; repair or replace alternator • Clean bulb and socket contacts and connections • Replace voltage regulator
Lights flicker	• Loose connection • Poor ground • Circuit breaker operating (short circuit)	• Tighten all connections • Run ground wire from light housing to car frame • Check connections and look for bare wires
Lights "flare"—Some flare is normal on acceleration—if excessive, see "Lights Burn Out Quickly"	• High voltage setting	• Replace voltage regulator
Lights glare—approaching drivers are blinded	• Lights adjusted too high • Rear springs or shocks sagging • Rear tires soft	• Have headlights aimed • Check rear springs/shocks • Check/correct rear tire pressure
Turn Signals		
Turn signals don't work in either direction	• Blown fuse • Defective flasher • Loose connection	• Replace fuse • Replace flasher • Check/tighten all connections
Right (or left) turn signal only won't work	• Bulb burned out • Right (or left) indicator bulb burned out • Short circuit	• Replace bulb • Check/replace indicator bulb • Check/repair wiring
Flasher rate too slow or too fast	• Incorrect wattage bulb • Incorrect flasher	• Flasher bulb • Replace flasher (use a variable load flasher if you pull a trailer)
Indicator lights do not flash (burn steadily)	• Burned out bulb • Defective flasher	• Replace bulb • Replace flasher
Indicator lights do not light at all	• Burned out indicator bulb • Defective flasher	• Replace indicator bulb • Replace flasher

Troubleshooting Basic Turn Signal and Flasher Problems

Most problems in the turn signals or flasher system can be reduced to defective flashers or bulbs, which are easily replaced. Occasionally, problems in the turn signals are traced to the switch in the steering column, which will require professional service.
F = Front   R = Rear   • = Lights off   o = Lights on

Problem	Solution
Turn signals light, but do not flash	• Replace the flasher
No turn signals light on either side	• Check the fuse. Replace if defective. • Check the flasher by substitution • Check for open circuit, short circuit or poor ground
Both turn signals on one side don't work	• Check for bad bulbs • Check for bad ground in both housings
One turn signal light on one side doesn't work	• Check and/or replace bulb • Check for corrosion in socket. Clean contacts. • Check for poor ground at socket
Turn signal flashes too fast or too slow	• Check any bulb on the side flashing too fast. A heavy-duty bulb is probably installed in place of a regular bulb. • Check the bulb flashing too slow. A standard bulb was probably installed in place of a heavy-duty bulb. • Check for loose connections or corrosion at the bulb socket
Indicator lights don't work in either direction	• Check if the turn signals are working • Check the dash indicator lights • Check the flasher by substitution
One indicator light doesn't light	• On systems with 1 dash indicator: See if the lights work on the same side. Often the filaments have been reversed in systems combining stoplights with taillights and turn signals. Check the flasher by substitution • On systems with 2 indicators: Check the bulbs on the same side Check the indicator light bulb Check the flasher by substitution

CIRCUIT PROTECTION

Fuse Link

▶ **See Figure 20**

The fuse link is a short length of special, Hypalon (high temperature) insulated wire, integral with the engine compartment wiring harness and should not be confused with standard wire. It is sev-eral wire gauges smaller than the circuit which it protects. Under no circumstances should a fuse link replacement repair be made using a length of standard wire cut from bulk stock or from another wiring harness.

To repair any blown fuse link use the following procedure:

1. Determine which circuit is damaged, its location and the cause of the open fuse link. If the damaged fuse link is one of

REMOVE EXISTING VINYL TUBE SHIELDING
REINSTALL OVER FUSE LINK BEFORE CRIMPING
FUSE LINK TO WIRE ENDS

TAPE

TAPE OR STRAP

TYPICAL REPAIR USING THE SPECIAL #17 GA. (9.00" LONG-YELLOW) FUSE LINK REQUIRED FOR THE AIR/COND. CIRCUITS

FUSE LINK

TAPE OR STRAP

TYPICAL REPAIR FOR ANY IN-LINE FUSE LINK USING THE SPECIFIED GAUGE FUSE LINK FOR THE SPECIFIC CIRCUIT

TAPE

TYPICAL REPAIR USING THE EYELET TERMINAL FUSE LINK OF THE SPECIFIED GAUGE FOR ATTACHMENT TO A CIRCUIT WIRE END

TAPE

(3) FUSE LINKS

TYPICAL REPAIR ATTACHING THREE LIGHT GAUGE
FUSE LINKS TO A SINGLE HEAVY GAUGE FEED WIRE

TAPE

BUTT CONNECTOR
FOR 10 OR 12 GA. WIRE

DOUBLED WIRE CRIMPED

#10 OR 12 GA. WIRE

LIGHT GAUGE WIRE

BUTT CONNECTOR
FOR #14 OR 16 WIRE

FUSIBLE LINK REPAIR PROCEDURE

Fig. 20 Repairing the fusible links

three fed by a common No. 10 or 12 gauge feed wire, determine the specific affected circuit.

2. Disconnect the negative battery cable.

3. Cut the damaged fuse link from the wiring harness and discard it. If the fuse link is one of three circuits fed by a single feed wire, cut it out of the harness at each splice end and discard it.

4. Identify and procure the proper fuse link and butt connectors for attaching the fuse link to the harness.

5. To repair any fuse link in a 3-link group with one feed:

   a. After cutting the open link out of the harness, cut each of the remaining undamaged fuse links close to the feed wire weld.

   b. Strip approximately ½ in. (12.7mm) of insulation from the detached ends of the two good fuse links. Then insert two wire ends into one end of a butt connector and carefully push one stripped end of the replacement fuse link into the same end of the butt connector and crimp all three firmly together.

➡**Care must be taken when fitting the three fuse links into the butt connector as the internal diameter is a snug fit for three wires. Make sure to use a proper crimping tool. Pliers, side cutters, etc. will not apply the proper crimp to retain the wires and withstand a pull test.**

   c. After crimping the butt connector to the three fuse links, cut the weld portion from the feed wire and strip approximately ½ in. (12.7mm) of insulation from the cut end. Insert the stripped end into the open end of the butt connector and crimp very firmly.

   d. To attach the remaining end of the replacement fuse link, strip approximately ½ in. (12.7mm) of insulation from the wire end of the circuit from which the blown fuse link was removed, and firmly crimp a butt connector or equivalent to the stripped wire. Then, insert the end of the replacement link into the other end of the butt connector and crimp firmly.

   e. Using rosin core solder with a consistency of 60 percent tin and 40 percent lead, solder the connectors and the wires at the repairs and insulate with electrical tape.

6. To replace any fuse link on a single circuit in a harness, cut out the damaged portion, strip approximately ½ in. (12.7mm) of insulation from the two wire ends and attach the appropriate replacement fuse link to the stripped wire ends with two proper size butt connectors. Solder the connectors and wires and insulate with tape.

7. To repair any fuse link which has an eyelet terminal on one end such as the charging circuit, cut off the open fuse link behind the weld, strip approximately ½ in. (12.7mm) of insulation from the cut end and attach the appropriate new eyelet fuse link to the cut stripped wire with an appropriate size butt connector. Solder the connectors and wires at the repair and insulate with tape.

8. Connect the negative battery cable to the battery and test the system for proper operation.

➡**Do not mistake a resistor wire for a fuse link. The resistor wire is generally longer and has print stating 'Resistor-don't cut or splice.'**

When attaching a single No. 16, 17, 18 or 20 gauge fuse link to a heavy gauge wire, always double the stripped wire end of the fuse link before inserting and crimping it into the butt connector for positive wire retention.

Fuse Box Location

- 1975 and later Pacer: On the left of the glove box
- 1975–78 Gremlin and Hornet: Next to the parking brake mechanism
- 1975–78 Except Pacer, Gremlin and Hornet: In the glove box
- 1979–88 All models: Next to the parking brake mechanism

TRAILER WIRING

Wiring the vehicle for towing is fairly easy. There are a number of good wiring kits available and these should be used, rather than trying to design your own.

All trailers will need brake lights and turn signals as well as tail lights and side marker lights. Most areas require extra marker lights for overwide trailers. Also, most areas have recently required back-up lights for trailers, and most trailer manufacturers have been building trailers with back-up lights for several years.

Additionally, some Class I, most Class II and just about all Class III trailers will have electric brakes. Add to this number an accessories wire, to operate trailer internal equipment or to charge the trailer's battery, and you can have as many as seven wires in the harness.

Determine the equipment on your trailer and buy the wiring kit necessary. The kit will contain all the wires needed, plus a plug adapter set which includes the female plug, mounted on the bumper or hitch, and the male plug, wired into, or plugged into the trailer harness.

When installing the kit, follow the manufacturer's instructions.

The color coding of the wires is usually standard throughout the industry. One point to note: some domestic vehicles, and most imported vehicles, have separate turn signals. On most domestic vehicles, the brake lights and rear turn signals operate with the same bulb. For those vehicles with separate turn signals, you can purchase an isolation unit so that the brake lights won't blink whenever the turn signals are operated, or, you can go to your local electronics supply house and buy four diodes to wire in series with the brake and turn signal bulbs. Diodes will isolate the brake and turn signals. The choice is yours. The isolation units are simple and quick to install, but far more expensive than the diodes. The diodes, however, require more work to install properly, since they require the cutting of each bulb's wire and soldering in place of the diode.

One, final point, the best kits are those with a spring loaded cover on the vehicle mounted socket. This cover prevents dirt and moisture from corroding the terminals. Never let the vehicle socket hang loosely; always mount it securely to the bumper or hitch.

WIRING DIAGRAMS

WIRE COLOR CHART

BLACK	BLK	LIGHT GREEN	LT GRN
BROWN	BRN	ORANGE	ORG
BLUE	BLU	PINK	PNK
DARK BLUE	DK BLU	PURPLE	PPL
DARK GREEN	DK GRN	RED	RED
GREEN	GRN	TAN	TAN
GRAY	GRY	WHITE	WHT
LIGHT BLUE	LT BLU	YELLOW	YEL

Sample diagram—how to read and interpret wiring

WIRING DIAGRAM SYMBOLS

BATTERY CONNECTOR OR SPLICE CIRCUIT BREAKER CAPACITOR COIL DIODE FUSE FUSIBLE LINK GROUND LED

RESISTOR SINGLE FILAMENT BULB DUAL FILAMENT BULB HEATING ELEMENT SOLENOID OR COIL VARIABLE RESISTOR CRYSTAL POTENTIOMETER HORN OR SPEAKER

ALTERNATOR DISTRIBUTOR ASSEMBLY IGNITION COIL SPARK PLUG STEPPER MOTOR HEAT ACTIVATED SWITCH RELAY

NORMALLY OPEN SWITCH NORMALLY CLOSED SWITCH GANGED SWITCH 3-POSITION SWITCH REED SWITCH MOTOR OR ACTUATOR SPEED SENSOR JUNCTION BLOCK MODEL OPTIONS BRACKET

Common wiring diagram symbols

Fig. 21 Engine wiring—1975 Gremlin, Hornet, Matador and Pacer

Fig. 22 Chassis wiring—1975–77 Gremlin, Hornet, Matador and Pacer

Fig. 23 Chassis wiring—1975-77 Gremlin, Hornet, Matador and Pacer (continued)

Fig. 24 Engine wiring—1976–77 Gremlin, Hornet, Matador and Pacer

Fig. 25 Chassis wiring—1978 Gremlin, Hornet, Matador and Pacer

Fig. 26 Engine wiring—1978 Gremlin and Matador and 1978–79 Concord, spirit, Pacer and AMX

Fig. 27 Chassis wiring—1979 Concord, Pacer and AMX

Fig. 28 Chassis wiring—1978–80 Concord, Pacer, Spirit, Gremlin, Matador, AMX and 1980 Eagle

Fig. 29 Engine wiring—1980 Concord, Pacer, Spirit, Eagle and AMX

Fig. 30 Engine wiring—1980–81 Concord, Spirit and 1981 SX4 and Eagle 2.5L engines

Fig. 31 Chassis wiring—1980–81 Concord, Pacer, Spirit, Eagle, AMX and SX4

Fig. 32 Engine wiring—1981 Concord, Spirit, Eagle and SX4 4.2L engines

Fig. 33 Engine wiring—1981–83 Concord, Spirit and SX4 and 1981–88 Eagle

Fig. 34 Engine wiring—1982 Concord and Spirit and 1982–83 Eagle and SX4 2.5L engines

Fig. 35 Engine wiring—1982-83 Concord, Spirit, Eagle and SX4 4.2L engines

Fig. 36 Chassis wiring—1982–83 Concord, Spirit, Eagle and SX4

Fig. 37 Engine wiring—1984 Eagle 2.5L engine

Fig. 38 Chassis wiring—1984–88 Eagle

Fig. 39 Engine wiring—1984–88 Eagle 4.2L engine

MANUAL TRANSMISSION 7-2
UNDERSTANDING THE MANUAL
  TRANSMISSION 7-2
IDENTIFICATION 7-2
ADJUSTMENTS 7-2
  LINKAGE 7-2
  REMOVAL & INSTALLATION 7-5
PACER OVERDRIVE UNIT 7-7
IDENTIFICATION 7-7
  REMOVAL & INSTALLATION 7-7
CLUTCH 7-8
UNDERSTANDING THE CLUTCH 7-8
ADJUSTMENTS 7-8
  PEDAL FREE-PLAY 7-8
  REMOVAL & INSTALLATION 7-10
AUTOMATIC TRANSMISSION 7-21
UNDERSTANDING AUTOMATIC
  TRANSMISSIONS 7-21
  TORQUE CONVERTER 7-21
  PLANETARY GEARBOX 7-21
  SERVOS & ACCUMULATORS 7-22
  HYDRAULIC CONTROL
    SYSTEM 7-22
TRANSMISSION 7-23
  REMOVAL & INSTALLATION 7-23
ADJUSTMENTS 7-31
  LOW & REVERSE BAND 7-31
  LOW & REVERSE BAND 7-32
  KICK-DOWN BAND 7-32
  SHIFT LINKAGE 7-32
  THROTTLE LINKAGE 7-32
NEUTRAL SAFETY/BACK-UP LIGHT
  SWITCH 7-33
  TESTING 7-33
  REMOVAL & INSTALLATION 7-33
TRANSFER CASE 7-37
IDENTIFICATION 7-37
TRANSFER CASE 7-37
  REMOVAL & INSTALLATION 7-37
DRIVELINE 7-39
DRIVESHAFT AND U-JOINTS 7-39
  REMOVAL & INSTALLATION 7-39
  U-JOINT OVERHAUL 7-41
EAGLE FRONT AXLE 7-45
AXLE, SHAFT, SEAL AND
  BEARING 7-45
  REMOVAL & INSTALLATION 7-45
REAR AXLE 7-46
IDENTIFICATION 7-46
AXLE SHAFT, BEARING AND SEAL 7-46
  REMOVAL & INSTALLATION 7-46
SPECIFICATION CHARTS
  MANUAL TRANSMISSION
    APPLICATION CHART 7-19
  AUTOMATIC TRANSMISSION
    APPLICATION CHART 7-23
  TRANSFER CASE APPLICATION
    CHART 7-37
TROUBLESHOOTING CHARTS
  MANUAL TRANSMISSION AND
    TRANSFER CASE 7-17

BASIC CLUTCH PROBLEMS 7-20
BASIC AUTOMATIC TRANSMISSION
  PROBLEMS 7-35
TRANSMISSION FLUID
  INDICATIONS 7-35
LOCKUP TORQUE CONVERTER
  SERVICE DIAGNOSIS 7-36
BASIC DRIVESHAFT PROBLEMS 7-44

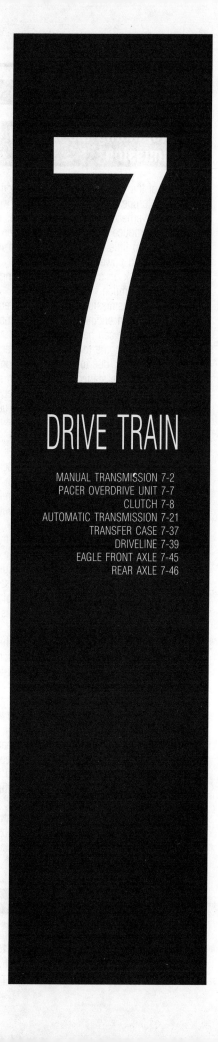

7
DRIVE TRAIN

MANUAL TRANSMISSION 7-2
PACER OVERDRIVE UNIT 7-7
CLUTCH 7-8
AUTOMATIC TRANSMISSION 7-21
TRANSFER CASE 7-37
DRIVELINE 7-39
EAGLE FRONT AXLE 7-45
REAR AXLE 7-46

MANUAL TRANSMISSION

Understanding the Manual Transmission

Because of the way an internal combustion engine breathes, it can produce torque (or twisting force) only within a narrow speed range. Most overhead valve pushrod engines must turn at about 2500 rpm to produce their peak torque. Often by 4500 rpm, they are producing so little torque that continued increases in engine speed produce no power increases.

The torque peak on overhead camshaft engines is, generally, much higher, but much narrower.

The manual transmission and clutch are employed to vary the relationship between engine RPM and the speed of the wheels so that adequate power can be produced under all circumstances. The clutch allows engine torque to be applied to the transmission input shaft gradually, due to mechanical slippage. The vehicle can, consequently, be started smoothly from a full stop.

The transmission changes the ratio between the rotating speeds of the engine and the wheels by the use of gears. 4-speed or 5-speed transmissions are most common. The lower gears allow full engine power to be applied to the rear wheels during acceleration at low speeds.

The clutch driveplate is a thin disc, the center of which is splined to the transmission input shaft. Both sides of the disc are covered with a layer of material which is similar to brake lining and which is capable of allowing slippage without roughness or excessive noise.

The clutch cover is bolted to the engine flywheel and incorporates a diaphragm spring which provides the pressure to engage the clutch. The cover also houses the pressure plate. When the clutch pedal is released, the driven disc is sandwiched between the pressure plate and the smooth surface of the flywheel, thus forcing the disc to turn at the same speed as the engine crankshaft.

The transmission contains a mainshaft which passes all the way through the transmission, from the clutch to the driveshaft. This shaft is separated at one point, so that front and rear portions can turn at different speeds.

Power is transmitted by a countershaft in the lower gears and reverse. The gears of the countershaft mesh with gears on the mainshaft, allowing power to be carried from one to the other. Countershaft gears are often integral with that shaft, while several of the mainshaft gears can either rotate independently of the shaft or be locked to it. Shifting from one gear to the next causes one of the gears to be freed from rotating with the shaft and locks another to it. Gears are locked and unlocked by internal dog clutches which slide between the center of the gear and the shaft. The forward gears usually employ synchronizers; friction members which smoothly bring gear and shaft to the same speed before the toothed dog clutches are engaged.

Identification

A lightweight Warner SR4 4-speed was introduced in six cylinder models in late 1976 and is used in all 1980–81 models. The four cylinder uses a Warner HR-1 4-speed transmission through 1979. The SR4 transmission has a cast aluminum case and extension housing, while the HR-1 has a cast iron case and an aluminum extension housing. The SR4 and HR-1 have internal, non-adjustable shift linkage. In 1982 a new Warner (T4) four speed and an optional Warner (T5) five speed transmission were introduced. Both are lightweight and feature an integral mounted shift mechanism.

➡ **SR4 and HR-1 transmissions have metric fasteners in most threaded holes.**

An identification tag, containing Warner and American Motors part numbers, is located at the rear of the transmission. The Warner model number is also usually cast into the side of the case.

The model 150T 3-speed transmission was also used through 1979. A nine character identification code is stamped on the left front case flange, but does not give the model number.

The 150T can readily be identified by its nine bolt top cover which is narrower in the front. Unlike the Warner transmissions, it does not have a drain plug: lubricant is drained by removing the lower extension housing bolt. Warner 3-speeds have a rectangular top cover, usually with four or six bolts.

Adjustments

LINKAGE

Pacer

COLUMN SHIFT

1. Detach the shift rods from the shift levers. Insert a 3/16 in. (4.76mm) drill through the column shift lever holes.
2. Shift into Reverse and lock the column with the ignition key. Position the First/Reverse shift lever in Reverse.
3. Adjust the shift rod trunnion to a free pin fit in the outer shift lever. Tighten the trunnion locknuts.
4. Unlock the column and move the gearshift to Neutral. Both of the transmission out shift levers should be in the Neutral detent.
5. Repeat Step 3 for the Second/Third shift rod trunnion.
6. Withdraw the drill from the column levers. Shift through all gears and check for a free crossover into Neutral.
7. Shift into Reverse and lock the column. The column should lock without any binding.

FLOOR SHIFT

1. Place the transmission shift levers in Neutral.
2. Loosen the Second/Third transmission lever attaching nut and adjusting bolt.
3. With the First/Reverse shift rod in the Neutral position, align the Second/Third shift rod so that its notch is exactly aligned with the notch in the First/Reverse shift rod.
4. Tighten the adjustment bolt and attaching nut.
5. Shift through all of the gears being particularly careful for binding in the First-to-Second shift.
6. To adjust the back-up light switch, loosen the jam nuts and then slide the switch forward or backward, as necessary. Tighten the jam nuts.

Except Pacer

COLUMN SHIFT
▶ **See Figure 1**

1. Disconnect the shift rods from the transmission shift levers. Insert a ³⁄₁₆ in. (4.76mm) drill through the column shift lever holes.

2. Shift into Reverse and lock the column with the ignition key. Position the transmission First/Reverse shift lever in Reverse.

3. Adjust the shift rod trunnion to a free pin fit in the transmission shift lever. Tighten the trunnion locknuts.

4. Unlock the column and move the gearshift to Neutral. Both of the transmission shift lever should be in the Neutral detent.

5. Repeat Step 3 for the Second/Third shift rod trunnion.

6. Remove the drill from the column levers. Shift through all gears and check for a free crossover into Neutral.

7. Shift into Reverse and lock the column. The column should lock without any binding.

3-SPEED FLOORSHIFT
▶ **See Figure 2**

1. Place the transmission shift levers in their neutral positions.

2. Loosen the second/third lever adjuster.

3. Keeping the first/reverse shift rod and transmission lever in the neutral position, align the second/third rod so the shift notch is exactly aligned with the first/reverse shift notch. Tighten the adjuster.

4. Operate the linkage and check for full engagement of all gears and a smooth crossover from first to second.

5. If there is a reverse lockup rod to the steering column, loosen both of the locknuts about ½ in. (12.7mm) each. Shift into reverse and lock the column. You may have to rotate the lever at the bottom of the column up into the locked position. Tighten the lower locknut until it contacts the trunnion. Tighten the upper locknut while holding the trunnion centered. Unlock the column and shift through gears. Shift into reverse and lock the binding.

Fig. 1 On column shift models, make sure the shift levers are properly aligned

Fig. 2 Exploded view of the three-speed floor shift linkage components

REMOVAL & INSTALLATION

Except Eagle

➡**Open the hood to avoid damage when the rear cross-member is removed. If the overdrive and transmission are to be separated, first engage then disengage the overdrive with the clutch pedal depressed and the engine running.**

1. Matchmark the driveshaft and rear axle yoke for correct installation. Split the rear universal joint and slide the driveshaft off the back of the transmission. Support the transmission with a jack.

2. Detach the column shift mechanism linkage from the transmission, and disconnect the clutch linkage and speedometer cable; disconnect the back-up light switch wiring, and TCS switch wiring, also.

On a floorshift, remove the shift lever. Remove the boot and unbolt the lever. Detach the column reverse lockup rod. Pull the lever and gauge out together. Support the engine.

3. Disconnect the overdrive wiring. Remove the rear transmission support cushion bolts. Also remove the starter on four cylinder models.

4. On Pacers with overdrive, remove the cotter pin from the parking brake equalizer and disconnect the front cable from the equalizer. Remove the cable adjuster and hooks from the floorpan bracket and lower equalizer and rear brake cables to provide clearance. Also, remove the ground strap from the floorpan.

➡**On V8 models with dual exhaust or dual catalytic converters, exhaust pipes must be disconnected from manifolds and lowered to gain working clearance.**

5. On HR1s, remove the throwout lever protective boot and disengage the clutch cable from the lever. Also remove the inspection cover at the front of the clutch housing.

6. Remove the transmission support crossmember except on Pacers; remove the crossmember with the transmission on those models. Remove the two lower studs which hold the transmission to the bell housing and replace these two studs with two long pilot studs on 150Ts and SR4s. On the HR1, remove the catalytic converter support bracket attaching bolts from the transmission rear support.

7. Remove the two top studs and slide the transmission assembly along the pilot studs and out of the car. On HR1s, support the engine and remove the clutch housing to engine bolts and remove the clutch and transmission as an assembly.

To install:

1. Fill the slots in the inner groove of the throwout bearing with light temperature grease and soak the crankshaft pilot bushing wick in engine oil. Fit the throwout bearing and the sleeve assembly in the clutch fork. Center the bearing over the clutch lever. Shift 150Ts and SR4s into first gear.

2. Install two pilot studs in the clutch housing, instead of the lower clutch housing cap screws on 150Ts and SR4s.

3. Carefully slide the transmission into place. Be careful not to damage the clutch driven plate splines while mating them with the transmission input shaft. It may be necessary to raise the front of the engine for the HR1.

4. Install the upper screws, which attach the case to the housing. Remove the pilot studs and install the lower cap screws.

5. If the car is equipped with a floor shift, install the shift lever retainer and shift rods, if removed.

6. Attach the speedometer cable, connect the back-up light switch wires and the Transmission Controlled Spark (TCS) wire, if so equipped. On the HR1, connect the clutch cable and adjust as necessary. Also install the inspection cover and the catalytic converter bracket bolts.

7. Raise the transmission. Attach the rear crossmember and support to the transmission. Fasten the crossmember to the side sills and finger-tighten the bolts. Install and tighten the crossmember-to-support bolts. Tighten the crossmember stud nuts. Install the parking brake cables and ground strap on Pacer.

8. Attach the exhaust pipes to the exhaust manifolds, on V8 engines, if they were removed.

9. Install the front U-joint yoke on the transmission. Do the same for the rear U-joint at the differential. Be sure the alignment marks made earlier line up.

10. Connect the shift rods on the column shift transmissions and the reverse lockup rod on the floorshift transmission. Check the transmission oil level and add lubricant, as needed.

11. Remove the supports and lower the car.

12. Install the shift lever if the car is a floorshift transmission.

13. Adjust the shift linkage, if it was disturbed.

1980–81 Eagle

1. Shift the transmission into neutral.

2. Remove the screws attaching the gearshift lever bezel and boot to the floorpan.

3. Slide the bezel and boot upward on the gearshift lever to provide access to the lever attaching bolts.

4. Remove the bolts attaching the gearshift lever to the lever mounting cover on the transmission adapter housing and remove the gearshift lever.

5. Remove the bolts attaching the gearshift lever mounting cover to the transmission adapter and remove the mounting cover to provide access to the transfer case upper mounting stud nut in the transmission adapter housing.

6. Remove the nut from the transfer case upper mounting stud located inside the transmission adapter housing.

7. Raise the automobile.

8. Remove the skid plate.

9. Remove the speedometer adapter retainer bolt and remove the retainer, adapter, and cable. Discard the adapter O-ring and plug the adapter opening in the transfer case to prevent excessive oil spillage.

➡**Mark the position of the speedometer adapter for assembly alignment reference before removing it.**

10. Mark the driveshafts and axle yokes for assembly alignment reference and disconnect the driveshafts at the transfer case.

11. Disconnect the back-up lamp switch wire.

12. Place a support stand under the engine.

13. Support the transmission and transfer case using a transmission jack.

14. Remove the rear crossmember.

15. Remove the catalytic converter bracket from the transfer case.

16. Remove the bolts attaching the transmission to the clutch housing.

17. Remove the transmission and transfer case as assembly.

18. Remove the nuts from the transfer case mounting studs and remove the transmission from the transfer case.

To install:

19. Install the transmission on the transfer case. Install and tighten all the transfer case mounting stud nuts to 26 ft. lbs.

20. Support the transmission/transfer case assembly on a transmission jack.

21. Align the transmission clutch shaft with the throwout bearing and clutch disc splines and seat the transmission against the clutch housing.

22. Install and tighten the transmission-to-clutch housing attaching bolts to 55 ft. lbs.

23. Connect the driveshafts to the transfer case yokes. Tighten the clamp strap bolts to 15 ft. lbs.

24. Install the rear crossmember. Tighten the crossmember attaching bolts to 30 ft. lbs.

25. Connect the back-up lamp switch wire.

26. Install the replacement O-ring on the speedometer adapter and install the adapter and cable, and the retainer. Tighten the retainer bolt to 100 in. lbs.

✳✳ WARNING

Do not attempt to reuse the original adapter O-ring. The ring is designed to swell in service to improve its sealing qualities, and could be cut or torn during installation if reuse is attempted.

27. Attach the catalytic converter bracket to transfer case. Tighten the retaining nuts to 26 ft. lbs.

28. Check and correct the lubricant levels in the transmission and transfer case if necessary.

29. Install the skid plate. Tighten the skid plate attaching bolts to 30 ft.lb. torque.

30. Remove the stand used to support the engine and remove the transmission jack if not removed previously.

31. Lower the automobile.

32. Clean the mating surfaces of the gearshift lever mounting cover and the transmission adapter housing.

33. Apply RTV type sealant to the gearshift lever mounting cover and install the cover on the transmission adapter housing. Tighten the cover bolts to 13 ft. lbs.

34. Install the gearshift lever on the mounting cover. Be sure the lever is engaged with the shift rail before tightening the lever attaching bolts. Tighten the lever attaching bolts to 18 ft. lbs.

35. Position the gearshift lever boot and bezel in the floorpan and install the bezel attaching screws.

1982–88 Eagle

▶ See Figure 3

1. Shift the transmission into Neutral.

2. Remove the screws attaching the gearshift lever bezel and boot to the floorpan.

3. Slide the bezel and boot upward on the gearshift lever to provide access to the lever attaching bolts.

4. Remove the bolts attaching the gearshift lever to lever mounting cover on transmission adapter housing and remove the gearshift lever.

5. Remove the bolts attaching the gearshift lever mounting cover to the transmission adapter, and remove the mounting cover to provide access to the transfer case upper mounting stud nut in the transmission adapter housing.

6. Remove the nut from the transfer case upper mounting stud located inside the transmission adapter housing.

Fig. 3 The transfer case upper mounting bolt is located under the lever cover—Eagle models

7. Raise the automobile.

8. Remove the skid plate.

9. Remove the speedometer adapter retainer bolt and remove the retainer, adapter, and cable. Discard the adapter O-ring and plug the adapter opening in the transfer case to prevent excessive oil spillage.

➡ **Mark the position of the speedometer adapter for assembly alignment reference before removing it.**

10. Mark the driveshafts and axle yokes for assembly alignment reference and disconnect the driveshafts at the transfer case.

11. Disconnect the back-up lamp switch wire.

12. Place a support stand under the engine.

13. Support the transmission and transfer case using a transmission jack.

14. Remove the rear crossmember.

15. Remove the catalytic converter bracket from the transfer case and the brace rod from the bracket.

16. Remove the bolts attaching the transmission to the clutch housing.

17. Remove the transmission and transfer case as assembly.

18. Remove the nuts from the transfer case mounting studs and remove the transmission from the transfer case.

To install:

19. Install the transmission on transfer case. Install and tighten all the transfer case mounting stud nuts to 26 ft. lbs.

20. Support the transmission/transfer case assembly on a transmission jack.

21. Align the transmission clutch shaft with the throwout bearing and clutch disc splines and seat the transmission against the clutch housing.

22. Install and tighten the transmission-to-clutch housing attaching bolts to 55 ft. lbs.

23. Connect the driveshafts to the transfer case yokes. Tighten the clamp strap bolts to 15 ft. lbs.

24. Install the brace rod and the rear crossmember. Tighten the attaching bolts to 30 ft. lbs.

25. Connect the back-up lamp switch wire.

26. Install a replacement O-ring on the speedometer adapter

and install the adapter and cable, and retainer. Tighten the retainer bolt to 100 inch lbs.

27. Attach the catalytic converter bracket to the transfer case. Tighten the retaining nuts to 26 ft. lbs.
28. Check and correct the lubricant levels in the transmission and transfer case, if necessary.

29. Install the skid plate. Tighten the skid plate attaching bolts to 30 ft.lb. torque.
30. Remove the stand used to support the engine and remove the transmission jack if not removed previously.
31. Lower the automobile.
32. Clean the mating surfaces of the gearshift lever mounting cover and the transmission adapter housing.
33. Apply RTV type sealant to the gearshift lever mounting cover and install the cover bolts to 13 ft. lbs.
34. Install the gearshift lever on the mounting cover. Be sure the lever is engaged with the shift rail before tightening the lever attaching bolts. Tighten the lever attaching bolts to 18 ft. lbs.
35. Position the gearshift lever boot and bezel in the floorpan and install the bezel attaching screws.

PACER OVERDRIVE UNIT

Identification

The Laycock de Normanville overdrive unit for the Pacer is an electro-hydraulic actuated, planetary gear type, mounted to a special adapter at the rear of the transmission.

When the overdrive is in the direct drive position (overdrive switched off), and the car is driven forward, power from the transmission mainshaft is transmitted through the freewheel rollers and unidirectional clutch to the overdrive output shaft. When the car is backing up or during periods of engine braking, torque is transmitted through the clutch sliding member which is held by spring pressure against the tapered portion of the output shaft. When the overdrive is actuated, the clutch sliding member is pressed by hydraulic pressure against the brake disc (ring), which locks the sun wheel. As a result, the output shaft of the overdrive rotates at a higher speed than the mainshaft, thereby accomplishing a 30% reduction in engine speed in relation to vehicle speed.

The overdrive is actuated by a switch located beneath the steering wheel. This switch energizes a solenoid on the overdrive unit, via a switch on the transmission, which is cut in only when Third gear is engaged. The solenoid has two windings: a heavy control winding and a lower current, hold winding. When actuated, the control winding opens the overdrive control valve, whereupon the control winding is cut off and the valve is held in the open position by the hold winding. The control valve regulates the pressurized oil flow from the cam operated pump to the hydraulic pistons which operate the overdrive clutch sliding member.

REMOVAL & INSTALLATION

▶ **See Figure 4**

➡**To facilitate removal, the vehicle should first be driven in Third gear with the overdrive engaged, and then coasted for a few seconds with the overdrive disengaged and the clutch pedal depressed.**

1. Remove the transmission from the vehicle as previously outlined in the Transmission removal and installation procedure in this section.
2. Disconnect the solenoid cables.
3. If the overdrive unit has not already been drained, remove the six bolts and the overdrive oil pan.

Fig. 4 The overdrive unit is coupled to the transmission with an adapter—Pacer models

✳✳ CAUTION

Be careful to avoid spilling hot transmission fluid on your skin.

4. Remove the bolts which retain the overdrive unit to the transmission intermediate flange. Pull the unit straight to the rear until it clears the transmission mainshaft.

To install:

5. Reverse the above procedure to install. Install the overdrive oil pan with a new gasket. After installation of the transmission and overdrive assembly, fill the transmission (which automatically fills the overdrive), to the proper level with the correct lubricant. Check the lubricant level in the transmission after driving 6–9 miles.

CLUTCH

Understanding the Clutch

The purpose of the clutch is to disconnect and connect engine power at the transmission. A vehicle at rest requires a lot of engine torque to get all that weight moving. An internal combustion engine does not develop a high starting torque (unlike steam engines) so it must be allowed to operate without any load until it builds up enough torque to move the vehicle. To a point, torque increases with engine rpm. The clutch allows the engine to build up torque by physically disconnecting the engine from the transmission, relieving the engine of any load or resistance.

The transfer of engine power to the transmission (the load) must be smooth and gradual; if it weren't, drive line components would wear out or break quickly. This gradual power transfer is made possible by gradually releasing the clutch pedal. The clutch disc and pressure plate are the connecting link between the engine and transmission. When the clutch pedal is released, the disc and plate contact each other (the clutch is engaged) physically joining the engine and transmission. When the pedal is pushed in, the disc and plate separate (the clutch is disengaged) disconnecting the engine from the transmission.

Most clutch assemblies consists of the flywheel, the clutch disc, the clutch pressure plate, the throw out bearing and fork, the actuating linkage and the pedal. The flywheel and clutch pressure plate (driving members) are connected to the engine crankshaft and rotate with it. The clutch disc is located between the flywheel and pressure plate, and is splined to the transmission shaft. A driving member is one that is attached to the engine and transfers engine power to a driven member (clutch disc) on the transmission shaft. A driving member (pressure plate) rotates (drives) a driven member (clutch disc) on contact and, in so doing, turns the transmission shaft.

There is a circular diaphragm spring within the pressure plate cover (transmission side). In a relaxed state (when the clutch pedal is fully released) this spring is convex; that is, it is dished outward toward the transmission. Pushing in the clutch pedal actuates the attached linkage. Connected to the other end of this is the throw out fork, which hold the throw out bearing. When the clutch pedal is depressed, the clutch linkage pushes the fork and bearing forward to contact the diaphragm spring of the pressure plate. The outer edges of the spring are secured to the pressure plate and are pivoted on rings so that when the center of the spring is compressed by the throw out bearing, the outer edges bow outward and, by so doing, pull the pressure plate in the

same direction away from the clutch disc. This action separates the disc from the plate, disengaging the clutch and allowing the transmission to be shifted into another gear. A coil type clutch return spring attached to the clutch pedal arm permits full release of the pedal. Releasing the pedal pulls the throw out bearing away from the diaphragm spring resulting in a reversal of spring position. As bearing pressure is gradually released from the spring center, the outer edges of the spring bow outward, pushing the pressure plate into closer contact with the clutch disc. As the disc and plate move closer together, friction between the two increases and slippage is reduced until, when full spring pressure is applied (by fully releasing the pedal) the speed of the disc and plate are the same. This stops all slipping, creating a direct connection between the plate and disc which results in the transfer of power from the engine to the transmission. The clutch disc is now rotating with the pressure plate at engine speed and, because it is splined to the transmission shaft, the shaft now turns at the same engine speed.

The clutch is operating properly if:

1. It will stall the engine when released with the vehicle held stationary.

2. The shift lever can be moved freely between 1st and reverse gears when the vehicle is stationary and the clutch disengaged.

Adjustments

PEDAL FREE-PLAY

4-121 Engine

▶ **See Figure 5**

The clutch pedal free-play is adjusted by varying the length of the control cable. The preferred free-play is 1⅛ in. (28.6mm).

1. To adjust the cable, loosen the cable locknut at the rear of the cable and pull the cable forward until the free-play is eliminated from the throwout lever.

2. Rotate the adjuster nut toward the rear of the cable until the nut tabs contact the clutch housing.

3. Release the cable housing and turn the adjuster nut until the tabs engage the slots on the clutch housing.

4. Tighten the clutch cable locknut. Recheck clutch pedal free-play.

Fig. 5 Clutch linkage assembly—1977–79 4-121 engine

6-Cylinder and V8 Engines

▶ **See Figure 6**

A free-play measurement of ⅞-1⅛ in. (22.23–28.6mm) is acceptable. Adjust the free-play by varying the length of the bellcrank-to-throwout lever rod. Lengthen to reduce and shorten to increase free-play. The easiest way to measure free-play is to hold a yardstick alongside the clutch pedal and press the pedal down until you can feel spring tension.

➡**The 1981 and later 6-cylinder models and all 4-150 and 4-151 models have a hydraulic clutch which requires no adjustment.**

➡**Several different clutch assemblies have been used over the years. For correct clutch identification, see the accompanying illustrations.**

Fig. 6 Exploded view of the clutch pedal and linkage components on 6 and 8-cylinder engines through 1980

REMOVAL & INSTALLATION

4-121 Engine

▸ See Figures 7 and 8

✲✲ CAUTION

The clutch driven disc may contain asbestos, which has been determined to be a cancer causing agent. Never clean clutch surfaces with compressed air! Avoid inhaling any dust from any clutch surface! When cleaning clutch surfaces, use a commercially available brake cleaning fluid.

1. Remove the transmission.
2. Mark the clutch cover and flywheel for reassembly. Remove the cover and driven plate by loosening the bolts alternately and in several stages to avoid cover distortion.

Inspect the flywheel surface for heat cracks, scoring, or blue heat marks. Check the flywheel capscrews for proper torque. It will be necessary to lock-up the flywheel ring gear with a block or flywheel holding clamp tool before tightening these capscrews.

To install:

3. Align the driven plate and the cover on the flywheel with the marks made during removal and install the cover bolts finger-tight. Make sure the cover is engaged with the flywheel dowel pins.
4. Using a clutch alignment tool, align the driven plate. Tighten the cover bolts to 23 ft. lbs.
5. Install the transmission and the clutch housing assembly. It may be necessary to raise the front of the engine.

Fig. 7 Clutch driven plate used on 4-121 engines— 1977–79 models

Fig. 8 Clutch pressure plate used on 1977–79 4-121 engines with HR-1 4-speed transmission and all 1980–82 4-cylinder engines

6. Position the rear crossmember on the side sills and finger-tighten the bolts. Install the transmission-to-crossmember bolts. Tighten the crossmember nuts.

7. The remainder of the installation is the reverse of removal. Be sure, when installing the gearshift lever that the shift rail insert is facing straight down and the offset on the side of the lever fork is facing the right side of the extension housing before installing the lever.

4-150 Engine

▶ **See Figures 9 and 10**

✳✳ CAUTION

The clutch driven disc may contain asbestos, which has been determined to be a cancer causing agent. Never clean clutch surfaces with compressed air! Avoid inhaling any dust from any clutch surface! When cleaning clutch surfaces, use a commercially available brake cleaning fluid.

1. Remove the transmission.
2. Remove the starter.
3. Remove the throwout bearing and sleeve assembly.
4. Remove the bell housing.
5. Mark the clutch cover, pressure plate and the flywheel with a center punch so that these parts can be later installed in the same position.
6. Remove the clutch cover-to-flywheel attaching bolts. When removing these bolts, loosen them in rotation, one or two turns at a time, until the spring tension is released. The clutch cover is a steel stamping which could be warped by improper removal procedures, resulting in clutch chatter when reused.

Fig. 9 Exploded view of the 9 inch clutch assembly—1975–76 models

Fig. 10 Exploded view of the 10 inch clutch assembly—1975–76 models

To install:

7. Remove the clutch assembly from the flywheel.
8. The clutch release bearing (throwout bearing) is lubricated at time of assembly and no attempt should be made to lubricate it. Put a small amount of grease in the pilot bushing.
9. Install the driven plate with the short end of the hub toward the flywheel. Use a spare transmission mainshaft or an aligning arbor to align the pressure plate assembly and the driven plate.
10. Leave the arbor in place while tightening the pressure plate screws evenly a turn or two at a time. Torque the bolts to 40 ft. lbs.
11. Install the bellhousing. Torque the bolts to 40 ft. lbs.
12. Install the throwout bearing and sleeve assembly.
13. Install the starter.
14. Install the transmission.

4-151 Engine

▶ **See Figure 11**

✳✳ CAUTION

The clutch driven disc may contain asbestos, which has been determined to be a cancer causing agent. Never clean clutch surfaces with compressed air! Avoid inhaling any dust from any clutch surface! When cleaning clutch surfaces, use a commercially available brake cleaning fluid.

1. Remove the starter, disconnect the slave cylinder spring at the throwout lever, and remove the transmission.
2. Remove the clutch housing to engine bolts. Remove the housing.

Fig. 11 Typical clutch driven disc used on 4-151 engines

3. Remove the throwout bearing.

4. Matchmark the clutch cover and flywheel for installation. Loosen the clutch cover bolts alternately and evenly, to avoid distortion, and remove the clutch cover and disc.

5. Inspect the parts for signs of overheating (blue color), scoring, or abnormal wear. Overheated parts should be replaced. Deep scoring or wear may require replacement of the disc and cover, and refacing or replacement of the flywheel.

To install:

6. Place the disc and cover on the flywheel, aligning the marks made previously if the same cover is being used. Be sure the cover is engaged with the dowel pins. Install the cover bolts finger-tight.

7. Align the disc with an alignment tool.

8. Tighten the cover bolts alternately and evenly to 23 ft. lbs. Remove the alignment tool.

9. Install the throwout bearing, clutch housing, and transmission. The housing-to-engine bolts and transmission-to-housing bolts should be tightened to 54 ft. lbs.

6 and 8-Cylinder Engines

▶ **See Figures 12, 13 and 14**

1. Remove the transmission and the starter.

2. Disconnect the clutch linkage at the release lever.

3. Remove the capscrews that hold the bellhousing (clutch housing) to the engine. It may be necessary to more the rear of the engine up or down to gain wrench clearance.

➡**Any shims between the housing and engine must be replaced in exactly the same place to prevent misalignment.**

Fig. 12 Clutch pressure plate for all 1977–78 models with SR4 4-speed transmission; 1979–80 6 and 8-cylinder Pacer, Concord and AMX models with SR4 4-speed transmission; 1982 6-cylinder Spirit and Concord models

4. Remove the throwout lever, washer, bearing and sleeve assembly.

5. Matchmark the clutch cover, pressure plate, and flywheel before removal to ensure proper balance.

6. Loosen each clutch cover capscrew a few turns at a time until spring tension is released, then remove the cover, pressure plate, and disc.

To install:

7. Check the pilot bushing in the end of the crankshaft for scoring or looseness. If it is necessary to replace the bushing, use either an expanding end slide hammer or a suitable tap. Screwing the tap into the bore until it bottoms will force the bushing out. Another way to remove the bushing is to pack it and the crankshaft cavity with grease, then insert the clutch shaft aligning tool (dummy pilot shaft) into the bushing and tap it with a soft hammer. The bushing will be pushed out. It is important to clean out all the grease.

Lubricate the bushing with grease before installing the clutch.

Fig. 13 Typical clutch driven disc used on 6 and 8-cylinder engines—1977–82 models

Sometimes there is a lubricating wick, which should be soaked in engine oil, then placed in the crankshaft cavity.

8. Inspect the flywheel surface for heat cracks, scoring, or blue heat marks. Check the flywheel capscrews for proper torque (105 ft. lbs.). It will be necessary to lock-up the flywheel ring gear with a block or flywheel holding clamp tool before tightening these capscrews.

The throwout (release) linkage consists of a forked, pivoted lever contacting the bearing at one end and the linkage pushrod on the other. A return spring keeps the lever in contact with the ball pivot.

The throwout bearing itself is prelubricated and cannot be re-packed if dry. A bad bearing results in uneven clutch pedal pressure and a grinding, rattling noise when the pedal is depressed. Replace any noisy throwout bearings as soon as is practicable to prevent disintegration and possible transmission or clutch damage.

9. Slide the new clutch disc onto the transmission input shaft to check for binding. Remove any burrs from either the splines or hub using emery paper, then clean with a safe solvent.

10. Place the clutch disc against the flywheel and secure it by inserting a dummy pilot shaft (such shafts, made of wood, are

CLUTCH COVER

DIAPHRAGM SPRING

PRESSURE PLATE

Fig. 14 Clutch pressure plate for all 1977–78 3-speed models; 1979 6-cylinder Spirit with 150T 3-speed or SR4 4-speed transmission; 1980 6-cylinder Spirit with 4-speed transmission; 1981 6-cylinder models; 1982 6-cylinder Eagle models

available from automotive jobbers) or an old transmission input shaft.

11. Place the new pressure plate (it's always a good policy to replace the pressure plate when installing a new disc) in position, after first making sure that the clutch disc is facing the proper direction (the flywheel side is marked), and that the matchmarks are aligned if the old pressure plate is used.

12. Install all the capscrews finger-tight. Tighten the screws a little at a time, working around the pressure plate to avoid distorting it, to 40 ft. lbs. Remove the pilot shaft.

➡**Do not depress the clutch pedal until the transmission is installed or the throwout bearing will fall out.**

13. Install the clutch housing, throwout bearing and transmission. Hook up the clutch linkage and check the adjustment.

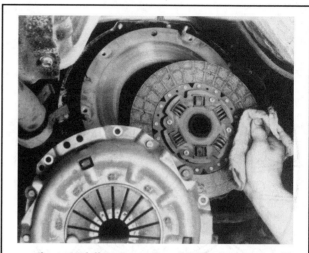

. . . then carefully remove the clutch and pressure plate assembly from the flywheel

Typical clutch alignment tool, note how the splines match the transmission's input shaft

Check across the flywheel surface, it should be flat

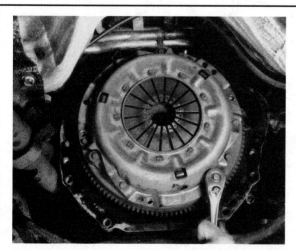

Loosen and remove the clutch and pressure plate bolts evenly, a little at a time . . .

If necessary, lock the flywheel in place and remove the retaining bolts . . .

. . . then remove the flywheel from the crankshaft in order replace it or have it machined

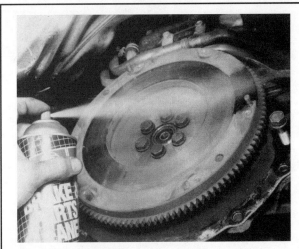

Be sure that the flywheel surface is clean, before installing the clutch

Upon installation, it is usually a good idea to apply a thread-locking compound to the flywheel bolts

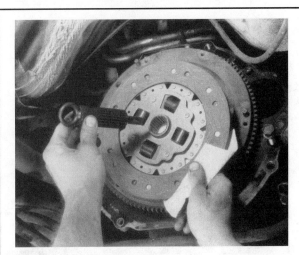

Install a clutch alignment arbor, to align the clutch assembly during installation

Check the pressure plate for excessive wear

Clutch plate installed with the arbor in place

Clutch plate and pressure plate installed with the alignment arbor in place

Install the clutch assembly bolts and tighten in steps, using an X pattern

Pressure plate-to-flywheel bolt holes should align

Be sure to use a torque wrench to tighten all bolts

You may want to use a thread locking compound on the clutch assembly bolts

View of the clutch and pressure plate assembly

Troubleshooting the Manual Transmission and Transfer Case

Problem	Cause	Solution
Transmission shifts hard	• Clutch adjustment incorrect • Clutch linkage or cable binding • Shift rail binding	• Adjust clutch • Lubricate or repair as necessary • Check for mispositioned selector arm roll pin, loose cover bolts, worn shift rail bores, worn shift rail, distorted oil seal, or extension housing not aligned with case. Repair as necessary.
	• Internal bind in transmission caused by shift forks, selector plates, or synchronizer assemblies • Clutch housing misalignment • Incorrect lubricant • Block rings and/or cone seats worn	• Remove, dissemble and inspect transmission. Replace worn or damaged components as necessary. • Check runout at rear face of clutch housing • Drain and refill transmission • Blocking ring to gear clutch tooth face clearance must be 0.030 inch or greater. If clearance is correct it may still be necessary to inspect blocking rings and cone seats for excessive wear. Repair as necessary.
Gear clash when shifting from one gear to another	• Clutch adjustment incorrect • Clutch linkage or cable binding • Clutch housing misalignment • Lubricant level low or incorrect lubricant • Gearshift components, or synchronizer assemblies worn or damaged	• Adjust clutch • Lubricate or repair as necessary • Check runout at rear of clutch housing • Drain and refill transmission and check for lubricant leaks if level was low. Repair as necessary. • Remove, disassemble and inspect transmission. Replace worn or damaged components as necessary.
Transmission noisy	• Lubricant level low or incorrect lubricant • Clutch housing-to-engine, or transmission-to-clutch housing bolts loose • Dirt, chips, foreign material in transmission • Gearshift mechanism, transmission gears, or bearing components worn or damaged • Clutch housing misalignment	• Drain and refill transmission. If lubricant level was low, check for leaks and repair as necessary. • Check and correct bolt torque as necessary • Drain, flush, and refill transmission • Remove, disassemble and inspect transmission. Replace worn or damaged components as necessary. • Check runout at rear face of clutch housing
Jumps out of gear	• Clutch housing misalignment • Gearshift lever loose • Offset lever nylon insert worn or lever attaching nut loose • Gearshift mechanism, shift forks, selector plates, interlock plate, selector arm, shift rail, detent plugs, springs or shift cover worn or damaged • Clutch shaft or roller bearings worn or damaged	• Check runout at rear face of clutch housing • Check lever for worn fork. Tighten loose attaching bolts. • Remove gearshift lever and check for loose offset lever nut or worn insert. Repair or replace as necessary. • Remove, disassemble and inspect transmission cover assembly. Replace worn or damaged components as necessary. • Replace clutch shaft or roller bearings as necessary

Troubleshooting the Manual Transmission and Transfer Case (cont.)

Problem	Cause	Solution
Jumps out of gear (cont.)	• Gear teeth worn or tapered, synchronizer assemblies worn or damaged, excessive end play caused by worn thrust washers or output shaft gears	• Remove, disassemble, and inspect transmission. Replace worn or damaged components as necessary.
	• Pilot bushing worn	• Replace pilot bushing
Will not shift into one gear	• Gearshift selector plates, interlock plate, or selector arm, worn, damaged, or incorrectly assembled	• Remove, disassemble, and inspect transmission cover assembly. Repair or replace components as necessary.
	• Shift rail detent plunger worn, spring broken, or plug loose	• Tighten plug or replace worn or damaged components as necessary
	• Gearshift lever worn or damaged	• Replace gearshift lever
	• Synchronizer sleeves or hubs, damaged or worn	• Remove, disassemble and inspect transmission. Replace worn or damaged components.
Locked in one gear—cannot be shifted out	• Shift rail(s) worn or broken, shifter fork bent, setscrew loose, center detent plug missing or worn	• Inspect and replace worn or damaged parts
	• Broken gear teeth on countershaft gear, clutch shaft, or reverse idler gear	• Inspect and replace damaged part
	Gearshift lever broken or worn, shift mechanism in cover incorrectly assembled or broken, worn damaged gear train components	• Disassemble transmission. Replace damaged parts or assemble correctly.
Transfer case difficult to shift or will not shift into desired range	• Vehicle speed too great to permit shifting	• Stop vehicle and shift into desired range. Or reduce speed to 3–4 km/h (2–3 mph) before attempting to shift.
	• If vehicle was operated for extended period in 4H mode on dry paved surface, driveline torque load may cause difficult shifting	• Stop vehicle, shift transmission to neutral, shift transfer case to 2H mode and operate vehicle in 2H on dry paved surfaces
	• Transfer case external shift linkage binding	• Lubricate or repair or replace linkage, or tighten loose components as necessary
	• Insufficient or incorrect lubricant	• Drain and refill to edge of fill hole with SAE 85W-90 gear lubricant only
	• Internal components binding, worn, or damaged	• Disassemble unit and replace worn or damaged components as necessary
Transfer case noisy in all drive modes	• Insufficient or incorrect lubricant	• Drain and refill to edge of fill hole with SAE 85W-90 gear lubricant only. Check for leaks and repair if necessary. Note: If unit is still noisy after drain and refill, disassembly and inspection may be required to locate source of noise.

Troubleshooting the Manual Transmission and Transfer Case (cont.)

Problem	Cause	Solution
Noisy in—or jumps out of four wheel drive low range	• Transfer case not completely engaged in 4L position	• Stop vehicle, shift transfer case in Neutral, then shift back into 4L position
	• Shift linkage loose or binding	• Tighten, lubricate, or repair linkage as necessary
	• Shift fork cracked, inserts worn, or fork is binding on shift rail	• Disassemble unit and repair as necessary
Lubricant leaking from output shaft seals or from vent	• Transfer case overfilled	• Drain to correct level
	• Vent closed or restricted	• Clear or replace vent if necessary
Lubricant leaking from output shaft seals or from vent (cont.)	• Output shaft seals damaged or installed incorrectly	• Replace seals. Be sure seal lip faces interior of case when installed. Also be sure yoke seal surfaces are not scored or nicked. Remove scores, nicks with fine sandpaper or replace yoke(s) if necessary.
Abnormal tire wear	• Extended operation on dry hard surface (paved) roads in 4H range	• Operate in 2H on hard surface (paved) roads

Manual Transmission Application Chart

Transmission Types	Years	Models
HR-1	1978–79	All models w/4-121
Tremec T-150 3-sp	1975–76	All except 6-cylinder Gremlin
	1977–78	Standard on all 6-cylinder models
	1979	Spirit w/6-232
Warner SR-4 4-sp	1977–78	Optional on all 6-cylinder models
	1979	All except 6-232 Spirit & models w/4-121
	1980–82	Standard on all models*
Warner T-4 4-sp	1982–88	Standard on all models*
Warner T-5 5-sp	1982–88	Optional on all models
	1987	Standard on all models
Warner T-14 3-sp	1975–76	Gremlin w/ 6-cylinder engine

*1982 models may come equipped with either the SR-4 or T-4, depending on availability. Make sure you know which one you have, in as much as the SR-4 uses GL-5 85W-90 gear oil and the T-4 uses Dexron® II ATF fluid. The easiest way to tell is by shift pattern: The SR-4 reverse position is to the extreme left; the T-4 reverse is to the extreme right.

Troubleshooting Basic Clutch Problems

Problem	Cause
Excessive clutch noise	Throwout bearing noises are more audible at the lower end of pedal travel. The usual causes are: • Riding the clutch • Too little pedal free-play • Lack of bearing lubrication A bad clutch shaft pilot bearing will make a high pitched squeal, when the clutch is disengaged and the transmission is in gear or within the first 2″ of pedal travel. The bearing must be replaced. Noise from the clutch linkage is a clicking or snapping that can be heard or felt as the pedal is moved completely up or down. This usually requires lubrication. Transmitted engine noises are amplified by the clutch housing and heard in the passenger compartment. They are usually the result of insufficient pedal free-play and can be changed by manipulating the clutch pedal.
Clutch slips (the car does not move as it should when the clutch is engaged)	This is usually most noticeable when pulling away from a standing start. A severe test is to start the engine, apply the brakes, shift into high gear and SLOWLY release the clutch pedal. A healthy clutch will stall the engine. If it slips it may be due to: • A worn pressure plate or clutch plate • Oil soaked clutch plate • Insufficient pedal free-play
Clutch drags or fails to release	The clutch disc and some transmission gears spin briefly after clutch disengagement. Under normal conditions in average temperatures, 3 seconds is maximum spin-time. Failure to release properly can be caused by: • Too light transmission lubricant or low lubricant level • Improperly adjusted clutch linkage
Low clutch life	Low clutch life is usually a result of poor driving habits or heavy duty use. Riding the clutch, pulling heavy loads, holding the car on a grade with the clutch instead of the brakes and rapid clutch engagement all contribute to low clutch life.

AUTOMATIC TRANSMISSION

Understanding Automatic Transmissions

The automatic transmission allows engine torque and power to be transmitted to the rear wheels within a narrow range of engine operating speeds. It will allow the engine to turn fast enough to produce plenty of power and torque at very low speeds, while keeping it at a sensible rpm at high vehicle speeds (and it does this job without driver assistance). The transmission uses a light fluid as the medium for the transmission of power. This fluid also works in the operation of various hydraulic control circuits and as a lubricant. Because the transmission fluid performs all of these functions, trouble within the unit can easily travel from one part to another. For this reason, and because of the complexity and unusual operating principles of the transmission, a very sound understanding of the basic principles of operation will simplify troubleshooting.

TORQUE CONVERTER

The torque converter replaces the conventional clutch. It has three functions:

1. It allows the engine to idle with the vehicle at a standstill, even with the transmission in gear.

2. It allows the transmission to shift from range-to-range smoothly, without requiring that the driver close the throttle during the shift.

3. It multiplies engine torque to an increasing extent as vehicle speed drops and throttle opening is increased. This has the effect of making the transmission more responsive and reduces the amount of shifting required.

The torque converter is a metal case which is shaped like a sphere that has been flattened on opposite sides. It is bolted to the rear end of the engine's crankshaft. Generally, the entire metal case rotates at engine speed and serves as the engine's flywheel.

The case contains three sets of blades. One set is attached directly to the case. This set forms the torus or pump. Another set is directly connected to the output shaft, and forms the turbine. The third set is mounted on a hub which, in turn, is mounted on a stationary shaft through a one-way clutch. This third set is known as the stator.

A pump, which is driven by the converter hub at engine speed, keeps the torque converter full of transmission fluid at all times. Fluid flows continuously through the unit to provide cooling.

Under low speed acceleration, the torque converter functions as follows:

The torus is turning faster than the turbine. It picks up fluid at the center of the converter and, through centrifugal force, slings it outward. Since the outer edge of the converter moves faster than the portions at the center, the fluid picks up speed.

The fluid then enters the outer edge of the turbine blades. It then travels back toward the center of the converter case along the turbine blades. In impinging upon the turbine blades, the fluid loses the energy picked up in the torus.

If the fluid was now returned directly into the torus, both halves of the converter would have to turn at approximately the same speed at all times, and torque input and output would both be the same.

In flowing through the torus and turbine, the fluid picks up two types of flow, or flow in two separate directions. It flows through the turbine blades, and it spins with the engine. The stator, whose blades are stationary when the vehicle is being accelerated at low speeds, converts one type of flow into another. Instead of allowing the fluid to flow straight back into the torus, the stator's curved blades turn the fluid almost 90° toward the direction of rotation of the engine. Thus the fluid does not flow as fast toward the torus, but is already spinning when the torus picks it up. This has the effect of allowing the torus to turn much faster than the turbine. This difference in speed may be compared to the difference in speed between the smaller and larger gears in any gear train. The result is that engine power output is higher, and engine torque is multiplied.

As the speed of the turbine increases, the fluid spins faster and faster in the direction of engine rotation. As a result, the ability of the stator to redirect the fluid flow is reduced. Under cruising conditions, the stator is eventually forced to rotate on its one-way clutch in the direction of engine rotation. Under these conditions, the torque converter begins to behave almost like a solid shaft, with the torus and turbine speeds being almost equal.

PLANETARY GEARBOX

The ability of the torque converter to multiply engine torque is limited. Also, the unit tends to be more efficient when the turbine is rotating at relatively high speeds. Therefore, a planetary gearbox is used to carry the power output of the turbine to the driveshaft.

Planetary gears function very similarly to conventional transmission gears. However, their construction is different in that three elements make up one gear system, and, in that all three elements are different from one another. The three elements are: an outer gear that is shaped like a hoop, with teeth cut into the inner surface; a sun gear, mounted on a shaft and located at the very center of the outer gear; and a set of three planet gears, held by pins

The torque converter housing is rotated by the engine's crankshaft, and turns the impeller—The impeller then spins the turbine, which gives motion to the turbine shaft, driving the gears

in a ring-like planet carrier, meshing with both the sun gear and the outer gear. Either the outer gear or the sun gear may be held stationary, providing more than one possible torque multiplication factor for each set of gears. Also, if all three gears are forced to rotate at the same speed, the gearset forms, in effect, a solid shaft.

Most automatics use the planetary gears to provide various reductions ratios. Bands and clutches are used to hold various portions of the gearsets to the transmission case or to the shaft on which they are mounted. Shifting is accomplished, then, by changing the portion of each planetary gearset which is held to the transmission case or to the shaft.

SERVOS & ACCUMULATORS

The servos are hydraulic pistons and cylinders. They resemble the hydraulic actuators used on many other machines, such as bulldozers. Hydraulic fluid enters the cylinder, under pres-

Planetary gears in the minimum reduction (drive) range. The ring gear is allowed to revolve, providing a higher gear ratio

Planetary gears work in a similar fashion to manual transmission gears, but are composed of three parts

Servos, operated by pressure, are used to apply or release the bands, to either hold the ring gear or allow it to rotate

Planetary gears in the maxium reduction (low) range. The ring gear is held and a lower gear ratio is obtained

sure, and forces the piston to move to engage the band or clutches.

The accumulators are used to cushion the engagement of the servos. The transmission fluid must pass through the accumulator on the way to the servo. The accumulator housing contains a thin piston which is sprung away from the discharge passage of the accumulator. When fluid passes through the accumulator on the way to the servo, it must move the piston against spring pressure, and this action smooths out the action of the servo.

HYDRAULIC CONTROL SYSTEM

The hydraulic pressure used to operate the servos comes from the main transmission oil pump. This fluid is channeled to the various servos through the shift valves. There is generally a manual shift valve which is operated by the transmission selector lever and an automatic shift valve for each automatic upshift the transmission provides.

➡**Many new transmissions are electronically controlled. On these models, electrical solenoids are used to better control the hydraulic fluid. Usually, the solenoids are regulated by an electronic control module.**

There are two pressures which affect the operation of these valves. One is the governor pressure which is effected by vehicle speed. The other is the modulator pressure which is effected by intake manifold vacuum or throttle position. Governor pressure rises with an increase in vehicle speed, and modulator pressure rises as the throttle is opened wider. By responding to these two pressures, the shift valves cause the upshift points to be delayed with increased throttle opening to make the best use of the engine's power output.

Most transmissions also make use of an auxiliary circuit for downshifting. This circuit may be actuated by the throttle linkage the vacuum line which actuates the modulator, by a cable or by a solenoid. It applies pressure to a special downshift surface on the shift valve or valves.

The transmission modulator also governs the line pressure, used to actuate the servos. In this way, the clutches and bands will be actuated with a force matching the torque output of the engine.

Transmission

REMOVAL & INSTALLATION

1975–76 Models

1. Disconnect the fan shroud (if equipped).
2. Disconnect the transmission fill tube at the upper bracket.
3. Raise the car on hoist.

✳✳ WARNING

It is necessary that the hood be open to avoid damage to the hood and air cleaner when the rear crossmember is removed.

4. Remove the inspection cover from the front of the converter housing.
5. Rotate the torque converter until the drain plug is accessible. Remove the plug and drain the converter.
6. Remove the transmission fill tube.

Automatic Transmission Application Chart

Transmission	Years	Models
Chrysler 727	1975–76	All w/8-360, 8-401
	1977	Optional on 8-304 HD
		All 8-360
	1978	Optional on 6-258 HD and Fleet uses
		All 8-360
Chrysler 904	1975–77	All w/6-cylinder
	1978–79	All 4- and 6-cylinder engines
	1980	All except Eagle
	1981	All 4-cylinder use a wide ratio version
		6-cylinder, except Eagle, use a standard ratio
	1982	All 4-cylinder models
		6-cylinder, except Eagle, use a lock-up torque converter
	1983	All 4-cylinder models
		6-cylinder, except Eagle and Concords built for fleet sales, use a lock-up torque converter
Chyrsler 998	1975–79	All w/8-304
	1980	All Eagle
	1981–82	6-cylinder Eagle
	1983	6-cylinder Eagle
		Concord sedan and wagon built for fleet sales use a lock-up torque converter
	1984	4-cylinder models use a wide ratio version
		6-cylinder models use a lock-up torque converter
	1985–88	All models use a lock-up torque converter

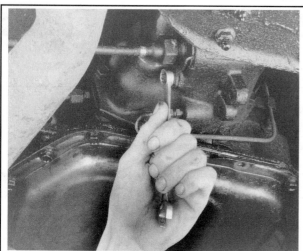

Use a wrench to unfasten the speedometer cable retaining clip

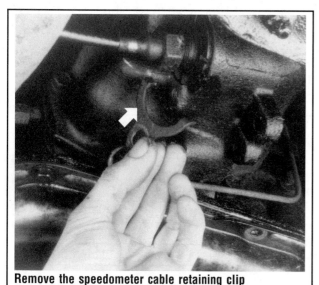

Remove the speedometer cable retaining clip

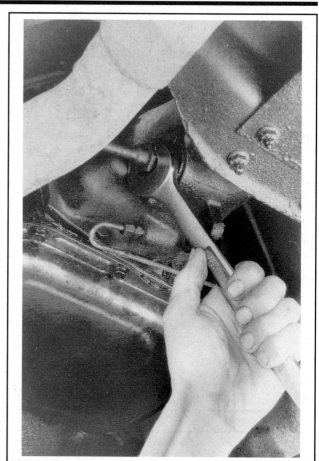

Unbolt the retaining nut and disengage the speedometer cable from the transmission

7. Remove the starter.

8. Mark the rear universal joint and yoke for alignment reference during installation.

9. Remove the driveshaft.

10. Disconnect the catalytic converter(s) (if equipped) and front exhaust pipes to provide working clearance.

11. Disconnect the front exhaust pipe brace from the transmission.

12. Disconnect the speedometer cable, throttle and shift linkage, neutral safety, TCS switch wires, fluid cooler lines, and the governor pressure oil line from the transmission to the TCS control switch.

13. Mark the converter drive plate and converter for alignment reference during installation.

14. Remove the bolts which attach the converter to the drive plate.

15. Place the transmission jack under the transmission.

16. Remove the crossmember from the side sill and rear support cushion.

17. Remove the support cushion and adapter from the extension housing.

18. Remove the bolts which attach the transmission to the engine.

19. Move the transmission and converter a sufficient distance to clear the crankshaft.

20. Maintain pressure against the converter and lower the assembly until the transmission housing clears the engine.

To install:

21. If the torque converter is removed, insert Pump Aligning Tool J-24033 (Models 904-998), J-24045 (Model 727) or other equivalents into the pump.

22. Engage the pump rotor.

23. Rotate the tool until the drilled holes in the tool are vertical.

24. Remove the tool.

25. Rotate the converter until the pump drive slots are vertical, and carefully install the converter into pump.

26. Place the assembly on a transmission jack.

27. Raise the transmission assembly and align the converter with the drive plate. Refer to the marks made during removal.

28. Raise the transmission and slide it forward.

29. Raise, lower, or tilt the transmission to align the converter housing pilot holes with the dowels in the engine.

30. Install the two lower converter housing attaching bolts and pull the housing up snugly.

31. Install the remaining attaching bolts.

32. Tighten all the converter housing attaching bolts to 28 ft. lbs.

33. Install the rear crossmember, rear support cushion and adapter.

34. Remove the transmission jack.

35. Install the screws which attach the torque converter to the drive plate.

36. Install the drain plug.

37. Install the inspection cover.

38. Install the starter.

39. Connect the neutral safety switch, TCS switch, throttle and shift linkages, fluid cooler lines, and speedometer cable.

40. Install the transmission filler tube in the transmission.

41. Install the driveshaft. Refer to the alignment marks made during removal.

42. Connect the front exhaust pipes, catalytic converter(s) (if equipped), and lower the car.

43. Connect the filler tube upper bracket.

44. Fill the transmission to the correct level.

45. Adjust the manual throttle linkage.

46. Road test the car for proper transmission operation.

1977–79 Models

4-121 ENGINE

1. Open the hood.

☀☀ WARNING

The hood must remain open to avoid damaging the hood and air cleaner when the rear crossmember is removed.

2. Disconnect the fan shroud.

3. Remove the bolt attaching the transmission filler tube to the rear of the engine.

4. Place the gearshift lever in Neutral.

5. Raise and support the car on jackstands.

6. Mark the driveshaft and yoke for assembly alignment reference.

7. Remove the driveshaft.

8. Remove the starter motor.

9. Remove the speedometer adapter and cable assembly. Cover the adapter bore in the case after removal.

10. Disconnect the gearshift and throttle linkage. On cars with column shift, remove the bolt attaching the linkage bellcrank bracket to the converter housing.

11. Remove the cover at the front of the converter housing.

12. Mark the converter drive plate and converter for assembly alignment reference.

13. Remove the bolts attaching the converter to the drive plate. Rotate the crankshaft and drive plate using a ratchet handle and socket or box end wrench on the crankshaft front pulley bolt to gain access to the drive plate-to-converter bolts.

➡**The crankshaft pulley bolt is a metric size and requires a 24mm socket or wrench. However, a ¹⁵⁄₁₆ in. (23.8mm) socket or wrench may also be used.**

14. Support the transmission using a transmission jack. Retain the transmission on the jack using a safety chain.

15. Lower the transmission slightly and disconnect the oil cooler lines at the transmission.

16. Remove the bolt attaching the rear support cushion to the rear support cushion bracket (bracket is attached to transmission extension housing).

17. Remove the rear crossmember-to-frame side sill attaching nuts and remove the crossmember and support cushion as assembly.

18. Place the support stand under the front of the engine.

19. Remove the bolts attaching the catalytic converter support bracket to the transmission.

20. Remove the bolts attaching the transmission and filler tube to the engine.

➡**The transmission-to-engine blockbolts are metric size bolts.**

21. Move the transmission and converter rearward until clear of the crankshaft.

22. Hold the converter in position and lower the transmission until the converter housing clears the engine.

☀☀ WARNING

If the transmission was removed to correct a malfunction that generated sludge or heavy accumulations of metal or friction material particles, the oil cooler and cooler lines must be thoroughly flushed and the torque converter replaced. Do not attempt to flush the converter if it is contaminated.

To install:

23. If the torque converter was removed, insert Pump Aligning Tool J-24033 or its equivalent into the pump rotor and engage the tool slots with the pump rotor drive lugs.

24. Rotate the aligning tool until the hole in tool is vertical then remove the tool.

25. Rotate the converter until the pump drive slots in the converter hub are vertical.

26. Carefully insert the converter hub into the oil pump. Be sure the drive lugs of the pump inner rotor are completely engaged with the drive slots in the converter hub.

27. Raise the transmission and align the converter with the drive plate. Refer to the alignment marks made during removal.

28. Move the transmission forward and raise, lower, or tilt the transmission to align the converter housing pilot holes with the dowels in the engine block.

➡**If the downward angle at the rear of the engine is not sufficient to permit transmission installation, raise the front of the engine to increase the downward angle.**

29. Install two, transmission-to-engine lower attaching bolts and tighten the bolts to pull the transmission to the engine.

30. Install the drive plate-to-converter attaching bolts. Tighten them to 26 ft. lbs.

31. Install the remaining transmission-to-engine attaching bolts. Tighten the bolts to 54 ft. lbs.

32. Connect the oil cooler lines.

33. Raise the transmission, position the rear crossmember, in-

stall the crossmember attaching nuts and tighten the nuts to 30 ft. lbs.

34. Install the rear support cushion-to-support cushion bracket bolt and tighten the bolt to 49 ft. lbs.

35. Remove the safety chain and transmission jack.

36. Install the cover at the front of the converter housing.

37. Install the starter motor.

38. Connect the neutral start switch wires to the switch terminal.

39. Connect the gearshift and throttle linkage. On cars with column shift, position the linkage bellcrank bracket on the converter housing and install the bracket attaching bolt.

40. Install the speedometer cable and adapter assembly. Be sure the adapter is correctly indexed.

41. Install the catalytic converter support bracket bolt.

42. Lower the car.

43. Fill the transmission to the correct fluid level.

44. Adjust the gearshift lever, then the throttle linkage.

➡**The gearshift lever adjusting trunnion is located on the steering column shift lever.**

45. Road test the car to check transmission operation.

6- AND 8-CYLINDER ENGINES

1. Disconnect the fan shroud if equipped.
2. Disconnect the transmission fill tube at the upper bracket.
3. Open the hood.

❊❊ WARNING

It is necessary that the hood be open to avoid damaging the hood and air cleaner when the rear crossmember is removed.

4. Raise and support the car on jackstands.

5. Remove the inspection cover from the converter housing.

6. On 6-cylinder cars, remove the screws attaching the clamp to the exhaust pipe support bracket and slide the clamp off the bracket.

7. Remove the transmission fill tube.

8. Mark the driveshaft and rear axle yoke for assembly alignment reference.

9. Remove the driveshaft.

10. On 8-cylinder cars, disconnect the exhaust pipes at the exhaust manifolds.

11. Remove the speedometer adapter and cable assembly. Cover the adapter bore in the case after adapter removal.

12. Disconnect the gearshift and throttle linkage.

13. Disconnect the wires at the neutral start switch.

14. Disconnect the TCS switch oil line at the transmission fitting.

15. Mark the converter drive plate and converter for assembly alignment reference.

16. Remove the bolts attaching the converter to the drive plate. Rotate the crankshaft and drive plate using the ratchet handle and socket on the crankshaft front pulley bolt to gain access to the drive plate bolts.

17. Support the transmission using a transmission jack. Retain the transmission on the jack using a safety chain.

18. Lower the transmission slightly and disconnect the oil cooler lines at the transmission.

19. Remove the bolts attaching the rear support cushion to the transmission.

20. Remove the rear crossmember-to-frame side sill attaching nuts and remove the crossmember. On Pacers, remove the ground strap.

21. Remove the bolts attaching the converter support bracket to the transmission.

22. Remove the bolts attaching the transmission to the engine.

23. Move the transmission and converter rearward to clear the crankshaft.

24. Hold the converter in position and lower the assembly until the converter housing clears the engine.

❊❊ WARNING

If the transmission was removed to correct a malfunction that generated sludge or heavy accumulations of metal particles or friction material, the oil cooler and cooler lines must be flushed thoroughly and the torque converter replaced. Do not attempt to flush the converter if it is contaminated.

To install:

25. If the torque converter was removed, insert Pump Aligning Tool J-24033 or its equivalent in the pump rotor until the rotor drive lugs engage the slots in tool.

26. Rotate the tool until the drilled hole in the tool is vertical and remove the tool.

27. Rotate the converter until the pump drive slots in the converter hub are vertical and carefully insert the converter hub into the pump. Be sure the drive lugs of the pump inner rotor are properly engaged in the drive slots of the converter hub.

28. Raise the transmission and align the converter with the drive plate. Refer to the assembly alignment marks.

29. Pull the transmission forward.

30. Raise, lower, or tilt the transmission to align the converter housing pilot holes with the dowels in the engine.

31. Install the two converter housing lower attaching bolts and tighten the bolts to pull the housing to the engine.

32. Install the drive plate-to-converter attaching bolts.

33. Install the remaining converter housing-to-engine attaching bolts and tighten all bolts to 28 ft. lbs.

34. Connect the oil cooler lines.

35. Install the rear support cushion on the transmission.

36. Raise the transmission, position the rear crossmember, and install the crossmember attaching nuts. On Pacers, install the ground strap.

37. Remove the safety chain and transmission jack.

38. Install the inspection cover.

39. On 6-cylinder cars, install the exhaust pipe support bracket.

40. Install the starter.

41. Connect the wires to the neutral switch.

42. Connect the gearshift and throttle linkage.

43. Install the speedometer cable and adapter assembly. Be sure the adapter is correctly indexed.

44. Install the driveshaft. Refer to the alignment marks made during removal.

45. On 8-cylinder cars, connect the front exhaust pipes and the catalytic converter support bracket bolts.

46. Lower the car.
47. Fill the transmission to the correct level.
48. Adjust the gearshift selector lever linkage.
49. Road test the car to check transmission operation.

1980–81 Models

4-151 ENGINE

1. Open the hood.

✳✳ WARNING

The hood must remain open to avoid damaging the hood and air cleaner when the rear crossmember is removed.

2. Disconnect the fan shroud.
3. Remove the bolt attaching the transmission fill tube to the engine.
4. Place the gearshift lever in Neutral.
5. Raise and support the car on jackstands.
6. Mark the driveshaft and yoke for assembly alignment reference. On Eagle models, also remove the skid plate.
7. Remove the driveshafts.
8. Remove the starter motor. On Eagle models, also remove the stiffening braces.
9. Remove the speedometer adapter and cable assembly. Cover the adapter bore after removal.
10. Disconnect the gearshift and throttle linkage. On automobiles with column shift, remove the bolt attaching linkage bellcrank bracket to the converter housing.
11. Remove the cover at the front of the converter housing.
12. Mark the converter drive plate and the converter for assembly alignment reference.
13. Remove the bolts attaching the converter to the drive plate. Rotate the crankshaft and drive plate using the ratchet handle and socket or box end wrench on the crankshaft front pulley bolt to gain access to the drive plate plate-to-converter bolts.

➡The crankshaft pulley bolt is a metric size bolt.

14. Support the transmission using a transmission jack. Retain the transmission on the jack using a safety chain.

➡On Eagle models, both the transmission and transfer case must be properly supported on the transmission jack and retained with a safety chain.

15. Disconnect the oil cooler lines at the transmission.
16. Remove the bolt attaching the rear support cushion to the rear support cushion bracket (bracket is attached to transmission extension housing).
17. Remove the rear crossmember attaching nuts and remove the crossmember and support cushion as assembly.
18. Place a support stand under the front of the engine.
19. Remove the bolts attaching the catalytic converter support bracket to the transmission, if equipped.
20. Remove the fill tube.
21. Remove the bolts attaching the transmission to the engine.

➡The transmission-to-engine blockbolts are metric size bolts.

22. Move the transmission (and transfer case, if equipped) and converter rearward until clear of the crankshaft.
23. Hold the converter in position and lower the transmission until the transmission converter housing clears the engine.

✳✳ WARNING

If the transmission was removed to correct a malfunction that generated sludge or heavy accumulations of metal or friction material particles, the oil cooler and cooler lines must be thoroughly flushed and the torque converter replaced. Do not attempt to flush the converter if it is contaminated.

To install:
24. If the torque converter was removed, insert Pump Aligning Tool J-24033 or its equivalent into the pump rotor and engage the tool slots with the pump rotor drive lugs.
25. Rotate the aligning tool until the hole in the tool is vertical, then remove the tool.
26. Rotate the converter until the pump drive slots in the converter hub are vertical.
27. Carefully insert the converter hub into the oil pump. Be sure the drive lugs of the pump inner rotor are completely engaged with the drive slots in the converter hub.
28. Raise the transmission and align the converter with the drive plate. Refer to the alignment marks made during removal.
29. Move the transmission forward and raise, lower, or tilt the transmission to align the transmission converter housing dowel holes with the dowels in the engine block.

➡If the downward angle at the rear of the engine is not sufficient to permit transmission installation, raise the front of the engine to increase the downward angle.

30. Install two transmission-to-engine lower attaching bolts and tighten the bolts evenly to pull the transmission to the engine.
31. Install the drive plate-to-converter attaching bolts. Tighten the bolts to 40 ft. lbs.

➡Coat the threads of the drive plate-to-converter attaching bolts with Loctite®271 or equivalent.

32. Install the remaining transmission-to-engine attaching bolts. Tighten the bolts to 54 ft. lbs.
33. Connect the oil cooler lines.
34. Install rear crossmember and support cushion. Tighten attaching nuts to 30 ft. lbs.
35. Install the rear support cushion-to-support cushion bracket bolt. Tighten the bolt to 48 ft. lbs.
36. Remove the safety chain and transmission jack.
37. Install the converter housing inspection cover.
38. Install the starter motor. On Eagle models also install the stiffening brace and skid plate.
39. Connect the neutral start switch wires to the switch terminal.
40. Connect the gearshift and throttle linkage. On automobiles with column shift, position the linkage bellcrank bracket on the converter housing and install the bracket attaching bolt.

41. Install the speedometer cable and adapter assembly. Be sure the adapter is correctly indexed.
42. Connect the catalytic converter, if equipped. On Eagle models, add the correct quantity of transfer case lubricant.
43. Lower the automobile.
44. Fill the transmission to the correct fluid level.
45. Check and adjust the gearshift lever and throttle linkage if necessary.

➡**The gearshift lever adjusting trunnion is located at the lower end of the steering column.**

46. Road test the automobile to check transmission operation.

6-258 ENGINES

1. Disconnect the fan shroud, if equipped.
2. Disconnect the transmission fill tube at the upper bracket.
3. Open the hood.

✳✳ WARNING

It is necessary that the hood be open to avoid damaging the hood and air cleaner when the rear crossmember is removed.

4. Raise and support the automobile on jackstands.
5. Remove the inspection cover from the converter housing.
6. On Spirit and Concord, remove the screw attaching the exhaust pipe clamp to the exhaust pipe support bracket and slide the clamp off the bracket.
7. Remove the transmission fill tube.
8. Remove the starter. On Eagle models, also remove the stiffening braces.
9. Mark the driveshaft(s) and yoke(s) for assembly alignment reference.
10. Remove the driveshaft(s).
11. On Eagle models, disconnect the exhaust pipe and move it aside for working clearance.
12. Remove the speedometer adapter and cable assembly. Discard the adapter and cable seals, they are not reuseable. Cover the adapter bore after removal.
13. Disconnect the gearshift and throttle linkage.
14. Disconnect the wires at the neutral start switch.
15. Mark the converter drive plate and converter for assembly alignment reference.
16. Remove the bolts attaching the converter to the drive plate. Rotate the crankshaft and drive plate using a ratchet handle and socket on the crankshaft from the pulley bolt to gain access to the drive plate bolts.
17. On Eagle models, remove the skid plate and stiffening brace.
18. Support the transmission (and transfer case on Eagle models) using a transmission jack. Retain the transmission on the jack using a safety chain.
19. Disconnect the oil cooler lines at the transmission.
20. Remove the bolts attaching the rear support cushion to the transmission.
21. Remove the rear crossmember.
22. Remove the bolts attaching the transmission to the engine.

23. Move the transmission and converter rearward to clear the crankshaft.
24. Hold the converter in position and lower the transmission assembly until the converter housing clears the engine.

✳✳ WARNING

If the transmission was removed to correct a malfunction that generated sludge or heavy accumulations of metal particles or friction material, the oil cooler and cooler lines must be flushed thoroughly and the torque converter replaced. Do not attempt to flush the converter if it is contaminated.

To install:

25. If the torque converter was removed, insert Pump Aligning Tool J-24033 or its equivalent in the pump rotor until the rotor drive lugs engage the slots in the tool.
26. Rotate the tool until the drilled hole in the tool is vertical and remove the tool.
27. Rotate the converter until the pump drive slots in converter hub are vertical and carefully insert the converter hub into the pump. Be sure the drive lugs of the pump inner rotor are properly engaged in the drive slots of the converter hub.
28. Raise the transmission (and transfer case on Eagle models) and align the converter with the drive plate. Refer to the assembly alignment marks.
29. Move the transmission forward.
30. Raise, lower, or tilt the transmission to align the converter housing pilot holes with the dowels in the engine block.
31. Install two transmission lower attaching bolts and tighten the bolts evenly to pull the transmission to the engine.
32. Install the drive plate-to-converter attaching bolts.
33. Install the remaining transmission attaching bolts and tighten all bolts to 28 ft. lbs.
34. Connect the oil cooler lines.
35. Install the rear support cushion on the transmission, if removed.
36. Install the rear crossmember.
37. Remove the safety chain and transmission jack.
38. Install the inspection cover.
39. On Spirit and Concord, install the exhaust pipe clamp on the support bracket.
40. Install the starter. On Eagle models, also install the stiffening braces.
41. Connect the wires to the neutral switch.
42. Connect the gearshift and throttle linkage.
43. Install the speedometer cable and adapter assembly. Be sure the adapter is correctly indexed.
44. On Eagle models, connect the exhaust pipes, attach the stiffening brace and install the skid plate.
45. Install the driveshaft(s). Refer to the alignment marks made during removal. On Eagle models, add the correct quantity of transfer case lubricant.
46. Lower the automobile.
47. Fill the transmission to correct level.
48. Check and adjust the gearshift and throttle linkage if necessary.
49. Road test the automobile to check transmission operation.

1982 Models

4-151 ENGINE

1. Open the hood.

✳✳ WARNING

The hood must remain open to avoid damaging the hood and air cleaner when the rear crossmember is removed.

2. Disconnect the fan shroud.
3. Remove the bolt attaching the transmission fill tube to the engine.
4. Place the gearshift lever in Neutral.
5. Raise and support the automobile on jackstands.
6. Mark the driveshaft and yoke for assembly alignment reference. On Eagle models, also remove the skid plate.
7. Remove the driveshafts.
8. On Eagle models, disconnect the exhaust system at the exhaust manifold, loosen the exhaust system hangers and move the exhaust system as necessary to gain work space.
9. Remove the starter motor. On Eagle models, also remove the stiffening braces.
10. Remove the speedometer adapter and cable assembly. Cover the adapter bore after removal.
11. Disconnect the gearshift and throttle linkage. On automobiles with column shift, remove the bolt attaching the linkage bellcrank bracket to the converter housing.
12. Remove the cover at the front of the converter housing.
13. Mark the converter drive plate and converter for assembly alignment reference.
14. Remove the bolts attaching the converter to the drive plate. Rotate the crankshaft and drive plate using a ratchet handle and socket or box end wrench on the crankshaft front pulley bolt to gain access to the drive plate-to-converter bolts.

➡**The crankshaft pulley bolt is a metric size bolt.**

15. Support the transmission using a transmission jack. Retain the transmission on the jack using a safety chain.

✳✳ CAUTION

On Eagle models, both the transmission and transfer case must be properly supported on the transmission jack and retained with a safety chain.

16. Disconnect the oil cooler lines at the transmission.
17. Remove the bolt attaching the rear support cushion to the rear support cushion bracket (bracket is attached to transmission extension housing).
18. Remove the rear crossmember attaching nuts and remove the crossmember and support cushion as assembly.
19. Place the support stand under the front of the engine.
20. Remove the bolts attaching the catalytic converter support bracket to the transmission, if equipped.
21. Remove the fill tube.
22. Remove the bolts attaching the transmission to the engine.

➡**The transmission-to-engine blockbolts are metric size bolts.**

23. Move the transmission (and transfer case, if equipped) and converter rearward until clear of the crankshaft.
24. Hold the converter in position and lower the transmission until the transmission converter housing clears the engine.

✳✳ WARNING

If the transmission was removed to correct a malfunction that generated sludge or heavy accumulations of metal or friction material particles, the oil cooler and cooler lines must be thoroughly flushed and the torque converter replaced. Do not attempt to flush the converter if it is contaminated.

To install:

25. If the torque converter was removed, insert Pump Aligning Tool J-24033 or its equivalent into the pump rotor and engage the tool slots with the pump rotor drive lugs.
26. Rotate the aligning tool until the hole in tool is vertical, then remove the tool.
27. Rotate the converter until the pump drive slots in the converter hub are vertical.
28. Carefully insert the converter hub into the oil pump. Be sure the drive lugs of the pump inner rotor are completely engaged with the drive slots in the converter hub.
29. Raise the transmission and align the converter with the drive plate. Refer to the alignment marks made during removal.

✳✳ CAUTION

On Eagle models, both the transmission and transfer case must be supported on a transmission jack and retained with a safety chain.

30. Move the transmission forward and raise, lower, or tilt the transmission to align the transmission converter housing dowel holes with the dowels in the engine block.

➡**If the downward angle at the rear of the engine is not sufficient to permit transmission installation, raise the front of the engine to increase the downward angle.**

31. Install two transmission-to-engine lower attaching bolts and tighten the bolts evenly to pull the transmission to the engine.
32. Install the drive plate-to-converter attaching bolts. Tighten the bolts to 40 ft. lbs.

➡**Coat the threads of the drive plate-to-converter attaching bolts with Loctite®271, or equivalent.**

33. Install the remaining transmission-to-engine attaching bolts. Tighten the bolts to 54 ft. lbs.
34. Connect the oil cooler lines.
35. Install the driveshaft using the reference marks made during disassembly.
36. Install the rear crossmember and support cushion. Tighten the attaching nuts to 30 ft. lbs.
37. Install the rear support cushion-to-support cushion bracket bolt. Tighten the bolt to 48 ft. lbs.
38. Remove the safety chain and transmission cover.

39. Install the converter housing inspection cover.
40. Install the starter motor. On Eagle models also install the stiffening brace and skid plate.
41. Connect the neutral start switch wires to the switch terminal.
42. Connect the gearshift and throttle linkage. On automobiles with column shift, position the linkage bellcrank bracket on the converter housing and install the bracket attaching bolt.
43. Install the speedometer cable and adapter assembly. Be sure the adapter is correctly indexed.
44. Connect the catalytic converter, if equipped. On Eagle models, add the correct quantity of transfer case lubricant.
45. Lower the automobile.
46. Fill the transmission to the correct fluid level.
47. Check and adjust the gearshift lever and throttle linkage, if necessary.

➡**The gearshift lever adjusting trunnion is located at the lower end of the steering column.**

48. Road test the automobile to check transmission operation.

6-258 ENGINE

1. Disconnect the fan shroud, if equipped.
2. Disconnect the transmission fill tube at upper bracket.
3. Open the hood.

❊❊ WARNING

It is necessary that the hood be open to avoid damaging the hood and air cleaner when the rear crossmember is removed.

4. Raise and support the car on jackstands.
5. Remove the inspection cover from the converter housing.
6. On Spirit and Concord, remove the screw attaching the exhaust pipe clamp to the exhaust pipe support bracket and slide the clamp off the bracket.
7. Remove the transmission fill tube.
8. Remove the starter. On Eagle models, also remove the stiffening braces.
9. Mark the driveshaft(s) and yoke(s) for assembly alignment reference.
10. Remove the driveshaft(s).
11. On Eagle models, disconnect the exhaust pipe and move it aside for working clearance.
12. Remove the speedometer adapter and cable assembly. Discard the adapter and cable seals, they are not reuseable. Cover the adapter bore after removal.
13. Disconnect the gearshift and throttle linkage.
14. Disconnect the wires at the neutral start switch.
15. Mark the converter drive plate and converter for assembly alignment reference.
16. Remove the bolts attaching the converter to the drive plate. Rotate the crankshaft and drive plate using a ratchet handle and socket on the crankshaft front pulley bolt to gain access to the drive plate bolts.
17. On Eagle models, remove the skid plate and stiffening braces.

❊❊ CAUTION

Support the transmission (and transfer case on Eagle models) using a transmission jack. Retain the transmission on the jack using a safety chain.

18. Disconnect the oil cooler lines at the transmission.
19. Remove the bolts attaching the rear support cushion to the transmission.
20. Remove the rear crossmember.
21. Remove the bolts attaching the transmission to the engine.
22. Move the transmission and converter rearward to clear the crankshaft.
23. Hold the converter in position and lower the transmission assembly until the converter housing clears the engine.

To install:
24. If the torque converter was removed, insert Pump Aligning Tool J-24033 or its equivalent in the pump rotor until the rotor drive lugs engage the slots in the tool.
25. Rotate the tool until the drilled hole in the tool is vertical and remove the tool.
26. Rotate the converter until the pump drive slots in the converter hub are vertical and carefully insert the converter hub into the pump. Be sure the drive lugs of the pump inner rotor are properly engaged in the drive slots of the converter hub.
27. Raise the transmission (and transfer case on Eagle models) and align the converter with the drive plate. Refer to the assembly alignment marks.
28. Move the transmission forward.
29. Raise, lower, or tilt the transmission to align the converter housing pilot holes with the dowels in the engine block.
30. Install the two transmission lower attaching bolts and tighten the bolts evenly to pull the transmission to the engine.
31. Install the drive plate-to-converter attaching bolts.
32. Install the remaining transmission attaching bolts and tighten all bolts to 28 ft. lbs.
33. Connect the oil cooler lines.
34. Install the rear support cushion on the transmission, if removed.
35. Install the rear crossmember.
36. Remove the safety chain and transmission jack.
37. Install the inspection cover.
38. On Spirit and Concord, install the exhaust pipe clamp on the support bracket.
39. Install the starter. On Eagle models, also install the stiffening braces.
40. Connect the wires to the neutral switch.
41. Connect the gearshift and throttle linkage.
42. Install the speedometer cable and adapter assembly. Be sure the adapter is correctly indexed.
43. On Eagle models, connect the exhaust pipes, attach the stiffening brace and install the skid plate.
44. Install the driveshaft(s). Refer to the alignment marks made during removal. On Eagle models, add the correct quantity of transfer case lubricant.
45. Lower the automobile.
46. Fill the transmission to the correct level.
47. Check and adjust the gearshift and throttle linkage, if necessary.
48. Road test the automobile to check transmission operation.

Adjustments

LOW & REVERSE BAND

All 904; 1978 and Later 998

♦ **See Figure 15**

1. Drain the fluid and remove the pan.
2. On 6-cylinder models:
    a. Remove the adjusting screw locknut.
    b. Tighten the adjusting screw to 41 inch lbs.
  On some early Pacers, and all 998, torque the screw to 72 inch lbs.
    c. Back the adjusting screw out 7 turns. (3¼ turns on early 1975 Pacers).

d. Hold the adjusting screw, install the locknut, and tighten the locknut to 35 ft. lbs.

➡**Heavy duty fleet versions of the 258 six and 304 V8 use the same transmission as the 360 and 401 V8. Thus, these models would follow the adjustment procedure for the 360 and 401 V8.**

3. On V8 models:
    a. Loosen the locknut and back it off 5 turns.
    b. Tighten the adjusting screw to 72 inch lbs.
    c. Back the adjusting screw out 4 turns with the 304 V8 and 2 turns with the 360 and 401 V8's.
    d. Hold the adjusting screw and tighten the locknut to 35 ft. lbs.
4. Install the pan with a new gasket. Tighten the screws to 150 in.lb. Fill the transmission as explained in Section 1.

TO COOLER   KICKDOWN BAND ADJUSTING SCREW

FROM COOLER

THROTTLE LEVER

GEARSHIFT CONTROL LEVER

NEUTRAL START SWITCH

Fig. 15 Common automatic transmission adjustment points and controls

LOW & REVERSE BAND

All 727 and 1975–77 998

◆ **See Figure 16**

1. Raise the car, drain the transmission, and remove the pan.
2. Loosen the locknut on the adjusting screw and back off the locknut about 5 turns. Be sure the adjusting screw is free to turn.
3. Tighten the adjusting screw to exactly 72 inch lbs. of torque.
4. Back off the adjusting screw exactly to specification. Hold the adjusting screw to keep it from turning and tighten the locknut to 30–35 ft. lbs.
   - 998 4 turns
   - 727 2 turns
5. Install the pan using a new gasket. Tighten the pan bolts to 150 inch lbs. Refill the transmission with DEXRON®II fluid.

KICK-DOWN BAND

The adjustment screw for the kickdown band is located on the left side of the transmission, above the throttle and manual linkage levers.

1. Loosen the locknut and back it off 5 turns.
2. Using a torque wrench, tighten the screw to 72 inch lbs.

3. Back off the adjusting screw:
   - 998 and 727, 1972–77 2½ turns
   - 904 2 turns
   - 998, 1978 and later 2 turns
   1978 2½ turns
4. Hold the adjusting screw and tighten the locknut to 29 ft. lbs.

SHIFT LINKAGE

The function of this adjustment is to make sure that the transmission is fully engaged in each range position. If this is not the case, there could be severe damage due to slippage.

1. With the engine off, place the selector in Park and the transmission shifting lever in the Park detent.
2. Adjust the shift rod, as necessary, for a free pin fit.
3. See that the steering column lock and the Neutral safety switch operate properly.

THROTTLE LINKAGE

This adjustment positions a valve which controls shift speed, shift firmness, and part-throttle downshift sensitivity.

Fig. 16 Location of the low and reverse band adjusting screw locations

All Except 4-151 Engines

1. Detach the throttle control rod spring and hook it so that the throttle control lever is held forward against its stop.
2. Block the choke open and set the carburetor throttle linkage off the fast idle cam.

➡️**On models with a throttle solenoid valve, energize the solenoid and open the throttle halfway so that the solenoid will lock and then return the throttle to the idle position.**

3. Loosen, but do not remove, the retaining bolt on the throttle control rod adjusting link.
4. On V8's, remove the spring clip and nylon washer; leave them in place on sixes.
5. On sixes, pull on the end of the link to remove all lash. On V8s, push on the end of the link to remove all lash.
6. Tighten the retaining bolt while performing Step 5.
7. Replace the throttle control rod spring in its original location. On V8s, install the nylon washer and spring clip on the retaining rod before replacing the spring.

4-151 Engines
▶ **See Figure 17**

1. Remove the air cleaner.
2. Remove the spark plug separator from the throttle cable bracket and move the separator and bracket out of the way.
3. Raise the car and support it on jackstands. Remove the strut rod bushing heat shield from the bottom of the transmission and hold the throttle control lever rearward against its stop using a spring.
4. Lower the car and block the choke open, then set the carburetor linkage completely off the fast idle cam.
5. Turn the ignition key to the ON position to energize the throttle stop solenoid.
6. Unlock the throttle control cable by releasing the T-shaped clamp. Release the clamp by prying it up with a screwdriver.

7. Grasp the cable outer sheath and pull it and the cable forward to remove any load on the throttle cable bellcrank, which is part of the carburetor linkage.
8. Adjust the cable by moving the cable.

Neutral Safety/Back-up Light Switch

This switch prevents the engine from being started in any transmission position other than Neutral or Park. It also operates the back-up lights.

On all American Motors cars, a combination back-up light/Neutral safety switch is mounted on the left side of the transmission case. This switch cannot be adjusted; failure requires replacement.

TESTING

1. Unfasten the wiring connector from the switch.
2. Use a 12V test lamp to check for continuity between the center pin of the switch and the transmission case. The lamp should light only in Park or Neutral.
3. If the lamp lights in other positions, check the transmission linkage adjustments before replacing the switch.
4. To test the backup light function of the switch repeat Step 2 by bridging the outside pins to test continuity. The lamp should light only in Reverse. There should not be continuity from either of the pins to the case.

REMOVAL & INSTALLATION

▶ **See Figure 18**

1. Place a container under the switch to catch transmission fluid. Unscrew the switch.

Fig. 17 Release the T-shaped clamp with a prytool to unlock the throttle control cable—4-cylinder engine models

Fig. 18 The pan must be removed to gain access to the neutral safety and back-up light switch

1. Electrical connection
2. Neutral safety switch

Disengage the electrical connection from the neutral safety switch

Use a ratchet and socket to loosen the switch . . .

2. Shift to Park and then Neutral while checking to see that the operating fingers for the switch are centered in the case opening.

3. Screw a new switch and a new seal into the transmission. Tighten the switch to 24 ft. lbs.

4. Retest continuity. Add to the transmission fluid, as required. See Section 1 for details.

. . . then unscrew the switch the rest of the way by hand and remove the switch from the transmission

Troubleshooting Basic Automatic Transmission Problems

Problem	Cause	Solution
Fluid leakage	• Defective pan gasket	• Replace gasket or tighten pan bolts
	• Loose filler tube	• Tighten tube nut
	• Loose extension housing to transmission case	• Tighten bolts
	• Converter housing area leakage	• Have transmission checked professionally
Fluid flows out the oil filler tube	• High fluid level	• Check and correct fluid level
	• Breather vent clogged	• Open breather vent
	• Clogged oil filter or screen	• Replace filter or clean screen (change fluid also)
	• Internal fluid leakage	• Have transmission checked professionally
Transmission overheats (this is usually accompanied by a strong burned odor to the fluid)	• Low fluid level	• Check and correct fluid level
	• Fluid cooler lines clogged	• Drain and refill transmission. If this doesn't cure the problem, have cooler lines cleared or replaced.
	• Heavy pulling or hauling with insufficient cooling	• Install a transmission oil cooler
	• Faulty oil pump, internal slippage	• Have transmission checked professionally
Buzzing or whining noise	• Low fluid level	• Check and correct fluid level
	• Defective torque converter, scored gears	• Have transmission checked professionally
No forward or reverse gears or slippage in one or more gears	• Low fluid level	• Check and correct fluid level
	• Defective vacuum or linkage controls, internal clutch or band failure	• Have unit checked professionally
Delayed or erratic shift	• Low fluid level	• Check and correct fluid level
	• Broken vacuum lines	• Repair or replace lines
	• Internal malfunction	• Have transmission checked professionally

Transmission Fluid Indications

The appearance and odor of the transmission fluid can give valuable clues to the overall condition of the transmission. Always note the appearance of the fluid when you check the fluid level or change the fluid. Rub a small amount of fluid between your fingers to feel for grit and smell the fluid on the dipstick.

If the fluid appears:	It indicates:
Clear and red colored	• Normal operation
Discolored (extremely dark red or brownish) or smells burned	• Band or clutch pack failure, usually caused by an overheated transmission. Hauling very heavy loads with insufficient power or failure to change the fluid, often result in overheating. Do not confuse this appearance with newer fluids that have a darker red color and a strong odor (though not a burned odor).
Foamy or aerated (light in color and full of bubbles)	• The level is too high (gear train is churning oil)
	• An internal air leak (air is mixing with the fluid). Have the transmission checked professionally.
Solid residue in the fluid	• Defective bands, clutch pack or bearings. Bits of band material or metal abrasives are clinging to the dipstick. Have the transmission checked professionally.
Varnish coating on the dipstick	• The transmission fluid is overheating

Lockup Torque Converter Service Diagnosis

Problem	Cause	Solution

No lockup	• Faulty oil pump
	• Sticking governor valve
	• Valve body malfunction
	    (a) Stuck switch valve
	    (b) Stuck lockup valve
	    (c) Stuck fail-safe valve
	• Failed locking clutch
	• Leaking turbine hub seal
	• Faulty input shaft or seal ring
		• Replace oil pump
		• Repair or replace as necessary
		• Repair or replace valve body or its
		   internal components as neces-
		   sary
		
		• Replace torque converter
		• Replace torque converter
		• Repair or replace as necessary

Will not unlock	• Sticking governor valve
	• Valve body malfunction
	    (a) Stuck switch valve
	    (b) Stuck lockup valve
	    (c) Stuck fail-safe valve
		• Repair or replace as necessary
		• Repair or replace valve body or its
		   internal components as neces-
		   sary

Stays locked up at too low a speed in direct	• Sticking governor valve
	• Valve body malfunction
	    (a) Stuck switch valve
	    (b) Stuck lockup valve
	    (c) Stuck fail-safe valve
		• Repair or replace as necessary
		• Repair or replace valve body or its
		   internal components as neces-
		   sary

Locks up or drags in low or second	• Faulty oil pump
	• Valve body malfunction
	    (a) Stuck switch valve
	    (b) Stuck fail-safe valve
		• Replace oil pump
		• Repair or replace valve body or its
		   internal components as neces-
		   sary

Sluggish or stalls in reverse	• Faulty oil pump
	• Plugged cooler, cooler lines or
	   fittings
	• Valve body malfunction
	    (a) Stuck switch valve
	    (b) Faulty input shaft or seal
	       ring
		• Replace oil pump as necessary
		• Flush or replace cooler and flush
		   lines and fittings
		• Repair or replace valve body or its
		   internal components as neces-
		   sary

Loud chatter during lockup engagement (cold)	• Faulty torque converter • Failed locking clutch • Leaking turbine hub seal	• Replace torque converter • Replace torque converter • Replace torque converter

Vibration or shudder during lockup engagement	• Faulty oil pump
	
	• Valve body malfunction
	
	• Faulty torque converter
	• Engine needs tune-up
		• Repair or replace oil pump as nec-
		   essary
		• Repair or replace valve body or its
		   internal components as neces-
		   sary
		• Replace torque converter
		• Tune engine

Vibration after lockup engagement	• Faulty torque converter • Exhaust system strikes underbody • Engine needs tune-up • Throttle linkage misadjusted	• Replace torque converter • Align exhaust system • Tune engine • Adjust throttle linkage

Vibration when revved in neutral
Overheating: oil blows out of dip stick tube or pump seal
	• Torque converter out of balance
	• Plugged cooler, cooler lines or fit-
	   tings
	• Stuck switch valve
		• Replace torque converter
		• Flush or replace cooler and flush
		   lines and fittings
		• Repair switch valve in valve body
		   or replace valve body

Shudder after lockup engagement	• Faulty oil pump
	• Plugged cooler, cooler lines or
	   fittings
	• Valve body malfunction
	
	• Faulty torque converter
	• Fail locking clutch
	• Exhaust system strikes underbody
	• Engine needs tune-up
	• Throttle linkage misadjusted
		• Replace oil pump
		• Flush or replace cooler and flush
		   lines and fittings
		• Repair or replace valve body or its
		   internal components as neces-
		   sary
		• Replace torque converter
		• Replace torque converter
		• Align exhaust system
		• Tune engine
		• Adjust throttle linkage

TRANSFER CASE

Identification

An identifiction tag is usually located on the rear half of the transfer case. This tag specifies the transfer case model number and assembly number.

Transfer Case Application Chart

Transfer Case Type	Years	Models
New Process NP-207	1987–88	All models
Warner Quadra-Trac®	1976–79	Standard on CJ-7 w/automatic trans.

Transfer Case

REMOVAL & INSTALLATION

With Manual Transmission

◆ **See Figures 19 and 20**

➡**Steps 1 through 6, below, pertain to models with the SR-4 transmission only.**

1. Shift the transmission into Neutral.
2. Remove the screws attaching the gearshift lever bezel to the floorpan or console, if equipped.
3. Side the bezel and boot upward on the gearshift to provide access to the lever attaching bolts.
4. Remove the bolts attaching the gearshift lever to the lever

MANUAL TRANSMISSION

Fig. 20 Location of the manual transmission brace, bracket and related components

Fig. 19 Remove the gearshift cover and unfasten the transfer case upper mounting nut

mounting cover on the transmission adapter housing and remove the lever.

5. Remove the bolts attaching the gearshift lever mounting cover to the transmission adapter housing and remove the cover.
6. Remove the nut from the transfer case mounting stud located inside the transmission adapter housing.
7. Raise the automobile.
8. Remove the skid plate and rear brace rod at the transfer case.
9. Remove the speedometer adapter retainer attaching bolt and remove the retainer, adapter, and cable. Plug the adapter opening in the transfer case to prevent excessive oil spillage.

➡**Mark the position of the speedometer adapter for assembly reference before removing it.**

10. Mark the driveshafts and axle yokes for assembly alignment reference and disconnect the driveshafts at the transfer case.

11. On 1982 models, remove the transfer case shift motor vacuum harness.

12. Support the transfer case with a transmission jack.

13. Remove the nuts from the transfer case mounting stud nuts. Remove the transfer case.

To install:

14. Align the transmission output and transfer case input shafts and install the transfer case on the transmission adapter housing.

15. Install and tighten the transfer case mounting stud nuts to 33 ft.lb. torque.

16. Remove the jack used to support the transfer case.

17. Align and connect the driveshafts to the axle yokes. Tighten the clamp strap bolts to 15 ft. lbs. torque.

18. Install the replacement O-ring on the speedometer adapter and install the adapter and cable and retainer. Tighten the retainer bolt to 100 inch lbs.

✳✳ WARNING

Do not attempt to reuse the original adapter O-ring. The O-ring is designed to swell in service to improve its sealing qualities and could be cut or torn during installation if re-use is attempted.

19. Install the skid plate and rear brace rod. Torque the retaining bolts to 30 ft. lbs.

20. On 1982 models, install the transfer case shift motor vacuum harness.

21. Check and correct the lubricant levels in the transmission and transfer case if necessary.

22. Lower the automobile.

➡**Steps 23 through 26, below, pertain to models with the SR-4 transmission only.**

23. Install the nut on the transfer case mounting stud located inside the transmission adapter housing. Tighten the nut to 33 ft. lbs.

24. Install the gearshift lever on the mounting cover on the transmission adapter housing.

25. Install the gearshift lever on the mounting cover. Be sure lever is engaged with the shift rail before tightening the lever attaching bolts.

26. Position the gearshift lever boot and bezel on the floorpan or console, if equipped, and install the bezel attaching screws.

With Automatic Transmission
▸ **See Figure 21**

1. Raise the automobile.

2. Support the engine and transmission with a support stand or transmission jack.

3. Disconnect the catalytic converter support bracket at the adapter housing.

4. Remove the skid plate and rear brace rod at the transfer case.

5. Remove the speedometer cable and adapter from the transfer case. Discard the adapter O-ring; it is not reusable.

6. Mark the driveshafts and transfer case yokes for assembly reference.

Fig. 21 Automatic transmission brace, bracket and retainer locations

7. Disconnect the driveshafts at the yokes. Secure the shafts to the underside of the automobile.

8. Disconnect the gearshift and throttle linkage at the transmission.

9. Lower the rear crossmember.

10. Remove the transfer case-to-adapter housing stud nuts and remove the transfer case.

To install:

11. Install the transfer case on the adapter housing. Do not damage the output shaft splines during installation.

12. Install the transfer case-to-adapter housing stud nuts. Tighten the nuts to 33 ft. lbs. torque

13. Install the rear crossmember. Tighten the crossmember attaching nuts to 30 ft. lbs. torque.

14. Install the rear brace rod.

15. Remove the transmission jack or support stand.

16. Connect the gearshift and throttle linkage to the transmission.

17. Connect the driveshafts. Tighten the clamp strap bolts to 15 ft.lb. torque.

18. Install a new O-ring on the speedometer adapter and install the adapter and cable in the transfer case.

➡**Do not attempt to reuse the old adapter O-ring. The O-ring is designed to swell in service to provide improved sealing qualities and could be cut or torn if reinstallation is attempted.**

19. Install the skid plate and stiffening brace, if equipped. Tighten the retaining bolts to 30 ft. lbs.

20. Connect the catalytic converter support bracket to the adapter housing.

21. Check and adjust the transfer case lubricant level and transmission linkage adjustments if necessary.

22. Lower the automobile.

DRIVELINE

Driveshaft and U-Joints

◆ **See Figures 22 and 23**

Two types of driveshafts are used, designated types 1 and 2, depending on the type of bearing cap retaining ring. See the illustration.

REMOVAL & INSTALLATION

Except Eagle

1. Mark the rear universal joint yoke and bearing retainers so that you can reinstall them in their original positions.
2. Remove the U-bolts, being careful not to lose the round

Fig. 22 Exploded view of a common type 1 driveshaft assembly

Fig. 23 Exploded view of a type 2 driveshaft assembly

Unfasten the U-bolt retaining nuts . . .

. . . then remove the U-bolts from the driveshaft

Hold the U-joint caps and remove the driveshaft from the vehicle

Use tape to hold the U-joint caps in place to prevent loss of the needle bearings inside the caps

bearing retainer caps, which are filled with little needle bearings. Don't make any attempt to remove the large nut holding the yoke to the front of the rear axle assembly.

3. Slide the driveshaft back and remove it.

To install:

4. On installation, slide the front yoke on the transmission output shaft splines far enough to align the rear universal joint.

5. Align the marks you made in Step 1.

6. Install the rear U-bolts and tighten them evenly to 15 ft. lbs. A torque wrench isn't essential here, but remember that 15 ft. lbs. isn't very much. You can crush the bearings and retainer caps if you get carried away.

Eagle

♦ See Figure 24

➡Both driveshafts are secured at the transfer case end and the axle yoke end by straps. The straps are retained by Torx head bolts.

Fig. 24 Exploded view of the Eagle driveshaft components

1. Shift into Neutral. Raise and support the car.

2. Matchmark the driveshaft(s) at the transfer case and axle yoke for alignment reference.

3. Remove the retaining straps with a Torx bit tool of the proper size. Remove the driveshaft(s).

4. To install, align the matchmarks made during removal to assure proper balance. Seat the universal joints in the yokes and install the straps, tightening to 17 ft. lbs.

U-JOINT OVERHAUL

➡The four end bearings or roller retainers are held in the yoke ends by snaprings on the front U-joint. The rear U-joint has 4 retainers held by U-bolts.

1. The snaprings can be pried out with a screwdriver.

2. Place the assembly in a vise with a 9/16 in. socket against the bearing retainer on one side and a 1⅛ in. socket against the yoke on the other side.

3. Tighten the vise slowly; the bearing retainer will be forced out into the big socket.

4. Clamp the protruding bearing retainer gently in the vise and remove it. Watch our for the little needle bearings inside.

5. Remove the other bearings retainers in the same way.

To install:

6. Wash all the parts in a safe solvent and check carefully for wear. These parts aren't very expensive and aren't serviced often, so replace any doubtful parts. The 4-armed part is called a cross or a spider.

7. Pack enough high quality grease into each bearing retainer so that you can install the needle bearings without them falling out.

8. Install the cross into the yoke and put the end bearing retainer in place.

9. Place the yoke in a vise and press the bearing retainer, using a 9/16 in. socket, past the outside of the yoke.

10. Install the snaprings, making sure that they are securely seated.

Check the CV-boot for wear

Removing the outer band from the CV-boot

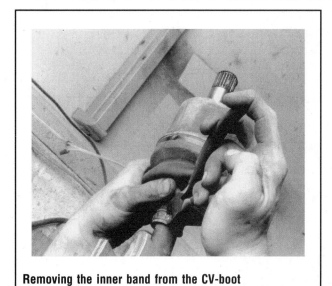

Removing the inner band from the CV-boot

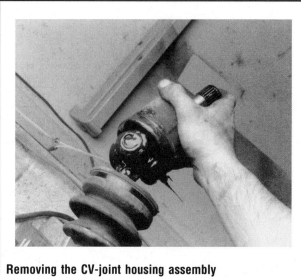

Removing the CV-joint housing assembly

Removing the CV-boot from the joint housing

Removing the CV-joint

Clean the CV-joint housing prior to removing boot

Inspecting the CV-joint housing

Removing the CV-joint outer snapring

Removing the CV-joint assembly

Checking the CV-joint snapring for wear

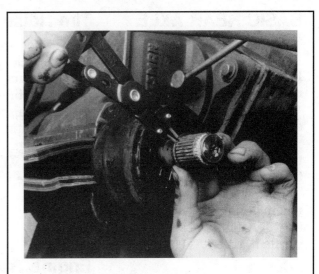

Removing the CV-joint inner snapring

CV-joint snapring (typical)

Installing the CV-joint assembly (typical)

BASIC DRIVESHAFT PROBLEMS

Problem	Cause	Solution
Shudder as car accelerates from stop or low speed	• Loose U-joint • Defective center bearing	• Replace U-joint • Replace center bearing
Loud clunk in driveshaft when shifting gears	• Worn U-joints	• Replace U-joints
Roughness or vibration at any speed	• Out-of-balance, bent or dented driveshaft • Worn U-joints • U-joint clamp bolts loose	• Balance or replace driveshaft • Replace U-joints • Tighten U-joint clamp bolts
Squeaking noise at low speeds	• Lack of U-joint lubrication	• Lubricate U-joint; if problem persists, replace U-joint
Knock or clicking noise	• U-joint or driveshaft hitting frame tunnel • Worn CV joint	• Correct overloaded condition • Replace CV joint

BASIC REAR AXLE PROBLEMS

First, determine when the noise is most noticeable.

Drive Noise: Produced under vehicle acceleration.

Coast Noise: Produced while the car coasts with a closed throttle.

Float Noise: Occurs while maintaining constant car speed (just enough to keep speed constant) on a level road.

Road Noise

Brick or rough surfaced concrete roads produce noises that seem to come from the rear axle. Road noise is usually identical in Drive or Coast and driving on a different type of road will tell whether the road is the problem.

Tire Noise

Tire noises are often mistaken for rear axle problems. Snow treads or unevenly worn tires produce vibrations seeming to originate elsewhere. **Temporarily inflating the tires to 40 lbs will significantly alter tire noise, but will have no effect on rear axle noises** (which normally cease below about 30 mph).

Engine/Transmission Noise

Determine at what speed the noise is most pronounced, then stop the car in a quiet place. With the transmission in Neutral, run the engine through speeds corresponding to road speeds where the noise was noticed. Noises produced with the car standing still are coming from the engine or transmission.

Front Wheel Bearings

While holding the car speed steady, lightly apply the footbrake; this will often decease bearing noise, as some of the load is taken from the bearing.

Rear Axle Noises

Eliminating other possible sources can narrow the cause to the rear axle, which normally produces noise from worn gears or bearings. Gear noises tend to peak in a narrow speed range, while bearing noises will usually vary in pitch with engine speeds.

EAGLE FRONT AXLE

Axle, Shaft, Seal and Bearing

REMOVAL & INSTALLATION

▶ **See Figure 25**

➡**The procedure for replacing the axle shafts and seals on 4-wheel drive models calls for removal of the axle first.**

1. Raise and support the front of the car. Install protectors over the halfshaft boots. Remove the halfshaft-to-axle flange bolts, and tie the halfshafts out of the way.

2. Matchmark the driveshaft and the axle yoke. Remove the driveshaft.

3. Support the axle on stands. Remove the five axle-to-engine mounting bolts.

4. Lower the axle partway and remove the vent hose. Remove the axle.

5. Remove the differential cover and drain the oil. Remove the axle shaft C-clips.

6. Remove the axle shafts.

7. Carefully remove the shaft seal using a screwdriver.

8. Two different bearings are used; the left side uses a ball bearing, and the right side uses a needle bearing. The ball bearing may be removed using a brass drift and a hammer. The nee-

Front Drive Axle Application Chart

Axle Type	Years	Models
Dana 30	1971–88	All models

1. Half-shaft assembly
2. Axle mounting brackets
3. Vent hose
4. Pinion and front bearing cup
5. Washer
6. Yoke and seal
7. Outer boot and retainer
8. Rzeppa joint assembly
9. Spindle
10. Half-shaft
11. Inner boot and retainer
12. Tri-pot joint assembly
13. Tri-pot housing
14. Axle shaft (short)
15. Ball bearing and seal
16. Axle housing
17. Axle shaft (long)
18. Needle bearing and seal
19. Preload shim
20. Washer
21. Depth shim
22. Pinion rear bearing and cup
23. Slinger
24. Pinion gear
25. Cover
26. Differential bearing and cup
27. Differential pinion and thrust washer
28. Pinion mate shaft
29. Side gear, thrust washer and lockring
30. Bearing cap
31. Ring gear
32. Differential case

Fig. 25 Exploded view of the Eagle front drive axle components

dle bearing should be removed using a needle bearing removal too.

➡**If the proper bearing removal tool is not available, remove the differential and remove the needle bearing using $^{15}/_{16}$ in. socket and a 3 ft. ratchet extension.**

To install:

9. Install the bearings, using drivers of the appropriate type and size.

10. Oil the lips of the new seal and install into the housing using a driver of the correct size.

REAR AXLE

Identification

Two sizes of differential assemblies are used on American Motors cars; 7$^9/_{16}$ in. (192mm) and 8$^7/_8$ in. (225mm) ring gear units. A twin-grip limited slip differential is available as an option on both units.

Rear Axle Application Chart

Axle Type	Years	Models
AMC 7$^9/_{16}$" ring gear	1984–88	All models
AMC 8$^7/_8$" ring gear	1973–83	All models

A letter code used to identify the axle ratio will be found on most differentials, stamped on the right axle tube housing boss, on the rear side, adjacent to the dowel hole. Some earlier cars have either a metal tag attached to one of the bolts of the differential housing cover or the code letter stamped on the right differential housing cover flange. It may be necessary to remove the cover from the differential to locate the letter. The codes and the axle ratio are listed in dealer parts books and shop manuals.

➡**The 7$^9/_{16}$ in. (192mm) axle can be identified by the cover mounted filler plug, and the 8$^7/_8$ in. (225mm) axle by the front filler on the housing.**

Axle Shaft, Bearing and Seal

REMOVAL & INSTALLATION

◆ See Figures 26 and 27

1. The hub and drum are separate units and are removed after the wheel is removed. The hub and axle shaft are serrated together on the taper. An axle shaft key assures proper alignment during assembly.

2. With the wheel on the ground and the parking brake applied, remove and discard the axle shaft nut cotter pin and remove the nut. Raise the car and remove the wheel. Release the parking brakes and remove the drum.

3. Attach a puller to the rear hub and remove the hub. The use of a 'Knock-out', or slide hammer, puller should be discouraged, since it may result in damage to the axle shaft or wheel bearings.

11. Install the axle shaft and C-clips.

12. Apply a bead of silicone seal to the differential cover and install the cover.

13. Fill the axle with 2.5 pints of 85W-90 GL-5 gear oil.

14. Move the axle into place under the car. Raise it sufficiently to connect the vent hose, then raise it fully into place and install the mounting bolts. Tighten to 50 ft. lbs.

15. Install the driveshaft, aligning the marks made during removal. Install the halfshaft to axle flange bolts, tightening to 45 ft. lbs.

4. Disconnect the parking brake cable at the equalizer.

5. Disconnect the brake tube at the wheel cylinder and remove the brake support plate assembly, oil seal, and axle shims. Note that the axle shims are located on the left side only.

6. Using a screw type puller, remove the axle shaft and bearings from the axle housing.

✳✳ WARNING

On Twin-Grip® axles, rotating the differential with one shaft removed will misalign the side gear splines, preventing installation of the replacement shaft.

7. Remove the axle shaft inner oil seal and install new seals at assembly.

8. The bearing is a press fit and should be removed with an arbor press.

To install:

9. The axle shaft bearings have no provision for lubrication after assembly. Before installing the bearings, they should be packed with a good quality wheel bearing lubricant.

10. Press the axle shaft bearings onto the axle shaft with the small diameter of the cone toward the outer (tapered) end of the shaft.

11. Soak the inner axle shaft seal in light lubricating oil. Coat the outer surface of the seal retainer with sealant.

12. Install the inner oil seal.

13. Install the axle shafts, indexing the splined end with the differential side gears.

14. Install the outer bearing cup.

15. Install the brake support plate. Sealant should be applied to the axle housing flange and brake support mounting plate.

16. Install the original shims, oil seal and brake support plate. Torque the nuts to 30–35 ft. lbs.

➡**The oil seal and retainer go between the axle housing flange and the brake support plate on 9 in. (228.6mm) brakes or 7$^9/_{16}$ in. (192mm) axle. On 10 in. (254mm) brakes or 8$^7/_8$ in. (225mm) axle, they go on the outside of the brake support plate.**

17. To adjust the axle shaft end-play, strike the axle shafts with a lead mallet to seal the bearings. Install a dial indicator on the brake support plate and check the play while pushing and pulling the axle shaft. End-play should be 0.004–0.008 in. (0.10–0.20mm), with 0.006 in. (0.15mm) desirable. Add shims to the left side only to decrease the play and remove shims to increase the play.

1. Bolt
2. Washer
3. Axle shaft oil seal and retainer assembly
4. Axle shaft bearing shim
5. Axle shaft bearing cup
6. Axle shaft bearing
7. Axle shaft
8. Axle shaft inner oil seal
9. Nut
10. Axle housing
11. Collapsible spacer
12. Pinion bearing cup-front
13. Pinion bearing-front
14. Pinion oil seal
15. Universal joint yoke
16. Pinion nut
17. Breather
18. Breather hose
19. Breather
20. Pinion depth adjusting shim
21. Pinion rear bearing cup
22. Pinion bearing-rear
23. Pinion gear
24. Differential bearing
25. Differential bearing cup
26. Differential bearing shim
27. Differential bearing cap
28. Differential bearing cap bolt
29. Ring gear
30. Differential case
31. Ring gear bolt
32. Differential pinion washer
33. Differential pinion
34. Differential side gear
35. Differential side gear thrust washer
36. Differential pinion shaft thrust block
37. Differential pinion shaft pin
38. Differential pinion shaft
39. Axle housing cover gasket
40. Axle housing cover
41. Axle identification tag
42. Bolt
43. Axle housing cover fill plug
44. Washer

Fig. 26 Exploded view of the 7 9/16 in. ring gear rear axle with a standard differential

1. Bolt
2. Washer
3. Axle shaft oil seal
4. Axle shaft bearing shim
5. Axle shaft bearing cup
6. Axle shaft bearing
7. Axle shaft
8. Axle shaft inner oil seal
9. Nut
10. Axle housing
11. Collapsible spacer
12. Pinion bearing cup-front
13. Pinion bearing-front
14. Pinion oil seal
15. Universal joint yoke
16. Pinion nut
17. Breather
18. Breather hose
19. Pinion depth
    adjusting shim
20. Pinion bearing cup-rear
21. Pinion bearing-rear
22. Pinion gear
23. Retainer clip
24. Differential side gear
25. Differential pinion shaft pin
26. Clutch cone
27. Differential case
28. Ring gear
29. Differential bearing
30. Differential bearing cup
31. Differential bearing shim
32. Differential bearing cap
33. Differential bearing cap bolt
34. Axle housing cover gasket
35. Axle housing cover
36. Axle identification tag
37. Bolt
38. Axle housing cover fill plug
39. Washer
40. Twin grip identification tag
41. Differential case bolt
42. Washer
43. Ring gear bolt
44. Differential case
45. Clutch cone
46. Differential side gear
47. Differential pinion thrust washer
48. Differential pinion
49. Retainer clip
50. Differential pinion shaft thrust block
51. Spring
52. Differential pinion shaft
53. Differential serviced
    as assembly only

Fig. 27 Exploded view of a Twin-Grip differential and related components

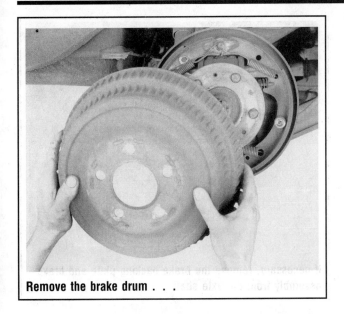

Remove the brake drum . . .

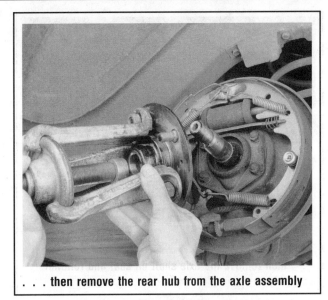

. . . then remove the rear hub from the axle assembly

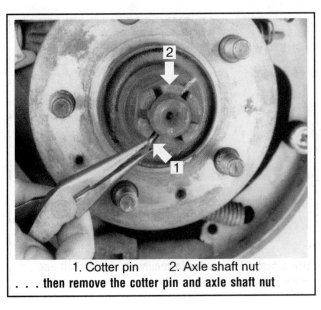

1. Cotter pin   2. Axle shaft nut
. . . then remove the cotter pin and axle shaft nut

Disconnect the parking brake cable at the equalizer

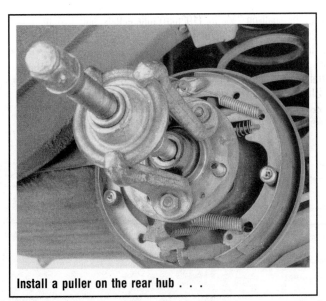

Install a puller on the rear hub . . .

1. Retaining bolts   2. Axle shaft oil seal retainer
Unfasten the axle shaft oil seal retainer bolts . . .

. . . then remove the axle shaft oil seal and retainer assembly

If necessary, remove the brake backing plate and brake assembly from the axle shaft

Remove the axle shaft bearing shim

1. Axle shaft   2. Bearings

Use a screw type puller to remove the axle shaft and bearings

18. Slide the hub onto the axle shafts aligning the serrations and the keyway onto the hub with the axle shaft key.

19. Replace the hub and drum, install the wheel, lower the car onto the floor and tighten the axle shaft nut to 250 ft. lbs. If the cotter pin hole is not aligned with a castellation on the nut, tighten the nut to the next castellation.

➡A new hub must be installed whenever a new axle shaft is installed.

20. Install two thrust washers on the shaft. Tighten the new hub onto the shaft until the hub is 1.19 in. (30.2mm) from the

end of the shaft on 7⁹⁄₁₆ in. (192mm) differentials, and 1.31 in. (33.2mm) on 8⁷⁄₈ in. (225mm) models. Remove the nut; remove one thrust washer. Install the nut and torque to 250 ft. lbs. New hubs do not have serrations on the axle shaft mating surface. The serrations are cut when the hub is installed to the axle shaft.

21. Connect the parking brake cable at the equalizer.

22. Connect the brake tube at the wheel cylinder and bleed the brakes.

WHEELS 8-2
WHEELS 8-2
　REMOVAL 8-2
　INSPECTION 8-2
　INSTALLATION 8-2
FRONT SUSPENSION 8-2
SHOCK ABSORBER 8-2
　REMOVAL & INSTALLATION 8-2
SPRING 8-6
　REMOVAL & INSTALLATION 8-6
UPPER CONTROL ARM 8-6
　REMOVAL & INSTALLATION 8-6
LOWER CONTROL ARM 8-9
　REMOVAL & INSTALLATION 8-9
BALL JOINTS 8-10
　INSPECTION 8-10
　REMOVAL & INSTALLATION 8-10
WHEEL BEARINGS 8-10
　INSPECTION 8-11
　ADJUSTMENT 8-11
FRONT END ALIGNMENT 8-11
　CASTER 8-11
　CAMBER 8-11
　TOE-IN 8-12
REAR SUSPENSION 8-14
SHOCK ABSORBER 8-16
　REMOVAL & INSTALLATION 8-16
LEAF SPRINGS 8-16
　REMOVAL & INSTALLATION 8-16
COIL SPRINGS 8-16
　REMOVAL & INSTALLATION 8-16
STEERING 8-19
STEERING WHEEL 8-19
　REMOVAL & INSTALLATION 8-19
TURN SIGNAL SWITCH, HAZARD
　SIGNAL AND LOCK CYLINDER 8-21
　REMOVAL & INSTALLATION 8-21
IGNITION SWITCH 8-22
　REMOVAL & INSTALLATION 8-22
MANUAL STEERING GEAR 8-22
　REMOVAL & INSTALLATION 8-22
　ADJUSTMENTS 8-25
POWER STEERING PUMP 8-26
　REMOVAL & INSTALLATION 8-26
POWER STEERING GEAR 8-28
　REMOVAL & INSTALLATION 8-28
　ADJUSTMENTS 8-44
　FLUID LEVEL & INITIAL
　　OPERATION 8-45
OUTER TIE RODS 8-46
　REMOVAL & INSTALLATION 8-46
INNER TIE RODS 8-48
　REMOVAL & INSTALLATION 8-48
COMPONENT LOCATIONS
　FRONT SUSPENSION COMPONENT
　　LOCATIONS—LATE MODEL
　　EAGLE 8-3
　FRONT SUSPENSION COMPONENT
　　LOCATIONS—EARLY MODEL
　　MATADOR 8-4
　REAR SUSPENSION COMPONENT

　　LOCATIONS—LATE MODEL
　　EAGLE 8-14
　REAR SUSPENSION COMPONENT
　　LOCATIONS—EARLY MODEL
　　MATADOR 8-15
SPECIFICATION CHARTS
　WHEEL ALIGNMENT
　　SPECIFICATIONS 8-12
TROUBLESHOOTING CHARTS
　BASIC STEERING AND SUSPENSION
　　PROBLEMS 8-30
　TROUBLESHOOTING THE STEERING
　　COLUMN 8-31
　TROUBLESHOOTING THE IGNITION
　　SWITCH 8-32
　TROUBLESHOOTING THE TURN
　　SIGNAL SWITCH 8-33
　TROUBLESHOOTING THE MANUAL
　　STEERING GEAR 8-35
　TROUBLESHOOTING THE POWER
　　STEERING GEAR 8-36
　TROUBLESHOOTING THE POWER
　　STEERING PUMP 8-38

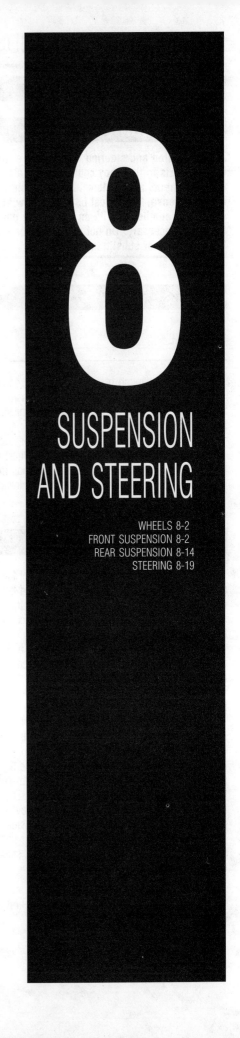

8

SUSPENSION
AND STEERING

WHEELS 8-2
FRONT SUSPENSION 8-2
REAR SUSPENSION 8-14
STEERING 8-19

WHEELS

✳✳ CAUTION

All suspension and steering fasteners are important attaching parts in that they could affect the performance of vital components and systems, and/or could result in major repair expense. They must be replaced with one of the same part number or with an equivalent part if replacement becomes necessary. Do not use a replacement part of lesser quality or substitute design.

Wheels

REMOVAL

1. Apply the parking brake and block the opposite wheel.
2. If equipped with an automatic transmission/transaxle, place the selector level in **P**; with a manual transmission/transaxle, place the shifter in Reverse.
3. If equipped, remove the wheel cover or hub cap.
4. Break loose the lug nuts. if a nut is stuck, never use heat to loosen it or damage to the wheel and bearings may occur. If the nuts are seized, one or two heavy hammer blows directly on the end of the bolt head usually loosens the rust. Be careful as continued pounding will likely damage the brake drum or rotor.
5. Raise the vehicle until the tire is clear of the ground. Support the vehicle safely using jackstands.
6. Remove the lug nuts and the tire and wheel assembly.

INSPECTION

Check the wheels for any damage. They must be replaced if they are bent, dented, heavily rusted, have elongated bolt holes, or have excessive lateral or radial runout. Wheels with excessive runout may cause a high-speed vehicle vibration.

Replacement wheels must be of the same load capacity, diameter, width, offset and mounting configuration as the original wheels. Using the wrong wheels may affect wheel bearing life, ground and tire clearance, or speedometer and odometer calibrations.

INSTALLATION

1. Lift the wheel onto the lugs.
2. Snug down the topmost nut, then snug down the rest of the nuts in a crisscross pattern.
3. Lower the vehicle and tighten the nuts securely.

FRONT SUSPENSION

The front suspension on all models except Pacer is an independent linked type with the coil springs located between seats in the wheelwell panels and seats in the upper control arms. Rubber insulators between the springs and seats reduce noise transmission to the body.

Direct acting, telescopic shock absorbers are located inside the coil springs and the control arms are attached to the body via rubber bushings.

The suspension system is a double ball joint design, both upper and lower control arms each having one joint.

On all models, strut rods serve to support the lower control arms. Stabilizer bars are used on some models.

The Pacer front suspension is different from all other AMC cars. The coil spring is mounted between the two control arms; seated at the bottom on the lower control arm and at the top in the suspension/engine mount crossmember. The crossmember is isolated from the rest of the body structure by rubber mounting points. The shock absorbers are mounted inside the coil spring. The steering knuckle is attached to the upper and lower control arms by upper and lower ball joints. A front stabilizer bar is optional.

➡The front end alignment must be checked after any disassembly procedure.

Shock Absorber

REMOVAL & INSTALLATION

➡When installing new shock absorbers, purge them of air by extending them in their normal position and compressing them while inverted. Do this several times. It is normal for there to be more resistance to extension than to compression.

Except Pacer

1. Remove the two lower shock absorber attaching nuts. Remove the washers and the grommets.
2. Remove the upper mounting bracket nuts and bolts.
3. Remove the bracket, complete with shock.
4. Remove the upper attaching nut and separate the shock from the mounting bracket.
5. For adjustable shocks: To adjust the shock, compress the piston completely. Holding the upper part of the shock, turn the shock until the lower arrow is aligned with the desired setting. A click will be heard when the desired setting is reached.

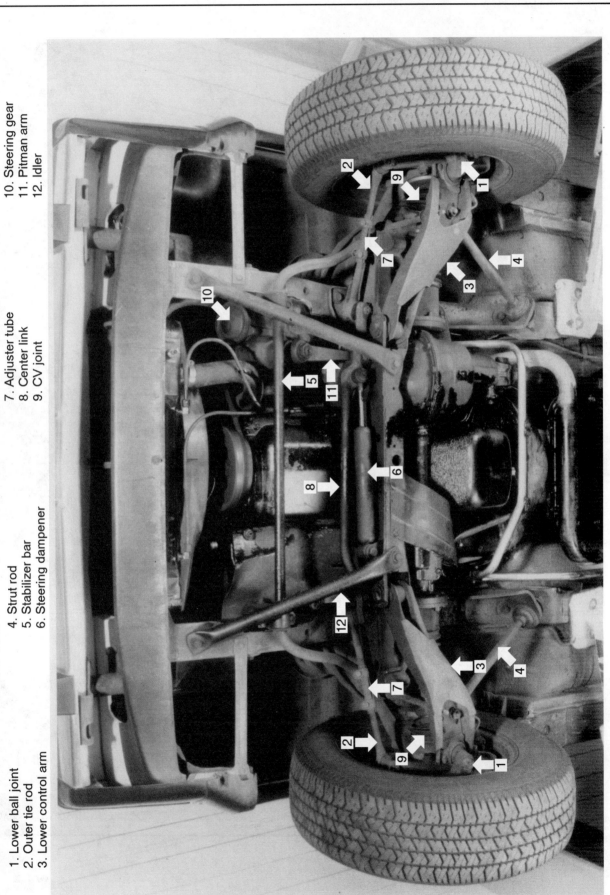

FRONT SUSPENSION COMPONENT LOCATIONS – LATE MODEL EAGLE

1. Lower ball joint
2. Outer tie rod
3. Lower control arm
4. Strut rod
5. Stabilizer bar
6. Steering dampener
7. Adjuster tube
8. Center link
9. CV joint
10. Steering gear
11. Pitman arm
12. Idler

FRONT SUSPENSION COMPONENT LOCATIONS - EARLY MODEL MATADOR

1. Strut rod
2. Lower control arm
3. Outer tie rod
4. Stabilizer bar
5. Center link
6. Pitman arm
7. Adjuster tube
8. Idler arm
9. Inner tie rod
10. Steering gear
11. Lower ball joints
12. Upper ball joints

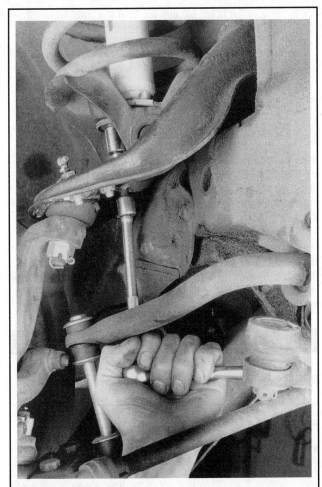

To remove the shock absorber, unfasten the lower mounting bolts . . .

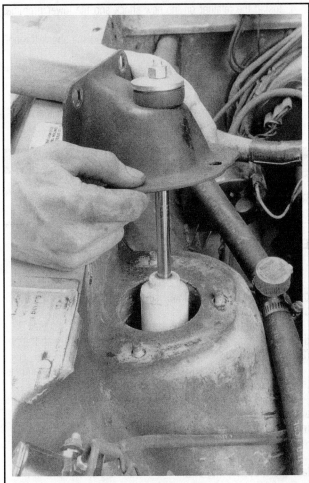

Remove the bracket and shock assembly, then separate the shock from the bracket

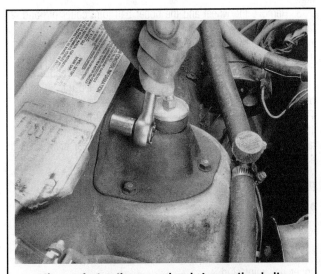

. . . then unfasten the upper bracket mounting bolts

To install:

1. Fit the grommets, washers, upper mounting bracket and nut on the shock, in the reverse order of removal. Tighten the nut to 8 ft.lb.

2. Fully extend the shock and install two grommets on the lower mounting studs.

3. Lower the shock through the hole in the wheel arch. Fit the lower attachment studs through the lower spring seat.

4. Install the grommets, washers, and nuts. Tighten the nuts to 15 ft.lb.

5. Secure the upper mounting bracket with its attachment nuts and bolts. Tighten them to 20 ft. lbs.

Pacer

1. Remove the shock absorber upper locknut.

2. Raise the car and remove the nuts from the lower shock absorber mounting studs.

3. Remove the shock along with the lower grommet and jounce bumper retainer from the shock absorber piston rod.

4. Install the retainer on the new shock and the lower grommet on the piston rod.

5. Extend the piston to full length and insert the shock through the lower control arm.

6. Install the locknuts on the lower mounting studs and lower the car.

7. Install the grommet, retainer, and locknut on the piston rod, making sure the grommet seats properly in the hole in the crossmember.

Spring

REMOVAL & INSTALLATION

Except Pacer

1. Remove the shock absorber.

2. Install a spring compressor through the upper spring seat opening and bolt it to the lower spring seat using the lower shock absorber mounting holes.

3. Remove the lower spring seat pivot retaining nuts, then tighten the compressor tool to compress the spring about 1" (25.4mm).

4. Jack up the front of the car and support it on axle stands at the subframe (allowing the control arms to hang free).

5. Remove the front wheel and pull the lower spring seat out away from the car, then slowly release the spring tension and remove the coil spring and lower spring seat.

To install:

1. Place the spring compressor through the coil spring and tape the rubber spring cushion to the small diameter end of the spring (upper).

2. Place the lower spring seat against the spring with the end of the coil against the formed shoulder in the seat. The shoulder and coil end face inwards, toward the engine, when the spring is installed.

3. Place the spring up against the upper seat, then align the lower spring seat pivot so that the retaining studs will enter the holes in the upper control arm.

4. Compress the coil spring and install the spring.

5. Then install the wheel and tire and lower the car to the floor (to place weight on suspension).

6. Install and tighten lower spring seat spindle retaining nuts and tighten them to 35 ft. lbs.

7. Remove the spring compressor and install the shock absorber.

Pacer

1. Disconnect the upper end of the shock absorber.

2. Raise the front end of the car and support it.

3. Disconnect the lower end of the shock absorber and remove it.

4. Disconnect the stabilizer bar at the lower control arm, if so equipped.

5. Remove the wheel, brake drum, or caliper and rotor. Do not allow the brake hose to support the weight of the caliper; use a length of wire to suspend the caliper from the frame.

6. Remove the two bolts that attach the steering arm to the steering knuckle and more the steering arm aside.

7. Use a spring compressor to compress the coil spring.

8. Remove the cotter pin and nut from the lower ball joint stud and disengage the stud from the steering knuckle with a puller.

9. Move the steering knuckle, steering spindle, and support plate, or anchor plate assembly, aside to provide working clearance. Do not allow the brake hose to support the weight of these components. Use wire to hand the components from the upper control arm.

10. Move the lower control arm aside and remove the spring.

11. Position the upper end of the spring in the spring seat of the front crossmember. Align the cut-off end of the bottom coil with the formed shoulder is the spring seat. The top coil is flat and does not use an insulator. Use a floor jack or jackstand to support the spring until the spring compressor is installed. Install the spring compressor.

12. Assemble the remaining components of the front suspension in the reverse order of removal. Tighten the ball joint stud nut to 75 ft. lbs., the steering arm-to-knuckle attaching bolts to 80 ft. lbs. through 1976, 55 ft. lbs. 1977 and later, the shock absorber lower mounting nuts to 20 ft. lbs., and the stabilizer bar locknut to 8 ft. lbs.

Upper Control Arm

REMOVAL & INSTALLATION

Except Pacer

▶ See Figures 1 and 2

1. Remove the shock absorber and compress the soil spring approximately 2 in. (51mm). Refer to the front spring removal and installation procedure in this section.

2. Jack up the front of the car and support the body on jackstands placed under the subframes (allow the control arms to hang free).

3. Remove the wheel and the upper ball joint cotter pin and retaining nut.

4. Separate the ball joint stud from the steering knuckle using a ball joint removal tool.

5. Remove the inner pivot bolts then remove the control arm.

6. To install, reverse the removal procedure. Do not tighten the pivot bolts nuts until the full weight of the car is on the wheels. The ball joint stud nut must be tightened to 40 ft. lbs., through 1975 and 75 ft. lbs. thereafter, the lower spring seat pivot retaining nuts to 35 ft. lbs., and the control arm inner pivot bolts to 45 ft. lbs. through 1976, 80 ft. lbs. 1977 and later.

Pacer

▶ See Figure 3

1. Raise and support the front of the vehicle.

2. Remove the wheel and tire.

3. Remove the cotter pin, locknut, and retaining nuts from the upper ball joint stud.

4. Loosen the stud from the steering knuckle with a ball joint removal tool.

5. Support the lower control arm with a floor jack.

6. Disengage the stud from the steering knuckle.

7. Remove the retaining nuts that attache the cross-shaft to the front crossmember and remove the upper control arm assembly.

GROMMET

UPPER MOUNTING
BRACKET

SPRING CUSHION

GROMMET

SPRING

SHOCK ABSORBER

SHOCK ABSORBER
LOWER MOUNTING
BRACKET

GROMMET

LOWER SPRING SEAT

GROMMET

SPRING SEAT
SPINDLE

BUSHING
RETAINER RING

CONTROL ARM
BUSHING (2)

UPPER
CONTROL ARM

UPPER CONTROL ARM
BALL JOINT

DUST COVER

STEERING
KNUCKLE PIN

IDENTIFICATION

THE COIL SPRING IS IDENTIFIED BY THE
LAST THREE NUMBERS ON THE TAG ATTACHED
TO THE SPRING

Fig. 1 Exploded view of the upper control arm and shock absorber mounting—except Eagle and Pacer

Fig. 2 Front suspension components—Eagle models

Fig. 3 Exploded view of the front suspension assembly—Pacer models

8. Install the upper control arm in the reverse order of removal, tightening the cross-shaft retaining nuts to 80 ft. lbs., the upper ball joint stud to 75 ft. lbs., and if new bushings were installed, tighten the nuts to 60 ft. lbs. after the car is lowered to the floor.

Lower Control Arm

REMOVAL & INSTALLATION

Except Eagle and Pacer

▶ **See Figure 4**

➡The inner end of the lower control arm is attached to a removable crossmember. The outer end is attached to the steering knuckle pin and ball joint assembly.

1. Jack up the car and support it on axle stands under the subframes.
2. Remove the brake drum or caliper and rotor from the spindle.
3. Disconnect the steering arm from the knuckle pin.
4. Remove the lower ball joint stud cotter pin and nut.
5. Separate the ball joint from the knuckle pin using a ball joint removal tool.
6. Disconnect the sway bar from the control arm.
7. Unbolt the strut rod.
8. Remove the inner pivot bolt and the control arm.
To install:
9. Reverse the removal procedure; do not tighten inner pivot bolt until car weight is on wheels. Tighten ball joint retaining nut to 40 ft. lbs. through 1976, 75 ft. lbs. thereafter, strut rod bolts to 75 ft. lbs., sway bar bolts to 8 ft. lbs., steering arm bolts to 65 ft. lbs. through 1979, 55 ft. lbs. thereafter, and control arm inner pivot bolt to 95 ft. lbs. through 1976, 110 ft. lbs. thereafter.

Fig. 4 Lower control assembly—except Eagle and Pacer models

Labels in figure:
STABILIZER BAR
STRUT ROD MOUNTING BRACKET
BUSHING (2 PIECE)
BUSHING (2 PIECE)
STRUT ROD
BUMPER MOUNTING BRACKET
LOWER CONTROL ARM
CROSSMEMBER
LOWER CONTROL ARM
LOWER BALL JOINT ASSEMBLY
BUMPER

Eagle

1. Remove the wheel cover. Remove and discard the cotter pin. Remove the nut lock and the hub pin.
2. Raise and support the front of the car. Remove the wheel. Remove the brake caliper from the knuckle and suspend it from the body of a length of wire; do not allow it to hand by the hose. Remove the rotor.
3. Remove the lower ball joint cotter pin and retaining nut. Discard the cotter pin.
4. Separate the ball joint stud from the steering knuckle using a ball joint removal tool.
5. Remove the halfshaft flange bolts and remove the half shaft.
6. Remove the strut rod-to-control arm bolts. Disconnect the stabilizer bar from the arm.
7. Remove the inner pivot bolt and remove the control arm.
To install:
8. Place the control arm into position and install the inner pivot bolt, but do not tighten the pivot bolt yet.
9. Install the ball joint stud into the steering knuckle. Install the nut and tighten to 75 ft. lbs. Continue to tighten until the holes align and install a new cotter pin.
10. Connect the stabilizer bar to the arm; tighten the bolts to 7 ft. lbs. Install the strut rod; tighten to 45 ft. lbs.
11. Install the halfshaft-to-axle flange bolts; tighten to 45 ft. lbs.
12. Place a jack under the lower control arm. Raise the jack carefully to compress the spring slightly. Tighten the control arm pivot bolt to 110 ft. lbs.
13. Install the rotor, caliper, and hub nut. Tighten the hub nut to 180 ft. lbs. Install the nut lock and a new cotter pin.
14. Install the wheel. Check and adjust the front end alignment as necessary.

Pacer

1. Disconnect the upper end of the shock absorber, raise the front end of the car and disconnect the lower end of the shock absorber and remove the shock absorber.
2. Disconnect the stabilizer bar at the lower control arm, if so equipped.
3. Remove the wheel, brake drum, or caliper and rotor. Do not allow the brake hose to support the weight of the caliper. Use wire to support it from the frame.
4. Remove the two bolts attaching the steering arm to the steering knuckle and more the steering arm aside.
To install:
5. Install a spring compressor and compress the spring.
6. Remove the cotter pin and nut from the lower ball joint stud. Remove the ball joint from the steering knuckle using a ball joint removal tool.
7. Move the steering knuckle assembly out of the way. Support the assembly with wire from the upper control arm.
8. Remove the two pivot bolts that attache the lower arm to the front crossmember and remove the lower control arm.
9. Install the lower control arm in the reverse order of removal, tightening the ball joint stud nut to 75 ft. lbs., the steering arm attaching bolts to 80 ft. lbs. through 1976, 55 ft. lbs. 1977 and later, the shock absorber lower attaching nuts to 20 ft. lbs., the stabilizer bar locknut to 8 ft. lbs., and lastly, after the car has been lowered to the ground with the wheel and tire installed, tighten the lower control arm pivot bolts to 95 ft. lbs. through 1976, and 110 ft. lbs. thereafter.

Ball Joints

INSPECTION

Except Pacer

➡**Be sure that the front wheel bearings are adjusted to specification before checking the upper ball joint.**

1. Jack up the front of the car and place jackstands under the frame side sills.

➡**The control arms must hang free if an accurate reading is to be obtained.**

2. Check the lower ball joints by grasping the lower portion of the wheel and pulling it in and out.

3. If there is noticeable lateral free-play, the lower ball joint is worn and must be replaced.

➡**The lower ball joints and control arms must be replaced as assemblies on Eagles.**

4. To check the condition of the upper ball joint, place a dial indicator with its plunger against the tire scrub bead (just outside the whitewall).

5. Move the upper portion of the wheel and tire toward the car's center, while watching the dial indicator.

6. Move the wheel and tire back out while watching the indicator.

7. The upper ball joint should be replaced it is total movement is greater than 0.160 in. (4.06mm).

➡**The upper ball joints and control arms must be replaced as assemblies on 1980 Eagles. On 1981 and later Eagles the upper ball joints are replaceable separately.**

Pacer

1. Check that the front wheel bearings are adjusted properly.
2. Remove the lubrication plug from the lower ball joints. Insert a piece of stiff wire until it contacts the ball. Mark the wire even with the edge of the plug hole.
3. Measure from the end of the wire to the mark. If it exceeds 7/16 in. (11.11mm), the ball joint should be replaced.
4. Place a jack under the lower control arm and lift the wheel off the floor.
5. Push the top of the tire in and out. If there is any looseness, replace the upper ball joint.
6. Pry the upper control arm up and down. If there is any looseness, replace the upper ball joint.

REMOVAL & INSTALLATION

➡**On Eagles, do not attempt to replace the ball joints separately. If the ball joints are worn, the control arms and ball joints must be replaced as complete assemblies.**

Lower Ball Joint

1. On all vehicles except Pacer, place a 2 in. × 4 in. × 5 in. (51mm × 102mm × 127mm) block of wood on the side sill so that it supports the control arm.

2. Jack up the front end of the car and place jackstands underneath the frame side sills to support the body.

3. Remove the wheel and the brake drum. On cars equipped with disc brakes, remove the caliper and rotor.

4. Disconnect the lower control arm strut rod, on models other than Pacer. Disconnect the stabilizer bar, if so equipped.

5. Separate the steering arm from the steering knuckle.

6. Remove the ball stud retaining nut, after removing its cotter pin.

7. Install a ball joint removal tool then loosen the ball stud in the knuckle pin. Leave the tool in place on the stud.

8. Place a jackstand under the lower control arm.

9. Chisel the heads off the rivets which secure the ball joint to the control arm. Use a punch to remove the rivets.

10. Remove the tool from the ball stud.

11. Remove the ball stud from the knuckle pin and remove the joint from the control arm.

To install:

1. Position the new ball joint so that its securing holes align with the rivet holes in the control arm.

2. Install the special 5/16 in. bolts, used to secure the ball joint, loosely.

❊ CAUTION

Use only the hardened 5/16 in. bolts supplied with the ball joint replacement kit; standard bolts are not strong enough.

3. Install the steering strut and stop on the lower control arm. Tighten their bolts to 75 ft. lbs.

4. Tighten the 5/16 in. ball joint securing bolts to 25 ft. lbs.

5. Apply chassis grease to the steering stops and fit the knuckle pin and retaining nut on the ball stud; tighten the nut to 40 ft. lbs. through 1976, 75 ft. lbs. through 1976, 75 ft. lbs. thereafter, and 75 ft. lbs. on all Pacers. Install a new cotter pin.

6. Complete the installation procedure in the reverse order of removal and then check front end alignment.

Upper Ball Joint

1. Perform Steps 1–3 of the lower ball joint removal procedure in this section.

➡**It is not necessary to remove the brake drum in Step 3. On 1981 and later Eagle models temporarily reinstall two lug nuts to retain each brake rotor. This eliminates repositioning rotors and calipers prior to reassembly.**

2. News, perform Steps 6–9 of the lower ball joint removal procedure to the upper ball joint.

3. Separate the upper ball joint from the knuckle pin.

To install:

1. Perform Steps 1–2 of the lower ball joint installation procedure.

2. Skip Step 3 and go on to Steps 4–5 of the lower ball joint installation procedure.

3. Complete the installation in the reverse order of removal and check front end alignment.

Wheel Bearings

4-wheel drive models have sealed, non-adjustable front hubs and bearings. There are darkened areas surrounding the bearing races in the hubs, which are the result of a heat treatment process; the darkened areas do not signify a defect.

INSPECTION

Check to see the inner cones of the bearings are free to 'creep' on the spindle. Polish and lubricate the spindle to allow 'creeping' movement and to keep rust from forming.

ADJUSTMENT

1. With the tire and wheel removed and the car supported by a suitable and safe means, remove the dust cover from the spindle.
2. Remove the cotter pin and nut retainer.
3. Rotate the wheel while tightening the spindle nut to 20–25 ft. lbs.

With new or freshly packed bearings, tighten the nut while gently spinning the wheel, then adjust the bearings

After the bearings are adjusted, install the dust cap by gently tapping on the flange—DO NOT damage the cap by hammering on the center

4. Loosen the spindle nut ⅓ of a turn.
5. Rotate the wheel while tightening the spindle nut to 6 inch lbs.
6. Fit the nut retainer over the spindle and align the slots in it with the cotter pin hole. Insert the cotter pin.
7. Install the dust cover.
8. Install the wheel assembly.

Front End Alignment

Correct alignment of the front suspension is necessary to provide optimum tire life and for proper and safe handling of the vehicle. Caster and camber cannot be set or measured accurately without professional equipment. Toe-in can be adjusted with some degree of success without any special equipment.

CASTER

Caster is the tilt of the front steering axis either forward or backward away from the vertical. A tilt toward the rear is said to be positive and a forward tilt is negative. Caster is calculated with a special instrument but one can see the caster angle by looking straight down from the top of the upper control arm. You will see that the ball joints are not aligned if the caster angle is more or less than 0 degrees. If the vehicle has positive caster, the lower ball joint would be ahead of the upper ball joint center line.

Caster angle affects straight line stability

CAMBER

Camber is the slope of the front wheels from the vertical when viewed from the front of the vehicle. When the wheels tilt outward at the top, the camber is positive. When the wheels tilt inward at the top, the camber is negative. The amount of positive and negative camber is measured in degrees from the vertical and the measurement is called camber angle.

Camber angle influences tire contact with the road

Toe-in

Toe-in means the distance between the wheels is closer at the front than at the rear of the wheels

TOE-IN

Toe-in is the amount, measured in a fraction of an inch, that the wheels are closer together in front than at the rear. Some vehicles are set with toe-out, that is, the wheels are closer together at the rear, than the front, to prevent excessive toe-in under power.

Wheel Alignment Specifications

AMX

Year	Caster (deg.) Range	Pref.	Camber (deg.) Range	Pref.	Toe-in (in.)	King Pin Incl. (deg.)
All	0 to 2½P	1¼P	0 to ¾P	⅜P	1/16 to 3/16	7¾

Gremlin/Hornet/Spirit/Concord

Year	Caster (deg.) Range	Pref.	Camber (deg.) Range	Pref.	Toe-in (in.)	King Pin Incl. (deg.)
1975–77	½N to ½P	0	①	②	1/16 to 3/16	7¾
1978	½P to 1½P	1P	①	②	1/16 to 3/16	7¾
1979–80	0 to 2½P	1¼P	0 to ¾P	⅜P	1/16 to 3/16	7¾
1981–82	0 to 2½P	1¼P	③	④	1/16 to 3/16	7¾
1983	3½P to 5P	4¼P	⑤	⑥	1/16 to 3/16	7¾

① Left: ⅛P to ⅝P
   Right: 0 to ½P
② Left: ⅜P
   Right: ¼P
③ Left: ⅛P to ¾P
   Right: ⅛P to ½P
④ Left: 7/16P
   Right: 5/16P
⑤ Left: ⅛P to ¾P
   Right: ⅛N to ½P
⑥ Left: 7/16P
   Right: 3/16P

Wheel Alignment Specifications

Matador

Year	Caster (deg.) Range	Pref.	Camber (deg.) Range	Pref.	Toe-in (in.)	King Pin Incl. (deg.)
1975–77	½P to 1½P	1P	①	②	¹⁄₁₆ to ³⁄₁₆	7¾
1978	0 to 2P	1P	①	②	¹⁄₁₆ to ³⁄₁₆	7¾

① Left: ⅛P to ⅝P
  Right: 0 to ½P
② Left: ⅜P
  Right: ¼P

Pacer

Year	Caster (deg.) Range	Pref.	Camber (deg.) Range	Pref.	Toe-in (in.)	King Pin Incl. (deg.)
1975–77	½P to 1½P	1P	①	②	¹⁄₁₆ to ³⁄₁₆	7¾
1978	1P to 3P	2P	①	②	¹⁄₁₆ to ³⁄₁₆	7¾
1979–80	1P to 3½P	2¼P	0 to ¾P	⅜P	¹⁄₁₆ to ³⁄₁₆	7¾

① Left: ⅛P to ⅝P
  Right: 0 to ½P
② Left: ⅜P
  Right: ¼P

Eagle

Year	Caster (deg.) Range	Pref.	Camber (deg.) Range	Pref.	Toe-out (in.)	King Pin Incl. (deg.)
1980	3P to 5P	4P	⅜N to ⅜P	0	¹⁄₁₆ to ³⁄₁₆	11½
1981–82	2P to 3P	2½P	⅛N to ⅝P	¼P	①	11½
1983	3P to 5P	2½P	⅛N to ⅝P	¼P	¹⁄₁₆ to ³⁄₁₆	11½
1984–88	2P to 3½P	2¾P	⅛N to ⅝P	¼P	¹⁄₁₆ to ³⁄₁₆	11½

① 1981: ¹⁄₁₆ to ³⁄₁₆
  1982: ¹⁄₁₆ out to ¹⁄₁₆ in

REAR SUSPENSION

REAR SUSPENSION COMPONENT LOCATIONS - LATE MODEL EAGLE

1. Shock absorbers
2. Leaf spring-to-axle U-bolts
3. Leaf springs
4. Axle assembly

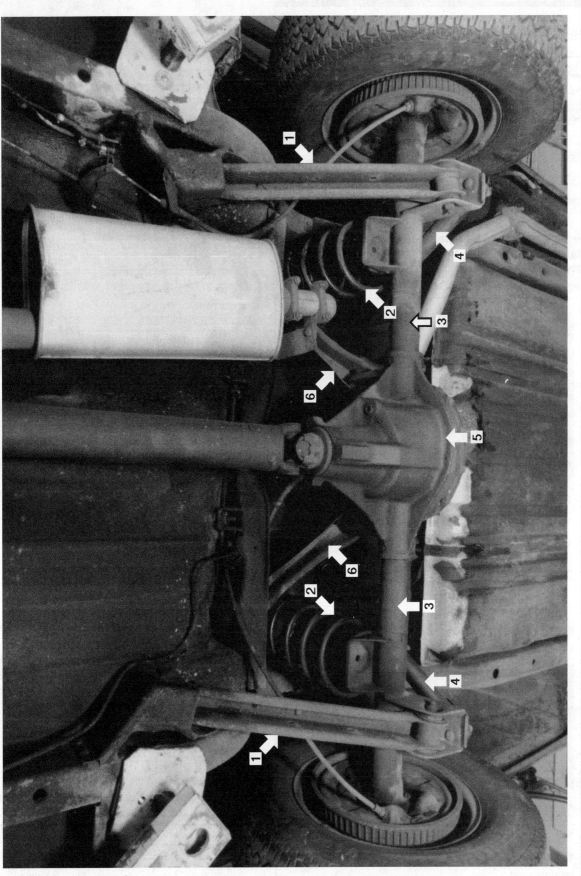

REAR SUSPENSION COMPONENT LOCATIONS - EARLY MODEL MATADOR

1. Lower control arm
2. Coil springs
3. Rear axle
4. Rear shock absorbers
5. Rear differential housing
6. Upper control arm

Shock Absorber

REMOVAL & INSTALLATION

➡**When installing new shocks purge them of air by repeatedly extending them in their normal position and compressing them while inverted. It is normal for there to be more resistance to extension than to compression.**

1. Support the rear axle with jacks or a lift; this allows the weight of the car to compress the rear spring.
2. Remove the lower shock attachment.
3. Remove the access plate on the rear underbody panel and remove the upper securing nut. It may be necessary to hold the top of the shock while unfastening the nut.

➡**Some models do not have an access plate. On these cars, remove the upper attachment plate complete as an assembly from under the car.**

. . . then remove the nut and washer

4. Remove the shock from under the car.
5. Installation is the reverse of removal.

Location of the rear shock absorber

Leaf Springs

REMOVAL & INSTALLATION

◆ See Figures 5, 6 and 7

1. Raise the car. Support the rear axle with jacks or a lift to take the load off the rear springs.
2. Disconnect the rear shock from the lower mounting stud.
3. Disconnect the axle U-bolts.
4. Remove the nut from the bolt which attaches the eye of the spring to the front mount. Remove the bolt.
5. On all except Pacer, remove the nuts from the rear shackle. Remove the shackle.
6. On the Pacer, remove the nuts from the rear hanger bracket on the frame sill and remove the spring. Remove the shackle after the spring is removed.
7. Installation is the reverse.

Coil Springs

REMOVAL & INSTALLATION

◆ See Figure 8

1. Raise the rear of the car and support the rear axle with jacks or a lift to take the load off the rear springs.
2. Disconnect the shock from the axle tube. Lower the axle to the fullest extent of its travel (limited by the control arms). Detach the upper control arms at the axle on 1975 and later models.
3. Pull down the axle tube to completely release the spring.
4. Reverse the above to install the spring. Torque the control arm pivot bolts to 45–80 ft. lbs. with the weight of the car on the springs.

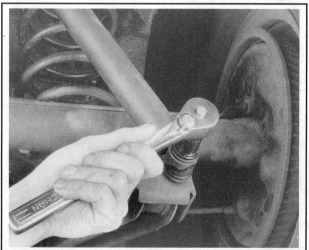

To remove the rear shock absorber, loosen the lower retaining nut . . .

Fig. 5 Exploded view of the leaf spring rear suspension—1975–76 models except Matador

Fig. 6 Rear suspension components—1977–82 models except Matador and Eagle

Fig. 7 Exploded view of the rear spring rear suspension assembly—Eagle models

Fig. 8 Rear suspension components—Matador models

STEERING

A collapsible, energy absorbing steering column is used. No service operations involving removal or disassembly of the steering column are given here. Such critical and delicate operations should be entrusted to qualified AMC service personnel.

Steering Wheel

REMOVAL & INSTALLATION

▶ **See Figures 9 and 10**

➡Some steering shafts have metric steering wheel nut threads. Metric shafts are identified by a groove running around the splines, and blue colored threads.

1. Disconnect the battery ground cable.
2. On wheels with horn button, remove the button by lifting up and pulling out.

3. On wheels with a horn bar, remove the screws from the back of the wheel and remove the bar. Do the same on rimblow wheels.
4. On rim-blow wheels, pull the wire out of the center connection.
5. Remove the nut and washer.
6. Install the bolts of a steering wheel puller into the tapped holes in the wheel and remove the wheel from the shaft.

Fig. 10 Use a puller to remove the steering wheel

Fig. 9 The metric steering shaft is identified by a groove running around the splines

To remove the steering wheel, first unfasten the horn pad retaining screws . . .

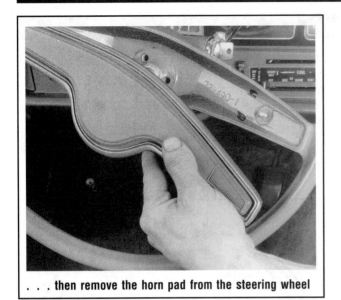

. . . then remove the horn pad from the steering wheel

Install a puller on the steering wheel . . .

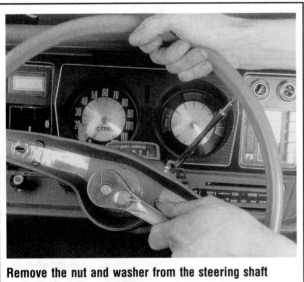

Remove the nut and washer from the steering shaft

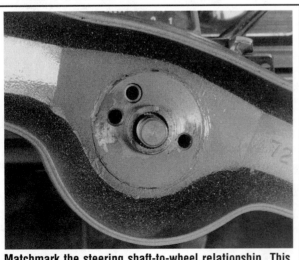

Matchmark the steering shaft-to-wheel relationship. This will aid in installation

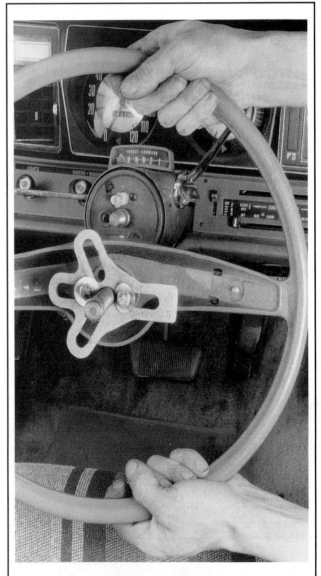

. . . then remove the steering wheel from the column

✳ CAUTION

Don't hammer on the steering wheel or the shaft. You could easily collapse your collapsible steering column.

To install:

7. Align the marks on the steering shaft and the wheel at the top.

8. Install the washer and nut and tighten the nut to 20 ft. lbs. This is a critical fastener; it must be torqued.

9. On wheels with a horn button, index the projection on the rubber retaining ring with the notch in the cup and push down to engage the ring.

10. On wheels with a horn bar, place the horn wire in the hole and secure it with the retainer and then install the screws. Do the same for rim-blow wheels.

11. Connect the battery cable.

Turn Signal Switch, Hazard Signal and Lock Cylinder

REMOVAL & INSTALLATION

▶ **See Figures 11, 12 and 13**

1. Disconnect the ground cable from the battery. On cars with tilt steering wheels, place the column in the straight position. Remove the steering wheel.

2. Loosen the anti-theft cover attaching screws and remove the cover from the column. Do not hammer on the shaft. Do not move the screws from the cover; they are attached to it with plastic retainers.

3. To remove the lockplate, a special compressor is required. This tool is an inverted U-shape with a hole for the shaft. The shaft nut is used to force it down. Depress the lockplate and pry the snapring from the groove in the steering shaft. Remove the tool, snapring, plate, turn signal cam, upper bearing preload spring, and thrust washer from the shaft.

Fig. 11 Use a suitable compressor tool to remove the lockplate from the steering column

Fig. 12 Turn signal switch mounting

Fig. 13 Removing the lock cylinder from the steering column

4. Place the turn signal lever in the right turn position and remove it.

5. Depress the hazard warning switch button and remove it, by rotating it counterclockwise. Remove the package tray (if equipped) and the lower trim panel.

6. Disconnect the wire harness connector block at its mounting bracket, which is located on the right side of the lower column. Remove the steering column mounting bracket attaching bolts. Remove the turn signal switch wiring harness protector from the bottom of the column.

➡️To aid in the removal and replacement of the directional switch harness, tape the harness connector to the wire harness to prevent snagging when removing the wiring harness assembly through the steering column. Prepare the new turn signal switch harness in the same manner for ease of installation.

7. On Gremlin, Hornet, Concord, and Spirit models equipped with a column mounted automatic transmission selector, use a paper clip to depress the locktab that holds the shift quadrant light wire in the connector block.

8. Remove the switch attaching screws. Withdraw the switch and wire harness from the column.

9. Insert the key into the lock cylinder and turn to the ON position. Remove the warning buzzer switch and the contacts as an assembly using needlenosed pliers. Take care not to let the contacts fall into the column.

10. Turn the key to the LOCK position and compress the lock cylinder retaining tab. Remove the lock cylinder. If the tab is not visible through the slot, knock the casting flash out of the slot.

To install:

1. Hold the lock cylinder sleeve and turn the lock cylinder clockwise (counterclockwise 1977 and later) until it contacts the stop.

2. Align the lock cylinder key with the keyway in the housing and slip the cylinder into the housing.

3. Lightly depress the cylinder against the sector, while turning it counterclockwise, until the cylinder and sector are engaged.

4. Depress the cylinder until the retaining tab engages, and the lock cylinder is secured.

5. Install the turn signal switch. Be sure that the actuating lever pivot is properly seated and aligned in the top of the housing boss, before installing it with its screws.

6. Install the turn signal lever and check the operation of the switch.

7. Install the thrust washer, spring and turn signal cancelling cam on the steering shaft.

8. Align the lockplate and steering shaft splines, and position the lockplate so that the turn signal camshaft protrudes from the 'dogleg' opening in the lockplate.

9. Use snapring pliers to install the snapring on the end of the steering shaft.

10. Secure the anti-theft cover with its screws.

11. Install the button on the hazard warning switch. Install the steering wheel, as detailed above.

Ignition Switch

REMOVAL & INSTALLATION

◆ See Figure 14

➡️The ignition switch on all models is mounted on the lower steering column tube and is connected to the lock cylinder via a lock rod.

1. Place the key in OFF/LOCK.
2. Remove the switch mounting screws.
3. Disconnect the lock rod, remove harness connector and switch.

Fig. 14 Ignition switch slider function locations

To install:

4. On the standard column, move the switch slide as far as it will go to the left (toward the wheel). On the tilt column, push the slide to the extreme right.

5. Position the lock rod into the hole on the switch slide.

6. Install the switch on the steering column. Be sure that the slide stays in its detent.

7. On the tilt column, do not tighten the mounting screws. Instead, push the switch down the column, away from the steering wheel. This will remove any slack from the lock rod.

8. Tighten the switch mounting screws.

Manual Steering Gear

REMOVAL & INSTALLATION

Except Pacer

◆ See Figures 15, 16 and 17

1. Remove the flexible coupling bolts.
2. Remove the pitman arm, using puller J-5566-04 or its equivalent.

Fig. 15 Use puller J-5566-04 or its equivalent to remove the pitman arm

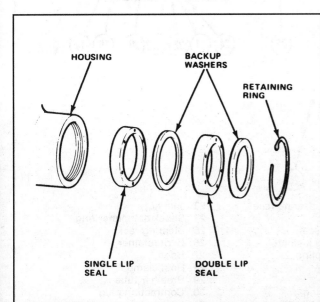

Fig. 16 Exploded view of the Pitman shaft seal assembly sequence

Fig. 17 Sectional view of the intermediate shaft and flexible coupling alignment

3. Remove the steering gear mounting screws and lower the steering gear.

To install:

1. Center the steering gear with the index mark up. The mark on the shaft of the flange must be aligned at assembly.

2. Insert the flexible coupling bolts into the shaft flange. Tighten the nuts to 20 ft. lbs. torque and the pinch bolt 30 ft. lbs.

3. Tighten the gear mounting screws to 65 ft. lbs. and the Pitman arm nut to 115 ft. lbs.

➡**After tightening the Pitman shaft nut, stake the thread at nut with a center punch to insure nut retention. Whenever the steering gear assembly is removed for replacement or overhaul, or the mounting bolts are loosened for any reason, the steering column MUST be realigned to the gear assembly. Slight misalignment of the steering column may cause increased steering effort and additional wear to the steering components.**

Pacer

GEAR ASSEMBLY

1. Unlock the steering column.

2. Raise and support the front of the car.

3. Remove the screws attaching the reinforcement brace to the front crossmember and the left engine support bracket and remove the brace.

4. Remove the flexible coupling pinch bolt and disengage the flexible coupling from the steering gear pinion shaft.

5. Remove the cotter pins and nuts from the tie rod ends.

6. Disconnect the rod ends using tool J-26951 or its equivalent.

7. Remove the bolts attaching the steering gear mounting clamp to the right side of the front crossmember.

➡**Before removing the bolts, loosen them slightly to minimize clamp distortion.**

8. Remove the steering gear housing-to-crossmember nuts. Remove the bolts, washers, sleeves, and grommets using a blunt punch.

9. Rotate the bottom of gear housing toward the front of the car until the pinion shaft is approximately parallel with the skid plate. Slide the gear assembly toward the right side of the car until the housing and tube clear the mounting plate and remove the steering gear assembly.

To install:

10. Assemble the grommets, sleeves, and washers and install them on the steering gear. The sleeves will hold the grommets in place during assembly.

11. Position the steering gear assembly on the crossmember. Install the tube and housing from the right side of the car. During installation, keep the pinion shaft approximately parallel with the mounting plate.

12. Install the mounting clamp-to-crossmember attaching bolts. Hand-tighten the bolts only.

13. Install the steering gear housing-to-crossmember attaching bolts, washers, and nuts and tighten them to 60 ft. lbs. torque.

14. Tighten the mounting clamp-to-crossmember attaching bolts to 50 ft. lbs. torque.

15. Connect the tie rod ends to the steering arms. Tighten the nuts to 50 ft. lbs. torque and install the replacement cotter pins.

16. Align the flat spline on the pinion shaft with the flat on the flexible coupling and install the coupling on the shaft. Install the pinch bolt and tighten it to 30 ft. lbs. torque.

17. Install the bolts attaching the reinforcement brace to the front crossmember and the engine support bracket. Tighten the bolts to 30 ft. lbs. torque.

18. Remove the supports and lower the car.

19. Check and correct the toe-in adjustment if necessary.

RUBBER BOOT
◆ See Figures 18, 19 and 20

1. Raise and support the front end of the car.

2. Cut and remove the boot clamps from the boot adjacent to the mounting clamp.

3. Mark the position of the adjuster tube and tie rod for assembly reference.

4. Loosen the adjuster tube clamp bolts and unthread the tube from tie rod.

5. Remove the boot.

1. Tie rod seal
2. Tie rod end
3. Adjuster tube
4. Mounting grommet
5. Mounting clamp
6. Tube and housing assembly
7. Upper pinion bushing
8. Lower thrust bearing race
9. Lower thrust bearing
10. Pinion shaft
11. Upper thrust bearing
12. Upper thrust bearing race
13. Adjuster plug
14. Pinion shaft seal
15. Adjuster plug locknut
16. Flexible coupling
17. Pinch bolt
18. Set screw
19. Tie rod housing
20. Inner tie rod
21. Ball seat
22. Ball seat spring
23. Jam nut
24. Shock dampener ring
25. Steering rack
26. Boot retainer
27. Boot
28. Boot clamp
29. Breather tube
30. Contraction plug
31. Lower pinion bushing
32. Preload spring

Fig. 18 Exploded view of the manual steering assembly—Pacer models

Fig. 19 Use tool J-26951 or its equivalent to disconnect the tie rod end from the manual steering gear—Pacer

Fig. 20 Manual steering gear mounting and components—Pacer models

✳✳ CAUTION

Do not allow the protective boot to become cut or torn during service operations. A damaged boot will expose the gear internal components to dirt, foreign material, and road splash resulting in premature wear.

    6. Remove the bolts attaching the mounting clamp to the front crossmember. Loosen the bolts before removing to minimize clamp distortion.
    7. Remove the clamp and grommet using a twisting, pulling motion.

To install:
    8. Install a replacement clamp and grommet. Align the hole in the grommet with the breather tube.
    9. Install the mounting clamp attaching bolts. Tighten the bolts to 50 ft. lbs. torque.
    10. Install the boot. Align the hole in the boot with the breather tube.
    11. Install the boot clamps. Position the ear of the clamps ¾ in. (19.05mm) from the breather tube. Compress the clamps using tool J-22610 or its equivalent.
    12. Install the adjuster tube on the tie rod and tighten the clamp bolts to 22 ft. lbs. torque.

➥**At least three threads should be visible at each end of adjuster tube. The number of threads per side should not differ by more than three.**

    13. Remove the supports, lower the car, and correct the toe-in as necessary.

BREATHER TUBE

    1. Raise and support the front of the car.
    2. Cut and remove the large diameter boot clamps from the boots.
    3. Slide the boots away from the breather tube and remove the tube.
To install:
    4. Install the replacement breather tube. Align the holes in the boots with the tube.
    5. Position the boots on the flanges at each end of the tube and housing and install the boot clamps. Position the clamp ear ¾ in. (19.05mm) from the breather tube. Tighten the clamps using tool J-22610 or its equivalent.
    6. Remove the supports and lower the car.

FLEXIBLE COUPLING

    1. Remove the nuts attaching the coupling to the intermediate shaft flange and compress the shaft to provide working clearance.
    2. Remove the coupling pinch bolt using ⁷⁄₁₆ in., 12 point socket or box end wrench and remove the coupling.
    3. Install the replacement coupling (flat-to-flat) and install the pinch bolt. Tighten the bolt to 30 ft. lbs. torque.
    4. Connect the intermediate shaft to the coupling and tighten the nuts to 25 ft. lbs. torque.

ADJUSTMENTS

Except Pacer

✳✳ CAUTION

Adjustments to the steering gear must be made only in the sequence given here or the steering gear will be damaged. That is, you must do the worm bearing preload adjustment before the sector and ball nut backlash adjustment, and you must do them both.

WORM BEARING PRELOAD
♦ **See Figures 21 and 22**

    1. Disconnect the battery ground cable.
    2. Remove the Pitman arm (the arm on the steering box) nut and mark the relationship of the arm to the shaft.

Fig. 21 Use a torque wrench to measure the manual steering gear Pitman shaft over-center torque drag adjustment

Fig. 22 Worm bearing preload adjustment on the manual steering gear

3. Use a puller to remove the pitman arm from the shaft.

4. Loosen the pitman shaft adjusting screw locknut and back off the adjusting screw (the small adjusting screw on the cover) a few turns.

5. Remove the horn button or bar.

6. Gently turn the steering wheel in one direction until it can't go any further, then turn it back half a turn.

✳✳ CAUTION

If you turn the steering wheel hard against the stop with the linkage disconnected, you will damage the steering gear.

7. Attach a torque wrench with a maximum reading of 50 in. lbs. or less to the steering wheel nut. Turn the wheel through a quarter turn with the wrench. The torque reading should be 5–8 in. lbs.

8. To adjust, loosen the big worm bearing adjuster locknut with a brass drift and hammer. Turn the adjuster plug (viewed from underneath) clockwise to increase the preload.

9. Tighten the locknut to 50 ft. lbs. and recheck the preload.

10. Go on to the next adjustment.

SECTOR AND BALL NUT BACKLASH

1. Turn the wheel gently from full right stop to full left stop and count the total number of turns stop-to-stop.

2. Turn back half the number of turns to the center position, then turn half a turn past the center position.

3. Use the torque wrench on the steering wheel nut to turn the gear through the center of travel. The torque required should be 4–10 in. lbs. The sum of this torque and that measured after worm bearing preload adjustment must not exceed 16 in. lbs.

4. To adjust, turn the adjusting screw on the cover. Tighten the locknut and recheck the torque or force required.

5. Replace the pitman arm on the shaft, aligning the marks you made back in Step 2 of worm bearing preload adjustment.

6. Tighten the pitman arm nut to 115 ft. lbs. and stake it to the shaft. This is a critical fastener; it must be torqued. To stake the nut means to slightly distort its inner edge by use of a punch or chisel.

7. Replace the horn button or bar and battery ground cable.

Power Steering Pump

REMOVAL & INSTALLATION

4-150, 6-232, 258 and 8-304, 360 and 401 Engines

1. Place a drip pan under the pump.

2. Disconnect both hoses at the pump and plug them.

3. It may be necessary to remove the air pump drive belt. Your might also have to remove the steering pump pulley. On cars with A/C, it may be necessary to remove the compressor drivebelt and pulley.

4. Remove the pump mounting nuts and washers from behind.

5. On 6-cylinder engines, loosen the pump bracket pivot bolts. On V8 engines, remove the front pump mounting bracket.

6. Remove the pump drive belt and the pump. If the pulley was removed, torque the nut to 60 ft. lbs.

To install:

7. Install the pump to the engine.

8. Install the hoses.

9. Fill the reservoir with the proper fluid as described in Section 1.

10. Turn the pump pulley counterclockwise (front view) until no more bubbles appear.

11. Install the drive belt and adjust it. Some general thoughts

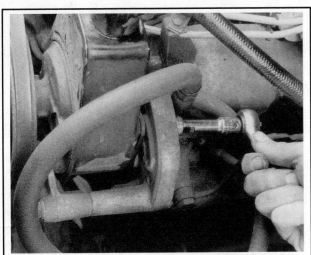

To remove the power steering pump, unfasten the retaining bolts and disconnect the drive belt

on drive belt tightening are given in Section 3 under the alternator removal and installation procedure. Most pumps have a boss behind the pulley so that you can apply tension with a 1⅝ in. (41mm) open end wrench.

12. Install and adjust the air pump belt.

13. Bleed the system by raising the front of the car and turning the wheels from side-to-side without hitting the stops for a few minutes. Check the level frequently.

4-121 Engine

1. Remove the adjuster locknuts and lockwashers retaining the pump and pivot bracket to the pump mounting bracket. The lower adjuster is accessible from underneath car.

➡**Except for the adjuster locknuts, all of the pump mounting bolts are metric sizes. The adjuster locknuts are loosened and tightened using a ⁹⁄₁₆ in. box end wrench having a 45° offset.**

2. Move the pump toward the engine and remove the pump belt.

3. Loosen the return hose clamp and slide the clamp back along the hose.

4. Pull the pump forward and disconnect both hoses.

5. Remove the bolts attaching the pump front mounting bracket to the rear mounting bracket and the engine block. Remove the pump, pivot bracket and front mounting bracket as an assembly.

6. Position the pump, front mounting bracket, and pivot bracket on the rear mounting bracket and connect the pressure and return hoses to the pump. Tighten the pressure hose fitting to 38 ft.lb. torque.

7. Install the front bracket-to-rear bracket bolts. Tighten the bolts to 25 ft. lbs. torque. Tighten the front bracket-to-engine blockbolt to 16 ft. lbs. torque.

8. Slide the return hose clamp into position and tighten the hose clamp.

9. Install the adjuster locknuts and lockwashers.

10. Adjust the pump belt.

4-151 Engine

1. Remove the ambient air induction hose and remove the adjusting bracket nut/bolts.

2. Move the pump toward the engine and remove the pump belt.

3. Loosen the return hose clamp and slide the clamp back along the hose.

4. Pull the pump forward and disconnect both hoses. The pressure hose has an 18mm metric fitting.

5. Remove the bolts attaching the pump front mounting bracket to the rear mounting bracket and the engine block. Remove the pump, pivot bracket, and front mounting bracket as an assembly.

6. Position the pump and mounting brackets on the engine. Connect the pressure and return hoses to the pump. Tighten the pressure hose fitting to 38 ft. lbs. torque.

7. Install the bracket and bracket bolts/nuts. Tighten the bolts to 25 ft. lbs. torque.

8. Adjust the pump belt tension.

Remove the pump from the vehicle

Power Steering Gear

REMOVAL & INSTALLATION

Except Pacer

1. Place the wheels in a straight ahead position.
2. Position a drain pan under the steering gear.
3. Disconnect the hoses at gear. Raise and secure the hoses above the pump fluid level to prevent excessive oil spillage, and cap ends of the hoses to prevent the entry of dirt.
4. Remove the flexible coupling-to-intermediate shaft attaching nuts.
5. Raise the automobile on hoist. On Eagle models, remove:
   a. skid plate, if equipped.
   b. left side crossmember-to-sill support brace.
   c. stabilizer bar brackets from frame.
6. Paint alignment marks on the pitman arm and the pitman shaft for assembly reference.
7. Remove the pitman arm using Puller Tool J-5566-04 or its equivalent.
8. Remove the steering gear mounting bolts and remove the steering gear.

To install:

1. Center the steering gear. Turn the stub shaft (using flexible coupling) from stop-to-stop and count the total number of turns; then turn it back from either stop, one-half the total number of turns to center the gear. At this pint, the flat on the stub shaft should be facing upward.
2. Align the flexible coupling and intermediate shaft flange.
3. Install the gear mounting bolts in the gear, install the spacer on the gear, and mount the gear on the frame side sill. Tighten the gear mounting bolts to 65 ft. lbs. torque.
4. Install and tighten the flexible coupling nuts to 25 ft. lbs. torque.
5. Install the pitman arm. Index the arm to the shaft using the alignment marks made during removal.
6. Install the pitman arm nut. Tighten the nut to 115 ft. lbs. torque and stake the nut to the pitman shaft in one place.

❈❈ CAUTION

The pitman arm nut must be staked to the shaft to retain it properly.

7. On Eagle models, install:
   a. stabilizer bar brackets.
   b. left side crossmember-to-sill support brace.
   c. skid plate, if equipped.
8. Lower the automobile.
9. Align the flexible coupling, if necessary. Refer to Flexible Coupling Adjustment.
10. Fill the pump reservoir with power steering fluid and bleed the air from the system.

Pacer

GEAR ASSEMBLY

▶ **See Figures 23, 24 and 25**

1. Unlock the steering column.
2. Raise and support the front of the car.

Fig. 23 Power steering gear removal—Pacer models

Fig. 24 Power steering gear and mounting components—Pacer models

Fig. 25 Power steering gear mounting—Pacer models

3. Remove the screws attaching the reinforcement brace to the front crossmember and the left engine support bracket and remove the brace.

4. Disconnect the stabilizer bar at the left side lower control arm, if equipped.

5. Remove the bolts attaching the stabilizer bar mounting clamps to the frame rail brackets and move the bar away from the front crossmember.

6. Place a support under the stabilizer bar to prevent damaging the bolt attaching the bar to the right side lower control arm.

7. Remove the left side frame rail clamp brackets.

8. Position a drain pan under the steering gear housing and disconnect the power steering hoses at the gear housing. Cap the hoses and plug the gear to prevent the entry of dirt.

9. Remove the flexible coupling pinch bolt and disengage the flexible coupling from the steering gear pinion shaft.

10. Remove and discard the cotter pins from the tie rod end retaining nuts.

11. Disconnect the tie rod ends using tool J-26951.

12. Remove the bolts attaching the steering gear mounting clamp to the crossmember.

✳✳ CAUTION

Before removing the bolts, loosen them slightly to minimize clamp distortion.

13. Remove the steering gear housing-to-crossmember attaching bolt nuts.

14. Remove the bolts, washers, sleeves and grommets from the steering gear housing using a blunt punch.

15. Rotate the bottom of the gear housing toward the front of the car until the pinion shaft is approximately parallel with the skid plate. Slide the gear assembly toward the right side of car until the housing and tube clear the mounting plate and remove the steering gear assembly.

16. Assemble and install the grommets, sleeves, and washers on the steering gear. The sleeves will hold the grommets in place during assembly.

17. Position the steering gear assembly on the crossmember. Install the gear from the driver's side of the car.

➡ **When installing the gear, keep the pinion shaft approximately parallel with the mounting plate.**

18. Install the mounting clamp bolts. Hand-tighten the bolts only.

19. Install the steering gear housing-to-crossmember attaching bolts, washers, and nuts and tighten them to 60 ft. lbs.

20. Tighten the mounting clamp bolts to 48 ft. lbs.

21. Connect the tie rod end to the steering arms. Tighten the tie rod end retaining nuts to 50 ft. lbs. and install the replacement cotter pints.

22. Align the flat spline of the steering gear pinion shaft with the index flat of the flexible coupling and install the coupling on pinion shaft. Install the pinch bolt and tighten it to 30 ft. lbs.

23. Install the bolts attaching the reinforcement bracket to the front crossmember and engine support bracket. Tighten the bolts to 30 ft. lbs.

24. Connect the power steering hoses to the gear housing. Be sure that the hoses do not touch the brace or crossmember.

25. Install the left side frame rail clamp brackets.

26. Position the stabilizer bar on the frame rail brackets and install the mounting clamp colts. Hand-tighten only.

27. Install the bolts, washers, and grommets attaching the stabilizer bar to the left side lower control arm.

28. Tighten the stabilizer bar mounting clamp bolts to 18 ft. lbs.

29. Remove the supports and lower the car.

30. Fill the power steering pump reservoir with power steering fluid.

31. Operate the engine until the fluid reaches normal operating temperature. Turn the wheel right and left several times (do not hold the wheel against the steering stops). Stop the engine and check the fluid level. Add fluid as necessary.

Troubleshooting Basic Steering and Suspension Problems

Problem	Cause	Solution
Hard steering (steering wheel is hard to turn)	• Low or uneven tire pressure • Loose power steering pump drive belt • Low or incorrect power steering fluid • Incorrect front end alignment • Defective power steering pump • Bent or poorly lubricated front end parts	• Inflate tires to correct pressure • Adjust belt • Add fluid as necessary • Have front end alignment checked/adjusted • Check pump • Lubricate and/or replace defective parts
Loose steering (too much play in the steering wheel)	• Loose wheel bearings • Loose or worn steering linkage • Faulty shocks • Worn ball joints	• Adjust wheel bearings • Replace worn parts • Replace shocks • Replace ball joints
Car veers or wanders (car pulls to one side with hands off the steering wheel)	• Incorrect tire pressure • Improper front end alignment • Loose wheel bearings • Loose or bent front end components • Faulty shocks	• Inflate tires to correct pressure • Have front end alignment checked/adjusted • Adjust wheel bearings • Replace worn components • Replace shocks
Wheel oscillation or vibration transmitted through steering wheel	• Improper tire pressures • Tires out of balance • Loose wheel bearings • Improper front end alignment • Worn or bent front end components	• Inflate tires to correct pressure • Have tires balanced • Adjust wheel bearings • Have front end alignment checked/adjusted • Replace worn parts
Uneven tire wear	• Incorrect tire pressure • Front end out of alignment • Tires out of balance	• Inflate tires to correct pressure • Have front end alignment checked/adjusted • Have tires balanced

Troubleshooting the Steering Column

Problem	Cause	Solution
Will not lock	• Lockbolt spring broken or defective	• Replace lock bolt spring
High effort (required to turn ignition key and lock cylinder)	• Lock cylinder defective • Ignition switch defective • Rack preload spring broken or deformed • Burr on lock sector, lock rack, housing, support or remote rod coupling • Bent sector shaft • Defective lock rack • Remote rod bent, deformed • Ignition switch mounting bracket bent • Distorted coupling slot in lock rack (tilt column)	• Replace lock cylinder • Replace ignition switch • Replace preload spring • Remove burr • Replace shaft • Replace lock rack • Replace rod • Straighten or replace • Replace lock rack
Will stick in "start"	• Remote rod deformed • Ignition switch mounting bracket bent	• Straighten or replace • Straighten or replace
Key cannot be removed in "off-lock"	• Ignition switch is not adjusted correctly • Defective lock cylinder	• Adjust switch • Replace lock cylinder
Lock cylinder can be removed without depressing retainer	• Lock cylinder with defective retainer • Burr over retainer slot in housing cover or on cylinder retainer	• Replace lock cylinder • Remove burr
High effort on lock cylinder between "off" and "off-lock"	• Distorted lock rack • Burr on tang of shift gate (automatic column) • Gearshift linkage not adjusted	• Replace lock rack • Remove burr • Adjust linkage
Noise in column	• One click when in "off-lock" position and the steering wheel is moved (all except automatic column) • Coupling bolts not tightened • Lack of grease on bearings or bearing surfaces • Upper shaft bearing worn or broken • Lower shaft bearing worn or broken • Column not correctly aligned • Coupling pulled apart • Broken coupling lower joint • Steering shaft snap ring not seated • Shroud loose on shift bowl. Housing loose on jacket—will be noticed with ignition in "off-lock" and when torque is applied to steering wheel.	• Normal—lock bolt is seating • Tighten pinch bolts • Lubricate with chassis grease • Replace bearing assembly • Replace bearing. Check shaft and replace if scored. • Align column • Replace coupling • Repair or replace joint and align column • Replace ring. Check for proper seating in groove. • Position shroud over lugs on shift bowl. Tighten mounting screws.
High steering shaft effort	• Column misaligned • Defective upper or lower bearing • Tight steering shaft universal joint • Flash on I.D. of shift tube at plastic joint (tilt column only) • Upper or lower bearing seized	• Align column • Replace as required • Repair or replace • Replace shift tube • Replace bearings
Lash in mounted column assembly	• Column mounting bracket bolts loose • Broken weld nuts on column jacket • Column capsule bracket sheared	• Tighten bolts • Replace column jacket • Replace bracket assembly

Troubleshooting the Steering Column (cont.)

Problem	Cause	Solution
Lash in mounted column assembly (cont.)	• Column bracket to column jacket mounting bolts loose	• Tighten to specified torque
	• Loose lock shoes in housing (tilt column only)	• Replace shoes
	• Loose pivot pins (tilt column only)	• Replace pivot pins and support
	• Loose lock shoe pin (tilt column only)	• Replace pin and housing
	• Loose support screws (tilt column only)	• Tighten screws
Housing loose (tilt column only)	• Excessive clearance between holes in support or housing and pivot pin diameters	• Replace pivot pins and support
	• Housing support-screws loose	• Tighten screws
Steering wheel loose—every other tilt position (tilt column only)	• Loose fit between lock shoe and lock shoe pivot pin	• Replace lock shoes and pivot pin
Steering column not locking in any tilt position (tilt column only)	• Lock shoe seized on pivot pin	• Replace lock shoes and pin
	• Lock shoe grooves have burrs or are filled with foreign material	• Clean or replace lock shoes
	• Lock shoe springs weak or broken	• Replace springs
Noise when tilting column (tilt column only)	• Upper tilt bumpers worn	• Replace tilt bumper
	• Tilt spring rubbing in housing	• Lubricate with chassis grease
One click when in "off-lock" position and the steering wheel is moved	• Seating of lock bolt	• None. Click is normal characteristic sound produced by lock bolt as it seats.
High shift effort (automatic and tilt column only)	• Column not correctly aligned	• Align column
	• Lower bearing not aligned correctly	• Assemble correctly
	• Lack of grease on seal or lower bearing areas	• Lubricate with chassis grease
Improper transmission shifting— automatic and tilt column only	• Sheared shift tube joint	• Replace shift tube
	• Improper transmission gearshift linkage adjustment	• Adjust linkage
	• Loose lower shift lever	• Replace shift tube

Troubleshooting the Ignition Switch

Problem	Cause	Solution
Ignition switch electrically inoperative	• Loose or defective switch connector	• Tighten or replace connector
	• Feed wire open (fusible link)	• Repair or replace
	• Defective ignition switch	• Replace ignition switch
Engine will not crank	• Ignition switch not adjusted properly	• Adjust switch
Ignition switch wil not actuate mechanically	• Defective ignition switch	• Replace switch
	• Defective lock sector	• Replace lock sector
	• Defective remote rod	• Replace remote rod
Ignition switch cannot be adjusted correctly	• Remote rod deformed	• Repair, straighten or replace

Troubleshooting the Turn Signal Switch

Problem	Cause	Solution
Turn signal will not cancel	• Loose switch mounting screws • Switch or anchor bosses broken • Broken, missing or out of position detent, or cancelling spring	• Tighten screws • Replace switch • Reposition springs or replace switch as required
Turn signal difficult to operate	• Turn signal lever loose • Switch yoke broken or distorted • Loose or misplaced springs • Foreign parts and/or materials in switch • Switch mounted loosely	• Tighten mounting screws • Replace switch • Reposition springs or replace switch • Remove foreign parts and/or material • Tighten mounting screws
Turn signal will not indicate lane change	• Broken lane change pressure pad or spring hanger • Broken, missing or misplaced lane change spring • Jammed wires	• Replace switch • Replace or reposition as required • Loosen mounting screws, reposition wires and retighten screws
Turn signal will not stay in turn position	• Foreign material or loose parts impeding movement of switch yoke • Defective switch	• Remove material and/or parts • Replace switch
Hazard switch cannot be pulled out	• Foreign material between hazard support cancelling leg and yoke	• Remove foreign material. No foreign material impeding function of hazard switch—replace turn signal switch.
No turn signal lights	• Inoperative turn signal flasher • Defective or blown fuse • Loose chassis to column harness connector • Disconnect column to chassis connector. Connect new switch to chassis and operate switch by hand. If vehicle lights now operate normally, signal switch is inoperative • If vehicle lights do not operate, check chassis wiring for opens, grounds, etc.	• Replace turn signal flasher • Replace fuse • Connect securely • Replace signal switch • Repair chassis wiring as required
Instrument panel turn indicator lights on but not flashing	• Burned out or damaged front or rear turn signal bulb • If vehicle lights do not operate, check light sockets for high resistance connections, the chassis wiring for opens, grounds, etc.	• Replace bulb • Repair chassis wiring as required

Troubleshooting the Turn Signal Switch (cont.)

Problem	Cause	Solution
Instrument panel turn indicator lights on but not flashing (cont.)	• Inoperative flasher • Loose chassis to column harness connection • Inoperative turn signal switch • To determine if turn signal switch is defective, substitute new switch into circuit and operate switch by hand. If the vehicle's lights operate normally, signal switch is inoperative.	• Replace flasher • Connect securely • Replace turn signal switch • Replace turn signal switch
Stop light not on when turn indicated	• Loose column to chassis connection • Disconnect column to chassis connector. Connect new switch into system without removing old. Operate switch by hand. If brake lights work with switch in the turn position, signal switch is defective. • If brake lights do not work, check connector to stop light sockets for grounds, opens, etc.	• Connect securely • Replace signal switch • Repair connector to stop light circuits using service manual as guide
Turn indicator panel lights not flashing	• Burned out bulbs • High resistance to ground at bulb socket • Opens, ground in wiring harness from front turn signal bulb socket to indicator lights	• Replace bulbs • Replace socket • Locate and repair as required
Turn signal lights flash very slowly	• High resistance ground at light sockets • Incorrect capacity turn signal flasher or bulb • If flashing rate is still extremely slow, check chassis wiring harness from the connector to light sockets for high resistance • Loose chassis to column harness connection • Disconnect column to chassis connector. Connect new switch into system without removing old. Operate switch by hand. If flashing occurs at normal rate, the signal switch is defective.	• Repair high resistance grounds at light sockets • Replace turn signal flasher or bulb • Locate and repair as required • Connect securely • Replace turn signal switch
Hazard signal lights will not flash—turn signal functions normally	• Blow fuse • Inoperative hazard warning flasher • Loose chassis-to-column harness connection • Disconnect column to chassis connector. Connect new switch into system without removing old. Depress the hazard warning lights. If they now work normally, turn signal switch is defective. • If lights do not flash, check wiring harness "K" lead for open between hazard flasher and connector. If open, fuse block is defective	• Replace fuse • Replace hazard warning flasher in fuse panel • Conect securely • Replace turn signal switch • Repair or replace brown wire or connector as required

Troubleshooting the Manual Steering Gear

Problem	Cause	Solution
Hard or erratic steering	• Incorrect tire pressure	• Inflate tires to recommended pressures
	• Insufficient or incorrect lubrication	• Lubricate as required (refer to Maintenance Section)
	• Suspension, or steering linkage parts damaged or misaligned	• Repair or replace parts as necessary
	• Improper front wheel alignment	• Adjust incorrect wheel alignment angles
	• Incorrect steering gear adjustment	• Adjust steering gear
	• Sagging springs	• Replace springs
Play or looseness in steering	• Steering wheel loose	• Inspect shaft spines and repair as necessary. Tighten attaching nut and stake in place.
	• Steering linkage or attaching parts loose or worn	• Tighten, adjust, or replace faulty components
	• Pitman arm loose	• Inspect shaft splines and repair as necessary. Tighten attaching nut and stake in place
	• Steering gear attaching bolts loose	• Tighten bolts
	• Loose or worn wheel bearings	• Adjust or replace bearings
	• Steering gear adjustment incorrect or parts badly worn	• Adjust gear or replace defective parts
Wheel shimmy or tramp	• Improper tire pressure	• Inflate tires to recommended pressures
	• Wheels, tires, or brake rotors out-of-balance or out-of-round	• Inspect and replace or balance parts
	• Inoperative, worn, or loose shock absorbers or mounting parts	• Repair or replace shocks or mountings
	• Loose or worn steering or suspension parts	• Tighten or replace as necessary
	• Loose or worn wheel bearings	• Adjust or replace bearings
	• Incorrect steering gear adjustments	• Adjust steering gear
	• Incorrect front wheel alignment	• Correct front wheel alignment
Tire wear	• Improper tire pressure	• Inflate tires to recommended pressures
	• Failure to rotate tires	• Rotate tires
	• Brakes grabbing	• Adjust or repair brakes
	• Incorrect front wheel alignment	• Align incorrect angles
	• Broken or damaged steering and suspension parts	• Repair or replace defective parts
	• Wheel runout	• Replace faulty wheel
	• Excessive speed on turns	• Make driver aware of conditions
Vehicle leads to one side	• Improper tire pressures	• Inflate tires to recommended pressures
	• Front tires with uneven tread depth, wear pattern, or different cord design (i.e., one bias ply and one belted or radial tire on front wheels)	• Install tires of same cord construction and reasonably even tread depth, design, and wear pattern
	• Incorrect front wheel alignment	• Align incorrect angles
	• Brakes dragging	• Adjust or repair brakes
	• Pulling due to uneven tire construction	• Replace faulty tire

Troubleshooting the Power Steering Gear

Problem	Cause	Solution
Hissing noise in steering gear	• There is some noise in all power steering systems. One of the most common is a hissing sound most evident at standstill parking. There is no relationship between this noise and performance of the steering. Hiss may be expected when steering wheel is at end of travel or when slowly turning at standstill.	• Slight hiss is normal and in no way affects steering. Do not replace valve unless hiss is extremely objectionable. A replacement valve will also exhibit slight noise and is not always a cure. Investigate clearance around flexible coupling rivets. Be sure steering shaft and gear are aligned so flexible coupling rotates in a flat plane and is not distorted as shaft rotates. Any metal-to-metal contacts through flexible coupling will transmit valve hiss into passenger compartment through the steering column.
Rattle or chuckle noise in steering gear	• Gear loose on frame • Steering linkage looseness • Pressure hose touching other parts of car • Loose pitman shaft over center adjustment **NOTE:** A slight rattle may occur on turns because of increased clearance off the "high point." This is normal and clearance must not be reduced below specified limits to eliminate this slight rattle. • Loose pitman arm	• Check gear-to-frame mounting screws. Tighten screws to 88 N·m (65 foot pounds) torque. • Check linkage pivot points for wear. Replace if necessary. • Adjust hose position. Do not bend tubing by hand. • Adjust to specifications • Tighten pitman arm nut to specifications
Squawk noise in steering gear when turning or recovering from a turn	• Damper O-ring on valve spool cut	• Replace damper O-ring
Poor return of steering wheel to center	• Tires not properly inflated • Lack of lubrication in linkage and ball joints • Lower coupling flange rubbing against steering gear adjuster plug • Steering gear to column misalignment • Improper front wheel alignment • Steering linkage binding • Ball joints binding • Steering wheel rubbing against housing • Tight or frozen steering shaft bearings • Sticking or plugged valve spool • Steering gear adjustments over specifications • Kink in return hose	• Inflate to specified pressure • Lube linkage and ball joints • Loosen pinch bolt and assemble properly • Align steering column • Check and adjust as necessary • Replace pivots • Replace ball joints • Align housing • Replace bearings • Remove and clean or replace valve • Check adjustment with gear out of car. Adjust as required. • Replace hose
Car leads to one side or the other (keep in mind road condition and wind. Test car in both directions on flat road)	• Front end misaligned • Unbalanced steering gear valve **NOTE:** If this is cause, steering effort will be very light in direction of lead and normal or heavier in opposite direction	• Adjust to specifications • Replace valve

Troubleshooting the Power Steering Gear (cont.)

Problem	Cause	Solution
Momentary increase in effort when turning wheel fast to right or left	• Low oil level • Pump belt slipping • High internal leakage	• Add power steering fluid as required • Tighten or replace belt • Check pump pressure. (See pressure test)
Steering wheel surges or jerks when turning with engine running especially during parking	• Low oil level • Loose pump belt • Steering linkage hitting engine oil pan at full turn • Insufficient pump pressure • Pump flow control valve sticking	• Fill as required • Adjust tension to specification • Correct clearance • Check pump pressure. (See pressure test). Replace relief valve if defective. • Inspect for varnish or damage, replace if necessary
Excessive wheel kickback or loose steering	• Air in system • Steering gear loose on frame • Steering linkage joints worn enough to be loose • Worn poppet valve • Loose thrust bearing preload adjustment • Excessive overcenter lash	• Add oil to pump reservoir and bleed by operating steering. Check hose connectors for proper torque and adjust as required. • Tighten attaching screws to specified torque • Replace loose pivots • Replace poppet valve • Adjust to specification with gear out of vehicle • Adjust to specification with gear out of car
Hard steering or lack of assist	• Loose pump belt • Low oil level **NOTE:** Low oil level will also result in excessive pump noise • Steering gear to column misalignment • Lower coupling flange rubbing against steering gear adjuster plug • Tires not properly inflated	• Adjust belt tension to specification • Fill to proper level. If excessively low, check all lines and joints for evidence of external leakage. Tighten loose connectors. • Align steering column • Loosen pinch bolt and assemble properly • Inflate to recommended pressure
Foamy milky power steering fluid, low fluid level and possible low pressure	• Air in the fluid, and loss of fluid due to internal pump leakage causing overflow	• Check for leak and correct. Bleed system. Extremely cold temperatures will cause system aeration should the oil level be low. If oil level is correct and pump still foams, remove pump from vehicle and separate reservoir from housing. Check welsh plug and housing for cracks. If plug is loose or housing is cracked, replace housing.
Low pressure due to steering pump	• Flow control valve stuck or inoperative • Pressure plate not flat against cam ring	• Remove burrs or dirt or replace. Flush system. • Correct
Low pressure due to steering gear	• Pressure loss in cylinder due to worn piston ring or badly worn housing bore • Leakage at valve rings, valve body-to-worm seal	• Remove gear from car for disassembly and inspection of ring and housing bore • Remove gear from car for disassembly and replace seals

Troubleshooting the Power Steering Pump

Problem	Cause	Solution
Chirp noise in steering pump	• Loose belt	• Adjust belt tension to specification
Belt squeal (particularly noticeable at full wheel travel and stand still parking)	• Loose belt	• Adjust belt tension to specification
Growl noise in steering pump	• Excessive back pressure in hoses or steering gear caused by restriction	• Locate restriction and correct. Replace part if necessary.
Growl noise in steering pump (particularly noticeable at stand still parking)	• Scored pressure plates, thrust plate or rotor • Extreme wear of cam ring	• Replace parts and flush system • Replace parts
Groan noise in steering pump	• Low oil level • Air in the oil. Poor pressure hose connection.	• Fill reservoir to proper level • Tighten connector to specified torque. Bleed system by operating steering from right to left—full turn.
Rattle noise in steering pump	• Vanes not installed properly • Vanes sticking in rotor slots	• Install properly • Free up by removing burrs, varnish, or dirt
Swish noise in steering pump	• Defective flow control valve	• Replace part
Whine noise in steering pump	• Pump shaft bearing scored	• Replace housing and shaft. Flush system.
Hard steering or lack of assist	• Loose pump belt • Low oil level in reservoir **NOTE:** Low oil level will also result in excessive pump noise • Steering gear to column misalignment • Lower coupling flange rubbing against steering gear adjuster plug • Tires not properly inflated	• Adjust belt tension to specification • Fill to proper level. If excessively low, check all lines and joints for evidence of external leakage. Tighten loose connectors. • Align steering column • Loosen pinch bolt and assemble properly • Inflate to recommended pressure
Foaming milky power steering fluid, low fluid level and possible low pressure	• Air in the fluid, and loss of fluid due to internal pump leakage causing overflow	• Check for leaks and correct. Bleed system. Extremely cold temperatures will cause system aeriation should the oil level be low. If oil level is correct and pump still foams, remove pump from vehicle and separate reservoir from body. Check welsh plug and body for cracks. If plug is loose or body is cracked, replace body.
Low pump pressure	• Flow control valve stuck or inoperative • Pressure plate not flat against cam ring	• Remove burrs or dirt or replace. Flush system. • Correct
Momentary increase in effort when turning wheel fast to right or left	• Low oil level in pump • Pump belt slipping • High internal leakage	• Add power steering fluid as required • Tighten or replace belt • Check pump pressure. (See pressure test)
Steering wheel surges or jerks when turning with engine running especially during parking	• Low oil level • Loose pump belt • Steering linkage hitting engine oil pan at full turn • Insufficient pump pressure	• Fill as required • Adjust tension to specification • Correct clearance • Check pump pressure. (See pressure test). Replace flow control valve if defective.

RUBBER BOOT

▶ See Figure 26

1. Raise and support the front end of the car.
2. Cut and remove the boot clamps from the boot adjacent to the mounting clamp.
3. Mark the position of the adjuster tube on the inner tie rod for assembly reference.
4. Loosen the adjuster tube inboard clamp bolt and unthread the tube from the inner tie rod.
5. Remove the bolts attaching the mounting clamp to the front crossmember. Loosen both bolts before removing them to minimize clamp distortion.
6. Remove the protective boot.

✳✳ CAUTION

Do not allow the protective boot to become cut, torn, or damaged during service operations. A damaged boot will expose the gear internal components to dirt, foreign material and road splash resulting in premature wear.

7. Remove the clamp and grommet using a twisting, pulling motion.

8. Install the replacement clamp and grommet. Align the hole in the grommet with the breather tube.
9. Install the boot. Align the hole in the boot with the breather tube.
10. Install the boot clamps. Position the clamp ear ¾" (19.05mm) from the breather tube. Tighten the clamps using tool J-22610.
11. Install the adjuster tube on the tie rod and tighten the clamp bolts to 14 ft.lb. torque.

➡**At least three threads should be visible at each end of adjuster tube. The number of threads per side should not differ by more than three.**

12. Install and tighten the mounting clamp bolts to 48 ft.lb. torque.
13. Remove the supports, lower the car, and correct the toe-in as necessary.

BREATHER TUBE

1. Raise and support the front of the car.
2. Cut and remove the large diameter boot clamps from the boots.
3. Slide the boots away from the breather tube and remove the tube.

Fig. 26 Cross-sectional view of the rubber boot and tie rod ends—Pacer power steering

To install:

4. Install the replacement breather tube. Align the holes in the boots with the tube.

5. Position the boots on the flanges at each end of the tube and housing and install the boot clamps. Position the clamp ear ¾ in. (19.05mm) from the breather tube. Tighten the clamps using tool J-22610 or its equivalent.

6. Remove the supports and lower the car.

FLEXIBLE COUPLING

1. Remove the nuts attaching the coupling to the intermediate shaft flange and compress the shaft to provide working clearance.

2. Remove the coupling pinch bolt using a ⁷/₁₆ in., 12 point socket or box end wrench and remove the coupling.

3. Install the replacement coupling (flat-to-flat) and install the pinch bolt. Tighten the bolt to 30 ft. lbs. torque.

4. Connect the intermediate shaft to the coupling. Tighten the nuts to 25 ft. lbs. torque.

OIL LINE

1. Raise and support the front of the car.

2. Remove the oil lines.

3. Install the replacement oil lines. Tighten the fittings to 30 ft.lb. torque.

4. Apply the parking brake, shift the transmission into Park or Neutral (on manual transmission) and start the engine. Turn the steering wheel right and left several times and check for leaks at the oil line fittings. If leaks are not evident, proceed to the next step. If leaks are evident, tighten the fittings and check again. If leaks persist, remove and replace the steering gear assembly.

5. Remove the supports and lower the car. Add power steering fluid as necessary.

BULKHEAD SEAL

▶ **See Figures 27 thru 32**

1. Raise and support the front of the car.

2. Disconnect the tie rod end connected to the tube side of the rack from the steering arm using tool J-26951.

3. Remove the mounting clamp bolts.

4. Remove the clamps from the boot at the tube-end of the gear and slide the boot away from the end of tube.

❊❊ CAUTION

Do not allow the protective boot to become cut or torn during service operations. A damaged boot will expose the gear internal components to dirt, foreign material and road splash resulting in premature wear.

5. Remove the large boot clamp at the housing end of the gear.

6. If the flat on the rack teeth is not visible, pull back the boot at the housing end of the gear and turn the steering wheel (to rotate the pinion) and extend the rack until the flat is accessible.

Fig. 28 Use tool J-25509 to install the outer bulkhead on the rack

Fig. 27 The hose clamps must be removed from the bulkhead so that it can be removed

Fig. 29 Use a 11/4 in. open end wrench and a plastic hammer to install the outer bulkhead in the tube

Fig. 30 Installing the hose clamp and rubber seal on the bulkhead connector

1. Flexible coupling-to-intermediate shaft attaching bolt
2. Lockwasher
3. Nut
4. Pinch bolt
5. Flexible coupling
6. Adjuster plug locknut
7. Adjuster plug assembly
8. Adjuster plug O-ring
9. Oil lines
10. Valve body seal rings
11. Valve body O-rings
12. Valve body
13. Spool valve damper O-ring
14. Spool valve
15. Torsion bar bushing (included in stub shaft)
16. Torsion bar seal ring (included in stub shaft)
17. Torsion bar (included in stub shaft)
18. Drive pin (included in stub shaft)
19. Stub shaft

Fig. 31 Exploded view of the power steering gear assembly—Pacer models

20. Drive pin (included in stub shaft)
21. Power steering hoses
22. Mounting bolt
23. Washer
24. Preload spring
25. Grommet
26. Bushing
27. Steering linkage (assembled)
28. Rack bushing
29. Grommet
30. Washer
31. Nut
32. Steering rack
33. Rack piston
34. Outer bulkhead O-ring
35. Bulkhead retaining ring
36. Jam nut
37. Ball seat
38. Inner tie rod
39. Inner tie rod housing
40. Boot clamp
41. Boot
42. Adjuster tube clamp bolt
43. Adjuster tube clamp
44. Adjuster tube
45. Tie rod end
46. Lube plug
47. Tie rod end seal
48. Tie rod end-nut
49. Cotter pin

50. Adjuster tube clamp nut
51. Boot clamp
52. Tie rod housing setscrew
53. Ball seat spring
54. Shock dampener ring
55. Outer bulkhead and seal assembly
56. Inner bulkhead
57. Breather tube
58. Rack piston seal ring
59. Contraction plug
60. Lower pinion bushing
61. Housing (included in tube and housing assembly)
62. Nut
63. Washer
64. Grommet
65. Mounting clamp
66. Bolt
67. Mounting grommet
68. Inner rack seal
69. Tube and power cylinder (included in tube and housing assembly)
70. Upper pinion bushing
71. Pinion shaft seal (lip type)
72. Support washer
73. Conical thrust bearing race
74. Thrust bearing
75. Drive pin (included in stub shaft)
76. Shaft cap (included in stub shaft)
77. Torsion bar bushing (included in stub shaft)

Fig. 32 Power steering gear assembly component list—Pacer models

7. Slide the shock dampener ring off the jamnut.
8. Loosen the jamnut using an open end wrench. Also use an open end wrench on the rack flat to prevent the rack from turning.

❋❋ CAUTION

Do not allow the rack to turn when loosening the jamnut. If the rack turns, the gear internal components could be damaged. Place an open end wrench over the flat adjacent to the rack teeth to prevent the rack from turning.

9. Loosen the setscrew in the tie rod housing, unthread the housing from the rack and remove the tie rod assembly, inner tie rod ball seat, and ball seat spring.
10. Turn the jamnut counterclockwise until it is one thread away from the end of the rack and reinstall the shock dampener ring on the jamnut.

❋❋ CAUTION

Do not remove the jamnut and shock dampener ring from the rack at this time. The jamnut and shock dampener ring will function as a stop when the bulkhead is removed.

11. Remove the bulkhead retaining ring from the end of the tube by inserting the pin punch through the access hole in the end of tube to force the retaining ring out of its groove. Place a screwdriver blade under the ring and pry the ring from tube.
12. Remove the bulkhead assembly as follows:
    a. Clean the rack and bulkhead area of the tube with a shop cloth.
    b. Position the small piece of rubber over the access hole in tube and secure the rubber with a wormdrive type hose clamp.

c. Position the drain pan under the tube end of the gear and wrap shop cloths around the rack and tube to prevent excessive oil spillage.
    d. Start the engine and turn the steering wheel to the left until the stop is contacted. Oil pressure will force the outer bulkhead out of the tube. Stop the engine immediately when the oil pressure forces the bulkhead out of the tube.
13. Remove the jamnut and shock dampener ring.
14. Remove and discard the outer bulkhead.

➡**Do not remove the inner bulkhead and do not remove the seals from the outer bulkhead. The outer bulkhead, bulkhead seal, and O-ring are serviced as an assembly only.**

15. Remove the hose clamp and small piece of rubber from the tube.
   To install:
16. Inspect the tube bore and bulkhead snapring groove area in the tube for nicks and scratches. Remove the nicks and scratches using a crocus cloth or 600 grit emery cloth. Remove the burrs and sharp edges from the shoulder at the threaded end of rack, using an emery cloth, crocus cloth, or small fine tooth file. Burrs must be removed to avoid damaging the bulkhead seal during installation.
17. Lubricate the replacement outer bulkhead and bulkhead seal with power steering fluid.
18. Lubricate the replacement outer bulkhead O-ring seal with power steering fluid and install the seal on the bulkhead.
19. Place Seal Protector Tool J-25509 over the rack threads and install the outer bulkhead on the rack.
20. Install the outer bulkhead in the tube using a 1¼ in. open end wrench and a plastic hammer.
21. Seat the outer bulkhead in the tube using a brass drift.
22. Install the bulkhead retaining ring. Position the gap in the

retaining ring ½ in. (12.7mm) away from the access hole in the tube.

✳✳ CAUTION

Do not scratch or damage the surface of the rack when using the open end wrench to seat the bulkhead.

23. Wipe the bulkhead area dry.
24. Fill the power steering pump reservoir with fluid and start engine.
25. Turn the steering wheel left and right several times and check for leaks. If leaks are not evident, proceed to the next step.
26. Install the shock dampener ring and jamnut on the rack.
27. Install the mounting clamp and grommet on the tube. Position the clamp on the crossmember and install the clamp but do not tighten the clamp attaching bolts.
28. Apply a liberal quantity of waterproof, EP-type, lithium base chassis lubricant to the inner tie rod ball seat and the ball end of the inner tie rod. Pack the tie rod housing with the same lubricant and apply a heavy coat of lubricant to the rack teeth.
29. Install the ball seat spring in the end of the rack and install the ball seat.
30. Assemble the inner tie rod and tie rod housing and install them on the rack.
31. Hand-tighten the tie rod housing on the rack while rocking the tie rod to prevent grease lock.
32. Back the tie rod housing off approximately ⅛ turn.
33. Tighten the tie rod housing setscrew to 9 ft.lbs. torque.
34. Tighten the jamnut to 60 ft.lb. torque. Use an open end wrench on the rack flat to prevent the rack from turning.

✳✳ CAUTION

Do not allow the rack to turn when tightening the jamnut. If the rack turns, gear internal components could be damaged. Place an open wrench over the flat adjacent to the rack teeth to prevent the rack from turning.

35. Check the inner tie rod movement. The tie rod most rock and turn freely in the housing to ensure proper operation.
36. Install the shock dampener ring over the jamnut.
37. Position the breather tube in the mounting grommet.
38. Install the protective boot over the end of the tube. Be sure the boot is fully seated in the tube undercut and that the hole in the boot is aligned with the breather tube.
39. Install the boot clamps. Tighten the clamps using tool J-22610.
40. Tighten the mounting clamp bolts to 48 ft.lb. torque.
41. Connect the tie rod end to the steering arm and install the tie rod end nut. Tighten the nut to 50 ft.lb. torque and install the replacement cotter pin.
42. Remove the supports and lower the car.
43. Check and correct the power steering system fluid level as necessary. Refer to Fluid Level and Initial Operation.

ADJUSTMENTS

Except Pacer

Because of the complexity involved in adjusting worm bearing preload and pitman shaft overcenter drag torque plus the friction effect produced by hydraulic fluid, the power steering gear must be adjusted off the automobile only.

The power steering gear requires two adjustments which are: worm bearing preload and pitman shaft overcenter drag torque.

Worm bearing preload is controlled by the amount of compression force exerted on the conical worm bearing thrust races by the adjuster plug.

Pitman shaft overcenter torque is controlled by the pitman shaft adjuster screw which determines the clearance between the rack piston and pitman shaft sector teeth.

✳✳ CAUTION

The following adjustment procedures must be performed exactly as described and in the sequence outlined. Failure to do so can result in damage to the gear internal components and improper steering response. Always adjust worm bearing preload first, then adjust pitman shaft overcenter drag torque.

WORM BEARING PRELOAD

◆ **See Figures 33, 34 and 35**

1. Seat the adjuster plug firmly in the housing using Spanner Tool J-7624 or its equivalent. Approximately 20 ft. lbs. torque is required to seat the housing.
2. Place an index mark on the gear housing opposite one of the holes in the adjuster plug.
3. Measure back (counterclockwise) 3/16 in. to ¼ in. (4.7 to 6.3mm) from the index mark and remark the housing.
4. Turn the adjuster plug counterclockwise until the hole in the plug is aligned with the second mark on the housing.
5. Install the adjuster plug locknut and tighten it to 85 ft. lbs. torque. Be sure the adjuster plug does not turn when tightening the locknut.
6. Turn the stub shaft clockwise to the stop, then turn the shaft back ¼ turn.
7. Using an in.lb. torque wrench with a maximum capacity of 50 in. lbs. and a twelve point deep socket, measure the torque required to turn the stub shaft. Take a reading with the beam of the torque wrench at, or near, the vertical position while turning the stub shaft at an even rate.

Fig. 33 Make a mark on the power steering gear housing next to the hole in the adjuster . . .

Fig. 34 . . . then make a second mark 3/16–1/4 in. from the first on models through 1979 and 1/2 in. on 1980–82 models

Fig. 36 Use a torque wrench to measure the Pitman shaft over-center torque drag on power steering gears

Fig. 35 Use a torque wrench to measure the wormshaft bearing preload on power steering gears

8. Record the torque reading. The torque required to turn the stub shaft should be 4–10 in. lbs. If the reading is above or below the indicated torque, the adjuster plug may not be tightened properly or may have turned when the locknut was tightened, or the gear may be assembled incorrectly, or the thrust bearings and races may be defective.

PITMAN SHAFT OVERCENTER DRAG TORQUE

♦ See Figure 36

1. Turn the pitman shaft adjuster screw counterclockwise until fully extended, then turn it back ½ turn clockwise.
2. Rotate the stub shaft from stop-to-stop and count the total number of turns.
3. Starting from either stop, turn the stub shaft back ½ the total number of turns. This is the gear center.

➡ When the gear is centered, the flat on the stub shaft should face upward and be parallel with the side cover and the master spline on the pitman shaft should be in line with the adjust screw.

4. Install an in.lb. torque wrench with a maximum capacity of 50 in. lbs. and a twelve point deep socket on the stub shaft. Place the torque wrench in the vertical position to take the reading.
5. Rotate the torque wrench 45° to each side of center and record the highest drag torque measured on or near the center.
6. Adjust the overcenter drag torque by turning the pitman shaft adjusting screw clockwise until the desired drag torque is obtained. Adjust the drag torque to the following limits:
   • On new steering gears, add 4 to 8 in. lbs., torque to the previously measured worm bearing preload torque, but do not exceed a combined total of 18 in. lbs. drag torque.
   • On used steering gears (400 or more miles), add 4 to 5 in.lb. torque to the previously measured worm bearing preload torque but do not exceed a combined total of 14 in. lbs. drag torque.
7. Tighten the pitman shaft adjusting screw locknut to 35 ft. lbs. torque after adjusting the overcenter drag torque.
8. Install the gear as outlined in Steering Gear Installation.
9. Fill the pump reservoir and bleed the gear and pump as outlined in Fluid Level and Initial Operations after completing the overcenter drag torque adjustment.

FLUID LEVEL & INITIAL OPERATION

1. Fill the pump reservoir.
2. Operate the engine until the power steering fluid reaches normal operating temperature of approximately 170°F (77°C), then stop the engine.
3. Turn the wheels to the full left turn position and add power steering fluid to the COLD mark on the dipstick.
4. Start the engine, operate it at hot idle speed and recheck fluid level. Add fluid, if necessary, to the COLD mark on the dipstick.

5. Bleed the system by turning the wheels from side to side without hitting the stops. Fluid with air in it will have a milky appearance. Air must be eliminated from the fluid before normal steering action can be obtained.

6. Return the wheels to the center position and operate the engine for an additional 2 to 3 minutes, then stop the engine.

7. Road test the automobile to make sure the steering functions normally and is free of noise.

8. Check the fluid level. Add fluid as required to raise the level to the HOT mark on the dipstick after the system has stabilized at its normal operating temperature.

Outer Tie Rods

REMOVAL & INSTALLATION

Except Pacer

◗ See Figures 37 and 38

1. Raise and support the front of the car.
2. Remove the cotter pin and retaining nut from the tie rod end stud.

Fig. 37 Steering linkage assembly—except Eagle and Pacer

Fig. 38 Exploded view of the steering linkage—Eagle models

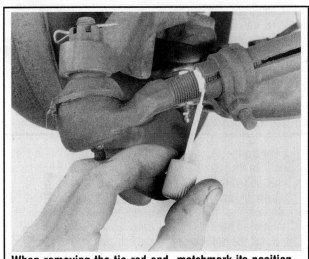

When removing the tie rod end, matchmark its position to the adjuster tube to aid during installation

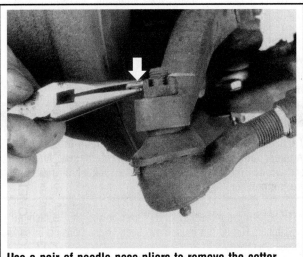

Use a pair of needle nose pliers to remove the cotter pin . . .

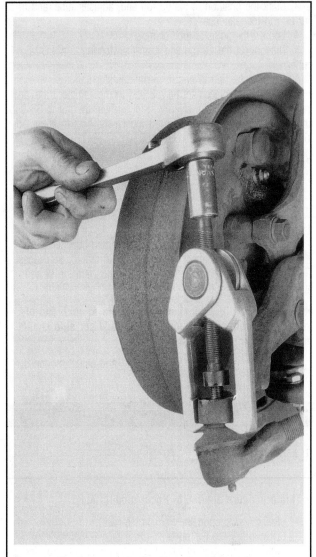

Use a puller to separate the tie rod end from the steering knuckle

. . . then remove the retaining nut

Loosen the adjuster tube clamps and unthread the tie rod end

3. Mark the position of the tie rod end, adjuster tube, and inner tie rod for reference.

4. Loosen the adjuster tube clamps.

5. Disconnect the tie rod end from the steering arm with a puller.

6. Remove the tie rod end from the adjuster tube.

7. Install the replacement tie rod end in the adjuster tube, and insert the end stud in the steering arm. Tighten the nut to 35 ft.lb. and install a new cotter pin. Do not loosen the nuts to align. Adjust the toe-in and tighten the clamps.

Pacer

1. Raise and support the front of the car.

2. Disconnect the tie rod end using tool J-26951.

3. Mark the position of the adjuster tube and tie rod end for assembly reference.

4. Remove and separate the tie rod ends and adjuster tubes.

5. Install the replacement tie rod ends and the adjuster tubes. Tighten the tube clamp bolts to 22 ft.lb. torque and the tie rod nuts to 50 ft.lb. torque.

➡**At least three threads should be visible at each end of the adjuster tubes. The number of threads per side should not differ by more than three.**

6. Remove the supports, lower the car, and adjust the toe-in as necessary.

Inner Tie Rods

REMOVAL & INSTALLATION

➡**This procedure applies to Pacer models only.**

1. Raise and support the front of the car.

2. Disconnect the tie rod ends using tool J-26951.

3. Mark the position of the adjuster tube and inner rod for assembly reference.

4. Loosen the adjuster tube inboard clamp bolt and unthread the adjuster tube and tie rod end from the inner tie rod assembly.

5. Cut and remove the large boot clamp and move the boot aside.

❋❋ CAUTION

Do not allow the protective boot to become cut or torn during service operations. A damaged boot will expose the gear internal components to dirt, foreign material, and road splash resulting in premature wear.

6. Slide the shock dampener ring off the jamnut.

7. Loosen the jamnut. Use an open end wrench to loosen the jamnut and place another open end wrench on the rack flat (adjacent to rack teeth) to prevent the rack from turning.

❋❋ CAUTION

If the rack is allowed to turn when loosening the jamnuts, the gear internal components could be damaged. An open end wrench must be used to hold the rack when loosening the jamnut.

8. Loosen the setscrew in the tie rod housing, unthread the housing from the rack and remove the inner tie rod, tie rod housing, inner tie rod ball seat, and ball seat spring.

9. Liberally apply a waterproof, EP-type, lithium base chassis lubricant to all replacement inner tie rod assembly wear surfaces. Pack the tie rod housing with the same lubricant.

10. Install the ball seat spring and ball seat in the end of the rack.

11. Assemble the inner tie rod and housing and install them on the rack.

12. Hand-tighten the tie rod housing while rocking the tie rod to prevent grease lock; then, back the housing off ⅛ turn (45°). The tie rod must rock and turn freely in the housing.

13. Tighten the tie rod housing setscrew to 9 ft. lbs. torque.

14. Tighten the jamnut to 60 ft. lbs. torque. Use an open end wrench to loosen the jamnut and place another open and wrench on the rack flat (adjacent to rack teeth) to prevent the rack from turning.

❋❋ CAUTION

If the rack is allowed to turn when tightening the jamnut, the gear internal components could be damaged. An open end wrench must be used to hold the rack when tightening the jamnut.

15. Check the movement of the inner tie rod after tightening the jamnut. The tie rod must move freely in the housing to ensure proper operation.

16. Slide the shock dampener ring over the jamnut.

17. Install the boot on the inner tie rod and tube or housing. Align the breather tube with the hole in the boot and install the boot clamps. Position the ear of large clamp ¾″ (19.05mm) from the breather tube. Compress the clamps using Tool J-22610.

18. Thread the adjuster tube and tie rod end assembly on the inner tie rod. Refer to the alignment marks made at disassembly.

19. Tighten the adjuster tube bolts to 22 ft. lbs. torque.

20. Connect the tie rod ends to the steering arms. Tighten the tie rod end nuts to 50 ft. lbs. torque and install replacement cotter pins.

21. Remove the supports, lower the car, and adjust the toe-in as necessary.

BRAKE OPERATING SYSTEM 9-2
BASIC OPERATING PRINCIPLES 9-2
    DISC BRAKES 9-2
    DRUM BRAKES 9-3
    POWER BOOSTERS 9-3
ADJUSTMENTS 9-3
    DRUM BRAKES 9-3
    DISC BRAKES 9-4
MASTER CYLINDER 9-4
    REMOVAL & INSTALLATION 9-4
    OVERHAUL 9-5
    BLEEDING 9-6
    BRAKE WARNING LIGHT
    SIGNAL 9-6
POWER BOOSTER 9-7
    REMOVAL & INSTALLATION 9-7
FRONT DRUM BRAKES 9-8
BRAKE DRUMS 9-9
    REMOVAL & INSTALLATION 9-9
    INSPECTION 9-10
BRAKE SHOES 9-10
    REMOVAL & INSTALLATION 9-10
WHEEL CYLINDERS 9-13
    OVERHAUL 9-13
WHEEL BEARINGS 9-15
    REMOVAL, PACKING &
    INSTALLATION 9-15
FRONT DISC BRAKES 9-15
DISC BRAKE PADS 9-15
    REMOVAL & INSTALLATION 9-15
BRAKE CALIPER 9-22
    REMOVAL, INSTALLATION,
    OVERHAUL 9-22
BRAKE DISC (ROTOR) 9-26
    REMOVAL & INSTALLATION 9-26
    INSPECTION 9-26
WHEEL BEARINGS 9-28
    REMOVAL, PACKING, &
    INSTALLATION 9-28
    ADJUSTMENT 9-30
REAR DRUM BRAKES 9-31
BRAKE DRUMS 9-32
    REMOVAL & INSTALLATION 9-32
    INSPECTION 9-32
BRAKE SHOES 9-32
    REMOVAL & INSTALLATION 9-32
WHEEL CYLINDERS 9-34
    OVERHAUL 9-34
HUBS AND BEARINGS 9-34
    REMOVAL & INSTALLATION 9-34
PARKING BRAKE 9-36
CABLES 9-36
    REMOVAL & INSTALLATION 9-36
    ADJUSTMENT 9-36
COMPONENT LOCATIONS
  FRONT DRUM BRAKE
    COMPONENTS 9-8
  REAR DRUM BRAKE
    COMPONENTS 9-31

SPECIFICATION CHARTS
  BRAKE SPECIFICATIONS 9-40
TROUBLESHOOTING CHARTS
  TROUBLESHOOTING THE BRAKE
    SYSTEM 9-41

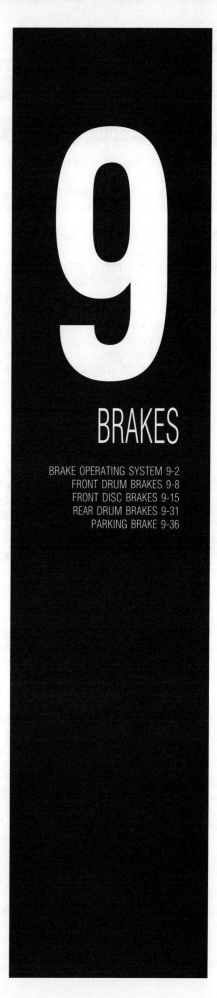

9

BRAKES

BRAKE OPERATING SYSTEM 9-2
FRONT DRUM BRAKES 9-8
FRONT DISC BRAKES 9-15
REAR DRUM BRAKES 9-31
PARKING BRAKE 9-36

BRAKE OPERATING SYSTEM

Basic Operating Principles

Hydraulic systems are used to actuate the brakes of all modern automobiles. The system transports the power required to force the frictional surfaces of the braking system together from the pedal to the individual brake units at each wheel. A hydraulic system is used for two reasons.

First, fluid under pressure can be carried to all parts of an automobile by small pipes and flexible hoses without taking up a significant amount of room or posing routing problems.

Second, a great mechanical advantage can be given to the brake pedal end of the system, and the foot pressure required to actuate the brakes can be reduced by making the surface area of the master cylinder pistons smaller than that of any of the pistons in the wheel cylinders or calipers.

The master cylinder consists of a fluid reservoir along with a double cylinder and piston assembly. Double type master cylinders are designed to separate the front and rear braking systems hydraulically in case of a leak. The master cylinder coverts mechanical motion from the pedal into hydraulic pressure within the lines. This pressure is translated back into mechanical motion at the wheels by either the wheel cylinder (drum brakes) or the caliper (disc brakes).

Steel lines carry the brake fluid to a point on the vehicle's frame near each of the vehicle's wheels. The fluid is then carried to the calipers and wheel cylinders by flexible tubes in order to allow for suspension and steering movements.

In drum brake systems, each wheel cylinder contains two pistons, one at either end, which push outward in opposite directions and force the brake shoe into contact with the drum.

In disc brake systems, the cylinders are part of the calipers. At least one cylinder in each caliper is used to force the brake pads against the disc.

All pistons employ some type of seal, usually made of rubber, to minimize fluid leakage. A rubber dust boot seals the outer end of the cylinder against dust and dirt. The boot fits around the outer end of the piston on disc brake calipers, and around the brake actuating rod on wheel cylinders.

The hydraulic system operates as follows: When at rest, the entire system, from the piston(s) in the master cylinder to those in the wheel cylinders or calipers, is full of brake fluid. Upon application of the brake pedal, fluid trapped in front of the master cylinder piston(s) is forced through the lines to the wheel cylinders. Here, it forces the pistons outward, in the case of drum brakes, and inward toward the disc, in the case of disc brakes. The motion of the pistons is opposed by return springs mounted outside the cylinders in drum brakes, and by spring seals, in disc brakes.

Upon release of the brake pedal, a spring located inside the master cylinder immediately returns the master cylinder pistons to the normal position. The pistons contain check valves and the master cylinder has compensating ports drilled in it. These are uncovered as the pistons reach their normal position. The piston check valves allow fluid to flow toward the wheel cylinders or calipers as the pistons withdraw. Then, as the return springs force the brake pads or shoes into the released position, the excess fluid reservoir through the compensating ports. It is during the time the pedal is in the released position that any fluid that has leaked out of the system will be replaced through the compensating ports.

Dual circuit master cylinders employ two pistons, located one behind the other, in the same cylinder. The primary piston is actuated directly by mechanical linkage from the brake pedal through the power booster. The secondary piston is actuated by fluid trapped between the two pistons. If a leak develops in front of the secondary piston, it moves forward until it bottoms against the front of the master cylinder, and the fluid trapped between the pistons will operate the rear brakes. If the rear brakes develop a leak, the primary piston will move forward until direct contact with the secondary piston takes place, and it will force the secondary piston to actuate the front brakes. In either case, the brake pedal moves farther when the brakes are applied, and less braking power is available.

All dual circuit systems use a switch to warn the driver when only half of the brake system is operational. This switch is usually located in a valve body which is mounted on the firewall or the frame below the master cylinder. A hydraulic piston receives pressure from both circuits, each circuit's pressure being applied to one end of the piston. When the pressures are in balance, the piston remains stationary. When one circuit has a leak, however, the greater pressure in that circuit during application of the brakes will push the piston to one side, closing the switch and activating the brake warning light.

In disc brake systems, this valve body also contains a metering valve and, in some cases, a proportioning valve. The metering valve keeps pressure from traveling to the disc brakes on the front wheels until the brake shoes on the rear wheels have contacted the drums, ensuring that the front brakes will never be used alone. The proportioning valve controls the pressure to the rear brakes to lessen the chance of rear wheel lock-up during very hard braking.

Warning lights may be tested by depressing the brake pedal and holding it while opening one of the wheel cylinder bleeder screws. If this does not cause the light to go on, substitute a new lamp, make continuity checks, and, finally, replace the switch as necessary.

The hydraulic system may be checked for leaks by applying pressure to the pedal gradually and steadily. If the pedal sinks very slowly to the floor, the system has a leak. This is not to be confused with a springy or spongy feel due to the compression of air within the lines. If the system leaks, there will be a gradual change in the position of the pedal with a constant pressure.

Check for leaks along all lines and at wheel cylinders. If no external leaks are apparent, the problem is inside the master cylinder.

DISC BRAKES

Instead of the traditional expanding brakes that press outward against a circular drum, disc brake systems utilize a disc (rotor) with brake pads positioned on either side of it. An easily-seen analogy is the hand brake arrangement on a bicycle. The pads squeeze onto the rim of the bike wheel, slowing its motion. Automobile disc brakes use the identical principle but apply the braking effort to a separate disc instead of the wheel.

The disc (rotor) is a casting, usually equipped with cooling fins between the two braking surfaces. This enables air to circulate between the braking surfaces making them less sensitive to heat buildup and more resistant to fade. Dirt and water do not drastically affect braking action since contaminants are thrown off by the centrifugal action of the rotor or scraped off the by the pads. Also, the equal clamping action of the two brake pads tends to ensure uniform, straight line stops. Disc brakes are inherently self-adjusting. There are three general types of disc brake:

1. A fixed caliper.
2. A floating caliper.
3. A sliding caliper.

The fixed caliper design uses two pistons mounted on either side of the rotor (in each side of the caliper). The caliper is mounted rigidly and does not move.

The sliding and floating designs are quite similar. In fact, these two types are often lumped together. In both designs, the pad on the inside of the rotor is moved into contact with the rotor by hydraulic force. The caliper, which is not held in a fixed position, moves slightly, bringing the outside pad into contact with the rotor. There are various methods of attaching floating calipers. Some pivot at the bottom or top, and some slide on mounting bolts. In any event, the end result is the same.

DRUM BRAKES

Drum brakes employ two brake shoes mounted on a stationary backing plate. These shoes are positioned inside a circular drum which rotates with the wheel assembly. The shoes are held in place by springs. This allows them to slide toward the drums (when they are applied) while keeping the linings and drums in alignment. The shoes are actuated by a wheel cylinder which is mounted at the top of the backing plate. When the brakes are applied, hydraulic pressure forces the wheel cylinder's actuating links outward. Since these links bear directly against the top of the brake shoes, the tops of the shoes are then forced against the inner side of the drum. This action forces the bottoms of the two shoes to contact the brake drum by rotating the entire assembly slightly (known as servo action). When pressure within the wheel cylinder is relaxed, return springs pull the shoes back away from the drum.

Most modern drum brakes are designed to self-adjust themselves during application when the vehicle is moving in reverse. This motion causes both shoes to rotate very slightly with the drum, rocking an adjusting lever, thereby causing rotation of the adjusting screw. Some drum brake systems are designed to self-adjust during application whenever the brakes are applied. This on-board adjustment system reduces the need for maintenance adjustments and keeps both the brake function and pedal feel satisfactory.

POWER BOOSTERS

Virtually all modern vehicles use a vacuum assisted power brake system to multiply the braking force and reduce pedal effort. Since vacuum is always available when the engine is operating, the system is simple and efficient. A vacuum diaphragm is located on the front of the master cylinder and assists the driver in applying the brakes, reducing both the effort and travel he must put into moving the brake pedal.

The vacuum diaphragm housing is normally connected to the intake manifold by a vacuum hose. A check valve is placed at the point where the hose enters the diaphragm housing, so that during periods of low manifold vacuum brakes assist will not be lost.

Depressing the brake pedal closes off the vacuum source and allows atmospheric pressure to enter on one side of the diaphragm. This causes the master cylinder pistons to move and apply the brakes. When the brake pedal is released, vacuum is applied to both sides of the diaphragm and springs return the diaphragm and master cylinder pistons to the released position.

If the vacuum supply fails, the brake pedal rod will contact the end of the master cylinder actuator rod and the system will apply the brakes without any power assistance. The driver will notice that much higher pedal effort is needed to stop the car and that the pedal feels harder than usual.

Vacuum Leak Test

1. Operate the engine at idle without touching the brake pedal for at least one minute.
2. Turn off the engine and wait one minute.
3. Test for the presence of assist vacuum by depressing the brake pedal and releasing it several times. If vacuum is present in the system, light application will produce less and less pedal travel. If there is no vacuum, air is leaking into the system.

System Operation Test

1. With the engine **OFF**, pump the brake pedal until the supply vacuum is entirely gone.
2. Put light, steady pressure on the brake pedal.
3. Start the engine and let it idle. If the system is operating correctly, the brake pedal should fall toward the floor if the constant pressure is maintained.

Power brake systems may be tested for hydraulic leaks just as ordinary systems are tested.

Adjustments

DRUM BRAKES

◆ **See Figure 1**

The drum brakes are self adjusting and do not normally require attention. However, if the brakes are disassembled, they must be adjusted upon assembly; or, if necessary, the brakes may be manually adjusted during the course of normal service.

1. Remove the rubber plug from the access slot on the backing plate.

➡**It may be easier to perform Step 1 with the drum removed; however, be sure that the drum is installed properly before beginning adjustment.**

2. Rotate the starwheel with a prytool or an adjoining tool until the wheel will not rotate.
3. Mark the starwheel and back it off one complete revolution.

➡**In order to back off the starwheel it may be necessary to use a piece of ⅛ in. (3mm) welding rod to hold the adjusting lever off the adjusting screw.**

4. Install the rubber plug in the access slot.
5. Make 10–15 hard applications of the brakes while backing the car up and then road test the car.

Fig. 1 A tool inserted through the access slot in the backing plate may be used to adjust the drum brakes

DISC BRAKES

The front disc brakes require no adjustment as hydraulic pressure maintains the proper brake pad-to-disc contact at all times.

➡**Because of this, the brake fluid level should be checked regularly (see Section 1).**

Master Cylinder

REMOVAL & INSTALLATION

◆ **See Figure 2**

1. Detach the front and rear brake lines from the master cylinder. On cars with drum brakes, the check valves will keep the fluid from draining our of the cylinder. If the car has disc brakes, one of both of the outlets must be plugged, to prevent fluid loss.

2. Remove the nuts which attach the master cylinder to the firewall of the power brake booster.

Fig. 2 Exploded view of a common master cylinders components

Use a line wrench to loosen the fuel line-to-master cylinder nuts

Disengage the fuel lines from the master cylinder

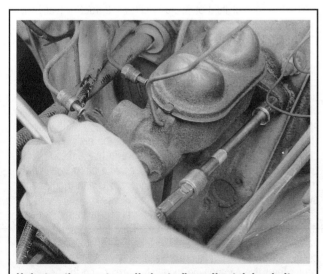
Unfasten the master cylinder-to-firewall retaining bolts

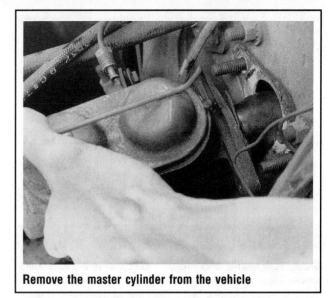
Remove the master cylinder from the vehicle

3. On cars that don't have power brakes, detach the pedal push-rod from the brake pedal.

4. Remove the master cylinder from the car.

5. Installation is the reverse of removal. Bleed the brake system once the master cylinder has been installed.

OVERHAUL

If the master cylinder leaks externally, or if the pedal sinks while being held down, the master cylinder is worn. There are three possible solutions:

    a. Buy a new master cylinder.

    b. Trade the old one in on a rebuilt unit.

    c. Rebuild the old one with a rebuilding kit.

1. Remove the cylinder from the car and drain the brake fluid.

2. Mount the cylinder in a vise so that the outlets are up and remove the seal from the hub.

3. Remove the stop screw from the bottom of the front reservoir.

4. Remove the snapring from the front of the bore and remove the primary piston assembly.

5. Remove the secondary piston assembly using compressed air or a piece of wire. Cover the bore opening with a cloth to prevent damage to the piston.

6. Clean the metal parts in brake fluid and discard all rubber parts.

7. Inspect the bore for damage or wear, and check the pistons for damage and proper clearance in the bore.

8. If the bore is only slightly scored or pitted it may be honed. Always use hones that are in good condition and completely clean the cylinder with brake fluid when honing is completed. If there is any evidence of contamination in the master cylinder, the entire hydraulic system should be flushed and refilled with clean brake fluid. Blow out all passages with compressed air.

9. Install new secondary seals in the two grooves in the flat end of the front piston. The lips of the seals will be facing away front each other.

10. Install a new primary seal and the seal protector on the op-

posite end of the front piston with the lips of the seal facing outward.

11. Coat the seals with brake fluid. Install the spring on the front piston with the spring retainer in the primary seal.

12. Insert the piston assembly, spring end first, into the bore and use a wooden rod to seat it.

13. Coat the rear piston seals with brake fluid and install them into the piston grooves with the lips facing the spring end.

14. Assemble the spring onto the piston and install the assembly into the bore spring first. Install the snapring.

15. Hold the piston assembly at the bottom of the bore and install the stop screw. Install a new seal on the hub. Bleed the cylinder as shown, before installation. Install the cylinder on the car. Bleed the system of air.

✳✳ WARNING

Clean, high quality brake fluid is essential to the safe and proper operation of the brake system. You should always buy the highest quality brake fluid that is available. If the brake fluid becomes contaminated, drain and flush the system, then refill the master cylinder with new fluid. Never reuse any brake fluid. Any brake fluid that is removed from the system should be discarded.

BLEEDING

The purpose of bleeding brakes is to expel air trapped in the hydraulic system. The system must be bled whenever the pedal feels spongy, indicating that compressible air has entered the system. It must also be bled whenever the system has been opened or leaking. You will need a helper for this job.

➡**When bleeding brakes the stem on the front of the brake combination valve must be held out 0.060 in. (1.52mm).**

1. Clean the bleed screw at each wheel.
2. Attach a small rubber hose to one of the bleed screws and place the end in a container of brake fluid.

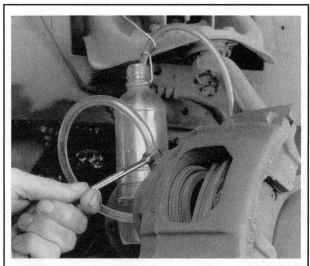

Bleeding the front disc brakes

Loosen the bleeder screw, press the brake pedal to the floor, then close the bleeder screw

3. Fill the master cylinder with brake fluid. Check the level often during bleeding. Pump up the brake pedal and hold it.

4. Open the bleed screw about ¼ turn, press the brake pedal to the floor, close the bleed screw, and slowly release the pedal. Continue until no more air bubbles are forced from the cylinder on application of the brake pedal.

5. Repeat the procedure on the remaining wheel cylinders. Disc brakes may be bled in the same manner as drum brakes, except that:

1. It usually requires a longer time to bleed a disc brake thoroughly.

2. The disc should be rotated to make sure that the piston has returned to the unapplied position when bleeding is completed and the bleed screw closed.

BRAKE WARNING LIGHT SIGNAL

▶ **See Figures 3 and 4**

The warning light on the dashboard is activated by a differential pressure switch located below the master cylinder. The signal indicates a loss of fluid pressure in either the front or rear brakes, and warns the driver that a hydraulic failure has occurred.

The pressure differential warning valve is a housing with the brake warning light switch mounted centrally on top. Directly below the switch is a bore containing a piston assembly. The piston assembly is located in the center of the bore and kept in that position by equal fluid pressure on either side. Fluid pressure is provided by two brake lines, one coming from the rear brake system and one from the front brakes. If a leak develops in either system (front or rear), fluid pressure to that side of the piston will decrease or stop causing the piston to move in that direction. The plunger on the end of the switch engages with the piston. When the piston moves off center, the plunger moves and triggers the switch to activate the warning light on the dash.

After repairing and bleeding any part of the hydraulic system the warning light may remain on due to the pressure differential valve remaining in the off-center position. All models have a self-centering valve. After repairs or bleeding have been performed, center the valve by applying moderate pressure on the brake pedal. This will turn on the light.

Fig. 3 Typical combination valve components—except Pacer models

Fig. 4 Cross-sectional view of a pressure differential valve—Pacer models

➡Front wheel balancing, on the car, of cars equipped with disc brakes may also cause a pressure differential in the front branch of the system.

Power Booster

REMOVAL & INSTALLATION

▶ See Figures 5 and 6

1. Disconnect the power booster clevis pin or the pushrod, depending on which type of unit is used.
2. Remove the vacuum hose from the power unit.

Fig. 5 Common power brake booster and master cylinder assembly—Pacer models

Fig. 6 Power brake booster and master cylinder assembly used on all models except Pacer

3. Unbolt and remove the master cylinder from the booster. It is not necessary to disconnect the brake lines from the master cylinder. There should be enough play in the lines to move the cylinder aside.
4. Unbolt and remove the booster from the firewall.
5. Installation is the reverse of removal. Torque the booster-to-dash nuts to 30 ft. lbs.

❋❋ WARNING

Some cars have two holes in the brake pedal for the pushrod. On cars with power brakes, use the lower hole.

FRONT DRUM BRAKES

FRONT DRUM BRAKE COMPONENTS

1. Shoe guide plate
2. Primary shoe
3. Secondary shoe
4. Adjuster cable
5. Adjuster cable guide
6. Primary return spring
7. Secondary return spring
8. Holddown spring
9. Holddown pin
10. Adjuster lever
11. Adjusting screw assembly
12. Adjuster spring

Typical front drum brake components

Brake Drums

REMOVAL & INSTALLATION

1. Remove the wheel cover, except on models with styled wheels which have the lug nuts exposed, and loosen the lug nuts.
2. Set the parking brake, block the rear wheels, and raise the front of the car, supporting it with jackstands.

✳✳ CAUTION

Be sure that the car is securely supported.

3. Remove the lug nuts and the wheel.
4. Loosen the brake adjusting starwheel by removing the plug from the adjusting slot and inserting a thin screwdriver into the hole to push the adjusting lever away from the wheel.

. . . then remove the cotter pin with a pair of needlenose pliers

Typical front brake drum

Remove the bearing nut and washer . . .

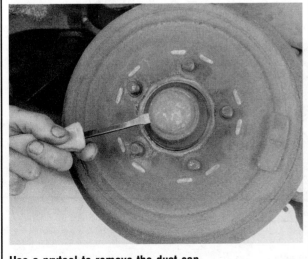

Use a prytool to remove the dust cap. . .

. . . then remove the outer wheel bearing

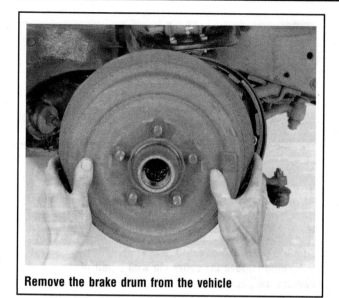

Remove the brake drum from the vehicle

5. Insert a brake adjusting tool into the hole and rotate the star-wheel so that the shoes contract.

➡**It may not always be necessary to back off on the adjuster in order to remove the drum.**

6. Remove the dust cover, grease cap, cotter pin, nut retainer, nut and the outer wheel bearing.

7. Remove the drum from the spindle.

8. Installation is performed in the reverse of or removal. Pack and adjust the wheel bearing as indicated in the wheel bearing procedure outlined in this section. Adjust the brakes, as outlined at the beginning of this chapter, after completing the drum installation.

INSPECTION

1. Clean the drum.

2. Inspect the drum for scoring, grooves, cracks, and out-of-roundness.

3. Light scoring may be removed by dressing the drum with fine emery cloth.

4. Heavy scoring will require the use of a brake lathe to turn the drum. The service limit of the drum inside diameter is 0.060 in. (1.524mm) over standard diameter.

Brake Shoes

REMOVAL & INSTALLATION

◗ **See Figure 7**

➡**If you are not thoroughly familiar with the procedure involved with brake shoe replacement, disassemble and assemble one side at a time, leaving the other side intact as a reference.**

Fig. 7 Exploded view of the self-adjusting front drum brake components

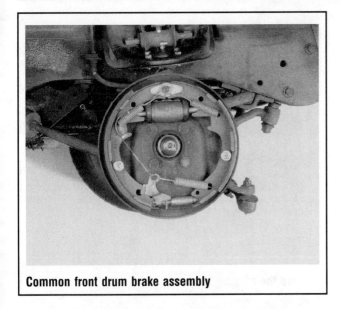

Common front drum brake assembly

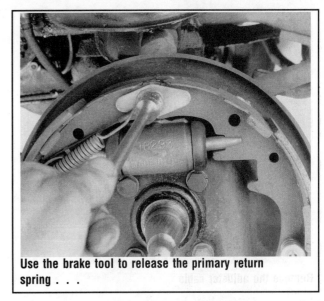

Use the brake tool to release the primary return spring . . .

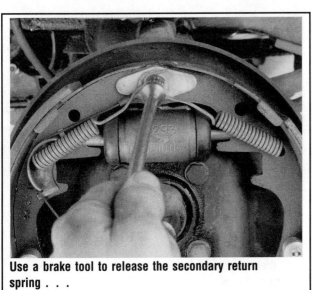

Use a brake tool to release the secondary return spring . . .

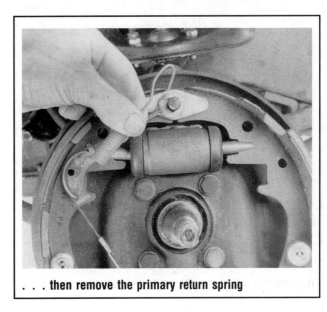

. . . then remove the primary return spring

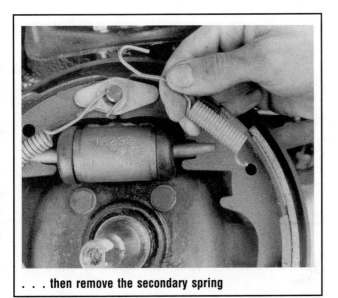

. . . then remove the secondary spring

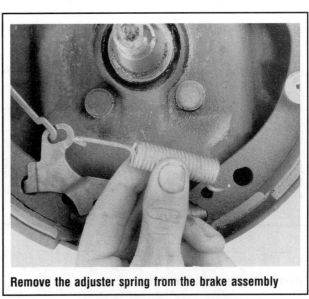

Remove the adjuster spring from the brake assembly

Remove the adjuster cable

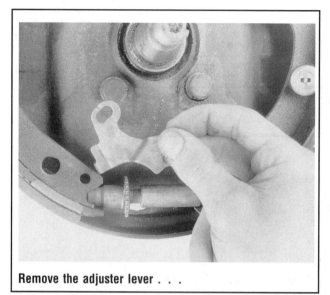

Remove the adjuster lever . . .

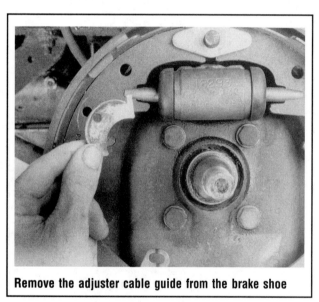

Remove the adjuster cable guide from the brake shoe

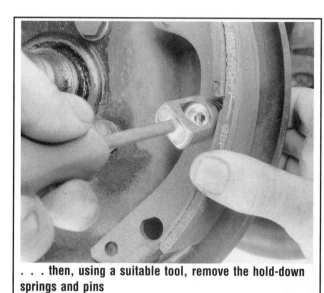

. . . then, using a suitable tool, remove the hold-down springs and pins

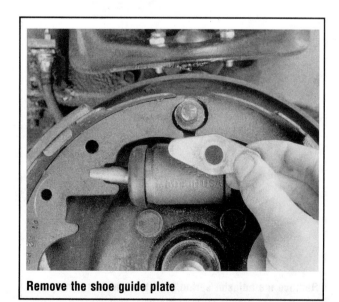

Remove the shoe guide plate

Remove the adjusting screw assembly and the brake shoes

1. Remove the brake drum.

Do not depress the brake pedal once the drum has been removed.

2. Remove the adjusting lever tang from the hole in the secondary shoe by grabbing the lever with a pair of pliers.
3. Place a wheel cylinder clamp over the wheel cylinder to retain its piston while the brake shoes are removed.
4. Unfasten the return springs with a brake springs removal tool by twisting them off the anchor pin.
5. Carefully remove the secondary shoe return spring, the adjusting cable, primary shoe return spring, the cable guide, the adjusting lever and spring in that order.

Be careful that all of the components of the brake do not fly out at once when the spring tension is being released.

6. Unfasten the hold-down springs and withdraw the shoes. Be careful not to get grease on the lining surfaces of the shoes.

To install:

➡**Always replace the shoes and linings on both wheels of the same axle; do not replace the shoes and linings on one side only.**

1. If there is any grease contamination, clean all of the parts, except the drums, with mineral spirits. If there is brake fluid contamination, use alcohol to clean the parts. Then clean all parts, including the drums with soap and water.
2. Polish the legs on the brake support plate with fine emery cloth. If there are any grooves on the support plate which limit shoe movement, the plate must be replaced (do not attempt to regrind).
3. Lubricate the ledges on the support plate, anchor pin, adjusting cable guide, adjusting screw threads and the pivot with molybdenum disulfide grease.
4. Place the shoes on the support plate and retain them with the hold-down springs.

➡**The following sequence is for 10 in. (254mm) brakes; reverse Steps 5 and 6 for 9 in. (228.6mm) brakes.**

5. Fit the adjusting cable eyelet over the anchor pin.
6. Install one end of the primary return spring in the primary shoe and the other end over the anchor pin with the brake spring tool.
7. Install the adjusting cable guide.
8. Fit the secondary shoe return spring in the same manner in which you installed the primary spring.
9. Install the adjusting screw assembly at the base of the brake shoe. Place the small hooked end of the adjusting spring into the large hole in the primary shoe.
10. Fit the large hooked end of the adjusting spring into the hole in the adjusting lever.

11. Engage the hooked end of the adjusting cable with the adjusting lever and place the cable over the cable guide.

Be sure that the adjusting cable is not twisted and that it cannot ride out of the guide.

12. Hook the tang on the adjusting lever into the large hole at the base of the secondary shoe by grasping the lever with pliers and pulling it into place.
13. Adjust the brakes and install the drums, as detailed elsewhere in this chapter.

Wheel Cylinders

OVERHAUL

▶ **See Figure 8**

1. Raise the vehicle on a hoist and remove the wheel and drum from the brake to be serviced.
2. Remove the brake shoes and clean the backing plate and wheel cylinder.
3. Disconnect the brake line from the brake hose. Remove the brake hose retainer clip at the frame bracket and remove the hose

Fig. 8 Exploded view of common wheel cylinder components

from the wheel cylinder. (On the rear brakes it will only be necessary to remove the line from the cylinder).

4. Remove the cylinder mounting bolts and remove the cylinder.

5. Remove the boots from the cylinder ends and discard. Remove the pistons, remove and discard the seal cups, and remove the expanders and spring.

6. Inspect the bore and pistons for damage or wear. Damaged pistons should be discarded, as they cannot be reconditioned. Slight bore roughness can be removed using a brake cylinder hone or crocus cloth. (Cloth should be rotated in the bore under finger pressure. Do not slide lengthwise.) Use only lint free cloth for cleaning.

7. Clean the cylinder and internal parts using only brake fluid or denatured alcohol.

On rear drum brakes, it is only necessary to remove the brake line from the wheel cylinder

On front drum brakes, remove the brake line from the brake hose . . .

. . . then remove the brake hose retainer clip

Loosen the brake hose-to-wheel cylinder nut . . .

. . . then disconnect the brake hose from the wheel cylinder

8. Insert the spring expander assembly. Lubricate all rubber parts using only fresh brake fluid.

9. Install new cups with the seal lips facing inward.

10. Install the pistons and rubber boots. Install the cylinder on the car in the reverse order or removal. Bleed the cylinder (see the preceding 'Bleeding' section).

FRONT DISC BRAKES

Disc Brake Pads

REMOVAL & INSTALLATION

✳✳ WARNING

To prevent paint damage from brake fluid, be sure to remove part of the brake fluid (don't reuse it) from the master cylinder and keep the master cylinder covered. Do not allow the cylinder to drain too low or air will be pumped into the system.

Unfasten its retaining bolts and remove the wheel cylinder from the backing plate

Wheel Bearings

REMOVAL, PACKING & INSTALLATION

1. The outer bearing is removed as part of the brake drum removal procedure.

2. Use a brass drift to remove the inner bearing and cup from the hub.

3. For installation and packing refer to wheel bearing procedure in the front disc brake portion of this section.

Adjustment

The bearing adjustment procedure for models equipped with front drum brakes is the same as for the disc brake equipped models. Refer to the wheel bearing procedure in the front disc brakes portion of this section.

1975–81 Models

EXCEPT PACER

◆ **See Figures 9, 10, 11 and 12**

1. Raise the front of the car and remove the front wheels.

2. Working on only one brake at a time, remove the caliper guide pins and positioners which attach the caliper to the adapter. Lift the caliper away from the disc.

3. Remove (and discard) the positioners and inner bushings from the guide pins, and the outboard bushings from the caliper.

4. Slide the disc pads out of the caliper, and carefully push the piston back into the bore. Later models have anti-rattle clips. Note their positions before removing them.

CALIPER ANCHOR PLATE

CALIPER

SCREW

SPRING

SPINDLE

INBOARD BRAKESHOE

CLIP

SUPPORT KEY

SEAL

SEAL

PISTON

DUST SEAL

BEARING

OUTBOARD BRAKESHOE

SPLASH SHIELD

RACE

NUT

NUT LOCK

RACE

WASHER

BEARING

COTTER PIN

SEAL

GREASE CUP

HUB AND ROTOR

Fig. 9 Exploded view of the front disc brake components—all 1975–76 models

Fig. 10 Front disc brake component locations—1977–78 Matador models

Fig. 11 Front disc brake components—1977–81 models except Matador and Eagle

Fig. 12 Exploded view of the front disc brake components—1980–81 Eagle models

Typical front disc brake assembly used on AMC models

Use a ratchet and socket to remove the caliper guide pins . . .

. . . then remove the caliper from the rotor

Remove the disc pads from the rotor

To install:

5. Lubricate the new outboard bushings and work them into position from the outboard side of the caliper.

6. Slide the new disc pads into position (outboard pad in the retaining spring) and carefully slide the caliper assembly over the rotor.

7. Lubricate and install the new inner bushings in the caliper. Install the new positioners on the guide pins with the open ends toward the outside.

8. Install the assembled guide pins from the inboard side and press while threading the pin into the adapter. Use extreme care to avoid crossing the threads. Tighten the caliper guide pins to 26 ft. lbs. Be sure that the tabs of the positioners are over the machined surfaces of the caliper.

✳✳ WARNING

Clean, high quality brake fluid is essential to the safe and proper operation of the brake system. You should always buy the highest quality brake fluid that is available. If the brake fluid becomes contaminated, drain and flush the system, then refill the master cylinder with new fluid. Never reuse any brake fluid. Any brake fluid that is removed from the system should be discarded.

9. Check the brake fluid level and add fluid if necessary. Pump the brake pedal to seat the linings against the disc. Replace the wheels and road test the car.

PACER

✳✳ WARNING

To prevent paint damage from leaking brake fluid, remove about ⅔ of the brake fluid from the larger reservoir (supplying the front brakes) in the master cylinder, and keep the cylinder reservoir covered. Do not allow the reservoir level to get too low or air will enter the hydraulic system, necessitating bleeding. Do not reuse the removed brake fluid.

1. Remove the hub caps and loosen the front wheel lug nuts slightly. Firmly apply the parking brake and block the rear wheels.

2. Raise the front of the car and install jackstands beneath the front jacking points or lower control arms. Remove the front wheels.

3. Working on only one caliper at a time, bottom the caliper piston in its bore by carefully inserting a screwdriver between the piston and the inboard shoe and prying back on the piston.

➡**Take care not to damage the rubber piston seals. If the piston cannot be bottomed with a screwdriver, a large C-clamp will suffice.**

4. Using a ¼ in. hex key or Allen wrench, remove the caliper support key retaining screw.

5. Remove the caliper support key and support spring using a drift pin and hammer. Lift the caliper assembly off its anchor plate and over the rotor (disc).

➡**Do not allow the caliper to hang by its flexible brake hose. Use a piece of heavy wire to suspend the caliper from the coil spring until you are ready to reinstall it.**

6. Remove the inboard brake shoe from the anchor plate. Remove the inboard brake shoe anti-rattle spring from the inboard shoe, noting its position for reassembly.

7. Remove the outboard brake shoe from the caliper, rapping lightly with a hammer, if necessary, to free it from the caliper.

8. Wipe the inside of the caliper free of all accumulated brake pad dust, road dirt and other foreign material with a clean, dry rag.

➡**Do not blow the caliper clean with compressed air, as this may dislodge the rubber dust cover.**

Check the piston seals for evidence of leakage from the piston bore, and overhaul the caliper if necessary. Clean all rust and dirt from the abutment (sliding), surfaces of the caliper and caliper anchor plate using a wire brush and crocus cloth. Then, lightly grease the sliding surfaces with white grease to ensure that the sliding motion of the caliper is not impaired.

To install:

9. Install the inboard brake shoe anti-rattle spring on the rear flange of the inboard brake shoe, making sure that the looped section of the clip is facing away from the rotor.

10. Install the assembled inboard brake shoe and anti-rattle spring in the caliper anchor plate, taking care not to dislodge the anti-rattle spring during installation.

11. Install the outboard brake shoe in the caliper, making sure to seat the shoe flange fully into the outboard arms of the caliper.

12. Install the caliper assembly over the rotor and into position in the anchor plate. Exercise extreme care when installing the caliper not to tear or dislodge the piston dust cover on the inboard brake shoe.

13. Align the caliper assembly with the abutment surfaces of the anchor plate and insert the caliper support key and support spring between the abutment surfaces at the rearward end of the caliper and anchor plate. Then, using a hammer and drift pin, drive the caliper support key and spring into position. Install the support key retaining screw and tighten to 15 ft. lbs.

✳✳ WARNING

Clean, high quality brake fluid is essential to the safe and proper operation of the brake system. You should always buy the highest quality brake fluid that is available. If the brake fluid becomes contaminated, drain and flush the sys-

tem, then refill the master cylinder with new fluid. Never re-use any brake fluid. Any brake fluid that is removed from the system should be discarded.

14. Fill the master cylinder reservoir to within ¼ in. (6mm) of the rim. Press the brake pedal firmly several times to seat the shoes.

15. Install the wheels and lower the car. Road test the car after rechecking the fluid level and checking for firm brake pedal.

1982–86 Models
▶ **See Figures 13 and 14**

1. Drain about ½ the fluid from the master cylinder.
2. Remove the hub cap and loosen the wheel retaining nuts.
3. Raise and support the automobile.
4. Remove the front wheels.
5. Work on one caliper at a time only.
6. Press the caliper piston to the bottom of the piston bore using a screwdriver. If the piston cannot be bottomed using a screwdriver, use a C-clamp.
7. Remove the caliper mounting pins using a 7mm hex or Allen wrench.
8. Lift the caliper assembly out of the anchor plate and off the rotor.
9. Suspend the caliper from the coil spring using a heavy wire. Do not let the brake hose support the weight of the caliper.
10. Remove the outboard brake shoe from the anchor plate while holding the anti-rattle clip against the caliper anchor plate. Note the position of the anti-rattle clip for assembly reference.
11. Remove the inboard brake shoe from the anchor plate and remove the anti-rattle clip.

✳✳ WARNING

The abutment surfaces of the caliper and anchor plate must be clean, smooth, and lightly lubricated with molybdenum disulfide grease before brake shoe and caliper installation. Rust, corrosion, or foreign material on the abutment surfaces will impair the sliding action of the brake shoes in the anchor plate.

To install:

12. Install the anti-rattle clip on the trailing end of the anchor plate being sure the split end of the clip faces away from the rotor.

13. Install the inboard brake shoe in the caliper anchor late while holding the anti-rattle clip in place.

14. Install the outboard brake shoe in the caliper anchor plate while holding the anti-rattle clip in place.

15. Install the caliper over the rotor and into position in the anchor plate.

16. Install the caliper mounting pins and tighten them to 26 ft. lbs.

✳✳ WARNING

Be very careful to avoid tearing or dislodging the dust boot when installing the caliper. A damaged boot will expose the caliper piston to road splash resulting in corrosion and eventual piston seizure.

MOUNTING
PIN

BLEEDER
SCREW AND
COVER

BUSHING

CALIPER
ANCHOR
PLATE

CALIPER

BRAKE HOSE

ADAPTER
BRACKET

WASHER

SEAL

PISTON

DUST
BOOT

ANTI RATTLE
CLIP

INBOARD
BRAKESHOE

OUTBOARD BRAKE SHOE

BEARING

SEAL

CUP

SPINDLE

WHEEL STUD

NUT

NUT LOCK

O-RING

SPLASH
SHIELD

CUP

BEARING

WASHER

GREASE CAP

COTTER PIN

HUB AND ROTOR
ASSEMBLY

Fig. 13 Exploded view of the front disc brake components—1982–83 Spirit and Concord models

Fig. 14 Exploded view of the front disc brake assembly—1982–88 Eagle models

---

✳✳ WARNING

Clean, high quality brake fluid is essential to the safe and proper operation of the brake system. You should always buy the highest quality brake fluid that is available. If the brake fluid becomes contaminated, drain and flush the system, then refill the master cylinder with new fluid. Never re-use any brake fluid. Any brake fluid that is removed from the system should be discarded.

---

17. Fill both master cylinder reservoirs to within ¼ in. (6.3mm) of the rim.

18. Press firmly on the brake pedal several times to seat the brake shoes.

19. Install the wheels and tires and lower the automobile.

20. Check the fluid level in the master cylinder and correct it if necessary.

✳✳ CAUTION

Check for a firm brake pedal and proper brake operation before moving the automobile.

Brake Caliper

REMOVAL, INSTALLATION, OVERHAUL

1975–81 Models

EXCEPT PACER

1. Raise the front of the car and remove the front wheels.
2. Working on one side at a time only, disconnect the brake

hose from the steel brake line and cap the fittings. Remove the U-shaped retainer from the hose fitting (if it has one).

3. Remove the caliper mounting bolts (locating pins) and positioners and lift the caliper away from the disc.

4. Clean the holes in the caliper ears, and wipe all dirt from the mounting bolts. If the bolts are corroded or damaged they should be replaced.

5. Remove the shoe support springs from the piston.

6. Remove the rubber bushings from the grooves in the caliper ears.

7. Remove the brake hose, drain the brake fluid, and clean the outside of the caliper.

8. Pad the inside of the caliper with towels and direct compressed air into the brake fluid inlet hole to remove the piston.

✳✳ CAUTION

To prevent damage to the piston use just enough air pressure to ease it out of the bore. Do not attempt to catch or protect the piston with your hand since this may cause serious injury.

9. Use a prytool to pry the boot out of the caliper. Avoid scratching the bore.

10. Remove the piston seal from its groove in the caliper bore. Do not use a metal tool of any type for this operation.

11. Blow out all passages in the caliper and bleeder valve. Clean the piston and piston bore with fresh brake fluid.

12. Examine the piston for scoring, scratches, or corrosion. If any of these conditions exist the piston must be replaced, as it is plated and cannot be refinished.

13. Examine the bore for the same defects. Light rough spots may be removed by rotating crocus cloth, using finger pressure, in the bore. Do not polish with an in and out motion or use any other abrasive. Piston-to-bore clearance should be 0.002–0.006 in. (0.051–0.152mm).

To install:

14. Lubricate the piston bore and the new rubber parts with fresh brake fluid. Position the seal in the piston bore groove.

15. Lubricate the piston with brake fluid and assemble the boot into the piston groove so that the fold faces the open end of the piston.

16. Insert the piston into the bore, taking care not to unseat the seal.

17. Force the piston to the bottom of the bore. (This will require a force of 50–100 lbs.). Seat the boot lip around the caliper counterbore. Proper seating of the boot is very important for sealing out contaminants.

18. Install the brake hose into the caliper using a new copper gasket.

19. Lubricate the rubber bushings. Install the bushings in the caliper ears.

➡**Lubrication of the bushings is essential to ensure the proper operation of the sliding caliper design.**

20. Install the shoe support spring in the piston.

21. Install the disc pads in the caliper and remount the caliper on the hub. Refer to the disc brake pad removal and installation procedure in this section.

✳✳ WARNING

Clean, high quality brake fluid is essential to the safe and proper operation of the brake system. You should always buy the highest quality brake fluid that is available. If the brake fluid becomes contaminated, drain and flush the system, then refill the master cylinder with new fluid. Never reuse any brake fluid. Any brake fluid that is removed from the system should be discarded.

22. Reconnect the brake hose to the steel brake line. Install the retainer clip. Bleed the brakes.

23. Replace the wheels, check the brake fluid level, check the brake pedal travel, and road test the vehicle.

PACER

1. Remove the caliper as outlined under Steps 1–7 of the disc brake pad removal and installation procedure in this section.

2. Place a clean piece of paper on your work area to put the parts of the caliper on while it is being disassembled.

3. Drain the brake fluid from the caliper by opening the bleeder plug.

4. Place the caliper assembly in a vise with padded jaws.

✳✳ WARNING

Do not overtighten the vise; too much pressure will cause distortion of the caliper bore.

5. Using compressed air, remove the piston from the caliper bore. Be careful not to damage the piston or the bore. Leave the dust boot in the caliper groove while the piston is being removed.

6. Take the caliper out of the vise and withdraw the dust boot.

7. Work the piston seal out of its groove in the piston bore with a small, pointed wooden or plastic stick. Do not use a screwdriver or other metallic tool to remove the seal as it could damage the bore. Throw the old seal away.

8. Unscrew the bleeder plug.

9. Clean all of the parts in brake fluid (do not use solvent) and wipe them dry with a clean, lint free cloth. Dry the passages and bores with compressed air.

Check the cylinder bore for scoring, pitting, and/or corrosion. If the caliper bore is deeply scored or corroded, replace the entire caliper.

If it is only lightly scored or stained, polish with crocus cloth. Use finger pressure to rotate the crocus cloth in the cylinder bore. Any black stains found in the bore are caused by seals and are harmless.

✳✳ WARNING

Do not slide the crocus cloth in and out of the bore. Do not use any other type of abrasive material.

Check the piston. If it is pitted, scored, or worn, it should be replaced with a new one.

Check the piston-to-bore clearance with a feeler gauge. It should be 0.002–0.006 in. (0.051–0.152mm). If it is more than this, replace the caliper assembly.

To install:

1. Dip a new piston seal in clean brake fluid. Position the seal in one area of the groove in the cylinder bore and gently work it into place around the groove until it is seated. Be sure that your fingers are clean before touching the seal.

➡**Never reuse an old piston seal.**

2. Coat a new piston boot with clean brake fluid. Work it into the outer groove of the bore with your fingers until it snaps into place. Don't worry if the boot seems too large for the groove; once seated, it will fit properly. Check the boot, by running your forefinger around the inside of it, to be sure that it is correctly installed.

3. Coat the piston with plenty of brake fluid. Spread the boot with your fingers and insert the piston into it.

4. Depress the piston until it bottoms in the bore.

✳✳ WARNING

Apply uniform force to the piston or it will crack.

5. Install the caliper assembly as outlined under Steps 9–15 of the disc brake pad removal and installation procedure.

1982–86 Models
▶ **See Figure 15**

1. Drain and discard ⅔ of the brake fluid from the master cylinder reservoir serving the front disc brakes. Do not drain the reservoir completely.

2. Remove the hub cap and loosen wheel retaining nuts.

3. Raise and support the automobile.

4. Remove the front wheels.

5. Work on one caliper at a time.

6. Wipe all dirt and grease from the caliper brake hose fitting using a shop cloth.

7. Disconnect the brake line at the caliper and discard the hose fitting washer. Cover the open end of the hose with tape or a clean shop cloth.

8. Remove the caliper and brake shoes as outlined in Brake Shoe Replacement.

9. Clean the caliper exterior with brake cleaning solvent.

Fig. 15 Pad the inside of the caliper with towels and use compressed air to remove the caliper piston

10. Drain the remaining fluid from the caliper and place the caliper on a clean work surface.

11. Pad the caliper interior with clean shop cloths.

✳✳ CAUTION

Do not, under any circumstances, place your fingers in front of the piston in an attempt to catch or protect it. In addition, use only enough air pressure to ease the piston out of the bore. Excessive air pressure can eject the piston with enough force to cause damage or injury.

12. Insert the air nozzle into the caliper fluid inlet hole and slowly apply just enough air pressure to ease the piston out of the bore.

13. Remove and discard the dust boot. Use a screwdriver to pry the boot from the bore. Do not scratch the piston bore during boot removal.

14. Remove and discard the piston seal. Use a pencil or similar wood implement to remove the seal.

✳✳ WARNING

Remove the seal using a pencil, wooden stick, piece of plastic, or similar tool only. Do not use a metal tool or similar object to remove the seal, as the bore could be scored.

15. Remove the bleeder screw.

16. Remove and discard the plastic sleeves and rubber bushings from the caliper mounting ears.

Inspect the caliper piston. Replace the piston if nicked, scratched, corroded, or if the protective plating has worn off.

✳✳ WARNING

Do not attempt to refinish the piston in any way. The outside diameter is the sealing surface and is manufactured to very close tolerances. Removal of the nickle-chrome protective plating will lead to pitting, corrosion, and eventual piston seizure.

Inspect the piston bore. Replace the caliper if the bore is nicked, scratched, worn, cracked, or badly corroded. However, minor stains or corrosion can be removed using crocus cloth.

✳✳ WARNING

Do not use emery cloth or similar abrasives on the piston bore. If the bore does not clean up with crocus cloth, replace the caliper. Clean the caliper thoroughly with brake fluid or brake cleaning solvent if the bore was polished.

17. Lubricate the piston bore and replacement seal with brake fluid.

To install:

▶ **See Figures 16, 17 and 18**

18. Install the seal in the bore groove. Work the seal into the groove using fingers only.

19. Lubricate the piston with the brake fluid.

20. Install the replacement dust boot on the piston. Slide the metal retainer portion of the seal over the open end of the piston

Fig. 16 Lubricate the dust boot with new brake fluid, then install it on the piston

Fig. 17 Position the dust boot so that its metal retainer is flush with the rim of the caliper piston

Fig. 18 Use tool J-33028 or its equivalent to seat the dust boot properly in the counterbore

and pull the seal rearward until the rubber boot lip seats in the piston groove.

21. Push the metal retainer portion of the boot forward until the retainer is flush with the rim at the open end of the piston and the seal fold snaps into place.

22. Insert the piston into the bore and into the piston seal. Do not unseat the seal.

23. Press the piston to the bottom of the bore using a hammer handle.

24. Seat the metal retainer portion of the dust boot in the counterbore at the upper end of the piston bore using Tool J-33028 or its equivalent.

25. Install the bleeder screw. Tighten the screw securely but not to the required torque until the brakes have been bled.

26. Install the replacement plastic sleeves and rubber bushings in the caliper mounting ears.

27. Check the rotor for face run-out, thickness variation, deep scores, cracks, and broken ventilating ribs.

28. Install the brake shoes and caliper as outlined under Brake Shoe Replacement.

29. Install a replacement washer on the brake hose fitting and connect the hose to the caliper. Tighten the fitting to 25 ft. lbs. torque.

30. Fill the master cylinder to within ¼ in. (6.3mm) of the reservoir rims and bleed the brakes as outlined under Brake Bleeding.

31. After bleeding, press the brake pedal firmly several times to seat the brake shoes. Recheck the master cylinder fluid level and correct it if necessary.

32. Install the wheels and tighten the retaining nuts to 75 ft. lbs. torque.

33. Lower the automobile.

❊❊ CAUTION

The metal portion of the dust boot must be seated evenly and below the face of the caliper.

❊❊ CAUTION

Check for a firm brake pedal and proper brake operation before moving the automobile.

Brake Disc (Rotor)

REMOVAL & INSTALLATION

Except Eagle

1. Raise the front end and remove the wheel.
2. Remove the caliper and adapter assembly. Details are given earlier.
3. Wire the caliper to the suspension to prevent straining the brake line.
4. Remove the grease cap, cotter pin, nut, and washer front the wheel spindle.

After removing the caliper and brake pads, the brake rotor (disc) may be removed from the spindle

5. Pull the disc out slightly and push it back. Remove the outer wheel bearing.

✳✳ WARNING

Keep your greasy hands off the disc surface!

6. Remove the hub and disc.
7. Make sure that the grease in the hub is clean, that the wheel bearings are both packed with grease, and that the disc surfaces are clean.

✳✳ WARNING

Use only grease specified for disc brake use. Ordinary grease will melt and ooze all over the braking surfaces, ruining the friction pads.

8. Slide the hub and disc onto the spindle.
9. Install the outer bearing, washer, and nut. Adjust the wheel bearings as described later in this section. Install the cotter pin.

10. Clean the grease cap and coat the inside with grease. Don't pack it full. Install it.
11. Replace the caliper.
12. On replacing the wheel, torque the nuts to 75 ft. lbs.

➡**You may feel a little silly torquing wheel nuts, but this is important to prevent distorting the disc.**

Eagle

1. Loosen the wheel retaining nuts.
2. Raise and support the automobile.
3. Remove the front wheels.
4. Remove the caliper assembly but do not disconnect the brake line. Suspend the caliper from a wire hook attached to the front spring. Do not let the brake hose support the weight of the caliper.
5. Remove the rotor. Pull the rotor straight off of the hub.
6. Install the rotor on the hub.
7. Install the caliper.
8. Install the wheel. Tighten the wheel retaining nuts to 75 ft. lbs.
9. Lower the automobile.

✳✳ CAUTION

Check for a firm brake pedal and proper brake operation before moving the automobile.

INSPECTION

▸ See Figures 19, 20 and 21

The disc can be checked for runout (wobble) and thickness variations with a dial indicator and a micrometer while mounted on the car, or in a lathe. Runout should not exceed 0.005 in. (0.127mm) and thickness variation should not exceed 0.001 in. (0.025mm). The disc can be machined, but the final thickness must be at least 0.940 in. (23.876mm).

MAXIMUM RUNOUT
0.003 INCH

Fig. 19 Use a dial indicator to check the rotor lateral run-out

SURFACE MUST BE SQUARE WITH CENTERLINE TO 0.010 INCH

CENTERLINE

MOUNT ON BEARING CUPS WHEN MEASURING

Fig. 20 Check that the hub-to-bore run-out is within specifications

Fig. 21 Use a micrometer on a few different positions to check the thickness variation of the rotor

➡These are the factory's specifications; some state inspection laws aren't this lenient.

Wheel Bearings

REMOVAL, PACKING, & INSTALLATION

1. Use the Brake Disc Removal and Installation procedure to remove the bearings.
2. Remove the inner bearing.
3. Clean the bearings thoroughly in a safe solvent. Check their condition, but don't spin them any more than is absolutely necessary.
4. Replace the seal on assembly.
5. Make sure that the inner cones of the bearings are free to creep (move slowly) on the spindle. This adds to the life of the bearings.

If difficulty is encountered, gently tap on the pliers with a hammer to help free the cotter pin

Pry the dust cap from the hub taking care not to distort or damage its flange

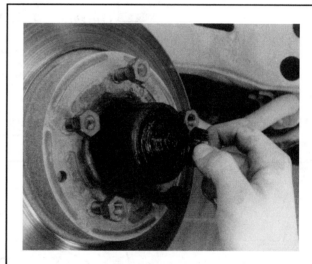

Loosen and remove the castellated nut from the spindle

Once the bent ends are cut, grasp the cotter pin and pull or pry it free of the spindle

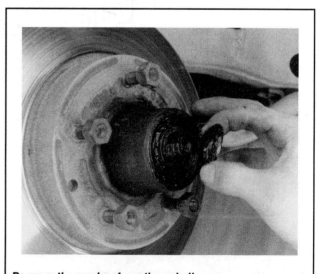

Remove the washer from the spindle

With the nut and washer out of the way, the outer bearings may be removed from the hub

With the seal removed, the inner bearing may be withdrawn from the hub

Pull the hub and inner bearing assembly from the spindle

Thoroughly pack the bearing with fresh, high temperature wheel-bearing grease before installation

Use a small prytool to remove the old inner bearing seal

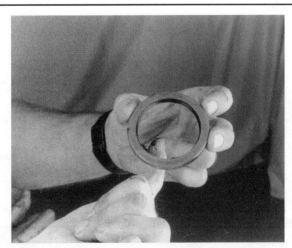

Apply a thin coat of fresh grease to the new inner bearing seal lip

Use a suitably sized driver to install the inner bearing seal to the hub

After the bearings are adjusted, install the dust cap by gently tapping on the flange—DO NOT damage the cap by hammering on the center

With new or freshly packed bearings, tighten the nut while gently spinning the wheel, then adjust the bearings

6. Pack both wheel bearings using wheel bearing grease made for disc brakes. Ordinary grease will melt and ooze out, ruining the pads. Place a healthy glob of grease in the palm of one hand and force the edge of the bearing into it so that the grease fills the bearing. Do this until the whole bearing is packed. Grease packing tools are available which make this job a lot less messy.

7. Install the inner bearing and seal.

8. Use the Brake Disc Removal and Installation procedure to replace the bearings and disc.

ADJUSTMENT

1. Raise the front wheel off the floor.

2. Remove the grease cap and cotter pin.

3. To seat the bearings, tighten the wheel spindle nut to 20–25 ft. lbs. while turning the wheel.

4. Loosen the nut ⅓ turn. Tighten the nut to 2–10 inch lbs.

5. If there is a nut retainer, place it on the nut with the slots of the retainer aligned with the spindle cotter pin hole. Install a new cotter pin and the dust cap.

REAR DRUM BRAKES

REAR DRUM BRAKE COMPONENTS

1. Shoe guide plate
2. Adjuster cable
3. Primary shoe
4. Secondary shoe
5. Adjuster cable guide
6. Primary return spring
7. Secondary return spring
8. Parking brake strut
9. Parking brake strut spring
10. Hold down pin
11. Hold down spring
12. Hold down spring caps
13. Adjuster lever
14. Adjuster spring
15. Adjusting screw assembly
16. Parking brake lever

Typical rear drum brake components

Brake Drums

REMOVAL & INSTALLATION

➡**Release the parking brake before attempting rear drum removal.**

1. Remove the wheel cover and loosen the lug nuts. Remove the cotter key and the axle shaft nut.

➡**If the car is equipped with styled wheels, it will be necessary to raise the car and remove the wheel first.**

2. Block the front wheels, raise the car, and support it with jackstands.

❊❊ CAUTION

Be sure that the car is securely supported.

3. Remove the wheel.
4. Unfasten the three screws which secure the brake drum and withdraw the drum.

❊❊ WARNING

Do not depress the brake pedal once the drum has been removed.

5. Installation is performed in the reverse order of removal.

INSPECTION

Rear drum inspection procedures and specifications are identical to those given in the front drum brake inspection procedure in this section.

Brake Shoes

REMOVAL & INSTALLATION

The removal and installation procedure for the rear brake shoes is similar to that for the front shoes. The only differences are: the parking brake lever must be removed from (and installed on) the secondary shoe and the parking brake strut spring assembly must be removed from (and installed), between the shoes.

Common rear drum brake assembly

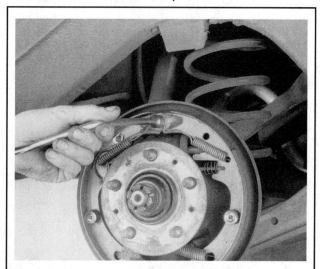
Use a brake tool to release the return springs . . .

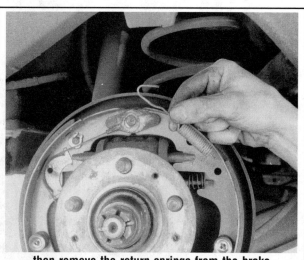
. . . then remove the return springs from the brake assembly

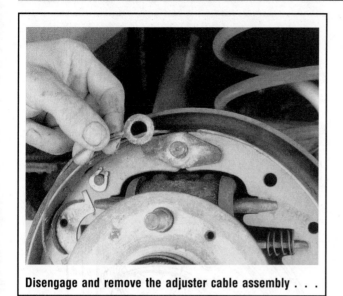

Disengage and remove the adjuster cable assembly . . .

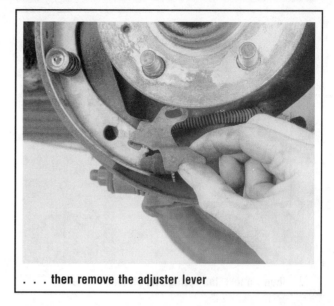

. . . then remove the adjuster lever

. . . then remove the shoe guide plate

Remove the adjusting screw assembly

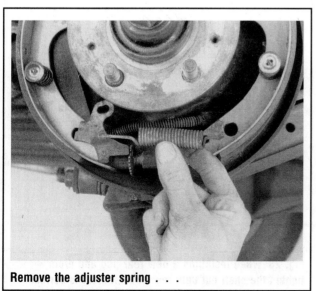

Remove the adjuster spring . . .

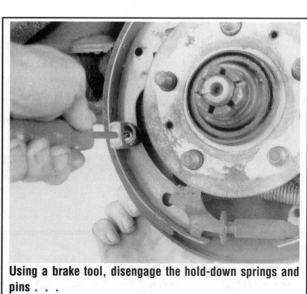

Using a brake tool, disengage the hold-down springs and pins . . .

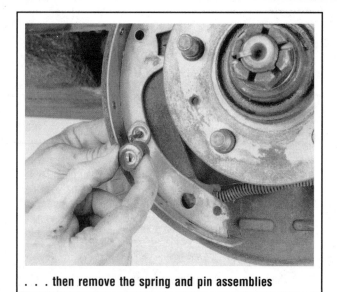

. . . then remove the spring and pin assemblies

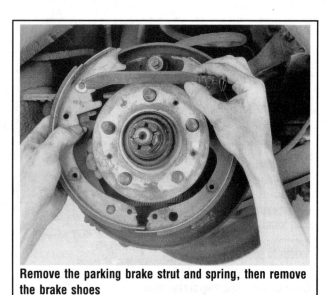

Remove the parking brake strut and spring, then remove the brake shoes

Wheel Cylinders

OVERHAUL

The servicing procedures for the rear wheel cylinders are identical to those for the front cylinders previously described.

Hubs and Bearings

REMOVAL & INSTALLATION

▶ See Figures 22 and 23

The rear axle splines cut serrations into the inner diameter of the rear wheel hub. If the hub is to be removed, matchmark the hub to the axle so that the job of aligning the serrations and

Fig. 22 Use a suitable puller to remove the rear hub

Fig. 23 When installing a new rear hub and drum, tighten the shaft nut until the measurement is correct

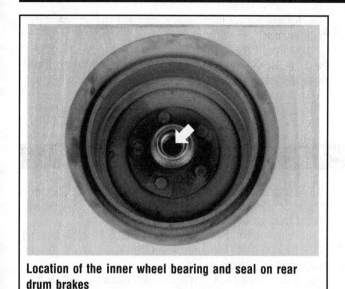

Location of the inner wheel bearing and seal on rear drum brakes

Use a seal installer and mallet to install the inner bearing seal in the drum

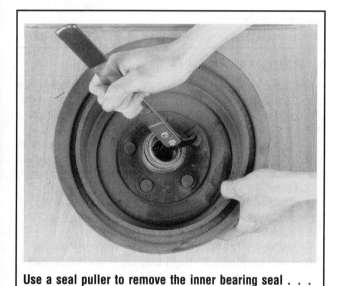

Use a seal puller to remove the inner bearing seal . . .

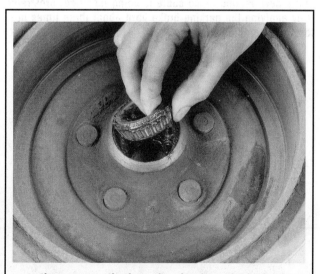

. . . then remove the inner bearing from the brake drum

splines will be easier. If this is not done, the axle will cut new splines which may be so near the old that the hub will move on the axle with resultant damage to the hub, axle, and differential gears.

When a new hub is installed, the serrations will be cut in the hub as it is installed on the shaft.

If a new axle shaft is installed, a new hub, without serrations, must be installed. And old shaft with a new hub also is an allowable combination.

1. Remove the wheel and brake drum as detailed above.
2. Matchmark the hub and axle shaft.
3. Attach a suitable puller to the wheel hub to remove it.

✳✳ WARNING

Do not use a knockout type puller on the end of the axle shaft, as this could damage the wheel bearings or the thrust blocks. Use a screw type puller.

4. Inspect the hub for faulty lug studs, a worn keyway or center bore, and damaged serrations. Replace the hub and drum if any of these are present or if it is cracked.

➡The hub and drum must both be replaced if either one is defective.

5. Installation, if the old hub and drum are being replaced, is performed in the reverse order of removal. Tighten the axle shaft nut to 250 ft. lbs. with the weight of the car resting on the rear wheels.

➡Be sure to align the matchmarks made during removal.

A new hub and drum assembly must be installed in the following order:

1. Align the hub keyway with the key on the axle shaft.
2. Slide the hub and drum onto the axle shaft as far as they will go.
3. Fit two well lubricated thrust washers over the axle shaft and install the axle shaft nut.
4. Install the wheel and lug nuts, remove the jackstands, and lower the car.

5. Tighten the axle shaft nut until the distance from the outer face of the hub to the outer end of the axle shaft is one of the following:

- 7⁹⁄₁₆ in. (192mm) differential—1.7 in. (43.18mm)
- 8⁷⁄₈ in. (225mm) differential—1.30 in. (33.02mm)

➡**If the hub is not pressed in to the proper specifications, the splines will be improperly cut.**

PARKING BRAKE

Cables

REMOVAL & INSTALLATION

Left Rear Cable

1. Raise the vehicle and support it securely by the frame. Loosen the adjusting nut and compress the retainer fingers at the equalizer lever to loosen the cable.
2. Disconnect the cable at the connector and then remove it from the equalizer.
3. Mark the relationship between the wheel and axle flange and remove the wheel. Remove the brake drum.
4. Using an appropriate tool, disconnect and remove the primary shoe return spring and parking brake strut.
5. Compress the retainer fingers and loosen the cable housing at the backing plate. Then, disconnect the cable from the parking brake lever and remove it.
6. Install a new cable in reverse order, checking carefully that it is properly routed and securely retained. Adjust the parking brake.

Right Rear Cable

1. Raise the vehicle and support it securely by the frame. Remove the adjusting nut at the equalizer lever. Compress the fingers of the retainers and then loosen the cable housing from the retainers at the frame and at the axle housing retaining clip.
2. Mark the relationship between the wheel and axle flange and then remove the wheel. Remove the brake drum as described above.

6. Remove the nut front the axle shaft and take off one of the thrust washers.
7. Reinstall the axle shaft nut and tighten it to 250 ft. lbs. If the cotter key cannot be inserted, tighten the nut to the next castellation and install the key.

3. Using an appropriate tool, disconnect and remove the primary shoe return spring and parking brake strut. Remove the secondary brake shoe hold-down spring.
4. Compress the retainer fingers and loosen the cable housing at the backing plate. Then, disconnect the cable from the parking brake lever and remove it.
5. Install a new cable in reverse order, checking carefully that it is properly routed and securely retained. Adjust the parking brake.

ADJUSTMENT

▶ **See Figures 24, 25 and 26**

The rear brakes serve a dual purpose. They are used as service brakes and as parking brakes. To obtain proper adjustment of the parking brake, the service brakes must first be properly adjusted as outlined earlier.

1. Apply the parking brake 4 clicks from the fully released position.
2. Raise and support the vehicle.
3. Loosen the locknut at the equalizer.
4. Tighten or loosen the adjusting nut until a moderate drag is felt when the rear wheels are rotated forward.
5. Tighten the locknut.
6. Release the parking brake and rotate the rear wheels. No drag should be felt. If even a light drag is felt, readjust the parking brake.
7. Lower the vehicle.

➡**If a new parking brake cable is being installed, prestretch it by applying the parking brake hard about three times before making adjustments.**

Fig. 24 Parking brake assembly components—1975 models except Pacer

Fig. 25 Exploded view of the parking brake assembly—1976–88 models except Pacer

MOUNTING STUD LOCKNUT (2)

LEVER ASSEMBLY

PARKING BRAKE WARNING
LIGHT SWITCH

MOUNTING BOLT (2)

RELEASE CABLE AND
HANDLE ASSEMBLY

CABLE ADJUSTER AND HOOKS

LOCKNUT

BRACKET

RETURN SPRING

FRONT PARKING
BRAKE CABLE

EQUALIZER

EQUALIZER
BRACKET

CLIP

RIGHT REAR
CABLE

BRACKET

CLIP

LEFT REAR
CABLE

Fig. 26 Parking brake assembly components—Pacer models

Raise the rear of the vehicle and support it with jackstands

Tighten the locknut at the equalizer until a slight drag is felt when the wheels are rotated forward

Brake Specifications
Gremlin/Hornet/Spirit/Concord/Pacer/AMX

Years	Master Cyl. Bore	Brake Disc			Brake Drum		Wheel Cyl. or Caliper Bore	
		Original Thickness	Minimum Thickness	Maximum Run-out	Orig. Inside Dia.	Max. Wear Limit	Front	Rear
1975–76	①	1.190	1.120	0.003	②	③	④	⑤
1977	1.000	0.880	0.810	0.003	10.000	10.060	2.600	0.812
1978	0.945	0.880	0.810	0.003	⑥	⑥	2.600	⑦
1979–80	0.945	0.880	0.810	0.003	⑥	⑥	2.600	⑧
1981–83	0.945	0.880	0.810	0.003	⑨	⑨	2.600	0.945

① Non-power and power drum, and power disc: 1.0000
　Power disc: 1.0625
② 6-cyl.: 9.000
　8-cyl.: 10.000
③ 6-cyl.: 9.060
　8-cyl.: 10.060
④ Drum brakes, wheel cylinder dia.:
　　6-cyl. 1⅛
　　8-cyl. 1³⁄₁₆
　Disc brakes, caliper bore: 3.100
⑤ Gremlin: ⅞
　Hornet 6-cyl.: 1³⁄₁₆
　Hornet 8-cyl.: ⅞

⑥ 4-cyl.: 9.000; 9.060 max.
　All others: 10.000; 10.060 max.
⑦ 4-cyl.: 0.940
　All others: 0.812
⑧ 4-cyl.: 0.945
　AMX: 0.945
　Pacer/Spirit/Concord 6- and 8-cyl.: 0.810
⑨ All except Station Wagon: 9.000; 9.060 max.
　Station Wagon: 10.000; 10.06 max.

Brake Specifications
Matador

Years	Master Cyl. Bore	Brake Disc			Brake Drum		Wheel Cyl. or Caliper Bore	
		Original Thickness	Minimum Thickness	Maximum Run-out	Orig. Inside Dia.	Max. Wear Limit	Front	Rear
1975–76	①	1.190	1.120	0.003	10.000	10.060	3.100	②
1977	③	1.190	1.120	0.003	10.000	10.060	3.100	②
1978	1.125	1.190	1.120	0.003	10.000	10.060	3.100	②

① Non-power: 1¹⁄₁₆
　Power: 1⅛
② Except Station Wagon: ⅞
　Station Wagon: ¹⁵⁄₁₆
③ Non-power: 1.000
　Power: 1.125

Eagle

Years	Master Cyl. Bore	Brake Disc			Brake Drum		Wheel Cyl. or Caliper Bore	
		Original Thickness	Minimum Thickness	Maximum Run-out	Orig. Inside Dia.	Max. Wear Limit	Front	Rear
1980–88	0.940	0.880	0.810	0.003	10.000	10.060	2.600	0.945

Troubleshooting the Brake System

Problem	Cause	Solution
Low brake pedal (excessive pedal travel required for braking action.)	• Excessive clearance between rear linings and drums caused by inoperative automatic adjusters	• Make 10 to 15 alternate forward and reverse brake stops to adjust brakes. If brake pedal does not come up, repair or replace adjuster parts as necessary.
	• Worn rear brakelining	• Inspect and replace lining if worn beyond minimum thickness specification
	• Bent, distorted brakeshoes, front or rear	• Replace brakeshoes in axle sets
	• Air in hydraulic system	• Remove air from system. Refer to Brake Bleeding.
Low brake pedal (pedal may go to floor with steady pressure applied.)	• Fluid leak in hydraulic system	• Fill master cylinder to fill line; have helper apply brakes and check calipers, wheel cylinders, differential valve tubes, hoses and fittings for leaks. Repair or replace as necessary.
	• Air in hydraulic system	• Remove air from system. Refer to Brake Bleeding.
	• Incorrect or non-recommended brake fluid (fluid evaporates at below normal temp).	• Flush hydraulic system with clean brake fluid. Refill with correct-type fluid.
	• Master cylinder piston seals worn, or master cylinder bore is scored, worn or corroded	• Repair or replace master cylinder
Low brake pedal (pedal goes to floor on first application—o.k. on subsequent applications.)	• Disc brake pads sticking on abutment surfaces of anchor plate. Caused by a build-up of dirt, rust, or corrosion on abutment surfaces	• Clean abutment surfaces
Fading brake pedal (pedal height decreases with steady pressure applied.)	• Fluid leak in hydraulic system	• Fill master cylinder reservoirs to fill mark, have helper apply brakes, check calipers, wheel cylinders, differential valve, tubes, hoses, and fittings for fluid leaks. Repair or replace parts as necessary.
	• Master cylinder piston seals worn, or master cylinder bore is scored, worn or corroded	• Repair or replace master cylinder
Decreasing brake pedal travel (pedal travel required for braking action decreases and may be accompanied by a hard pedal.)	• Caliper or wheel cylinder pistons sticking or seized	• Repair or replace the calipers, or wheel cylinders
	• Master cylinder compensator ports blocked (preventing fluid return to reservoirs) or pistons sticking or seized in master cylinder bore	• Repair or replace the master cylinder
	• Power brake unit binding internally	• Test unit according to the following procedure: (a) Shift transmission into neutral and start engine (b) Increase engine speed to 1500 rpm, close throttle and fully depress brake pedal (c) Slow release brake pedal and stop engine (d) Have helper remove vacuum check valve and hose from power unit. Observe for backward movement of brake pedal. (e) If the pedal moves backward, the power unit has an internal bind—replace power unit

Troubleshooting the Brake System (cont.)

Problem	Cause	Solution
Spongy brake pedal (pedal has abnormally soft, springy, spongy feel when depressed.)	• Air in hydraulic system	• Remove air from system. Refer to Brake Bleeding.
	• Brakeshoes bent or distorted	• Replace brakeshoes
	• Brakelining not yet seated with drums and rotors	• Burnish brakes
	• Rear drum brakes not properly adjusted	• Adjust brakes
Hard brake pedal (excessive pedal pressure required to stop vehicle. May be accompanied by brake fade.)	• Loose or leaking power brake unit vacuum hose	• Tighten connections or replace leaking hose
	• Incorrect or poor quality brakelining	• Replace with lining in axle sets
	• Bent, broken, distorted brakeshoes	• Replace brakeshoes
	• Calipers binding or dragging on mounting pins. Rear brakeshoes dragging on support plate.	• Replace mounting pins and bushings. Clean rust or burrs from rear brake support plate ledges and lubricate ledges with molydisulfide grease. **NOTE:** If ledges are deeply grooved or scored, do not attempt to sand or grind them smooth—replace support plate.
	• Caliper, wheel cylinder, or master cylinder pistons sticking or seized	• Repair or replace parts as necessary
	• Power brake unit vacuum check valve malfunction	• Test valve according to the following procedure: (a) Start engine, increase engine speed to 1500 rpm, close throttle and immediately stop engine (b) Wait at least 90 seconds then depress brake pedal (c) If brakes are not vacuum assisted for 2 or more applications, check valve is faulty
	• Power brake unit has internal bind	• Test unit according to the following procedure: (a) With engine stopped, apply brakes several times to exhaust all vacuum in system (b) Shift transmission into neutral, depress brake pedal and start engine (c) If pedal height decreases with foot pressure and less pressure is required to hold pedal in applied position, power unit vacuum system is operating normally. Test power unit. If power unit exhibits a bind condition, replace the power unit.
	• Master cylinder compensator ports (at bottom of reservoirs) blocked by dirt, scale, rust, or have small burrs (blocked ports prevent fluid return to reservoirs).	• Repair or replace master cylinder **CAUTION:** Do not attempt to clean blocked ports with wire, pencils, or similar implements. Use compressed air only.
	• Brake hoses, tubes, fittings clogged or restricted	• Use compressed air to check or unclog parts. Replace any damaged parts.
	• Brake fluid contaminated with improper fluids (motor oil, transmission fluid, causing rubber components to swell and stick in bores	• Replace all rubber components, combination valve and hoses. Flush entire brake system with DOT 3 brake fluid or equivalent.
	• Low engine vacuum	• Adjust or repair engine

Troubleshooting the Brake System (cont.)

Problem	Cause	Solution
Grabbing brakes (severe reaction to brake pedal pressure.)	• Brakelining(s) contaminated by grease or brake fluid	• Determine and correct cause of contamination and replace brakeshoes in axle sets
	• Parking brake cables incorrectly adjusted or seized	• Adjust cables. Replace seized cables.
	• Incorrect brakelining or lining loose on brakeshoes	• Replace brakeshoes in axle sets
	• Caliper anchor plate bolts loose	• Tighten bolts
	• Rear brakeshoes binding on support plate ledges	• Clean and lubricate ledges. Replace support plate(s) if ledges are deeply grooved. Do not attempt to smooth ledges by grinding.
	• Incorrect or missing power brake reaction disc	• Install correct disc
	• Rear brake support plates loose	• Tighten mounting bolts
Dragging brakes (slow or incomplete release of brakes)	• Brake pedal binding at pivot	• Loosen and lubricate
	• Power brake unit has internal bind	• Inspect for internal bind. Replace unit if internal bind exists.
	• Parking brake cables incorrectly adjusted or seized	• Adjust cables. Replace seized cables.
	• Rear brakeshoe return springs weak or broken	• Replace return springs. Replace brakeshoe if necessary in axle sets.
	• Automatic adjusters malfunctioning	• Repair or replace adjuster parts as required
	• Caliper, wheel cylinder or master cylinder pistons sticking or seized	• Repair or replace parts as necessary
	• Master cylinder compensating ports blocked (fluid does not return to reservoirs).	• Use compressed air to clear ports. Do not use wire, pencils, or similar objects to open blocked ports.
Vehicle moves to one side when brakes are applied	• Incorrect front tire pressure	• Inflate to recommended cold (reduced load) inflation pressure
	• Worn or damaged wheel bearings	• Replace worn or damaged bearings
	• Brakelining on one side contaminated	• Determine and correct cause of contamination and replace brakelining in axle sets
	• Brakeshoes on one side bent, distorted, or lining loose on shoe	• Replace brakeshoes in axle sets
	• Support plate bent or loose on one side	• Tighten or replace support plate
	• Brakelining not yet seated with drums or rotors	• Burnish brakelining
	• Caliper anchor plate loose on one side	• Tighten anchor plate bolts
	• Caliper piston sticking or seized	• Repair or replace caliper
	• Brakelinings water soaked	• Drive vehicle with brakes lightly applied to dry linings
	• Loose suspension component attaching or mounting bolts	• Tighten suspension bolts. Replace worn suspension components.
	• Brake combination valve failure	• Replace combination valve
Chatter or shudder when brakes are applied (pedal pulsation and roughness may also occur.)	• Brakeshoes distorted, bent, contaminated, or worn	• Replace brakeshoes in axle sets
	• Caliper anchor plate or support plate loose	• Tighten mounting bolts
	• Excessive thickness variation of rotor(s)	• Refinish or replace rotors in axle sets
Noisy brakes (squealing, clicking, scraping sound when brakes are applied.)	• Bent, broken, distorted brakeshoes	• Replace brakeshoes in axle sets
	• Excessive rust on outer edge of rotor braking surface	• Remove rust

Troubleshooting the Brake System (cont.)

Problem	Cause	Solution
Noisy brakes (squealing, clicking, scraping sound when brakes are applied.) (cont.)	• Brakelining worn out—shoes contacting drum of rotor	• Replace brakeshoes and lining in axle sets. Refinish or replace drums or rotors.
	• Broken or loose holdown or return springs	• Replace parts as necessary
	• Rough or dry drum brake support plate ledges	• Lubricate support plate ledges
	• Cracked, grooved, or scored rotor(s) or drum(s)	• Replace rotor(s) or drum(s). Replace brakeshoes and lining in axle sets if necessary.
	• Incorrect brakelining and/or shoes (front or rear).	• Install specified shoe and lining assemblies
Pulsating brake pedal	• Out of round drums or excessive lateral runout in disc brake rotor(s)	• Refinish or replace drums, re-index rotors or replace

EXTERIOR 10-2
DOORS 10-2
  REMOVAL & INSTALLATION 10-2
  ADJUSTMENT 10-2
MANUAL DOOR LOCKS 10-3
  REMOVAL & INSTALLATION 10-3
POWER DOOR LOCKS 10-3
  REMOVAL & INSTALLATION 10-3
HOOD 10-3
  REMOVAL & INSTALLATION 10-3
  ALIGNMENT 10-5
LIFTGATE 10-7
  REMOVAL & INSTALLATION 10-7
  ALIGNMENT 10-15
TAILGATE 10-17
  REMOVAL & INSTALLATION 10-17
  ADJUSTMENT 10-18
WINDSHIELD 10-18
  REMOVAL 10-18
  INSPECTION 10-19
  INSTALLATION 10-19
REAR WINDOW GLASS 10-22
  REMOVAL & INSTALLATION 10-22
MANUAL TAILGATE WINDOW 10-23
  REMOVAL & INSTALLATION 10-23
ELECTRIC TAILGATE WINDOW 10-23
  REMOVAL & INSTALLATION 10-23
INTERIOR 10-24
DOOR PANELS 10-24
  REMOVAL & INSTALLATION 10-24
MANUAL DOOR GLASS AND
  REGULATOR 10-26
  REMOVAL & INSTALLATION 10-26
ELECTRIC WINDOW MOTOR 10-37
  REMOVAL & INSTALLATION 10-37
ELECTRIC TAILGATE WINDOW
  MOTOR 10-38
  REMOVAL & INSTALLATION 10-38
POWER SEAT MOTOR 10-38
  REMOVAL & INSTALLATION 10-38
HEADLINER 10-38
  REMOVAL & INSTALLATION 10-38
TROUBLESHOOTING CHARTS
  HOW TO REMOVE STAINS FROM
    FABRIC INTERIOR 10-40

10

BODY AND TRIM

EXTERIOR 10-2
INTERIOR 10-24

EXTERIOR

Doors

REMOVAL & INSTALLATION

1. Match the hinge-to-body and hinge-to-door locations. Either support the door on jackstands or have somebody hold it for you.
2. On models with a center door check, push in on the claw and pull out the stopper pin. Alternatively, unbolt the door check from the door.

→**Depending on equipment, it may be necessary to disconnect various wires running into the door.**

3. Remove the lower hinge-to-door bolts.
4. Remove the upper hinge-to-door bolts and lift the door off the hinges.
5. If the hinges are being replaced, remove them from the door pillar.

To install:

6. Install the door and hinges with the bolts finger-tight.
7. Adjust the door and tighten the hinge bolts.
8. Install the door check.

ADJUSTMENT

▶ **See Figures 1, 2 and 3**

When checking door alignment, look carefully at each seam between the door and body. The gap should be constant and even all the way around the door. Pay particular attention to the door

Fig. 2 Loosen the door striker bolts, hold the handle in the open position and close the door. The striker will move into the correct position

Fig. 3 Location of the striker plate and lower block

Fig. 1 The doors can be adjusted by loosening the bolts and moving the door to the desired position

seams at the corners farthest from the hinges; this is the area where errors will be most evident. Additionally, the door should pull against the weatherstrip when latched to seal out wind and water. The contact should be even all the way around and the stripping should be about half compressed.

The position of the door can be adjusted in three dimensions:

fore and aft, up and down, in and out. The primary adjusting points are the hinge-to-body bolts. Apply tape to the fender and door edges to protect the paint. Two layers of common masking tape works well. Loosen the bolts just enough to allow the hinge to move. With the help of an assistant, position the door and re-tighten the bolts. Inspect the door seams carefully and repeat the adjustment until correctly aligned.

The in-out adjustment (how far the door "sticks out" from the body) is adjusted by loosening the hinge-to-door bolts. Again, move the door into place, then retighten the bolts. This dimension affects both the amount of crush on the weatherstrips and the amount of "bite" on the striker.

Further adjustment for closed position and smoothness of latching is made at the latch plate or striker. This piece is located at the rear edge of the door and it attached to the bodywork; it is the piece the latch engages when the door is closed.

Although the striker size and style may vary between models or from front to rear, the method of adjusting it is the same:

1. Loosen the large cross-point screw(s) holding the striker. Know in advance that these bolts will be very tight; an impact screwdriver is a handy tool to have for this job. Make sure you are using the proper size bit.

2. With the bolts just loose enough to allow the striker to move if necessary, hold the outer door handle in the released po-sition and close the door. The striker will move into the correct lo-cation to match the door latch. Open the door and tighten the mounting bolts. The striker may be adjusted towards or away from the center of the car, thereby tightening or loosening the door fit. The striker can be moved up and down to compensate for door position, but if the door is correctly mounted at the hinges this should not be necessary.

➥**Do not attempt to correct height variations (sag) by ad-justing the striker.**

3. Additionally, some models may use one or more spacers or shims behind the striker. These shims may be removed or added in combination to adjust the reach of the striker.

4. After the striker bolts have been tightened, open and close the door several times. Observe the motion of the door as it en-gages the striker; it should continue its straight-in motion and not deflect up or down as it hits the striker.

5. Check the feel of the latch during opening and closing. It must be smooth and linear, without any trace of grinding or bind-ing during engagement and release.

It may be necessary to repeat the striker adjustment several times (and possibly re-adjust the hinges) before the correct door to body match is produced.

Manual Door Locks

REMOVAL & INSTALLATION

Lock Cylinder

1. Remove the rubber sealer along the rear edge of the door to expose the lock cylinder retainer.
2. Remove the retainer with a small prybar.
3. Remove the lock cylinder and extension rod from the out-side of the door.

4. Installation is the reverse of removal.

Latch and Control Linkage

1. Remove the door trim panel and water shield.
2. Remove the lock cylinder.
3. Remove the bolts from the control assembly. Push it into the door and lower it to the bottom.
4. Disconnect the control arm from the door latch and remove the control assembly through the access hole in the bottom of the door.
5. Remove the bolts attaching the door latch to the door panel. Push the latch in and turn it 90° to free it from the lock lever rod. Remove it through the lower access hole.
6. Installation is the reverse of removal.

Power Door Locks

REMOVAL & INSTALLATION

Switch

1. Disconnect the battery ground.
2. Remove the door trim panel and watershield.
3. Remove the switch housing from the inner door panel.
4. Disconnect the wiring and pry up the switch retaining clips. Remove the switch.
5. Installation is the reverse of removal.

Actuator Motor

1. Disconnect the battery ground.
2. Remove the door trim panel and watershield.
3. Using a ¼ in. drill bit, drill out the motor mounting rivets.
4. Disconnect the motor actuator rod from the bellcrank.
5. Disconnect the wires from the motor and lift the motor from the door.
6. Installation is the reverse of removal. Use ¼-20 × ½ in. bolts and locknuts in place of the rivets.

Hood

REMOVAL & INSTALLATION

Except Pacer

▶ **See Figure 4**

➥**If the hood is properly aligned, prior to removal, match-mark the position of the hinges and hood reinforcement.**

1. Raise the hood fully.
2. Disconnect the underhood light wire.
3. Matchmark the hood-to-hinge position.
4. While your assistant supports the hood, remove the hood-to-hinge bolts and lift off the hood.
5. Installation is the reverse of removal. Torque the bolts to 23 ft. lbs.

Fig. 4 Exploded view of the hood and fender components—except Pacer models

Matchmark the position of the hood to the hinge . . .

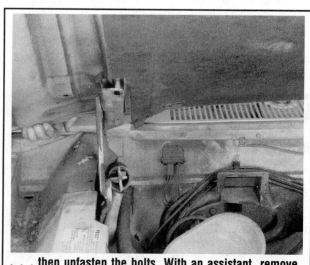

. . . then unfasten the bolts. With an assistant, remove the hood from the vehicle

Pacer

◆ **See Figure 5**

➡️If the hood is properly aligned, prior to removal, match-mark the position of the hinges and hood reinforcement.

1. Raise the hood fully.
2. Disconnect the underhood light wire.
3. Unbolt the grille from the hood.
4. Matchmark the hood-to-hinge position.
5. While your assistant supports the hood, remove the hood-to-hinge bolts and lift off the hood.
6. Installation is the reverse of removal. Torque the bolts to 23 ft. lbs.

Fig. 5 Hood and front fender components—Pacer models

ALIGNMENT

◆ **See Figures 6, 7, 8, 9 and 10**

➡️Hood hinge mounting holes are oversized to permit movement for hood alignment. If the hood is to be moved to either side, the hood lock striker, hood lever lock and safety hook assembly must first be loosened.

1. Loosen the hinge mounting bolts slightly on one side and tap the hinge in the direction opposite to that in which the hood is to be moved.
2. Tighten the bolts.
3. Repeat this procedure for the opposite hinge.
4. Check that the lock striker, lever lock and safety hook are properly adjusted to ensure positive locking.
5. If the rear edge of the hood is not flush with the cowl, add or subtract shims (caster and chamber adjusting shims will work) or flat washers between the hinge and the hood at the rear bolt (hood too low) or front bolt (hood too high).

Fig. 6 Loosen the hood hinge bolts to adjust the hood forwards and backwards

Fig. 7 To adjust the hood vertically, turn the stop screws at the front and or rear of the hood

Fig. 8 The hood pin can be adjusted to ensure it locks properly

Fig. 9 Loosen the hinge-to-body bolts and move the hood up and down to adjust the rear height of the hood

Fig. 10 The hood lock base can also be adjusted to ensure positive lock engagement

Liftgate

REMOVAL & INSTALLATION

Sportabout

1. Open the liftgate fully.
2. Remove the anti-rattle pin.
3. Remove the upper trim molding and disconnect the defroster grid wires. Tape the ends to the glass.
4. Unbolt the supports and fold them downward.

✳✳ WARNING

Never unbolt the supports unless the liftgate is fully opened. In any other position, the supports are under tension.

5. Close the liftgate in the locked position.
6. From inside, remove the liftgate-to-hinge screws.
7. Unlock the liftgate and remove it.
To install:
8. Position the liftgate in the opening and lock it.
9. If removed, place the rubber gaskets on the hinges and insert the hinges boss into the gate.
10. Install the hinge-to-gate screws about ¾ of the way.

11. From outside, unlock and fully open the liftgate. Allow it to slide down on the hinges.
12. Tighten the hinge screws to 11 ft.lbs.
13. Connect the defroster grid wires.
14. Install the molding.
15. Install the supports.
16. Install and adjust the anti-rattle pin.
17. Adjust the liftgate fit as described earlier.

Gremlin
▶ **See Figures 11 amd 12**

1. Remove the upper center and corner finish moldings.
2. Open the liftgate fully.
3. Unbolt the supports and fold them downward.

✳✳ WARNING

Never unbolt the supports unless the liftgate is fully opened. In any other position, the supports are under tension.

4. Close the liftgate in the locked position.
5. Lower the headliner and remove the nut from the hinge studs.
6. Remove the hinge reinforcements.
7. Disconnect the defroster grid wires. Tape the ends to the glass.
8. Unlock the liftgate and remove it.

Fig. 11 Exploded view of the Gremlin liftgate components—1975–77 models

Fig. 12 Liftgate component locations—1978 Gremlin models

To install:

9. Position the liftgate in the opening and lock it.

10. If removed, place the rubber gaskets on the hinges and insert the studs into the gate.

11. Install the hinge reinforcements onto the studs.

12. Tighten the hinge nuts to 11 ft. lbs.

13. Connect the defroster grid wires.

14. Install the headliner.

15. Install the supports.

Pacer Sedan

▶ **See Figure 13**

1. Open the liftgate.

2. Remove the rear upper finish molding.

3. Disconnect the rear window defogger and tape the wire ends to the glass.

4. Remove the right and left headliner upper rear finish moldings.

5. Remove the liftgate trim panel.

6. Disconnect the wires from the wiper motor.

7. Tie a length of string to the motor wiring and pull the wiring from the liftgate.

➡**You'll use the string to guide the wiring into position during installation.**

8. Disconnect the washer hose from the nozzle tube.

9. Remove the retainer clips from the ball stud sockets on the liftgate.

10. With the liftgate fully open, pull the supports off of the ball studs. Swing the supports down and out of the way.

✳✳ WARNING

Never attempt to remove the supports with the lift gate closed or partially closed! Closing the liftgate puts the supports under tremendous pressure!

11. Close the liftgate.

12. Remove the hinge-to-body nuts. Keep track of the shim pack for each hinge.

13. Unlatch the tailgate and remove it.

To install:

14. Installation is the reverse of removal. Torque the hinge nuts to 12 ft. lbs. Don't lose the shims. Make sure they are placed under their respective hinges.

15. Adjust the liftgate as necessary.

Fig. 13 Exploded view of the liftgate assembly—Pacer models

Pacer Wagon
♦ **See Figure 14**

1. Open the liftgate.
2. Remove the rear upper finish molding.
3. Remove the right and left headliner upper rear finish moldings.
4. Disconnect the rear window defogger and tape the wire ends to the glass.
5. Carefully pull down the rear edge of the headliner and disconnect the liftgate harness from the body harness.
6. Remove the nuts attaching the liftgate harness tube to the body.
7. Remove the liftgate harness.
8. Disconnect the washer hose from the nozzle tube.
9. Remove the retainer clips from the ball stud sockets on the liftgate.
10. With the liftgate fully open, pull the supports off of the ball studs. Swing the supports down and out of the way.

✳✳ WARNING

Never attempt to remove the supports with the lift gate closed or partially closed! Closing the liftgate puts the supports under tremendous pressure!

11. Close the liftgate.
12. Remove the hinge-to-body nuts. Keep track of the shim pack for each hinge.
13. Unlatch the tailgate and remove it.
To install:
14. Installation is the reverse of removal. Torque the hinge nuts to 12 ft. lbs. Don't lose the shims. Make sure they are placed under their respective hinges.
15. Adjust the liftgate as necessary.

Fig. 14 Pacer wagon liftgate component locations

Spirit, Eagle SX/4 and AMX
▶ **See Figures 15 and 16**

1. Open the liftgate.
2. Remove the rear upper finish molding.
3. Disconnect the rear window defogger and tape the wire ends to the glass.
4. Remove the retainer clips from the ball stud sockets on the liftgate.
5. With the liftgate fully open, pull the supports off of the ball studs. Swing the supports down and out of the way.

✳✳ WARNING

Never attempt to remove the supports with the lift gate closed or partially closed! Closing the liftgate puts the supports under tremendous pressure!

6. Close the liftgate.
7. Remove the hinge-to-body nuts. Keep track of the shim pack for each hinge.
8. Unlatch the tailgate and remove it.

To install:

9. Installation is the reverse of removal. Torque the hinge nuts to 12 ft. lbs. Don't lose the shims. Make sure they are placed under their respective hinges.
10. Adjust the liftgate as necessary.

Fig. 15 Exploded view of the liftgate assembly—Spirit and AMX models

Fig. 16 Liftgate component locations—Spirit models

Concord and Eagle Hatchback

▶ **See Figure 17**

1. Open the liftgate.
2. Remove the rear upper finish molding.
3. Disconnect the rear window defogger and tape the wire ends to the glass.
4. Remove the retainer clips from the ball stud sockets on the liftgate.
5. With the liftgate fully open, pull the supports off of the ball studs. Swing the supports down and out of the way.

❈❈ WARNING

Never attempt to remove the supports with the lift gate closed or partially closed! Closing the liftgate puts the supports under tremendous pressure!

6. Close the liftgate.
7. Remove the hinge-to-body nuts. Keep track of the shim pack for each hinge.
8. Unlatch the tailgate and remove it.

To install:

9. Installation is the reverse of removal. Torque the hinge nuts to 12 ft. lbs. Don't lose the shims. Make sure they are placed under their respective hinges.
10. Adjust the liftgate as necessary.

Fig. 17 Exploded view of the liftgate components—Hornet and Concord hatchback models

Concord and Eagle Wagon

◆ See Figure 18

1. Open the liftgate.
2. Remove the rear upper finish molding.
3. Disconnect the rear window defogger and tape the wire ends to the glass.
4. Remove the retainer clips from the ball stud sockets on the liftgate.
5. With the liftgate fully open, pull the supports off of the ball studs. Swing the supports down and out of the way.

6. Close the liftgate.
7. Remove the hinge-to-body nuts. Keep track of the shim pack for each hinge.
8. Unlatch the tailgate and remove it.

Fig. 18 Hornet and Concord hatchback station wagon liftgate components

To install:

9. Installation is the reverse of removal. Torque the hinge nuts to 12 ft. lbs. Don't lose the shims. Make sure they are placed under their respective hinges.

10. Adjust the anti-rattle pin for proper fit. Adjust the liftgate as necessary.

ALIGNMENT

Sportabout

1. Remove the anti-rattle pin and striker.
2. Remove the rear finish moldings.
3. Loosen the hinge-to-body nuts.
4. Move the liftgate to obtain the proper fit.
5. Tighten the nuts to 11 ft. lbs.
6. Install the moldings, striker and anti-rattle pin.

Pacer Sedan

FRONT SURFACE ADJUSTMENT

1. Open the liftgate.
2. Remove the rear upper finish molding.
3. Remove the right and left headliner upper rear finish moldings.
4. Remove the retainer clips from the ball stud sockets on the liftgate.
5. With the liftgate fully open, pull the supports off of the ball studs. Swing the supports down and out of the way.

❄❄ WARNING

Never attempt to remove the supports with the lift gate closed or partially closed! Closing the liftgate puts the supports under tremendous pressure!

6. Close the liftgate.
7. Remove the hinge-to-body nuts. Keep track of the shim pack for each hinge.
8. Unlatch the tailgate and lift it at the leading edge, supporting it with wood blocks.
9. Loosen the hinge-to-liftgate screws.
10. Install or remove shims as required, between the hinge and liftgate, to obtain the desired gap.
11. Tighten the screws to 12 ft. lbs.
12. Remove the blocks and position the liftgate in its opening.
13. Position the hinge-to-body shim packs and install the nuts. Torque the nuts to 12 ft. lbs.
14. Install the rear upper finish molding.
15. Open the liftgate and install the supports and clips.
16. Adjust the striker and tighten the bolts to 52 ft. lbs.

REAR SURFACE ADJUSTMENT

1. Remove the striker.
2. Move the liftgate rear surface downward by placing a wood block on top of the body opening drain trough and carefully hammering the trough downward.
3. Move the liftgate rear surface up by placing a wood block under the drain trough and carefully hammering the trough upward.
4. Install the striker and adjust it for proper latching and alignment. Tighten the striker bolts to 52 ft. lbs.

Pacer Wagon

GAP ADJUSTMENT

1. Open the liftgate.
2. Remove the rear upper finish molding.
3. Remove the right and left headliner upper rear finish moldings.
4. Remove the retainer clips from the ball stud sockets on the liftgate.
5. With the liftgate fully open, pull the supports off of the ball studs. Swing the supports down and out of the way.

❄❄ WARNING

Never attempt to remove the supports with the lift gate closed or partially closed! Closing the liftgate puts the supports under tremendous pressure!

6. Close the liftgate.
7. Loosen the hinge-to-body nuts. Keep track of the shim pack for each hinge.
8. Install or remove shims as required, between the hinge and body, to obtain the desired gap.
9. Tighten the screws to 12 ft. lbs.
10. Tighten the nuts to 12 ft. lbs.
11. Install the rear upper finish molding.
12. Open the liftgate and install the supports and clips.
13. Adjust the striker and tighten the bolts to 52 ft. lbs.

FRONT SURFACE ADJUSTMENT

1. Open the liftgate.
2. Remove the rear upper finish molding.
3. Remove the retainer clips from the ball stud sockets on the liftgate.
4. With the liftgate fully open, pull the supports off of the ball studs. Swing the supports down and out of the way.

❄❄ WARNING

Never attempt to remove the supports with the lift gate closed or partially closed! Closing the liftgate puts the supports under tremendous pressure!

5. Close the liftgate.
6. Remove the hinge-to-body nuts, keeping track of the shim packs for each hinge.
7. Open the liftgate at the leading edge and support it with wood blocks.
8. Loosen the hinge-to-liftgate screws. Keep track of the shim pack for each hinge.
9. Install or remove shims as required, between the hinge and liftgate, to obtain the desired gap.
10. Tighten the screws to 12 ft. lbs.
11. Tighten the nuts to 12 ft. lbs.
12. Install the rear upper finish molding.
13. Open the liftgate and install the supports and clips.
14. Adjust the striker and tighten the bolts to 52 ft. lbs.

Spirit, Eagle SX/4 and AMX

SIDE GAP ADJUSTMENT

1. Remove the anti-rattle pin and striker.
2. Remove the rear upper finish molding.

3. Remove the retainer clips from the ball stud sockets on the liftgate.

4. With the liftgate fully open, pull the supports off of the ball studs. Swing the supports down and out of the way.

✳✳ WARNING

Never attempt to remove the supports with the lift gate closed or partially closed! Closing the liftgate puts the supports under tremendous pressure!

5. Close the liftgate.

6. Loosen the hinge-to-body nuts. Keep track of the shim pack for each hinge.

7. Install or remove shims as required, between the hinge and body, to obtain the desired gap.

8. Tighten the screws to 12 ft. lbs.

9. Tighten the nuts to 12 ft. lbs.

10. Install the rear upper finish molding.

11. Open the liftgate and install the supports and clips.

12. Install the anti-rattle pin. Adjust the striker and tighten the bolts to 52 ft. lbs.

FRONT GAP ADJUSTMENT

1. Open the liftgate.

2. Remove the rear upper finish molding.

3. Remove the retainer clips from the ball stud sockets on the liftgate.

4. With the liftgate fully open, pull the supports off of the ball studs. Swing the supports down and out of the way.

✳✳ WARNING

Never attempt to remove the supports with the lift gate closed or partially closed! Closing the liftgate puts the supports under tremendous pressure!

5. Disconnect the rear defogger wires and tape the wire ends to the glass.

6. Close the liftgate.

7. Remove the hinge-to-body nuts, keeping track of the shim packs for each hinge.

8. Open the liftgate at the leading edge and support it with wood blocks.

9. Loosen the hinge-to-liftgate screws. Keep track of the shim pack for each hinge.

10. Install or remove shims as required, between the hinge and liftgate, to obtain the desired gap.

11. Tighten the screws to 12 ft. lbs.

12. Tighten the nuts to 12 ft. lbs.

13. Install the rear upper finish molding.

14. Open the liftgate and install the supports and clips.

15. Connect the rear defogger wires.

16. Adjust the anti-rattle pin for proper fit. Tighten the screws to 25 in. lbs. Adjust the striker and tighten the bolts to 52 ft. lbs.

Concord and Eagle Hatchback

SIDE GAP ADJUSTMENT

1. Remove the anti-rattle pin and striker.

2. Remove the rear upper finish molding.

3. Remove the retainer clips from the ball stud sockets on the liftgate.

4. With the liftgate fully open, pull the supports off of the ball studs. Swing the supports down and out of the way.

✳✳ WARNING

Never attempt to remove the supports with the lift gate closed or partially closed! Closing the liftgate puts the supports under tremendous pressure!

5. Close the liftgate.

6. Loosen the hinge-to-body nuts. Keep track of the shim pack for each hinge.

7. Install or remove shims as required, between the hinge and body, to obtain the desired gap.

8. Tighten the screws to 12 ft. lbs.

9. Tighten the nuts to 12 ft. lbs.

10. Install the rear upper finish molding.

11. Open the liftgate and install the supports and clips.

12. Install the anti-rattle pin. Adjust the striker and tighten the bolts to 52 ft. lbs.

FRONT GAP ADJUSTMENT

1. Open the liftgate.

2. Remove the rear upper finish molding.

3. Remove the retainer clips from the ball stud sockets on the liftgate.

4. With the liftgate fully open, pull the supports off of the ball studs. Swing the supports down and out of the way.

✳✳ WARNING

Never attempt to remove the supports with the lift gate closed or partially closed! Closing the liftgate puts the supports under tremendous pressure!

5. Disconnect the rear defogger wires and tape the wire ends to the glass.

6. Close the liftgate.

7. Remove the hinge-to-body nuts, keeping track of the shim packs for each hinge.

8. Open the liftgate at the leading edge and support it with wood blocks.

9. Loosen the hinge-to-liftgate screws. Keep track of the shim pack for each hinge.

10. Install or remove shims as required, between the hinge and liftgate, to obtain the desired gap.

11. Tighten the screws to 12 ft. lbs.

12. Tighten the nuts to 12 ft. lbs.

13. Install the rear upper finish molding.

14. Open the liftgate and install the supports and clips.

15. Connect the rear defogger wires.

16. Adjust the anti-rattle pin for proper fit. Tighten the screws to 25 in.lb. Adjust the striker and tighten the bolts to 52 ft. lbs.

Concord and Eagle Wagon

GAP ADJUSTMENT

1. Remove the anti-rattle pin and striker.

2. Remove the rear upper finish molding.

3. Remove the retainer clips from the ball stud sockets on the liftgate.

4. With the liftgate fully open, pull the supports off of the ball studs. Swing the supports down and out of the way.

WARNING

Never attempt to remove the supports with the lift gate closed or partially closed! Closing the liftgate puts the supports under tremendous pressure!

5. Close the liftgate.
6. Loosen the hinge-to-body nuts. Keep track of the shim pack for each hinge.
7. Install or remove shims as required, between the hinge and body, to obtain the desired gap.
8. Tighten the screws to 12 ft. lbs.
9. Tighten the nuts to 12 ft. lbs.
10. Install the rear upper finish molding.
11. Open the liftgate and install the supports and clips.
12. Install the anti-rattle pin. Adjust the striker and tighten the bolts to 52 ft. lbs.

REAR SURFACE ADJUSTMENT

1. Remove the striker.
2. Move the liftgate rear surface downward by placing a wood block on top of the body opening drain trough and carefully hammering the trough downward.
3. Move the liftgate rear surface up by placing a wood block

under the drain trough and carefully hammering the trough upward.
4. Install the striker and adjust it for proper latching and alignment. Tighten the striker bolts to 10 ft. lbs.

Tailgate

REMOVAL & INSTALLATION

Dual Tailgate

♦ See Figure 19

1. Open the tailgate vertically.
2. Remove the torsion rod retainer clip.
3. Use locking pliers to twist the torsion rod a little bit counterclockwise, and pull the torsion rod out of the right lower hinge.

CAUTION

Never try to pull the torsion rod out when the tailgate is opened horizontally!

1. Tailgate support cable
2. Left upper half hinge and eccentric roller pin assembly
3. Left upper body half hinge and latch assembly
4. Left upper hinge horizontal latch release bellcrank
5. Left latch release rod
6. Release rod clip
7. Horizontal remote control
8. Horizontal release handle
9. Right latch release rod
10. Rlease rod clip
11. Vertical release remote control
12. Vertical release bellcrank
13. Vertical release handle
14. Tailgate latch assembly
15. Latch striker and bracket assembly
16. Right lower half hinge and latch assembly
17. Right lower body half hinge and latch assembly
18. Upper latch to lower hinge latch release cable
19. Glass operated safety release rod
20. Torsion rod retainer clip
21. Torsion rod
22. Left lower hinge assembly door half
23. Left lower hinge assembly body half

Fig. 19 Exploded view of the tailgate components—Matador wagon models

4. Pivot the torsion rod away from the body.

5. Close the tailgate, then open it horizontally.

6. Open the rear compartment, remove the plastic liner screws, lift the liner and disconnect the wiring harness at the tailgate.

7. Support the weight of the tailgate on some kind of stand, or have a couple of friends hold it.

8. Disconnect the support cable from the left upper hinge.

9. Disengage the right lower hinge by manually tripping the latch.

10. Trace the outline of the left lower hinge on the tailgate inner panel.

11. Unbolt the left lower hinge from the inner panel and remove the tailgate.

12. Installation is the reverse of removal. Adjust the tailgate for fit as necessary.

ADJUSTMENT

Left Upper Hinge

1. Remove the striker pin from the right upper bracket.

2. Loosen the eccentric roller pin setscrew in the body half of the left upper hinge.

3. Insert a screwdriver in the slot in the bottom of the pin.

4. Rotate the pin in the desired direction.

5. Tighten the setscrew.

6. Install the striker pin at the right pillar bracket and adjust it up or down to allow the pin to enter the latch in the center of the opening.

Right Lower Hinge

1. Remove the striker pin from the right upper bracket.

2. Loosen the body half of the right lower hinge.

3. Adjust the hinge to provide smooth vertical and horizontal operation.

4. Tighten the body half hinge bolts.

5. Install the striker pin at the right pillar bracket and adjust it up or down to allow the pin to enter the latch in the center of the opening.

Windshield

➡ **Bonded windshields require special tools and special removal procedures to be performed to ensure the windshield will be removed without being broken. For this reason we recommend that you refer all removal and installation to a qualified technician.**

✳✳ CAUTION

Always wear heavy gloves and safety glasses when handling glass to reduce the risk of injury.

When replacing a cracked windshield, it is important that the cause of the crack be determined and the condition corrected, before new glass is installed. The cause of the crack may be an obstruction or a high spot somewhere around the flange of the opening; cracking may not occur until pressure from the high spot or obstruction becomes particularly high due to winds, extremes of temperature or rough terrain.

When a windshield is broken, the glass may have already fallen or been removed from the weatherstrip. Often, however, it is necessary to remove a cracked or otherwise imperfect windshield that is still intact. In this case, it is a good practice to crisscross the glass with strips of masking tape before removing it; this will help hold the glass together and minimize the risk of injury.

If a crack extends to the edge of the glass, mark the point where the crack meets the weather strip (use a piece of chalk to mark the point on the cab, next to the weatherstrip). Later, examine the window flange for a cause of the crack which started at the point marked.

The higher the temperature of the work area, the more pliable the weather strip will be. The more pliable the weather strip, the more easily the windshield can be removed.

There are two methods of windshield removal, depending on the method of windshield replacement chosen. When using the short method of installation, it is important to cut the glass from the urethane adhesive as close to the glass as possible. This is due to the fact that the urethane adhesive will be used to provide a base for the replacement windshield.

When using the extended method of windshield replacement, all the urethane adhesive must be removed from the pinchweld flange so, the process of cutting the window from the adhesive is less critical.

REMOVAL

▶ **See Figures 20 and 21**

1. Place a protective covering around the area where the glass will be removed.

2. Remove the windshield wiper arms, the cowl vent grille, the windshield supports, the rear view mirror and the interior garnish moldings.

3. Remove the exterior reveal molding and glass supports from the windshield.

4. Using the hot knife cut the windshield from the urethane adhesive. If the short method of glass replacement is to be used,

Fig. 20 Common windshield mounting

Fig. 21 Use a hot knife to cut the windshield adhesive

keep the knife as close to the glass as possible in order to leave a base for the replacement glass.

5. With the help of an assistant, remove the glass.

6. If the original glass is to be reinstalled, place it on a protected bench or a holding fixture. Remove any remaining adhesive with a razor blade or a sharp scraper. Any remaining traces of adhesive material can be removed with denatured alcohol or lacquer thinner.

➡**When cleaning the windshield glass, avoid contacting the edge of the plastic laminate material (on the edge of the glass) with a volatile cleaner. Contact may cause discoloration and deterioration of the plastic laminate. DO NOT use a petroleum based solvent such as gasoline or kerosene; the presence of oil will prevent the adhesion of new material.**

INSPECTION

Inspection of the windshield opening, the weather strip and the glass may reveal the cause of a broken windshield; this can help prevent future breakage. If there is no apparent cause of breakage, the weatherstrip should be removed from the flange and the flange inspected. Look for high weld or solder spots, hardened spot welds sealer, or any other obstruction or irregularity in the flange. Check the weatherstrip for irregularities or obstructions in it.

Check the windshield to be installed to make sure that it does not have chipped edges. Chipped edges can be ground off, restoring a smooth edge to the glass and minimizing concentrations of pressure that cause breakage. Remove no more than necessary, in an effort to maintain the original shape of the glass and the proper clearance between it and the flange of the opening.

INSTALLATION

▶ **See Figures 22, 23, 24 and 25**

Short Method

1. Apply masking across the windshield pillar-to-windshield opening, then cut the tape and remove the windshield.

2. Using an alcohol dampened cloth, clean the metal flange surrounding the windshield opening. Allow the alcohol to air dry.

3. Using the pinchweld primer found in the service kit, apply it to the pinchweld area. DO NOT let any of the primer touch the exposed paint or damage to the finish may occur; allow five minutes for the primer to dry.

4. Cut the tip of the adhesive cartridge approximately ³⁄15 inch (5mm) from the end of the tip.

5. Apply the adhesive first in and around the spacer blocks. Apply a smooth continuous bead of adhesive into the gap between the glass edge and the sheet metal. If necessary use a flat bladed tool to paddle the material into position. Sbe sure that the adhesive contacts the entire edge of the glass and extends to fill the gap between the glass and the solidified urethane base.

6. With the aid of a helper, position the windshield on the filler strips against the two support spacers.

➡**The vehicle should not be driven and should remain at room temperature for six hours to allow the adhesive to cure.**

FOR EXTENDED METHOD POSITION
FILLER STRIP ON GLASS
(POSITION FILLER STRIP ON BODY
FOR SHORT METHOD)

APPLY PRIMER TO INNER
SURFACE AND EDGE
OF GLASS

ANTENNA LEAD
WIRE TAPED

6 mm (1/4")

OMIT PRIMER AND ADHESIVE FOR
100 mm (4") BOTH SIDES OF ANTENNA LEAD WIRE

Fig. 22 Apply primer to the windshield as shown

FOR EXTENDED METHOD ENLARGE
NOZZLE BY CUTTING OUT MATERIAL
WITHIN SCORE LINES

MASKING TAPE
6 mm (1/4") FROM
GLASS EDGE

10 mm (3/8")

ADHESIVE
CAULKING
MATERIAL

5 mm (3/16")

Fig. 23 Applying sealant to the windshield

ADHESIVE
CAULKING
MATERIAL

TRIM

OPERATION A

PRIME

OPERATION B

APPLY

OPERATION C

FLAT STICK

WORK
INTO
JOINTS

OPERATION D

Fig. 24 Trim the sealant to accept the reveal trim molding

GUIDE GLASS ALONG REAR
EDGE OF FRONT FENDER

PIGTAIL LEAD
TAPED TO GLASS

Fig. 25 With an assistant, install the glass into the frame

7. Spray a mist of water onto the urethane. Water will assist in the curing process. Dry the area where the reveal molding will contact the body and glass.

8. Install new reveal moldings. Remove the protective tape covering the butyl adhesive on the underside of the molding. Push the molding caps onto each end of one of the reveal moldings. press the lip of the molding into the urethane adhesive while holding it against the edge of the windshield. Take care to seat the molding in the corners. The lip must fully contact the adhesive and the gap must be entirely covered by the crown of the molding. Slide the molding caps onto the adjacent moldings. Use tape to hold the molding in position until the adhesive cures.

9. Install the wiper arms and the interior garnish moldings.

➡**The vehicle should not be driven and should remain at room temperature for six hours to allow the adhesive to cure.**

Extended Method

1. Using a strip filler, install the sealing strip onto the pinchweld flange. The joint of the molding should be located at the bottom center of the molding.

2. Apply masking tape across the windshield pillar-to-windshield opening, then cut the tape and remove the windshield.

3. Using an alcohol dampened cloth, clean the metal flange surrounding the windshield opening. Allow the alcohol to air dry.

4. Using the pinchweld primer, found in the service kit, apply it to the pinchweld area. DO NOT let any of the primer touch the exposed paint for damage to the finish may occur; allow five minutes for the primer to dry.

5. With the aid of an assistant, position the windwhield on the filler strips against the two support spacers.

6. Cut the tip of the adhesive cartridge approximately ⅜ in. from the end of the tip.

7. Apply the adhesive first in and around the spacer blocks. Apply a smooth continuous bead of adhesive into the gap between the glass edge and the sheet metal. If necessary, use a flat bladed tool to paddle the material into position. Be sure that the adhesive contacts the entire edge of the glass and extends to fill the gap between the glass and the primed sheet metal.

➡**The vehicle should not be driven and should remain at room temperature for six hours to allow the adhesive to cure.**

8. Spray a mist of warm or hot water onto the urethane. Water will assist in the curing process. Dry the area where the reveal molding will contact the body and glass.

9. Install the reveal molding onto the windshield and remove the masking tape from the inner surface of the glass.

10. Press the lip of the molding into the urethane adhesive while holding it against the edge of the windshield. Take care to seat the molding in the corners. The lip must fully contact the adhesive and the gap must be entirely covered by the crown of the molding. Use tape to hold the molding in position until the adhesive cures.

11. Install the wiper arms and the interior garnish moldings.

Rear Window Glass

REMOVAL & INSTALLATION

All Except the Spirit Hatchback and Eagle SX/4

➡**These models use a butyl tape retention method for rear window glass installation. An electric hot knife, tool J-24709-01 or equivalent, is necessary for this procedure. Also, an assistant would be very helpful.**

1. Cover all adjacent areas, both exterior and interior.
2. If equipped, remove the wiper arm.
3. Remove all finish moldings around the glass.
4. If equipped, disconnect the wires from the rear defogger and tape the ends to the glass.

➡**Use extreme care to avoid and scratching or damage to the defogger grid!**

5. Using the hot knife, insert the blade under the edge of the glass. Cut the material as close as possible to the inside surface of the glass.

➡**Clean the hot knife blade with steel wool while it is still warm.**

6. Slowly push the glass outward along the top with your feet until the butyl tape stretches 1–2 in. Have an assistant cut the tape with a scissors, completely around the glass. Use wood blocks to keep the glass from touching the adhesive as the tape is being cut, or it will immediately restick.

7. When the glass is out, remove all traces of the butyl tape from the glass opening and ball it up to lift off any remaining deposits. Use 3M General Purpose Adhesive Cleaner, or equivalent, to clean up the area.

To install:

8. Make sure that there is no molding- or metal-to-glass interference.

9. Make sure that all molding clips are properly positioned and not broken.

10. Repair any broken weld studs.

11. The two rubber spacer blocks below the glass at the outer ends must be in position to prevent the glass from settling and breaking.

12. Make sure that the anti-squeak protector is in position on the lower flange.

13. Using spacer blocks, temporarily position the glass in the opening.

14. Center the glass to achieve equal spacing all around.

15. Using masking tape at the bottom center or at the rubber spacers, and extending it over the body panels, mark the glass-to-body position for permanent installation.

16. Cut the tape just below the glass and remove the glass.

17. Clean the pinchweld and glass thoroughly. It must be clean and dry.

18. Apply a thin, uniform, ½ in. wide coat of butyl tape primer on both the pinchweld flange and the glass edge, and allow it to dry for 10 minutes.

19. Apply butyl tape to the pinchweld flange, midway up the right side, flush with the edge of the flange.

➡**If you're using a butyl tape kit with an integral sponge rubber filler, make sure that the filler is flush with the edge of the flange.**

20. Strip off the paper as the tape is applied. Cut the tape at 45° angles downward and to the outside, and butt the ends of the tape firmly to prevent leaks.

21. Place the glass in the opening, aligning it exactly with the tape markers you previously made. **Be exact!** The primer will adhere to the butyl tape on contact!

22. Firmly press the glass against the butyl tape with hand pressure.

23. Carefully trim excess primer with a razor blade.

24. Clean the glass and surrounding area with 3M General Purpose Adhesive Cleaner, or equivalent.

25. Recheck the glass-to-butyl tape contact, applying additional hand pressure as needed. Dull spots indicate poor contact.

26. Apply 3M Windshield Sealer, or equivalent, to any open spots.

27. Install all previously removed parts.

Spirit Liftback and Eagle SX/4

➡**The rear window on these models is retained by a rubber channel.**

1. Cover all adjacent areas.
2. Remove the wiper arm and motor.
3. From inside, peel the rubber channel down while pushing outward on the glass.

➡**If the rubber channel is bonded to the pinchweld, spray a generous amount of 3M Release Agent, or equivalent, between the rubber channel and body. Allow 2–3 minutes for the stuff to work.**

4. Once the glass has been pushed away from the upper flange area, pull the window assembly up and out of the lower flange area.

5. Remove all sealer from the flange with 3M General Purpose Adhesive Cleaner, or equivalent.

6. Install the rubber channel on the glass.

7. Lubricate the rubber channel liberally with soapy water and position the assembly in the body opening.

8. Using a small wood spatula, pry the rubber channel over the pinchweld flange while an assistant pushes inward on the glass.

9. Apply 3M Windshield sealer, or equivalent, between the channel and glass using a hand applicator gun.

10. Wipe off surplus sealer.

11. Install the wiper motor and arm.

Manual Tailgate Window

REMOVAL & INSTALLATION

1. Open the tailgate.
2. Remove the trim panel.
3. Raise the glass completely.
4. Slide the glass assembly to disengage the regulator arms from the glass bottom channel and remove the glass.
5. If the glass is stuck in the down position due to a defective regulator:
   a. Remove the access holes covers.
   b. Remove the regulator handle assembly.
   c. Drill out the regulator pinion shaft housing rivets.
   d. Pull the shaft housing free and lift the glass from the tailgate.
6. Installation is the reverse of removal.
7. Align the glass as necessary by loosening the glass slide channel screws and moving the glass as needed to obtain proper fit. Tighten the screws.

Electric Tailgate Window

REMOVAL & INSTALLATION

1. Open the tailgate.
2. Remove the control handles and trim panel.
3. Raise the glass completely.

➡**To raise the glass with the tailgate open, manually depress the safety switch, mounted on the left auxiliary floor panel, and turn the key to the right.**

4. Slide the glass assembly to disengage the regulator arms from the glass bottom channel and remove the glass.

5. If the glass is stuck in the down position due to a defective regulator:
   a. Remove the access holes covers.
   b. Remove the regulator handle assembly.
   c. Drill out the regulator pinion shaft housing rivets.
   d. Pull the shaft housing free and lift the glass from the tailgate.

To install:
6. Installation is the reverse of removal.
7. Align the glass as necessary by loosening the glass slide channel screws and moving the glass as needed to obtain proper fit. Tighten the screws.
8. Installation is the reverse of removal.
9. Align the glass as necessary by loosening the glass slide channel screws and moving the glass as needed to obtain proper fit. Tighten the screws.

INTERIOR

Door Panels

REMOVAL & INSTALLATION

♦ **See Figure 26**

1. Loosen the screws and remove the door handle and window handle.
2. Remove the arm rest, and, if equipped, the assist handle.

3. Remove the screws securing the bottom of the trim panel to the door.
4. Using a wide-bladed tool, carefully pry out the panel-to-door frame clips. Pry right at the clip and not between them, to avoid damaging the panel.
5. Remove the trim panel. Replace any damaged clips.
6. Installation is the reverse of removal.

Fig. 26 Exploded view of the door components—Gremlin, Hornet, Concord, AMX and Eagle

1. Allen wrench   2. Window handle

Use an Allen wrench to remove the window handle retainer . . .

. . . then remove the handle from the door panel

1. Trim piece   2. Retaining screws

Remove the trim piece to gain access to the arm rest retaining screws

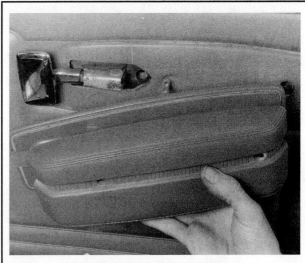

Remove the arm rest from the door panel

Use a screwdriver to remove the screws at the front of the arm rest . . .

Remove the door panel retaining screws . . .

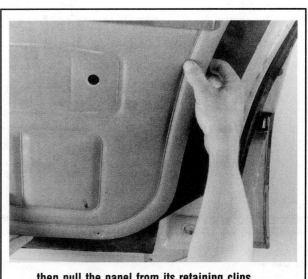

. . . then remove the retaining screws from the side

. . . then pull the panel from its retaining clips

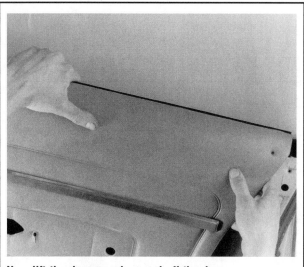

Now lift the door panel up and off the door

Manual Door Glass and Regulator

REMOVAL & INSTALLATION

Front Door

GREMLIN, HORNET, SPIRIT, CONCORD, AMX, PACER AND EAGLE

▶ **See Figures 27 thru 33**

1. Remove the inner glass weatherstripping.
2. Remove the door panel and water dam.
3. Position the glass so that the screws are visible through the upper access holes in the door panel.
4. Using masking tape, tape the glass to the top of the window frame to keep it from falling.
5. Remove the front screw and wave washer.
6. Remove the rear screws.

Fig. 27 Door glass and regulator components—Gremlin, Hornet, Concord, Eagle and AMX

Fig. 28 Front door glass and hardware components—Gremlin, Hornet, Concord, AMX and Eagle

Fig. 29 Glass and hardware assembly—Pacer models with a vent window

Fig. 30 Exploded view of the door assembly—Pacer

Fig. 31 Glass and hardware assembly—Pacer models without a vent window

Fig. 32 Removing the door glass—Concord and Eagle

Fig. 33 Exploded view of the door assembly—Concord

7. Hold the glass, remove the tape and roll the regulator all the way down.

8. Lower the glass, tilt it towards the hinge side of the door and pull it out.

9. Installation is the reverse of removal. When installing the glass, keep it towards the outside of the frame. Tighten the screws to 40 in. lbs.

MATADOR COUPE

♦ **See Figures 34 and 35**

1. Remove the inner glass weatherstripping.
2. Remove the door panel and water dam.

3. Loosen the door glass retaining brackets.
4. Remove the up-stops from the window.
5. Support the glass and remove the nuts attaching the glass to the guide plate.
6. Lift the glass out of the door.
7. Installation is the reverse of removal. Tighten all fasteners to 70 in. lbs.

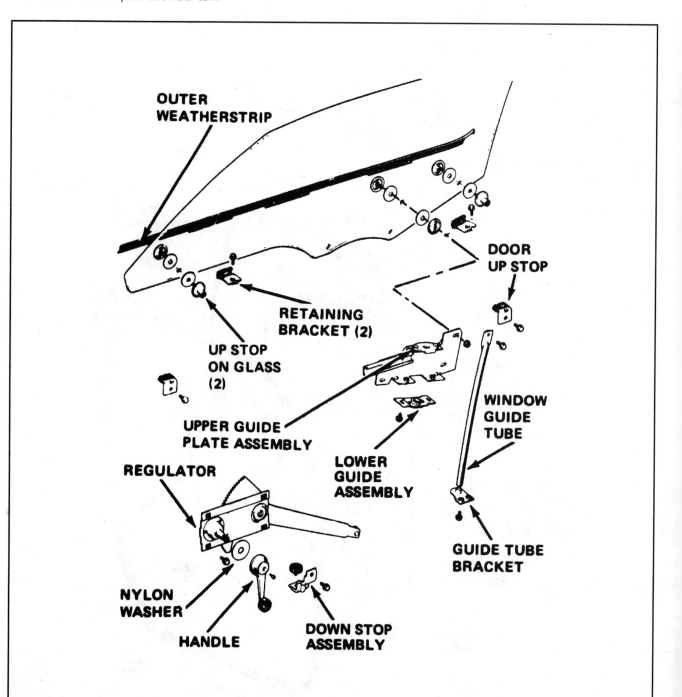

Fig. 34 Exploded view of the glass and hardware—Matador coupe

Fig. 35 Exploded view of the door components—Matador coupe

MATADOR SEDAN AND WAGON

♦ **See Figures 36, 37, 38 and 39**

1. Remove the door trim panel and water dam.
2. Raise the glass to about 1 in. from the top of the frame.
3. Tape the glass to the top of the frame to keep it from falling.
4. Remove the regulator.
5. Remove the channel aluminum frame lower adjustable mounting stud nut.
6. Insert a screwdriver through the lower mounting hole and into the stud mounting hole in the bracket.
7. Push the aluminum frame outward to clear the inner door panel.
8. Push the frame rearward to disengage the channel from the glass.

➡**During all this pushing and sliding, remember that the channel is aluminum and can be easily deformed!**

9. Remove the tape from the glass.
10. Slide the glass out of the channel and lift it from the door.

11. Installation is the reverse of removal. Torque all fasteners to 70 in. lbs.

Rear Door

HORNET

1. Remove the door trim panel and water dam.
2. Position the glass so that the retaining screws are visible and remove them.
3. Push the glass away from the roller guide plate assembly and pull the tang on the plate out of the hole in the lower window channel.
4. Slide the roller guide plate assembly down.
5. Lower the glass to the stop.
6. Tilt the glass towards the latch side of the door and disconnect the regulator arm roller from the glass bottom channel.
7. Pull the glass straight up and out of the door.
8. Installation is the reverse of removal. Torque the fasteners to 40 in. lbs.

Fig. 36 Front door components—Matador sedan and station wagon

Fig. 37 Removing the door window regulator—Matador sedan and wagon

Fig. 38 Exploded view of the door glass hardware—Matador sedan and station wagon

Fig. 39 Cross-sectional view of the joint cover molding—Matador station wagon

MATADOR (SEDAN AND WAGON), CONCORD AND EAGLE
▶ See Figures 40 and 41

1. Remove the door trim panel and water dam.
2. Remove the rubber seal from the frame.
3. Roll the glass up all the way and slide it towards the hinge side to disconnect the rear regulator arm.
4. Raise and tilt the rear of the glass rearwards to disconnect the front arm.
5. Remove the glass.
6. Installation is the reverse of removal. Torque the fasteners to 90 in.lb.

Fig. 40 Exploded view of the rear door components—Matador sedan and station wagon

Fig. 41 Rear door glass and hardware assembly—Hornet, Concord and Eagle models

Electric Window Motor

REMOVAL & INSTALLATION

1975–79 Models

FRONT DOOR

1. Raise the window to the full up position.
2. Disconnect the battery ground cable.
3. Remove the control switch panel.
4. Remove the door trim panel and water dam.

5. Insert a small drift into the hole in the door panel to hold the glass in the up position.
6. Remove the regulator slide channel attaching screws and the regulator attaching screws.
7. Remove the lower division channel screw.
8. Move the regulator channel assembly arms forward and then back to disconnect them from the glass bottom channel.
9. Disconnect the wiring at the motor.
10. Move the regulator arms up and out through the opening in the door panel.
11. Slide the regulator motor and regulator between the inner panel and the division channel to remove it from the door.
12. Installation is the reverse of removal.

REAR DOOR

1. Raise the window to the full up position.
2. Disconnect the battery ground cable.
3. Remove the control switch panel.
4. Remove the door trim panel and water dam.
5. Insert a small drift into the hole in the door panel to hold the glass in the up position.
6. Remove the regulator slide channel attaching screws and the regulator attaching screws.
7. Disconnect the wiring at the motor.
8. Disconnect the remote control rod at the latch.
9. Move the regulator channel assembly arms forward and then back to disconnect them from the glass bottom channel.
10. Move the regulator arms up and out through the opening in the door panel.
11. Slide the regulator motor and regulator between the inner panel and the division channel to remove it from the door.
12. Installation is the reverse of removal.

1980–88 Models

1. Disconnect the battery ground.
2. Remove the door trim panel.
3. Squeeze the cable coupling retainer and pull down on the cable to free it from the regulator drive.
4. Using a 1/4 in. drill bit, drill out the motor mounting rivets, disconnect the wires at the motor and lift it from the door.
5. Installation is the reverse of removal. Use 1/4-20 × 1/2 in. screws to replace the rivets.

Electric Tailgate Window Motor

REMOVAL & INSTALLATION

1. Remove the glass.
2. Remove the access hole covers.
3. Using the key switch, move the regulator arms to a horizontal position.
4. Disconnect the motor wire.
5. Matchmark the regulator position on the mounting panel.
6. Remove the regulator mounting bolts and remove the regulator and motor.
7. Installation is the reverse of removal. Torque the fasteners to 70 in. lbs.

Power Seat Motor

REMOVAL & INSTALLATION

1. Disconnect the battery ground.
2. Remove the bolts holding the seat assembly to the floor pan.
3. Tilt the seat and disconnect the wiring harness.
4. Remove the seat assembly.
5. Invert the seat on a clean surface.
6. Remove the attaching bolts and lift out the seat motor. Disconnect the wiring and cables.
7. Installation is the reverse of removal.

➡If the seat transmission fails, it is not replaceable. The entire seat adjuster assembly will have to be replaced.

Headliner

REMOVAL & INSTALLATION

Gremlin, Hornet, Concord and Eagle Sedans

◆ See Figure 42

1. Remove the sun visors.
2. Remove the windshield moldings and end caps.
3. Remove the rear window moldings and end caps.
4. Remove the plastic trim strip and cap retainers.
5. Remove the dome light.
6. Remove the coat hooks.
7. On Hornet sedans, remove the 4 top screws from the roof extension trim panels.
8. Insert a length of cord in the top hole of each panel and tie them together to hold the panels at a 45° angle.

STEP 1-PUSH CLIP DOWN

STEP 2-SLIDE CLIP TO RIGHT AND UP

STEP 3-ENGAGE CLIP IN UPPER SLOT

Fig. 42 Installing the J-molding retaining clips

9. Insert a screwdriver blade under the right side J-molding. Locate and pry out the 3 snap-in clips that retain the J-molding to the roof rail.

10. Lower the headliner on the right side and disengage the left side by raising it up and out of the J-molding.

11. Remove the headliner.

12. Installation is the reverse of removal. Check the accompanying illustration to see how the clips should be repositioned.

AMX, Concord Hatchback, Concord Wagon, Eagle Wagon, Hornet Sportabout, Hatchback, Spirit Liftback and SX/4

1. Remove the sun visors.
2. Remove the windshield moldings and end caps.
3. Remove the rear window moldings and end caps.
4. Remove the plastic trim strip and cap retainers.
5. Remove the dome light.
6. Remove the coat hooks.
7. Insert a length of cord in the top hole of each panel and tie them together to hold the panels at a 45° angle.
8. Insert a screwdriver blade under the right side J-molding. Locate and pry out the 3 snap-in clips that retain the J-molding to the roof rail.
9. Lower the headliner on the right side and disengage the left side by raising it up and out of the J-molding.
10. Remove the headliner through the liftgate.
11. Installation is the reverse of removal. Check the accompanying illustration to see how the clips should be repositioned.

Matador Coupe

1. Remove the sunvisors, front and rear finish moldings, coat hooks, B-pillar trim attaching screws and dome lamp.
2. Insert a screwdriver blade between the retainer and roof rail. Rotate the screwdriver to pop the clips out of the holes in the roof rail. Remove the retainers on either he left or right side.
3. Lower the headliner and remove it through the door.

➡**There are two slotted holes in the headliner retainer, one above the other. A barb on the clip is engaged in the lower hole when the headliner is removed from the car. The clips must be positioned to engage the upper holes in all headliner retainers before installing the headliner.**

4. Center the headliner in the car.
5. Insert the left edge into the retainer and, while holding it there, grasp the headliner through the dome light opening to guide the right edge into the retainers.
6. Using the sunvisor holes as guides, center the headliner fore and aft.
7. Push up on the J-molding at each clip location to engage the barbs on the clips with the lower holes in the headliner retainers.
8. Install all the other parts.

Matador Sedan

FRONT SECTION

1. Remove the sunvisors, front and rear finish moldings, coat hooks, B-pillar trim attaching screws and dome lamp.
2. On the 4-door Sedan, remove the:

   a. Front seat
   b. Right front door
   c. Steering wheel

3. On Sedans, remove the rear window finish molding.
4. On Wagons, remove the joint cover molding. The molding is retained by spring steel clips which snap over an embossment in the roof rafter.
5. On Wagons, remove the J-molding screw and joint cover and pry the ends of the headliner joint cover from the J-moldings.
6. Pry the molding downward at the rear side to disengage the retaining clips from the embossment on the roof support rafter. The clips will remain in the molding.
7. Insert a screwdriver under the J-molding and slide it along the right roof rail, prying out each clip as you come to it.
8. Lower the headliner on the right side and disengage the left side of the headliner by carefully raising it up and out of the J-molding.
9. On models which use adhesive as a retaining agent, break the adhesive bond carefull, or use an adhesive disolver.
10. Tip the headliner diagonally and remove it through the door on Sedans, or through the tailgate on Wagons.

➡**There are two slotted holes in the headliner retainer, one above the other. A barb on the clip is engaged in the lower hole when the headliner is removed from the car. The clips must be positioned to engage the upper holes in all headliner retainers before installing the headliner.**

11. Installation is the reverse of removal. Use the openings in the headlier to center it during installation. Push up on the J-molding at each clip location to engage the barbs on the clips with the lower holes in the headliner retainers.

REAR SECTION

1. Remove the joint cover molding, tailgate opening header molding and J-moldings above the rear quarter windows.
2. Remove the headliner through the tailgate opening.
3. Installation is the reverse of removal.

Eagle Kammback, Pacer and Spirit Sedan

1. Remove the sunvisors, sunvisor brackets and top and corner windshield finish moldings.
2. Remove the liftgate finish moldings and dome lamp.
3. Remove the right and left side finish moldings.
4. Insert a screwdriver blade between the retainer and roof rail. Rotate the screwdriver to pop the clips out of the holes in the roof rail. Remove the retainers on either he left or right side.
5. Lower the headliner on the left side and disengage the right side by raising up and out of the retainers.
6. Remove the headliner through the liftgate opening.

➡**There are two slotted holes in the headliner retainer, one above the other. A barb on the clip is engaged in the lower hole when the headliner is removed from the car. The clips must be positioned to engage the upper holes in all headliner retainers before installing the headliner.**

7. Installation is the reverse of removal. Use the openings in the headliner to center it during installation. Push up on the J-molding at each clip location to engage the barbs on the clips with the lower holes in the headliner retainers.

How to Remove Stains from Fabric Interior

For rest results, spots and stains should be removed as soon as possible. Never use gasoline, lacquer thinner, acetone, nail polish remover or bleach. Use a 3' x 3" piece of cheesecloth. Squeeze most of the liquid from the fabric and wipe the stained fabric from the outside of the stain toward the center with a lifting motion. Turn the cheesecloth as soon as one side becomes soiled. When using water to remove a stain, be sure to wash the entire section after the spot has been removed to avoid water stains. Encrusted spots can be broken up with a dull knife and vacuumed before removing the stain.

Type of Stain	How to Remove It
Surface spots	Brush the spots out with a small hand brush or use a commercial preparation such as K2R to lift the stain.
Mildew	Clean around the mildew with warm suds. Rinse in cold water and soak the mildew area in a solution of 1 part table salt and 2 parts water. Wash with upholstery cleaner.
Water stains	Water stains in fabric materials can be removed with a solution made from 1 cup of table salt dissolved in 1 quart of water. Vigorously scrub the solution into the stain and rinse with clear water. Water stains in nylon or other synthetic fabrics should be removed with a commercial type spot remover.
Chewing gum, tar, crayons, shoe polish (greasy stains)	Do not use a cleaner that will soften gum or tar. Harden the deposit with an ice cube and scrape away as much as possible with a dull knife. Moisten the remainder with cleaning fluid and scrub clean.
Ice cream, candy	Most candy has a sugar base and can be removed with a cloth wrung out in warm water. Oily candy, after cleaning with warm water, should be cleaned with upholstery cleaner. Rinse with warm water and clean the remainder with cleaning fluid.
Wine, alcohol, egg, milk, soft drink (non-greasy stains)	Do not use soap. Scrub the stain with a cloth wrung out in warm water. Remove the remainder with cleaning fluid.
Grease, oil, lipstick, butter and related stains	Use a spot remover to avoid leaving a ring. Work from the outisde of the stain to the center and dry with a clean cloth when the spot is gone.
Headliners (cloth)	Mix a solution of warm water and foam upholstery cleaner to give thick suds. Use only foam—liquid may streak or spot. Clean the entire headliner in one operation using a circular motion with a natural sponge.
Headliner (vinyl)	Use a vinyl cleaner with a sponge and wipe clean with a dry cloth.
Seats and door panels	Mix 1 pint upholstery cleaner in 1 gallon of water. Do not soak the fabric around the buttons.
Leather or vinyl fabric	Use a multi-purpose cleaner full strength and a stiff brush. Let stand 2 minutes and scrub thoroughly. Wipe with a clean, soft rag.
Nylon or synthetic fabrics	For normal stains, use the same procedures you would for washing cloth upholstery. If the fabric is extremely dirty, use a multi-purpose cleaner full strength with a stiff scrub brush. Scrub thoroughly in all directions and wipe with a cotton towel or soft rag.

GLOSSARY

AIR/FUEL RATIO: The ratio of air-to-gasoline by weight in the fuel mixture drawn into the engine.

AIR INJECTION: One method of reducing harmful exhaust emissions by injecting air into each of the exhaust ports of an engine. The fresh air entering the hot exhaust manifold causes any remaining fuel to be burned before it can exit the tailpipe.

ALTERNATOR: A device used for converting mechanical energy into electrical energy.

AMMETER: An instrument, calibrated in amperes, used to measure the flow of an electrical current in a circuit. Ammeters are always connected in series with the circuit being tested.

AMPERE: The rate of flow of electrical current present when one volt of electrical pressure is applied against one ohm of electrical resistance.

ANALOG COMPUTER: Any microprocessor that uses similar (analogous) electrical signals to make its calculations.

ARMATURE: A laminated, soft iron core wrapped by a wire that converts electrical energy to mechanical energy as in a motor or relay. When rotated in a magnetic field, it changes mechanical energy into electrical energy as in a generator.

ATMOSPHERIC PRESSURE: The pressure on the Earth's surface caused by the weight of the air in the atmosphere. At sea level, this pressure is 14.7 psi at 32°F (101 kPa at 0°C).

ATOMIZATION: The breaking down of a liquid into a fine mist that can be suspended in air.

AXIAL PLAY: Movement parallel to a shaft or bearing bore.

BACKFIRE: The sudden combustion of gases in the intake or exhaust system that results in a loud explosion.

BACKLASH: The clearance or play between two parts, such as meshed gears.

BACKPRESSURE: Restrictions in the exhaust system that slow the exit of exhaust gases from the combustion chamber.

BAKELITE: A heat resistant, plastic insulator material commonly used in printed circuit boards and transistorized components.

BALL BEARING: A bearing made up of hardened inner and outer races between which hardened steel balls roll.

BALLAST RESISTOR: A resistor in the primary ignition circuit that lowers voltage after the engine is started to reduce wear on ignition components.

BEARING: A friction reducing, supportive device usually located between a stationary part and a moving part.

BIMETAL TEMPERATURE SENSOR: Any sensor or switch made of two dissimilar types of metal that bend when heated or cooled due to the different expansion rates of the alloys. These types of sensors usually function as an on/off switch.

BLOWBY: Combustion gases, composed of water vapor and unburned fuel, that leak past the piston rings into the crankcase during normal engine operation. These gases are removed by the PCV system to prevent the buildup of harmful acids in the crankcase.

BRAKE PAD: A brake shoe and lining assembly used with disc brakes.

BRAKE SHOE: The backing for the brake lining. The term is, however, usually applied to the assembly of the brake backing and lining.

BUSHING: A liner, usually removable, for a bearing; an anti-friction liner used in place of a bearing.

CALIPER: A hydraulically activated device in a disc brake system, which is mounted straddling the brake rotor (disc). The caliper contains at least one piston and two brake pads. Hydraulic pressure on the piston(s) forces the pads against the rotor.

CAMSHAFT: A shaft in the engine on which are the lobes (cams) which operate the valves. The camshaft is driven by the crankshaft, via a belt, chain or gears, at one half the crankshaft speed.

CAPACITOR: A device which stores an electrical charge.

CARBON MONOXIDE (CO): A colorless, odorless gas given off as a normal byproduct of combustion. It is poisonous and extremely dangerous in confined areas, building up slowly to toxic levels without warning if adequate ventilation is not available.

CARBURETOR: A device, usually mounted on the intake manifold of an engine, which mixes the air and fuel in the proper proportion to allow even combustion.

CATALYTIC CONVERTER: A device installed in the exhaust system, like a muffler, that converts harmful byproducts of combustion into carbon dioxide and water vapor by means of a heat-producing chemical reaction.

CENTRIFUGAL ADVANCE: A mechanical method of advancing the spark timing by using flyweights in the distributor that react to centrifugal force generated by the distributor shaft rotation.

CHECK VALVE: Any one-way valve installed to permit the flow of air, fuel or vacuum in one direction only.

CHOKE: A device, usually a moveable valve, placed in the intake path of a carburetor to restrict the flow of air.

CIRCUIT: Any unbroken path through which an electrical current can flow. Also used to describe fuel flow in some instances.

CIRCUIT BREAKER: A switch which protects an electrical circuit from overload by opening the circuit when the current flow exceeds a predetermined level. Some circuit breakers must be reset manually, while most reset automatically.

COIL (IGNITION): A transformer in the ignition circuit which steps up the voltage provided to the spark plugs.

COMBINATION MANIFOLD: An assembly which includes both the intake and exhaust manifolds in one casting.

COMBINATION VALVE: A device used in some fuel systems that routes fuel vapors to a charcoal storage canister instead of venting them into the atmosphere. The valve relieves fuel tank pressure and allows fresh air into the tank as the fuel level drops to prevent a vapor lock situation.

COMPRESSION RATIO: The comparison of the total volume of the cylinder and combustion chamber with the piston at BDC and the piston at TDC.

CONDENSER: 1. An electrical device which acts to store an electrical charge, preventing voltage surges. 2. A radiator-like device in the air conditioning system in which refrigerant gas condenses into a liquid, giving off heat.

CONDUCTOR: Any material through which an electrical current can be transmitted easily.

CONTINUITY: Continuous or complete circuit. Can be checked with an ohmmeter.

COUNTERSHAFT: An intermediate shaft which is rotated by a mainshaft and transmits, in turn, that rotation to a working part.

CRANKCASE: The lower part of an engine in which the crankshaft and related parts operate.

CRANKSHAFT: The main driving shaft of an engine which receives reciprocating motion from the pistons and converts it to rotary motion.

CYLINDER: In an engine, the round hole in the engine block in which the piston(s) ride.

CYLINDER BLOCK: The main structural member of an engine in which is found the cylinders, crankshaft and other principal parts.

CYLINDER HEAD: The detachable portion of the engine, usually fastened to the top of the cylinder block and containing all or most of the combustion chambers. On overhead valve engines, it contains the valves and their operating parts. On overhead cam engines, it contains the camshaft as well.

DEAD CENTER: The extreme top or bottom of the piston stroke.

DETONATION: An unwanted explosion of the air/fuel mixture in the combustion chamber caused by excess heat and compression, advanced timing, or an overly lean mixture. Also referred to as "ping".

DIAPHRAGM: A thin, flexible wall separating two cavities, such as in a vacuum advance unit.

DIESELING: A condition in which hot spots in the combustion chamber cause the engine to run on after the key is turned off.

DIFFERENTIAL: A geared assembly which allows the transmission of motion between drive axles, giving one axle the ability to turn faster than the other.

DIODE: An electrical device that will allow current to flow in one direction only.

DISC BRAKE: A hydraulic braking assembly consisting of a brake disc, or rotor, mounted on an axle, and a caliper assembly containing, usually two brake pads which are activated by hydraulic pressure. The pads are forced against the sides of the disc, creating friction which slows the vehicle.

DISTRIBUTOR: A mechanically driven device on an engine which is responsible for electrically firing the spark plug at a predetermined point of the piston stroke.

DOWEL PIN: A pin, inserted in mating holes in two different parts allowing those parts to maintain a fixed relationship.

DRUM BRAKE: A braking system which consists of two brake shoes and one or two wheel cylinders, mounted on a fixed backing plate, and a brake drum, mounted on an axle, which revolves around the assembly.

DWELL: The rate, measured in degrees of shaft rotation, at which an electrical circuit cycles on and off.

ELECTRONIC CONTROL UNIT (ECU): Ignition module, module, amplifier or igniter. See Module for definition.

ELECTRONIC IGNITION: A system in which the timing and firing of the spark plugs is controlled by an electronic control unit, usually called a module. These systems have no points or condenser.

END-PLAY: The measured amount of axial movement in a shaft.

ENGINE: A device that converts heat into mechanical energy.

EXHAUST MANIFOLD: A set of cast passages or pipes which conduct exhaust gases from the engine.

FEELER GAUGE: A blade, usually metal, of precisely predetermined thickness, used to measure the clearance between two parts.

FIRING ORDER: The order in which combustion occurs in the cylinders of an engine. Also the order in which spark is distributed to the plugs by the distributor.

FLOODING: The presence of too much fuel in the intake manifold and combustion chamber which prevents the air/fuel mixture from firing, thereby causing a no-start situation.

FLYWHEEL: A disc shaped part bolted to the rear end of the crankshaft. Around the outer perimeter is affixed the ring gear. The starter drive engages the ring gear, turning the flywheel, which rotates the crankshaft, imparting the initial starting motion to the engine.

FOOT POUND (ft. lbs. or sometimes, ft.lb.): The amount of energy or work needed to raise an item weighing one pound, a distance of one foot.

FUSE: A protective device in a circuit which prevents circuit overload by breaking the circuit when a specific amperage is present. The device is constructed around a strip or wire of a lower amperage rating than the circuit it is designed to protect. When an amperage higher than that stamped on the fuse is present in the circuit, the strip or wire melts, opening the circuit.

GEAR RATIO: The ratio between the number of teeth on meshing gears.

GENERATOR: A device which converts mechanical energy into electrical energy.

HEAT RANGE: The measure of a spark plug's ability to dissipate heat from its firing end. The higher the heat range, the hotter the plug fires.

HUB: The center part of a wheel or gear.

HYDROCARBON (HC): Any chemical compound made up of hydrogen and carbon. A major pollutant formed by the engine as a byproduct of combustion.

HYDROMETER: An instrument used to measure the specific gravity of a solution.

INCH POUND (inch lbs.; sometimes in.lb. or in. lbs.): One twelfth of a foot pound.

INDUCTION: A means of transferring electrical energy in the form of a magnetic field. Principle used in the ignition coil to increase voltage.

INJECTOR: A device which receives metered fuel under relatively low pressure and is activated to inject the fuel into the engine under relatively high pressure at a predetermined time.

INPUT SHAFT: The shaft to which torque is applied, usually carrying the driving gear or gears.

INTAKE MANIFOLD: A casting of passages or pipes used to conduct air or a fuel/air mixture to the cylinders.

JOURNAL: The bearing surface within which a shaft operates.

KEY: A small block usually fitted in a notch between a shaft and a hub to prevent slippage of the two parts.

MANIFOLD: A casting of passages or set of pipes which connect the cylinders to an inlet or outlet source.

MANIFOLD VACUUM: Low pressure in an engine intake manifold formed just below the throttle plates. Manifold vacuum is highest at idle and drops under acceleration.

MASTER CYLINDER: The primary fluid pressurizing device in a hydraulic system. In automotive use, it is found in brake and hydraulic clutch systems and is pedal activated, either directly or, in a power brake system, through the power booster.

MODULE: Electronic control unit, amplifier or igniter of solid state or integrated design which controls the current flow in the ignition primary circuit based on input from the pick-up coil. When the module opens the primary circuit, high secondary voltage is induced in the coil.

NEEDLE BEARING: A bearing which consists of a number (usually a large number) of long, thin rollers.

OHM: (Ω) The unit used to measure the resistance of conductor-to-electrical flow. One ohm is the amount of resistance that limits current flow to one ampere in a circuit with one volt of pressure.

OHMMETER: An instrument used for measuring the resistance, in ohms, in an electrical circuit.

OUTPUT SHAFT: The shaft which transmits torque from a device, such as a transmission.

OVERDRIVE: A gear assembly which produces more shaft revolutions than that transmitted to it.

OVERHEAD CAMSHAFT (OHC): An engine configuration in which the camshaft is mounted on top of the cylinder head and operates the valve either directly or by means of rocker arms.

OVERHEAD VALVE (OHV): An engine configuration in which all of the valves are located in the cylinder head and the camshaft is located in the cylinder block. The camshaft operates the valves via lifters and pushrods.

OXIDES OF NITROGEN (NOx): Chemical compounds of nitrogen produced as a byproduct of combustion. They combine with hydrocarbons to produce smog.

OXYGEN SENSOR: Used with the feedback system to sense the presence of oxygen in the exhaust gas and signal the computer which can reference the voltage signal to an air/fuel ratio.

PINION: The smaller of two meshing gears.

PISTON RING: An open-ended ring which fits into a groove on the outer diameter of the piston. Its chief function is to form a seal between the piston and cylinder wall. Most automotive pistons have three rings: two for compression sealing; one for oil sealing.

PRELOAD: A predetermined load placed on a bearing during assembly or by adjustment.

PRIMARY CIRCUIT: The low voltage side of the ignition system which consists of the ignition switch, ballast resistor or resistance wire, bypass, coil, electronic control unit and pick-up coil as well as the connecting wires and harnesses.

PRESS FIT: The mating of two parts under pressure, due to the inner diameter of one being smaller than the outer diameter of the other, or vice versa; an interference fit.

RACE: The surface on the inner or outer ring of a bearing on which the balls, needles or rollers move.

REGULATOR: A device which maintains the amperage and/or voltage levels of a circuit at predetermined values.

RELAY: A switch which automatically opens and/or closes a circuit.

RESISTANCE: The opposition to the flow of current through a circuit or electrical device, and is measured in ohms. Resistance is equal to the voltage divided by the amperage.

RESISTOR: A device, usually made of wire, which offers a preset amount of resistance in an electrical circuit.

RING GEAR: The name given to a ring-shaped gear attached to a differential case, or affixed to a flywheel or as part of a planetary gear set.

ROLLER BEARING: A bearing made up of hardened inner and outer races between which hardened steel rollers move.

ROTOR: 1. The disc-shaped part of a disc brake assembly, upon which the brake pads bear; also called, brake disc. 2. The device mounted atop the distributor shaft, which passes current to the distributor cap tower contacts.

SECONDARY CIRCUIT: The high voltage side of the ignition system, usually above 20,000 volts. The secondary includes the ignition coil, coil wire, distributor cap and rotor, spark plug wires and spark plugs.

SENDING UNIT: A mechanical, electrical, hydraulic or electromagnetic device which transmits information to a gauge.

SENSOR: Any device designed to measure engine operating conditions or ambient pressures and temperatures. Usually electronic in nature and designed to send a voltage signal to an on-board computer, some sensors may operate as a simple on/off switch or they may provide a variable voltage signal (like a potentiometer) as conditions or measured parameters change.

SHIM: Spacers of precise, predetermined thickness used between parts to establish a proper working relationship.

SLAVE CYLINDER: In automotive use, a device in the hydraulic clutch system which is activated by hydraulic force, disengaging the clutch.

SOLENOID: A coil used to produce a magnetic field, the effect of which is to produce work.

SPARK PLUG: A device screwed into the combustion chamber of a spark ignition engine. The basic construction is a conductive core inside of a ceramic insulator, mounted in an outer conductive base. An electrical charge from the spark plug wire travels along the conductive core and jumps a preset air gap to a grounding point or points at the end of the conductive base. The resultant spark ignites the fuel/air mixture in the combustion chamber.

SPLINES: Ridges machined or cast onto the outer diameter of a shaft or inner diameter of a bore to enable parts to mate without rotation.

TACHOMETER: A device used to measure the rotary speed of an engine, shaft, gear, etc., usually in rotations per minute.

THERMOSTAT: A valve, located in the cooling system of an engine, which is closed when cold and opens gradually in response to engine heating, controlling the temperature of the coolant and rate of coolant flow.

TOP DEAD CENTER (TDC): The point at which the piston reaches the top of its travel on the compression stroke.

TORQUE: The twisting force applied to an object.

TORQUE CONVERTER: A turbine used to transmit power from a driving member to a driven member via hydraulic action, providing changes in drive ratio and torque. In automotive use, it links the driveplate at the rear of the engine to the automatic transmission.

TRANSDUCER: A device used to change a force into an electrical signal.

TRANSISTOR: A semi-conductor component which can be actuated by a small voltage to perform an electrical switching function.

TUNE-UP: A regular maintenance function, usually associated with the replacement and adjustment of parts and components in the electrical and fuel systems of a vehicle for the purpose of attaining optimum performance.

TURBOCHARGER: An exhaust driven pump which compresses intake air and forces it into the combustion chambers at higher than atmospheric pressures. The increased air pressure allows more fuel to be burned and results in increased horsepower being produced.

VACUUM ADVANCE: A device which advances the ignition timing in response to increased engine vacuum.

VACUUM GAUGE: An instrument used to measure the presence of vacuum in a chamber.

VALVE: A device which control the pressure, direction of flow or rate of flow of a liquid or gas.

VALVE CLEARANCE: The measured gap between the end of the valve stem and the rocker arm, cam lobe or follower that activates the valve.

VISCOSITY: The rating of a liquid's internal resistance to flow.

VOLTMETER: An instrument used for measuring electrical force in units called volts. Voltmeters are always connected parallel with the circuit being tested.

WHEEL CYLINDER: Found in the automotive drum brake assembly, it is a device, actuated by hydraulic pressure, which, through internal pistons, pushes the brake shoes outward against the drums.

ADD-ON ELECTRICAL EQUIPMENT   6-12
ADJUSTMENTS (AUTOMATIC TRANSMISSION)   7-31
   KICK-DOWN BAND   7-32
   LOW & REVERSE BAND   7-31
   LOW & REVERSE BAND   7-32
   SHIFT LINKAGE   7-32
   THROTTLE LINKAGE   7-32
ADJUSTMENTS (BRAKE OPERATING SYSTEM)   9-3
   DISC BRAKES   9-4
   DRUM BRAKES   9-3
ADJUSTMENTS (CLUTCH)   7-8
   PEDAL FREE-PLAY   7-8
   REMOVAL & INSTALLATION   7-10
ADJUSTMENTS (IDLE SPEED AND MIXTURE)   2-29
   1975–79 6-CYLINDER AND V8 ENGINES   2-30
   1980 6-CYLINDER AND V8 ENGINES   2-33
   1981–82 6-CYLINDER AND V8 ENGINES   2-33
   1983 4-150 ENGINES   2-34
   1983–84 6-258 ENGINE   2-34
   4-121 ENGINES   2-29
   4-151 ENGINES   2-29
ADJUSTMENTS (MANUAL TRANSMISSION)   7-2
   LINKAGE   7-2
   REMOVAL & INSTALLATION   7-5
AIR CLEANER   1-26
   REMOVAL & INSTALLATION   1-26
AIR CONDITIONING   1-39
   DISCHARGING, EVACUATING & CHARGING   1-42
   GENERAL SERVICING PROCEDURES   1-40
   ISOLATING THE COMPRESSOR   1-42
   SAFETY PRECAUTIONS   1-39
   SYSTEM INSPECTION   1-41
AIR CONDITIONING COMPRESSOR   3-51
   REMOVAL & INSTALLATION   3-51
AIR INJECTION SYSTEM   4-9
   DESCRIPTION   4-9
   REMOVAL & INSTALLATION   4-10
   TROUBLESHOOTING   4-11
AIR POLLUTION   4-2
ALTERNATOR   3-11
   ALTERNATOR PRECAUTIONS   3-11
   BELT TENSION ADJUSTMENT   3-14
   REMOVAL & INSTALLATION   3-11
ALTERNATOR AND REGULATOR SPECIFICATIONS   3-14
AMERICAN MOTORS BREAKERLESS INDUCTIVE DISCHARGE IGNITION
  SYSTEM   2-18
   COMPONENTS   2-18
   DESCRIPTION & OPERATION   2-18
   DIAGNOSIS & TESTING   2-19
   DISTRIBUTOR OVERHAUL   2-19
AMERICAN MOTORS SOLID STATE IGNITION (SSI) SYSTEM   2-20
   DESCRIPTION & OPERATION   2-20
   TESTING   2-20
ANTI-DIESELING SOLENOID   4-19
   TESTING   4-19
AUTOLITE/MOTORCRAFT 2100 AND 2150 CARBURETORS   5-14
   ADJUSTMENT   5-14
   DESCRIPTION   5-14
AUTOLITE/MOTORCRAFT 4300 AND 4350 4-BBL CARBURETORS   5-20
   ADJUSTMENTS   5-22
   DESCRIPTION   5-20
AUTOMATIC TRANSMISSION   7-21
AUTOMATIC TRANSMISSION (FLUIDS AND LUBRICANTS)   1-59
   FLUID & FILTER CHANGE   1-60
   FLUID LEVEL CHECK   1-59
AUTOMATIC TRANSMISSION APPLICATION CHART (SPECIFICATION
  CHARTS)   1-18
AUTOMATIC TRANSMISSION APPLICATION CHART (SPECIFICATION
  CHARTS)   7-23
AUTOMOTIVE EMISSIONS   4-3
AUTOMOTIVE POLLUTANTS   4-2

MASTER

INDEX

HEAT TRANSFER 4-3
TEMPERATURE INVERSION 4-2
AVOIDING THE MOST COMMON MISTAKES 1-2
AVOIDING TROUBLE 1-2
AXLE SHAFT, BEARING AND SEAL (REAR AXLE) 7-46
REMOVAL & INSTALLATION 7-46
AXLE, SHAFT, SEAL AND BEARING (EAGLE FRONT AXLE) 7-45
REMOVAL & INSTALLATION 7-45
BALL JOINTS 8-10
INSPECTION 8-10
REMOVAL & INSTALLATION 8-10
BASIC AUTOMATIC TRANSMISSION PROBLEMS 7-35
BASIC CLUTCH PROBLEMS 7-20
BASIC DASH GAUGE PROBLEMS 6-33
BASIC DRIVESHAFT PROBLEMS 7-44
BASIC FUEL SYSTEM DIAGNOSIS 5-2
BASIC FUEL SYSTEM PROBLEMS 5-33
BASIC LIGHTING PROBLEMS 6-42
BASIC OPERATING PRINCIPLES 9-2
DISC BRAKES 9-2
DRUM BRAKES 9-3
POWER BOOSTERS 9-3
BASIC STEERING AND SUSPENSION PROBLEMS 8-30
BASIC TIRE PROBLEMS 1-51
BASIC TURN SIGNAL AND FLASHER PROBLEMS 6-43
BASIC WHEEL PROBLEMS 1-51
BASIC WINDSHIELD WIPER PROBLEMS 6-27
BATTERY (ENGINE ELECTRICAL) 3-23
REMOVAL & INSTALLATION 3-23
BATTERY (ROUTINE MAINTENANCE) 1-31
BATTERY FLUID 1-31
CABLES 1-33
CHARGING 1-34
GENERAL MAINTENANCE 1-31
REPLACEMENT 1-34
BATTERY, STARTING AND CHARGING SYSTEMS 3-4
BASIC OPERATING PRINCIPLES 3-4
BELTS 1-35
ADJUSTING 1-36
INSPECTION 1-35
REMOVAL & INSTALLATION 1-36
BLOWER MOTOR 6-12
REMOVAL & INSTALLATION 6-12
BODY LUBRICATION AND MAINTENANCE 1-78
BODY DRAIN HOLES 1-78
DOOR HINGES & HINGE CHECKS 1-78
LOCK CYLINDERS 1-78
TAILGATE 1-78
BOLTS, NUTS AND OTHER THREADED RETAINERS 1-8
BOOTS 1-39
INSPECTION 1-39
BRAKE CALIPER 9-22
REMOVAL, INSTALLATION, OVERHAUL 9-22
BRAKE DISC (ROTOR) 9-26
INSPECTION 9-26
REMOVAL & INSTALLATION 9-26
BRAKE DRUMS (FRONT DRUM BRAKES) 9-9
INSPECTION 9-10
REMOVAL & INSTALLATION 9-9
BRAKE DRUMS (REAR DRUM BRAKES) 9-32
INSPECTION 9-32
REMOVAL & INSTALLATION 9-32
BRAKE MASTER CYLINDER 1-64
FLUID LEVEL CHECK 1-64
BRAKE OPERATING SYSTEM 9-2
BRAKE SHOES (FRONT DRUM BRAKES) 9-10
REMOVAL & INSTALLATION 9-10
BRAKE SHOES (REAR DRUM BRAKES) 9-32

REMOVAL & INSTALLATION 9-32
BRAKE SPECIFICATIONS 9-40
BREAKER POINTS AND CONDENSER 2-11
DESCRIPTION & OPERATION 2-11
DWELL ADJUSTMENT 2-16
REMOVAL & INSTALLATION 2-12
CABLES 9-36
ADJUSTMENT 9-36
REMOVAL & INSTALLATION 9-36
CAMSHAFT 3-93
REMOVAL & INSTALLATION 3-93
CAMSHAFT SPECIFICATIONS 3-32
CAPACITIES CHART 1-83
CARBURETOR SPECIFICATIONS 5-30
CARBURETORS 5-4
OVERHAUL 5-6
REMOVAL & INSTALLATION 5-4
CARTER BBD 2-BBL CARBURETOR 5-10
ADJUSTMENT 5-10
CARTER YF CARBURETOR 5-6
ADJUSTMENTS 5-9
DESCRIPTION 5-6
CARTER YFA CARBURETOR 5-28
ADJUSTMENT 5-29
CATALYTIC CONVERTER (ELECTRONIC ENGINE CONTROLS) 4-29
OPERATION 4-29
CATALYTIC CONVERTER (EXHAUST SYSTEM) 3-114
REMOVAL & INSTALLATION 3-114
CHECKING ENGINE COMPRESSION 3-30
CHOKE HEAT BY-PASS VALVE (CHBPV) 4-30
OPERATION 4-30
CIRCUIT PROTECTION 6-44
CLUTCH 7-8
COIL SPRINGS 8-16
REMOVAL & INSTALLATION 8-16
COMPONENT LOCATIONS
EMISSION COMPONENT LOCATIONS—EARLY MODEL V8 ENGINE 4-6
EMISSION COMPONENT LOCATIONS—LATE MODEL INLINE ENGINE 4-7
FRONT DRUM BRAKE COMPONENTS 9-8
FRONT SUSPENSION COMPONENT LOCATIONS—EARLY MODEL MATADOR 8-4
FRONT SUSPENSION COMPONENT LOCATIONS—LATE MODEL EAGLE 8-3
MAINTENANCE COMPONENT LOCATIONS—EARLY MODEL V8 ENGINE 1-24
MAINTENANCE COMPONENT LOCATIONS—LATE MODEL INLINE ENGINE 1-25
REAR DRUM BRAKE COMPONENTS 9-31
REAR SUSPENSION COMPONENT LOCATIONS—EARLY MODEL MATADOR 8-15
REAR SUSPENSION COMPONENT LOCATIONS—LATE MODEL EAGLE 8-14
CONTROL HEAD 6-18
REMOVAL & INSTALLATION 6-18
CONTROL UNIT 4-28
REMOVAL & INSTALLATION 4-28
COOLANT 1-61
COOLANT LEVEL CHECK 1-61
DRAINING, FLUSHING & REFILLING 1-62
COOLING 1-74
ENGINE 1-74
TRANSMISSION 1-74
CRANKCASE EMISSION CONTROLS 4-5
OPERATION 4-5
REMOVAL & INSTALLATION 4-8
TESTING 4-8

CRANKCASE EMISSIONS 4-5
CRANKSHAFT 3-109
    CLEANING & INSPECTION 3-110
    INSTALLATION 3-111
    REMOVAL 3-109
CRANKSHAFT AND CONNECTING ROD SPECIFICATIONS 3-33
CRANKSHAFT PULLEY (VIBRATION DAMPER) 3-78
    REMOVAL & INSTALLATION 3-78
CYLINDER HEAD 3-61
    REMOVAL & INSTALLATION 3-61
DELCO HIGH ENERGY IGNITION (HEI) SYSTEM 2-21
    COMPONENT REPLACEMENT 2-23
    HEI SYSTEM PRECAUTIONS 2-21
    TROUBLESHOOTING THE HEI SYSTEM 2-22
DESCRIPTION 3-23
    4-121 ENGINE 3-23
    4-150 ENGINE 3-25
    4-151 ENGINE 3-25
    6-232 AND 258 ENGINES 3-27
    8-304, 360 AND 401 ENGINES 3-27
DISABLING THE INTERLOCK SYSTEM 6-34
DISC BRAKE PADS 9-15
    REMOVAL & INSTALLATION 9-15
DISTRIBUTOR 3-6
    INSTALLATION 3-8
    REMOVAL 3-6
DISTRIBUTOR CONTROLS 4-15
    DUAL DIAPHRAGM DISTRIBUTOR TEST 4-15
DO'S 1-7
DON'TS 1-8
DOOR PANELS 10-24
    REMOVAL & INSTALLATION 10-24
DOORS 10-2
    ADJUSTMENT 10-2
    REMOVAL & INSTALLATION 10-2
DRIVE AXLES 1-65
    DRAIN & REFILL 1-66
    FLUID LEVEL CHECK 1-65
DRIVELINE 7-39
DRIVESHAFT AND U-JOINTS 7-39
    REMOVAL & INSTALLATION 7-39
    U-JOINT OVERHAUL 7-41
EAGLE FRONT AXLE 7-45
ELECTRIC ASSIST CHOKE 4-19
    OPERATION 4-19
    TESTING 4-19
ELECTRIC TAILGATE WINDOW 10-23
    REMOVAL & INSTALLATION 10-23
ELECTRIC TAILGATE WINDOW MOTOR 10-38
    REMOVAL & INSTALLATION 10-38
ELECTRIC WINDOW MOTOR 10-37
    REMOVAL & INSTALLATION 10-37
ELECTRONIC ENGINE CONTROLS 4-20
ELECTRONIC IGNITION 2-18
EMISSION COMPONENT LOCATIONS—EARLY MODEL V8 ENGINE 4-6
EMISSION COMPONENT LOCATIONS—LATE MODEL INLINE
    ENGINE 4-7
EMISSION CONTROL SYSTEMS USAGE 4-8
EMISSION CONTROLLED DISTRIBUTOR VACUUM APPLICATION CHART
    FOR VEHICLES EQUIPPED WITH TCS 4-18
EMISSION CONTROLS 4-5
ENGINE (ENGINE MECHANICAL) 3-34
    REMOVAL & INSTALLATION 3-34
ENGINE (SERIAL NUMBER IDENTIFICATION) 1-16
    4-121 ENGINE 1-16
    4-150 ENGINE 1-16
    4-151 ENGINE 1-16
    6-232 & 258 ENGINES 1-17
    8-304, 360, 401 ENGINES 1-17
ENGINE APPLICATION CHART 1-17
ENGINE ELECTRICAL 3-2
ENGINE MECHANICAL 3-23
ENGINE MECHANICAL PROBLEMS 3-117
ENGINE OIL 1-53
    OIL & FILTER CHANGE 1-54
    OIL LEVEL CHECK 1-53
ENGINE OVERHAUL TIPS 3-27
    INSPECTION TECHNIQUES 3-28
    OVERHAUL TIPS 3-29
    REPAIRING DAMAGED THREADS 3-29
    TOOLS 3-28
ENGINE PERFORMANCE (TROUBLESHOOTING CHARTS) 3-120
ENGLISH TO METRIC CONVERSION CHARTS 1-88
ENTERTAINMENT SYSTEMS 6-24
EVAPORATIVE EMISSIONS 4-5
EXHAUST GAS RECIRCULATION (EGR) SYSTEM 4-11
    OPERATION 4-11
    REMOVAL & INSTALLATION 4-14
EXHAUST GASES 4-3
    CARBON MONOXIDE 4-4
    HYDROCARBONS 4-3
    NITROGEN 4-4
    OXIDES OF SULFUR 4-4
    PARTICULATE MATTER 4-4
EXHAUST MANIFOLD 3-48
    REMOVAL & INSTALLATION 3-48
EXHAUST MANIFOLD HEAT VALVE 1-34
    SERVICING 1-34
EXHAUST SYSTEM 3-112
EXPLANATION OF TROUBLE CODES GM C-4 AND CCC
    SYSTEMS 4-26
EXTERIOR 10-2
FASTENERS, MEASUREMENTS AND CONVERSIONS 1-8
FIRING ORDER 2-8
FLUID DISPOSAL 1-52
FLUIDS AND LUBRICANTS 1-52
FLYWHEEL/FLEXPLATE AND RING GEAR 3-112
    REMOVAL & INSTALLATION 3-112
FRONT DISC BRAKES 9-15
FRONT DRIVE AXLE APPLICATION CHART 1-19
FRONT DRUM BRAKE COMPONENTS 9-8
FRONT DRUM BRAKES 9-8
FRONT END ALIGNMENT 8-11
    CAMBER 8-11
    CASTER 8-11
    TOE-IN 8-12
FRONT EXHAUST PIPE (HEAD PIPE) 3-113
    REMOVAL & INSTALLATION 3-113
FRONT HUB AND WHEEL BEARINGS 1-69
    ADJUSTMENT 1-69
FRONT SUSPENSION 8-2
FRONT SUSPENSION COMPONENT LOCATIONS—EARLY MODEL
    MATADOR 8-4
FRONT SUSPENSION COMPONENT LOCATIONS—LATE MODEL
    EAGLE 8-3
FUEL AND OIL RECOMMENDATIONS 1-53
FUEL FILTER 1-28
    REMOVAL & INSTALLATION 1-28
FUEL PUMP 5-2
    REMOVAL & INSTALLATION 5-2
    TESTING 5-3
FUEL RETURN SYSTEM 4-30
    OPERATION 4-30
FUEL SYSTEM 5-2
FUEL TANK 5-33
FUEL TANK SENDING UNIT 5-34

REMOVAL & INSTALLATION 5-34
FUEL TANK VAPOR EMISSION CONTROL SYSTEM 4-20
    OPERATION 4-20
    TROUBLESHOOTING 4-20
FUEL VAPOR CANISTER 1-30
    SERVICING 1-30
FUSE BOX LOCATION 6-45
FUSE LINK 6-44
GENERAL ENGINE SPECIFICATIONS 3-31
GENERAL INFORMATION (ELECTRONIC ENGINE CONTROLS) 4-20
    ACTIVATING THE TROUBLE CODE 4-26
    AMERICAN MOTORS FEEDBACK SYSTEM 4-23
    BASIC TROUBLESHOOTING 4-24
    COMPUTER COMMAND CONTROL (CCC) SYSTEM 4-22
    COMPUTER CONTROLLED CATALYTIC CONVERTER (C-4)
      SYSTEM 4-21
GENERAL INFORMATION (EXHAUST SYSTEM) 3-112
GENERAL INFORMATION (VALVE LASH) 2-27
    ADJUSTMENT 2-27
GENERAL RECOMMENDATIONS 1-73
HANDLING A TRAILER 1-74
HEADLIGHTS 6-34
    REMOVAL & INSTALLATION 6-34
HEADLINER 10-38
    REMOVAL & INSTALLATION 10-38
HEATER CORE 6-14
    REMOVAL & INSTALLATION 6-14
HEATING AND AIR CONDITIONING 6-12
HEI PLUG WIRE RESISTANCE CHART 2-7
HITCH (TONGUE) WEIGHT 1-73
HOLLEY 5210-C CARBURETOR 5-26
    ADJUSTMENTS 5-26
HOOD 10-3
    ALIGNMENT 10-5
    REMOVAL & INSTALLATION 10-3
HOSES 1-37
    INSPECTION 1-37
    REMOVAL & INSTALLATION 1-38
HOW TO BUY A USED VEHICLE 1-79
HOW TO REMOVE STAINS FROM FABRIC INTERIOR 10-40
HOW TO USE THIS BOOK 1-2
HUBS AND BEARINGS 9-34
    REMOVAL & INSTALLATION 9-34
IDENTIFICATION (MANUAL TRANSMISSION) 7-2
IDENTIFICATION (PACER OVERDRIVE UNIT) 7-7
    REMOVAL & INSTALLATION 7-7
IDENTIFICATION (REAR AXLE) 7-46
IDENTIFICATION (TRANSFER CASE) 7-37
IDLE SPEED AND MIXTURE 2-29
IGNITION COIL 3-5
    REMOVAL & INSTALLATION 3-5
IGNITION MODULE 3-6
    REMOVAL & INSTALLATION 3-6
IGNITION SWITCH 8-22
    REMOVAL & INSTALLATION 8-22
IGNITION TIMING 2-24
INDUSTRIAL POLLUTANTS 4-2
INNER TIE RODS 8-48
    REMOVAL & INSTALLATION 8-48
INSTRUMENT AND SWITCHES 6-27
INSTRUMENT CLUSTER 6-27
    REMOVAL & INSTALLATION 6-27
INTAKE MANIFOLD 3-43
    REMOVAL & INSTALLATION 3-43
INTERIOR 10-24
JACKING 1-76
JACKING PRECAUTIONS 1-77
JUMP STARTING A DEAD BATTERY 1-75

JUMP STARTING PRECAUTIONS 1-75
JUMP STARTING PROCEDURE 1-76
LEAF SPRINGS 8-16
    REMOVAL & INSTALLATION 8-16
LIFTGATE 10-7
    ALIGNMENT 10-15
    REMOVAL & INSTALLATION 10-7
LIGHTING 6-34
LOCKUP TORQUE CONVERTER SERVICE DIAGNOSIS 7-36
LOWER CONTROL ARM 8-9
    REMOVAL & INSTALLATION 8-9
MAINTENANCE COMPONENT LOCATIONS—EARLY MODEL V8
  ENGINE 1-24
MAINTENANCE COMPONENT LOCATIONS—LATE MODEL INLINE
  ENGINE 1-25
MAINTENANCE OR REPAIR? 1-2
MANUAL DOOR GLASS AND REGULATOR 10-26
    REMOVAL & INSTALLATION 10-26
MANUAL DOOR LOCKS 10-3
    REMOVAL & INSTALLATION 10-3
MANUAL STEERING GEAR (FLUIDS AND LUBRICANTS) 1-67
MANUAL STEERING GEAR (STEERING) 8-22
    ADJUSTMENTS 8-25
    REMOVAL & INSTALLATION 8-22
MANUAL TAILGATE WINDOW 10-23
    REMOVAL & INSTALLATION 10-23
MANUAL TRANSMISSION 7-2
MANUAL TRANSMISSION (FLUIDS AND LUBRICANTS) 1-57
    FLUID CHANGE 1-58
    FLUID LEVEL CHECK 1-57
MANUAL TRANSMISSION AND TRANSFER CASE 7-17
MANUAL TRANSMISSION APPLICATION CHART (SPECIFICATION
  CHARTS) 1-18
MANUAL TRANSMISSION APPLICATION CHART (SPECIFICATION
  CHARTS) 7-19
MANUAL TRANSMISSION FLUID RECOMMENDATIONS 1-58
MASTER CYLINDER 9-4
    BLEEDING 9-6
    BRAKE WARNING LIGHT SIGNAL 9-6
    OVERHAUL 9-5
    REMOVAL & INSTALLATION 9-4
MIXTURE CONTROL SOLENOID 4-28
    REMOVAL & INSTALLATION 4-28
MOTOR 6-24
    REMOVAL & INSTALLATION 6-24
MUFFLER 3-113
    REMOVAL & INSTALLATION 3-113
NATURAL POLLUTANTS 4-2
NEUTRAL SAFETY/BACK-UP LIGHT SWITCH 7-33
    REMOVAL & INSTALLATION 7-33
    TESTING 7-33
OIL PAN 3-72
    REMOVAL & INSTALLATION 3-72
OIL PUMP 3-75
    REMOVAL & INSTALLATION 3-75
OIL VISCOSITY SELECTOR 1-53
OUTER TIE RODS 8-46
    REMOVAL & INSTALLATION 8-46
OXYGEN SENSOR 4-28
    REMOVAL & INSTALLATION 4-28
PACER OVERDRIVE UNIT 7-7
PARKING BRAKE 9-36
PCV SYSTEM 1-29
    REMOVAL & INSTALLATION 1-29
PISTON AND RING SPECIFICATIONS 3-33
PISTONS AND CONNECTING RODS 3-98
    CHECKING CYLINDER BORE 3-103
    CYLINDER HONING 3-102

INSPECTION 3-100
INSTALLATION 3-105
MEASURING THE OLD PISTONS 3-102
PISTON PIN REPLACEMENT 3-99
PISTON RING REPLACEMENT 3-105
REMOVAL 3-98
RING TOLERANCES 3-104
SELECTING NEW PISTONS 3-102
POINT TYPE IGNITION 2-11
POWER BOOSTER 9-7
REMOVAL & INSTALLATION 9-7
POWER DOOR LOCKS 10-3
REMOVAL & INSTALLATION 10-3
POWER SEAT MOTOR 10-38
REMOVAL & INSTALLATION 10-38
POWER STEERING GEAR 8-28
ADJUSTMENTS 8-44
FLUID LEVEL & INITIAL OPERATION 8-45
REMOVAL & INSTALLATION 8-28
POWER STEERING PUMP 8-26
REMOVAL & INSTALLATION 8-26
POWER STEERING RESERVOIR 1-68
PREVENTIVE MAINTENANCE CHART 1-86
PRINTED CIRCUIT BOARD 6-32
REMOVAL & INSTALLATION 6-32
PUSHING AND TOWING 1-73
RADIATOR 3-53
REMOVAL & INSTALLATION 3-53
RADIO 6-24
REMOVAL & INSTALLATION 6-24
REAR AXLE 7-46
REAR AXLE APPLICATION CHART 1-19
REAR DRUM BRAKE COMPONENTS 9-31
REAR DRUM BRAKES 9-31
REAR EXHAUST PIPE OR TAILPIPE 3-113
REMOVAL & INSTALLATION 3-113
REAR MAIN BEARING OIL SEAL 3-107
REMOVAL & INSTALLATION 3-107
REAR SUSPENSION 8-14
REAR SUSPENSION COMPONENT LOCATIONS—EARLY MODEL
MATADOR 8-15
REAR SUSPENSION COMPONENT LOCATIONS—LATE MODEL
EAGLE 8-14
REAR WINDOW GLASS 10-22
REMOVAL & INSTALLATION 10-22
RECOMMENDED EQUIPMENT CHECKLIST 1-75
REGULATOR 3-14
REMOVAL & INSTALLATION 3-14
ROCHESTER E2SE CARBURETOR 5-23
ADJUSTMENTS 5-25
ROCKER SHAFTS AND ROCKER STUDS 3-39
REMOVAL & INSTALLATION 3-39
ROUTINE MAINTENANCE 1-24
SAFETY PRECAUTIONS 6-2
SEAT BELT/STARTER INTERLOCK SYSTEMS 6-34
SERIAL NUMBER IDENTIFICATION 1-14
SERVICING YOUR VEHICLE SAFELY 1-7
SHOCK ABSORBER (FRONT SUSPENSION) 8-2
REMOVAL & INSTALLATION 8-2
SHOCK ABSORBER (REAR SUSPENSION) 8-16
REMOVAL & INSTALLATION 8-16
SIGNAL AND MARKER LIGHTS 6-35
REMOVAL & INSTALLATION 6-35
SPARK PLUG WIRES 2-7
REMOVAL & INSTALLATION 2-7
TESTING 2-7
SPARK PLUGS 2-2
INSPECTION & GAPPING 2-6

REMOVAL & INSTALLATION 2-2
SPARK PLUG HEAT RANGE 2-2
SPARK PLUGS AND WIRES 2-2
SPECIAL TOOLS 1-6
SPECIFICATIONS CHARTS
ALTERNATOR AND REGULATOR SPECIFICATIONS 3-14
AUTOMATIC TRANSMISSION APPLICATION CHART 1-13
AUTOMATIC TRANSMISSION APPLICATION CHART 7-23
BRAKE SPECIFICATIONS 9-40
CAMSHAFT SPECIFICATIONS 3-32
CARBURETOR SPECIFICATONS 5-30
CONVERSION FACTORS 1-13
CRANKSHAFT AND CONNECTING ROD SPECIFICATIONS 3-33
EMISSION CONTROL SYSTEMS USAGE 4-8
EMISSION CONTROLLED DISTRIBUTOR VACUUM APPLICATION
CHART FOR VEHICLES EQUIPPED WITH TCS 4-18
ENGINE APPLICATION CHART 1-13
FRONT DRIVE AXLE APPLICATION CHART 1-13
GENERAL ENGINE SPECIFICATIONS 3-31
HEI PLUG WIRE RESISTANCE CHART 2-7
MANUAL TRANSMISSION APPLICATION CHART 1-13
MANUAL TRANSMISSION APPLICATION CHART 7-19
PISTON AND RING SPECIFICATIONS 3-33
REAR AXLE APPLICATION CHART 1-13
STANDARD AND METRIC CONVERSION FACTORS 1-13
STANDARD TORQUE SPECIFICATIONS AND FASTENER
MARKINGS 1-10
STARTER SPECIFICATIONS 3-22
TORQUE SPECIFICATIONS 3-34
TRANSFER CASE APPLICATION CHART 1-13
TRANSFER CASE APPLICATION CHART 7-37
TUNE-UP SPECIFICATIONS 2-9
USING A VACUUM GAUGE 3-116
VALVE SPECIFICATIONS 3-32
WHEEL ALIGNMENT SPECIFICATIONS 8-12
SPRING 8-6
REMOVAL & INSTALLATION 8-6
SPROCKETS 3-93
REMOVAL & INSTALLATION 3-93
STANDARD AND METRIC CONVERSION FACTORS 1-13
STANDARD AND METRIC MEASUREMENTS 1-12
STANDARD TORQUE SPECIFICATIONS AND FASTENER
MARKINGS 1-10
STARTER 3-14
COMPONENT REPLACEMENT 3-15
OVERHAUL 3-19
REMOVAL & INSTALLATION 3-14
STARTER SPECIFICATIONS 3-22
STEERING 8-19
STEERING WHEEL 8-19
REMOVAL & INSTALLATION 8-19
STEPPER MOTOR 4-29
REMOVAL & INSTALLATION 4-29
TAILGATE 10-17
ADJUSTMENT 10-18
REMOVAL & INSTALLATION 10-17
TANK ASSEMBLY 5-33
DRAINING 5-33
REMOVAL & INSTALLATION 5-33
THERMOSTAT 3-42
REMOVAL & INSTALLATION 3-42
THERMOSTATICALLY CONTROLLED AIR CLEANER SYSTEM
(TAC) 4-14
OPERATION 4-14
TROUBLESHOOTING 4-14
TIMING 2-24
INSPECTION & ADJUSTMENT 2-25
TIMING BELT 3-89

REMOVAL & INSTALLATION 3-89
TIMING CASE COVER 3-79
 REMOVAL & INSTALLATION 3-79
TIMING CHAIN/GEAR AND SPROCKET/PULLEY 3-85
 REMOVAL & INSTALLATION 3-85
TIPS 1-80
 ROAD TEST CHECKLIST 1-82
 USED VEHICLE CHECKLIST 1-80
TIRE SIZE COMPARISON CHART 1-52
TIRES AND WHEELS 1-47
 CARE OF SPECIAL WHEELS 1-50
 INFLATION & INSPECTION 1-48
 TIRE DESIGN 1-48
 TIRE ROTATION 1-47
 TIRE STORAGE 1-48
TOOLS AND EQUIPMENT 1-3
TORQUE 1-9
 TORQUE ANGLE METERS 1-12
 TORQUE WRENCHES 1-11
TORQUE SPECIFICATIONS 3-34
TRAILER TOWING 1-73
TRAILER WEIGHT 1-73
TRAILER WIRING 6-45
TRANSFER CASE 7-37
TRANSFER CASE (FLUIDS AND LUBRICANTS) 1-67
TRANSFER CASE (TRANSFER CASE) 7-37
 REMOVAL & INSTALLATION 7-37
TRANSFER CASE APPLICATION CHART (SPECIFICATION
 CHARTS) 7-37
TRANSFER CASE APPLICATION CHART (SPECIFICATION
 CHARTS) 1-19
TRANSMISSION (AUTOMATIC TRANSMISSION) 7-21
 REMOVAL & INSTALLATION 7-23
TRANSMISSION (SERIAL NUMBER IDENTIFICATION) 1-17
 AUTOMATIC 1-17
 MANUAL 1-17
TRANSMISSION CONTROLLED SPARK (TCS) SYSTEM 4-16
 OPERATION 4-16
 TESTING 4-17
TRANSMISSION FLUID INDICATIONS 7-35
TROUBLESHOOTING 6-3
 BASIC TROUBLESHOOTING THEORY 6-4
 TEST EQUIPMENT 6-4
 TESTING 6-6
TROUBLESHOOTING BASIC POINT-TYPE IGNITION SYSTEM
 PROBLEMS 2-17
TROUBLESHOOTING CHARTS
 BASIC AUTOMATIC TRANSMISSION PROBLEMS 7-35
 BASIC CLUTCH PROBLEMS 7-20
 BASIC DASH GAUGE PROBLEMS 6-33
 BASIC DRIVESHAFT PROBLEMS 7-44
 BASIC FUEL SYSTEM PROBLEMS 5-33
 BASIC LIGHTING PROBLEMS 6-42
 BASIC STEERING AND SUSPENSION PROBLEMS 8-30
 BASIC TIRE PROBLEMS 1-51
 BASIC TURN SIGNAL AND FLASHER PROBLEMS 6-43
 BASIC WHEEL PROBLEMS 1-51
 BASIC WINDSHIELD WIPER PROBLEMS 6-27
 CAPACITIES CHART 1-83
 ENGINE MECHANICAL PROBLEMS 3-117
 ENGINE PERFORMANCE 2-36
 ENGINE PERFORMANCE 3-120
 ENGLISH TO METRIC CONVERSION CHARTS 1-88
 EXPLANATION OF TROUBLE CODES GM C-4 AND CCC
  SYSTEMS 4-26
 HOW TO REMOVE STAINS FROM FABRIC INTERIOR 10-40
 LOCKUP TORQUE CONVERTER SERVICE DIAGNOSIS 7-36
 MANUAL TRANSMISSION AND TRANSFER CASE 7-17

OIL VISCOSITY SELECTOR 1-53
PREVENTIVE MAINTENANCE CHART 1-86
RECOMMENDED EQUIPMENT CHECKLIST 1-75
TIRE SIZE COMPARISON CHART 1-52
TRANSMISSION FLUID INDICATIONS 7-35
TROUBLESHOOTING BASIC POINT-TYPE IGNITION SYSTEM
 PROBLEMS 2-17
TROUBLESHOOTING THE BRAKE SYSTEM 9-41
TROUBLESHOOTING THE HEATER 6-13
TROUBLESHOOTING THE IGNITION SWITCH 8-32
TROUBLESHOOTING THE MANUAL STEERING GEAR 8-35
TROUBLESHOOTING THE POWER STEERING GEAR 8-36
TROUBLESHOOTING THE POWER STEERING PUMP 8-38
TROUBLESHOOTING THE STEERING COLUMN 8-31
TROUBLESHOOTING THE TURN SIGNAL SWITCH 8-33
TROUBLESHOOTING THE BRAKE SYSTEM 9-41
TROUBLESHOOTING THE HEATER 6-13
TROUBLESHOOTING THE IGNITION SWITCH 8-32
TROUBLESHOOTING THE MANUAL STEERING GEAR 8-35
TROUBLESHOOTING THE POWER STEERING GEAR 8-36
TROUBLESHOOTING THE POWER STEERING PUMP 8-38
TROUBLESHOOTING THE STEERING COLUMN 8-31
TROUBLESHOOTING THE TURN SIGNAL SWITCH 8-33
TUNE-UP SPECIFICATIONS 2-9
TURN SIGNAL SWITCH, HAZARD SIGNAL AND LOCK CYLINDER 8-21
 REMOVAL & INSTALLATION 8-21
**UNDERSTANDING AND TROUBLESHOOTING ELECTRICAL
SYSTEMS 6-2**
UNDERSTANDING AUTOMATIC TRANSMISSIONS 7-21
 HYDRAULIC CONTROL SYSTEM 7-22
 PLANETARY GEARBOX 7-21
 SERVOS & ACCUMULATORS 7-22
 TORQUE CONVERTER 7-21
UNDERSTANDING BASIC ELECTRICITY 6-2
 AUTOMOTIVE CIRCUITS 6-3
 CIRCUITS 6-2
 SHORT CIRCUITS 6-3
 THE WATER ANALOGY 6-2
UNDERSTANDING ELECTRICITY 3-2
 BASIC CIRCUITS 3-2
 TROUBLESHOOTING 3-3
UNDERSTANDING THE CLUTCH 7-8
UNDERSTANDING THE MANUAL TRANSMISSION 7-2
UPPER CONTROL ARM 8-6
 REMOVAL & INSTALLATION 8-6
USING A VACUUM GAUGE 3-116
VACUUM DIAGRAMS 4-31
VACUUM SWITCH 4-28
 REMOVAL & INSTALLATION 4-28
VACUUM THROTTLE MODULATING SYSTEM (VTM) 4-15
 ADJUSTMENT 4-16
 OPERATION 4-15
 TESTING 4-16
VALVE LASH 2-27
VALVE SEATS 3-72
 INSPECTION AND REFACING 3-72
VALVE SPECIFICATIONS 3-32
VALVES AND SPRINGS 3-66
 INSPECTION & REFACING 3-69
 INSTALLATION 3-72
 LAPPING 3-71
 REFACING 3-70
 REMOVAL 3-66
 VALVE SPRING TESTING 3-71
VEHICLE (SERIAL NUMBER IDENTIFICATION) 1-14
 1975–80 MODELS 1-14
 1981–88 MODELS 1-15
WATER PUMP 3-56

REMOVAL & INSTALLATION 3-56
WHEEL ALIGNMENT SPECIFICATIONS 8-12
WHEEL BEARINGS (FRONT DISC BRAKES) 9-28
  ADJUSTMENT 9-30
  REMOVAL, PACKING, & INSTALLATION 9-28
WHEEL BEARINGS (FRONT DRUM BRAKES) 9-15
  REMOVAL, PACKING & INSTALLATION 9-15
WHEEL BEARINGS (FRONT SUSPENSION) 8-10
  ADJUSTMENT 8-11
  INSPECTION 8-11
WHEEL CYLINDERS (FRONT DRUM BRAKES) 9-13
  OVERHAUL 9-13
WHEEL CYLINDERS (REAR DRUM BRAKES) 9-34
  OVERHAUL 9-34
WHEELS 8-2
WHEELS (WHEELS) 8-2

INSPECTION 8-2
INSTALLATION 8-2
REMOVAL 8-2
WHERE TO BEGIN 1-2
WINDSHIELD 10-18
  INSPECTION 10-19
  INSTALLATION 10-19
  REMOVAL 10-18
WINDSHIELD WIPERS 6-24
WINDSHIELD WIPERS (ROUTINE MAINTENANCE) 1-43
  ELEMENT (REFILL) CARE & REPLACEMENT 1-43
WIPER LINKAGE 6-27
  REMOVAL & INSTALLATION 6-27
WIRING DIAGRAMS 6-46
WIRING HARNESSES 6-8
  WIRING REPAIR 6-8